SHAKESPEARE A
THE IDEA OF LATE W

According to the idea of 'late style', in their last few years, certain great artists, writers or composers enter a rejuvenated phase of serene, abstract, archaic or childlike creativity, a phenomenon held to result from the proximity of death. Gordon McMullan reads late style, however, not as a transhistorical phenomenon but as a critical construct, taking Shakespeare as his exemplar. He maps the development of the idea of 'late Shakespeare' from the later eighteenth century to the present, showing the mismatch between what he calls the 'discourse of lateness' and the actual conditions of production and of authorship in early modern theatre and suggesting the generativity of the idea of late Shakespeare for late work by subsequent writers (notably, James and Conrad). In the course of his analysis, he addresses subjects from gerontology to anti-Stratfordianism and from art history to eschatology, highlighting the negotiations required to sustain the discourse of lateness and demonstrating the ongoing productivity of 'late Shakespeare' for the self-fashioning of actors, directors and critics. In the process, he offers the first full critique of the idea of late style, which will be of interest not only to literature specialists but also to art historians and musicologists and to anyone curious about the relationship of creativity to old age and death.

GORDON MCMULLAN is Professor of Shakespeare and Early Modern Drama at King's College London. He taught at the University of Newcastle from 1989, moving to King's in 1995. He has been a Leverhulme Fellow (2002–3) and has held visiting fellowships at the Huntington Library, the University of Newcastle NSW, and the Humanities Research Centre of the Australian National University. His books include *The Politics of Unease in the Plays of John Fletcher* (1994), the Arden Shakespeare edition of *Henry VIII* and *Reading the Medieval in Early Modern England* (co-edited with David Matthews, Cambridge, 2007). A founding general editor of Arden Early Modern Drama, he has acted as textual consultant to RSC productions and has spoken about Shakespeare and theatre on BBC radio.

SHAKESPEARE AND THE IDEA OF LATE WRITING

Authorship in the Proximity of Death

GORDON McMULLAN

CAMBRIDGE UNIVERSITY PRESS
Cambridge, New York, Melbourne, Madrid, Cape Town, Singapore,
São Paulo, Delhi, Dubai, Tokyo, Mexico City

Cambridge University Press
The Edinburgh Building, Cambridge CB2 8RU, UK

Published in the United States of America by Cambridge University Press, New York

www.cambridge.org
Information on this title: www.cambridge.org/9780521158008

© Gordon McMullan 2007

This publication is in copyright. Subject to statutory exception
and to the provisions of relevant collective licensing agreements,
no reproduction of any part may take place without the written
permission of Cambridge University Press.

First published 2007
Reprinted 2009
First paperback edition 2010

A catalogue record for this publication is available from the British Library

ISBN 978-0-521-86304-9 Hardback
ISBN 978-0-521-15800-8 Paperback

Cambridge University Press has no responsibility for the persistence or
accuracy of URLs for external or third-party internet websites referred to in
this publication, and does not guarantee that any content on such websites is,
or will remain, accurate or appropriate.

*In memory of
Sasha Roberts (1966–2006),
Shakespearean and salsa dancer*

Contents

Acknowledgements		*page* ix
Introduction		1
1	Shakespeare and the idea of late writing: authorship in the proximity of death	24
	1.1 *La dernière période*	24
	1.2 Late style in the wake of war: Neumann, Broch, Adorno	32
	1.3 The shapes of lateness	42
	1.4 Late Shakespeare	50
	1.5 Shakespeare and the idea of late writing	60
2	The Shakespearean caesura: genre, chronology, style	65
	2.1 A question of genre	66
	2.2 A question of chronology	78
	2.3 A question of style	104
3	The invention of late Shakespeare: subjectivism and its discontents	127
	3.1 'Dramatick perfection': Malone and the establishment of a chronology	128
	3.2 Inventing late Shakespeare from Coleridge to Dowden	136
	3.3 The backlash: (post)subjectivism from Strachey to Bond	160
	3.4 'A certain mastery': Henry James and the elusive late Shakespeare	168
4	Last words/late plays: the possibility and impossibility of late Shakespeare in early modern culture and theatre	190
	4.1 Premodern endings	193
	4.2 The Shakespearean swan song	202
	4.3 Last words	215
	4.4 Late style and the conditions of theatrical production in early modern London	225

5 How old is 'late'? Late Shakespeare, old age, *King Lear*   259
   5.1 Old-age style   260
   5.2 Old-age style without old age   271
   5.3 Shakespeare's middle years   284
   5.4 'I have a journey, sir, shortly to go': *King Lear* as a late play   294
   5.5 Kings and desperate men   314

6 *The Tempest* and the uses of late Shakespeare in the theatre: Gielgud, Rylance, Prospero   318
   6.1 Theatre of complicity   320
   6.2 Lateness and the mid-life crisis   327
   6.3 Performing late selfhood: Gielgud, Prospero, Shakespeare   331
   6.4 Authorship and authenticity: Rylance, Prospero, Shakespeare   337
   6.5 Postscript: late style in Australia: Bell, Prospero, Shakespeare   350

Notes   354
Index   394

Acknowledgements

I have been fortunate, writing this book, both in the friends who encouraged me and in the institutions that supported me. Successive heads of the Department of English at King's College London – John Stokes, Ann Thompson and Clare Lees – have endorsed my requests for research leave, thereby prompting the generosity of four institutions: King's itself; the Leverhulme Trust, which gave me an invaluable period of sustained library time at the outset; the Arts and Humanities Research Council, which funded a crucial semester's leave at the end; and the Humanities Research Centre at the Australian National University in Canberra, which offered the perfect writing environment. I'd like also to thank librarians in three places: the National Library of Australia in Canberra; the Folger Shakespeare Library in Washington DC, where in a visit of a few days I benefited from the advice of Georgianna Ziegler and Erin Blake; and the incomparable British Library in St Pancras, especially Barbara Ryglowska and the staff in Rare Books, the venue for the bulk of my work on this project.

My individual debts are substantial and I hope the reader will forgive a lengthy set of acknowledgements. First of all, I'd like to thank Sarah Stanton at Cambridge University Press, who has been magnificently supportive throughout, coping calmly with RAE-induced angst. I want too to thank the anonymous readers for the Press for their support and also Rosemary Williams for her precise and generous copy-editing. I'd also like to thank colleagues both at King's – Clare Brant, Richard Kirkland, Alan Marshall, Clare Pettitt, Max Saunders, Ishtla Singh, Anna Snaith, Mark Turner, Shamoon Zamir and, above all, Sonia Massai – and at other University of London colleges – Tim Armstrong, Rachael Gilmour, Helen Hackett, Tom Healy and Sue Wiseman – for their patience in face of my tendency to turn all conversations into seminars on late style. And I'd like especially to thank Richard Proudfoot, who poured out valuable suggestions. I also wish to thank colleagues elsewhere who listened to versions of chapters, especially at Keele University (where I spoke on Julie Sanders's invitation) and also at the Universities of Cambridge, Melbourne, Nevada at Reno, Newcastle, Newcastle NSW, Oxford, Queensland, St Andrews, Sussex, Sydney and Tasmania. Ceri Sullivan e-mailed regularly with ideas and moral support. Juliane Wünsch provided translations of German material on late style. Bettina Schergaut, Clare McManus, Howard Marchitello, Sam Smiles and Jim Shapiro read chunks of the final draft and gave advice: naturally, I blame them for every error that remains. I'm grateful, too, to the following: Katherine Baxter, A. R. Braunmuller, Martin Butler, Tom Cain, Kate Chedgzoy, Warren Chernaik, Chris Clark, Marilyn Corrie, Line Cottegnies, Nicky Cotton, Anisha Dasgupta, Allison Deutermann, Tim Dolin, Gareth Edwards, Keir Elam, Markman Ellis, Ruth Evans, Jennifer Forsyth, Michael Gamer, Anne Goldgar, Susan Green, Paul Hamilton, Judith Hawley, Philip Horne, Alice Hunt, J. Paul Hunter, Annie Janowitz, David Johnson, John Jowett, Margaret Kean, M. J. Kidnie, James Knowles, Courtney Lehmann, Sara Lodge, Raphael Lyne, Gail Marshall, Sermin Meskill, Glenn Most, Subha Mukherji, Irene Musumeci, Kate Newey, Ladan Niayesh, Michelle O'Callaghan, Francis O'Gorman, Kevin de Ornellas, Simon Palfrey, Mike Pincombe, Adrian Poole, Bryony Randall, Sophie Ratcliffe, Kellie Robertson, Miri Rubin, Lacy Rumsey, Marie Rutkoski, Jim Shapiro, Cathy Shrank, Catherine Silverstone, Boika Sokolova, Patrick Spottiswoode, Adam Steinhouse, Alison Stenton, Emma Sutton, Gary Taylor, Suzanne Trill, John Watkins, Valerie Wayne and George Younge. Peter Holland and Stephen Orgel kindly invited me to speak at one of their Huntington theatre-history conferences, where Roy Ritchie was his usual vastly hospitable self. Russ McDonald generously let me read *Shakespeare's Late Style* in typescript. Margreta de Grazia went out of her way to help me secure funding for the last months of writing. In 2003, I examined a PhD thesis on the late plays by Jonathan Hartwell of the Shakespeare Institute and I would like to record my debt to his extraordinary endnotes and bibliography. And if it hadn't been for David Bergeron's superb teaching on the 'Late Shakespeare' course I took when on a graduate exchange programme at the University of Kansas in 1984–5, I would surely never have written this book.

I would like to offer warm thanks too to Ian Donaldson and his colleagues in Canberra, especially Caroline Turner and also Leena Messina and Judy Buchanan, for their hospitality during my time as a Visiting Research Fellow at the HRC in winter 2006. I hugely appreciated conversations there with my fellow fellows and especially with Tim Duff and Ann Jones. Particular thanks go to Kylie Message for tolerating my wittering about rosellas and currawongs and to Alison Procter for the fish song and that roo. Thanks also to Kate Flaherty, Penny Gay, John Potts, Jeni Porter and Mitchell Dean in Sydney; Rohan Mead, Tania de Jong, Paul Salzman, Stephanie Trigg, Joel Trigg and Mark Williams in Melbourne; and Philip, Jenna and Sylvia Mead in Hobart.

My mother, Muriel McMullan, has had to be very patient with me while this book was in progress, as has my aunt, Hilda Brooks, a talent they have both spent the last forty-five years honing. I may not always succeed in showing them that I'm grateful, but I am.

Julia Banister made the late phase of this book far more fun than it should have been.

In loose given-name alphabetical order, thanks must also go to Allison Sneider for chardonnay in Houston; to Amanda, Adrian and Louis O'Callaghan for greyhounds and (finally) Cru; to Bernhard Klein for Augustiner and that game at the Westfalenstadion; to Bettina Schergaut for TWA; to Clara Calvo for flamingoes and de Lempicka; to Clare McManus for Anfield tickets and faith in Rafa and Stevie G; to David Kastan (and to Jane and Marina) for Forest and Fino; to David Matthews (who detests verbose acknowledgements sections) and Anke Bernau for FMCs above Canal Street; to Emily Wade for kayaking in Austin and that tan suitcase in DC; to Eric Rasmussen for sixty-one lunchbags and lunch at *Le Manoir*; to Farah Karim-Cooper for tapas and for being the perfect collaborator on the King's/Globe MA; to Gill Plain and James McKinna for coping with the espresso explosion; to Lynne Vallone and Howard Marchitello for blue birds, green snakes and G&Ts; to Ina Habermann and to Bernhard and David for silent storms, leech-gatherers and Faugères; to Jane Kingsley-Smith for helping me distinguish varieties of wren; to Jonathan Hope and Jennifer Smith for getting the tides right off Campbeltown; to Jonathan Sawday and Ruth Evans for Whitsundays sailing; to Karl Horton and Naomi Fiss for smoked salt, Zuni and (controversially) atavism (grim); to Larry Scanlon for Complete Moral Collapse; to Lucy Munro for B&F at the White Bear; to Paula de Pando, who lives in Triana, where it never rains, for the best bread-and-butter in the world; to Peter and Annie Holbrook for dinner at Anise and lunch in New Farm; to Peter Shaw and Michael Croft for a bottle of 'Bonzo' and for Michael's glorious cooking (I did mention Stravinsky, Peter, so you won't have to 'tweak my academic nose'); to Rohan Mead and Tania de Jong for shacks and shells on the Mornington Peninsula; to Sam Smiles for guiding me through the minefield; to Sonia Massai for transforming life on the

Strand (and to Cosimo Pacciani for Fiorentina and a *bistecca alla fiorentina*); to Suzanne and Philip Gossett for *Boris Godunov* in Florence, *La Clemenza di Tito* in Sydney and *saltimbocca* on the Via Panisperna; to Tiffany Stern for Glyndebourne, Rex Stout and this book's structure; and, unalphabetically, to Roxy Beaujolais and her staff (especially Terry and also Tom Paine) for making The Seven Stars ('Because they are not eight') the best pub in London.

What a sociable book it turned out to be.

London and Canberra, 2001–2006

Introduction

This was the fatal period of that virtuous fabric.[1]

More are men's ends marked than their lives before.[2]

In his mischievous essay, '*Tempest* in a Teapot', Tony Dawson draws attention to the stories that are told about the end of Shakespeare's career and to the reductive effect these stories invariably have.[3] He announces without preamble that he thinks *The Tempest* 'Shakespeare's most consistently overrated play' ('*Tempest* in a Teapot', 61) and points out that this is a direct result of the play's privileged position as the last Shakespeare wrote, that in view of 'the importance of chronology in the assessment of Shakespeare's plays' the fact that *The Tempest* 'comes at the end of Shakespeare's career means that it will be read retrospectively, as climactic' (ibid., 61). Resisting this tendency, he points both to the actual absence of evidence for determining which of the three plays *Cymbeline*, *The Winter's Tale* and *The Tempest*, all apparently written in 1610 or 1611, was truly the last of Shakespeare's solo-written plays and to the tactics critics deploy in order to ensure that, of the three, it is *The Tempest* which retains that status by default, thereby sustaining the standard assumption that the play is intrinsically autobiographical. He notes that *Cymbeline*, for one, is often treated – on a purely impressionistic basis – 'as an apprentice work in comparison with *The Winter's Tale* and *The Tempest*' and is therefore 'seen usually as written earlier than they', an entirely imaginary priority constructed simply because, as Dawson puts it, 'we do not like to imagine *Cymbeline* as Shakespeare's last complete play' (ibid., 62). And he offers an alternative vision of the end of Shakespeare's career, helpfully providing a page or two of anxious dialogue between Hemmings and Condell by way of support and asking

what is wrong with imagining Shakespeare's career trailing off, going from bad to worse, from *The Tempest* to *Cymbeline* and parts of *Henry VIII*, before being judiciously terminated by his worried partners in The King's Men, who perhaps asked young Fletcher to do what he could to make the old master's new texts acceptable to their increasingly perplexed audiences? (ibid., 62–3)[4]

Having posed the question, he provides the obvious answer: 'Well, we all *know* what is wrong with thinking this way – we have too great an investment (personal, academic, and ideological) to make it desirable' (ibid., 63).

That investment, I wish to argue, is made not only in *The Tempest* or in the plays known collectively as 'late Shakespeare' but in the overarching idea underpinning claims that certain creative artists have a distinguishable 'late phase' or 'late period' at the end of their careers, and in the privileged place that the idea of late writing occupies in the critical imagination. It is important to be aware that when we refer to Shakespeare's last romances or tragicomedies as his 'late plays' and to his final playwriting years as his 'late phase', we are neither simply affirming chronology nor rehearsing an understanding of the creative process that would have been familiar to Shakespeare himself. Nor, again, are we working on a premise applicable only to the study of Shakespeare. We are, rather, invoking a general history of critical analysis, a history that starts with the establishment of style as the organic product not of an epoch but of the life and will of a given artist. This organic understanding of style, which emerged from the biological thought of certain German Romantic philosophers and which transformed critical attitudes in the early nineteenth century, continues to provide the basic foundation of everyday thinking about creativity even now, despite the best efforts of poststructuralism and postmodernism to dislodge it. The field that received the initial impact of this new understanding of the work of art was not, as it happens, literary criticism but musicology, and it was almost immediately (if stutteringly and locally to begin with) that the idea of the 'late work' began to emerge as a way to make sense of the last compositions of certain composers – principally, to begin with, Beethoven and Mozart. The fundamental change wrought by Romantic philosophy was the assertion of a direct connection between the progress of the artist's life and of that artist's style from youth to maturity. The invention of late style was, and remains, supplementary to this vision of the creative life – supplementary, that is, both in the straightforward sense of 'additional' and in the slightly more elusive deconstructive sense in which, by claiming finally to complete something previously considered complete, the supplement demonstrates the impossibility of completion. But it is at the same time central to that vision, because the artist's late period is held to fulfil the cycle or to endorse the trajectory (depending on the metaphor deployed) of the extraordinary creative life. As such, rather than being of merely peripheral interest, the idea of late style is in fact synecdochic of the biographical urge in general, and any critique of late style must therefore also involve a critique of the central place biography still occupies in the critical process.

Wilfully, I will indulge in a little life-writing of my own. I first began to address the idea of late style when I was asked, a little over a decade ago, if I would be interested in editing *Henry VIII* for the Arden Shakespeare series. *Henry VIII* (or *All is True*, as it was known when first performed) offers, as I was already aware, a classic instance of the anxiety of the supplement. Postdating *The Tempest*, it was in all likelihood the penultimate play in which Shakespeare had a hand, first performed in June 1613 and responsible – through the misfiring of a cannon that was to mark the King's entrance to a banquet – for burning down the first Globe theatre, the original 'Shakespeare's Globe', in an event described in humorously eschatological terms by the courtly gossip Sir Henry Wotton. 'This was the fatal period of that virtuous fabric', he noted, tongue a fair way into cheek, 'wherein yet nothing did perish but wood and straw, and a few forsaken cloaks; only one man had his breeches set on fire, that would perhaps have broiled him, if he had not by the benefit of a provident wit put it out with bottle ale' (Wotton, *Letters*, 2: 33). *Henry VIII* is thus in several disconnected ways a 'late play'. It is a play which verges on the end of things, marking a moment of dissolution that is both personal and institutional and thus, finally, eschatological. It is also, curiously, a play which, despite the various reports of the burning down of the Globe and its central place in that event, leaves surprisingly little trace of its existence, in Shakespearean criticism at least. Tracking its critical history in order to construct an introduction for my edition, I found myself becoming increasingly frustrated by the play's absence from books both on Shakespeare's history plays and on his late plays. The former omission I felt I could understand (although that didn't stop it irritating me): postdating the previous Shakespearean history play, *Henry V*, by fourteen years and entirely out of rhythm with it and with the other plays dramatising an historical sovereign's reign, *Henry VIII* has generally appealed even less to critics than has *King John*, the other Shakespearean history play generally considered three companion-pieces short of a tetralogy. Nineteenth-century critics tended to assume that both plays were written at the same time in the wake of the major historical cycles as a kind of double afterthought, and they still tend to be treated, at least tacitly, as displaced and somewhat dysfunctional twins. The Signet Shakespeare edition, for instance (like the Garland collection of critical essays on the plays), bundles these two belated histories together as no-hopers between a single set of artistically underwhelming covers.

The omission of *Henry VIII* from books on the history plays was, then, relatively understandable. Its concomitant omission from books on the late plays, on the other hand, seemed to me to be thoroughly baffling. Why, I wondered, when they address Shakespeare's final years, do critics (with a few honourable exceptions, but only a few) focus solely on the four plays dating from 1608 to 1611 – that is, *Pericles*, *The Winter's Tale*, *Cymbeline* and *The Tempest* (and often, in fact, on only three of these, casting *Pericles* adrift) – and not the two (or three) plays that postdate them – *Henry VIII*, *Cardenio* (lost but perhaps not wholly irrecoverable) and *The Two Noble Kinsmen*? It seemed clear that this selectivity was not arbitrary, that there were in fact several explanations, each of which had a distinct bearing on the overarching idea of 'late work'. First, there was, as Dawson has reminded us, the matter of the privileged status of *The Tempest* in the minds of critics as Shakespeare's self-consciously 'last' play. Second, there was the difficulty critics still have in coming to terms with the notion of Shakespearean collaboration, since each of the post-*Tempest* plays is demonstrably co-written. And third, there were the problems these plays present, being in various ways noticeably different from their immediate predecessors, for any attempt to offer a clearcut, overarching definition of 'late Shakespeare'. Even critics apparently uncomfortable with the premises of subjectivism – by which I mean readings that assume a direct relationship between the state of mind of the author at a given moment and the nature of his output at that moment – persisted in an unspoken sentimental belief that *The Tempest* represents Shakespeare's valedictory gesture, his 'farewell to the stage', reading Prospero as the playwright's *alter ego*. Any play that postdated *The Tempest*, therefore, was considered *de trop*, in frankly poor taste, as unappealing as an ageing pop star's comeback tour. Moreover, the collaborative authorship of these plays – *Pericles* written with George Wilkins, *Cardenio*, *Henry VIII* and *The Two Noble Kinsmen* with John Fletcher – created severe and specific problems for subjectivism. After all, if you don't know which line was written by which playwright, how can you reach useful biographical conclusions? And, in any case, how can a play actually be a *late* play if it is also, for one of its two authors, an *early* play (as is the case with the Fletcher collaborations)? These are not comfortable questions for anyone keen to sustain the idea of late Shakespeare and they are therefore customarily ducked.

As I worked on *Henry VIII*, then, I became increasingly aware that it is impossible to separate 'late Shakespeare' from a certain supra-individual conception of lateness, universal in supposed scope but vaguely defined and contradictory – a conception which seemed to me to a certain extent both to produce and to be produced by the idea of a specifically *Shakespearean* lateness. The idea of late writing or late style was created neither by nor for Shakespeare: it emerged in the first instance, I suggest, within musicology and was only later applied to literary texts and to fine art (though this statement should be qualified with reference to Vasari's account of the style of Titian's last paintings, to which I will return). But it undoubtedly developed, at least in anglophone culture, quite specifically by way both of critical accounts of Shakespeare's later career and of the tendency of subsequent writers self-consciously to look to Shakespeare for precedents for their own late work. The idea of 'late Shakespeare', in other words, contributed to the establishment of what I will call a *discourse of lateness* – that is, a construct, ideological, rhetorical and heuristic, a function not of life or of art but of the practice of reading or appreciating certain texts within a set of predetermined parameters. The history of Shakespearean criticism foregrounds the attribution to late style of the status of a kind of apotheosis, an almost mystical seal attached to the life of a genius, and readings and appropriations of the late plays continue to provide instances both of the persistence of lateness as a controlling concept in the contemporary default understanding of the creative process and of the utility of the established understanding of Shakespearean lateness for the construction by others of modern and postmodern creative selfhoods. I aim here both to chart the construction of the idea of a Shakespearean late phase and its impact on subsequent models of lateness and to demonstrate the inadequacy of the idea of late style as a means of understanding a group of plays created in the conditions of early modern English professional theatre. By situating a particular set of late works in their historical and institutional context and by assessing the limitations of our current understanding of the function of the word 'late' in the phrase 'late style', I hope to offer a case study for a critique of the overarching, interdisciplinary concept.

My subject, then, is late style; my exemplar Shakespeare. And the question I wish to ask is this. What difference does it make to think about late Shakespeare in the context of the general understanding of late style?

Before I proceed, however, I wish to make a few matters clear. First and foremost, I want to emphasise that this is not a book about Shakespeare's late plays. It is, rather, a book about a particular critical *idea* of Shakespeare's late plays and, by extension, about the late work of a highly select cohort of writers, artists and composers who have come to be considered geniuses. It is, in other words, a reception history, an account of the process through which a group of plays came to be understood in certain ways, not a critical assessment that addresses them one by one in the classic manner, relying on close analysis for support in the development of a reading of those plays. I may one day write that book, but this is not it. In any case, in its function as a critique of the persistent determination of Shakespeareans to read the work through the unfolding of the life, this book need not, in a sense, be about the late plays at all. It could equally easily be a book about readings of Shakespeare's early comedies as apprentice works – there is, as Kenneth Clark once argued, 'nothing more mysterious than the power of an aged artist to give life to a blot or scribble; it is as inexplicable as the power of a young poet to give life to a word' – or of his major tragedies as instances of the maturity of a great writer.[5] It could, in other words be a book about any given set of plays as they are assessed in relation to the period of the playwright's life in which they were written. That said, the idea of late writing brings with it certain resonances which make it an especially productive object of critical attention – more so, arguably, than either 'early work' or 'mature work' – for a study of this kind, resonances which cover a lot of ground both spiritual and material, from teleology to gerontology, from theatre history to connoisseurship. But, principally, the idea of late writing offers a critical focus for our persistent belief in genius, for our insistence on the centrality of biography to critical analysis, and thus for the way we treat the relationship between creator and creation in all fields of artistic endeavour, enabling us to examine the interaction between an artist's work and the conditions within which the artistic career is achieved, and to assess the extent to which the artist in question is able to determine his or her future reputation and thus dictate to posterity.

My second caveat is that this is not a book about style. Or, rather, it is not a book that offers sustained stylistic analyses of the Shakespearean (or any other) late work. I have been unusually fortunate in the writing of this book that my work has run alongside that of Russ McDonald on his *Shakespeare's Late Style* and I am indebted to his detailed and precise account of the technicalities of that style. I have chosen the term 'late writing' in my title rather than 'late style' per se because it seems to me that the concept of lateness, though grounded in assumptions about poetic or painterly style, is by no means limited to questions of stylistics and I wish to make this apparent. Shakespeare's last plays unquestionably mark a change in style, one which McDonald describes closely and which is in various ways different from his former styles – though it is not as uniform and consistent a style as some would wish, and it comes under considerable pressure as soon as more plays than the 'central' three (or four) are acknowledged as constituents of 'late Shakespeare'. My interest, however, lies primarily not with the minutiae of that style as it emerges but with the way in which the recognition of a stylistic shift in late Shakespeare stems from, and to a certain extent produces, an overarching understanding of late style as transcending time and place. I wish, in other words, to analyse the way in which certain habits of pen or mind have, through a process of critical construction over time, metamorphosed into a transhistorical, transcultural phenomenon.

Thirdly, in the context of questions of close reading and of stylistic analysis, it is perhaps worth stating immediately that this book is not a contribution to the so-called 'new formalism'. By this I do not mean, I should point out, that I object to close reading as a fundamental procedure in the interpretation of texts – on the contrary, close reading remains for me an essential first step for any historical, material or cultural reading – though this book, as I have noted, happens to offer little in the way of close readings of plays. Rather I refer to the tendency in recent years of certain critics, mostly in the United States, capitalising both upon the ebbing of the tide of New Historicism and upon certain received notions about the late plays as highly aestheticised works, to deploy those plays in order to make large and retrograde claims for the ahistoricity of art. This book sets out to demonstrate the contingency both of creative work and of such claims. It is highly unfortunate for the late plays that, for reasons I will in due course examine, they have become directly associated with the aesthetic at the expense of the historical. Criticism over the last twenty or so years, kickstarted in the mid-eighties by postcolonial readings of *The Tempest*, has worked hard to redress that balance, situating the late plays in their ideological and material contexts and demonstrating the various ways in which traditional formalist assumptions about the plays, about their underlying serenity and their essential or theological qualities, elided a wide range of political complexities and severities. At the same time, however, New Historicist criticism – followed in the late nineties by analyses of the affective qualities of early modern theatre – perhaps unwittingly sustained the aesthetic associations of the late plays by dwelling on the sense of wonder that, it is held, is their controlling emotion.[6]

Partly as a result of this, the late plays have been particularly prominent in recent years as exemplary texts for the exponents of what has become known as the new formalism. In readings of this kind, the plays become the embodiment of the purity of Shakespeare's engagement with high matters of style and emotion and thus serve as a bulwark against the philistine forces of materialist theory. This position, I would argue, has its roots in the idea of late style itself – in, for instance, Henry James's celebration of *The Tempest* as Shakespeare's 'high testimony to th[e] independent, absolute value of Style'.[7] The late plays are thus regularly detached from the material and institutional conditions in which they were produced and are presented instead as the direct manifestation of the author's mind at the point of particular clarity and perspective that is only achievable by certain artists at the very end of the journey. The word 'late' itself locates the plays strictly in their relationship to a particular authorial chronology, ignoring context. Thus our persistence in reading these plays as 'late plays' can provide an opening for the reversal of much that has been gained in the understanding of early modern drama through the turn to history and to materiality. Failure fully to interrogate the given of lateness – to understand the origins of the association of these plays with transcendence and essentialism – opens the plays up to analyses that use them as a stalking horse for attacks on a swathe of valuable developments in criticism in the late twentieth and early twenty-first century.[8] They deserve better, frankly.

I wish to offer a fourth caveat – addressing one of the most sensitive issues with which a student of late style is obliged to engage – by stating right away that this is not a book about writing in old age. It has become very clear to me in the course of writing this book that many people have a deep-seated belief in the special quality of late work, particularly when it is defined as work produced in old age. When, over the course of the last four or five years, I have discussed the question of late style with others, my interlocutors have often been happy enough for me to explain the problems I have with the idea of late Shakespeare, but they have tended to draw the line when I turn to the work of their favourite ageing artist or composer and suggest the inadequacy of the idea for understanding those works, or when I suggest that the larger concept of lateness is itself a critical construct. I can understand this very readily. After all, a great deal of the pleasure I have had in writing this book has been in discovering for the first time for myself some of the profoundly accomplished and moving works produced by artists, composers and writers in old age: Rembrandt's overwhelming *Lucretia* in the Minneapolis Institute of Art, say (which kept me transfixed when I should probably have been attending papers at the Shakespeare Association conference that had brought me to Minnesota), or Strauss's magnificent *Four Last Songs* as sung by Elisabeth Schwarzkopf (to which I was first directed by Jonathan Dollimore) or, in an entirely different location and tradition, the remarkable works of art produced, in an eight-year period beginning when she was seventy-eight, by the Aboriginal artist Emily Kame Kngwarreye (in particular, the abstract and diffuse paintings of the 'Last Series', introduced to me in Canberra by Caroline Turner). These are truly astonishing works of art and their status is unquestioned: it is what is *said* about them as exemplars of a perceived transhistorical phenomenon that at times can be debatable.

Clearly, for creative artists in any genre, old age can produce a profound concentration, an intense focus of attention and a tendency to look back over the career that preceded, and enabled the particular form of, that attention, and it is undeniable that work produced in old age frequently embodies certain characteristics. Robert Butler's notion of the life review, for instance, 'in which older people feel forced to confront the ghosts of their past in order to make peace with themselves', is a useful point of reference for critical studies of work produced in old age.[9] In this book, though, I focus not on these characteristics per se but on the accretions and associations superimposed upon them, on the conflation of the idea of an 'old-age style' with the broader category of late style – that is, with work produced at the end of the artistic life *at whatever age* – and on the underlying assumption of universal application that seems always to characterise analyses of late work, preferring to examine rather than to elide the impact of contingencies and complicities on the ascription of a late style. In other words, my interest lies in the construction of the myth of late style and in the impact of that myth on the work of a writer, not in the nature of creativity in old age. Others have written and are writing specifically about old-age style and about the interrelations of gerontology and criticism, and although I will touch on that work in Chapter 5, it is not my intention in this book directly to work within the field of humanistic gerontology as delineated by Thomas Cole, Robert Kastenbaum and Ruth Ray in their *Handbook of the Humanities and Aging*.[10] Nevertheless, it seems to me that Kathleen Woodward is right when she claims that the repression of ageing is an intrinsic component of contemporary western culture, and I would argue that the concept of late style is designed less to celebrate than to *deny* the difference represented by old age and to substitute for it a myth of synchrony, a projection of a transcendent late style that is the same for all supreme creative artists at all times, opening up access for a handful of geniuses to a world of archetypes beyond history and chronology, which has nothing to do with the ageing process.

My critical scepticism, then, is directed not at certain celebrated works produced in old age but rather at the overarching metaphysical category said to tie them together (and to tie them to certain works produced at the ends of creative lives where the artists in question did not live into old age) and at the process through which that category is applied in ways that, I would argue, obfuscate rather than illuminate the achievements of ageing artists. Late style is precisely *not* limited to writing in old age, and in Chapter 5 I will suggest a series of ways in which *Altersstil* and *Spätstil* (the canonical German terms for 'old-age style' and 'late style') are by no means synonymous. It seems to me, on the contrary, essential to distinguish between 'old-age style' and 'late style' because the importance accorded to late work is not always the product of a privileging of old age per se (even the old age of a genius) but rather of a celebration of a particular liminality – of, that is, the proximity of death. Late work is, in other words, borderline activity, a creative response to death, a kind of eschatology. Since death does not always wait patiently for old age, the significance of late work can be said to lie in its primary relationship to death, not in its contingent relationship to old age, and the attribution of a late period to an artist who dies in middle age or even in late youth causes distinct problems for any attempt to equate 'late style' and 'old-age style'. Moreover, the late phase is something attributed by critics only to a very few creative artists, a limited handful of acknowledged geniuses. Death comes to all of us; old age to most; a late phase – in the sense in which it has been applied to composers, artists and writers – to very few indeed.

This is not, then, a book written about or against old age. That said, it is a book about a topic more often than not discussed, understandably enough, by critics late in life. Edward Said is the most recent instance, concluding his career with a book on endings as he began it with one on beginnings, and celebrating in particular the resistant strain in late writing, writing that refuses to go gently into the night. It would seem self-evident that someone who has lived a long time and experienced a long career has the potential for greater empathy with a creative artist at the end of life than does someone only a certain way along that road. But personal engagement of this kind has disadvantages as well as advantages. Whichever stage of life you discuss (and this seems especially true of the end of life), you are bound to feel as if you understand it better when you inhabit it yourself – 'That is why,' Havelock Ellis said of Michelangelo, 'his later work fascinates us endlessly as, slowly, after many years, enlightened by the long course of our own experience, we begin at last to understand what it means' – yet you are also likely to identify with it in a way that may well make you complicit in its construction and in the elisions it effects.'[11] It is perhaps predictable that C. J. Sisson, best known for his mocking attack on biographical readings of Shakespeare in a British Academy lecture of 1934, should ease gradually away from the hardline position he had adopted at the age of forty-nine to a softer stance at sixty-five (when he described his earlier attack as an 'extreme of resistance') and then to what was in effect a wholesale retraction right at the end of his life: Samuel Schoenbaum cites a late unpublished lecture in which Sisson writes that it 'is a poor, cool, and distant critical embrace of literature that forgets, or ignores, the life-blood of a man that runs through the veins of his created works', thereby implicitly criticising his younger self.[12] By contrast, one of the very best and most clear-eyed essays on lateness, that of Catherine Soussloff on late Bernini, was written by an assistant professor at the outset of her career.[13] As far as the present book is concerned, I should state that I drafted this preface at the age of forty-three, which might perhaps, for some, make any attempt on my part to write authoritatively on the subject of late style somewhat questionable. This may well be true, but I feel obliged to point out that forty-three happens also to have been Shakespeare's age when he wrote *Pericles*, the first of his so-called 'late plays'. Whether this coincidence helps or hinders my understanding of lateness, this book's readers will have to decide for themselves.[14]

I am of course performing here a standard act of critical iconoclasm, the kind of manoeuvre rehearsed repeatedly in cultural studies over the last half-century, in noting and assessing the contradictions both in a particular critical concept treated as transhistorical and transcultural and in the application of that concept to the work of a canonical writer. And like all analyses of this kind, my reading opens itself up to an obvious critique: that in focussing on a canonical artist and on a concept applied only to canonical artists across the range of genres, I am myself part of the industry that produces and sustains the canon. I can't deny this. But the fact is that late style – and this is one of the principal reasons for the oblique relationship this study bears to the field of literary gerontology, which by definition seeks the characteristic features of *all* writing produced in old age, not just an atypical fraction – is an élite concept, a way of distinguishing a creative elect, and it is therefore impossible to analyse the concept outside the framework of the most rigorously restrictive and exclusive of canons. This does not entail acceptance of such a canon or of the premises for the formation of that canon, and I hope my scepticism about the value and applicability of the classic concept of late style will defend me from any such charge. On the contrary, my work fits, I hope, with that of others sceptical about the shaping of Shakespeare as author – Margreta de Grazia on canon-construction, Jeffrey Masten on collaboration, Jonathan Bate on genius – and my immediate influences run from Barbara Hodgdon's exemplary refusal, in *The End Crowns All*, to separate performance studies from literary criticism, via Samuel Schoenbaum's seminal work on the varying shapes given to Shakespeare's life by biographers (it is impossible to work on this topic without ending up repeating Schoenbaum almost verbatim in places), to the considerable impact on our understanding of specifically theatrical authorship of work on the early modern repertory by Roslyn Knutson, Scott McMillin and Sally-Beth MacLean, Mary Bly and, most recently, Lucy Munro. I also touch on the debate over Shakespeare's 'literariness' recently reignited by Lukas Erne's fine book *Shakespeare as Literary Dramatist*, work which includes, *inter alia*, Patrick Cheney's series of monographs on the self-conscious construction of authorship by early modern canonical writers, the most recent being an account of Shakespeare. This work demonstrates a range of possibilities for writerly self-consciousness in early modern England and I have learned a great deal from it about the place of theatre in relation to inherited ideas of artistic self-fashioning, an issue I discuss in Chapter 4. At the same time, my discussion here will, I hope, give a moment's pause to those who are tempted to take Erne's book – as Erne himself does not wish to do – as support for the (re)construction of an untheatrical Shakespeare.

I find it curious that – despite recent developments in the humanistic study of ageing – nobody has yet produced a comprehensive critique of the idea of late style. This book, I should hastily add, is not that comprehensive account. It is, rather, a preliminary and fragmentary investigation into and meditation upon the idea of 'late style' or 'late work' as it has been deployed in the criticism of one representative instance of late writing. Still, if there is no ur-text on this topic, certain critical works inevitably assume prominence in the thinking of anyone engaged with questions of late style. Laurence Lipking's *The Life of the Poet* and Michael Millgate's *Testamentary Acts* are notable instances, each addressing aspects of literary lateness in a way that is highly productive for their successors. Kenneth Clark's *The Artist Grows Old* is, of course, a landmark moment in the assessment of old-age style in the field of art. Kenneth Muir's *Last Periods of Shakespeare, Racine and Ibsen* and David Grene's *Reality and the Heroic Pattern: Last Plays of Ibsen, Shakespeare, and Sophocles* serve as classic statements of late style as a transhistorical phenomenon. An implicit underpinning to the kind of work I am performing here, it almost goes without saying, is Frank Kermode's *The Sense of an Ending*, in which he articulates the larger picture into which the study of late style inevitably fits (though he offers relatively little of specific interest to the Shakespearean, writing as he does for the most part about fiction and discussing Shakespeare only briefly and the late plays not at all). And there is also, as I have mentioned already, Edward Said's late writing on the subject of late style, expounded in a series of reviews and articles before his death, and then published in its most extensive form in the posthumous *On Late Style*, which appeared as I was drafting this introduction.[15] Said's work on the subject is characteristically engaging and polemical, but it is not a critique of the idea of lateness: on the contrary, it is a celebration of a certain manifestation of lateness – lateness as difficult, irascible, resistant, unreconciled.

Lateness is an unusual concept in its deployment across the full range of disciplines in the humanities: highly influential in musicology, a little more quietly or uncertainly so in literary criticism, and perhaps most prominent of all in art history, and this breadth of application makes life hard for anyone working on the subject whose training lies, as most people's does, in a sub-branch of a single discipline. The concept of late style emerged, as I have noted, from early nineteenth-century German and French biographies of composers – Beethoven, mainly, but also (slightly bewilderingly) Mozart – and developed in part as a way to address the writing of the ageing Goethe. Art history, having in a sense – through Vasari's observations about the changes in Titian's painterly style in the latter stages of his life – initiated the whole thing, returned very late in the day but has subsequently engaged so extensively with late style as to make the concept effectively its own. Asked cold to name representative late stylists, people tend to come up with a longer list of painters than they do of writers or composers. Titian, Rembrandt and Turner are most frequently mentioned; Picasso, too, seems to fit the bill. Meanwhile, Beethoven remains the principal exemplar for musicologists, not only of late style in general but of late style viewed in a particular way as difficult, profound, an acquired taste, as (in Said's sense) resistant. Yet for a different understanding of lateness – the customary understanding, that is, of late work as serene, redemptive, spiritual – and for English and American *literary* history, which came a little belatedly to the table of lateness, the central figure is that of Shakespeare, the most apparently uncontroversial instance of a great writer with a classic late style. The absence of controversy about this is curious, bearing in mind the highly awkward and fractured relationship that exists between the specifics of late Shakespeare and the larger understanding of late style. It is that relationship that I take as my exemplar here.

This book is, then, by its nature, interdisciplinary, even as it remains very clearly not the work of an art historian or a musicologist but of a literary scholar with a specialism in early modern theatre. My understanding of the late plays depends, however, upon an awareness of the larger picture of late style, and it therefore necessitates my stepping regularly outside the immediate field of Shakespeare studies in order to make connections between the ways in which literary critics read late Shakespeare and those in which art historians read the late work of a painter such as Rembrandt or musicologists that of Beethoven. Much of the most productive material on late style, in any case, comes from beyond the borders of literary criticism. The recent and welcome Getty collection, *Late Thoughts*, edited by Karen Painter and Thomas Crow, for instance (which appeared just before the present book went to press), addresses questions of late style in music and art, but not in literature.[16] Art history is, it is clear, especially productive for the student of lateness. Apart from Clark's *The Artist Grows Old*, there is Hugo Munsterberg's later, more upbeat development of Clark's argument in *The Crown of Life*, as well as the exploratory 1987 issue of *Art Journal* dedicated to old-age style (in which Soussloff's essay on Bernini appeared) and an accumulating series of exhibitions and catalogues on the late work of Picasso, Titian, Klee, Goya and many others. Sam Smiles's work in progress on the development of the idea of late style in art history, *The Late Work of Artists*, promises to be the fullest account to date, taking Turner as its principal test case.[17] Musicologists, too, continue to produce accounts of the late styles of composers, recent instances of which include Joseph N. Straus's *Stravinsky's Late Music* and Maynard Solomon's acclaimed *Late Beethoven*, which are instructively different in their approaches to the same issue. Ian Bent's casually brilliant parenthetical explanations of the origins of style as an object of musicological study in Volume 1 of his *Music Analysis in the Nineteenth Century* made a great deal clear to me that had previously been anything but, and my debt will be obvious, most notably in Chapter 3.[18] As will be apparent almost immediately in Chapter 1, Theodor W. Adorno's fragmentary but hugely important essays on late Beethoven, in all their opaque, aphoristic and at times internally inconsistent brilliance, have made a profound and, at times, uncomfortable, impact, as they must on any analyst of late work. And Philip Gossett's forthcoming work on the contradictory ways in which commentators have understood the end of the life of Rossini promises to extend the debate in productive ways.[19]

Not that you need to be a professional art historian or musicologist to register the role of late style in the way in which creative careers are publicly represented. It has been almost impossible in Britain in recent years to go

Introduction 15

to an art exhibition that is not fundamentally monographic – constructed, that is, as a linear account of the career of an individual artist – and which does not inevitably conclude with a room displaying the 'late work' of that artist. The National Gallery's remarkable Titian exhibition in 2003 is a good case in point. From the wall labels, the visitor learned that '[b]y the 1560s Titian liked to emphasise, even exaggerate, his advanced years', that the 'blurred definition' of *Virgin and Child* (c. 1565–70) is 'typical of Titian's late painting style, which became remarkably free in his old age', that the 'slashed and bleeding tree trunks and lightly sketched foliage' of *St Jerome in Penitence* (1575) and the 'vigorous brushwork and expressive use of colour' of *Tarquin and Lucretia* (1571) are 'characteristic of Titian's remarkable late style', while at the same time 'Titian's very loose handling of the paint, particularly evident in the atmospheric forest landscape' in *The Death of Actaeon* (c. 1565–76) 'has prompted much debate as to whether this work is in fact finished'. All of these observations – even the last of them, which potentially undermines the premise – simply assume that Titian's late style is a fact rather than an interpretation, that a late style is something that can be definitively delineated.

Again, the centenary celebrations of both Mozart and Shostakovich on BBC Radio 3 in 2006 made clear to me how strong a guiding force the idea of late style remains in the public dissemination of classical music. Mozart's *Requiem*, of course, has a substantial recent history as an exemplar of late style in the shape of the mythologising work done by Peter Shaffer's *Amadeus*, both in the theatre and on screen. And one of the most moving concerts broadcast in the 2006 Shostakovich season was a performance by the Hallé Orchestra in Manchester of two magnificent, brooding (yet at times playful) late works, the Fifteenth (and last) Symphony, Op. 141, and the *Suite on Verses of Michelangelo*, Op. 145a, both described for the listener as instances of the composer's great late style. Listening to this concert made me realise that my own interest in lateness had in fact originally been piqued long before I began work on *Henry VIII* when, sitting in Liverpool's Philharmonic Hall as a gloom-obsessed fifteen-year-old, I first heard and loved the Michelangelo Verses – a doubly late work, since it was written not long before Shostakovich's death and is based on poems written by Michelangelo when he was in his eighties.[20] Two decades later, a reading of Said's *Musical Elaborations*, in which he touches on the debate over late Beethoven, struck a similar chord. Thinking about Said's writing about Adorno's writing about Beethoven, I came to realise that where Said (and Adorno) *believed* at a certain level in an overarching and perhaps transcendent concept of late style, I was – for all that I found instances of late work such as that of Shostakovich profoundly moving – more sceptical of the overall idea and wanted to investigate it more closely by way of the reception history of the writer on whom I am professionally most focussed. At the same time, even as I began to recognise the motivations for the writing of this book, I became increasingly aware that the self-consciousness of an autobiographical explanation of the kind I have so far been making is itself symptomatic of the problems I am addressing. If there is one inevitable outcome of work on late style, it would seem, that outcome is complicity – critical complicity with authorial self-fashioning, which itself becomes a kind of self-fashioning for the critic too. As with life-writing, then, so with the discourse of lateness: an account of late work is always also an account of the analyst of late work, at whatever stage of life that analyst has reached.

On one point, books on Shakespeare's late plays are agreed: that they are in fact *late* plays. In this book, by contrast, I ponder the word 'late' and its meanings and by extension question the critical assumption (mainly unspoken nowadays) that Shakespeare's late plays are instances of a transhistorical category known as 'late writing'. My argument, simply, is that while artists of the highest ability frequently (though by no means invariably) develop a new and striking style in their latter years, lateness as a critical category is a construct, not a given, and it is this construct, not the varied reality of late creativity, that has shaped the general understanding of late works. Late style is perhaps the last of the great overarching critical ideas to be brought before the jury of theoretical or posttheoretical scepticism, as a sub-category of, but nonetheless distinct from, the Romantic concept of Genius. Its origins, arguably, go right back to classical Greece and Rome, but it did not take recognisable form, as I have suggested, until the early nineteenth century, as a direct product of Romanticism's urge to root stylistic development in the life of the individual genius rather than in period and context. Thus while Shakespeare would have been aware of a range of ways to understand the latter part of a life, especially of a creative life, he would not for a moment have understood the kinds of claim that were made for his last plays by Edward Dowden in the 1870s and by scores of critics in Dowden's wake. This does not of course mean that all the critics who have read Shakespeare's last plays as late work have necessarily been wrong to do so – to object purely on grounds of anachronism would be equivalent to arguing that one cannot learn anything about Shakespeare by way of the work of Marx or Freud or Derrida because these writers happen to postdate him – but I would argue that their persistent presumption, explicit or implicit, that lateness is natural, universal and transhistorical has led to a consistent misreading of those plays. I hope that by the time you reach the end of this book you will agree.

A terminological point. In the course of this book, I use the terms 'late style', 'late writing' and 'lateness' to refer to the alleged phenomenon whose history I am recounting. The last of these terms is a way to delineate the idea as a whole and to evade the specificity of the words 'style' and 'writing', but I connect it to the arguably overused term 'discourse' in order to express my belief that lateness has come to signify a general understanding of the progress of the artistic life and the relationship of that life to textual production that overlaps with, but is not identical with, subjectivism. 'Late writing' per se works well enough, of course, for literary endeavour and for musical composition but is not so helpful when applied to fine or plastic art, and since I am intent on demonstrating that late style cannot adequately be studied in one artistic discipline to which it has been applied without reference being made to the other disciplines within which it has also been deployed, I am aware of its limitations. 'Late style', on the other hand, seems to imply something functioning solely within the field of form and is thus sometimes too restrictive in relation to the larger issue I am analysing, which is thematic as well as formal. The connected term 'late manner' I use only occasionally, by and large in certain precise historical or formal contexts, principally to echo later nineteenth-century artists such as Henry James, for whom 'the late manner' was a default term meaning the style of the last phase of a genius.

A further and more important terminological point, also a caveat. One outstanding problem will inevitably arise in any history of late style to create difficulties for a critic who is trying to negotiate the concept's limitations, a problem that is particularly difficult to address both because it is pervasive and because, technically, it is a sin of omission rather than of commission. It is a problem that ought by now to be clear from my deliberately specific pronoun usage – namely, the problem of the *gendering* of late style. Gender offers the most obvious immediate critical blind spot in studies of late style: there is no clearer indication of the limitations and fundamental context-boundedness of the discourse of lateness than its systematic exclusion of women. As the various lists offered by critics make immediately apparent, women have no place in the ranks of late stylists, just as they have no place (or at best a highly circumscribed place) in the larger concept – genius – of which late style is a sub-category. Attempts are occasionally made, slightly defensively, to make exceptions for writers such as Jane Austen and Virginia Woolf, but these cases are somehow never entirely straightforward. The instance of Woolf raises the difficult issue of the relationship of late style to suicide; that of Austen requires an overt deployment of critical selectivity in order to foreground *Persuasion* as a possible exemplar of late style while avoiding the problem of the un-late qualities apparent in the later, unfinished *Sanditon*.[21] Where such problems tend to be resolved by critics dealing with male artists, they seem, with regard to women, to remain open, making an unqualified ascription of a late style to a woman writer, artist or composer even more unlikely than an ascription of genius. The gendering of lateness thus forces analysts of late style into a doubly questionable theoretical stance, since not only are they, by definition, obliged to focus solely on canonical artists, they are also obliged to study male artists only. This is not to say that women artists, writers and composers have not produced remarkable work late in life, but rather that critics have effectively never attributed the cachet of late style to that work.

Art exhibitions offer an obvious instance of this. It is currently near-inevitable that monographic shows should conclude with a 'late room' in which the final work of the artist is celebrated as evidence of sublime creative ability producing, at the very end of the life, consummate achievements offering a certain transcendence of the material and conventional. An interesting recent exception to this rule was the exhibition of the work of Tamara de Lempicka at the Royal Academy in 2004 which, while clearly a standard monographic show in every other way (except, of course, in having a woman artist as its subject), treated the latter section of her life not as a period of transcendent achievement but rather of decline into sentiment and loss of clarity. Yet even a cursory viewing of the work made it apparent that very little undue effort would be required to read Lempicka differently, assimilating her late paintings of nuns and children into a classic description of lateness as spiritual expression and/or as a return to the concerns of childhood.[22] But this was not done (and to argue that she did not have a late style because she was not a genius would simply be to beg the question), and it is not generally done either in exhibitions or in critical accounts of women artists – not least, of course, because so few woman artists in history have had the means or opportunity to develop a large enough body of work over a long enough career for the attribution of a late phase.[23] This absence of a discourse of female lateness serves not only to underline the rigid gendering of the category but also to demonstrate in an exemplary way, despite the relentless rhetoric of transcendence that characterises accounts of late work, both that late style is a timebound cultural product, not a natural phenomenon, and that that timeboundedness is, as a matter of course, elided by critics.

Psychoanalysis appears to bear some of the responsibility for this lacuna. Kathleen Woodward, working within the emerging field of literary gerontology, began her career with a psychoanalytic account of the late work of key (male) American modernist poets but has, over time, become increasingly sceptical of the Freudian attitude both towards old age and, specifically, towards older women, reaching the point of arguing that psychoanalysis is itself 'complicit with our culture's repression of aging' and tracing that complicity in part to Freud's own gender politics.[24] In *Aging and its Discontents*, Woodward cites *The Interpretation of Dreams* as a case in point, remarking on the relentless negativity of Freud's terms for describing older women. 'She was', Freud writes of a female figure in one of his dreams, 'of an age not far from the time of the decay of feminine beauty', which he a little later describes as 'elderly'.[25] In a much later essay, written when Freud was himself in his late seventies, we see how early, for Freud, female ageing appears to commence when he compares the potential impact of analysis on men and on women:

A man of about thirty strikes us as a youthful, somewhat unformed individual, whom we expect to make powerful use of the possibilities for development opened up to him by analysis. A woman of the same age, however, often frightens us by her psychical rigidity and unchangeability. Her libido has taken up final positions and seems incapable of exchanging them for others. There are no paths open to further development.[26]

As Woodward observes, '[t]he ideal Freudian (analytical) woman is young, under thirty' (Woodward, *Aging*, 193), not older, more experienced, more established in her views. The attitude to the older woman apparent here would seem to make the attribution of a late style to women artists by critics with Freudian allegiances somewhat unlikely. That said, psychoanalysis in its various forms does in fact underpin a good deal of work on creativity in old age, with Jungian archetypes frequently providing a basic premise for assertions about the breaking through into essence effected by late work – though these archetypes themselves betray a certain intrinsic misogyny. Behind the account of late style offered by the Jungian psychologist Erich Neumann, for instance, lies a central archetype – that of the 'Great Old Man' or, as he calls it elsewhere, the 'Wise Old Man' – which, along with certain secondary figures, notably those of the 'Great Mother' and the 'Young Beloved Woman', is held to shape the life of the individual in ways beyond his or her control. These models, in which men are old and wise while women are either objects of desire or sources of reproduction, suggest the strain involved in the construction of a discourse of lateness from the materials both of psychoanalysis and of mysticism, even as exponents of both appear drawn to that discourse.

Perhaps surprisingly, feminist critics, though offering substantial critiques of the gendering of genius, have not to date worked specifically to resist the basic misogyny of accounts of late style. Though she is, of course, not necessarily representative, Hélène Cixous, for instance, in her characteristically elliptical way, is surprisingly uninclined to offer a critique of the patriarchal nature of the discourse of lateness. On the contrary, she appears almost inclined to celebrate it. 'I have always dreamed', she writes,

about the last text of a great writer. A text written with final energies, the last breath. On the last day before death, the author sits on the edge of the earth, feet light in the infinite air, and looks at the stars. [...] The last day is beautiful for those who know how to live it, it is one of the most beautiful days of life. On that particular day [...] one sees the world through the eyes of the gods: I am finally going to become a part of the worldly mysteries.[27]

For Cixous,

[t]he ultimate works are brief and burning, like the fire that reaches toward the stars. Sometimes they are only one line. They are works written with extraordinary tenderness. Works of gratitude: for life, for death. For it is also as a result of death and *thanks to* death that we discover the splendor of life. It is death that makes us remember the treasures life contains, with all its living misfortunes and its pleasures. ('The Author in Truth', 137)

And she turns not, as you might expect, to a woman artist (Anguissola might arguably have worked for her, or Kollwitz, perhaps) for her demonstration but to Rembrandt as mediated by Genet:

In his very beautiful texts on Rembrandt, Genet says [...] that the trajectory of Rembrandt's works began with gilding, by covering over with gold, and then by burning the gold, consuming it, to attain the gold-ash with which the last paintings are painted.

It is only at the end of a superhuman human-going-to-the-depths-of-the-fathoming-of-life-and-back that one will be able to cease gilding everything. [...] And then one can begin to adore.[28]

And she continues her analysis by focussing on a phrase scribbled down in his last hours by Kafka –

a phrase that fell from his hand, from his man's hand at the moment he was not striving to be a writer, the moment he was Franz Kafka himself, beyond books. [... D]eprived of his voice, as he was dying, Kafka scribbled down, on scraps of paper, what was passing through his mind: and those who were with him at the moment of his passing collected those scraps of paper that are for me the most beautiful books in the world. Perhaps these so very delicate phrases, these phrases of a dying man, are the equivalent, extremely rare in writing, of what is much more frequent in painting: the last paintings. It's at the end, at the moment when one had attained the period of relinquishing, of adoration, and no longer of gilding, that miracles happen. (Cixous, 'The Last Painting', 116–17)

Cixous is here using the discourse of lateness in order to interrogate Romantic attitudes to authorship; yet, for all that her consummate irony allows her to twist and turn her way through a minefield of assumptions, her admiration for the particular late style that is most poignantly expressive of that questionable category remains somehow uncritical and her world of late stylists surprisingly male.

There have, though, been exceptions to the rule of the exclusion of women from the ranks of late stylists, as there have been exceptions to their general exclusion from the ranks of genius. An early instance can be found in an 1877 review of George Eliot's *Daniel Deronda* in which the (male) reviewer defends her against certain critical charges and equates her late work with that of Shakespeare, Beethoven and Turner. 'If', the reviewer argues,

in the objection which has been brought against her recent style there be any portion of truth, it will be found in the circumstance that an occasional sentence becomes laboured, and perhaps overloaded in her effort to charge it fully and accurately with its freight of meaning.[29]

But, he goes on to point out,

[t]he manner of few great artists – if any – becomes simpler as they advance in their career, that is, as their ideas multiply, as their emotions receive more numerous affluents from the other parts of their being, and as the vital play of their faculties with one another becomes swifter and more intricate. (361)

And this, he argues, is clearly the case with Eliot: 'When the sustained *largo* of the sentences of *Daniel Deronda* is felt after the crude epigrammatic smartnesses of much of the writing in [her early novel] *Scenes of Clerical Life* we perceive [. . .] a preponderance of gain over loss' (362). *Daniel Deronda* is thus 'a homage to the emotions rather than to the intellect of man', possessing 'an impassioned aspect, an air of spiritual prescience, far more than the exactitude of science' and 'the main forces which operate in it' are 'sympathies, aspirations, ardours, and ideas chiefly as associated with these' (362). This 'spiritual prescience' stems directly from the place of the novel at the end of the curve of Eliot's career.

The reviewer here, treating Eliot as the equal of Shakespeare, is none other than Edward Dowden, the first critic fully to delineate a Shakespearean late style and the starting point for all work on the subject. Dowden is an obvious target for attacks on the naïver forms of critical subjectivism and he serves also as a focus for the postmodern distaste for Victorian criticism. It is therefore both useful and important to begin with a reminder that his work, in its day, had a quality of radicalism. At the same time, Dowden's reading of the late plays, for all that we cannot assess it now without a sense of the distance that has been covered in criticism in the course of a century and a quarter, continues, as I will show, to underpin the discourse of lateness in Shakespearean studies and thus a considerable portion of the field as a whole. A critique is therefore essential – one, however, which is careful to situate Dowden's intervention within the larger picture of the development of the discourse of lateness and which thus both gives him his considerable due and underlines the need to be aware of problems inherent in the critical assumptions underlying his arguments. For postmodern critics – and I include myself in this category – to disparage Dowden without being aware of the danger of unwittingly sharing certain of his basic premises could look a good deal like bad faith.

In this book, I address the idea of late style as it has been deployed in the case of Shakespeare from Dowden onwards (and, for that matter, from well before Dowden) and I seek to demonstrate three things. At the most basic level, I wish to show that 'late Shakespeare' is a term which, while it delineates a small group of texts located chronologically within the career of a single playwright, is an instance of a far more broadly deployed understanding of 'late style' or 'old-age style', an understanding which is presented as transcultural and transhistorical in scope but which was in fact first constructed in the conditions of emerging Romanticism and is capable of being fully understood only within that context. I argue that this construct, despite having recognisable roots in early modern culture, would have been incomprehensible to Shakespeare and his contemporaries. And I argue that the subjectivist premise of 'late Shakespeare' – the assumption that the development of the work derives from and maps the development of the personality – fundamentally misrepresents the processes of production of early modern theatre. Developing these three fundamental points, I wish to argue that the particular understanding of late Shakespeare sustained by several generations of Shakespeareans, while somewhat belated in the general history of the discourse of lateness, has in fact been instrumental in the construction and development of that discourse – that late Shakespeare has, in other words, both been constructed by and contributed to the construction of the idea of late writing – and, finally, that late Shakespeare has provided and continues to provide opportunities for creative artists, critics and theatre professionals self-consciously to construct their own careers by way of the idea of late writing.

CHAPTER 1

Shakespeare and the idea of late writing: authorship in the proximity of death

He saw the distinguished thing coming, faced it, and received it with words worthy of all his dealings with life.[1]

> O, but they say the tongues of dying men
> Enforce attention, like deep harmony.[2]

1.1 *LA DERNIÈRE PÉRIODE*

The Musée Picasso in Paris, housed within the elegant Hôtel Salé in the Marais, offers visitors a representative, chronologically ordered selection of the artist's works – his personal collection, as it happens, subsequently augmented to fill gaps in the narrative – which charts the linear development of an exemplary creative genius, each room representing the successive 'periods' of Picasso's artistic life. These visitors learn, if they did not already know, that Picasso lived a very long time. And if they anticipate a certain decline, weariness or loss of control in his work by the time he reached his ninetieth year, then they find that they have to think again. The wall label in Room 20 – which covers the last eleven years of the artist's life, from 1962 to 1973, a phase described simply as 'La dernière période' ('The last period') – reads as follows:

The last works painted by Picasso, when he was over ninety years old, reflect an extraordinary renaissance, a renewal of figurative language which appears to be a plea for the rediscovered lyrical power of the painted image. The bright, blazing colours, the vehemence of the paint brush forming figures in frenzied swirls or large daubs with splashes and impasto, reveal the vitality and dynamism of an artist for whom painting was more than ever a living matter. Picasso in his old age gave an accomplished example of a return to the 'childhood' of art. [...] From the dramatic portrait of the old painter to the one of the young artist, the entire life of Picasso is summarized in a creative apotheosis forecasting the trends of contemporary painting.[3]

Ostensibly, this account presents Picasso as *sui generis*, as an unparallelled artistic genius whose transcendent abilities are confirmed by a spectacular burst of late generativity, a unique explosion of creativity in the twilight years that provides both a completion of the circle of the artistic life and a prophecy of the future of art. On closer inspection, however, it almost imperceptibly acknowledges, by describing Picasso as an 'accomplished' rather than a unique example of an artist renewing art in old age, that this is not entirely the case, that he is not a lone instance of this phenomenon. In fact, were you to read this account of late Picasso alongside descriptions of the late work of other artists, writers or composers also considered geniuses, you would find a range of parallels that make it not simply a stand-alone account of the output of an individual artist at a particular period of his life but a classic description of late style as a final flowering, a last surge of creative energy in the face of death.

The lives of artists, writers and composers are, like their works, typically understood episodically and progressively, as having beginnings, middles and endings, and for a range of reasons the latter in particular have taken on particular significance as validation of the entire career. This has, in a sense, been true since classical times. The idea of the *cursus*, the *rota Virgilii*, the poetic career running from pastoral via eclogue to epic, is an obvious instance of an artistic teleology, a way of mapping the creative life as a development towards a generic consummation, with a powerful and sustained impact – making Pope, for instance, centuries later, anxious that, despite all his achievements, he had never completed his projected epic and creating lasting problems for Milton scholarship in negotiating the work subsequent to *Paradise Lost*. This is a teleology which is willed – doubly willed, in a way, since a sixteenth- or seventeenth-century writer following the Virgilian path is deliberately and self-consciously reworking an already deliberate and self-conscious career structure: the imitator, like Virgil himself, produces something knowing, something that makes a clear statement to his readers. It is, in Pierre Bourdieu's terms, a form of position-taking, a conscious writerly trajectory.[4]

The last years of certain major creative artists in the western canonical tradition, however, have been taken by critics in the course of the last two centuries as instances of something quite different from the genre-based poetic progress for which Virgil's career is the guiding example. They are read as exemplars of a phenomenon both personal and impersonal, a shared, transhistorical and apparently *involuntary* phenomenon – that of 'late writing' or 'late style', terms which signify the qualities associated with a last brief period of renewed energy that comes *after* the major achievements of the life of a creative artist in any discipline, extending, completing and validating that life. This is, of course, a characterisation of the artistic life that depends upon a biographical imperative in the ordering of the creating subject, a linear narrative and a clear sense that the works of the last years of certain artists are qualitatively and stylistically distinct from those artists' earlier work (though often reminiscent of the very earliest work) and are marked by a manner – an accomplished, sometimes serene, sometimes irascible, manner – felt in some way to reach 'beyond the subjective'. Late-period work is typically depicted not as a steady development towards an epic climax in the way of the Virgilian model, but as a kind of coda, a supplementary phase of the creative life manifesting itself at the same time as a renewal, a rediscovery, a renaissance, characterised in particular ways, by a looseness of facture, a tendency towards intense colour or expression, a certain difficulty and abstraction of manner, and by a distinct style which is in a way childlike and yet at the same time – and this is frequently the key authenticator of true lateness – predictive of styles yet to be established by the artist's successors, of future developments in the particular art form in question – as work, in other words, that stands outside its own time. Late work is not generically bound; it is personal, essential, autobiographical; it is a supplement to the main body of the artist's work which is also a fulfilment of that work; at the same time, it has ramifications beyond the personal, expressing a sense of epochal lateness or of a going beyond the possibilities of the current moment or, combining the two, of a certain paradoxical prolepsis in its finality.

The Musée Picasso wall label does precisely this work, claiming Picasso's last eleven years as a classic instance of this phenomenon – one known, because of the prominence with which it has figured in German critical culture, by the ostensibly interchangeable terms *Altersstil/Alterswerk* ('old-age style'/'old-age work') or *Spätstil/Spätwerk* ('late style'/'late work'). It describes this period as a time of renewal which is also a recapitulation of earlier styles and subject matter, expressed with a childlike simplicity and a certain looseness of painterly technique indicative of a mythopoeic tendency, a whittling down to basics, a return not only to the artist's youth but also to the youth of art which is at the same time a looking forward to the future after the artist's death and a kind of self-portraiture which is also a process of citation. It serves, in other words, as a validation of Picasso's artistic genius. The key requirements for the attribution of a late style are a life of demonstrable artistic achievement and a marked shift in tone or style between the mid- or mature-period works and those delineated as 'late', such that the later works are highly distinct in relation both to the artist's prior work and to the epoch in which he works. Context and contingency have little relevance: late work appears to be a phenomenon that transcends boundaries of culture, location and chronology, manifesting itself in remarkably similar ways at different times and in different places, and the work is validated because it both marks the end of a celebrated creative life and offers the possibility of transcendence of current conditions. This identity of manifestation, whether in the late work of a dramatist in ancient Greece or a painter in modern France, seems to claim for late style a kind of synchronic quality, an opening up of a window onto a phenomenon residing outside history. At the same time, while the features of the late phases of different artists will be recognisably similar, there will be certain differences of emphasis in individual cases, so that the late productions of creative artists as different in personality, medium, era and context as, say, Rembrandt, Henry James and Stravinsky have been read equally for their distinctiveness in relation to the individual's earlier work and for their particular quality as 'late writing', and the late work itself has been defined in a range of ways which are by no means always compatible. What holds the idea together, overriding the differences between individual cases, is the assumption that genius is an accomplishment or gift that, rather than fading, blooms in the shadow of death.

The differences are nonetheless instructive. As far as Rembrandt is concerned – who, along with Beethoven and Shakespeare, is the most frequently cited exemplar of late style – the emphasis tends to fall on old age, self-knowledge and a certain splendid artistic isolation, and also on the development of style both in terms of a craggy roughness of stroke and of the transformation of treatment over time – that is, on the way in which the painter sees the same things (notably his own face) across the course of his life. Alongside this, there is in Rembrandt studies an emphasis on authenticity and connoisseurship: one demonstrates one's delicacy of taste (which one shares with the artist) by being able to distinguish in certain precise ways a given painter's handling of a subject from that of others, and one of the styles most typically addressed as the terrain of the connoisseur is the late style, the difficulty of which, along with its tendency to play fast and loose with convention, make it, for the neophyte, the least accessible of styles (along, arguably, with the early style, in which the potential for eventual greatness can be seen only by those with particular insight). This marks the clearest distinction between the model of generic development offered by the *rota Virgilii* – anyone, it is assumed, can recognise the formulaic features of epic – and the subtler, less tangible qualities of the late style.[5]

In the case of Henry James, who actively propagated the equation of lateness with a certain sophistication of sensibility, there is also a focus on connoisseurship and on style itself – on the long, convoluted sentences that characterise the last novels and that have frequently, since James's death, been the target of parody – but the principal interest lies in the question of revision, of the shaping of the earlier work from the later perspective and of the institutionalisation of that revising tendency in the New York Edition, and with the determination of James to establish and complete that monument to his own lifetime achievement. In regard to Stravinsky, on the other hand, the critical emphasis has tended to rest on the sharpness of the change in style in his work in the early 1950s, the abandonment of the neoclassicism he had championed for thirty years and the wholly unexpected turn in his last years – a period described by a recent commentator as a 'second spring, a late flowering of compositional activity' – to the twelve-tone compositional technique associated with Schoenberg, whose music had previously been anathema to him.[6]

In each of these cases, the critics make certain assumptions about what constitutes a late style, assumptions about personality, trajectory, clarity of vision, renewal, about the relationship of the late work to the early work, about the ways in which the late work both differs from the creative exemplar's previous writing or composing or painting and is at the same time a logical resolution of that work. For the artists in question, the proximity of death is held to provoke a surge of transformative creative energy, and the work done in the last phase, while embodying a self-conscious return to certain aspects of their earliest work, is read as marking a fundamental break with the prior artistic achievement.[7] It is clear that each instance, notwithstanding differences in emphasis, is subsumed to a larger understanding of the style associated with late-period creativity, an overarching premise that elides distinctions and determines how the individual late style will be read.

A paradigmatic instance of the understanding of late work as it was constituted early in the twentieth century can be found in Havelock Ellis's *Impressions and Comments* of 1924 (hereafter 'Ellis'). In an extended entry dating from four years earlier, Ellis describes his visit to the newly established Musée Rodin, which, like the Picasso museum, is a permanent retrospective created from the artist's personal collection and established in a grand Parisian property in the wake of his death. He writes of the profound impact Rodin's late work has had upon him. 'I spent an afternoon before leaving Paris at the old Hôtel de Biron,' he reports, 'where the almost complete work of Rodin is now admirably displayed', and he adds:

What here interested me most was the final development of his art in the last sculptures of his old age, because this was new to me; he had not reached that stage when I saw him at work in the little studio in a remote district of Paris, where at that time he sought seclusion, far from the showplace in the Rue de l'Université. (Ellis, 4)

Rodin's late sculptures have 'a distinct character of their own as a group. They are effaced, the details are smoothed out, as it were washed away by the action of running water, so that only the largest and simplest harmonies of line and form remain' (ibid.). Ellis sees these late sculptures both as a supplement to the main body of Rodin's work and as a clear stylistic endpoint:

> With this final development the large sweep of Rodin's art was completed. There was no further development possible. He began as a minute realist and in that early stage his work even caused offence because it was said to be merely photographic. Then, during the greater and most active part of his career, he developed his characteristic style of deliberate exaggeration, the heightening of natural proportions for the ends of art, the play of light and shade. Finally that stage, too, passed away, and this last period arrived of large simple masses, softened and alleviated of all semblance to reality, gliding into a vast dim dream. (Ellis, 4–5)

For Ellis, then, Rodin's career can be divided into three distinct phases – early, mature and late – and the late work has passed beyond the style of the productions of his maturity, moving into a dreamlike world detached both from representation and from conscious artifice. Moreover, he reads Rodin's late sculpture as an instance of a larger phenomenon, asking 'Have not all the supreme artists tended to follow a like course?' and treating the acquisition of a late style as evidence of the sculptor's genius, since that final change of course, one that makes 'no further development possible', is not something available to 'the lesser artists, the artists of talent' who can only seek 'ever further to emphasise the vision of the world which they set out to present' (Ellis, 5). Lateness, in its crowning finality, is evidence of genius, not of mere talent. 'Look at Michelangelo', urges Ellis, seeking unassailable evidence:

> In that little chapel in Florence devoted to the last stage of his art, one of the shrines of the creative human spirit, we seem to see the marble itself bursting into a life so significant because not completely disentangled out of the obscure depths of Nature from which it draws that life. (ibid., 6)

Late style, for Ellis, pushes beyond representation until it is caught up in nature itself, fading back from the details of human existence.

He expands his claims for the function of late style as a key indicator of genius by pointing out its disciplinary range, noting that 'it is not only among artists in this medium [that is, sculpture] that we find the same course of development' (Ellis, 6–7) but in many forms of creativity. He cites as evidence of this Titian in whose paintings in old age the splendours of that master's earlier works are forgotten in the attainment of a subdued and clouded glory which rises to still greater heights', along with 'Rembrandt, whose art reached its climax as it passed away in the golden haze which, to memory, seems to fill the Hermitage', and he then leaps forward in time to 'think of Turner, whose early genius of the earth, sober and sombre, leapt up to heaven at last in mist and flame' (ibid., 6–7). Nor, he adds, 'is it in painting only. It is so also in poetry', and he turns to the texts which offer, for him as for so many others, the primary instance of poetic late style: Shakespeare's late plays. 'Look', he demands,

at the last plays of Shakespeare, so loose and undramatic, so flowing or so broken, so full of exquisite music of the spirit more than of poetic form, of a heavenly atmosphere refined beyond any that was ever breathed on earth and yet so humanly tender. (ibid., 7)

This unsurpassed poet – Shakespeare is here very distinctly a poet and not a playwright, since the late plays, for Ellis, are 'undramatic' – finds a 'music of the spirit' that he shares not with his contemporaries (there is no mention of Jonson, say, or Webster) but with later poets, specifically Romantic poets – with Shelley, for instance, 'who completed a large cycle of art in a short time, and wrote at last [...] only with water and fire' or, 'within a yet greater and yet shorter cycle', with Keats (ibid.). These poets, though writing at different times and in different circumstances, share a certain refinement, a certain cyclical or evolutionary quality, an elemental force that lifts them above the merely representative and enables them to find the equivalent in words to a late Turner sunrise or storm. And, with the critic taking interdisciplinary allusion and creative anachronism a logical stage further (as appears to happen with particular regularity in readings of late Turner), late style and the language of impressionism begin to seem unavoidably interlocked when Ellis writes of 'mist and flame', 'water and fire', or a 'golden haze', as if it is the discoveries of Cézanne or Monet that have opened up a subsequent understanding of what was already there in the late work of their predecessor.

Ellis remarks on the persistent inadequacy of critical methodology for understanding late work. 'The critics', he says

have always stumbled a little over this final phase of supreme genius. They used to think that Michelangelo's last work was unfinished. They still often think that what we must recognise in such a manifestation is lassitude, a failure of energy, a weakening grasp of brain or hand. (ibid., 7–8)

This, for him, is a misreading, although he acknowledges the 'element of truth in such criticism' before converting that acknowledgement into a peroration on the subject of late style as the outcropping of strength through weakness: 'Let us not forget', he exhorts his reader, 'that it is the mark of high genius, less to display athletically Titanic strength than to be able to use weakness to reach divine ends' (ibid., 8). The aim of the 'music of the spirit' is, after all, to step beyond the representational, and late style best permits this. The power of true art, Ellis suggests, is thus 'supremely visible in the typical last phase of the highest genius': yes, he acknowledges,

[t]he artist has lost his early power of realistic grip and with it lost also his early taste for such power. But he has lost it only to attain a wider and deeper and more symbolic mastery of the world. He no longer cares for the mere literal imagery of a scene he will leave so soon. But he cares more than he has ever before cared for its essence, and he is conscious of that essence with a delicacy of sensitive perception he never before possessed. (ibid.)

This sensitivity of perception eases the late artist beyond the quotidian world until he can assume a detached, hieratic stance: 'He is no longer concerned with things; they are receding from his view. As he rises above the earth, like Elijah in his chariot of fire, he now sees it only in the distance' (ibid.). Late style is thus the final form of expression prior to the dissolution of the material.

For Ellis, then – as for the scores of others who have reverently delineated its contours in art, in music and in literature – late style is evidence of creativity that escapes the attempts of the earthbound to define it, of genius rising above the historical and the cultural to stand as proof of the possibility of creative redemption. It reflects a moving beyond the material world into the realm of spirit, a translation only possible for the supremely gifted. Its serenity of tone, perhaps paradoxically, is also its difficulty, evidence of the impenetrable mastery of the accomplished artist in his last days. It offers a point of access to essence, a way to move beyond actuality to archetype, beyond the quotidian to the symbolic. It is both timeless and uninterested in disciplinary distinction, appearing with equal force in painting, in sculpture, in poetry, in drama and in music from classical times to the present – in every period and field, in other words, of serious artistic endeavour – a phenomenon equally associated with Titian and with Turner, with Shakespeare and with Shelley, with Bach and with Bartók. There is perhaps a certain disciplinary hierarchy – discussions such as Ellis's frequently begin with an instance from art or from music and only then draw in literary figures, invariably including Shakespeare – and there do appear to be limitations on the temporal reach of lateness – only in literature are late styles attributed to pre-Renaissance material – but whatever priority or chronology is asserted, the practical differences between musical, artistic and literary style are elided until there is a phenomenon common to all, a distinct stylistic development that is evidence at the same time of the transcendence of individual circumstances and of the particular qualities of the individual in whose late work this style is uncovered.

1.2 LATE STYLE IN THE WAKE OF WAR: NEUMANN, BROCH, ADORNO

Ellis is by no means alone in his understanding of late style. The middle of the twentieth century saw a significant flurry of enthusiasm for the late productions of certain artists. The naïve, quasi-theological understanding of late style we see in Ellis – already by the 1920s something of a critical commonplace – begins to take on subtler contours, to develop in the context of more rigorous theorising, in the immediate postwar period. The work of three writers in particular – the psychologist Erich Neumann, the novelist Hermann Broch and the cultural theorist Theodor W. Adorno – taken as a developing set (though not in strict chronological order), serves to demonstrate both the broad shared parameters and the considerable ramping up of theoretical sophistication in the analysis of late style that had taken place by the late 1940s. The first of these writers, Neumann, is in a way too critically eccentric to count as a theorist per se of lateness – certainly when considered alongside a figure such as Adorno, so profoundly aware of his philosophical inheritance and so inherently sceptical of broad-brush assessments of cultural phenomena – but he marks a particular approach to the idea of late style which has a long reach, an understanding premised on a certain wilful naïvety. Drawing heavily on the work of C. G. Jung, Neumann emphasises the centrality of the archetype to the process of artistic creativity and he celebrates late style principally for its function as a means of access to the essential and the transcendental, reading lateness as a means of escape from contingency. 'One of the principal functions of all art,' he explains, is

to set in motion the archetypal reality of the transpersonal within the individual and on the highest level of artistic experience to bring the individual himself to transcendence – that is, to raise him above time and epoch and also above the limited eternity realized in any limited archetypal form – to lead him to the timeless radiant dynamic that is at the heart of the world.[8]

In order to explain this artistic 'transcendence', Neumann turns to the particular achievement of certain artists in old age, arguing that

[t]he struggle of these great men with the powers inside them and the times outside them seems to result in a statement which transcends the artistic and symbolic reality of their creative life. In music, painting, sculpture, and poetry they penetrate to the archetypal transcendence which is the inner life of the world. What speaks to us from a self-portrait of the aged Rembrandt, from the end of *Faust*, Part II, from Shakespeare's last plays or Titian's late paintings, from *The Art of Fugue* or a late Beethoven quartet, is a strange transfiguration, a break-through into the realm of essence. And this transfiguration is independent of content, form, matter, or style, although the transcendence of form would seem to be one of its elements. ('Art and Time', 103)

This description is characteristic of writing on late work both in its grouping of unquestioned canonical geniuses across time – Titian, Shakespeare, Rembrandt, Bach, Goethe, Beethoven – and in its basic premise that late work goes beyond the subjective, beyond the material, to a higher truth available only to certain individuals late in life. It is also characteristic of work on late style – whether or not that work is overtly dependent upon Jung – in the Jungian inflection of its emphasis on archetypal forms and in its basic uncritical acceptance of the idea that late style brings with it a form of transcendence.

Neumann offers a frankly mystical understanding of lateness. The 'secret alchemy' in the late work of great artists, he argues, 'achieves a synthesis of the numinosum at the heart of nature and psyche', explaining that '[t]hese aged masters seem to have attained the image and likeness of a primal creative force, prior to the world and outside the world, which, though split from the very beginning into the polarity of nature and psyche, is in essence one divided whole'.[9] In so doing, they have stepped outside the material and the timebound to achieve transcendence and thus their art 'no longer relates either consciously or unconsciously to any historical time; the solitary monologue of these "extreme" works is spoken, as it were, into the void' (ibid., 104). And, he adds, 'one cannot quite tell whether it is a monologue or a dialogue between man and the ultimate' (ibid.). The result is an objectivity beyond culture. The late artistic work

is no longer oriented toward the world or man, the ego or the collective, security or insecurity; instead, the creative act which mysteriously creates form and life in nature as in the human psyche seems to have perceived itself and to shine forth with its own incandescence. The creative impulse seems to have liberated itself. United on the plane of artistic-creation, the self which man experiences within him and the world-creative self which is manifested outwardly achieve the transparency of symbolic reality. (ibid., 105)

Late work thus attests to a freedom from material realities and restrictions that is possible only towards the end of the artist's life. Context is entirely secondary, is in a sense simply left behind.

For Neumann, the great artist's life comprises three phases, the first two of which are shared by all artists: 'He begins by responding to a creative impulse within him, which [...] strives to find form of whatever kind. Then, maturing, he grows into the contingency of his epoch; through study, he becomes the heir and son of his cultural tradition' (Neumann, 102). But the great artist can be distinguished because he goes a stage further, a stage in which he no longer has the company of others:

[W]hether the artist grows slowly away from the tradition of his time or passes over it at one bound and brings the new element the epoch lacked, ultimately, if he does not stop at the stage of representation of the cultural canon – and no truly great artist has ever done so – he finds himself alone. He is alone regardless of whether he is worshipped as an Olympian, whether he is an organist respected in a small circle, or whether he ends in deafness, poverty, or madness. (ibid., 102–3)

This final phase marks truly great art, since '[i]n the creative solitude of the Great Old Men the limitations of the epoch are passed over; they have escaped the prison of time and the ego-bound consciousness' (ibid., 104). In this phase, 'the creative integration of the personality transcends the contingency of any time-bound form' (ibid.) and critical analysis is thus in a sense disabled. In Neumann's assumptions about the individual's ability to transcend contingency and about the isolation of the great artist from the mass of humanity is apparent his fundamental dependence upon certain Romantic notions of selfhood, as it is in the basic assumption he makes about the efficacy of the idea of genius and in the wilful dismissal of context and history entailed by his reading of the sources and manifestations of artistic creativity. Neumann's work thus offers one polarity in the discourse of lateness, in which late style is evidence of a breakthrough into the extra-temporal world of archetypes that is the preserve of only the most individual of artists, even as their very individuality is at the same moment dissolved into the archetype, vanishing even as it is revealed.

Neumann's contemporary Hermann Broch – best known for his massive, groundbreaking novel *The Death of Virgil*, which both explores and self-consciously embodies the idea of late style, both personal and epochal – offers in his critical writing an understanding of lateness that is, in several ways, very close kin to Neumann's own, though Broch does not have Neumann's particular inclination towards Jungian archetypes. Instead, he outlines the common factors in the life and work of the handful of artists to whom late styles have traditionally been ascribed. Firstly, each of the careers in question is marked by a 'sharp stylistic break', a caesura or rupture in their mode of expression, which is 'not merely a development in the original direction' but rather expresses a dissatisfaction with the reach of the artists' previous styles.[10] This caesura is marked by 'the reaching of a new level of expression', he notes,

> such as the old Titian's discovery of the all-penetrating light which dissolves the human flesh and the human soul to a higher unity; or such as the finding by Rembrandt and Goya, both at the height of their manhood, of the metaphysical surface which underlies the visible in man and thing, and which nevertheless can be painted; or such as the *Art of the Fugue* which Bach in his old age dictated without having a concrete instrument in mind, because what he had to express was either beneath or beyond the audible surface of music; or such as the last quartets of Beethoven, in which he – only then in his fifties but already near to death – found the way from earthly music to the music of the infinite; or such as Goethe's last writings, the final scenes of *Faust* for instance, where the language discloses its own mysteries and, therefore, those of all existence. ('Mythical', 10–11)

This rupture, this profound shift of mode, is characterised, secondly, by what Broch calls 'a kind of *abstractism* in which the expression relies less and less on the vocabulary, which finally becomes reduced to a few prime symbols, and instead relies more and more on the syntax' (ibid., 11). Defining art as, at its core, the negotiation and manipulation of convention, he argues that this abstractism marks the artist's refusal to be 'content with the conventional vocabulary provided him by his epoch' (ibid., 12). The impulse of the late artist is to transcend the personal and instead to seek to express the epochal, and in order to do so the artist must find a way to step beyond his own epoch through stylistic development. In a clear statement of the selectivity of genius, Broch argues that this can be realised

> only by the artist of old age. The other, who remains bound to his conventional vocabulary, seduced by the known richness of its content – a Frans Hals or a Thomas Wolfe – though he may enlarge his art more and more, reaching a boundless abundance, is never able to achieve his real goal: one cannot capture the universe by snaring its atoms one by one; one can only capture it by showing its basic and essential principles. [...] And here the abstractism of such ultimate principles joins hands with the abstractism of the technical problem: this union constitutes the 'style of old age'. (ibid., 12–13)

And he explains that

> [t]he artist who has reached such a point is beyond art. He still produces art, but all the minor and specific problems, with which art in its worldly phase usually deals, have lost interest for him; he is interested neither in the 'beauty' of art, nor in the

effect which it produces on the public: although more the artist than any other, his attitude approximates that of the scientist, with whom he shares the concern for expressing the universe; however, since he remains an artist, his abstractism is not that of science but – surprisingly enough – very near to that of myth. (ibid.)

The true late stylist, then, for Broch as for Neumann, is typified by his detachment from the world and is thus able to lift himself beyond convention: as a result, the artistic style he produces is one of abstraction, of a freedom from the concrete – a language, finally, of myth.

Behind the arguments of Broch and Neumann (and of their recent interpreter Edward Said) and underpinning this sense of late art as epochal, while at the same time in a range of ways contradicting both, lies the fragmentary, challenging work of Theodor W. Adorno on the idea of late style, which is by far the most significant and far-reaching theoretical meditation on the subject to date.[11] As critic after critic has pointed out, Adorno's own style is sufficiently opaque and he appears to contradict himself in enough ways that a thorough analysis of his musical writings would be a major project in itself, and a grasp of his understanding of late style is made still more difficult by the fact that he never addressed the question directly or in a sustained way, that his assertions about the late style of Beethoven (for it is always *à propos* of Beethoven that Adorno discusses lateness) appear in a series of essays and fragments and comprise at best work towards a book on the subject that he never wrote (fragments of which were eventually assembled in thematic order by Rolf Tiedemann).[12] This, it could be argued, is only appropriate, given Adorno's understanding of the inevitable orientation of late style toward silence – a logical extension of Ellis's receding late artist – a silence mediated en route by sketches, fragments and incomplete components that never add up to a whole because the whole itself would embody the totalising tendency of ideology that late style resists. The fragmentary nature of the work, however, is by no means the only problem provoked by Adorno's understanding of late style, raising as it does a remarkable series of points that anyone attempting to delineate either a given late style or any sense of an overarching idea of lateness is obliged to address.

Adorno's principal emphasis lies with what I have called the *caesura*, the firm shift of style marking the beginning of a given late period. 'A theory of the very late Beethoven', he states, 'must start from the decisive boundary dividing it from the earlier work – the fact that in it nothing is immediate, everything is refracted, significant, withdrawn from appearance and in a sense antithetical to it' (*Beethoven*, 136). This postboundary work is difficult, compressed, resistant – characteristics that are, for Adorno, common to all late styles, fending off not only ideas of organic, linear growth but also of general access. 'The maturity of the late works of important artists is not like the ripeness of fruit', he argues in the famous opening passage of his essay, noting that

[a]s a rule, these works are not well rounded, but wrinkled, even fissured. They are apt to lack sweetness, fending off with prickly tartness those interested merely in sampling them. They lack all that harmony which the classicist aesthetic is accustomed to demand from the work of art, showing more traces of history than of growth. (ibid., 123)

The accepted explanation for this, Adorno notes,

is that they are products of a subjectivity or, still better, of a 'personality' ruthlessly proclaiming itself, which breaks through the roundedness of form for the sake of expression, exchanging harmony for the dissonance of its sorrow and spurning sensuous charm under the dictates of the imperiously emancipated mind. The late work is thereby relegated to the margins of art and brought closer to documentation. Accordingly, references to Beethoven's biography and fate are seldom absent from discussions of his last works. It is as if, in face of the dignity of human death, art theory wanted to forfeit its rights and abdicate before reality. (ibid.)

This, for Adorno, is the basic error made in accounts of late style. Faced with the extraordinary nature of that style – and for Adorno, as should by now be clear, there is in Beethoven's late style 'something extraordinary, and of an extreme seriousness of a kind hardly to be found in any other music' (*Beethoven*, 186) – and needing an explanation for it, critics turn straight away to the facts of the life, 'escap[ing]', in Adorno's words, 'into biography, trying to explain the sense of the extraordinary by the life of the old Beethoven, his illness, his difficulties with his nephew and all those things' (ibid., 186–7). It is against such biographical readings that Adorno writes when he analyses late Beethoven.

Adorno thus rejects subjectivism, dismissing, as part of his overarching emphasis on 'mediation', the idea that late style is the expression of personality.[13] By extension, he rejects the general idea of late work as subjective expression, since the late compositions refuse to be made into the obvious products of Beethoven's anger or his artistic ruthlessness or whatever else biographers have associated with them. 'By declaring mortal subjectivity the substance of the late work', he argues, subjectivism 'hopes to gain awareness of death directly in the work of art' (Adorno, 125). This, he says, 'remains the deceptive summit of its metaphysics' (ibid.). 'To be sure', he continues, 'it perceives the disruptive force of subjectivity in the late work of art. But it looks in the opposite direction to that in which this force is acting; it looks for it in the expression of subjectivity itself' (ibid.). This, however, 'as something mortal, and in the name of death, vanished from the work of art in reality' (ibid.). Thus, for Adorno,

> [t]he force of subjectivity in late works is the irascible gesture with which it leaves them. It bursts them asunder, not in order to express itself but, expressionlessly, to cast off the illusion of art. Of the works it leaves only fragments behind, communicating itself, as if in ciphers, only through the spaces it has violently vacated. Touched by death, the masterly hand sets free the matter it previously formed. The fissures and rifts within it, bearing witness to the ego's finite impotence before Being, are its last work. (ibid.)

Thus, he proceeds, the conventions are

> no longer imbued and mastered by subjectivity, but left standing. As subjectivity breaks away from the work, they are split off. As splinters, derelict and abandoned, they finally themselves become expression; expression no longer of the isolated ego but of the mythical nature of the creature and its fall, the stages of which the late works mark out symbolically, as if in moments of pausing. (ibid.)

This process, which lies at the heart of Adorno's analysis, produces a particular style in which 'there is altogether something like a tendency towards dissociation, decay, dissolution, but not in the sense of a process of composition which no longer holds things together: the dissociation and disintegration themselves become artistic means' (*Beethoven*, 189). Adorno's stress here on the role of convention (an emphasis that he drew in part from Lukács and Benjamin) stems from his recognition that its deployment undermines the thrust of subjectivist reading which wants the composer to be expressing himself all the time, not working within inherited parameters. It is as if, on the contrary, Beethoven is deliberately foregrounding convention. Where, for Broch, late stylists are in conflict with convention, for Adorno, on the contrary, the late style is embodied in the actual conventions themselves, since that style is in thrall to death and death empties out the subjective, leaving behind *only* convention, 'convention [...] made visible in unconcealed, untransformed bareness' (ibid., 124). Late style is a fleeting moment prior to death, captured at the exact point at which the subjective breaks away, departs into exile. The irascibility or abruptness of late work he reads as the trace of subjectivity at the moment of its departure: this impulse leaves the conventions standing, but standing 'vacated' as shattered fragments. Thus the 'fissures and rifts' in Beethoven's late work, which Adorno sees paradoxically not as markers of loss but as a 'surplus of material', are the ego's last efforts before death. The conventional aspects of late work become expression, but symbolic expression of the myth of humanity, not a sustaining of individual ego. An artist's late style, in the end, is not the late style of that artist. Rather, the artist is what the late style leaves behind.

In this context, the 'abbreviation' of Beethoven's late style, the fragmentation and the caesurae that, for Adorno, characterise that style, can be read as the outcome not of a desire to transcend convention but rather, by contrast, of liberation from the illusion that the subjective could ever master convention. The caesurae 'are those moments of breaking free' which mark the end of expression – 'the work falls silent as it is deserted, turning its hollowness outward' (Adorno, 126) – and which thus reflect at the level of detail the caesura within the artist's life, the moment of the turn away from representation that decisively marks the beginning of the late phase. This liberation Adorno associates, it is important to note, not only with Beethoven but with late style as a general phenomenon. Of the *Six Bagatelles for Piano*, Op. 126, for instance, he writes that their 'strange brevity [...] reveals at the same time the curious contraction, and the tendency towards the inorganic, which gives access to the innermost secret not only of the late Beethoven but perhaps of every great late style' (*Beethoven*, 130), and he proceeds to define that secret. 'The late Beethoven's demand for truth', he argues,

> rejects the illusion of the identity of subjective and objective, which is almost the same thing as the classicist idea. A polarization results. Unity is transcended, yielding fragmentariness. In the last quartets this is achieved by the abrupt, unmediated juxtaposing of bare axiomatic motifs and polyphonic complexes. The rift between the two, which proclaims itself, turns the impossibility of aesthetic harmony into aesthetic content, failure in the highest sense into a yardstick of success. (ibid., 152)

In this sense, late style is, for Adorno, not just the endpoint of a linear sequence but a critique of the mature or middle style and of any style that maintains the illusion that a synthesis of subjective and objective, expression and form, can be sustained. '[T]o retain their status as authentic art', Rose Subotnik tells us in her reading of Adorno, 'the works of Beethoven's late style had to replace synthesis as their formal content with the impossibility of synthesis; in effect their aesthetic content had to become the impossibility of aesthetic wholeness and harmony'.[14] Adorno's choice of a telling counterpart for the artists at the moment of recognition of this impossibility is of particular interest for students of late Shakespeare. It is, he argues, '[a]t this point in the career of the artist' that 'the truth content of art whose vehicle was integration turns against art': '[i]t is precisely at these turning points that art has had some of its greatest moments'.[15] 'What pressures artists into making such about-faces', Adorno notes, 'is the realization that their works are overloaded with elements of organization and control'; as a result, he suggests, 'they put aside the magic wand, as does Prospero, Shakespeare's mouthpiece in *The Tempest*' (Adorno, *Aesthetic*, 67). 'Before he reaches this disintegrative truth', however, 'the artist must traverse the field of integration with its triumphs and defeats' (ibid.). It is only the artists of considerable achievement, the Beethovens and the Shakespeares, therefore, who can achieve the late style, and it is one of the latter's last characters, Prospero, who embodies that achievement – a perhaps surprisingly conventional turn in Adorno's otherwise wilfully obtuse account of lateness.

In trying to pinpoint what it is that makes this late style, this 'disintegrative truth', so distinct, Adorno emphasises the obtuseness, the 'enigma', of the late style, listing some of its varying and at times contradictory characteristics: a 'tendency to polyphony', a '*bare* quality', 'popular-song banality', an 'unsublimated, *un*assimilated "folksiness"', an echo of 'something long *past*, forgotten, entirely remote from the present, and therefore infinitely *touching*', along with a 'sombre, threatening quality' (Adorno, *Beethoven*, 127; the italics are Adorno's). Elsewhere, he writes of what he calls the 'moment of distress in late Beethoven' and of, by contrast, 'gruff humour as a means of transcending form', a carnivalesque impulse he calls 'the ogre', which is a somewhat reluctantly positive version of the irascibility that results from the dissociation of subjective and objective (ibid., 136). And just as it seems apparent that these characteristics are those specifically of Beethoven himself, Adorno notes that they are nothing of the sort: they are, rather, those of late style in general. The turn back to past forms, for instance, is not the sole preserve of the late Beethoven: he shares this 'archaizing tendency [...] with the late style of almost all great composers from Bach to Schoenberg', and Adorno adds that

[a]ll of them, as exponents of the bourgeois spirit, reached its limit, without being able to transcend it while using the resources of the bourgeois world; the suffering inflicted by the present forced each of them to fall back on something from the past as a sacrifice to the future. (ibid., 153)

This turn to the archaic marks a recognition by the supremely accomplished artist that representation cannot, in the end, sustain subjectivity:

The compulsion of identity is broken and the conventions are its fragments. The music speaks the language of the archaic, of children, of savages and of God, but not of the individual. All the categories of the late Beethoven are challenges to idealism – almost to 'spirit.' Autonomy is no more. (ibid., 157)

The subjective is replaced by atavistic, archetypal forms, the earliest, simplest conventions, that do not, as Neumann would claim, provide access to the synthesis of subjective and objective, but instead do the precise opposite, filling the void left in the wake of the failure of that synthesis. Subotnik argues that, for Adorno,

> the third-period subject [...] sees through its own developmental omnipotence as nothing but an arbitrary, externally derived convention; and the explicit return of the convention proper to prominence in the third-period style constitutes clear evidence for Adorno that the subject has entered into, and therefore abdicated from, the superior force of external reality. The subject has not only failed to assimilate convention, a collective invention, into the individual artistic fantasy, instead allowing 'bald', recurring conventions to break apart the smooth harmony of the artistic façade, but it has declared its impotence before all objective reality, nature as well as society, and thus defined itself by acknowledging indirectly its own death. ('Adorno's Diagnosis', 259)

The resignation from the subjective is an acknowledgement of death, of the subject's impotence in the face of the inevitability of dissolution.

What this leaves behind, and thus what characterises late creativity, is (and this is as close to Neumann as Adorno comes) a kind of typology:

> [E]ach individual part stands not for itself but as a representative of its type, its category, a situation which indeed comes very close to the allegorical. Here, *only* types are invented, everything singular being set down as a sign for them; and, conversely, the force of each individual element lies in the fact that it is replete with its type, is no longer itself. [...] Moreover, the style of every great artist's old age has something of this [including] the much-observed predilection of the late Goethe for the typical. Technically, therefore, the 'typicality' of the themes, and so on, of the late Beethoven needs to be demonstrated. (Adorno, *Beethoven*, 160)

These late styles share a tendency towards monumentalism. In the wake of contraction, abbreviation and the caesura there remains only emptiness, but paradoxically that emptiness is itself a kind of mark: '[t]he empty phrase is set in place as a monument to what has been – a monument in which subjectivity is petrified' (ibid., 126). '[T]he late style', Adorno tells us, 'is the self-awareness of the insignificance of the individual, existent. Herein lies the relationship of the late style to *death*' (ibid., 161; Adorno's italics). Late style is thus a memorialising of subjectivity in the recognition of its absence – the precise opposite of subjective expression per se, but not unlike it in the sense that it has become a fossil or trace of its earlier form.

It is 'classicity burst into fragments' (ibid., 134). In late Beethoven, says Adorno, 'there is no longer any "fabric"': '[a]t the very place once occupied by dynamic totality, there is now fragmentation' (Adorno, 137). There are thus two antithetical premises here, but no synthesis: 'The fragmented landscape is objective, while the light in which it glows is subjective' (Adorno, 126). Beethoven refuses to bring about a 'harmonious synthesis' of these opposed elements: 'As a dissociative force he tears them apart in time, perhaps in order to preserve them for the eternal' (ibid.). 'In the history of art', Adorno concludes, 'late works are the catastrophes' (ibid.).

Late style becomes here both a much darker, more forbidding phenomenon and a far more substantial philosophical proposition than it appears in Neumann's account of genius establishing transparent access to freely available archetypes. It provides no access to the transcendent in any positive sense. On the contrary, its appearance is evidence of a kind of exalted failure at the end of the artistic life to achieve resolution and its resigned quality reflects the recognition of that failure. Yet Adorno's analysis of late style shares with those of Broch and Neumann the same basic premise: that late work is a form of eschatology. Because the late style results from the dissolution of the individual, it is impossible to separate individual from epochal lateness, even though late style does not solely manifest itself at the ends of eras. This might not in a way matter, of course, if with Herbert Butterfield you hold that '[e]very instant is "eschatological"'.[16] For Butterfield, writing like Broch and Neumann in the immediate aftermath of a world war, this condition is uncomfortably apparent: every moment brings with it the possibility of death. Epochs can end at any time and individual and epochal lateness become inseparable. If, however, we seek clearly to differentiate an artist's late work from his earlier work, this conflation of temporal difference into the single moment is a significant challenge because it suggests that *all* artistic work is, in a certain way, late work.

1.3 THE SHAPES OF LATENESS

The escalation of the stakes in the analysis of late style from Ellis to Adorno is quite bewildering, especially considering that only thirty or so years separate the two accounts. Both celebrate late style as a hallmark of genius, both see something profound and distinct in late work, something that refuses to be bound by circumstance and moment. Ellis's is a gentler vision, an evocation of the splendour that crowns artistic consummation and passes into a golden redemptive haze. Adorno provides a far more complex and provocative theoretical analysis that sees late style as fundamental to a grasp of the relationship of art and epoch, reading late work as the sharpest, most dissonant, most critical possible mode of expression while nonetheless insisting, in effect, on its impossibility as style. It is not the slightest bit surprising, then, that the general understanding of late work that persists to the present – the one that surfaces regularly enough in exhibition catalogues, theatre programmes, newspaper articles and so on – remains far closer to that of Ellis than to that of Adorno. The Musée Picasso's celebration of the artist's late style as a 'renaissance', a 'renewal', a rediscovery of the 'lyrical power of the painted image', is, for instance, worlds apart from Adorno's account of late Beethoven – which is itself a celebration in a sense, but a paradoxical celebration of a profound loss, a sort of critical mourning – and the museum wall-label text has no sense of Adorno's treatment of the late apotheosis as marking at the same time the end of expression, the end of all artistic possibilities. The sense of energy in the completion of the creative cycle at the end of the life offered by that text, while closely compatible with the celebration of artistic fulfilment in Ellis's vision of the 'music of the spirit', the leaping up heavenwards in flame, that for him characterises late style, is a very long way indeed from Adorno's understanding of the same phenomenon as the fragmentary residue of convention in the wake of the shattering of the subjective. Picasso's late style is represented as an optimistic upward curve, an expression of future possibilities that death will not be able to arrest. Adorno's late Beethoven seeks a future too, but he does so by way of crisis, and the future he seeks is embodied in subsequent music, notably that of Schoenberg, and only then by way of the acceptance of the final impossibility of artistic synthesis.

Nonetheless, it is clear that all of these accounts of late style, from Ellis to Adorno, from Neumann to the Musée Picasso wall-label text, agree on certain fundamental tenets. Adorno's starting point, like that of Ellis, is the fissure or caesura in Beethoven's output, the profound shift that takes place somewhere in the stylistic space between the Ninth Symphony and the late quartets, the 'decisive boundary dividing it from the earlier work'. His sense of this caesura is characteristically complex – he qualifies his definition of late style by way of a discussion of certain of Beethoven's later works (the *Missa Solemnis* being the principal instance) that are, in the words of Tiedemann, encapsulating Adorno's point, 'late work without late style' – but it is a caesura nonetheless, marking a profound change in

Beethoven's music even if the actual moment of change is impossible to pinpoint. A new style emerges, a style described in a range of ways as both extraordinary and unexpected, one aspect of which, for Adorno as for the others, is the role of late work as a return to something earlier, even to something frankly primitive, along perhaps with a tendency towards typology or, more intrusively, mythopoeia. In each case, the late style is read as proleptic, as 'a creative apotheosis' which 'forecast[s]' later developments in the history of its discipline. There is, in other words, in late work, it is claimed, a broad and radical perspective, that of an artistic achievement which sweeps both back to the distant past and forward to a perhaps equally distant future. Late work celebrates and summarises (or, perhaps, in Adorno's terms, offers a critique of) what precedes it, offering a glimpse of a future that is always paradoxically in fact a past. And the standard terms, the common features, of late style emerge as a certain abstraction or looseness and a detachment, a dreamlike quality, that is read on the one hand by Neumann and Broch as a penetration of the superficial leading to a transcendence of the materials of art, a synthesis of subjective and objective, of personality and form, and on the other by Adorno as a failure to achieve any such transcendence, a failure which is itself in a certain way nonetheless a transcendence, but of self rather than world. Late style is marked by the adoption of a new and distinctive tone that is described in various contradictory ways as, on the one hand, difficult and opaque and, on the other, serene and resigned. It is a phenomenon common to a range of élite artists across time and space, which even the Musée Picasso wall-label text acknowledges in its description of the late work as an 'accomplished example' of the end of a creative life, despite its urge to celebrate Picasso as unique in his late generativity. Only Adorno qualifies this in a fundamental way – and even he repeats the phrase 'in the late work of great artists' sufficiently frequently for us to recognise that he accepts late style as a transhistorical, transcultural phenomenon, even if the history that is being transcended has a difficult teleology.

At the same time, it becomes increasingly clear that contradiction and paradox are also basic elements in accounts of late style. Picasso we have seen described as offering in his late work both 'an accomplished example of a return to the "childhood" of art' and 'a creative apotheosis forecasting the trends of contemporary painting' – a return, that is, to something prior which is at the same time a looking forward. Broch and Adorno understand late work as the product of an individual of extraordinary talent and, at the same time, as the expression of an epoch, the reflection of extraordinary times. Again, it seems clear that late style emerges involuntarily from within the genius in his last years as a hallmark of his abilities, yet in the example of Henry James we have seen a late stylist who, by way of a careful and deliberate process of revision, makes clear the self-consciousness of his lateness. Late style is either, as for Sophocles, Titian or Goethe, the product of unarguable old age or, for Goya or Beethoven and all the more outrageously for Mozart or Shelley, of a proximity to death that precedes the onset of old age per se. And it is either the crowning of the career, a consummation of a lifetime of artistic experience only available to the true artist, or a supplement that postdates the major achievements, offering an unexpected extension of an apparently complete career that appears in certain ways to question that completion.

It is thus possible to outline a series of binaries through which the unease that characterises analyses of late style might be negotiated:

personal/impersonal
individual/epochal
involuntary/knowing
serene/irascible
childlike/difficult
archaic/proleptic
old age/proximity to death
completion/supplement

Each of these constituent binaries both helps define late style and offers an obstacle to the clarity of that definition and thus to the attribution of a late style to a given artist. In their graphic expression of the negotiations and elisions required in order to establish a definition of this kind and of the attributions that that definition would make possible, they demonstrate the difficulty faced by critics in their attempts to delineate late style as a generally applicable, transhistorical phenomenon. They are not, as will be clear, uniformly direct antonyms, but they represent substantive disagreements among critics over the potential of late style as a productive category, and the sheer breadth of issues they broach is itself an index of the problems that would need to be overcome in order to establish an unequivocal definition of late style.

On closer inspection, they can perhaps be broken down into smaller and more manageable groupings that establish the key issues at stake. *Personal/impersonal* and *individual/epochal*, for instance, arguably address the same question – the extent, that is, to which a late style is generated from within or is the product of forces beyond the artist's control. The pairing *involuntary/knowing* can perhaps be grouped here too, although it will remain fairly unstable since an involuntary late style might either be one of which the artist remains wholly unaware or one which takes the artist by surprise, and a knowing late style might either be one which is self-consciously willed and constructed or one to which, after initial surprise, the artist finds himself adapting. The binaries *serene/irascible, childlike/difficult* and *archaic/proleptic* could also arguably be viewed as three versions of the same issue, expressing the difference between a late style seen either as a calm return to an innocent past or as a resistance to finality which, in its very violence, hints at what is to come. This is a fundamental divide in late-style criticism. Rejecting the standard presumption of decay or decline in the work of old age, critics, as we have seen, construct two diametrically opposed constituent moods for late work: the option of serenity – Rodin's work 'gliding', in Ellis's words, 'into a vast dim dream' or the 'heavenly atmosphere' of Shakespeare's last plays – and the option of difficulty or irascibility – the 'sombre, threatening quality', the 'lack of sweetness', that Adorno attributes to the late Beethoven and in general to late work. The former reads late style as the expression of a stepping beyond the material, a final renunciation of the things of the world and a finding of peace in the prospect of the spiritual, all of which have their final embodiment in the abstraction of late style. The latter offers a revisionist understanding of late style as the expression of a refusal to resign, of a resistance to the giving up of selfhood required to achieve transcendence, of a resentment of the cutting off of artistic possibilities imperiously required by death. For Kenneth Muir, for instance, W. B. Yeats belongs only to a second tier of late stylists – he 'falls a little below the greatest' – because, although '[h]is last period represents a Herculean effort to rise above his previous limitations and [...] gave rise to some wonderful poetry, wider in its range and more profound than anything he had written before', thereby demonstrating the attainment of a certain 'wisdom', in the end he 'lacks serenity'.[17] Adorno, by contrast, regards this absence of serenity as characteristic of true late works: 'they are the products of a subjectivity [...] which breaks through the roundedness of form for the sake of expression, exchanging harmony for the dissonance of its sorrow' (*Beethoven*, 123). Resolution of this fundamental difference appears unlikely.

That said, the most recent interpreter of lateness, Edward Said – in an analysis performed principally, as I have noted, as a reading of Adorno – sees the absence of such resolution as a cause for celebration. Writing of the 'prerogative of late style' to 'render disenchantment and pleasure without resolving the contradiction between them', Said argues that '[w]hat holds them in tension, as equal forces straining in opposite directions, is the artist's mature subjectivity, stripped of hubris and pomposity, unashamed either of its fallibility or of the modest assurance it has gained as a result of age and exile'.[18] This unresolved polarisation of disenchantment and pleasure opens up, for Said, the possibility of a certain dialogic: of reading late style, with Adorno, as consisting of both options in, as it were, rapid succession – as the flash of recognition of the impossibility of a synthesis of subjective and objective that simultaneously induces silence. It could in this light be argued that the serenity of late style is in the end not so distant as might be supposed from its irascibility, an argument that has in fact held a quiet currency since attributions of late style were first made early in the nineteenth century. An account of Goethe's last work written around the time of his death, for instance, outlines not only the peace of mind the great writer had achieved but also the considerable effort required by the ageing poet to sustain that peace of mind. The writer notes the contrast between physical frailty and mental agility that was characteristic of Goethe in his old age:

He had no longer the bodily strength of his manhood, nor the same power of undergoing fatigue, and he had outlived those ties of heart and head which bound him to so many great men who were no more. But his mind remained acute, observant, creative to the end; – its activity stopped only at the point where his physical strength failed him, and this was as great as it could be at his age.[19]

At the same time, the writer notes the mental discipline that allowed for this passive intellectual stability:

It has been truly remarked that he avoided conversation on painful or agitating subjects; but this did not arise from feebleness or pusillanimity; it was the result of reflection, and of the highest degree of self-knowledge. Intensely susceptible, as we have remarked, to all impressions; subjugated by any new and striking ideas, he had above any man to dread those which might have turned him aside from his track, and given up his immense imagination to uncurbed wanderings. (Anon., *Notes on Goethe*, 81–2)

The substantial conscious effort required by Goethe to maintain tranquillity, to keep his 'immense imagination' from disturbance, and the consequent need to avoid certain contingencies and external influences suggest the narrowness of the border between late serenity and its ostensible polar opposite expressed in the poet's raging against the dying of the light.

Not that critics, by and large, show much interest in a synthesis of this kind. Accounts of a given late style tend to come down firmly on one side or the other, with national tradition visibly influencing the choice. German writers characteristically concentrate on Beethoven for their assessments of the tenets of late style and treat their composer as the classic instance of the grim, isolated artist resisting the oncoming end. For anglophone criticism, however, a different exemplar has been at the heart of developments in the discourse of lateness since the mid-nineteenth century and that is Shakespeare, whose late plays are cited invariably as the primary embodiment of the serene, spiritual version of late style. At first sight, however, the two artists – the one writing plays in the early seventeenth century, the other writing music in the early nineteenth century – seem to have far more in common than this might suggest. Both are given distinct late periods marked by an abrupt, substantial and unexpected generic and formal shift and bounded by the brief space from this transformation to the end of the creative life. Both, in that last period, rather than declining into mediocrity, produce work that puzzles critics, who cannot with any ease explain the logic or cause of the shift, forcing them to seek explanations in biography. *The Tempest*, in particular, evokes a powerful sense, for critics, of Shakespeare's surging imagination as he contemplates retirement and eventual death, recapitulating the themes of his youth but opening up a brave new world of expression. The last string quartets of Beethoven, the *Grosse Fuge*, the final piano sonatas, all for their part evoke a similar sense of the composer's genius, also opening up new ways of imagining the medium out of which they are carved. The difference lies in the sharply distinguished tonality of the accounts offered of the two artists in their last days. Beethoven, resenting the imminence of dissolution, carves out with a ferocious fervour an artistic vision that goes beyond the materials and conditions of classical music and so enters uncharted creative waters. Shakespeare, calm now in the wake of the crisis embodied in the major tragedies, finds artistic expression for the mood that takes him away from the city and the theatre and into the Warwickshire countryside. Beethoven resists. Shakespeare accepts.

It is impossible to reproduce an account of this kind of the difference in tone between late Beethoven and late Shakespeare without a sense both of its profound artificiality and of its fundamental datedness. Yet it retains a remarkable critical currency nonetheless, both among non-specialists seeking a general exemplar of late style and among critics of the deepest and most specific experience. Not long before he died, Edward Said published a review of Maynard Solomon's *Late Beethoven* (subsequently reworked, in part, by Michael Wood in the process of editing the material that forms *On Late Style*) in which, approvingly citing Broch's list of key late stylists – Titian, Rembrandt, Goya, Bach, Beethoven, Goethe – he outlines the distinctive features of the last works of Beethoven. These, Said argues,

> form an identifiable group and show marked evidence of a considerable transformation in his actual compositional style from the romantic heroism of his middle-period works to a difficult, highly personal and (to the listener and even his contemporaries) a somewhat unattractive, not to say repellent, idiom.[20]

He goes on to quote Adorno's 'impossibly gnomic' account, as he puts it, of this 'repellent idiom', noting that 'late-style Beethoven is not, as one might expect, all about reconciliation and a kind of restful summing-up of a long, productive career', an alternative (and, implicitly, second-rate) manifestation of late style that is to be found, he argues, 'in Shakespeare's late romances like *The Tempest, The Winter's Tale* and *Cymbeline*, or in Sophocles' *Oedipus at Colonus*, where, to borrow from another context, ripeness is all'.[21] Shakespeare here becomes the primary exponent of late style understood as serene, as calm resignation or resolution. Said's own experience of exile and illness and his concomitant and characteristic desire not to go quietly seem, however, to have led him to champion not this serenity but the resistant, irascible late work of a Yeats or a Lampedusa: 'But what', he asks, 'of artistic lateness not as harmony and resolution but as intransigence, difficulty, and unresolved contradiction?', adding that he would like 'to explore the experience of late style that involves a nonharmonious, nonserene tension, and above all, a sort of deliberately unproductive productiveness going *against*' (*On Late Style*, 7). For Said, much of the appeal of Adorno's understanding of lateness was in the status of late style as writing in a kind of temporal exile: 'Adorno', he wrote, 'is very much a late figure because so much of what he does militated ferociously against his own time' (ibid., 22). In a tribute published shortly after Said's death, Jacqueline Rose, noting his insistence that '[i]nstead of the harmonious composure you might expect from someone at the end of his life, Beethoven's late compositions were marked by "intransigence and a sort of irascible transgressiveness"', observes that Said is here 'clearly describing himself'.[22] Whether or not this is precisely the case, there is no doubt that Said preferred his late artists to resist dissolution, to remain in exile, than to accept serenely the resolution of death. For Said, in the last few years of his life, Shakespeare stood for a particular form of late style for which he had, in both senses, very little time.

1.4 LATE SHAKESPEARE

When he returned to romance in his latest plays, it was as one who had earned the right to deal with life as he chose, because he knew it all, and had traversed it from surface to surface to centre. We may be grateful that he chose as he did. (J. W. Mackail)[23]

'In the history of every artist, and of every man', wrote Edward Dowden in 1875, introducing the discussion of the late plays in his book *Shakspere: A Critical Study of his Mind and Art*, 'there are periods of quickened existence, when spiritual discovery is made without an effort, and attainment becomes easy and almost involuntary.'[24] These periods, he argues, 'may be arrived at through prolonged moral conflict and victory, or through some sudden revelation of joy, or through supreme anguish and renouncement', and he adds that

> [w]hen a man has attained some high and luminous tableland of joy or of renouncement, when he has really transcended self, or when some one of the everlasting, virtuous powers of the world, – duty or sacrifice, or the strength of anything higher than oneself – has assumed authority over him, forthwith a strange, pathetic, ideal light is shed over all beautiful things in the lower world which has been abandoned. (Dowden, *Mind and Art*, 379)

That Shakespeare found a renewed and serene creative phase at the end of his life does not, then, for Dowden, make him unique. In fact, Dowden's vision appears, initially at least, to be wholly democratic, offering the possibility of spiritual attainment to one and all, although it rapidly becomes apparent that his main interest is not in fact in 'every man' but in the moment of final epiphany specifically as it manifests itself in the life of the creative artist. It is such 'epochs of spiritual discovery', we learn, that 'lie behind the art of the artist, it may be immediately, or it may be remotely, and out of these it springs' (ibid.). The immediacy of the expression of this new vision of the world depends substantially on genre and, for Dowden, revising the classical *rota*, it is dramatists who demonstrate the most mature responses. 'Lyrical writers', Dowden explains, 'usually utter themselves nearly at the moment when they are smitten with the sharp stroke of joy, or of pain', whereas dramatists 'utter themselves more often not upon the moment, but after an interval, during which self-possession and self-mastery have been attained' (ibid.). The premise of deferral in Dowden's opening statement is restated here: for the dramatist, expression is always belated, always at a distance from the experience being expressed. And the self-control of the dramatist, the ability to delay the climactic moment, the moment of the outcry, suggests the maturity of his technique.

Beginning his account of the late plays in this way, Dowden finds himself on the horns of a dilemma, torn between his desire to make Shakespeare unique and his underlying premise that the creative process adopts similar patterns for all artists. The argument of his book is that the plays directly reflect the development of Shakespeare's mind, that the work for the stage is the expression of his selfhood and of the experiences that serve both to confirm and develop that selfhood. At the same time, Dowden implicitly accepts that, for all that 'late Shakespeare' is the product of the end of a unique life, it is also part of a larger phenomenon, that of late style in general. Although he does not do so explicitly in his Shakespeare book, in the review of George Eliot he wrote two years later, as we have seen, he places a range of great artists, including '[t]he later sonatas of Beethoven' and '[t]he later landscapes of Turner', as well as Eliot's late writing, directly alongside 'the style of Shakspere's later plays' (Dowden, '*Deronda*', 361–2). Acknowledging that this phenomenon is shared with others, then, Dowden at the same time seeks to ensure that Shakespeare remains its most complete exemplar. Reworking his topographical language of height and depth, tableland and mountain, he argues that

> [g]reat artists belong ordinarily to one of two chief classes – the class of those whose virtue resides in breadth of common human sympathy, or of those who, excelling rather by height than breadth, attain to rare altitudes of human thought or human passion. For the one, the large table-land, with its wealth of various life, its substantial possessions, its corn, its shadow-casting trees, and lowing kine; for the other, the mountain-summit, its thrill, its prospect, its keen air, and its inspiration. (ibid., 348)

The greatest artists, he claims, unite these two classes and, '[o]f such, Shakspere may be considered the master and chief' (ibid., 349). No 'speculative summit more serene or of wider vision', he argues, 'has been attained by the foot of man than that of the great enchanter of the "Tempest", who is Shakspere himself looking down, detached and yet tender, upon the whole of human experience' (ibid.). Dowden specifies no particular timetable at this stage, but the individual's march through a faintly colonial landscape, his attaining of a spiritual 'tableland' through 'duty or sacrifice', perhaps through 'supreme anguish', and his subsequent 'renouncement' of the affairs of the world seems to imply the passing of a certain number of years. In the context of Dowden's understanding of expression as belated, renunciation is necessarily a late gesture, a stance that can be adopted only by those who have, over a sustained period, achieved something profound and have subsequently chosen to stand above and beyond that achievement. And it is of course late works of which Dowden writes here – late works to which he first gave a name, 'the Romances', and which are otherwise known as 'Shakespeare's late plays'.

Prompted by F. J. Furnivall, the guiding light of the recently formed New Shakspere Society, who was convinced that the production of a critical biography would transform Shakespearean studies (and whose preferred spelling of the playwright's name he adopts), Dowden set out to read the progress of the plays across the career as external evidence of the internal development of the playwright's mind. As he phrases it in his second chapter, deploying biological language inherited from Schelling and Goethe, he aims to 'observe, in some few of its stages of progress, the growth of [an] organism' – the organism in question being 'a dramatic poet'. All organisms are characterised by growth and development and Shakespeare is no different, progressing through phases of experience and mood:

Shakspere in 1590, Shakspere in 1600, and Shakspere in 1610, was one and the same living entity; but the adolescent Shakspere differed from the adult, and again from Shakspere in the supremacy of his ripened manhood, as much as the slender stem, graceful and pliant, spreading its first leaves to the sunshine of May, differs from the moving expanse of greenery, visible a century later, which is hard to comprehend and probe with the eye in its infinite details, multitudinous and yet one [...] – the tree which has a history, and bears in wrinkled bark and wrenched bough memorials of time and change, of hardship, and drought, and storm. (Dowden, *Mind and Art*, 42–3)

It is on this basis that he sets out to map each stage of the life, of which, for Dowden, there are four. The full schematic pattern is clearer in his 'Literature Primer' of two years later than it is in the fuller *Shakspere: His Mind and Art* (the 'Primer' had enormous influence and was reprinted regularly well into the twentieth century with additional bibliographies by Alfred Pollard), but it is clearly there in the earlier book, too. The first phase he calls 'In the workshop', the work of an 'industrious apprentice' displaying 'a quick enjoyment of existence'; the second 'In the world', featuring work which is 'strong and robust' and which begins 'to deal in an original and powerful way with the matter of history'; and the third 'Out of the depths', marking the grimmest period of the playwright's life, in which the grief caused by the deaths of his father and his son prompted him 'to inquire into the darkest and saddest parts of human life; to study the great mystery of evil'.[25]

The 'Fourth Period', which he sees as wholly distinct from the preceding phases, he calls 'On the heights,' reading it as a time in which the artist emerges with a 'clear and solemn vision' to produce plays in which 'there is a resolution of the dissonance, a reconciliation' expressed as a 'pathetic yet august serenity' (Dowden, *Mind and Art*, 403, 406, 380). 'The impression left upon the reader by Shakspere's last plays', he claims confidently, 'is that, whatever his trials and sorrows and errors may have been, he had come forth from them wise, large-hearted, calm-souled' (Dowden, 'Primer', 60). In this period, the dramatist created theatre quite different from anything that had gone before, plays characterised, in Dowden's words, by

a certain abandonment of the common joy of the world, a certain remoteness from the usual pleasures and sadnesses of life, and at the same time, all the more, [a] tender bending over those who are like children still absorbed in their individual joys and sorrows. (Dowden, *Mind and Art*, 415)

The mood of the plays as a group is central to his analysis of each:

The spirit of these last plays is that of serenity which results from fortitude, and the recognition of human frailty; all of them express a deep sense of the need of repentance and the duty of forgiveness. And they all show a delight in youth and the loveliness of youthful joy, such as one feels who looks on these things without possessing or any longer desiring to possess them. (Dowden, 'Primer', 60)

This godlike serenity had not come easily to Shakespeare but, emerging from the profound crisis which yielded *King Lear* and *Timon of Athens*, he found a new mood which 'demanded not a tragic issue' but rather 'an issue into joy and peace': the 'dissonance' that had characterised the tragedies would instead 'be resolved into a harmony, clear and rapturous, or solemn and profound [...] a reconciliation' (Dowden, *Mind and Art*, 406). In part, this was the result of Shakespeare's detaching himself from the theatre: for Dowden, *The Winter's Tale*, to take a particular late play, has a 'breezy air' which 'is surely that which blew over Warwickshire fields upon Shakspere now returned to Stratford; its country lads and lasses [...] are those with which the poet had in a happy spirit renewed his acquaintance' (Dowden, 'Primer', 151). But, above all, the final reconciliation was the logical endpoint of the Romantic understanding of the growth of genius, inflected with a Christian (or at least a post-Christian) urge for redemption. This was, then, both a period unique to Shakespeare, something that emerged from his particular experience of life – in other words, a very personal development – and at the same time a manifestation of a process that could have been expected from the very beginning, because it is in the nature of genius to develop in stages and because it would be unthinkable for the National Poet not to find salvation at the end. As Sir Walter Raleigh anxiously phrased it fifty years later, demonstrating a basic dependence upon Dowden's narrative,

[m]any a life has been wrecked on a tenth part of the accumulated suffering which finds a voice in the Tragedies. The Romances are our warrant that Shakespeare regained a perfect calm of mind. If *Timon of Athens* had been his last play, who could feel any assurance that he dies at peace with the world?[26]

The late plays here serve as reassurance to the concerned critic that Shakespeare left this world in the knowledge of his own salvation.

Dowden's delineation of a Shakespearean late phase is one of the most celebrated events in the history of Shakespeare criticism, a rare paradigm-shifting moment in which a new way of thinking about a given creative artist is expressed fully for the first time. The late Shakespeare that Dowden describes (and Raleigh echoes) became established as the primary exemplar within anglophone critical culture of the idea of the late phase as we have seen it described – as a period of serenity in the wake of struggle, a late resurgence of powers a few years before death, a kind of spiritual homecoming which is also an instance of great art's transcendence of the contingent. The shape of cutting-edge critical studies has changed so drastically since Dowden's day that it is extraordinarily difficult to recapture the freshness of the impact his work must have had, an impact apparent both in the refutations of his position offered by critics in the early twentieth century – the most significant being those of Lytton Strachey and C. J. Sisson – and in the persistence of Dowden's reading across that century and into the next.[27] Although in Chapter 3 I will outline the resistance to Dowden, I wish here to emphasise the extent to which, despite the various critiques that have been offered of it, Dowden's basic understanding of the late plays has continued to underscore readings of those plays right up to the present.

One exemplary instance of this can be found in the work of Russell Fraser, who in his 1992 quasi-biography *Shakespeare: The Later Years*, manages in one crisp paragraph to assemble most of the standard tenets of Shakespearean lateness:

Early in 1608 Shakespeare entered on his last phase with *Pericles, Prince of Tyre*. Forty-four this year, he had eight years left. Byron and Mozart died in their thirties, Shelley and Marlowe at twenty-nine, and Wordsworth, though living long, dwindled to 'Wordwords.' Shakespeare, luckier than some and more resourceful than others, got it all down, nothing left over. Toward the end he was putting out fresh shoots. Four romances and a coda record his final flowering, *Pericles* leading off. (Fraser, *Shakespeare*, 216)

Sailing blithely here between the Scylla and Charybdis of caesura and chronology, Fraser broad-brushes his argument, allowing the juxtapositions he effects with other writers and with a composer to do a good deal of silent work, implying certain things about late Shakespeare without actually stating them. This listing of parallel figures is a standard tactic both in general descriptions of late style (as we have seen in Ellis, Neumann and Broch) and in specific accounts of late Shakespeare. As Russ McDonald notes, '[a]n implausibly large number of critics find themselves unable to write about the last phase of Shakespeare's career without invoking the late years of Ibsen, Michelangelo or, invariably, Beethoven'.[28] McDonald is here referring less to Dowden's originary reading or to the aphoristic posturing of a Fraser than to certain mid-twentieth-century critics who insisted on reinforcing Shakespeare's claims to a late style by placing him alongside a series of other late stylists. Kenneth Muir's *Last Periods of Shakespeare, Racine, and Ibsen*, published almost a century after Dowden and still clearly indebted to his vision, is perhaps the most clearcut instance of this, though McDonald could equally easily be referring to David Grene's remarkably similar *Reality and the Heroic Pattern: Last Plays of Ibsen, Shakespeare, and Sophocles* of six years later (written, it seems, despite the obvious similarities of title and subject matter, in ignorance of Muir's earlier work) or, to a slightly lesser extent, to Cyrus Hoy's *The Hyacinth Room*. Muir, Grene and Hoy all deliberately juxtapose late Shakespeare with the late periods of other dramatists: Sophocles, Racine, Ibsen and Strindberg. Hoy self-consciously takes the title both for his book on genre in Shakespeare and for his particular chapter on the late plays not from Shakespeare himself but from Strindberg's *The Ghost Sonata*, making the connection direct by arguing that '[t]he closing moments of *The Ghost Sonata* amount to a dramatization of Prospero's famous words' at the end of *The Tempest*.[29] That these critics are dependent for their understanding of late Shakespeare upon an overarching concept of lateness is apparent in Muir's description of Beethoven's late music as 'an ideal example of the final achievement of a great artist, when he seems to acquire a new profundity, a new understanding, in making a last attempt to solve the enigma of life' (Muir, 3) and in his choice of Beethoven and Botticelli as parallel cases of artists who achieve 'joy' in the wake of 'a full realisation of human evil and suffering' which, for him, in a complex implicit evocation of Blake, is 'the innocence which follows experience, not that which precedes it' (Muir, 5). In so doing, Muir highlights the redemptive urge in post-Second-World-War late-play criticism, the quest for a happy ending which suggests that, for all that he dismisses Dowden as 'naïve', he retains a good deal of Dowden's understanding of late style.

For Muir, the connecting factor between the playwrights he analyses is that they each experienced 'something in the nature of a religious conversion' which for some 'involved a partial repudiation of their past work' but for others 'involved rather a reconsideration in light of their new vision of some of the themes which had obsessed them in their earlier years' (*Last Periods*, 113). For Hoy, in turn, at the end of the late plays,

> [t]he offenders rise above their offenses, and the injured rise above their injuries. In achieving so much, they come into possession of themselves, which here means that offenders and injured alike rise to a sense of their common humanity: of their shared capacity for giving joy and sorrow, for hurting and forgiving and being forgiven. (*Hyacinth Room*, 317)

Forgiveness thus becomes the central activity of the plays:

> [W]hat issues in a fully developed sense of tragic betrayal in *Hamlet* or *Lear*, or in Strindberg's *Father*, leads in the last plays of Shakespeare and of Strindberg to another and non-tragic sense of evil. In the last plays of Shakespeare, the innocent can cope with evil without being corrupted or destroyed by it. There, evil does not beget evil. What it elicits instead is a virtue of surpassing strength: a strength which quite confounds the guilty. (ibid., 301)

Everything, for Hoy, 'turns on the need, and the capacity for, forgiveness' (ibid., 301–2). This, naturally, has a distinct impact on the shape of the plays: 'Most of these last plays are not tragic', Muir notes, 'as though the poets, as they drew near to their eternal home, found the tragic interpretation of life no longer most valid for them' (*Last Periods*, 113). The theological lateness envisaged here is thus also a generic lateness: the mid-century late-play critics treat the plays as fundamentally *comic* in the sense that their shared teleology is redemption. Criticism of this kind – including, in particular, the parallel, explicitly Christian work on the late plays of Northrop Frye and G. Wilson Knight – is thus the equivalent in the conservative micro-climate of Shakespeare studies to the broader attention paid to late style in the postwar writings of Neumann, Broch and Adorno, though these late-play critics seem to have found a redemption in late work not so readily available to their philosophically more sophisticated German peers. Knight and Neumann would seem to have almost nothing in common as critics, yet they share a general tendency to mysticism which makes the late plays an obvious Shakespearean toehold for both, and it was Knight's Christian nationalism, despite its tangible eccentricity, that became enshrined as, in effect, the Shakespearean establishment's response to the end of the war.[30] Certainly, it is clear that the aftermath of war produced an enthusiasm for redemptive readings of the late plays conspicuous by its absence from the Shakespeare criticism of the immediate pre-war period.[31]

Readings of the late plays have of course moved a very long way since this mid-century celebration of Shakespearean lateness. In the seventies and eighties, the theoretical premises of Shakespeare criticism came under intense scrutiny from the structuralist and poststructuralist detachment of author from work, a development that put considerable pressure on subjectivist readings, and the early eighties saw a surge in historicised and gendered analyses that argued for a harsher understanding of the late plays' world, offering alternative readings of Prospero as an irascible colonist, of the problem of incest as the driving force of Pericles' tribulations, of Paulina's uneasy manipulation of events at the close of *The Winter's Tale*, of the casual violence of Guiderius and Arviragus and the abjection of Innogen in *Cymbeline* and of Theseus' tyranny towards Emilia and the sense of irreparable loss with which *The Two Noble Kinsmen* reaches its close. In each case, the plays appear less serene, less forgiveness-centred, more territorially troubling and patriarchally inflected, than they had to Muir's generation, undermining the belief that they form a seamless group characterised by a shared serenity and a distinct style underpinned by the development of Shakespeare's personality. Critical attitudes, though, die hard, and current introductions to and anthologies of criticism on the subject of the late plays, far from jettisoning the premises of these mid-century readings, seem in fact, sometimes unintentionally, to extend their impact right up to the present.

One representative recent anthology, which provides a fine selection of the best essays on the late plays from the eighties and nineties and helpfully demonstrates the developments in interpretation effected by way of historicist, materialist and feminist criticism, nonetheless makes clear, both in what its editor argues and in what he elides, the persistence of a discourse of Shakespearean lateness still bearing the hallmarks of Dowden. This, together with Said's representative positioning of the late plays as paradigmatically serene, suggests that the era of Dowden has not yet run its course. The editor of the collection in question, Kiernan Ryan, announces that he will take as his focus the 'four romances', noting that these are the plays 'most critics have in mind when they refer to the last plays of Shakespeare' and giving clear dates for each so as to establish as the correct chronological sequence the order in which he names them: *Pericles* he dates to 1607–8, *Cymbeline* to 1609–10, *The Winter's Tale* to 1610–11 and *The Tempest* to 1611.[32] 'Few would now dispute,' he claims, that the four plays with which this book is concerned were all written, in an evidently uninterrupted sequence, between 1607 and the end of 1611, and that the last of them, *The Tempest*, is also the last play in the canon attributable wholly to the hand of Shakespeare. (*Last Plays*, 4)

He acknowledges nonetheless that it would be possible to make '[a] strong case [...] for expanding this group to include *Henry VIII* (1612–13) and *The Two Noble Kinsmen* (1613)' but argues that 'on balance it seems wiser to regard them as beyond the remit of this book', offering four reasons for this decision: one, that they are collaborations; two, that the former at least 'can be more comfortably and more profitably housed with the histories'; three, that there has in any case not been enough decent criticism of either play for it to be worth putting any of it into the anthology; and four, most importantly, that the 'family resemblance' the collaborative *Pericles* shares with the other three 'romances' is harder to detect in the two final collaborations, leading him to omit them in the hope that 'what the book has gained in coherence and sharpness of focus should compensate in some measure for its failure to be comprehensive' (ibid., 1–2).

Ryan begins by noting 'how completely' readings of the late plays have changed with the rise of critical theory, which has dismantled '[t]he old historicist and humanist pieties' and rendered 'obsolete' readings of the plays as 'serene myths of redemption or edifying spiritual allegories' (ibid., 2). He notes too the underlying role of Dowden in the construction of these now-obsolete ideas of Shakespearean 'romance'. 'The last plays', he argues, 'began the [twentieth] century still in thrall to the late Victorian view of them bequeathed by Edward Dowden', who shared with 'his Edwardian successors' a 'post-Romantic belief in literature as a direct reflection of the author's mind' (Ryan, 6). Thus, for these critics, 'Prospero epitomized the personality of the Bard himself in his declining years, and the mood of mellow resignation and world-weary, wise serenity imputed to Shakespeare's surrogate was read back from *The Tempest* into the plays that immediately preceded it' (ibid., 6–7). Ryan makes his distaste for this Victorian tendency to read the plays as outcroppings of the Shakespearean psyche entirely clear. A couple of pages earlier, though, he had admitted that

> [i]t is tempting to speculate on the possibility that Shakespeare raided the resources of romance in order to wrestle with the demons spawned by his own domestic history. The peculiar intensity and resonance of these parables of expiation may owe much to their author's prospective retirement to dwell with the wife and daughters, and the lingering ghost of a beloved son, from whom his theatrical life in London had divorced him for so many years. No one will ever know

exactly how much, but the parallels between the plights of Pericles, Cymbeline, Leontes and Prospero and the family fortunes of the playwright viewed from this point in his life are too striking to dismiss as irrelevant to an appreciation of the plays. (ibid., 5)

'At the very least', he continues,

they serve to remind us, at a time when the author is too often reduced to a mere textual effect, that these works are the deliberate creations of a formidably complex individual, striving to give dramatic form and poetic expression to his deepest private fears and fantasies. (ibid.)

'Indeed', he adds, 'it might not be entirely fanciful to suppose that Shakespeare's dramatic refraction of his actual anxieties is one source of the plays' enigmatic aura' (ibid.). This is telling speculation, demonstrating as it does the persistence of subjectivism in late-play studies. Having rejected Dowden's sense of the relationship between playwright and play, Ryan now appears prepared to read the late plays, if not directly as 'reflections', then a little more obliquely as 'refractions', of the playwright's mind.

Ryan's account thus underlines the extent to which the premises of late-play studies have stayed much the same for a century and a quarter. The late plays are the 'four romances': *Pericles*, *The Winter's Tale*, *Cymbeline* and *The Tempest*, in that order, offering a clear and uncontentious chronology. They do not include, for a range of instructive reasons, either *Henry VIII* or *The Two Noble Kinsmen* (or, for that matter, *Cardenio*, which is rarely even mentioned). One of these plays, *Henry VIII*, can in any case be conveniently assigned to a different generic grouping, suggesting that it is genre rather than chronology that ties the plays together and perhaps also that the anthology might better have addressed a set of plays called 'Shakespeare's romances' than a potentially larger group called 'Shakespeare's last plays'. And of course *Henry VIII*, along with *The Two Noble Kinsmen*, can be excluded because both are collaborations and thus at best only half Shakespearean. The 'last plays', for Ryan as for Dowden, are 'last' precisely in their relation to Shakespeare and thus must be viewed primarily in that relation. The collaborative *Pericles* can be included because it has a distinct 'family resemblance' to the other three solo romances which the two later collaborations lack, family resemblance being key to the generic teleology of the late plays. Moreover, the absence of decent criticism of *Henry VIII* and *The Kinsmen* suggests that the source of the problem lies with the plays themselves rather than with the critics, since the clear implication is that, if these plays were any good, critics would by now have done some good work on them. And Ryan concludes by offering a final, rather curious, perspective redolent of the arguments of Neumann and others on the transcendent potential of the late plays. He briefly cites the work of Ernst Bloch, for whom the most significant quality of the finest creative endeavour is 'its power to recollect and raise to consciousness what has hitherto been unconscious, as its power to tap into a *future unconscious*, which lies over the horizon ahead of us rather than buried in the past behind us' (*Last Plays* 19). This 'future unconscious', we learn, 'is what Bloch calls the *Novum*. To gain a glimpse of it is to gain a glimpse of the prospective in the previous so strange and startling that it can be conveyed only in the occult aesthetic idiom devised by the innovative author' (ibid.). And Ryan sketches a Blochian reading of Shakespeare's late plays as writing that provides a glimpse of a creative future yet to be realised at the time of composition, writing which is the product both of the individual psyche of its author and of the collective unconscious which is history. Turning away from criticism that demonstrates 'a compulsion to translate the plays into a familiar idiom', to 'reduce them to a recognizable version of a creed, a period, a theory or a politics that is already known' – in other words, to historicise and/or theorise them – he looks forward to a reading which might 'stage through its engagement with [the late plays'] style and structure an open, unpredictable dialogue between then and now about what might be' (ibid.). This is in many ways an appealing project – and any reading which reduces a complex work of art to material for a reductive philosophy is, naturally, to be resisted – but the future perspective it seeks in the late plays is redolent all the same of the understanding of late style championed by critics such as Neumann and thus demonstrates the willingness even of the most theoretically and historically aware Shakespeareans to adopt in the case of the late plays readings that would appear questionable when applied to other phases of the career.

1.5 SHAKESPEARE AND THE IDEA OF LATE WRITING

I have a double – perhaps better, an intertwined – aim in this book, since I am writing both about Shakespeare and about lateness. Although the idea of late style was invented entirely independently of Shakespeare and of Shakespearean studies, an adequate understanding of late Shakespeare cannot be achieved, I wish to argue, without a critical engagement with the larger concept. That concept depends, as I have suggested, upon certain presumptions that, since they emerge from particular times and places yet are represented as universal and transcendent, require critical interrogation, and it seems logical to do so by way of a single test case, that of late Shakespeare. Moreover, since the idea of late style has developed – at least within literary studies – substantially through and for Shakespeare, late Shakespeare would appear to be an ideal exemplar. From Henry James to Mark Rylance, I will argue, creative artists have found in late Shakespeare a means through which to articulate the shape of their own careers and lives, offering them a manipulable paradigm that has been productive of further creativity. This suggests the flexibility and productivity both of the idea of lateness and of the Shakespeare canon as it has been constituted by critical activity, and the availability of both as vehicles for the development and expression of subsequent artistic endeavour beyond the bounds of each.

A number of key questions persist. To what extent is late style primarily a phenomenon of ageing? Or is it, rather, a phenomenon of the proximity of death whether or not the individual addressed reached old age? Is late style involuntary, something that, as it were, descends upon a creative individual out of the blue at a certain stage of his life? Or is it the product of contingencies, of medical conditions to be associated with old age, for instance, or of the psychological response to an awareness of the imminence or even simply the ongoing inevitability of death? These questions are essentially the same whether one is addressing a composer, a novelist or a painter, since the original premises have been applied equally, though at different times, in the fields of musicology, literary criticism and art history. In engaging with late Shakespeare in this book I will, I hope, tell a story of interest to anyone working on the late style of a canonical creative individual in any of these disciplines. Shakespeare criticism situates the late plays as late within Shakespeare's *œuvre*, but it also situates them, at least implicitly, within a larger understanding of late style. But that larger understanding raises difficulties for the project I have undertaken, not the least of which is the question of the actual possibility of a critique of this kind. The unquestioning transhistoricity of a Neumann or a Broch is, for a cultural critic, straightforward enough to address, but the far more complex and subtle (not to mention fragmented) analysis offered by Adorno makes any such critique far more problematic, if for no other reason than the seriousness with which he addresses his subject, forcing one to acknowledge the critical value of the very phenomenon whose existence one is questioning. Adorno thus haunts this book throughout, even when he receives no specific mention. The principal means through which I negotiate this haunting is my attempt to offer a history for the construction of the idea of late writing, a history in which Shakespeare, at least as much as Adorno's protagonist Beethoven, plays a major part. And in the course of mapping that history I address certain of Adorno's assumptions that make far less sense in relation to Shakespeare than they do in respect of Beethoven, suggesting not that this implies the inadequacy of Shakespeare as exemplar but rather that the counter-case implies the inadequacy of the shared concept.

In the end, late style, as I will suggest in particular in Chapter 4, is a form of commemoration. Walter Benjamin, Adorno's friend and colleague, cites in a different context an assertion about memory which seems to me to resonate also for the question of late style:

'A man who dies at the age of thirty-five,' said Moritz Heimann once, 'is at every point of his life a man who dies at the age of thirty-five.' Nothing is more dubious than this sentence – but for the sole reason that the tense is wrong. A man – so says the truth that was meant here – who died at thirty-five will appear to *remembrance* at every point in his life as a man who dies at the age of thirty-five. In other words, the statement that makes no sense for real life becomes indisputable for remembered life.[33]

Benjamin's point is highly salient for the analysis of late work, which presents two connected problems. If a creative artist dies unexpectedly, it will be up to others to determine whether or not he had a late style. If a creative artist dies in old age, having remained in command of his artistic faculties, it will be partly up to *him* to determine whether or not he had a late style, at least once the concept exists and he is working within the era of the discourse of lateness. In neither case is there anything 'natural' about the lateness in question. Either it is subsequently imposed by critics as a product of hindsight or it is consciously adopted by the artist in order to determine posterity's understanding of his work. It is the negotiation between the critical imposition and the artistic self-consciousness which is the most technically difficult issue to address in any overall critique of late style. Tracing the development and productivity of the idea of a specific Shakespearean lateness seems to me to provide an opportunity to negotiate this difficulty.

In the course of the following chapters, I will argue that late style is less a demonstrable phenomenon than a redemptive fantasy of rejuvenation, a form of wish-fulfilment shared by artists and critics which may at times approximate biographical truth but which is far more often the product either of the imposition of an understanding of the creative process inimical to the actual conditions in which the art works in question were produced or of complicity on the part of the artist, who consciously produces work that fulfils the criteria for the attribution of a late style. Focussing on Shakespeare as my exemplar, I will address first of all the problem of the caesura, of, that is, the difficulty of reconciling the clarity of delineation of a given late period with the evidence, arguing that although the critical history of the Shakespearean late plays demonstrates a clear consensus that they stand apart from the rest of Shakespeare's work chronologically, stylistically and generically, it is nonetheless remarkably difficult to find the 'decisive boundary', to use Adorno's term, upon which that history depends. I will then assess the formation in the early nineteenth century of the overarching discourse of lateness and I will map the place of Shakespeare in the development of that discourse in England both before and after Dowden, tracing the growth of Shakespearean lateness from the earliest chronology, that of Malone at the end of the eighteenth century, to the instructive anxiety of Henry James about Shakespearean lateness at the beginning of the twentieth, demonstrating the pervasiveness of the idea of late Shakespeare in anglophone literary culture and the repeated deployment of that idea in the self-conscious construction of late styles by subsequent writers.

Thereafter, moving back in time, I will address the possibility of a Shakespearean late style in the context of the culture and theatre of his time, arguing that the conditions for early modern playwriting were such that the subjectivist premise of the idea of late style is asymmetrical both to the possible understandings of artistic productivity available in the early modern period and to the modes of production in the early modern theatre. At the same time, I will argue, the seeds of future ideas of late creative selfhood can be found in early seventeenth-century English culture, noting that while Shakespeare would have been bewildered by Dowden's understanding of his last plays, he would nonetheless have had a strong sense both of the possibilities available for the narrative structuring of a life, and especially of a creative life, and of the particular importance of the endings of lives to that structuring process.

I will then address the vexed yet pivotal question of the relationship of late style to old age, considering the criteria for the establishment of a late period and examining the problem represented by the fact of Shakespeare's producing his 'late work' in middle age, and concluding by mapping the critical urge to rewrite *King Lear*, the quintessential Shakespearean play of old age, as a late play, despite its generic and chronological inappropriateness in relation to that grouping. And I will conclude the book as a whole by examining the generative appropriability of late Shakespeare in the late twentieth and early twenty-first centuries, demonstrating the utility for theatre professionals – my principal instances are Sir John Gielgud and Mark Rylance – of the idea of a Shakespearean late style as it is manifest in the traditional identification of Shakespeare and Prospero, arguing that the contours of a postmodern theatrical career can be delineated by way of a further identification, that of playwright, character and actor/director.

My overall question is simple: what difference does it make to think about late Shakespeare in the context of the overarching question of late writing or late style?

CHAPTER 2

The Shakespearean caesura: genre, chronology, style

Suddenly in 1608 there was a change.[1]

Late style is, I wish to argue, a concept creative artists and critics have together established in order to negotiate the proximity of death and, for this negotiation to begin in individual instances, certain conditions must be fulfilled and work done in order to establish the place of a given late style within the overarching concept. Part of that work, for the critic, involves easing readers past issues that might complicate the understanding of late style they have been encouraged to adopt as the embodiment of a certain transcendence – issues that include, as I have suggested, tone, contingency, complicity and gender. And part is the establishment in the individual case of the key criteria for the attribution of a late style. There are several such – a defensible argument that the work in question displays overwhelming evidence of genius is an obvious primary instance – but the single most basic criterion, the one from which the rest in a sense develop, is what I have called the *caesura*, that is, the point at which the mid- or mature-period style stops and the late style begins. Epochs, personal and social, must begin and end somewhere if they are to be distinguished and categorised, and one of the key issues in analyses of late work is the problematic idea of the divide between the late period and whatever came before it. We have seen that Adorno, while acknowledging the considerable problem posed by the compositions his editor Tiedemann calls 'late work without late style', insists nonetheless on the absolute abruptness of the change in style that marks the onset of the late phase of Beethoven. We have seen, too, that, for Broch, the late phase is marked by a 'sharp stylistic break, [...] not merely a development in the original direction' ('Mythical', 11).

This caesura depends first and foremost upon chronology. In the absence of an accepted, demonstrable order for the productions of a given artist, no periods of creativity, no beginning, middle or ending, can be ascribed to that artist and there can therefore be no late work. It also depends on certain changes both in style and in genre (notwithstanding Neumann's claim that the principal characteristic of late work is a transcendence of form), changes which demonstrate that the works in question fit together in a way that they do not with earlier works by the same author. Each of these criteria is interwoven with the others. Without a chronology, no clear lines can be drawn and thus stylistic or generic differences cannot be distinguished for discrete groups of works; stylistic and generic distinctions in turn reflect and feed into each other so that the one entails the other; and the chronology itself is sometimes determined, in the absence of external evidence, by way of generic and stylistic difference. None of these shared features necessarily leads to a conclusion about the works' status as the products of serene renunciation or irascible decline, though in the case of Shakespeare the issue of genre creates a certain amount of pressure in that regard because of the association critics habitually make between romance and reconciliation. But clarity in respect of each of the categories is required in order fully to determine the existence of a late style. In this chapter I will consider the place in late-play criticism of these three issues – genre, chronology and style – in order to assess both the evidence for and the obstacles to the establishment of a clearly delimited Shakespearean late phase.

2.1 A QUESTION OF GENRE

We have seen Adorno's emphasis on *catastrophe*, on lateness as discontinuity, as the ending that comes about as a result of sudden change; we have seen him fret over the relationship in Beethoven's late work between integration and disintegration – both, that is, between the fragmented nature of the individual components of a given late work and the unity that nonetheless characterises that work, and between the nature of the late works as embodiments of discontinuity within Beethoven's career and their inevitability as the concluding manifestation of that career as a whole. For all that he argues for overall coherence, however, the prompt for the debate Adorno sets up is the basic, tangible break that he believes the late works form with Beethoven's mid-period style. The same is of course true for Shakespeare. Dowden could never have marked out his period 'On the heights' and his category of 'Romance' had he not been able both to rely upon a chronology and to locate and specify certain significant stylistic and generic tendencies that mark out those plays from what preceded them and thus to establish a clear dividing line. The obstacles to this, however, are clear. There is nothing in the First Folio – which provides the only texts we have of *The Winter's Tale*, *Cymbeline*, *The Tempest* and *Henry VIII* and wholly omits *Pericles*, *Cardenio* and *The Two Noble Kinsmen* – to suggest a chronological mindset, nothing to offer a sense of 'early' or 'late'. If anything, the Folio might be seen wilfully to invert that pattern right from the start, beginning as it does with *The Tempest*, the play critics prefer to think of as the very last. The structure of the volume, moreover, does notoriously little to help students of the late plays, rejecting chronology as its governing principle and organising the plays into groups that disperse the late plays and thus deny them a separate, distinct generic identity. It may be that the First Folio was in some sense, as G. K. Hunter has suggested, 'a conspectus of a literary career [. . .] a set of plays to be read as authorial creations rather than theatrical documents, now open to detailed criticism, interpretative questioning and relevant annotation of meanings', but there are certain problems with this notion to which I will return in Chapter 4. And there is little, if anything, to suggest that the order of production informs the sequence in which the plays are presented, despite ingenious critical attempts to find logic in apparent arbitrariness, which consist mostly in variations on Dowden's observation that the Folio 'opens with The Tempest [and] closes with Cymbeline [and that t]he Winter's Tale is the last of the comedies, which all lie between this play and The Tempest', a 'circumstance', he concedes, that 'may have been a piece of accident', before adding 'but if so, it was a lucky accident'.[2]

Ryan, a century and a quarter later, as we have seen, though keen to emphasise the developments in interpretation of the late plays across time, in practice sustains Dowden's basic assumption that there are three unequivocal late plays – *The Winter's Tale*, *Cymbeline* and *The Tempest* – along with one prior collaboration, *Pericles*, which offers sufficient in the way of a 'family likeness' to make up a total of four but which is relatively marginal, both because of its status as a collaboration and because it is absent from the Folio (it only enters the canon in 1664 with the Third Folio). He acknowledges, as does Dowden in his 'Primer', that other, later plays exist, but he likewise excludes them from practical consideration. The plays both critics refer to as the 'late plays' or 'romances' are, they insist, quite different in kind from Shakespeare's other plays, marking a change in stance and direction that bears a distinct relation to the stage of life the playwright had reached at the time of writing: they share certain features with Shakespeare's work as a whole, of course, but the point of emphasis is their difference from the earlier work. Written between 1607 and 1611, these plays are typically treated as forming a coherent group, a trilogy or tetralogy on the model, implicitly, of the history plays, especially since both the first and second tetralogies can be regarded as variations on the theme of three-plus-one: the three parts of *Henry VI* plus *Richard III*, *Richard II* plus the three connected plays *1 & 2 Henry IV* and *Henry V* or, alternatively, *Henry V* plus the three connected plays *Richard II*, *1 & 2 Henry IV*. Whichever shape you impose – eliding such issues as the chronology of the *Henry VI* plays and the causal relationship of the two parts of *Henry IV* – you have either a three-plus-one or a straightforward four, and the late plays can be structured either way. Critics who have subscribed to the bare-minimum three-play group include, first and foremost, Dowden, who in the first edition of *Shakspere: His Mind and Art* treated *Cymbeline*, *The Winter's Tale* and *The Tempest* as a distinct group with shared characteristics, and, subsequently, as diverse a set of Shakespeareans as E. M. W. Tillyard, Robert Ornstein and, most recently, Robert Henke.[3] Dowden, starting out in this way as a three-play man, took a couple more years to accept *Pericles*, including it with the other three in the third edition of *Mind and Art* in 1877. Those who follow his revised line in accepting *Pericles* as an integral member of the four-play group include Derek Traversi, Frank Kermode, Douglas Peterson, Marco Mincoff, Ruth Nevo, Robert Adams, Maurice Hunt, Cynthia Marshall, Simon Palfrey and Alison Thorne.[4] All agree that the four plays share a coherent identity.

I argued in Chapter 1 that late work is not generically bound (for Ellis, the late plays are, for instance, simply 'undramatic'), but the general tendency of late-style critics – with the obvious exceptions of Adorno and Said – to find in late work such attributes as rejuvenation, reconciliation, resignation and redemption would appear to narrow the generic possibilities. For Kenneth Muir, writing in the mid-sixties at the high-water mark of the discourse of lateness and positing as the primary connection between a range of different late periods a process of religious or quasi-religious conversion late in life, the question of genre was essentially theological. 'Most of these last plays are not tragic', he noted, 'as though the poets, as they drew near to their eternal home, found the tragic interpretation of life no longer most valid for them' (Muir, 113). The late plays' generic coherence and their redemptive orientation were central tenets of mid-twentieth-century criticism, dominating late-play studies, as we have seen, until critics influenced by cultural and ideological theory began to re-read these plays as the products of more complex and oppressive social and, crucially, material forces than their predecessors would have cared to acknowledge. For Dowden, it was simple: the plays were 'romances', a term he had presumably picked up from Coleridge and Hazlitt.[5] 'There is', he argues simply,

> a romantic element about these plays. In all there is the same romantic incident of lost children recovered by those to whom they are dear – the daughters of Pericles and Leontes, the sons of Cymbeline and Alonso. In all there is a beautiful romantic background of sea or mountain. The dramas have a grave beauty, a sweet serenity, which seem to render the name 'comedies' inappropriate; we may smile tenderly, but we never laugh loudly, as we read them. Let us, then, name this group consisting of four plays, Romances. (Dowden, 'Primer', 55–6)

A range of twentieth-century critics, though sceptical of some aspects of his material, sustained and developed Dowden's argument. In the second half of the century, E. C. Pettet, Northrop Frye, Stanley Wells, Howard Felperin, Barbara Mowat, Robert Uphaus and others all championed 'romance' as the best way to sum up what was characteristic about this group of plays.[6] Pettet, for instance, noting Dowden's 'imprecise' use of the term and the 'half-apologetic air of vagueness about' Tillyard's observation in *Shakespeare's Last Plays* that 'when we call Shakespeare's last plays romances, I suppose we mean that his material is remote and improbable and that he uses the happy ending', sets out to clarify the romantic essence of the late plays (Pettet, *Romance Tradition*, 161; Tillyard, *Last*, 71). He notes, *inter alia*, that the plays all, '[w]ith the exception of *The Tempest*, whose plot cannot be ascribed to any known source [...] derive directly from one branch or another of romantic literature'; that the 'mass of incident, th[e] vigour and excitement of narrative, is characteristically romantic in that it is quite unhampered by any considerations of verisimilitude'; that 'particular romance conventions' recur throughout the plays; that 'the plays are characterised by the quality of movement and of abrupt changes of scene that we find so frequently in the romantic tale'; that Shakespeare in the last plays 'reverted, as he was compelled to by the romantic nature of his stories, to the type of character that is more than half pasteboard'; and that 'the setting [...] too, is unmistakeably romantic', by which he means both the plays' courtly context and their 'pastoralism' (*Romance Tradition*, 161, 163, 164, 166, 168, 169). For Felperin, echoing Pettet's resistance to vagueness, the late romances 'have received less than justice in this century, not so much because they have lacked sensitive readers as because those readers have lacked a working theory of romance'; at the same time, he admits that '[c]oming to terms with romance is a difficult task, precisely because romance, of all imaginative modes, is the most fundamental, universal, and heterogeneous' (*Shakespearean Romance*, vii, 7). Developing this premise, he defines romance very broadly indeed to include not only third-century classical romance – he cites Longus' *Daphnis and Chloe*, Heliodorus' *Aethiopica*, Achilles Tatius' *Clitophon and Leucippe* and Xenophon's *Ephesiaca* – and medieval chivalric romance – *Bevis of Hampton*, *Guy of Warwick*, Chaucer, Gower and Malory, *inter alia* – but also medieval mystery and morality plays – *The Castle of Perseverance*, *Pride of Life*, *Everyman* and *Mundus et Infans* – and plots the ways in which the late plays renegotiate the various forms of what he considers the same basic phenomenon. And he hints at debates to come when he argues that the plays are in a kind of productive conflict with the form on which they depend: 'The moral and mimetic dimension of Shakespearean romance comes into being through its stubborn refusal to accept and repeat the conventions of romance without revaluating them' (Felperin, 54). This is not yet a critique of the idea of Shakespearean romance, but it opens up the possibility of such a critique.[7]

Despite such warnings, recent critics continue in various ways to insist that the late plays are best described as 'romances'. For Elizabeth Bieman, '[t]he motif of transformation or metamorphosis, often from deathlike states to new life', which she considers the central motif of the last plays, 'prevails as constant in the otherwise protean literary genre, romance'.[8] Others are a little more circumspect, while nonetheless preferring 'romance' to any other candidate. Alison Thorne, though calling her 'New Casebook' collection 'Shakespeare's Romances', heavily qualifies the term in her helpful introduction. Noting the 'outpouring' in the seventies and eighties of 'scholarly monographs devoted to the task of explicating the peculiarities of the "romances" by reference to the generic conventions they deploy', she acknowledges that many studies of the late plays

> might be accused of overstating the explanatory power of such an approach, besides taking too little account of the provisionality of generic nomenclatures and the evidence that the literary conventions attached to the 'kinds' tended to be regarded (by the more talented writers at least) not as a binding set of rules, but, at most, as a starting-point for individual experimentation.[9]

But, she adds, '[h]andled cautiously with such provisos in mind [...] generic definitions can be a valuable analytical tool', providing, as they do, 'an indispensable frame of reference that allows us to trace how received forms are being invoked and manipulated in the "romances"' (*Shakespeare's Romances*, 4). Barbara Mowat too devotes the first section of her fine essay in Jean Howard and Richard Dutton's *Companion to Shakespeare's Works* to offering provisos, demonstrating her own critical development from her

A question of genre

early work on the late plays by explaining why she no longer sees 'romance' as an adequate descriptive term for these plays before proceeding to offer what is in fact the most convincing recent analysis of the plays *as* romances. She demonstrates the late plays' roots in the kinds of drama that frustrated Philip Sidney – 'all their plays be neither right tragedies, nor right comedies', he objected,

> mingling kings and clowns, not because the matter so carrieth it, but thrust in the clown by head and shoulders to play a part in majestical matters with neither decency nor discretion, so as neither the admiration nor commiseration, nor the right sportfulness, is by their mongrel tragicomedy obtained

– but which were visibly still alive and well on the early Jacobean stage, not least in the shape of the perennially popular *Mucedorus*, the most frequently reprinted of all plays in the period, known to have been performed at court in 1610 but in all likelihood revived a little prior to this – around 1606 – just in time to be an influence on late Shakespeare.[10]

Most recently, Helen Cooper, in her magisterial book *The English Romance in Time*, echoing Felperin, lists Geoffrey of Monmouth's *History*, Chaucer's *Canterbury Tales*, *Sir Gawain and the Green Knight*, *Bevis of Hampton*, *Guy of Warwick*, Malory's *Morte d'Arthur*, Spenser's *Faerie Queene*, Beaumont and Fletcher's *Philaster* and Shakespeare's late plays as all belonging to the same broad family as the continental *Amadis de Gaule*, *Celestina* or *Floris and Blancheflour*.[11] She negotiates the obvious problem of the sheer reach of this material by finessing genre through the term 'meme', coined by Richard Dawkins in *The Selfish Gene* to signify 'an idea that behaves like a gene in its ability to replicate faithfully and abundantly, but also on occasion to adapt, mutate, and therefore survive in different forms and cultures' (*English Romance*, 3). Cooper thus reads romance not as a genre but as a series of interconnected motifs that, taken together, evoke an understanding in the reader of the kind meant by Jauss when he coined the term 'horizon of expectation' (a term also deployed by Thorne).[12] As Barbara Fuchs puts it, '[c]ritics disagree about whether it is a genre or a mode, about its origins and history, even about what it encompasses. Yet, paradoxically, readers are often able to identify romance almost tacitly: they know it when they see it.'[13]

Such finessing is a response to the way in which 'romance' as a generic term designed to cohere the late plays – used, as we have seen, by the vast bulk of twentieth-century late-play critics – has over the last thirty years or so been found to be less than helpful for a range of good reasons. Partly this is, as Thorne notes, because of the discrepancies between the structure and action of individual plays and the expectations and characteristics of both classical and medieval romance as poetic genres; partly because the modern understanding of the word, unavoidably affected by the significance given to it in the late eighteenth and early nineteenth centuries, is so different from the early modern sense; and partly because of the modern association of 'romance' with certain kinds of popular paperback fiction. Diana Childress, in her landmark 1974 essay 'Are Shakespeare's Last Plays Really Romances?', argues that 'to apply the term "romance" to Shakespeare's later plays [...] as has so often been done, is not only anachronistic but also very misleading', and provides a helpful summary of the issues.[14] '[I]t is the later meanings added to "romance"', she argues, 'that have made the term so plastic. Any poet who draws his inspiration from medieval romance is assumed to be writing romances, even though he may be using romance materials to quite different ends – for an allegory, an epic, or a play' (ibid., 45–6). Childress lists a series of features that, for her, keep the late plays distinct from romance: irony, alienation, estranging humour, grotesquerie – in general, forms of distancing. All are elements that could, she acknowledges, be derived from or absorbed into romance, but for her it is Shakespeare's handling of these elements that stops his plays from being themselves romances. At the same time, the plays approximate to parody without actually becoming parodic: they can, she says, 'be produced as parodies on the stage, but that is only simplifying and flattening these plays to make them easier to digest. The optimistic endings – if they are optimistic – are not altogether satisfying, nor do I think they are intended to be satisfying' (ibid., 53). To call the plays 'romances', critics have suggested, is to presume their unqualified engagement with earlier textual forms, to leave the extent of their generic self-irony unaccounted for, and to assume that the plays as a group are characterised by the kind of benign simplicity that was once thought to be their hallmark but which recent readings – postcolonial readings of *The Tempest*, for instance – have suggested is simply not an adequate way to understand the impact of these plays in their first contexts. Once the ironic, referential and alienated nature of the deployment of romance material evident in the plays comes under scrutiny, in other words, it becomes harder and harder to think of the plays as themselves simply 'romances'.

Cooper develops this argument a little further by noting that the very last play in the sequence, *The Two Noble Kinsmen*, in its reworking of Chaucer, concludes in a manner that defies even the most enthusiastic optimist. While it is clear that the play, 'like its source, offers itself for recognition as romance[that is] a story of two young knights of high prowess who fall in love with the same woman', it is equally clear that

[t]hroughout the play [...] the authors home in on the elements Chaucer had made problematic, and intensify them. Love is presented not as an ideal but as an obsession. Same-sex friendship is called into question, except when its object (Emilia's childhood friend) is dead. The play's strong women speak of exercising their strength outside the action in terms of a martial acquaintance with slaughtered babies, and within it they are consistently cast as victims rather than agents. The lovers, for all their declarations of adoration, reveal themselves as callous sexual predators. (*English Romance*, 374)

There is little sign, for Cooper, then, in this latest of late plays, of the serene reconciliation, the happy ending, that brings closure to romance. In any case, Chaucer's *Knight's Tale*, the principal source, is itself, for her (she is, of course, best known as a Chaucerian), a long way from the mainstream of romance in its grimness, and by the time of *The Two Noble Kinsmen* the quest is no longer a possibility: 'Chaucer's Arcite laments that a man trying to find happiness in life is like a drunkard unable to find his way home', she notes, whereas 'Shakespeare's Theseus suggests that there is no home to be found, that life is a nightmare city where the streets themselves turn errancy into error' (Cooper, 375). Thus '[a]fter the wonder of the romances, their reunions and near-miraculous resurrections and recoveries, their prophesied workings out of all things for good', she observes, Shakespeare 'ends his career in the bleakness of a medieval romance that goes wrong' (ibid.) by writing a play that is hardly, in the final analysis, recognisable as belonging to the same genre. If, that is, 'romance' counts technically as a term for a dramatic genre at all. As Mowat notes, 'the category is strikingly absent from Polonius's comically comprehensive list of such genres, and, indeed, from Shakespeare's works generally' (Mowat, 133). For Childress, in the end, the late plays 'cannot fairly be called romances' (Childress, 53). Thus, while it is easy enough to see why, for Elizabeth Bieman, despite these various difficulties', 'romance' nonetheless 'more than compensates' (Bieman, xi), the term, for all of its obvious applicability, hardly, in Robert Henke's words, 'exhausts the plays' dramaturgy'.[15]

What, then, are the alternatives? There have been scores. As Gary Schmidgall observes, *The Tempest*, for one, has been read as 'morality play, initiation ritual, refinement of the *commedia dell'arte*, topical response to New World voyages [and] masque' and as 'hymeneal celebration, fairy tale, myth, or autobiographical palinode'.[16] One option is, simply enough, 'comedy', with the last plays read as the culmination of work begun in Shakespeare's youth and thus, rather than registering a clearcut late shift in generic engagement, marking a return to the forms and sources of some of his earliest work (*Pericles*, for instance, a return to the materials of *The Comedy of Errors*, *The Two Noble Kinsmen* to those of *A Midsummer Night's Dream*). Specifically, the late plays have been read as 'comedies of atonement', a form of the genre requiring the passing of a certain amount of time and thus in certain ways close kin to romance. But this reading has tended by and large, unsurprisingly, to be promoted, by critics from D. G. James to Howard Felperin, precisely *as* a sub-category of 'romance' rather than of 'comedy' per se, and it is clear enough that, both as a broad generic appellation and as a form we associate with Shakespeare's early-to-mid plays of festivity and generational negotiation, the term 'comedy' hardly begins to encompass the development in Shakespeare's formal technique by 1607 or 1608: to limit the late plays to a role as rehearsals of that earlier comic mode is to impose on them inappropriate restrictions. A far stronger contender is 'tragicomedy', a productively hybrid (and usefully vague) term of which Robert Henke has been the most recent proponent, building on work of some pedigree by Ashley Thorndike, Marvin Herrick, Frank Ristine, Joan Hartwig, Verna Foster and others in reading the late plays through the lens of the writings of the highly influential Italian theorist Giambattista Guarini, in which he defended the genre against charges that, in its hybridity, it constituted an unacceptable travesty of decorum.[17] Guarini argued for a generic flexibility rejected on classical grounds by his peers, reading tragicomedy as the legitimate offspring of the classical genres of tragedy and comedy, offering historically appropriate new possibilities for theatre, and he insisted that genre is not fixed but responsive to changing contexts. This makes the motivation for considering 'tragicomedy', rather than 'romance', as a cohering generic label for the last plays clear. As Hartwig observes (and as we have seen), '[a] certain uneasiness arises from viewing the plays in terms of the romance tradition alone because the strictures of classification occasionally impose limits on what Shakespeare was free to do with the romance conventions' (*Tragicomic Vision*, 11). Tragicomedy, on the other hand, is enough of a broad church to encompass the various generic traits critics have observed in the late plays which do not themselves constitute an adequate generic ascription and yet require acknowledgement and incorporation into whichever overarching identity is chosen, from pastoral to masque and from myth to morality.

Starting with Ristine, however (who is in fact evasive about the place of the Shakespearean late plays in his genealogy of the genre), these critics, even as they argue *for* 'tragicomedy' as the term best suited to the task of encompassing the complex intersection of generic, ideological, cultural and historical forces that combine to produce the last plays, are forced to acknowledge that Shakespeare's practice in those plays meshes at best uncomfortably both with Guarinian theory and with the contemporary practice of, on the one hand, Marston and, on the other, Fletcher – which in itself offers at best an equivocal relationship to Guarini – and thus compromises their choice.[18] Shakespeare did unquestionably write tragicomedies, plays which mix tragic and comic elements and which offer a range of political and aesthetic possibilities quite other than the conservatism traditionally assigned to them, but his experiments with plays that blend tragedy and comedy include material a long way beyond the scope of Guarini's ideas. As Bieman rightly notes, the principal problem with 'tragicomedy' as a label for the late plays is that the term will 'encompass also such comedies as, perhaps, *Much Ado About Nothing* and, certainly, *Measure for Measure*' and 'fits *The Tempest* only if we stretch the tale Prospero tells Miranda back into that undelineated "dark [...] abysm of time" that precedes the tightly unified action on the island stage' (*The Romances*, xi). Moreover, it was, in the end, the tragicomedies of his late co-adjutor Fletcher – ironic, various, unromantic, excessive – rather more than Shakespeare's own that set the agenda for the theatrical future both before and after the Civil War, an eventuality which does not provide, for Shakespeareans, the right comic outcome to the tragedy of the closing of the theatres and has, for the most part, been elided. Marston, Daniel, (Beaumont and) Fletcher and others were, in the second decade-and-a-half of the seventeenth century, experimenting with and creating a genre that reaches far beyond, and is ultimately shaped quite differently from, the Shakespearean late plays, which are simply one manifestation of a genre in, to use Ristine's term, 'transition'.

Thus critics seem largely to agree that the problems involved in calling the group of plays in the Shakespeare canon from *Pericles* to *The Two Noble Kinsmen* 'tragicomedies' or 'romances' are such that it is best to avoid doing so altogether. Both terms are seen as too limiting and exclusive adequately to embrace the plays' generic dependencies and possibilities, and each effectively undermines the other as an adequate denominator of the plays' generic orientation. 'Romance', while signalling certain key structural impulses that characterise the plays, is simply too all-encompassing a term to be of much use in understanding their specifics. 'Tragicomedy', too, is an inadequate term for these plays, if only because as a technical description it is broad enough to encompass plays within the canon such as *Measure for Measure* and *Troilus and Cressida* that fall beyond, and bear little modal resemblance to, the final group. And there is, as we have seen, little in the publication history of these plays to suggest that they were viewed as a generically coherent group by Shakespeare's contemporaries, except perhaps by Ben Jonson in the contemptuous lines of the Scrivener in *Bartholomew Fair*:

if there bee neuer a *Seruant-monster* i'the *Fayre*; who can help it? he sayes; nor a nest of *Antiques*? Hee is loth to make Nature afraid in his *Playes*, like those that beget *Tales, Tempests*, and such like *Drolleries*, to mix his head with other mens heeles, let the concupisence of *Iigges* and *Dances*, raigne as strong as it will amongst you.[19]

Moreover, both generic ascriptions – and I use 'ascription' deliberately for its echoes of authorship ascription, since it seems to me that at times the desire to establish a single, clear generic label for these plays is akin to the determination to prove that a given play was written by a single, clear, easily distinguishable individual – have, for a range of reasons, come to evoke a conservatism that many current critics would choose to reject, seeing no need to create readings which are, in David Norbrook's phrase, 'more royalist than the King's Men'.[20] 'Romance' in particular is lined up alongside the influence of the masque to ascribe a conservative politics to the plays, a tendency apparent, for instance, in David Bergeron's essay in the Dutton and Howard *Companion*: 'As spectacle complements state and majesty in masques,' we learn, 'so it completes romance in Shakespeare's last plays.'[21] The genre of the late plays is, in this reading, intrinsically aligned with royalist ideology. Yet, particularly by way of accounts of *The Tempest* which resist both the idea of the benign Prospero and the assumption that the play's deployment of the masque as a structural element is unironic, but also through, for instance, readings of *Cymbeline* in the context of the history of English nationhood, many critics have chosen to resist this equation of masque and romance as conservative forms and to emphasise instead the complexity and multiplicity of political viewpoint in the last plays (and, for that matter, in the masque, too). Equally, it is clear that although, as Henke notes, 'Italian tragicomedy was mainly a courtly phenomenon, and the powerful, mysterious, and providential harmonies wrought in the final act of tragicomedies like *Il Pastor Fido* surely reflected the power of ducal courts like that of Ferrara' (*Pastoral Transformations*, 24), and though Guarini's play directly inspired the first Jacobean foray into Italianate pastoral tragicomedy, Fletcher's *Faithful Shepherdess*, critics are understandably chary of imposing without qualification a political model of this kind onto the emergent English form.[22]

A question of genre

For these reasons, then, critics who happily refer to *Hamlet* as a tragedy or *Love's Labours Lost* as a comedy have in recent years avoided 'romance' and 'tragicomedy' (along with the hybrid, or fence-sitting, term 'romantic tragicomedy') as ways of gathering into a single group the plays *Pericles*, *Cymbeline*, *The Winter's Tale* and *The Tempest*, never mind *Henry VIII* and *The Two Noble Kinsmen*.[23] This is not always simply a ducking of the issue of genre. For Ruth Nevo, the plays, in their numinous lateness, have a *postgeneric* quality. 'In his later plays', she argues, performing the transhistorical, transdisciplinary comparison characteristic, as we have seen, of studies of late work, and echoing Ellis writing about the late Rodin and the late Michelangelo, 'Shakespeare, like late Yeats, like late Picasso, yields to his themes, loosens or even abandons the constraints of classical category and moves beyond genre towards an indeterminate mode akin to reverie' (*Other Language*, 6). For Nevo, chronology outweighs – supersedes, even – generic ascription: late style, is, for her, simply 'beyond genre'. Yet even as she turns for a parallel to her principal critical influence, Freud – suggesting, in a broadening of the applicability of 'late work', that '[t]here is a strange affinity between these strangely anguished "comedies" and Freud's late review of his own theories' in *Beyond the Pleasure Principle* – she contradicts herself, offering a clear demonstration of the difficulty of negotiating between the temporal manifestations of the transtemporal mode that is late style and the historically bound concept of genre (ibid., 6). *Beyond the Pleasure Principle*, she argues, is 'a melancholy disquisition, Freud's displaced mourning for his daughter, an oceanic death-wish fantasy' – that is, 'a tragicomedy' – and she adds that 'Shakespeare's tragicomedies are also essays beyond the pleasure principle and toward mourning' (ibid.). The urge to substitute for genre a lateness that transcends form thus appears to fall in on itself: as chronology reappears, it is almost immediately elided with tragicomedy, even in the midst of an attempt to move beyond generic terminology.

That said, Nevo is not alone in her desire to sidestep genre. A. D. Nuttall had already argued in 1966, in response to the debate over generic terminology, for the unique status of the late plays. 'There is', he claimed, 'a sense in which the last plays of Shakespeare are *sui generis*, so that any word would do (the blanker the better)'.[24] This sentiment is echoed in the recent work of Robert Henke, who – despite arguing vigorously for the relationship of the late plays to tragicomedy in the pastoral tradition – concludes that, in the end, '[a]s a label, the neutral term "late plays" is probably best, for there is always danger in announcing that one has finally discovered the true generic identity of these odd creations' (*Pastoral Transformations*, 31). Partisans for 'romance' seem equally inclined to adopt the 'neutral term'.

Barbara Mowat, for instance, despite her strong arguments for the nature of the plays as inheritors of Elizabethan dramatic romance, recognising that the various generic terms need to be treated with kid gloves and given very careful, historically aware definition, appears also to prefer 'late play' as a kind of default label for plays whose complex generic affiliations she is addressing: 'late' as a description of the plays has, for her, no more or less significance than it does in a phrase such as 'the late 1600s' and is thus, in Henke's word, 'neutral'. Yet, as I hope will by now be clear, 'late' is a word loaded with a specific critical history which brings with it a series of presumptions and elisions that arguably do far more than either of the terms 'romance' or 'tragicomedy' to limit our understanding of the last plays in the Shakespeare canon. To accept its 'neutrality', as Henke proposes we do, is to elide the convoluted history not only of late Shakespeare but also of the construction of the overarching idea of 'late work' or 'late style' across the disciplines. It is thus to nullify the logic of the word, as well as to ignore the fact that 'late play' automatically invokes the question of subjectivism, since it seeks the meaning of the play solely in its author, as if the playwright were the sole locus of meaning for a play produced for an acting company and an audience. 'Late' is not at all Nuttall's 'blanker, better' word: it is in fact just as loaded with prior and determining meaning as are 'romance' and 'tragicomedy'. 'Late play' is thus anything but a 'neutral term'.

2.2 A QUESTION OF CHRONOLOGY

There is nothing intrinsic to the process of playwriting that insists on a shared profile for a set of plays from a given period of a playwright's life. After all, few critics invited to take a five-year period from an earlier part of Shakespeare's life – 1600–1605, say – would wish to make overarching stylistic or generic claims or argue for the overall coherence of a group of plays that includes (on the basis of the chronology in the second edition of the *Oxford Shakespeare*) *Hamlet, Twelfth Night, Troilus and Cressida, Sir Thomas More, Measure for Measure* and *Othello*, along, perhaps, with *Timon of Athens* and the first version of *King Lear*. Clearly, in view of the immense stylistic and generic diversity among these plays, ways other than the simply chronological are required to order and assess them. The late plays, however, elicit a wholly different response, despite the fact that a good deal of selectivity is required – nothing like as much as would be needed for the 1600–1605 plays, but more than enough to put the practice under a good deal of pressure – before a coherent grouping can be achieved. The driving force of this different treatment is, in one form or another (no matter how well disguised), subjectivism, the placing of the life of the playwright at the centre of the understanding of his work which, as we have seen, tends to reach its most intense and exclusive pitch with late periods.

In any case, as Dawson points out in his *Tempest* essay, the precise chronology of these plays is far less clearcut than might be supposed. Just as there is no way of knowing the order in which the thirteen supposedly unfinished paintings left in Rembrandt's studio at his death might have been painted (or, for that matter, how long some of them had been sitting there prior to his death, finished or not), so there is no unequivocal external evidence to guarantee that *The Tempest* postdates *Cymbeline* and *The Winter's Tale*.[25] The dating of these plays depends in large part upon Simon Forman's diary: he saw *Cymbeline* probably in late April 1611 (no date is given but his account of the performance appears in sequence with later April events) and *The Winter's Tale* on 15 May 1611. This, however, does not necessarily reflect the order of composition since Forman also saw *Macbeth*, a play long established in the repertory, on 20 April 1611 and there is no evidence to suggest that the late-play performances he attended were necessarily first nights. Yet critics unanimously insist on taking the accepted order for these plays as a self-evident fact – or, at least, they did until the inversion of the order of *Cymbeline* and *The Winter's Tale* proposed by the editors of the *Oxford Shakespeare* in 1986 shook up their assumptions. And even the *Oxford Shakespeare* has no qualms about retaining *The Tempest* as the last of the four.

We do at least know that *Pericles* came first, since it was published in quarto form in 1609 and appears in the Stationers' Register for 20 May 1608, probably receiving its première around the same time.[26] But it is not impossible that over the next couple of years Shakespeare wrote his subsequent three plays in the order *The Tempest, Cymbeline, The Winter's Tale* or, alternatively, *The Winter's Tale, The Tempest, Cymbeline* – the latter being the order championed by Philip Edwards, swimming against the tide, who sees *Cymbeline* as at least as much 'a kind of farewell play' as he does *The Tempest*.[27] It is of course equally, but no more, possible that Shakespeare wrote these plays in the order *Cymbeline, The Winter's Tale, The Tempest*, as most of us, with the exception of Edwards, would, if we are honest, prefer. The point is that we do not actually know. Yet the insistent association, first made well prior to Dowden, of Shakespeare and Prospero as consummate creators giving up their respective arts (I will return to this in Chapter 3), requires that the order which concludes with *The Tempest* be the correct one. As Dowden noted,

> [i]t has been suggested that Prospero, the great enchanter, is Shakspere himself, and that when he breaks his staff, drowns his book, and dismisses his airy spirits, going back to the duties of his dukedom, Shakspere was thinking of his own resigning of his powers of imaginative enchantment, his parting from the theatre, where his attendant spirits had played their parts, and his return to Stratford. (Dowden, 'Primer', 150)

He accepts this without comment and it has remained, as Tony Dawson wryly notes, in the back of Shakespeareans' minds ever since, despite the current state of knowledge – that is, that there is no evidence with which to fix an unchallengeable order of composition for the three 'central' late Shakespeare plays and that, whichever of the three comes last, there are in any case three collaborations that postdate them. It remains entirely possible that the established order is in fact correct, but that does not redeem the inadequacy of the subjectivism that underpins the critical desire for this to be so and it cannot in any case, of course, erase the later collaborations.

The absence of clear external evidence for a late-play chronology calls for other means of entrenching the preferred order and, in the course of the twentieth century, a consensus emerged about the development of the late plays from initial experiment in a new form to final, consummate achievement in that form. Sir Arthur Quiller-Couch, writing in 1921 and neatly combining literary criticism with upper-class leisure pursuits, began the process in characteristic style: Shakespeare, he argued, 'in his later years essaying about the hardest technical difficulty a dramatist can propose to himself, and, beaten thrice – in *Pericles*, in *Cymbeline*, in *The Winter's Tale* – with a fourth and last shot, in *The Tempest* br[ought] down his quarry from the sky'.[28] Others, while not deploying the same unfortunate sporting metaphor, share this developmental view of the process, but begin to introduce distinctions between the first three plays. For J. M. Nosworthy, in his influential 1955 Arden *Cymbeline*, it was clear 'from the outset that *Pericles*, *Cymbeline*, and, to a certain but insignificant extent, *The Winter's Tale* were the pioneer colonizing efforts of a Shakespeare more completely without a reputable model than he had ever been', adding that '[w]e have only to set the play beside *The Tempest* to see how clumsy and palpable it all is' (edition, xxxi, xxxii). In his introduction, Nosworthy describes *Cymbeline* as an 'experimental romance', noting that, along with *Pericles*, it represents 'the first fruits of a new attempt' and thus was 'prone to partial or total failure' (ibid., xlix). '[T]he technical perfection of *The Tempest*,' Nosworthy adds, 'is generally admitted to verge on the miraculous, and we must be prepared for lapses at the experimental stage' (ibid.). Larry S. Champion similarly treats all of the late plays as versions of comedy, but where he presents *The Winter's Tale* and *The Tempest* as 'comedies of transformation', in an earlier chapter he uses Boas's term 'problem comedies' (already thoroughly outmoded by this time) to group *Pericles* and *Cymbeline* with *All's Well That Ends Well* and *Measure for Measure*, arguing that Shakespeare does not again achieve a 'comic [...] success commensurate with that of *Twelfth Night*' until he writes *The Winter's Tale* and *The Tempest*, treating the earlier plays as 'interim' efforts.[29] Champion holds that, as far as comedy was concerned, Shakespeare had a decade in the wilderness – a period presumably coinciding with Dowden's third period, 'Out of the depths' – and only re-emerged, a little rusty in respect of the form, with *Pericles* and *Cymbeline*. For Kenneth Muir, summing up in 1979, *Pericles* begins Shakespeare's experiments in the romance form and his work in this genre gradually improves with *Cymbeline* and then with *The Winter's Tale* until finally there is the climactic *Tempest*, 'the most structurally perfect of all Shakespeare's plays' (Muir, *Comic Sequence*, 150). The Oxford Shakespeare's inversion of *Cymbeline* and *The Winter's Tale* was a major setback for this viewpoint, but since the publication of the first edition, critics have worked hard to put *Cymbeline* back in its place, unearthing a series of topicalities to reconfirm that the play marks a transitional form between *Pericles* and *The Winter's Tale*. For Leeds Barroll, *Pericles* and *Cymbeline* form a 'first wave' of late plays – *Cymbeline* being most likely first performed at the Globe in the first half of 1610 and then at court at Christmas 1610–11 – and *The Winter's Tale* and *The Tempest* a second, the four split into two groups of two by the exigencies of plague-closure.[30] Valerie Wayne, in turn, for different reasons (using the awkward topicality of the Arbella Stuart elopement as a marker for the likelihood of performance), agrees that the play received its first court performance at Christmas 1610–11, but considers that it was written in mid-1610.[31] Either way, both find, in the absence of conclusive external evidence, contextual reasons for establishing a gap between *Cymbeline* and the 'second wave'. Both, however, are in the end reliant on inference rather than proof, and each may be susceptible to the longstanding critical characterisation of *Cymbeline* as an 'experimental' romance.

The desire for unity – at the level of the career as well as that of the single text – motivating the argument for an internal progression within the four 'romances' also manifested itself in the work of certain mid-twentieth-century critics in the form of an intermittent counter-current that took the idea of internal progression to the next logical stage, seeking coherence and development not just in a discrete group of plays but in Shakespeare's career as a whole. These critics in effect rejected the caesura by emphasising not change but continuity, arguing that the late plays, rather than representing a sharp fissure in Shakespeare's work, in fact fulfil the overall scheme of his writing life. For G. Wilson Knight, characteristically offering an extreme version of this reading, the late plays are the consummation of Shakespeare's steady development of a royalist-nationalist vision, the 'crowning act for which the Ariel of Shakespeare's art has been steadily, from play to play, disciplined and matured', the logical product of 'his whole life-work to this point'.[32] For Tillyard, on the other hand, late Shakespeare, rather than marking a clean break with what went before, is an extension of what he calls the 'tragic pattern', in which, for him, regeneration is inherent, and thus represents not a caesura but the ongoing development of a fundamental order – perhaps, finally, tragicomic rather than tragic – already apparent in the mid-period work (Tillyard, *Last*, 16–58, esp. 21). Knight and Tillyard may have read the career in different ways, but they agree on the evidence of continuity in the work from start to finish. And in the fullest of the postwar 'continuity' readings, Derek Traversi made it clear that he saw in Shakespeare's plays one long coherent unified artistic history, of which the late plays form not, as for some critics, 'a somewhat irrelevant appendix', but an integral part (*Last Phase* vii). 'Among the most fruitful aspects of recent Shakespearean criticism', he argued, 'has been the realization that there exists, behind the long and varied sequence of the plays, a continuous development of theme and treatment which makes it impossible to regard any of them, even the greatest, as mere isolated masterpieces. The last comedies, in particular, have gained enormously in stature from being read in the light of this understanding' (ibid., 1). Far from being a fresh development in Shakespeare's progress as a writer, then, the late plays, for these critics, represent an extension of the logic of the work so far – not an obvious extension, by any means, but one which, in hindsight, can be seen to provide genuine fulfilment of a consistent creative vision. It is thus clear that genre and chronology are joined at the hip.

The pivotal play for the mid-century critics, the play that underpins their claim for continuity between mature tragedies and late plays, was *King Lear*, which served both as Shakespeare's most complete tragedy and as the clearest precursor of the late plays (Traversi's book, for instance, mentions virtually no other play beyond the 'four romances' apart from *Lear*). Tillyard approvingly cites Dover Wilson's claim that '[t]he Lear that dies is not a Lear defiant, but a Lear redeemed' ('This last scene', wrote Dover Wilson elsewhere, 'reminds us, inevitably, of Calvary') and Knight, in *The Wheel of Fire*, offers one of the most notorious readings of *Lear*, arguing that Edmund, as he dies, 'recognizes love at last, its mystery, its power, its divinity' and asking of Lear's belief at the play's end that he sees Cordelia's lips move: 'What smiling destiny is this he sees at the last instant of racked mortality?'[33] Traversi concludes his map of the development of Shakespearean poetic expression in the tragedies with *King Lear*, reading the pattern he claims to see as steady movement away from convention towards a drama of 'personality,' in which '[t]he moral drama of the central figure finds full dramatic projection in the external events which he himself has, by an act of the will, set in motion' and so 'the events in turn acquire coherence and meaning through the relationship which binds them at every stage to the tensions which constitute the tragedy of the hero' (*Last Phase*, 14). The process is one in which psychology and event become one and the same, and *Lear* is the culmination of this process:

With *King Lear*, in so many ways Shakespeare's central masterpiece, these possibilities are at last fully realized. The integration of plot and character is more complete than ever before. There is a very real sense, indeed, in which the whole action of the tragedy might be described as a projection of the conflicting issues supremely present in the mind of the central figure. (ibid.)

'From this state of affairs', he suggests,

it is an easy and natural step to the deliberate abandonment of realism which is apparent in the last plays. [...] T]he tendency is [...] away from realism, towards a conception of the art of the theatre in which character and action alike are real in relation to the poetic unity to which they belong, and finally to that alone. (ibid., 18)

Thus, for Traversi, in the plots of the late plays,

the harmonizing theme first attempted in *King Lear* and there broken, after the brief restoration of the aged king to Cordelia, by the prevailing tragic development produces a conception of drama completely removed from realism and properly definable in symbolic terms. (ibid., 2)

The resistance to realism that the late plays represent, then, became, for postwar critics, a marker not of their difference from the mid-period plays but rather of their extension of the dramatic logic of those plays, with *King Lear* as the natural bridge between tragedy and romance.

Tillyard, Knight and Traversi argued their positions with great conviction, but they remained atypical of twentieth-century late-Shakespeare criticism in their rejection of the caesura. The vast majority of late-play critics argued, implicitly or explicitly, in a manner commensurate with analyses of late work in general, for a marked division between the late style and the work that preceded it. The continuity critics did so, too, in a way: their determination to demonstrate consistent development is a sustained attempt to explain away the differences they cannot actually deny between the late plays and the plays that preceded them. Most late-play critics, however, are only too keen to dwell on those differences. For them, if not for a Dover Wilson or a Tillyard, the points of divergence between the late plays and everything that came before are almost too obvious to mention and the existence of the caesura is simply taken for granted. Despite their opposed viewpoints, however, both sides are obliged to elide certain problematical matters so as to achieve a sense either of fissure or of continuity. If Traversi is to sustain a clear sense of progress across the career from the immature early plays to the fully mature and, finally, transcendent late plays – the internally coherent development, that is, of a poet, not of a professional playwright working in a commercial environment – he can acknowledge no breaks, fissures must be neatly smoothed over, and the final phase becomes, unsurprisingly, triumphantly universal. Writing of Cerimon's speech at Thaisa's revival, he argues that, at this point in the first play of the last phase,

a new, transhumanizing element (so to call it) enters explicitly into the verse, giving its full symbolic quality to what has now become the poetry of resurrection. This is perhaps the first time in Shakespeare that the full range of his mature poetry is lent to an effect so deliberately remote, so charged with a quality that can truly be described as supernatural, and yet so free from any suggestion of abstraction or strain. (*Last Phase*, 31)

The steady process of development leads, then, for Traversi, to the kind of claim for late transcendence that is, as we have seen, characteristic of accounts of late style. Yet he declines to relate the Shakespearean 'last phase' to any larger idea of late style – as if late Shakespeare stood alone – and so he cannot actually define what is 'late' about Shakespeare's 'late plays' because he does not move outside the four plays upon which he is insistently focussed, minimising context. The nearest he gets to acknowledging the possibility of any non-Shakespearean input at all into the construction of the late plays is the occasional passing mention of Beaumont and Fletcher (*Philaster* pops up momentarily in a footnote): there is no discussion at all, however, of the institutions – the company, the repertory – through and for which the plays came into existence.

Not that the caesura critics are any less inclined to limit the evidence. We have seen from the cases of Beethoven and Picasso the difficulties of hindsight and the clash between the critic's desire for a clearcut caesura and the actualities of a given life. One of the central issues in lateness studies, I have suggested, is the question of the return to the early, the argument that one of the key characteristics of late style – especially when equated with old-age style – is the tendency of creative artists late in life to turn back to the interests of their younger days – 'a sense' in Edward Said's words, 'of recapitulation and return for a long artistic trajectory' (*On Late Style*, 159). Robert Butler, as I have noted, argues that a key form of expression amongst older people is the 'life review' – work, that is, 'in which older people [. . .] confront the ghosts of their past in order to make peace with themselves' (Butler, *Life Review*, 66). For many late-play critics, noting the considerable evidence of return in the late plays, from the return of the protagonist to his point of origin to the generic return the plays themselves embody to a form of drama long out of fashion, this is precisely what Shakespeare is doing in his late work. *Pericles*, for instance, as we have seen, returns to the story of Apollonius of Tyre which Shakespeare had first broached in *The Comedy of Errors*; *The Tempest* considers once again the artistic possibilities premised by the work of Ovid and of Virgil; *Henry VIII* harks back to the form of the history play which Shakespeare had abandoned thirteen years earlier; *The Two Noble Kinsmen* returns to *The Knight's Tale*, Shakespeare's source for *A Midsummer Night's Dream*, presenting Theseus and Hippolyta once again and reworking the same situation for a darker purpose. Here, then, is a writer revising, rethinking, reassessing, turning back to the materials with which he forged the beginnings of his career and which are now rethought from the informed perspective of maturity and experience.

It would of course be absurd to deny that these plays mark a series of returns and revisions. 'The late plays', as Russ McDonald phrases it, 'feel almost obsessively reiterative.'[34] But it would be equally absurd to restrict Shakespearean return – as the caesura critics wished to do – only to the late plays. Nevo points out the obvious problem with the narrow association of the late plays and ideas of return, namely that

Shakespeare is *throughout* the most reiterative of poets – his returns and recurrences are as incessant as they are exfoliating and diversified; his imagination kindles afresh to each redevelopment of familiar components, or, perhaps it would be truer to say, every work leaves in its wake a detritus of un- or not yet resolved or integrated components which leads on to the next. (*Other Language*, 2; my emphasis)

Lawrence Danson echoes this, noting that Shakespeare's plays right across the career 'refer back and forth among themselves, endlessly invoking and endlessly complicating the genres they simultaneously inherit and make'.[35] This point – that *each stage* of Shakespeare's career, not just the late phase, is marked by processes of return and revision, which is, after all, a staple of Shakespearean criticism – has particular significance in view of the emphasis critics place on the supposed finality of the returns embodied in the late plays, on their role as evidence of the completion of the artistic circle. It is this presumption of return as evidence of finality that Nevo and Danson rightly question. For the former, Shakespeare's entire career is 'a palimpsest [...] upon which are inscribed again and again re-presentations of lived experience in the forms of art' (*Other Language*, 2–3), and return is thus one of the basic driving forces of the work throughout the playwright's life. That Nevo, a psychoanalytic critic, should foreground this issue is hardly surprising, but it remains a valuable corrective, all the same. She cites Freud's 'Little Hans' as a way to explain the returns inherent in romance: 'A thing which has not been understood inevitably reappears; like an unlaid ghost, it cannot be laid to rest until the mystery is solved and the spell broken' (ibid., 33). And she makes sense of the centrifugal-then-centripetal plots of the late plays by treating them as if they were dreams – dreams shared between playwright and audience, obeying structural conventions that map the psyche rather than reproducing literary or dramatic genre per se – and reading the individual play text 'as if it were a series of dreams one wished to interpret, dreams exhibiting the features that dreams exhibit: condensations, displacements, doublings, splittings, pictographs, and the cunning diversionary tactics of the covert will to reveal and to express' (ibid., 32). This is an attempt, as we have seen, to read the late plays as in a certain way *beyond genre*, to suggest that the quality of lateness in Shakespeare's romances is best understood as postconventionality, as the artistic representation of the workings of the psyche that has found a way to transcend formal expectations and conventions. In this, Nevo, though Freudian rather than Jungian in orientation, appears to converge with Neumann in her understanding of late style: her reading suggests that chronology is of secondary importance in the study of plays that reach beyond the here and now to represent the timeless structures of the mind. Nonetheless, her principal point remains valid. To limit the idea of return solely to the late plays and thus to imply that everything in the Shakespeare canon prior to that point operated on the basis of a kind of artistic linearity is to distort the complex dynamic of Shakespearean creativity, the repeated rethinking, reshaping, revising, that characterises all his plays.

If the question of return is central to lateness studies, then a further key issue – one that appears at its starkest in relation to chronology, since chronology is rarely either clearcut or objective and Shakespearean chronology is neither – is *selection*, the making of decisions about incorporation within and exclusion from a given set of works. The relationship between strict chronology and the grouping of the so-called 'late plays' is always strained and any reading of these plays will inevitably entail a degree of selection and omission. Endings, as we have seen, typically take on a particular burden of significance that puts great pressure on questions of sequence, and chronologies, having a symbiotic relationship with biography, tend to make clear their dependence upon teleologies. Tillyard, Traversi and Knight, driven by the urge for unity not only within individual works but also across the entire career, broke ranks in order to see the Shakespearean late style as the product not of fissure but of steady development towards poetic consummation. In the case of Knight, however, this led to an unexpected, if characteristically maverick, development – the addition of *Henry VIII* to the customary four-play schema – which had the potential to undermine the continuity argument even as it sought to extend it, since, though Knight's vision of the plays as a career-long Christian-nationalist project was enhanced by taking *Henry VIII*, with its ostensible celebration of royal power and succession within the expanding nation-state, as the final play, for each of the other continuity critics, dependent as they were on the identification of Shakespeare and Prospero and thus on the finality of *The Tempest*, this reordering was potentially disruptive. Knight's idiosyncrasy thus makes all too apparent the subjectivity of accounts dependent upon subjectivism, underlining the contingency of a given critic's choice of final play and in the process raising the considerable problem of the 'late-late' or 'post-late' plays – that is, the ostensible evidence of finality in *The Tempest* yet the contradictory evidence that Shakespeare was involved in the writing of three more plays thereafter – and thus of what might be called the 'double caesura', the career ending resonantly with *The Tempest* and then again, awkwardly and disruptively, with *The Two Noble Kinsmen*. While critics championing each of the three-, three-plus-one- or four-play patterns may disagree with each other over issues of priority and progression, they all tacitly agree in performing the same basic exclusion, silently or near-silently excising the three plays – one missing, *Cardenio*, and two extant, *Henry VIII* and *The Two Noble Kinsmen* – that unavoidably postdate *Pericles*, *Cymbeline*, *The Winter's Tale* and *The Tempest*, whichever order of priority is established for the 'central' group of four.

The question of the double caesura immediately invokes the twin problems of authorship and authenticity because the plays of the second caesura are all collaborations and acknowledging them, in their irreparable dual-authoredness, means that not only can we no longer pretend that there are no more plays after the four 'romances', we also cannot pretend (even defining dramatic authorship as narrowly as possible) that the 'late plays' are all entirely Shakespeare's. As a result, we not only lose the comfort of solo authorship and thus of the possibility of uniformity of purpose across the career of a single playwright, we also – crucially – lose the subjectivist logic of the word 'late'. After all, these plays may be 'late' Shakespeare but they are at the same time 'early' (or at least earlyish) Fletcher. This is a radical problem for subjectivism and cannot be overstated. Indeed, as I will argue in Chapter 4, the recognition of the collaborative basis of early modern theatrical production, whether broadly or narrowly conceived – that is, whether read as texts produced by, through and for a range of agents from the actor and the acting company to the audience and patron for whom they are written or as plays written by two or more collaborating playwrights – hacks savagely into the premises for subjectivism and thus into the very idea of late style. Collaboration has long been a dirty word in Shakespearean studies, and that is a gauge of the basic failure of Shakespeareans to come to grips with the nature of playwriting in Shakespeare's day. Nosworthy, discussing some of what he considers to be the less dramatically convincing moments in *Cymbeline*, notes dryly that at these moments '[s]ome editors and critics smell collaboration', thereby providing a classic statement of the disparagement of collaborative effort that underpinned late-play criticism across the twentieth century (Nosworthy, edition, xxviii). Recent work by Brian Vickers in summarising the ways in which the various 'co-authors' within the Shakespearean *œuvre* might be distinguished commendably confronts the fact of collaboration, but the term Vickers deploys – co-*author* – makes clear the teleology of his analysis (as of all authorial attribution work performed on the Shakespearean canon) in the distinguishing of the autonomous *author* Shakespeare as the determining presence in the sections of the plays considered to be his and thus in the reinstating of a degree of Shakespearean control over the collaborative work.[36]

This resentment of collaborative endeavour is invariably apparent in studies of *Henry VIII* and *The Two Noble Kinsmen*. As I have noted elsewhere, critics who like these plays have been happy to claim them for Shakespeare; those who don't have found it useful to be able to lay the blame on Fletcher.[37] And if two hands are acknowledged (as they have been since, in 1850, Tennyson and Spedding simultaneously divided *Henry VIII* between Shakespeare and Fletcher on the basis of their perceptions of the writers' respective styles and thus established a profile that has subsequently been refined but not substantially modified by more rigorously statistical attribution studies), then other means must be found to exonerate Shakespeare from such questionable behaviour. Sir William Bailey, for instance, writing at the turn of the century, dealt with this problem simply enough by inserting chronological distance and converting collaboration into revision by another, reading *Henry VIII* as the product of scenes written by Shakespeare back in Elizabeth's reign and reworked much later by Fletcher: 'After the production of "The Tempest"', he wrote confidently, 'there is no evidence whatever that Shakespeare wrote a line except to sign his will or some legal document.'[38] Bailey's confidence is misplaced, as most twentieth-century critics came to acknowledge; yet, while they accept the evidence for the post-*Tempest* collaborative work, they have nonetheless consistently sought reasons – sometimes contradictory reasons – to ignore that evidence. Tillyard, leaving *Henry VIII* out of his book on Shakespeare's histories just as he left it out of his book on the late plays, explained his decision by setting maturity and collaboration against each other, reading collaborative work as acceptable only in the apprentice:

I have omitted *Henry VIII*, not being convinced that Shakespeare wrote it all. The case of this play is quite different from that of *Henry VI*. In youthful work resemblances to predecessors or contemporaries are to be expected and are no argument for divided authorship; in mature work they are surprising and demand an explanation.[39]

The headmaster in Tillyard would dearly have liked to require the playwright to explain himself, reading late collaboration – unwittingly interestingly, in view of subsequent analyses of late style as the expression of a return to the interests of childhood or youth – as evidence of an unexpected and inappropriate loss of confidence. Kenneth Muir and Sean O'Loughlin, presaging Muir's better-known *Last Works of Shakespeare, Racine and Ibsen*, echo this concern, treating the collaborations as dotages:

The Shakespearean parts of *Henry VIII, The Two Noble Kinsmen*, and *Cardenio* were presumably written in retirement to help his fellows and John Fletcher to keep up with demand for new plays. In the two plays that survive intact, there are no passages that throw any fresh light on Shakespeare. There is only a repetition of the old themes in a weakened form. The trial-scene of Queen Katherine, for example, is a less powerful version of the trial of Hermione. Any detailed discussion of these plays is outside the purpose of this book.[40]

For Muir and O'Loughlin, the post-*Tempest* plays, since they must be acknowledged, can only be evidence of decline after the heights achieved in the late plays: certainly, they do not merit inclusion under that heading.

One way or another, the late collaborations must be sidelined and Shakespeare's input downplayed. The four 'romances', Robert Adams informs us – writing three years after the Oxford Shakespeare had eschewed the generic groupings familiar from standard 'complete works' such as the Riverside in favour of a carefully considered chronological order, thereby inevitably foregrounding the awkward existence of the post-*Tempest* plays – 'form a distinct group' and, while Shakespeare 'did some later collaborative writing with John Fletcher [. . .] at most his participation in the three post-romance plays was limited to particular scenes'.[41] Marco Mincoff finds a yet more succinct way to make the same point, describing *The Tempest* as 'Shakespeare's last *complete* drama' (*Things Supernatural*, 118; my italics) and thus, like Bailey, defining Fletcher less as Shakespeare's co-adjutor (to use Ben Jonson's term) than as his editor, tying together the unfinished scenes left behind by the great author, and treating collaboration as an aesthetically fragmented, temporally dislocated mode of writing, intrinsically both provisional and posterior. More recently, Cynthia Marshall, addressing *Pericles, Cymbeline, The Winter's Tale* and *The Tempest* as 'the last plays' and omitting the later collaborations entirely, implicitly acknowledges that she has allowed the premise of her book to override the evidence – 'Although literary biography is not my aim,' she claims, 'still there are inherent connections between an author's late works and certain typical thematic concerns, such as death and summation' – and she avoids distraction from these concerns by the simple expedient of mentioning no playwright other than Shakespeare in the entire course of her book.[42]

When they do acknowledge the late collaborations, critics tend either to choose their words with care or to establish myths to explain Shakespeare's working with someone else. For Russell Fraser, as we have seen, the shape of Shakespeare's late phase is clear: 'four romances and a coda form his final flowering' (*Later Years*, 216). Fraser's alliteration does a good deal of work here, uniting the four solo plays by leaving the 'coda' bereft of a key initial consonant and separating the three subsequent collaborations from the true canon, using a musical term to denote a structural component that allows for further development and at the same time provides completion while remaining supplementary. This offers a compact version of the various stories told of the end of the life which acknowledge but subordinate the post-late plays, ensuring that the group-of-four remains the principal focus of anyone considering the end of Shakespeare's career and that the collaborations can therefore be gently relegated to the status of afterthought. The standard version of the composition of the late plays thus emerges. Starting in late 1607 or early 1608, Shakespeare began work on what would become known as his late plays. He wrote *Pericles* first, probably with a lesser playwright called George Wilkins (who later capitalised on the connection by novelising the plot), and then, after a short pause for reflection, he wrote *Cymbeline* and *The Winter's Tale* in that order in 1610 before finishing his career the following year, resoundingly and self-consciously, with *The Tempest*, viewed (even if the critic generally otherwise steers clear of biography) as transparently autobiographical, with Prospero's drowning of his book, his considered and climactic exit from the island, marking the moment of Shakespeare's own retirement from the life of the urban playwright and his departure for the green fields of Stratford. But a year or so later, the peace of this rural retirement was disturbed – and generally this is attributed to the inability of his colleagues in the King's Company to cope without him, principally because of the inexperience of his nominated successor, John Fletcher – by the obligation to be involved in the writing of more plays. He is thus allowed to have collaborated on *Henry VIII*, the lost *Cardenio* and *The Two Noble Kinsmen* with Fletcher, fifteen years his junior, writing key scenes, perhaps providing the overarching structure, but by no means displaying a full commitment to the process and distinctly uninclined to return for longer than was necessary to his London life.[43] Finally, after *The Two Noble Kinsmen* and with the ongoing success of Fletcher's plays, Shakespeare could properly retire, returning to Stratford, obligations complete, never to write again.

This story makes sense of the material, by and large, and it offers a series of psychological explanations – explanations, that is, which provide psychological satisfaction not only for an imagined Shakespeare but also for those doing the imagining – for the playwright's actions in this last creative period of his life. It also allows for a quiet classification of the collaborative material as representing the second, third and fourth orders of Shakespearean lateness. *Pericles* is second-class, the next best thing to the three solo plays, since it most overtly shares their generic and stylistic tendencies; but the complexities of its textual history, its deliberately archaic language and the inescapability of the attribution of a substantial chunk of the play to a dramatist other than Shakespeare mean that it can never assume a status precisely parallel to the solo work. *Henry VIII* and *The Two Noble Kinsmen* form the third class of late play. Most commentators accept that both plays are collaborations with Fletcher (though there have been exceptions, most notably R. A. Foakes's determined attempt in his 1957 Arden edition to treat *Henry VIII* as solely Shakespeare's) and that the evidence suggests that the authorship was, broadly speaking, evenly shared.[44] That said, even those entirely happy to accept the plays' collaborative construction seek connections with the main body of the canon: Lois Potter, for instance, rekindles the caesura/continuity debate by arguing that *The Two Noble Kinsmen*, far from representing a break with Shakespeare's prior writing, is 'consistent with the classicizing tendency found in his plays from *Macbeth* onward' and that '[e]ven the sense of anticlimax at the end of 5.4 can be paralleled in other late Shakespeare plays'.[45] For most, however, *Henry VIII* and *Kinsmen* form at best a detached pairing, half in and half out of the canon, not least because their postdating *The Tempest* and thus spoiling the progression argument makes them more culpable than *Pericles*, easily dismissible as a (largely) failed experiment. Yet even *Henry VIII* and the *Kinsmen* appear canonical in comparison with *Cardenio*, the trickiest of all the late collaborations to negotiate for the obvious reason that it is no longer extant. We may have its ghost in the later *Double Falsehood*, but we do not (*pace* Charles Hamilton) have *Cardenio* itself.[46] It thus forms the fourth class of late play and can be ignored, as indeed it has been by all but the tiniest handful of critics, the one notable (and highly welcome) recent exception being Jennifer Richards's and James Knowles's collection *Shakespeare's Late Plays: New Readings*, which includes two essays on the play, one apiece by Julia Briggs and Richard Wilson.[47]

Not that *Pericles* – the second-class play – could be quite so easily disregarded: its awkward presence at the head of the four-play group necessarily required negotiation. Traversi, for instance, showing considerable sleight of hand, elides Wilkins's participation by setting authorship *against* authenticity. Writing about the protagonist's rediscovery of his father's armour, he argues that his 'words upon finding himself newly clothed in it have, whatever be their actual authorship, an authentic Shakespearean ring' (Traversi, 23–4), an assertion which plays havoc with each of his key terms, implying that the Wilkins sections are as fully Shakespearean as those of Shakespeare himself.[48] Russell Fraser, for his part, creates a rather complex, condensed narrative that allows him to dismiss Wilkins's input to *Pericles*. Eighteenth-century editors, he notes, attributed much of the play to a collaborator. Shakespeare, from this perspective, '[i]mproving the dialog, [...] augmented the "catastrophe," and was "most liberal of his aid" in Act V' (*Later Years*, 217). 'But this picture of the master adding "a few flowery lines"', he argues, echoing

Traversi, 'affronts sensibility. From the stunning first scene straight to the end, the design of *Pericles*, a grand conception, is Shakespeare's'. And he proceeds to express his disapproval of Shakespeare's taste in acquaintances: 'The author of *Measure for Measure*', he observes primly, 'wasn't choosy about the company he kept', adding that '[t]he collaborator who dropped his pronouns looks like George Wilkins', whom he describes as 'a hack writer' and brothel creeper 'whose dubious career and Shakespeare's intersected'. Then he accounts for the play itself:

Exploiting his Shakespeare connection, Wilkins reworked the play he and the eminent friend had made together. In 1608 he turned it into a prose romance, something like the rushed-into-print 'novel' that follows a popular movie. The play's 'true history', he called it, 'recently presented' by the King's Majesty's Players. Sprucing up his romance, he cribbed from another version of the Pericles story, in the public eye this year, thanks to a new edition. Next year came the play itself with its attribution on the titlepage to 'William Shakespeare'. Editors, accepting this badly printed quarto as the 'skeleton' of his *Pericles*, flesh it out with Wilkins' novel, a quarry of lines and phrases, some of them blank verse lines, omitted in the published play. One recent commentator sees a broken vase, not a few pieces missing, the rest roughly patched and glued together. But whatever its defects, the vase is still of great price. (ibid., 217–18)

Like Traversi, Fraser puts a good deal of effort into excising the collaborator while maintaining a belief in the evidence of genius that remains – a belief apparent in his conflation of Shakespeare and Henry James both in his use of the word 'master' and in what is perhaps, bearing in mind Fraser's regular comparison of late Shakespeare and late James, an oblique *Golden Bowl* reference in his metaphor for the text of *Pericles*. Simon Palfrey, in his fine book on the late plays, repeats this conflation of Shakespeare and James. Though he recognises the limitations of the tradition of working only with the first four (or three) late plays, he proceeds to do so nonetheless, offering a brief explanation for this decision:

I have chosen not to look in detail at *The Two Noble Kinsmen* and *Henry VIII*. The critical conventions surrounding the four earlier works require, I think, sustained challenge; sticking to the traditional group has helped define my work's scope. And indeed, if there is a generic link between *The Tempest* and *The Two Noble Kinsmen* [...] there is equally a link between the civic debates of *Pericles* and *Coriolanus*. [...] To go 'forward' in time, then, was no more tempting than to go 'backward': such a project is there to be done, but not quite here. (*Late Shakespeare*, 31)

The focus on the four-play group makes sense in view of Palfrey's principal aim of challenging the critical conventions associated with criticism of those plays, and his anti-chronological stance is refreshing, yet a few lines later he, like Fraser, slips into tellingly Jamesian language when he suggests, implying a less tactical dismissal of the plays of the second caesura, that 'there is enough missing from the two post-*Tempest* plays to suggest that Shakespeare knew that a certain mastery had been achieved' (ibid.).

It is Fletcher, as this suggests, rather than Wilkins, who troubles the critics most. Fraser works the aphoristic staccato of his manner especially hard when setting out to remove the threat of this notorious collaborator. 'Beaumont and Fletcher', he argues, implicitly echoing the Coleridgean charge that the pair 'catered' to an aristocratic audience happy with something less than art,

> hope to please everyone, giving offense to none. *Hamlet*, offending some, wrings out withers, but their revision of Shakespeare's play, appropriating the melancholy, turns it to laughter. In *Philaster*, or *Love Lies a-Bleeding*, the blood is wiped up in Act V. One of their kingly heroes falls in love with his sister. *Respice finem*, though: that wasn't his sister and the hero wasn't really a king. Mistaken identity occupies late Shakespeare too, and his sad but happy plays look like Beaumont and Fletcher in outline. Readers who don't discriminate between means and ends set him at the feet of his junior colleagues, an old dog learning new tricks. (*Later Years*, 231)

Fletcherian tragicomedy is thus spurned as mere crowd-pleasing and critics who think they see Fletcherian influence in the late plays of Shakespeare – who naturally never wrote plays with an audience in mind, or at least not one inclined to be pleased – are undiscriminating. The target here (other than the generally insensitive Shakespearean) is the turn-of-the-century critic Ashley Thorndike and those who echo his groundbreaking argument – the first genuine threat to Dowden's reading of the late plays as the products of Shakespeare's state of mind – that the impetus for the creation of the late plays can be found in the early tragicomedies written by Beaumont and Fletcher for the boy players.[49] Fraser dismisses this out of hand, refusing to entertain the distasteful image of Shakespeare learning from his juniors and inferiors, but Thorndike's argument – though overstated, in part because his relative dating of the plays in question is simply impossible to verify – has persisted, especially in relation to the marked similarities between *Philaster* and *Cymbeline*.[50] As Mincoff noted, Thorndike's case 'has not in fact been adequately refuted, and the usual argument with which it is rejected, which boils down to a confession of belief that genius cannot be influenced by mediocrity, is no argument at all' (*Things Supernatural*, 15). 'Still', he adds, 'there is a decided weakness in Thorndike's theory', which is that though 'he is at least partly right with regard to *Cymbeline*, he dismisses *Pericles* from the account too lightly, for its does provide a better point of departure for the romances as a whole than Beaumont's *Philaster*' (ibid.). It remains a chicken-and-egg debate, this, unresolvable until or unless the plays in question can be unequivocally dated; but Thorndike's basic point – that Shakespeare was 'constantly influenced by dramatic conditions and fashions and [...] was using and perfecting dramatic types which other men had originated' (*Influence*, 152) – runs directly counter to the subjectivism of the bulk of late-play criticism; and the extent of the threat offered to the idea of the autonomous Shakespeare by the image of his emulating the success of others, an image uncomfortably reinforced by his subsequent decision to write three plays in collaboration with Fletcher, is apparent in the effort Fraser expends to dismiss it. Evidence that collaborative production was the norm in the early modern theatre, that collaboration between Shakespeare and Fletcher is more to be expected than that Shakespeare should have written upwards of thirty plays entirely by himself, must be suppressed if the discourse of lateness is to be sustained and extended by way of the Shakespeare canon.[51]

The problem of collaboration, of the intrusion of another personality into the hermetic world of subjectivism, taken in conjunction with Thorndike's arguments for Fletcherian influence and the considerable critical debate they have subsequently provoked, indicates that chronology unavoidably introduces external factors, factors other than Shakespeare's own growth as a playwright and as a human being – factors, in other words, inimical to subjectivism. By the early twentieth century, several such factors had been established in order to explain the late-play caesura, a representative selection of which can be found in the fragmentary opening comments of Harley Granville Barker's 1930 preface to *Cymbeline* – a play, he observes, that 'is said to have been a product, probably the first, of Shakespeare's leisured retirement to Stratford' but which also seems to have been the product of a series of practical theatrical influences:

Professor Ashley Thorndike thinks it was written in emulation of Beaumont and Fletcher's successful *Philaster*. There are signs that it was intended for the 'private' theatre of the Blackfriars. More than one editor has scented a collaborator; the late Dr. Furness, in particular, put many of the play's weaknesses to this account. [...] The Folio labels it tragedy, but it is not; it is tragi-comedy rather, or romance.[52]

Barker casually outlines these possibilities without nailing his colours to any particular mast. Commenting on what he calls the play's 'sophisticated artlessness,' though, he reads the play specifically as late work, thereby implicitly sidelining the various material explanations for its oddness of tone:

> This art that displays art is a thing very likely to be to the taste of the mature and rather wearied artist. When you are exhausted with hammering great tragic themes into shape it is a relief to find a subject you can play with, and to be safely able to take more interest in the doing than the thing done. For once you can exercise your skill for its own sake. The pretty subject itself seems to invite a certain artlessness of treatment. But the product will have a sophisticated air about it. (*Prefaces*, 247)

Dowdenesque subjectivism thus persists here in a hybrid, slightly downbeat form, with an echo (in the idea of Shakespeare as 'wearied') of the best-known attack on Dowden, that of Lytton Strachey (to which I will return in Chapter 3). At the same time, institutional contexts clearly intrude upon the personal. The last plays are read, in a way familiar from Malone, as the product not of the practicalities of commercial theatre but rather of the tranquillity of a Stratford retirement; at the same time, the change in style they represent in Shakespeare's output marks them out as the product of the King's Men's occupation of the Blackfriars, a theatre markedly different in a range of ways from the Globe. Of the arguments for material influence Barker cites, this is the only one he does not attribute to others. Hybrid subjectivism thus suggests that the plays, as the product of Shakespeare's 'leisured retirement,' stand free from worldly input yet that they are written for a particular space either 'in emulation' of other writers or in collaboration with them – the latter, according to Furness at least, introducing 'weaknesses'.

Barker's preface is a convenient digest of the various contradictory options considered by critics after Dowden to account for the differences between the late plays and the rest of the canon: Shakespeare's alleged departure for Stratford and the mental and spiritual elbow-room this was thought to have given him; the effect of the acquisition of the Blackfriars on the repertory of the King's Men; the input of other playwrights in the form of collaboration (writing with Wilkins or Fletcher) or of influence; and the question of genre and the problematic terms 'tragicomedy' and 'romance'. Of these various possibilities, the explanation privileged by Barker is also the one which has had the most consistent longevity: the argument for the impact on Shakespeare's writing of the newly acquired theatre at the Blackfriars. G. E. Bentley, in the first issue of *Shakespeare Survey*, invented a narrative for this claim. Once they knew the Blackfriars was going to become available, he suggests, the core members of the company gathered for a series of 'conferences', in which they decided – partly because the new theatre was a risky proposition and they needed the playwright who knew the actors best to ensure its success, partly because the Globe 'could be left to take care of itself with an old repertory as the Blackfriars could not' and partly because they felt that Shakespeare, who had invested personally in the new space, would work hard to ensure that it ran smoothly – 'that William Shakespeare should write henceforth with the Blackfriars in mind and not the Globe'.[53] The logic of this is clear. For Bentley, '[n]o competent critic who has read carefully through the Shakespeare canon has failed to notice that there is something different about *Cymbeline*, *The Winter's Tale*, *The Tempest*, and *The Two Noble Kinsmen*' ('Blackfriars Theatre', 47–8). This 'difference' he attributes directly to the move to the Blackfriars, an attribution which

> accords with the known facts of theatre history, [...] with the biographical evidence of Shakespeare's long and close association with all the enterprises of the Lord Chamberlain's-King's men for twenty years [and] with his fabulously acute sense of the theatre and the problems of the actor; and it does no violence to his artistic integrity or to his poetic genius. (ibid., 48–9)

A straightforward enough story, if fictional.

The received wisdom for most of the second half of the twentieth century, this tale has, more recently, run into resistance. Andrew Gurr argues that 'too much has been made about the possible effects on Shakespeare's writing when, after a thirteen-year delay, the Blackfriars playhouse finally came into the possession of Shakespeare's company', not least because there are two obvious omissions from Bentley's list of plays whose 'difference' can be attributed to the acquisition of the indoor playhouse.[54] These are, first of all, *Pericles*, which unquestionably shares a great deal with the others but which unfortunately and inescapably pre-dates the company's occupation of the Blackfriars and, secondly, *Henry VIII*, which we know for certain was performed at the first Globe, not the Blackfriars, in June 1613, because it was responsible, as I noted in the Introduction, for the burning down of the theatre.[55] Still, it is hard to deny that *Henry VIII* exhibits a series of theatrical features consistent with those considered characteristic of the late plays (the features Irwin Smith calls 'Blackfriars Conventions'): dancing and masque-like events (Wolsey's party and Katherine's vision), the use of a descent (for the angels in the vision), the absence (notable in an ostensible 'history' play) of battles and some arguably rather claustrophobic action, all of which might reasonably be thought to point towards the Blackfriars as the expected venue, despite the evidence of at least one catastrophic performance at the Globe.⁵⁶ More to the point, the historical resonance of performance in the Blackfriars space was considerable, since the very same building had been used for the 1529 divorce hearing of Henry and Katherine of Aragon dramatised in 2.4, and the play makes sure nobody misses the connection: 'The most convenient place that I can think of / For such receipt of learning,' says King Henry, unnecessarily, at the end of 2.2, 'is Blackfriars' (2.2.136–7), making it hard to deny that the play was written with a view to performance in that space. At the same time, not only are we certain, because of the documentary evidence relating to the destruction of the theatre, that the play was performed at the Globe, we can also see certain characteristics that make it seem out of place as a Blackfriars play. It features not just 'hautboys' and 'cornets', instruments perhaps feasible for use in the low-key environment of the music room at the Blackfriars, but also trumpets, which are not thought to have been practical in such a confined space. Moreover, the Folio text's uniquely full stage directions – which do not derive (as John Jowett has persuasively argued *The Tempest*'s do) from later scribal embellishment but are drawn near-verbatim from Holinshed, a hybrid form of stage direction, in other words, at once literary and theatrical – make it clear that the play needs a considerable amount of stage-space.⁵⁷ The construction of a doubling chart for *Henry VIII* shows that the play in the form it exists in the Folio could not have been performed at the Blackfriars on a stage that was, to use Gurr's figures, perhaps twenty feet by sixteen compared with the Globe's forty-four feet by twenty-seven: twenty-four people need to process onto stage at once in the divorce–trial scene alone. In Gurr's evocative words, '[t]he smallish Blackfriars stage, already encumbered with fifteen stool-sitting gallants wearing ostrich-plumed hats and smoking long pipes, would not have taken large crowds easily' ('Tempest at Blackfriars', 97). Logical inferences thus include the presumption that *Henry VIII* was performed at both theatres; that it was written either with both playhouses in mind or first of all for the Blackfriars but with immediate adaptation for the Globe; and that the Folio text represents the spatially generous Globe version. Not that any of this can be proved. But we know that the company shifted to the five-act structure that had not been necessary for plays performed solely in an open-air theatre and that they installed a descent machine at the Globe in order to be able to replicate action possible at the Blackfriars but not previously feasible at the Globe; we also know that a clear divergence of repertory between the two theatres was still a few years off when the late plays were written, that Globe plays were adapted for the Blackfriars until a repertory specific to that space could be established. It certainly seems unlikely that the play as it exists in the First Folio and perhaps therefore as it was performed at the Globe can be identical with the play as it was performed at the Blackfriars. And since, as Tiffany Stern puts it in *Making Shakespeare*, '[w]hat works within a small artificially lit theatre can [...] be adapted to work outdoors on a large naturally lit stage [but] the reverse is not necessarily the case', it seems that the Folio text in all probability represents the spatially expanded Globe version of the play.[58] For Gurr, only *The Tempest*, of the entire canon, bears unequivocal signs – in its music and its clearcut five-act structure – of having been written specifically for the company's new space. If this is the case, and if therefore the other Folio late plays are Globe versions written for both theatres, then the blanket assumption that the Blackfriars provided a radical break in staging for the King's Company repertory and that this explains the 'difference' of the late plays is questionable. Replacing subjectivism with contingencies has not, then, proven a straightforward task.

I have dwelt momentarily on the question of the occupation of the Blackfriars, but, since Barker wrote his preface, further external factors have been examined as possible motivations for the change in style apparent in the late plays. These include, *inter alia*, the influence of forms of courtly drama, most notably the masque, on the shape the late plays adopt (an influence most apparent in *The Tempest* and *Henry VIII*, each of which features an actual formal dance sequence, but detectable also in the rest of the late plays) and the impact of the relentless plague closures in the period between the accession of James I and the burning down of the Globe in 1613.[59] The argument for the second of these as a factor in the shaping of the late period has been championed forcefully by Leeds Barroll, who began with the simple premise that 'an awareness of plague restrictions might alter our notions of when several Shakespeare plays were first presented on the London stage' and found himself subsequently addressing central issues in Shakespearean biography – issues which were almost immediately underlined by Mary Bly's account of the short-lived King's Revels company at the Whitefriars, in which she shows that, '[i]n essence, the company died of the plague'.[60] As Bly notes, '1607–8 were remarkably bad plague years' (*Queer Virgins*, 129), which is true enough; Barroll, however, shows that every year in the period 1603–10 was substantially, and in some cases devastatingly, affected by savage bouts of plague and thus by prolonged closure of the theatres. Things got very bad from the second half of 1606 onwards: the playhouses were closed for all but a couple of weeks in

1607, for all but three-and-a-half spring months in 1608, for the full twelve months of 1609 and for seven-and-a-half months in 1610. It must have been quite a shock to the acting companies, then, to find that they could perform every week of 1611 bar a mere six in February and March.[61]

The late plays – were it not for the likelihood that *Pericles* predates mid-1608 – could thus easily come to be seen as the post-plague plays, plays which in effect postdate the eighteen-and-a-half month period of consistent closure from July 1608 to January 1610 inclusive. Even accepting the priority of *Pericles*, it is hard to avoid the further implications of Barroll's argument about the impact of plague – namely, that the late-play caesura is the product not of a sudden shift of internal perspective on the part of the playwright but rather of a period of externally imposed theatrical inactivity. From this perspective, the issue of plague closure offers a point of conjunction with Thorndike, since the acquisition of the services of Beaumont and Fletcher by the King's Men follows hard on the reopening, in part, presumably, because of their established expertise in writing for the Blackfriars and in part because of the demise of certain children's companies – the King's Revels as a direct result of the plague, the Queen's Revels due to politics – and the result was *Philaster*, *The Maid's Tragedy* and *A King and No King*, all first performed between 1609 and 1611. It is thus worth noting that the late plays emerged after a sustained period of theatre closure that marked the collapse of a couple of companies which had effectively only just got going and which might have had a decent future if their moment had not coincided with an appallingly sustained period of plague, an eventuality which allowed the King's Men, whose resources gave them a considerable edge in times of hardship, to capitalise on others' losses.

Barroll deploys this information, curiously, neither to argue the strongest case available to him from the evidence he has isolated nor to use that evidence to modify the traditional late-play chronology. He claims, rather, that the plague closures suggest that *Pericles* and *Cymbeline* were produced 'between 1608 and 1610, prior to the cessation of plague (*Pericles* in 1608, [...] *Cymbeline* in 1610, prior to Simon Forman's viewing in 1611)' and that '*Winter's Tale* and *Tempest* may both be dated in 1611, with *Winter's Tale* appearing at the Globe shortly after it reopened' (*Politics, Plague*, 177–8). In other words, despite suggesting that 'Shakespeare's "final period" may be viewed [...] in terms of the pressure points that were produced by playhouse closings' (ibid., 178), Barroll resists the radical possibility offered by the relationship of closure and caesura, preferring instead to reiterate the standard two-plus-two pattern for the 'four' late

A question of chronology 101

plays and thus leave matters largely unchanged. In the end, his understanding of Shakespearean creativity remains that of the genius producing his art *despite* rather than *because of* operative conditions: 'It was an art', he concludes, 'that did not bloom and flourish naturally in the spring of an English cultural Renaissance, but an art that had to be wrested from and forged in the crucible of daunting social disruption, danger and indifference' (ibid., 209). Somewhere in there (and despite the enormous value of the evidence Barroll has provided in the cause of the resistance to subjectivism), Dowden's voice can still be heard.

Not that the material-condition arguments, finally, provide a clearcut alternative to a subjectivist understanding of the late-play caesura. Whatever view is taken of the impact on the company repertory of the new indoor venue, of court culture or of plague closure, the point is twofold: that impersonal factors of this kind run directly counter to the subjectivism that persistently underpins post-Dowden accounts of the late plays and yet that none of them individually seems to offer the clarity required for an adequately sharp caesura. The court masque did not impinge on the public theatre overnight in late 1607; the King's Men's reoccupation of the Blackfriars postdates *Pericles* and was, as Barroll has emphasised, grimly interrupted by plague closures; the precise relative dating of the Beaumont and Fletcher plays is still impossible to ascertain. The underlying problem lies not, however, I would argue, with the inadequacy of these material explanations when compared with the claims of subjectivism but rather with the idea of the caesura itself. There is, despite the general critical assumption of the clarity of the break, a perhaps surprisingly vague period of transition from the tragedies to the late plays. The second edition of the *Oxford Shakespeare* gives the following chronology for the years 1606 to 1616: *Timon of Athens* ('conjecturally assigned to 1605–6'), *Macbeth* ('composed probably in 1606'), *Antony and Cleopatra* (written 'no later than 1606'), *All's Well That Ends Well* (moved provocatively from its first-edition location between *Othello* and *Timon*, though with no explanation or exact date offered), *Pericles* (1607 or 1608), *Coriolanus* ('written around 1608'), *The Winter's Tale* ('perhaps' 1609–10, its precedence to *Cymbeline* due to unspecified 'stylistic evidence'), *The Tragedy of King Lear* (around 1610), *Cymbeline* ('stylistic evidence places the play in about 1610–11'), *The Tempest* ('it seems clear that Shakespeare wrote *The Tempest* during the later part of 1610 or 1611'), *Cardenio* (1612–13), *Henry VIII* (1613) and *The Two Noble Kinsmen* (also 1613). Both *Troilus and Cressida* and *Shakespeares Sonnets* were published in quarto in 1609 and

Shakespeare wrote the *impresa* for the earl of Rutland's appearance in the Accession Day festivities on 24 March 1613. The date of publication of the Sonnets has the potential to be profoundly disruptive of Shakespearean chronology, especially if, with Patrick Cheney in his recent *Shakespeare, National Poet-Playwright*, you choose to read Shakespeare's publications not as random afterthoughts but as highly significant, indeed structural, moments in the career. As Cheney notes, citing Katherine Duncan-Jones's biography *Ungentle Shakespeare*, the simultaneous publication of *Troilus* and the Sonnets makes us notice certain similarities between these apparently unconnected texts:

> both were printed by George Eld; they are 'the product of revision'; and they contain epistles that 'invite [...] comparison'. Moreover, play and poem alike offer 'a defamiliarizing re-fashioning' of literary tradition [...]; and both are 'deeply rooted in an awareness of death, and of the desperate struggle to make one's voice heard before disease destroys both pen and phallus'.[62]

Duncan-Jones, depending on the narrative she has already offered of a post-*Pericles* Shakespeare, ravaged by syphilis and knowing that his death could not be far off, reads the 1609 publications as a distinct late gesture (see Chapter 5, 290–91).

Of the material ordered by presumed date of composition, *Coriolanus* is the most obviously out of place – or at least it is out of place in respect of the clearcut generic caesura of tradition – as are Folio *Lear* (if the 1610 dating is correct) and the two published texts, *Troilus and Cressida* and *Shakespeares Sonnets*, though the latter two can be partially explained as earlier material reproduced. Not much can be done about *Coriolanus*, however, which could just as easily have been written in 1612 as in 1606 and has at different times been dated circumstantially to a range of options within those parameters, but which is most often associated with 1608 and is thus located between *Pericles* and the rest of the late plays despite bearing little apparent generic resemblance to them.[63] For Lee Bliss, noting the play's clear five-act structure and stage directions requiring not trumpets but cornets (wind instruments associated, as I have noted, with the indoor theatres), *Coriolanus* 'appears to be Shakespeare's first play written with the Blackfriars in mind as a possible venue', and she points out the possible connections between the play and other tragedies, notably Chapman's *Bussy D'Ambois*, first performed at the Blackfriars in its previous role as the home to the Children of the Queen's Revels (Bliss, ed., *Coriolanus*, 4–5). The Blackfriars was not, after all, as Lucy Munro has made clear, exclusively a venue for tragicomedy.[64]

A question of chronology 103

It is not just *Coriolanus*, either. Despite Barroll's attempts to isolate the four romances as a distinct set of plays divided into two groups of two, *Antony and Cleopatra*, *Timon of Athens*, *Coriolanus*, *Cardenio* and *The Two Noble Kinsmen* all haunt his last chapter: early on he notes that for *Antony and Cleopatra*, *Timon* and *The Two Noble Kinsmen*, 'there are no printing or performance records at all in Shakespeare's lifetime', allowing them to 'form no integral part of [his] narrative', but later he is obliged to admit that *Pericles* and *Antony and Cleopatra* were entered together in the Stationers' Register and, particularly uncomfortably, that *Timon* and *Coriolanus* may have 'filled th[e] gap of Shakespeare's time' he has posited in order to mark a clear boundary between *The Tempest* and the collaborations 'between 1611 and 1613' (*Politics, Plague*, 177, 207). In any case, the image of the contented (or weary) bard departing permanently for rural bliss in Stratford starts to look questionable when situated alongside certain items in the archives. One is the occasional evidence that Shakespeare, retaining his interests in the capital, moved regularly between Stratford and London. He was, for instance, in London in late spring 1612 to testify in the Belott–Mountjoy suit; and on 16 November 1614 Thomas Greene, Stratford's town clerk, who was in London to work against the proposed Welcombe enclosure, went to see Shakespeare, who had arrived in London the previous day, to discuss the case with him – both apparent evidence of a Shakespeare who is going about his normal business and thus neither ill nor gathering his thoughts for his impending death.[65] Another is his acquisition the previous March of the Blackfriars gatehouse apartment – part of the same former priory that housed the King's Men's newly occupied theatre – which had brought him to London to seal the mortgage deal and which, even if he had no intention of living in the property, suggests a man not quite finished with London. Samuel Schoenbaum's assumption that he bought it as an investment, based as it is on the premise that Shakespeare had by then 'retired to Stratford', raises the problem implicit in the word 'investment' for ideas of lateness in its suggestion that Shakespeare expected a fair few years yet of life. 'At most', Schoenbaum notes, crashing, amused, through a century of late-play criticism, 'in *The Tempest* he is saying *au revoir* rather than adieu' (*Documentary*, 228).

We can see, then, even from so necessarily limited an account, that for all sorts of reasons the idea of the caesura is highly problematic and that 'late Shakespeare', though ostensibly a purely chronological term, in fact functions in a manner sufficiently selective and exclusive as to be barely recognisable in that capacity, despite the temporal implications of the word 'late'.

In order to characterise a phase of Shakespeare's output in biographically derived terms, it seems, a range of omissions and elisions is required. Thus, in the end, in a magnificent paradox, the key premise for the establishment of a Shakespearean late period – chronology – becomes one of the principal obstacles to its continued value as a category. Pre-empting a great deal of later critical juggling and wishful thinking, Dowden, as we have seen, negotiated the awkwardness of the absence from the First Folio both of a sense of chronology and of a specific section entitled 'Romances' to complement 'Tragedies', 'Comedies' and 'Histories' as constituent generic components of the Shakespearean *œuvre* by suggesting that the locations within the existing sections of the three key romances (the Folio opens with *The Tempest* and closes with *Cymbeline* and the section of 'Comedies' concludes with *The Winter's Tale*), though ostensibly arbitrary, in fact quietly attest to their status as late writing, suggesting that 'our first and our last impression of Shakspere shall be that of Shakspere in his period of large, serene wisdom, and that in the light of the clear and solemn vision of his closing years all his writings shall be read' (Dowden, *Mind and Art*, 403). In this context of 'impressions', chronology, at the level of detail, becomes far less important than might be hoped. It is only the order of epochs within the overall life that matters, not the order within a given epoch of its constituent plays:

Whether Macbeth preceded Othello, or Othello Macbeth, need not greatly concern us [...] we do not understand Shakspere much the better when the question has been settled, than we did while the answer remained doubtful. Both plays belong, and they belong to the same degree, to one and the same period in the history of Shakspere's mind and art. (ibid., 379–80)

Internal order is thus determined by its value for the overall argument: 'it is The Tempest', notes Dowden, 'which gives its most perfect expression to the spirit that breathes through these three plays [*Cymbeline*, *The Tempest* and *The Winter's Tale*] which bring to an end the dramatic career of Shakspere; and therefore for us it is Shakspere's latest play' (ibid., 380). Chronology, in the end, the point of origin for any attribution of lateness, succumbs to purpose, rendering it a far-from-adequate premise for an alleged caesura.

2.3 A QUESTION OF STYLE

The question of 'late style' pivots, finally, as is only logical, on the issue of style itself, the sharp emergence of a new and distinct style being the key marker of caesura. Yet it is obvious that the simple fact of old age or proximity to death does not always produce work which can be characterised by the term 'late style'. Tiedemann, Adorno's editor, coined the deadpan phrase 'late work without late style' as a way to describe those of Beethoven's works – principally, the *Missa Solemnis* and the Ninth Symphony – that, though chronologically late in Beethoven's *œuvre*, do not, for Adorno, share to an adequate degree the distinctive characteristics of the late piano sonatas or quartets (though Adorno is inconsistent in his analysis, at times excluding the sonatas too from his account of the late style). Beethoven, in other words, despite the clarity of the stylistic caesura Adorno elsewhere claims for him, writes inconsistently in a 'late style'. Shakespeare appears a much more clearcut case. For all that the late Shakespearean caesura turns out, as we have seen, to be far more difficult to pin down generically and chronologically than might be expected, critics broadly agree that the late plays share a style that is noticeably distinct from any of Shakespeare's previous styles. And this kind of critical agreement is typical of discussions of the principal exemplars of late style across the disciplines: it is in fact in regard to the question of style itself – to, that is, a tangible change in technique in the latter part of the career – that each discipline makes its strongest claim.

Inevitably, though, there are material and terminological differences between the ways in which literary criticism, musicology and art history address the specifics of late style. A key term peculiar to art history, for instance, is 'loose facture'. Rembrandt is regularly cited, as we have seen, as a classic, perhaps *the* classic, exemplar of late style and the term and its synonyms are prominent in appreciations of his last paintings. Mariët Westermann, in a recent mainstream account, writes both of 'the evocative, non-descriptive quality of Rembrandt's late paintings' and the 'heavy, expressively worked paint', the 'craggy, gravelly [...] surfaces', that establish that quality.[66] 'His last self-portraits', she argues, 'owe much of their gravity to the dense and crusty character of this paint' – they 'depend' she says, 'on their rough surfaces for their full effect'– and she gives a personality to this style, describing it, in terms that Said would have appreciated, as 'singular and wilful' (*Rembrandt*, 310, 289). Looking closely at the magnificent late *Lucretia*, for instance, she notes the artist's technique: 'the rawness of the paint – pasted on thickly where there is substance, dragged across bare ground in shadow – registers Lucretia's pain' (ibid., 310). And she cites Houbraken, who evokes anecdotally the sheer physicality of Rembrandt's late style:

For many years he was so busy painting that people had to wait a long time for their pieces, even though he worked quickly, particularly in his last period, when his work, seen from nearby, would look as if it was smeared on with a trowel. Which is why, when people came to his studio and wanted to see his work at close range, he would pull them back saying 'the smell of paint will bother you'. It is also said that he once painted a portrait so thickly, that you could lift the painting from the ground by the nose. Thus you see also gems and pearls on jewels and turbans that are painted in such a raised manner that they look as if they have been modelled, a way of handling his pieces which makes them look strong even seen from afar.[67]

Houbraken's description has its most obvious recent counterpart in Simon Schama's account of the late style in his magisterial biography *Rembrandt's Eyes*. Writing of what he calls the 'revolutionary force and visionary courage of Rembrandt's last pictures', Schama notes – and it is worth, I think, quoting this fine passage at length – that

he ventures far beyond anything recognizable as conventional impasto laid on with a palette knife, creating, especially in the garments billowing from his figures, fantastic passages of sculpted pigment in which the ostensible shapes they are meant to describe – folds, pleats, swags, brocades – dissolve and collapse, actually seeming to occlude and obstruct, rather than assist, definition. The painting here is barely recognizable as brushwork at all, the tool of delivery by which it's been laid onto the canvas still completely unfathomable – neither brush nor palette knife, nor fingers dabbling in the oily pigment. From zone to zone, it varies radically in feel and texture where Rembrandt was evidently experimenting with different rates of drying and layering. In some passages, like the back of the man's cape in *The Jewish Bride*, the paint seems first thickly laid on and then thinned out, by scouring, scraping, or combing, giving the upper layer a fibrous, stringily matted feel. In other areas, the paint is muddily coagulate, puddled, dripped, and caked; in other spots, more granular and abraded; in other places again, it seems clayey and bricklike, as though kiln-roasted, the colors parched or flame-licked, fired tiles of pigment laid down like tesserae. In still other passages, the paint surface is worked into a scarred and cratered ground like the valley floor of one of Seghers's moonscapes, pitted and pimply with gritty excrescences. And there are places where it resembles a raggedly quilted fabric, the pieces of work loosely stitched together.[68]

Schama gives a magnificently textured description here, doing as much as any critic can in words to achieve an evocation of the physical form of the work, to establish the uniqueness of the late Rembrandt style. In order to do so, though, he – inevitably, it seems – offers a series of comparisons with other late styles. Rembrandt's late subject-matter, for instance, Schama acknowledges, was something he shared with Rubens: 'The chain of life, its profound, organic mystery, its vital pulse arising as desire, enacted in passion, and ending in abiding trust and companionship', Schama writes, 'was the subject both Rubens and Rembrandt chose to portray as the essence of humanity at the end of their lives' (*Rembrandt's Eyes*, 666). But, he adds immediately, the means by which the two artists expressed their vision of love's redemption could hardly have been more different. Rubens chose his lightest, most lyrical vein; brushes gripped painfully in his gout-tortured hands yet skimming over the surface of the canvas with the lithe agility of boyhood, the strokes silky, feathery, light, and delicate, something he might have learned from Titian. Rembrandt, of course, had taken his lessons from Titian, too. But in his last paintings, he set them aside. Instead of a broken manner, his love-painting has a massive, monumental quality; something as much hewn or graven as painted, the burning molten colors fused together into a solid block like some immense, glowing gem hardened in volcanic fire. (ibid., 666)

'In the most prodigious passages of his last paintings', Schama continues, Rembrandt produced 'the kind of work that went realms beyond the most radical and broken inventions of Titian and even the startling patch-and-daub painting of Velázquez' (ibid.). Thus, he concludes, '"Rough" or "broad" painting – the conventional art-historical terminology – is no longer adequate to characterize the revolutionary force and visionary courage of Rembrandt's last pictures' (ibid.). Rembrandt's late style, then, is different from that of others. Yet, even as he wrests Rembrandt to a higher plane, Schama – aware that the existence of a specific art-historical terminology for the style signifies a general discourse of artistic lateness – finds himself recalling the late work of others, if only in order, rather transparently, to diminish that work in the comparison. It is hard, after all, to imagine that many students of Titian would recognise the sum total of the impact of his late *Saint Jerome in Penitence*, say, or of *The Flaying of Marsyas* in Schama's dismissive 'broken'.

It is in fact almost impossible to find a description of the late style of a given artist without also finding a comparison with that of another. Hajo Düchting, offering an account of the late Miró, begins with a comparison which is dependent upon the assumption that late style is supra-individual. 'Miró's late abstract paintings', he argues,

are reminiscent of Klee, a modern painter whom Miró valued very much indeed and towards whom he had felt in many ways an affinity from the very beginning. However, unlike *Polyphonies*, which Klee painted in the Bauhaus days, there is no conscious dependence here, but rather a parallel artistic development that sprang from a similar power of imagination.[69]

It is a certain 'power of imagination' at the end of life that produces late style, then, and it is the shared impact of that imaginative quality that allows the borderlines between artistic disciplines to be breached and counterparts for terms such as 'loose facture' to be found for non-material art-forms. We have already seen in Havelock Ellis both the general applicability of these terms to artists other than Rembrandt – in his descriptions, for instance, of Titian's late paintings in which the splendours of that master's earlier works are forgotten in the attainment of a subdued and clouded glory which rises to still greater heights' or of 'Turner, whose early genius of the earth, sober and sombre, leapt up to heaven at last in mist and flame' – and the ease with which similar terminology can be deployed in respect of works beyond the realms of the discipline of art, as he slips from these imagistic accounts of artists to discussions of the 'water and fire' of Shelley's last poems and, of course, of Shakespeare's late plays, 'so loose and undramatic, so flowing or so broken, so full of exquisite music of the spirit more than of poetic form' (see Chapter 1, 29–30). In this context, Schama's terminology, far from confirming the uniqueness of the late Rembrandt style, is in real danger, despite his impeccable specificity, of making it sound very much akin to the late style of any other major creative artist.

It is the vague, elemental quality of what is being described that allows critical descriptions of work in wholly different art-forms produced at wholly different periods to appear so similar. Commentators on late style as a general phenomenon emphasise this quality. What is common, asks Broch, to the various examples of late work that he cites? The answer, as we have seen, is style, and a very particular style at that: 'All of them reveal a radical change in style, not merely a development in the original direction', he argues, 'and this sharp stylistic break can be described as a kind of *abstractism* in which the expression relies less and less on the vocabulary [...] and [...] more and more on the syntax' (Broch, 11). Abstraction, then, is key, a rejection of conventions of detail and specificity that for Broch defines the 'style of old age', a style which is at least as epochal as it is personal and which starts to look suspiciously like a series of proleptic glimpses of modernism. For Broch, as we have seen, this style, manifesting itself technically, is merely a symptom of something larger, something transhistorical: the artist, he argues, who is

graced and cursed with the 'style of old age' is not content with the conventional vocabulary provided him by his epoch. For to render the epoch, the whole epoch, he cannot remain within it; he must find a point beyond it. This often appears to him a technical problem, the problem of dissolving the existing vocabulary and, from its syntactical roots, forming his own. ('Mythical', 12)

Yet, Broch insists, the artist's 'real impulse goes beyond this – it goes to the universe; and the true piece of art, even though it be the shortest lyric, must always embrace the totality of the world' (ibid.). 'This', he adds, 'is felt by every true artist, but is creatively realized only by the artist of old age' (ibid.). The effect of this atemporality – of the general applicability of ideas of 'loose facture' and 'abstraction' to late work across the genres and centuries – is, paradoxically, then, both to diminish the uniqueness of the individual artists in question even as they are attributed a late style as a marker of that uniqueness and to reduce those artists to the status of more or less unwitting harbingers of modern art. I will return in due course to these questions – to the 'ownership' of late style; the question of whether, that is, a given artist's late style is that artist's unique style as it has developed for a range of reasons late in life or an instance of a general, transhistorical phenomenon known as 'late style' as it is channelled through the artist; and to the idea of late style as a kind of ongoing forerunner of the modern aesthetic. Neumann's language of the numinous and Broch's sense of the universal both insist that we address late style as a function of a supra-individual phenomenon, that we treat it as something effectively constant across time and space. Any counter-measure to this must therefore dwell on the specifics of a given late manner. What is needed are accounts of late styles that do not resolve into easy generalisations.

Broch, unsurprisingly, cites mainly German instances of achievement at this level – Bach, Beethoven, Goethe – but the principal exemplar for anglophone culture of this overarching late style has of course been Shakespeare. As we have seen in relation both to genre and to chronology, Shakespeare, like Beethoven, produced plays which critics might, following Tiedemann, call 'late works without late style', that is, plays other than the four 'romances' that occupy the same timeframe as those plays yet which are, to a greater or lesser extent, difficult to regard in the same tonal, stylistic or generic light – *Antony and Cleopatra* maybe, *Coriolanus* certainly, plus collaborative plays, *Timon of Athens*, *Henry VIII* or *The Two Noble Kinsmen* – which, taken together, suggest that Shakespearean lateness is less a question of genre or chronology than it is of a particular way with language and, above all, with verse. Which makes the question of style key. What *Pericles*, *The Winter's Tale*, *Cymbeline* and *The Tempest* have in common, we are repeatedly told, is a certain distinctive style, a style which is simultaneously characteristic both of that group of four plays and of late work in general. Yet pinning that style down has proved, over the years, a remarkably tough task. A range of critics has tried to sum up what is distinctive about the late Shakespearean language and, as often as not, these critics contradict each other. Some have discussed speech and meaning in the late plays without reflecting on the question of late style at all. For Maurice Hunt, for instance, language is not so much the vehicle as the shared theme of these four plays, which he collects under the title 'Shakespeare's Romance of the Word', arguing that renewed or redeemed language is itself the principal expression of transformation in the plays. The plays are 'linguistic explorations' which together form a group characterised by 'a consistent dramatic design' (*Shakespeare's Romance*, 13). Hunt's focus is distinctly literary-critical rather than stylistic: at no stage, in fact, does he discuss actual questions of style. Moreover, there is nothing in his account to tie the particular engagement of these plays with language to any larger issues of lateness. He reads the plays simply as 'great works of art', noting, for instance, that *The Winter's Tale* 'transcends conventional contexts, upon which it necessarily depends for its remarkable meanings, yielding at last a pure and powerful image for our understanding of it', but he does not relate this transcendence directly to the late technique (ibid., 108). The linguistic orientation of the plays, partially expressed as a question of style but principally as theme, he argues, unites them as 'romances of the word' but not as late plays per se. The collective term here for the plays – treated as a coherent group of four without mention of the collaborations (Wilkins and Fletcher do not appear in Hunt's index) – is 'romance' and the interest strictly thematic.

Most late-play critics, however, have read the language of the plays as, in one way or another, a tangible manifestation of their lateness and have thus written about them in terms broadly aligned with Broch and Ellis. It was critics in the mid-twentieth century, once again, who set the scene for subsequent readings. For Philip Edwards, in perhaps the simplest statement of the fundamental difference between late Shakespeare and everything that came before it, 'the Romances are written in a form of other-speaking'.[70] This quality of otherness is described, as we have seen, by Traversi as tending 'away from realism, towards a conception of the art of the theatre in which character and action alike are real in relation to the poetic unity to which they belong, and finally to that alone', such that the late plays are dependent upon 'a conception of drama completely removed from realism and properly definable in symbolic terms' (Traversi, 18, 2) – phrasing not unakin to that of Broch. Writing about *Cymbeline*, Traversi cites certain lines spoken by Posthumus:

> 'Tis still a dream, or else such stuff as madmen
> Tongue, and brain not; either both, or nothing,
> Or senseless speaking, or a speaking such
> As sense cannot untie. Be what it is,
> The action of my life is like it.   (*Cymbeline*, 5.5.239–43)

And he argues that '[t]he dream quality which characterizes so many utterances in Shakespeare's last plays is here bound up, linguistically

A question of style

speaking, with a sense of complexity, intricate uncertainty, which makes it something more than the merely poetic statement which it has so often felt to be', adding that '[j]ust as Prospero's famous vision of the dream fabric of our experienced world', which

> proceeds from his 'beating brain', is balanced against the immanent brutality of Caliban's design upon him in a way that forces reality upon us, so here the vivid energy of phrasing in 'tongue, and brain not,' and the intricate knottiness of 'senseless' opposed to 'sense' and 'speaking' to 'speaking,' corresponds to the felt pressure of reality. (*Last Phase*, 95)

This, however, is the point at which he parts company with Broch. The resistance to realism does *not*, for Traversi, produce abstraction. As we have seen, he argues that 'a new, transhumanizing element [...] enters explicitly into' the late-play verse, which thus becomes 'the poetry of resurrection', a poetry 'so charged with a quality that can truly be described as supernatural, and yet so free from any suggestion of abstraction or strain' (ibid., 31). For Traversi, then, abstraction is a symptom of strain, not serenity, and, despite the apparent similarity of his understanding of the nature of late work in general to that of Broch, he rejects the particular stylistic distinction made by the latter, the singling out of abstraction as a key attribute of the late style, as part of an underlying insistence on continuity and on redemptive purpose. The relationship between the general understanding of late style and specific accounts of the style of the late Shakespeare thus itself comes under a certain strain.

At least one mid-century critic, however, proved able to detach theological assumptions from stylistic analysis in providing an unusually concise description of the late style. For S. L. Bethell, in his 1956 edition of *The Winter's Tale*, the play's stylistic characteristics were clear:

> Rhythms for the most part are not smooth and regular as in the early plays, nor do they directly suggest the rhythms of ordinary speech as do those of Shakespeare's middle period. We are aware of the blank verse pattern and we can hear at the same time the tones of speech, but the total effect is new, a blank verse which is tense, springy, contorted. Among the means employed to achieve this are a daring use of harsh sound to express harsh feelings, the frequent omission of words properly required by the syntax [...] and a sometimes violent distortion of word order.[71]

In this brief but specific account, in which he addresses rhythm, versification, sound and syntax in turn to delineate what has changed since Shakespeare's 'middle period', Bethell describes not a vague and ethereal abstractism but rather a series of disruptions, disturbances and distortions – what Adorno might have called 'fissures and rifts' – in the smooth progress of the plays' language. It is as if Shakespeare were creating a synthesis of, moving a step beyond, the modulations both of speech and of dramatic verse, something fresh and at the same time taut – spring-loaded, as it were. What is key here is Bethell's eschewing of the impressionism of a Traversi for a harder, more precise analysis of individual stylistic features, one which seems to invite a fuller account elsewhere. Few critics, though, have taken the cue, most descriptions of the late style coming, like that of Bethell, from scholars making passing remarks about the characteristics of the late plays in the course of work targeted less at stylistic than at literary-critical analysis; only a handful of critics have attempted actual sustained analysis of the late style per se.[72]

By far the most sustained and convincing of these – coming exactly half a century after Bethell – is that of Russ McDonald in his invaluable *Shakespeare's Late Style*. He begins by offering a description of the late style in the Bethell mould, which deserves quoting in full:

The technical features that make Shakespeare's late style demanding can be enumerated in a few sentences. Ellipsis exerts a constant pressure on the sound and sense as the poet concentrates expression, omitting phonemic and verbal units that in an earlier phase of composition he would have retained. Connectives between clauses are sometimes removed, creating the effect of asyndeton: the words and phrases that remain make the verse sound unusually 'distilled'. Syntax becomes convoluted, often confusingly so, and even though word order in early modern English is much less standardized than it has since become, the number of deformed phrases, directional shifts, and intricately constructed sentences is exceptional for the period and exceptional for Shakespeare. Related to this grammatical complexity is the dependence on parenthesis, what one critic refers to as 'parenthomania, the alarming outbreak of brackets'. Repetition of various units – letters, words, phrases, rhythms – becomes more prominent and sometimes insistent, patterning heard clearly in the incantatory doublings in *Macbeth* and resounding most audibly in the extraordinary echoing effects of *The Tempest*. Blank verse, usually a guarantor of order and regularity, is now aggressively irregular, encompassing enjambments, light or weak endings, frequent stops or shifts of direction, and other threats to the integrity of the line. Metaphors tend to be introduced and often succeeded rapidly by others, not articulated at length. Finally, governing all these technical features is an insistent self-consciousness, an artist's playful delight in calling attention to his own virtuosity. (*Late Style*, 33)

McDonald takes each of the features he describes in turn as the basis for a chapter. Ellipsis, for instance, is key to the late-style effect: 'In seeking intensity', he argues, 'the mature Shakespeare experiments with a poetic method based on distillation and reduction' and on 'subordination and casting away' (ibid., 79). Florizel's lines at the start of the sheep-shearing

A question of style

scene are, he suggests, typical of this technique, the sense crammed into a smaller number of lines than might seem possible, offering a wealth of information heavily compressed:

> These your unusual weeds to each part of you
> Does give a life; no shepherdess, but Flora
> Peering in April's front. This your sheep-shearing
> Is as a meeting of the petty gods,
> And you the queen on't.   (*The Winter's Tale*, 4.4.1–5)

Another constituent characteristic of the late style is pleonasm. 'For all its fierce abridgements, the late line is also heavy with surplus', argues McDonald, especially at the level of verse: 'Shakespeare', he says, 'insists on crowding the condensed line with additional syllables' (*Late Style*, 96, 97). In the sheep-shearing speech, even as sense is compressed, the hypermetrical verse lines establish a structural tension with that compression: 'the speaker and auditor are confronted with so many syllables that the line requires a kind of auditory ellipsis in which unstressed syllables [...] huddle together in subjection to the stressed' (ibid., 96).

Further key characteristics include divagation and suspension, as '[t]he aggressively digressive syntax carries the listener on a winding and difficult semantic course, an apparently disordered collection of grammatical inversions, accumulated clauses, interpolations, unexpected breakings off', while 'in a striking number of instances, essential elements of grammar, particularly the verbal phrase, often the direct object, and sometimes even the subject, are withheld until the very end of the sentence' (ibid., 149). Innogen, impatient to meet Posthumus (or so she thinks) at Milford Haven, exemplifies this combination of digression and deferral:

> Read, and tell me
> How far 'tis thither. If one of mean affairs
> May plod it in a week, why may not I
> Glide thither in a day? Then, true Pisanio,
> Who long'st like me to see thy lord, who long'st –
> O let me bate – but not like me – yet long'st
> But in a fainter kind – O, not like me,
> For mine's beyond beyond; say, and speak thick –
> Love's counsellor should fill the bores of hearing,
> To th' smothering of the sense – how far it is
> To this same blessèd Milford. And by th' way
> Tell me how Wales was made so happy as
> T'inherit such a haven. But first of all,
> How we may steal from hence; and for the gap
> That we shall make in time from our hence-going

> And our return, to excuse; but first, how get hence.
> Why should excuse be born or ere begot?
> We'll talk of that hereafter. (*Cymbeline*, 3.2.49–66)

Underpinning the writing at the level of sound, even as the play as a whole serves as a kind of rehearsal of Shakespeare's earlier thematic engagements, is repetition. 'To listen carefully to the reiterative patterns that resound everywhere in these late texts', argues McDonald, 'is to perceive one of the primary sources of their poetic power' (*Late Style*, 181), and he maps the patterns of alliteration in Emilia's invocation at Diana's temple in *The Two Noble Kinsmen* –

> O sacred, shadowy, cold, and constant queen,
> Abandoner of revels, mute contemplative,
> Sweet, solitary, white as chaste, and pure
> As wind-fanned snow, who to thy female knights
> Allow'st no more blood than will make a blush,
> Which is their order's robe: I here, thy priest,
> Am humbled fore thine altar (5.3.1–7)

– or in the protagonist's disbelieving outburst at the climax of *Pericles* –

> O Helicanus, strike me, honoured sir,
> Give me a gash, put me to present pain,
> Lest this great sea of joys rushing upon me
> O'erbear the shores of my mortality
> And drown me with their sweetness. O, come hither,
> Thou that begett'st him that did thee beget,
> Thou that wast born at sea, buried at Tarsus,
> And found at sea again! – O Helicanus,
> Down on thy knees, thank the holy gods as loud
> As thunder threatens us, this is Marina! (sc. 21, 178–86)

– so as to underline the precise mechanics of the late style, manipulating his typeface – 'O *s*acred, *s*hadowy, <u>c</u>old and <u>c</u>onstant queen' or '**Th**o*u* that begett'st him **t**hat did **t**hee <u>beget</u>, / **Th**o*u* **t**hat wast born at sea, buried at Tarsus' (*Late Style*, 186–7) – in order to assist the reader to see the intricate patterns that emerge. McDonald thus provides by far the most thorough and detailed account of Shakespeare's late style to date, unpacking with great care the linguistic features shared between the plays of the final period.

Edward Said, as we have seen, at the end of his life championed a version of late style that he found vastly preferable to the consummate calm he saw, in accordance with critical tradition, as most fully embodied in late Shakespeare, asserting his preference for the furious, resistant lateness of a

A question of style

Beethoven or a Yeats. For him, the irascibility of lateness is embodied in the jaggedness and difficulty of style characteristically associated with late writing or late art, in its resistance to assimilation, and the Shakespearean tradition of finding resignation and acceptance in the late work frustrated him with its blandness, its refusal to rage at the dying of the light. A closer inspection of the technique of the late plays, however, might have given Said hope. Analysts of Shakespearean late style have in fact regularly been forced into uncomfortable negotiations between the biographical urge for serenity and the roughness and apparent wilful obscurity of the late-play verse, privileging the former over the latter to such an extent that a critic such as Said could turn as a matter of course to late Shakespeare as his prime exemplar of all he rejected in submissive, unresistant lateness. Yet the language of those critics who have moved beyond impressionism to a close analysis of stylistic detail suggests that this is a wholly misplaced understanding of the late Shakespearean style. As will by now be clear both from Bethell's brief and McDonald's far fuller account, once Shakespearean critics begin close analysis of the late style, the traditional Dowdenesque vocabulary of serenity and calm disperses with surprising rapidity.

The sheer intransigence and difficulty of the Shakespearean late style has been a significant ongoing challenge for critics writing broadly within the subjectivist tradition. Traversi, as we have seen, was forced to work quite hard to absorb the apparent strains of the late style into his balanced, redemptive account of the last plays and the terms deployed by Bethell express something quite other than serenity: the language of the plays, for him, is 'tense', 'contorted', 'harsh' and 'violent'. McDonald too emphasises, not always entirely willingly, the tensions that create the verbal effects he describes: 'aurally demanding and self-consciously artificial', the 'jerky, difficult', 'overloaded and repetitious', 'capricious', 'rhythmically demanding' late-play style, he observes, offers 'defiance of ready intelligibility', 'withholding [...] resolution' and becoming a 'syntactical thicket' (*Late Style* 113, 97, 108, 204, 77, 228). 'Suspicion of the word', he admits, having noted the 'destructive verbal illusions of the tragedies', 'haunt[s] plays like *The Winter's Tale* and *Henry VIII*, with its ironic alternative title, *All is True*, but distrust', he insists, 'is accompanied by resignation to or acceptance of such limitations' (ibid. 74). Yet there are clear signs of strain, as there were for Traversi, in the assimilation of the detailing of 'fissures and rifts' that dominate McDonald's four central descriptive chapters into his final evocative vision of the 'numinous' late plays as a whole (ibid. 253). The more we read these accounts, the less serene the plays appear, the more tension and violence of expression there appears to be in the late style.

The roughness of that style not only breaks up poetic sense and disperses the mists of serenity; it also threatens to fragment the late-play group, to create problems with assigning one single distinct style to these plays. Traversi, in his account of the *Winter's Tale* style – which he sees as 'characteristic of Shakespeare's late verse in its combination of freedom with a close subjection to the underlying development of meaning' (*Last Phase*, 166) – appears to accept a shared identity between the four 'romances' of which he writes, yet it soon becomes clear that he finds it rather difficult to incorporate *Cymbeline*, a play which for him seeks

> to secure an exploration of emotion that is not merely conventional, approaching it from a vast number of viewpoints and bringing these together in implied comparisons whose complexity is more than conventional. For the operation of artistic intuition, gathering up dissimilarities and fusing them into a superior unity which is, in this case, the entry into a new, richer life, this peculiar prose is a most suitable instrument. (ibid., 185)

F. C. Tinkler offers a darker rendering of this 'peculiar prose': for him, the writing 'has a hard corrugated texture' resulting 'from the persistent recreation of feelings in a particular kind of physical pain'.[73] The particular toughness and resistance of *Cymbeline*'s language seems, on close inspection, to be the cause of a deal of awkwardness in descriptions of the late style. Tellingly, *Cymbeline* is cited far more than any other play when evidence of a difficult, spiky late style is sought. J. W. Mackail writes not so much of a late-Shakespeare style but of a specific 'Cymbeline-style' and differentiates between it and what he calls 'the characteristic finished style of Shakespeare's mature work' (Mackail, 223), attributing the fragmentation of this individual late style to Shakespeare's easing back from full concentration as he nears retirement. For him, parenthomania is the clearest sign of a relaxation of full poetic powers:

> The most obvious note of this Cymbeline-style is the immense number of parentheses, and of parentheses within parentheses. It is as though Shakespeare's mind were working at its full compass – on three or four lines abreast as one might say – but not at its full tension or concentration in which the concurrent processes of thought become molten into one. He is writing with obvious pleasure, and obviously for his pleasure. The fires are drawn, and the beautifully adjusted engines go on running under a lower steam-pressure, and almost by their own momentum. (*Shakespeare's Romances*, 224)

The fragmentation of the late-Shakespearean sentence is thus the marker, for Mackail, of a relaxation of synthetic thinking. For McDonald, parenthesis of this kind is characteristic of all the late plays – he is careful to differentiate between parenthesis as a syntactical phenomenon and the

A question of style

penchant of the King's Men scribe Ralph Crane, responsible for the Folio late-play texts, for the insertion of round brackets – but the fact remains that, in the chapters on features such as ellipsis or divagation, he tends to turn to *Cymbeline* first when seeking lengthier passages in order to outline in detail the late-play style: the 'playful attitude towards style' that he describes 'seems to inform *Cymbeline* especially' (*Late Style*, 158).

For a number of late-play critics, then, the style of *Cymbeline* appears to an extent distinct from that of the others, the hardest both to pin down and to assimilate to the larger group, not least because of its multiplication of styles. For Brian Gibbons, *Cymbeline* 'is unique, even among Shakespeare's remarkably various works, for the heterogeneity of styles it employs'.[74] John Porter Houston, in an extended syntactical analysis, disagrees, but only partially: 'With *Cymbeline*', he argues, 'we reach a distinctive phase in Shakespeare's style, which is not simply a one-time experiment, relevant to that play alone, but also includes *The Winter's Tale* [...] and, in certain respects, extends even to *The Tempest*.'[75] For Houston, then, in a different take on the notion of late-Shakespearean experimentation, the *Cymbeline*-style spilt over into other plays, but not very far: his late-stylistic grouping emphasises *Cymbeline*, incorporates *The Winter's Tale*, somewhat grudgingly acknowledges certain aspects of *The Tempest* as belonging, and ignores the collaborative plays altogether. Even if Gibbons is exaggerating in calling *Cymbeline* unique, the difficulty of fixing a single distinct style for *one* of these plays, never mind the full set, seems roughly equivalent to the problems we have seen in the establishing of a fixed chronology.

Yet it is in this sense, arguably, that *Cymbeline*, in its very multiplicity, is in fact representative of the late plays as a whole. As McDonald admits of the late writing – even as he defines it as precisely as anyone has done to date – '[s]o varied and unpredictable is the verse that almost any generalization about its elements and their uses requires modification and, in some cases, contradiction as well' (McDonald, 34–5). This fragmentation of stylistic exemplars echoes the fragmentation of chronology we have already observed, the difficulty of pinning down a clearcut caesura dividing the late plays from what went before. McDonald notes that Bethell's description of late style in *The Winter's Tale* owes a good deal to A. C. Bradley's observations about later Shakespeare in his *Shakespearean Tragedy*, in which he notes that the style

becomes grander, sometimes wilder, sometimes more swelling, even tumid. It is also more concentrated, rapid, varied, and, in construction, less regular, not seldom twisted or elliptical. It is, therefore, not easy and lucid and in the more ordinary dialogue it is sometimes involved and obscure, and from these and other causes deficient in charm.[76]

This now seems familiar enough language to describe the difficult style of the late plays, but its particular interest stems from the two words I omitted at the beginning of the quotation: 'After *Hamlet*'. For Bradley, the Shakespearean late style he describes goes back as far as the turn of the century, encompassing *Macbeth*, *Antony and Cleopatra* and *Coriolanus* just as much as it does *Pericles*, *Cymbeline*, *The Winter's Tale* and *The Tempest*. We are back, then, perhaps unsurprisingly, to the vexed question of the caesura.

A book that stands almost entirely alone in the field of Shakespearean studies is George T. Wright's 1989 *Shakespeare's Metrical Art* and it is not hard to see why. Wright offers the kind of intense, technical assessment of Shakespearean verse that is beyond the majority of critics (including, I might add, the present writer), who lack his ear for the music of poetry or who simply find close reading or historicising more congenial practices. His purpose, as he states it at the start, is

> to describe the metrical system Shakespeare uses, particularly in his plays – the basic forms of his iambic pentameter line, its relation to other patterns (such as short lines, long lines, and prose), its changes over his career, and, most of all, the expressive gestures and powers this system provides for Shakespeare and his dramatis personae.[77]

The key interest of this for the analyst of late style lies in Wright's mapping of the 'changes over [Shakespeare's] career' in his deployment of verse form and in the conclusions he reaches about the late work. Though in several ways in tune with McDonald's account of late Shakespeare, Wright's assessment runs counter to it – and counter to most critics' assumptions about the late style – in one key respect, that of the caesura. He describes not a marked change around 1607, as might be anticipated, but rather a steady development in Shakespearean verse from the earliest plays to the latest. In effect, he maps the gradual growth, the gradual *ageing*, of Shakespeare as a versifier, even using as his metaphor the impact of the passing of time on the complexion: 'the lines', he says, writing of a speech in *Macbeth* but thinking ahead, 'continue to sound like iambic pentameter, but they seem cracked and weathered – like Hermione, showing their wrinkles, their lines of stress' (*Metrical Art*, 218–19). He is, however, getting a little ahead of himself in citing Hermione here, since there is further development beyond the period of the major tragedies. The 'counterpoint style' he has been describing is, he argues,

> far removed from that of the early plays, with their long, continuous lines and line-by-line accumulation of rhetorical segments. But Shakespeare was to go further still.

> In *Antony and Cleopatra, Coriolanus, Timon of Athens, Cymbeline*, and the first half of *The Winter's Tale*, he develops a yet more radical and jagged technique for posing antagonistic lengths of line and phrase against each other. Most of the previous plays, from *Richard II* to *Macbeth*, include numerous passages notable for their mellifluous phrasing and gracefully extended arguments. But, except for a few famous measures in *Antony and Cleopatra*, this later group of plays contains almost no set speeches likely to tempt the inveterate memorizer. (*Metrical Art*, 220)

What is fascinating about this description is that Wright, reclaiming the caesura as a feature of verse-form, appears to transfer the division between early and late from the career to the poetry, seeing in the late writing an emphasis on the line-break, on the fissure between phrases: 'Speech here', Wright argues, 'tends to be abrupt and agitated, the rift between phrase and line a constant feature of the verse', and he observes

> a notable increase in short phrases that constitute whole sentences or cola, a tactic which sharply increases the number of breaks in some lines. Instead of the long, magisterially controlled sentences that stride through the flowing lines of the middle plays, Shakespeare now allows his characters to speak in short bursts much of the time. (ibid.)

This development, he claims, is linear – 'The strangeness of this verse increases with each play in the series, at least up to *Cymbeline* and the first half of *The Winter's Tale*' (ibid.) – and, as parallel instances of the peculiar verse he sees as characteristic of this period, he compares passages from *Coriolanus* –

> Your voices? For your voices I have fought,
> Watched for your voices, for your voices bear
> Of wounds two dozen odd; battles thrice six
> I have seen and heard of for your voices, have
> Done many things, some less, some more. Your voices!   (2.3.126–30)

– and from *Cymbeline* –

> To lapse in fullness
> Is sorer than to lie for need, and falsehood
> Is worse in kings than beggars. My dear lord,
> Thou art one o'th' false ones. Now I think on thee
> My hunger's gone, but even before I was
> At point to sink for food.   (3.6.12–17)

Wright thus reads as a process of steady growth the development of the deployment of the pentameter across Shakespeare's life as he grows older and more experienced. In doing so, however, he does not differentiate between, on the one hand, *Antony and Cleopatra* and *Coriolanus* and, on the other, *Cymbeline* and at least the first half of *The Winter's Tale* – Wright is either unaware of or chooses to ignore the Oxford Shakespeare's inversion of the traditional order of *Cymbeline* and *The Winter's Tale* in their chronology – except inasmuch as each play demonstrates the linear development of Shakespeare's command of the form. He thus, in effect, diminishes, even dismisses, the possibility of finding a clearly distinguishable starting point for the 'late phase'. If there is a caesura of sorts in Wright's analysis, it falls not before *Pericles* – which hardly, as a collaboration, gets a mention (he omits *Henry VIII* and *The Two Noble Kinsmen* entirely) – or *Cymbeline* but halfway through *The Winter's Tale* and concludes with *The Tempest*. Style thus appears once more to be precisely as troublesome for the establishment of a clearly delineated late style as is chronology.

While there is undoubtedly a Shakespearean late style, then, in the sense that the plays at the end of the career manifest to a greater or lesser extent certain intense, fissured stylistic tendencies that cannot be found in the Elizabethan or earlier Jacobean plays, three key problems persist. The first of these is the difficulty of relating this Shakespearean late style to the larger discourse of lateness. The second is the difficulty of taking style as the principal criterion for the establishment of the caesura. And the third is the persistence of subjectivism even in the most purely stylistic of accounts. For all the formal specificity of McDonald's analysis, as the last sentence of his initial description of the late style – 'governing all these technical features is a pervasive self-consciousness, an artist's playful delight in calling attention to his own virtuosity' (33) – suggests, with its insistence on artistic self-awareness underpinning linguistic experimentation, he shows himself drawn, in identifying the source of that design, to a Brochian subjectivism: 'I propose', he writes, 'that we interpret the verbal obscurity and poetic difficulty of the late style as a function of Shakespeare's increasingly sophisticated way of thinking about the world, a stylistic manifestation of his ever developing view of human experience' (*Late Style*, 32). 'The difficulties of the late verse', he proceeds, 'attest to a straining after greater subtlety, an effort to represent many complex and at times virtually contradictory ideas' so that 'Shakespeare is frequently said to be deliberately seeking to intensify the virtual experience, trying to propel listeners beyond mere verbal denotation, contriving to make them participate in the feeling represented' (ibid.). Here McDonald echoes James Sutherland who, citing the syntactically awkward opening dialogue in *Cymbeline* –

FIRST GENTLEMAN	You do not meet a man but frowns. Our bloods
	No more obey the heavens than our courtiers
	Still seem as does the King.
SECOND GENTLEMAN	But what's the matter?
FIRST GENTLEMAN	His daughter, and the heir of's kingdom, whom
	He purposed to his wife's sole son – a widow
	That late he married – hath referred herself
	Unto a poor but worthy gentleman. She's wedded,
	Her husband banished, she imprisoned. All
	Is outward sorrow, though I think the King
	Be touched at very heart.
SECOND GENTLEMAN	None but the King?
FIRST GENTLEMAN	He that hath lost her, too. So is the Queen,
	That most desired the match. But not a courtier –
	Although they wear their faces to the bent
	Of the King's looks – hath a heart that is not
	Glad of the thing they scowl at (1.1.1–15)

– and sidestepping the process of the matching of voice to character that is fundamental to dramatic composition, suggests that 'the person who is thinking rapidly, breaking off, making fresh starts, and so on, is not the character, but Shakespeare himself'.[78]

This sense of the subordination of characterisation to the overarching dramatic purpose of the playwright has, as McDonald notes, been a persistent argument in descriptions of the late style – apparent, for instance, in the account given by Anne Barton of the style of *Pericles* and in John Porter Houston's important if neglected work on the Shakespearean sentence. As McDonald observes,

[a]n article of critical agreement is that the mature Shakespeare divides language from speaker, or at least the connection between style and character has been attenuated. [. . .] That Shakespeare learned, as he reached professional maturity in the mid-1590s, to make his speakers sound like themselves is one of the triumphs of his craft, one of the talents for which he is celebrated and by which he is differentiated from lesser dramatists. [. . .] However, about 1607 or so Shakespeare begins to weaken the link between speech and speaker. (*Late Style*, 33–4)

For Barton, Shakespeare in *Pericles* 'appears to be using Marina less as a character than as a kind of medium, through which the voice of the situation can be made to speak' and in *Cymbeline* he 'allows the wicked Queen [. . .] to speak of Britain in words that would not misbecome John of Gaunt', thus privileging purpose over characterisation; she cites both Bethell – for whom the late-play style represents 'Shakespeare's mind, not the character's; indeed, it draws our attention *away from* the speaker to what is spoken about' – and Charles Olson, for whom the late Shakespeare 'doesn't any longer bother to keep his music and thought inside the skin of the person and situation, able as he had been to make each person of his play make his or her individual self register its experience of reality'.[79] Houston argues that we must 'have recourse to the notion of some general design in the language of the play rather than to that of character or scene': he sees 'the generalisation in *Cymbeline* of relatively short sentences in patches' as 'part of a stylistic design independent of the expression of strong feelings or other common reasons one could find for them' (*Shakespearean Sentences*, 207, 200). And McDonald himself, aware though he is that most of the syntactically twisted passages he cites, those where the figures of speech he enumerates are most dominant, are moments of particular emotion for the speaker, moments of impatience, of frustration, of grief or of excitement, nonetheless echoes Houston's sense of an independent artistic design. Residually subjectivist criticism thus persists in seeking to account for the change of style evident in the late plays by turning to the idea of an overarching authorial style, despite the early modern understanding of style as a garment to be shrugged on or off. As John Hoskins put it, 'it may be that within this two hundred years we shall go through the whole body of rhetoric'; however, '[f]or my part', he continues blithely, 'I have used and outworn six several styles since I was first Fellow of New College, and am yet able to bear the fashion of writing company'.[80]

McDonald finds his preferred solution to the problem of the relationship of author to style by foregrounding genre. Refining his observation in an earlier essay on *The Winter's Tale* that 'even the syntax is tragi-comic', he argues that the style of the late plays is the product, finally, not of some kind of transcendent lateness but of genre.[81] His basic premise is that 'the distinctive properties discernible in the late verse are intimately related to the shift from tragedy to romance, that the altered style and new mode express Shakespeare's renewed sense of values and refreshed artistic purpose' (*Late Style*, 42). In other words, the complexities, the wanderings, the wavelike structure of the sentences can be dealt with because, with hindsight, they can be resolved into the play's concluding clarities. For McDonald, noting the frequency with which late Shakespearean sentences withhold significant grammatical elements and thus a final sense of meaning,

> Shakespeare regularly exaggerates the grammatical means of suspension so that sentences or passages in these late works engage, frustrate, and then finally satisfy the listener, often in an unexpected fashion. Likewise, in each case the significance of complex acts, whether linguistic or dramatic, is altered and clarified by a highly

theatrical conclusion, sometimes even a surprise ending. The romances offer a parallel between syntactical and narrative satisfaction, between small and large units of dramatic structure, and the nature of that correspondence is attributable to the altered conception of human experience generating Shakespeare's choice of stories and management of style. (ibid., 156)

Thus the stylistic idiosyncrasies of the late plays are a direct correlative of their generic underpinnings. 'Throughout the late verse', he notes,

the sentence itself becomes a kind of miniature romance narrative. The complex syntactical structures are animated by the same tension that obtains in the larger tale, the conflict between a desire for meaningful closure on the one hand and the stimulation of process on the other'. (ibid., 169)

The underpinning of this correlation remains subjectivist: it marks the fundamental change, a kind of refreshing, that takes place in Shakespeare's outlook in the aftermath of his composition of *King Lear* and *Timon of Athens*, that drives the parallel shift in genre and style. McDonald's analysis of grammatical and syntactical elements is anything but impressionistic and he has provided students of the late plays with an invaluable account of what it is, at the level of sentence, structure and versification, that makes the late plays distinct; yet not far beneath the surface there remains a certain subjectivism which, though it has shed the sublimated theology, is still in a residual sense redolent of Dowden. 'Finally', he writes, 'without falling into a sentimental reverie about the playwright as Prospero, it seems legitimate to speculate on' the extent to which the change in style 'has something to do with Shakespeare's awareness of, or disappointment at, or celebration of, his own professional end' (ibid., 180).

There is no doubt at all that the style of Shakespeare's later plays is markedly different from that of the plays which preceded them: by the end of his career, Shakespeare was writing in ways that would have been inconceivable to the youthful writer of *Love's Labour's Lost* or *The Two Gentlemen of Verona*. There is no doubt either that that style has certain specifiable characteristics. Yet, as with chronology, it refuses to offer a comfortable fit with the overarching discourse of lateness of which Shakespeare is supposed to be a central exemplar. As McDonald puts it with wry understatement, '[a] point of origin for the late Shakespearean style does not immediately present itself' (ibid., 42). As we have seen, he puts chronology under pressure both by beginning too early – the late style can, he says, be 'heard clearly in the incantatory doublings in *Macbeth*' (ibid., 33) and in any case, he notes, making a stylistic assertion that parallels Ruth Nevo's observations about the fundamental basis of

Shakespearean art in repetition and revision, 'since the late verse represents a metamorphosis or revision of earlier poetic practices, any decision about where to begin is to some degree arbitrary' (ibid., 42) – and by noting that the intertwining of generic and stylistic impetuses he has mapped from *Pericles* to *The Tempest* cannot be considered a 'final' style per se because of what came after *The Tempest*. Writing in a way reminiscent of Neumann of the 'numinous [. . .] world of Shakespearean romance', McDonald argues that 'Caliban's intimations of beauty and fulfilment in the world of dreams may stand as an image of this realm, the thousand twangling instruments as a synecdoche for Shakespeare's late style' (ibid., 253), but he also acknowledges that the collaborative post-*Tempest* plays, though sharing the idiosyncratic stylistic features he has so carefully delineated, take us in a quite different emotional direction.

Richard Proudfoot, in an important but underacknowledged essay, notes the difference between *The Two Noble Kinsmen* and the earlier late plays:

The Two Noble Kinsmen is unlike these plays in that the winning of love and the death of Arcite are juxtaposed at the end so that the overwhelming impression is not so much the value of love as its appalling cost. Not since *All's Well That Ends Well* had Shakespeare written a play whose conclusion leaves such a sense of unease. It is almost as if he was beginning once more to call in question the positive power of love. (Proudfoot, 'New Dramatists', 59)

Assuming the Oxford second-edition chronology to be correct, Proudfoot is here arguing that plays at both the very beginning and the very end of the late phase offer very little in the way of serenity, very little redemptive grace. McDonald, citing Proudfoot, acknowledges that in *The Two Noble Kinsmen*, as in *Henry VIII*, the affirmations that he has found in the plays up to *The Tempest* are no longer sustainable. 'Shakespeare's style still seems elliptical, roundabout, crowded, and extravagant', he argues, 'but the sense of possibility no longer seems to obtain. He seems to be changing his mind again' (McDonald, 254). This is a disarmingly frank way to conclude the book since it puts in jeopardy the argument of the whole. For McDonald, the stylistic characteristics of the late plays are the logical counterpart at word, sentence and paragraph level of the testing but heuristic wanderings, obfuscations and deferrals of the genre of romance and the expression of a shift of mood on the part of the playwright; if these post-romantic late plays, which have lost the heuristic drive, 'the sense of possibility', share the same basic stylistic tendencies, then that equation of mood, genre and technique must be threatened. It can, as McDonald is well aware, be decidedly tricky, when making an argument about the late plays, to depend upon fixed ideas of any kind, whether of genre, of chronology, or of style.

A question of style 125

Certain conclusions, then, present themselves in respect of the late style understood narrowly, as a technique of language, rather than broadly, as a phenomenon of old age or of the proximity of death. The first and most obvious is that, stylistically speaking, the plays of the last seven or eight years of Shakespeare's writing life (even if it is hard to be more specific than that) differ in tangible and demonstrable ways from those that precede them. Analyses such as those of Houston, Wright and McDonald, for all that they differ over boundaries and premises, agree on that. Secondly, and importantly, McDonald – detaching the stylistic difference of the late plays from the overarching idea of late style, noting the subsequent stylistic shift after *The Tempest* and attributing that change to the restless Shakespearean tendency always to seek new styles – acknowledges that there is nothing new or unique in the fact of a Shakespearean stylistic shift per se. Moreover, even as he offers a detailed sense of a common style amongst the late plays, he accepts that there is a good deal of evidence of collapse within the apparently crisp definition of the group: *Cymbeline*'s disproportionately frequent appearance as exemplar raises problems for the notion of a common late-play style and Wright's inability, on the basis of verse-form, to differentiate between *Coriolanus* and the various so-called 'romances' make arguments for an essential interconnection of style and genre in the late plays hard to sustain. As with chronology and genre, so, it seems, with style: the closer the analysis, the less certain the premises for a distinct and clearcut late-Shakespearean caesura.

'Suddenly in 1608 there was a change', claimed Kenneth Muir (Muir, *Comic Sequence*, 148). But it has become apparent that this is not the case. Adorno, writing about late style, insists, as we have seen, on the centrality of the caesura, the firm shift of style marking the beginning of a given late phase: 'A theory of the very late Beethoven', he argues, 'must start from the decisive boundary dividing it from the earlier work' (*Beethoven*, 136). For Shakespeare, it seems, Adorno would have been able to locate no such decisive boundary. Although the critical history of the late plays demonstrates a clear consensus that they stand apart from the rest of Shakespeare's work chronologically, stylistically and generically, it also makes clear the extent of the work – the evasions, elisions and omissions – required to create and sustain that consensus. As Suzanne Gossett says of *Pericles*,

> the 'lateness' paradigm is inadequate to describe a play which is not entirely by Shakespeare; on which Shakespeare worked when he was not yet forty-four years old; which reworks a plot that had already served as a frame for one of his earliest comedies; and which he may have been writing simultaneously with or shortly before *Coriolanus*, a play with ties to an entirely different section of Shakespeare's *oeuvre*. (Arden edition, 54)

In the rest of this book, I will argue that Gossett's caveat about the appropriateness of 'the "lateness" paradigm' as a way to understand *Pericles* can be extended to all the plays grouped as 'late' in Shakespeare's career. To that end, I will examine the construction of the idea of late Shakespeare, its origins and yet its impossibility in early modern culture, and I will consider the continued impact of that idea in criticism and in performance, seeking to make it as difficult as I can for Shakespeareans ever again to treat 'late play' as the 'neutral term'.

CHAPTER 3

The invention of late Shakespeare: subjectivism and its discontents

> Shakespeare is the only biographer of Shakespeare. [...] So far from Shakespeare's being the least known, he is the one person in all modern history fully known to us.[1]
>
> It is a preposterous kinde of writing to beginne the story of a great mans life, at the houre of his death.[2]
>
> For you yourself, sir, should be as old as I am – if, like a crab, you could go backward.[3]

Needless to say, the discourse of Shakespearean lateness did not emerge fully formed with one critic in the 1870s. I have so far described the general debt of late-style critics to Dowden and I have outlined the twentieth-century debates over the delimiting features of late Shakespeare. I want now, in the course of the next two chapters, going backward like Hamlet's crab, to trace the history of the possibility of late Shakespeare in the context of the larger history of the emergence of the general idea of late writing. By 'a history of the possibility', I mean, in part, a narrative of the development of the conditions for that emergence, one that will involve assessing the understanding available to Shakespeare and his contemporaries of the significance of last words and of last moments and the extent to which this understanding might inform the idea of late Shakespeare as it would in due course emerge. First of all, however, I will assess the formation in the early nineteenth century of the discourse of lateness as it is currently constituted and map the place of Shakespeare in the development of the idea of late style in England both before and after the pivotal moment marked by Dowden's *Shakspere: A Critical Study of His Mind and Art*, tracing the growth of Shakespearean lateness from the first chronology, that of Malone at the end of the eighteenth century, to the distinct and instructive anxiety of Henry James about Shakespearean lateness at the beginning of the twentieth. Shakespeare scholars will recognise that this necessitates, to a degree, traversing ground covered magnificently, though with a more general aim, a quarter of a century ago by Samuel Schoenbaum in *Shakespeare's Lives*, but it is an essential part of the story of late Shakespeare and cannot be omitted. I will proceed, in the next chapter, to outline the understanding available to Shakespeare and his audience of last things and last words – that is, to assess the extent to which an idea of late style might or might not have been imaginable in the first decade of the seventeenth century. The crablike chronology I am adopting may seem an odd – or, perhaps better, in acknowledgement of Patricia Parker's etymological excavations, a *preposterous* – way to proceed, but I hope that by the time you reach the end of Chapter 4 the logic of this reverse progress will be apparent. My basic contention, as will no doubt be already apparent, is that it is impossible to achieve an adequate assessment of Shakespearean lateness in isolation from a larger understanding of late style as an idea that, though it has certain roots in early modern culture, did not become fully possible until the early nineteenth century and that still to this day, despite its profound limitations as a way to understand the relationship of author and text, retains a remarkable authority.

3.1 'DRAMATICK PERFECTION': MALONE AND THE ESTABLISHMENT OF A CHRONOLOGY

There can be no late work without chronology. The idea of late style was, simply, not a possibility until critical attention first turned to the relationship between the life of the artist and the development of the work and thus to the question of the order in which that work was produced. The idea of the Shakespearean late style therefore cannot, practically speaking, predate the efforts of the barrister-turned-editor Edmond Malone to establish an order for the plays for the simple reason that nobody prior to Malone had made the effort to create a coherent and considered Shakespearean chronology. Lateness is a version, a sub-category, a refinement, of the idea of genius; as such, it derives from the Romantic conception of art as the product of the imagination of the creative individual. Shakespeare himself, I wish to argue, for all that he has been constructed subsequently as the archetypal creative genius, could have had no concept of late style per se and neither could his seventeenth- and most of his eighteenth-century interpreters, because they understood both style and last things quite differently from the ways in which these matters were subsequently comprehended. While early modern culture offers structures of thought that would in due course, as I will argue in Chapter 4, underpin the construction of an idea of late style, that idea itself – and this cannot be overstated – simply did not exist prior to the end of the eighteenth century. Malone's editorial predecessors had, it is true, from time to time voiced the belief that it might be of interest to know the order in which the plays were written, but they lacked adequate evidence to create a credible chronology and in any case they disagreed about the potential value for criticism of such information. If they shared an opinion on the subject, it was the assumption that the mature works were likely to be more sophisticated than the early simply because of the effects of increased experience on poetic accomplishment, Pope, for instance, arguing that 'the works of his riper years are manifestly raised above those of his former'.[4] But no critic prior to Malone put this assumption to the test – or, at least, the critics all presumed that there was insufficient evidence available to do so. In any case, they reasoned, if the compilers of the First Folio had considered chronology valuable, they would surely have presented the plays not according to broad generic groupings but in the order of first performance, as Ben Jonson had done in his *Works*.

Margreta de Grazia has done invaluable work in drawing our attention to Malone's role in the development of the modern understanding of Shakespeare by demonstrating that certain requirements now considered the basis for any adequate critical assessment of an author's work – authentic text, historical context, personal and artistic biography – only acquired that status in the wake of Malone's edition.[5] As she observes,

> [a]uthenticity, periodization, individuation, chronology, and even interpretation are the interlocked imperatives of the study of Shakespeare, the exemplary author of the English canon. Yet if they emerged in history, they cannot be the timeless necessities of Shakespeare study; rather they are the determinate needs of a specific historical situation. (*Verbatim*, 1)

Malone's own specific historical situation is made abundantly clear in a supportive letter he received from his friend the earl of Charlemont after expressing his fear of public ridicule for bothering to produce a painstakingly researched chronology. Charlemont – sharing A. W. Schlegel's recognition that '[i]t would be instructive in the highest degree, could we follow, step by step in his career, an author who at once founded and carried his art to perfection, and to go through his works in the order of time' – points out that '[t]he history of man is on all hands allowed to be the most important study of the human mind' and asks: '[W]hat is your chronological account of the writings of Shakespeare other than the history of the progress of the greatest genius that ever honoured and delighted human nature?'[6] Malone's quest for a Shakespearean chronology is thus a characteristic product of the Enlightenment, emerging from the concept of the temporal 'progress' of a 'genius' and the elevation of Shakespeare to the status of the 'greatest' such genius, and it is these ideas – becoming established by the late 1770s when Malone began work on an order for the plays, though to be embraced and delineated fully only with the development of Romanticism – that in the end required the invention of late Shakespeare.

For Malone, Shakespeare was simply unavailable for adequate analysis prior to the establishment of a sense of the totality of his life and achievement. 'In order fully to understand and appreciate Shakespeare', as Hardin Craig put it a century and a half later, restating Malone's logic, 'it is necessary to see him as a whole.'[7] Individual plays no longer stand alone as objects of critical analysis; they become fragments in a personal history. This is the first concrete evidence of a desire to think of the plays of Shakespeare in their relation to time and to each other and it provokes the creation of a biography. There had, of course, been accounts of the life of Shakespeare prior to Malone's chronology, from the brief summaries in Winstanley's *Lives of the Most Famous English Poets* (1687) and Langbaine's *Account of the English Dramatic Poets* (1691) to the first fully fledged 'life' which Nicholas Rowe appended to his 1709 edition of the plays and in which, for the first time, Shakespeare's retirement to Stratford is recounted.[8] But none of these attempted to read the life and the work in direct relation to each other. Placing Shakespeare in his overall historical and personal context helps the critic to locate him in time and space, but it provides no explanation for the differences either between his work and that of his contemporaries (who were, after all, operating under identical historical pressures) or within the course of his own work. A chronology, however, permits both a sense of the development of the playwright's work and the deployment of that work in the construction of a life, a life modelled on the progress of the creative output. For Malone, progress is central because it overrides contingency. Once a chronology was established, it could be seen that '[i]n both style and tone, the plays followed a generally steady and self-generated progression, independent of any contemporaneous historical events' (de Grazia, *Verbatim*, 145) – an argument sustained in the mid-twentieth century by the work of the continuity critics.

Style rather than genre, then, provided Malone with his primary focus. He held that apparent differences in verse technique between the various plays, taken together with whatever external evidence there was for the

Malone and the establishment of a chronology 131

dating of certain individual plays, might, if mapped correctly, tell the story of Shakespeare's progress as a poet and thus provide the basis for establishing an order of events. His particular interest lay with rhyme, or more particularly with the ratio of rhyming couplets to blank verse at a given stage of the career. 'It is not' he notes,

> merely the use of rhymes, mingled with blank verse, but their *frequency*, that is here urged, as a circumstance which seems to characterize and distinguish our poet's earliest performances. In the whole number of pieces which were written antecedent to the year 1600, and which, for the sake of perspicuity, have been called his *early compositions*, more rhyming couplets are found, than in all the plays composed subsequently to that year; which have been named his *late productions*. Whether in process of time, Shakspeare grew weary of the bondage of rhyme, or whether he became convinced of its impropriety in a dramatick dialogue, his neglect of rhyming (for he never wholly disused it) seems to have been *gradual*. As, therefore, most of his early productions are characterized by the multitude of similar terminations which they exhibit, whenever, of two early pieces it is doubtful which preceded the other, I am disposed to believe, (other proofs being wanting) that play in which the greater number of rhymes is found, to have been first composed.[9]

This, as Malone himself was to a certain extent aware, is a simplistic view of the place of rhyme in the development of Shakespearean verse, but it is clear that the word 'late' here holds no associations or implications other than simply to signify those plays which postdate 1600, lacking the elevated significance with which Dowden and subsequent critics would subsequently imbue it. That said, there is a sense from Malone's (flawed) logic of the development of rhyme ratios of a change in tone in the writing across the career, a change that stemmed, for Malone, from Shakespeare's feeling 'weary' of an aspect of his art, which is the first appearance in a critical discussion of the later plays of the word that would in due course become the keynote of Lytton Strachey's iconoclastic early-twentieth-century view of Shakespearean lateness. For Malone, though, Shakespeare's weariness with rhyme was a gradual, not a sudden, process, one which can first be seen around 1600 (a dating echoed in Bradley's later suggestion, which I noted in Chapter 2, that the late style began shortly after *Hamlet*) and thus cannot be taken as an early instance of the idea of a distinctive late phase, lacking as it does the identification of a caesura, of a sudden shift to a new genre. There is little more than the faintest embryo of lateness in Malone's understanding of the need for a chronology.

That said, Malone's premise for dating one of the plays, *Twelfth Night*, is of particular, if unexpected, interest for a study of the development of the idea of late Shakespeare, since not only did he place what now seems a classic instance of mid-period comedy right at the end of the playwright's career, he also gave a significant explanation for so doing. 'When Shakespeare quitted London and his profession, for the tranquillity of a rural retirement', he observed,

> it is improbable that such an excursive genius should have been immediately reconciled to a state of mental inactivity. It is more natural to conceive, that he should have occasionally bent his thoughts towards the theatre [. . .] and the interest of his associates whom he had left behind him to struggle with the capricious vicissitudes of publick taste. [. . .] To the necessity, therefore, of literary amusement to every cultivated mind, or to the dictates of friendship, or to both these incentives, we are perhaps indebted for the comedy of *Twelfth Night*; which bears evident marks of having been composed at leisure, as most of the characters that it contains, are finished to a higher degree of dramatick perfection, than is discoverable in some of our author's earlier comick performances.[10]

Malone was of course wrong in his dating of *Twelfth Night* – though, since it was not until 1831 that John Payne Collier unearthed the Manningham letter recounting the Middle Temple performance of 1602 and thus dated the play a full twelve years earlier, there was no evidence at the time to contradict him – and he eventually realised it: by 1821, he had changed his mind (frustratingly, he does not say why), ceding last place finally to *The Tempest*, a play that he was (correctly) convinced drew on and therefore must postdate the letter of William Strachey about the *Sea Venture* voyage and thus date from 1611 or thereabouts.[11] Even as he focusses his attention erroneously on *Twelfth Night* as the last play, however, there may, in the image of the poet 'bending his thoughts' from a distant location (though there is no suggestion of a desire to return from exile) and in the echo of the mage's reassurance to Alonso at the end of Act 5 that he will explain all 'at picked leisure', be a hint of the identification – later to become standard – of Shakespeare and Prospero. This was already, in any case, beginning to be implied by others. For John Gilbert Cooper, for instance, writing in 1755, Shakespeare is a magician of obvious power:

> For my Part, I am of opinion, that there is now living a Poet of the most genuine Genius this Kingdom ever produced, SHAKESPEAR alone excepted. By poetical Genius, I don't mean the meer talent of *making Verses*, but that glorious Enthusiasm of Soul, that *fine Frenzy*, as SHAKESPEAR calls it, *rolling from Heaven to Earth, from Earth to Heaven*, which, like an able Magician, can bring every Object of the Creation in any Shape whatever before the Reader's Eyes.[12]

It is a little odd that a direct association of playwright and character was not in fact made (in print, at least) until as late as 1838 by Thomas Campbell in his edition – 'Shakspeare, as if [. . .] inspired to typify himself, has made its hero a natural, a dignified, and benevolent magician' – but critics and poets had already begun to imply the identification of Prospero and Shakespeare long before a distinct understanding of the late plays had been established.[13]

It is the two plays *The Tempest* and *Twelfth Night*, then, that were most clearly associated, at the turn of the nineteenth century, with Shakespeare's last days. And in Malone's reasoning, however erroneous, for his late dating of *Twelfth Night* can be seen the emergence of two of the distinctive features of Shakespearean lateness as it would in due course be established. One is the association of the late plays with Shakespeare's retirement, not just reading *The Tempest* as a farewell to the stage but also treating the full set of late plays as proleptic of, if not the actual products of, the period after his departure from London. The other is the concomitant association of late Shakespeare with Stratford-upon-Avon, the town to which he returned at the end of his writing life, a connection we have seen emphasised by Dowden, for whom the 'breezy air' of *The Winter's Tale* 'is surely that which blew over Warwickshire fields upon Shakspere now returned to Stratford' (Dowden, 'Primer', 151). Stratford becomes for two reasons the characteristic locus of the later Shakespeare: it provides an appropriately green world into which the natural genius could retire – tangible evidence of the cyclical quality of the artistic life and the objective correlative of a sense of spiritual fulfilment at the end of the career – and, crucially, it enables the withdrawal of Shakespeare the poet from the grubby world of professional theatre. Malone's assumptions about the conditions for production of 'dramatick perfection' are obvious. Shakespearean theatre is first and foremost poetry, at its best when created at leisure in tranquillity, restricted otherwise by constant negotiation with 'the capricious vicissitudes of publick taste': 'dramatick perfection' is not the product of professional necessity but of casual literary 'amusement' in a context in which time is freely available. Shakespeare is thus converted into an eighteenth-century gentleman amateur, producing his most amusing work both to entertain himself and as a kind of gift to his former colleagues. This was certainly a notion that persisted. In the mid-nineteenth century, Thomas Carlyle bemoaned the fact that '[a]las, Shakspeare had to write for the Globe Playhouse: his great soul had to crush itself, as it could, into that and no other mould. It was with him, then, as it is with us all. No man works save under conditions.'[14] And for William Poel, at the end of the nineteenth century, seeking evidence in support of his own preference for fast-paced performance, '[t]here is no reason to suppose that Shakespeare ever divided his plays into scenes or acts, unless it were those that he wrote after he retired to Stratford. His plays bore signs, as did those of his contemporaries, of being written to be acted without a pause.'[15] The return to Stratford thus marked, for good or bad – your attitude depending on your preference for Shakespeare the playwright or Shakespeare the poet – a distinct move towards literariness. Yet even those who echoed Poel in firmly believing Shakespeare to be a man of the theatre persisted in succumbing to the myth of Stratford. Sir William Bailey, in his address to the newly formed Manchester Shakespeare Society in October 1902, while bluntly stating that Shakespeare 'wrote for the business of the theatre, not to create literature', nonetheless argued that 'gentle William simply wanted in the autumn of his life the peace of Prospero. He desired to end his days in serenity as a country gentleman at Stratford, in the midst of nature's innocence, beauty and melody' because his 'heart was with his immortal children away from the groundlings of the soiled city, for there with calm delight he could live in the family of his fancy'.[16]

As Jonathan Bate has shown, the close association of Shakespeare and Stratford draws on the development of the concept of genius from its classical signification of an attendant spirit associated with a particular location into the sense in which we now understand it as the ineffable quality that sets a tiny élite of creative artists apart, marking a creative ability stemming from a source other than the contingent. The late location is, then, in a certain way as important as the late work. Subsequent critics bewildered by Shakespeare's apparently voluntary return to Stratford – Halliwell-Phillips, say, or the Henry James of 'The Birthplace' (to which I will return in the final section of this chapter), for whom the attempt to ground the poet in the landscape only serves to make his identity less clear – appear to miss the point, but the critical necessity of the return to Stratford is clear from the moment Milton makes his distinction between Jonson the cosmopolitan classicist and Shakespeare the natural songbird, warbling his 'wood-notes wild' in his 'native' countryside. Already by the 1740s, half a century before Malone's agonising over dating, Joseph Warton had revived and extended Milton's nature-loving Shakespeare in verse which updates the point of comparison by replacing Jonson with Addison while also, as Bate notes, outrageously identifying Shakespeare with Christ, reshaping the eerie music of Prospero's island into an announcement of the Incarnation:

> What are the Lays of artful *Addison*,
> Coldly correct, to *Shakespeare*'s Warblings wild?
> Whom on the winding *Avon*'s willow'd Banks
> Fair Fancy found, and bore the smiling Babe

> To a close Cavern. (Still the Shepherds shew
> The sacred Place, whence with religious Awe
> They hear, returning from the Field at Eve,
> Strange Whisperings of sweet Music thro' the Air).[17]

In the eighteenth century, Bate argues, Shakespeare was seen 'as a country boy, a genius of the English earth, not a city man' – not, in other words, a man whose art could be delimited by the conditions of the London theatre – and he notes wryly that '[t]he enshrining of Stratford-upon-Avon as a site of pilgrimage has causes in aesthetic theory as well as effects in the emergent economy of tourism'.[18]

The final period of Shakespeare's life in Stratford thus complements the final period of the work, allowing lateness to be defined synecdochically, through the location of the last days of the National Poet, with England: it is Stratford's quintessential rural Englishness, finally, rather than cosmopolitan London, which embodies the late serenity of the master. Dowden sustains this argument when he suggests that '[t]here are moments when Shakspere was not wholly absorbed in his work as an artist at this period; it is as if he were thinking of his own life, or of the fields and streams of Stratford, and still wrote on' (Dowden, *Mind and Art*, 404), an only partial development from Furnivall's sentimental account of

> the poet's peaceful and quiet home-life again in Stratford, where he ends with his Prospero and Miranda, his Leontes finding again his wife and daughter in Hermione and Perdita; in whom we may fancy that the Stratford both of his early and late days lives again, and that the daughters he saw there, the sweet English maidens, the pleasant country scenes around him, passt as it were again into his plays. So that, starting with him in London, [...] we get him at last down quietly in his country home again, with the beauty of that country, wife and girl, and friends around him; with sheep-shearings to be talkt of, and Perdita with the Spring flowers to be lovd, and everything else serenely enjoyd; and so he ends his life.[19]

This fantasy is echoed repeatedly from here on by influential critics, not only by Dowden but also, later, by John Dover Wilson, who reads the late plays as being in fundamental harmony with Stratford's tranquillity, 'with its memories, its quiet pastures and wide skies, with all the wild life of bird and beast and flower, with the pleasant friendships and domesticities of the little town, with his house and garden, with his own family, and especially perhaps his younger daughter' (Wilson, *Essential*, 136–7) – this last, of course, being the source for each of the late-play daughters, Marina, Perdita, Innogen, Miranda, perhaps even the baby Elizabeth of *Henry VIII* (though hardly, one suspects, the Gaoler's Daughter of *The Two*

Noble Kinsmen). This, however, comes much later. In Malone's time, though the association of national genius with the power of the English landscape was developing rapidly, it was possible to resist the implications of Stratford.[20] Steevens, in whose 1778 edition Malone's *Attempt to Ascertain the Order in which the Plays Attributed to Shakspeare Were Written* first appeared, expressed by way of the question of return the limitations, for the late eighteenth century, of Shakespearean biography:

> As all that is known with any degree of certainty concerning Shakespeare, is – *that he was born at Stratford upon Avon, – married and had children there, – went to London, where he commenced actor, and wrote poems and plays, – returned to Stratford, made his will, died, and was buried,* – I must confess my readiness to combat every unfounded supposition respecting the particular occurrences of his life.[21]

Steevens here invokes the demonstrable lack of material evidence about the life in his day in order to damn the unhelpful tendency to speculate; there is no evidence yet either of the role Stratford would acquire in the Shakespearean trajectory or of the attribution of a particular mood or ethos – a serene return to the green places of his youth – to the playwright's last days and there is thus no sense yet of the Shakespearean late period as subsequently constructed.

3.2 INVENTING LATE SHAKESPEARE FROM COLERIDGE TO DOWDEN

Until and without Malone's painstaking work on chronology, then, there could be no late Shakespeare. It is from Malone that the structure of the Shakespearean career first emerged, a basis for understanding the creative life which would lead eventually, not far off a century later, to the establishment by Dowden of the idea of late Shakespearean romance. The first critic to suggest a Shakespearean career divided into periods with something approximating a late phase at the end was in fact Coleridge, but it is important, before turning to Coleridge's understanding of Shakespearean periodicity, to outline the context in which he was operating – to account, that is, for the very first attempts to delineate a late style. It is particularly important to note that the development in Titian's painterly style that Vasari saw in the later work, the earliest such account, is not in itself an ascription of a late style in the modern sense. 'His method of working in [his] last works', Vasari observes of Titian,

> is very different from the one he employed as a young man. While his early works are executed with a certain finesse and incredible care, and are made to be seen

both from close up and from a distance, his last works are executed with such large and bold brush-strokes and in such broad outlines that they cannot be seen from close up but appear perfect from a distance.[22]

'This technique', Vasari continues,

> explains why many, wishing to imitate Titian in this and to prove their expertise, have produced clumsy pictures, and this comes about because although many believe them to be executed without effort, the truth is very different and these artisans are very much mistaken, for it is obvious that his paintings are reworked and that he has gone back over them with colours many times, making his effort evident. (*Lives*, 504)

Clearly, Vasari sees a difference between the work of the young Titian and the old, but he belongs to an era that did not have a Romantic understanding of the origins of style and he makes, in Sam Smiles's words, 'none of the moves (descriptive, theoretical or biographical) a modern ascription of late style requires'.[23] His point is not that that Titian makes a classic late retreat from or dismissal of *disegno*, but rather, in fact, the opposite: that he maintains in these works the fundamental principles of art, something demonstrated by subsequent clumsy attempts at imitation that fail to realise the care and revision that has gone into producing the effects Vasari describes.

Vasari's account of late Titian in any case had little, if any, impact on the understanding of last works in general in the three centuries that followed. The dismissive clarity with which critics in the mid-eighteenth century, for instance, approached the last works of a given artist can be seen in the lugubrious description of the latter phases of the artistic career offered in Diderot and d'Alembert's *Encyclopedia* of 1765, which draws on a standard pattern most generally familiar from Victor Hugo's 'Preface to *Cromwell*', in which he reads individual human growth and epochal development as operating on an identical pattern. For Hugo, '[t]he human race as a whole has grown, has developed, has matured, like one of ourselves. It was once a child, it was once a man; we are now looking on at its impressive old age', and he maps the development of poetry on the basis of the 'three great ages of the world – primitive times, ancient times, modern times' as a progression from epic to ode to drama.[24] Resonantly, Hugo cites Shakespeare as the representative figure for the modern, dramatic age, and he offers a hint of what would later become one of the markers of the third or late style, the cyclical return to the style of youth: 'There is more than one connection between the beginning and the end', he writes, adding that 'the sunset has some features of the sunrise; the old man becomes a child once more' yet describing this last phase of life nonetheless as fundamentally melancholy, solemn and pensive. Diderot, for his part, pays no attention to this cyclical reading of the pattern of life, offering instead a cold linearity. 'Any one painter', Diderot baldly claims, 'has three successive manners, sometimes more', moving from the early and youthful to the mature and considered and then beginning the inevitable decline into artistic weakness:

> The first arises from the practice of imitating that of his master. Thus it is that from the works of a given [painter] one can tell that he comes from the school of this or that master. The second [*manner*] takes shape from his discovery that there are beauties in nature, and then the change is much for the better. But often, instead of substituting nature for the *manner* that he took over from his master, he opts for the *manner* of some other [painter] that he considers better. Finally, of the various defects by which his different *manners* have been marred, those of the [painter's] third [*manner*] are always still more exaggerated, and his last *manner* is always the worst.[25]

This is a blanket assertion and leaves no room for exceptions. It may well be in part, as Ian Bent suggests, Diderot's distaste for mannerism – itself a late phenomenon, epochally speaking, whose exponents in the generation that followed Titian, Raphael and Michelangelo deliberately drew on certain aspects of the late work of those artists for their self-consciously artificial style – that dictated his resistance to the last styles of the earlier masters.[26] Whatever the reason, the absence here of any sense that the late work can bring with it a positive shift of style suggests that the achievement of art criticism in first offering a recognisable description of a late style was subsequently lost, only to resurface fully in the early twentieth century.

Having been first into the field, in other words, the discipline of art history allowed itself to be passed by, and it would be several centuries before it recouped the loss this represents. It is, rather, in early nineteenth-century musicology that the modern understanding of late style began to take shape. It was, inevitably, Romanticism that informed this shift of attention, specifically the Romanticism of Fichte, Schelling and Goethe as expressed in the development of the idea of organic growth and the subsequent application of that idea to the particular growth seen in the mind and art of the individual artist. This understanding of creativity refused to differentiate the art from the artist; artistic development was understood to derive not from epoch, context or imitation of others but from the interior genius of the creative individual. The task of the critic thus became biographical and bibliographical, to chart the life and at the same time the chronology of the work, to treat each individual work as evidence of the growth of the artist. If artistic development was to be mapped in this way, then little could be achieved without access to the entire *œuvre*, and it was thus at this time that a series of projects was initiated for the publication of the complete works of certain key figures considered exemplary geniuses and thus for both chronological and biographical accounts of those figures.

The first musicologist to establish the outlines of something akin to a late period – and here I am drawing on the invaluable work of Ian Bent in making these materials accessible to the non-specialist – was the Italian Giuseppe Baini in his 1828 biography of Palestrina, in which it could be said that Vasari, after two and a half centuries of neglect, quietly reasserts control over the development of the idea of late style. Baini self-consciously reworked Vasari's understanding of style, drawing in particular on his account of the development of the styles of Raphael in the 1568 *Lives*, in order to map the life of Palestrina as a series of developing phases, intricately conceived and interwoven, the style of the work entwined with the development of the personality. Baini's approach became the model for subsequent biographers, one his successors would simplify and clarify. Baini outlines no fewer than ten distinct phases in the life of Palestrina, though forming what is in effect a three-part pattern: an early 'artificial' (that is, imitative) period, a mature 'natural' period and a final consummation. The sequence culminates in a last stylistic phase that marks the absolute height of Palestrina's powers. 'Finally', Baini recounts in a curiously gendered passage, Palestrina

> decided to espouse Nature [...] and his love, his attentions, her adornments, her beauty, his remorse for his transgressions before he met her, all this he painted with the vivid colours of a new style; a style however not simple, humble, abject, mediocre, temperate; but so noble, sublime and full of ideas, that never in my opinion has anyone been able continuously to sustain one so elevated.[27]

This new and culminatory style is

> serious, severe, dark and profound, very different from the preceding one. [... T]he words and meanings, though still distinctly intelligible, acquire that penetrating quality which persuades and moves as it delights, armed only with melody and harmony, and not needing stage, scenery, gesture, costumes and illusion. (Baini, *Memorie*, 430–1, Bent, *Fugue and Form*, 279)

In this final style, Palestrina had 'raised this type of music to the highest level of perfection' (*Memorie*, 432, *Fugue and Form*, 280) and there is thus no sense at all in Baini of anything subsequent to this achievement, nothing that conforms to the later expectations for a late style. Nonetheless, the profundity, the 'penetrating quality', and the shedding of the material machinery of performance attributed by Baini to this final phase clearly hint at future developments.

The simplest redaction of Baini's multi-phase structure and the first account to offer something recognisable to modern eyes as a late period – ironically, considering the age at death of its subject – comes with Alexander Ulïbïshev's *Nouvelle Biographie de Mozart* of 1843. A comparison of the accounts of Baini and Ulïbïshev underlines one of the ongoing problems in the analysis of late style: the question of the supplementarity of the late work. The three-stage model of the artistic life outlined by Diderot – the first stage embodying a learning process in which different styles are tested out; the second the culmination of that process in which the genius moves beyond the styles of others, substituting truth to 'nature' for inherited 'manner'; the third marking a decline from the peak – reappears, to an extent, in both Baini and Ulïbïshev, though the latter deliberately reduces Baini's ten phases to a vastly more manageable two. Baini's account, complex though it is, follows a relentless path of development to a high point and acknowledges no decline. Ulïbïshev, on the other hand, not only recounts what he sees as a phase of decline in Mozart but, crucially, also goes on to describe a final, unexpected burst of transcendent creativity *after* that period of decline, a reading of Mozart's career that has resonated to the present day, notably by way of Peter Shaffer's *Amadeus*. 'The last six months of Mozart's life', Ulïbïshev claims, 'were a period of superhuman creativity and angelic inspiration', and he tries to explain how this came about in someone who had died at the premature age of thirty-five:

He departed because his mission was completed; he gave up his art, but not before having attained the highest peaks. [. . .] He died young because his vital forces were exhausted by producing works of superhuman quality, of which his ageing genius would no longer have been capable, and his premature death was the condition of, and the price to be paid for, such work.[28]

Ulïbïshev here negotiates the problem of Mozart's age at death, explaining that the composer's life-work was already over and that he was exhausted by the production of certain key works. For Ulïbïshev, the creative soul could age at a different rate from the body, so while Mozart might have been young at the time of his death, his spirit had already grown old. 'If he had been able to glance calmly behind him, to look back over the prodigy's life he had led, cramming more than a century's worth of effort into ten years', writes Ulïbïshev, 'he would have understood his destiny' (Ulïbïshev, *Mozart*, 425). He waxes lyrical about the final period:

> We can say, speaking of the *Requiem*, that the composer's death holds nearly as high a place as his life in the annals of music. And, in effect, Mozart's long agony is characterised by a note of religious sublimity or of transcendent idealism [. . .] *The Magic Flute* and its overture, *Titus* and the *Requiem* – works which [. . .] begin with a separate piece, the *Ave verum Corpus* [. . .] a very simple chant, but melodious and well phrased [. . .] which seems very modern, you might say, at first sight. This it is, but it is also the highest kind of church music you could ever hear [. . .] what priestly seriousness and what seraphic blessedness![29]

And, with a nod to Baini, he adds: 'Palestrina, listening to [Mozart's music], would finally be able to say: Glory to the Lord! My work is complete. Now on earth we sing like the choir of the Chosen sing in heaven!' (Ulïbïshev, *Mozart*, 453). In this description lie the origins of the modern conception of late style (perhaps in particular of Adorno's formulation of that style in its emphasis on the proleptic modernity of Mozart's late work). For Ulïbïshev, the last music of Mozart is characterised by simplicity and transcendence, by a modernity which is yet also timeless, archaic and religious, offering a sense of fulfilment that even Palestrina, Baini's subject, would be able only to admire.

Baini's Palestrina and Ulïbïshev's Mozart both in their way, then, offer a sense of a late style, yet each critic defines the term in quite different ways. Baini offers the last work as a form of culmination, Ulïbïshev as a supplement that is also a kind of apotheosis. It is quite distinctly the latter which looks forward to the modern sense of lateness. Work from the peak of the artist's creativity, from his mature achievement, is not what is now meant by the 'late work', a phrase implying rather a period of creativity which *postdates* that peak, even (illogically) if that late work is seen by some critics as in certain ways surpassing the work customarily seen as the peak. Ulïbïshev offers a two- (or, more precisely, four-) part pattern that is both chiastic and reiterative, the decline mapped in the second part mirroring the ascent in the first, both parts ending with a burst of profound creative energy. In so doing he effectively pre-empts the four-period model that would in due course become the norm (youth, maturity, decline, rejuvenation), his ascent phase mapping the first period of growth and development, the culminating stage of that phase mapping the second period of maturity and artistic fulfilment, the decline phase mapping the third period of old age, and the final burst of 'angelic' energy at the end mapping the fourth or late period. It is this description of a final unexpected outpouring of genius in the wake of the decline into old age – of, in other words, transcendent supplementarity – and not Baini's model of organic, linear growth towards full achievement (a model still not so far from that of Virgil), which leads to the later formulation of late style not as culmination but as recapitulation, as a transcendent rounding off that stands apart from the principal achievement of the career, endorsing but not superseding that achievement.[30]

Up to a point, at least. Ulïbïshev may unwittingly have established the paradigm of supplementary lateness in his *Mozart*, but he had in fact, apparently paradoxically, fought hard against its development in the series of biographical accounts of Beethoven that appeared in the wake of Baini's *Palestrina*. These early biographers of Beethoven applied the familiar triple life-structure – youth, maturity, decline – to the career they were mapping, but they did so in markedly (and in some cases aggressively) different ways. The best known of the early biographers is Wilhelm von Lenz, whose idea of the 'third style' has underpinned all subsequent discussion of late Beethoven – including, importantly, that of Adorno – and retains a certain currency even now. But Lenz's biography was in fact preceded by three others – those of Johann Schlosser (1828), François-Joseph Fétis (1837) and Anton Schindler (1840) – and Lenz was subsequently hounded by Ulïbïshev for his supposed misunderstanding of the third or later style. As Bent notes, these biographers disagreed in their accounts over the primacy for structural purposes of the life or the work. Schindler (who had known Beethoven personally) divided the life into three roughly equal-sized sections based on external events rather than on stylistic changes within the work, thereby privileging the life, whereas Schlosser and Fétis chose to shape the life on the basis of developments in style. It was not until Lenz that a coherent sense of style as the key determinant of period was established or that the last period was given the qualities that critics came in due course universally to associate with the late style of a genius. That said, Schlosser associates certain characteristics with the third phase which would in due course be attributed instead to the fourth or late phase: retrospection, prophecy and a moving away from 'earthly burdens' towards the 'sun-filled transparent ether of eternal freedom' – terminology which, if it did not directly influence Dowden's later formulation of Shakespeare's late period, nonetheless offers a substantive context for that work. Schlosser's three-period pattern is in the process of becoming a four-period pattern, in other words, but has not yet quite done so.

It is ironic, then, that Lenz's principal opponent in establishing the canonical three-part pattern was none other than Ulïbïshev, since Lenz's innovation was to disregard the customary 'decadence' model for the third phase and to incorporate into that period the characteristics of the supplementary fourth phase of Ulïbïshev's Mozart. The eventual sense of the late period as both a logical extension and development of the career and a supplementary breaking out into a new style arguably originates in this debate between Lenz and Ulïbïshev, in which a curious struggle is evident between the assumption that the life can be – perhaps should be – divided into three periods and an underlying alternative four-part pattern with which it is partially at odds, a struggle apparent in Schlosser's deployment of the shape of Beethoven's Fifth Symphony as a pattern for 'the inner life of the composer'. Although Schlosser and his peers make no acknowledgement of it (and although three-part thinking is characteristic in general of the impact of Hegel), it is possible that what is happening here is the replication at the level of biography of the basic compositional pattern of Beethoven's era – that is, sonata form – and of the further development of that pattern with which Beethoven, though by no means its originator, is closely associated, namely, the addition of a substantial coda, a concluding section supplementary to, but also at the same time fulfilling, the basic form.[31]

Sonata form, at its simplest, comprises a three-part structure: statement or exposition (in which a musical idea is introduced), development (in which that idea is varied in a series of ways) and recapitulation (in which the original idea is restated, transformed into something more powerful by the musical process through which it has passed). This pattern – which I have stated as simply as possible, ignoring, for instance, the development through key changes that makes the conclusion a double return to both main theme and tonic – is fundamental to the music of these composers and is arguably transferred to their lives by the musicologists writing their first biographies, for whom thinking in this pattern would have been second nature. It provides a clear three-part pattern with a satisfying sense of resolution at the end which does not impose limitations on the process of development in the middle. Yet to the biographer of Beethoven, a four-part structure would be just as familiar as (is in fact simply a development of) this three-part pattern. Schlosser, seeking a musical model for Beethoven's life, reaches for the most familiar of his symphonies and reads it as directly parallel to the structure of that life. In the process, perhaps, the characteristics of the fourth or late period begin to emerge. Beethoven wrote unexpectedly lengthy codas which tend to do more work than had previously been associated with that final part of the sonata form, opening up new musical questions, turning to new keys, as well as turning back to the main theme. It could be argued that without Beethoven's particular compositional tendencies, the idea of late style would have developed very differently. Either way, what we see in the early biographers of composers is a negotiation between a three-part and a four-part pattern for the life that has never been fully resolved, an irresolution that perhaps underpins the perennial lack of clarity of accounts of late style.

It is Ulïbïshev's vast biography of Mozart, then, that marks the first appearance of the late phase in its modern form, with a distinct foretaste apparent in Baini's account of Palestrina. Subsequently, Lenz's biography of Beethoven consolidated and broadened the idea, though Lenz does not truly originate the three-part life, drawing in fact on Schlosser, Fétis and Schindler for his own synthesis. Musicology thus opens up the possibility of a general discourse of lateness, though the thinking about the relationship of style and life underpinning that possibility had already begun to influence attitudes to creativity in general. This is apparent in Hegel's observation that it was only in 'their mature manhood' that Goethe and Schiller 'presented us with creations profound, substantial, and the outcome of genuine inspiration, while no less thoroughly perfect in form', and that 'it was not till his old age that Homer devised and uttered his immortal songs' as well as in Goethe's self-consciousness about his own output in old age – 'I have to say', he acknowledges, 'that I really cannot complain about any lack of productivity in my old age', while at the same time admitting that 'what in my younger years I managed on a daily basis and in any context, I now achieve only from time to time and in favourable conditions' – despite the insistent claims of his early biographers for the unparallelled vigour of his last years.[32]

If it was natural for musicologists such as Ulïbïshev and Lenz to think in sonata form, then it is not entirely surprising that the first attempt to divide the Shakespearean career into periods, that of Coleridge, should look to drama for its model and read the life as a five-act play.[33] Coleridge had already in 1810 tentatively constructed a four-phase life, with the history plays added at the end and with no sense of a distinctive late period, but in a lecture of February 1819 – in which, the advertisement claimed, 'the Growth of SHAKSPEARE'S Genius' would be 'traced through *all* his Plays' and 'the probable order, in which they were composed, determined' – he offers a much fuller periodic structure for Shakespeare's career.[34] It is worth citing in full:

1. – Shakspear's Poems as prophetic of his Dramas: from the Lit. Life. Vol. I.
2. But if we are to be guided by internal evidence – and how little weight the external ought to have, I have shewn – his earliest dramatic attempt, prior in its first sketch at least to his Venus and Adonis, and probably planned before he

had left Stratford, is the Love's Labor Lost, Quart. 1598. Page (in Stockdales of 1807) 147.
3. Shortly after, I suppose the Pericles to have been first produced: from the *Pericles*, in Sharpe's Edition – blank Leaf to the Tit. Andron. –
4. And certain scenes in Jeronymo.
5. And in the same aera < the Winter's Tale, &> the Cymbeline, different from the Pericles by the entire Rifacciamento when Shak's celebrity as Poet and his Interest no less than his Influence as Manager enabled him to bring forward his laid-by Labor of Youth. –The example of Tit. Andron. most popular as well as Jeronymo in Shakspere's first Æra, but after by words of contempt, had led the young Dramatist to the lawless mixture of Dates & Manners –
6. As included in this æra I should place, 1. the Comedy of Errors (remarkable as being the only specimen of *poetical Farce* in our Language, that is, intentionally such. That all the distinct *kinds* of Drama, that might be educed a priori, have their representatives in his Works – Too many of B. and Fletcher's Com, Trag. & Tragi Comedies, and the greater number of Jonson's Comedies are Farce-plots.) 2. the All's well that ends well, originally intended as the Counterpart of L. Lab. Lost, and accordingly entitled Love's Labor Won – 3. The Taming of the Shrew. –and The Midshummer Night's Dream.
7. As concluding the Æra, the Much Ado About Nothing, and the Romeo and Juliet.

Second Æra.

8. The Richard the Second.
The King John.
The rifacciamento of the three parts of Henry VI – (reasons for refusing this to Sh.) and the Richard the Third –

The Third Æra

The Two Parts of Henry the IV.
Henry the 5.
The Merry Wives of Windsor
And, as a sort of Historical Mask or Shew Play, Henry the 8th –

Fourth Æra

gives all the graces and faculties of a genius in full possession and habit of power – peculiarly of the femine, *Lady*, character

The Tempest
The As you like it.
The Merchant of Venice.
The Twelfth Night –

and finally as its Summit, the Lear, the Hamlet, the Macbeth, and the Othello.

Fifth and last Æra

when the Energies of Intellect in the cycle of Genius were tho' in a richer and potenziated form becoming predominant over Passion and creative

> Self-modification – I am inclined to place < Meas. for Meas. Timon of Ath. (see Tr. and Cr.)> the Coriolanus, the Julius Caesar, Antony and Cleopatra, wth the Troilus and Cressida.[35]

Thus over half a century before Dowden, who tends to get the credit for dividing the career into periods, Coleridge offers a map of what he calls the 'æras' of Shakespeare's creative life, concluding with a last period characterised in certain ways as a phase in which, in the wake of a 'Fourth Æra' which displayed 'all the graces and faculties of a genius in full possession and habit of power', 'Intellect' now takes precedence 'over Passion and creative Self-modification'. In constructing his chronology, however, Coleridge was relying solely on

> the internal evidences furnished by the writings themselves, with no other positive *data* than the known facts, that the Venus and Adonis was printed in 1593, the Rape of Lucrece in 1594, and that the Romeo and Juliet had appeared in 1595, – and with no other presumptions than that the poems, his very first productions, were written many years earlier. (Coleridge, *Shakespeare Criticism*, vol. 1, 209)

In other words, he shows no awareness at all of Malone's painstakingly wrought chronology, producing a sequence which seems, to modern eyes, extraordinary, including in the last 'æra' several distinctly un-late plays, including *Measure for Measure, Julius Caesar, Antony and Cleopatra* and *Troilus and Cressida*. Despite his failure to choose his plays correctly, however, the language he uses, drawing on Schelling for the notion of 'potenziation', to describe the nature of his 'Fifth and last Æra' looks forward to Dowden's arguments for the progress from 'In the depths' to 'On the heights'. Coleridge may have got the order of the plays wrong, in other words, but he is characteristically ahead of the game nonetheless.

That said, though Coleridge was the first to map the life as a series of periods, the development of the idea was piecemeal: there is no more indication that Dowden was aware of Coleridge's periodisation than there is of Coleridge knowing Malone's chronology. There had, in any case, in the intervening years been several other attempts to negotiate the question of the relationship of life to work. And not only in the intervening years, either. Two years before Coleridge's lecture, Nathan Drake had divided the life into three distinct sections, concluding with 'Shakespeare in Retirement'. His 'Chronological Table' concludes with a run of plays relatively, if not entirely, familiar to modern eyes:

26	King Lear	1604
27	Cymbeline	1605
28	Macbeth	1606
29	Julius Caesar	1607
30	Antony and Cleopatra	1608
31	Coriolanus	1609
32	The Winter's Tale	1610
33	The Tempest	1611
34	Othello	1612
35	Twelfth Night	1613[36]

Drake acknowledges his dependence upon his immediate predecessors – 'the following Chronological Arrangement', he writes in his prefatory comments, 'which, though deviating, in several instances, from the chronologies of both Chalmers and Malone, will not, it is hoped, on that account be found needlessly singular, nor unproductive of a closer approximation to probability, and, perchance, to truth' (*Shakspeare and his Times*, 260) – and his list serves, in its relative accuracy, to underline the waywardness of Coleridge's various subjective chronologies.

It was not, as I have noted, until 1838 that the first direct equation of Shakespeare and Prospero as ageing magi heading into retirement was made in print – by Thomas Campbell in his edition of the plays – but it is worth being aware that this connection had already been made tacitly a good many years earlier by way of visual culture. The most prominent instance of this is Kent and Scheemakers's monument in Poets' Corner, Westminster Abbey, which dates from 1740 and features a casually posed Shakespeare leaning on a pile of books, his left hand pointing to a scroll inscribed with (mislineated) lines from Prospero's 'revels' speech which are clearly intended to be read self-reflexively:

> The Cloud capt Tow'rs,
> The Gorgeous Palaces,
> The Solemn Temples,
> The Great Globe itself,
> Yea all which it Inherit,
> Shall Dissolve;
> And like the baseless Fabrick of a Vision
> Leave not a wreck behind.

Another pre-Campbell rendering of Shakespeare as Prospero can be found, as William Pressly points out in his catalogue of paintings in the Folger

Library, in a design engraved by John Thurston for the title page of Thomas Tegg's 1812 edition of the plays. 'The vignette', Pressly notes, 'shows Prospero with Ariel, but the allusion, placed as it is as a preface to all the plays and not just to *The Tempest*, is to Shakespeare himself, with Ariel performing the role of the Muse of Inspiration.'[37] Likewise, an early nineteenth-century watercolour by William Marshall Craig presents an image of Shakespeare surrounded by his characters in which, as Pressly notes, 'Caliban is the most prominent, as Shakespeare is in the very act of calling him forth' (*Catalogue*, 12). Craig appears to draw upon the frontispiece, signed 'Richter', to a 1791 edition of the plays, which depicts Shakespeare asleep, reclined in his desk chair, with Caliban curled up to his right and, behind and around him, the *Macbeth* witches, *Dream* fairies, various kings, and the ghost of Hamlet's father.[38] Craig follows the same pattern, but the watercolour Shakespeare is more clearly associated with the character, with cloak and staff and in a stance akin to that of Prospero in a range of contemporary *Tempest* illustrations.[39] It would seem, in other words, that Campbell was stating something that had already become a commonplace.

There is perhaps a hint too, prior to Campbell, of the Shakespeare/Prospero identification in the writing of A. W. Schlegel, the Romantics' favourite German Shakespearean. In a discussion of irony dating from 1815, he argues that Shakespeare could, 'if he chose otherwise [...] destroy without compunction the beautiful, irresistibly attractive illusion which he had conjured up himself'.[40] The echo of Prospero's 'revels' speech here is hard to dismiss and, though Schlegel does not make the connection overtly, his observation may well have served as a prompt for Campbell. That said, prior to Malone's change of mind about his dating of *Twelfth Night* (and perhaps providing an impetus for that change of mind), Schlegel had declared himself less than convinced by the play's supposed finality, voicing in the process certain contemporary assumptions about the typical development of the artistic career: 'If this was really the last work of Shakspeare, as is affirmed,' he observed, 'he must have enjoyed to the last the same youthfulness of mind, and have carried with him to the grave the whole fulness of his talents' (*Vorlesungen*, 175). Reluctantly accepting Malone's dating, he wonders if the apparent youthfulness of *Twelfth Night* is perhaps a marker of Shakespeare's particular genius, his last work showing no signs of the decline in artistic merit Schlegel presumes to be the mark of the work of old age. But he continues to fret about the issue. Addressing the relative merits of *A Midsummer Night's Dream* and *The Tempest* (plays which particularly attracted the Romantics because of their overt imaginative qualities), he notes that *The Tempest* seems to be the product of the end of Shakespeare's life: 'most critics, on the supposition that the poet must have continued to improve with increasing maturity of mind, have given the last piece a great preference over the former'; but he adds: 'I cannot, however, altogether agree with them in this: the internal worth of these two works, in my opinion, are pretty equally balanced, and a predilection for the one or the other can only be governed by personal taste.'[41] The general assumption that a poet of Shakespeare's genius will 'improve with increasing maturity of mind' and therefore that the later works will be superior to the earlier does not wholly convince Schlegel, but he is willing to make an exception for true genius in old age. It is perhaps possible, then, to see in these comments of Schlegel's – even as he begins with a discussion of what we would consider the 'wrong' last play, *Twelfth Night* – an embryonic manifestation of the discourse of lateness. Moreover, there is in Schlegel an early hint of the generic connections that would in due course be drawn between the individual plays now grouped as the 'late plays'. Immediately after his discussion of *The Tempest* in the 'comedies' section of his book, he turns to *The Winter's Tale* and then to *Cymbeline*, making a direct comparison between Miranda and the royal brothers of the latter:

As Miranda's unconscious and unstudied sweetness is more pleasing than those charms which endeavour to captivate us by the brilliant decoration of the most refined cultivation, so in these two young men, to whom the chase has given vigour and hardihood, but who are unacquainted with their high destination, and have been always kept far from human society, we are equally enchanted by a *naïve* heroism which leads them to anticipate and to dream of deeds of valour, till an occasion is offered which they are irresistibly impelled to embrace. (*Vorlesungen*, 184–5)

It would be another fifty or more years before these thematic connections would be consolidated by the grouping of these plays as 'romances', but the potential for that association is arguably already apparent.

Before addressing the development of that grouping, however, it is worth pausing with Thomas Campbell because of the connection his identification of Shakespeare and Prospero offers between the developing discourse of lateness and the parallel idea of *lastness*, that is, of a certain apocalyptic consciousness manifesting itself within Romantic culture. Campbell's short poem 'The Last Man' is less well known now than Mary Shelley's novel of the same name (which is itself of course overshadowed by her

Frankenstein), but these two works, along with Byron's poem 'Darkness' and Beddoes's play *The Last Man*, mark the prominence that the theme of the last human being, the only survivor of war or famine, left behind grimly to contemplate the ruins of human society, held in the Romantic culture of the 1810s and 1820s; a fashion critics read in the context of the deaths of some of the more flamboyant Romantic writers and the political uncertainties that followed the defeat of Napoleon – as, in other words, a marker of the surviving poets' sense of their own epochal belatedness.[42] Building on earlier work by A. J. Sanbrook and Lee Sterrenberg, Fiona Stafford offers a full treatment of this phenomenon, plotting its development from Milton to H. G. Wells but principally demonstrating the scale of its impact on Romantic imaginings of the future.[43] She argues that 'writers of the eighteenth and nineteenth centuries were faced with an increasingly secular society and a future uncontrolled by providential destiny' and that '[a]s last things ceased to be associated with the collective, Apocalyptic ending of mankind', so 'the image of the last of the race as an isolated sufferer, burdened with memories, and cut off from others, became a common figure' (*Last of the Race*, 11). For the Romantics, the recognition of the irreversible linearity of time was painful and the myth of the last man embodied the simultaneous desire for a return to origins and a recognition that such a return is impossible. This paradox, Stafford argues, 'prompted a variety of responses, from the despair of Grainville and Beddoes, to the calm resignation or turbulent indignation of Byron and Martin, to the wilful refusal to accept the modern condition displayed by Campbell'; in each case, the writer expresses his or her despair of the condition of the present through the representation of lastness.[44] At the same time, the extraordinary comic-grotesque treatment of the topos by Thomas Hood in his poem 'The Last Man' shows, in Sara Lodge's words, that

> the dramatic solipsism of 'lastness' is hotly contested and often parodically undermined in the period, generally by writers who want to assert that the post-Romantic literary world is not as depleted as remnants of an earlier generation would like to believe.[45]

I am not, I should emphasise, suggesting a direct connection between Campbell's 'Last Man' and his identification of Prospero and Shakespeare – epochal lastness is by no means the same as the creative lateness whose development I am plotting – but the two arguably emerge from a connected fascination with the belated, perhaps stemming from Hegel's belief, famously summed up in his observation that the owl of Minerva flies only at dusk, that wisdom is hindsight, and polarised responses to 'lastness', from 'serene resignation' to 'turbulent indignation', appear to offer parallels to the varieties of tone attributed to late work. It is at least worth noting the phenomenon of the 'last man' as a general context for self-assertions of belatedness in the first quarter of the nineteenth century, not least because, as we have already seen, the borderline between the epochal and the personal within the discourse of lateness is always highly permeable.

Not that the development either of the identification of Shakespeare and Prospero or of Shakespearean lateness had much stability. A year after Campbell made his claim, Joseph Hunter published his *Disquisition on the Scene, Origin, Date, Etc. Etc. of Shakespeare's Tempest*, in which he disagreed far more bluntly than did Schlegel with the assumption that the play was Shakespeare's last. 'I have already announced to you what is my own impression', he writes, 'that this play is an early work', pointing out that, though, 'when the plays were first collected into a volume, the first place was assigned to *The Tempest*', it is nonetheless

difficult to discover a principle on which the arrangement was made; and it is not difficult to divine other reasons beside priority of composition for the place assigned to it. Yet it may seem strange that if it were the last work, it should first meet the eye in such a collection.[46]

Hunter rejects out of hand the emerging idea of a post-mature Shakespeare. 'Others', he writes, 'have discerned in the style and sentiment' of *The Tempest* 'marks of a period beyond the maturity of a Poet's life' (*Disquisition*, 63). 'But', he adds,

we see how extremely dubious and uncertain reasoning of this kind is, when we observe how often the most plausible conclusions of this kind have been dissipated by the discovery of some decisive evidence from without, fixing limits which no reasoning from the style or sentiments can justify any person in overleaping. (ibid., 63–4)

Footnoting Campbell, Hunter also rejects

what some persons have imagined they perceived in this play – intimations of its being a Poet's farewell, as if the retirement of Prospero were a kind of adumbration of the retirement of Shakespeare himself from the practice of the more innocent magic with which he had so long enchanted his countrymen.[47]

This dismissal of the identification of playwright and character is echoed a decade later by Henry Hudson, for whom Shakespearean solipsism is inconceivable. 'I can hardly think', he writes, 'that Shakespeare had any reference to himself in the passage [that is, the 'rough magic' speech], for, besides that he did not use to put his own feelings and purposes into the mouth of his characters, the doing so in this case would infer such a degree of self-exaltation as, it seems to me, his native and habitual modesty would scarce permit.'[48] 'Gentle' Shakespeare and the self-conscious appropriation of character for personal announcements are, for Hudson, incompatible.

Charles Knight, meanwhile, in his *Works* of 1841, reworking Malone's chronology with subjective abandon, had disagreed vehemently not only with the presumption that Shakespeare would speak through his character but also with the whole notion of a conscious farewell-to-art in mid-life. Shakespeare, he asserts, voicing an anxiety that would resonate down to Henry James and beyond, 'never could have contemplated, in health and intellectual vigour, any abandonment of that occupation which constituted his happiness and glory', adding that '[w]e have no doubt that he wrote on till the hour of his last illness'.[49] Knight seconds Hunter's resistance to the emerging chronology, making clear his understanding of the direction that the late work of genius will take and echoing Coleridge's 1810 order, seeing the culmination of the career not in the plays that would become known as the 'Romances' but in the Roman plays and arguing that the 'later plays [. . .] are unquestionably those in which the mighty intellect is more tasked than the unbounded fancy' and must 'present the philosophical and historical aspect of human affairs rather than the passionate and the imaginative' (edition, vol. 4, 126). Thus, for Knight, '[t]he Roman historical plays are [. . .] at the end of his career, as the English historical plays are at the beginning' (ibid.). His premise is both cyclical, as this suggests, and linear: 'The Roman plays denote', he argues, 'the growth of an intellect during five-and-twenty years' (ibid.). *The Tempest*, on the other hand, distinctly does not 'present the characteristics of the latest plays' because it blends the 'playfulness and beauty of the comedies [. . .] with the higher notes of passionate and solemn thought which distinguish the great tragedies', making it, for Knight, a mid-period play (ibid.). He accepts that '*The Winter's Tale* [. . .] was acted in 1611', noting that, '[c]omparing the style and rhythm of *The Tempest* with *The Winter's Tale*, we have little difficulty in believing that *The Winter's Tale* is the later play', and he argues for what he calls the 'probability' that *Pericles*, *Cymbeline* and *The Winter's Tale* 'were produced in their present form soon after the period of Shakspere's quitting the stage, about 1603; and perhaps before the production of "Macbeth", "Troilus and Cressida", "Henry VIII", and the Roman plays', adding that *The Tempest* 'belong[s] to the same cycle' (edition, vol. 4, 128). For Knight, then, in a curious blend of anti-theatricalism and rejection of Shakespearean retirement, the mature period – into which he grouped the four plays that would later become established as the final 'Romances' – began when Shakespeare ceased acting and the career was crowned with the grandeur of Roman history. In any case, as he shows in his biography of two years later, he was not at all convinced by readings that relate the art directly to the life: 'To one who is perfectly familiar with his works', he wrote of Shakespeare, 'they come more and more to appear as emanations of the pure intellect, totally disconnected from the personal relations of the being which produced them. Whatever might have been the wordly trials of such a mind, it had within itself the power of rising superior to every calamity.'[50] Knight thus looks forward here to the twentieth-century resistance to subjectivism.

By far the most fascinating of the constructions of the later Shakespeare between Campbell and Dowden, however, and one which both underlines the absence at this time of a standard chronology, demonstrating how malleable the life still was, and marks the emergence of the discourse of lateness in the middle of the century, is that of Hermann Ulrici in his 1846 book, *Shakespeare's Dramatic Art*. Ulrici offers what can perhaps best be described as an Old Testament vision of a late Shakespeare with a 'vivid faith in God's superintending and retributive providence', a reading of the end of the career apparently more in keeping with Edward Said's desire for a late refusal of reconcilation than with the theological optimism of a Dowden, and provides, in the process, an account of the language of the late plays that looks forward to the most recent accounts of the late style as fragmented and parenthetical.[51] He offers, in the Coleridgean manner, five epochs for the career. His 'Fourth Period', which runs from 1605 to 1609–10, consists of classical plays, offering an echo of the assumption both of Coleridge (in 1810, at least) and of Knight that these plays represent a culminating moment: *Julius Caesar* (which Ulrici dates to 1606), *Antony and Cleopatra* (1607), *Coriolanus* and *Troilus and Cressida* (both 1608). His Fifth Period, 'from 1609–10 to 1613–14', consists of nine plays: *Macbeth* and *Cymbeline* (both dated 1609–10), *The Winter's Tale* and *King John* (dated 1610–11), *The Tempest* (1611), *Othello* (1612) and, then, all in the period 1612–14, *Measure for Measure*, *Henry VIII* and, finally, *Timon of Athens*.

This final period seems to offer little, if any, hope. 'The shadows', Ulrici argues, 'have been continually thickening, until at last, in "Timon," the perfect night overtakes us' (*Dramatic Art*, 240). 'No one', he continues, 'could have painted misanthropy with such truth and force without having at some time or other experienced its bitter agony. Shakspeare's tone of mind must momentarily, at least, have been in unison with that of Timon' (ibid., 240–41). He notes that 'there were outward causes and reasons enough, not only in the last years of our poet's career, to embitter it' – everything, really, 'the memory [...] of his whole life' (ibid.) – and he argues that this final bitterness was severe:

He was doomed to look on, while that on which he had spent all his mental energy was profaned and blackened by rude hands; he was doomed to see genuine poetry, and with it the deep seriousness of the christian view of life, banished from the age. [...] Well, then, might the tone of his mind have sunk into the harsh dissonance which he seems to have laboured to embody in his last works, in order to shake it off from his own bosom. (*Dramatic Art*, 241–2)

The last plays, then – and *Timon* in particular – are both an expression and a displacement of late-life depression in both subject matter and, especially, technique. 'The style' of *Timon*, Ulrici argues, 'such is the stress and importance laid upon each word, might almost be called heavy. The thoughts are frequently huddled and packed together without order or connection; the turns are striking and sudden, while the abruptness and obscurity of the language are extreme' (ibid., 238). These stylistic observations lead him to place *Timon* at the end of the sequence: 'All these defects', he notes, 'force me to conjecture, that the piece may have wanted the author's last finishing touch, in consequence either of his retirement to Stratford, or his death' (ibid., 238–9). For Ulrici, then, it is grim Timon, not serene Prospero, who brings down the curtain.

Seeking the emergence of the late style, Ulrici foreshadows twentieth-century commentators in seeing *King Lear*, which he dates to 1605 – that is, at the end of the Third Period – as the key transitional play, one in which 'the tragic element, in spite of the terrific grandeur with which it is there invested, is, nevertheless, encircled with the same mild elegiac and brightening halo which plays around "Romeo and Juliet," "Richard the Second," and "Hamlet"' (ibid., 98). By contrast, 'in "Macbeth," and "Othello," the soothing and consolatory element is far from prominent, and in "Timon of Athens" is altogether absent' (ibid.). Thus the impetus for the tragedies and the late plays is one and the same. In a deeply negative Whig reading of seventeenth-century history which simultaneously ties late Shakespeare to and detaches it from the supposed 'decadence' of the drama following the death of Elizabeth, Ulrici sees the last plays as reflections of Shakespeare's deep disillusionment with the Jacobean world. 'In his later dramas', Ulrici argues,

there is mirrored a comparatively deeper and more serious view of life – bordering, perhaps, at times on severity and sternness. The source of this severer tone, as well

Inventing late Shakespeare from Coleridge to Dowden

as the cause of his return to Stratford, was [...] his dissatisfaction with the hostile tendency of the spirit of the age towards himself and his view of art, as well as a bitter regret for the political position of his country under James, and the evils which it was already suffering, and others which his prophetic eye too surely foresaw. (*Dramatic Art*, 118)

There is, it seems, little prospect of redemption in this fifth and final phase.

Yet, just as Ulrici appears committed to an unyieldingly grim account of the end of Shakespeare's career, he outlines a reading of the final period which reveals very clearly the state of development of the discourse of lateness in the mid-nineteenth century. '[T]his growing severity of view', he argues,

must have had its principal source [...] in the feeling which invariably wins upon every true and artistic genius in the evening of life, when he has experienced in his own person, that the best and highest of human existence is but the sport of this earthly temporality – a drop in the ocean of infinity – not independent in itself, but existent only in order to perish and to be glorified hereafter: a feeling which we meet with in some of the greatest painters of the fifteenth and sixteenth centuries, and which Shakspeare himself has so beautifully expressed in some of his later pieces; as, for instance, in the passage of the "Tempest," afterwards inscribed on his monument in Westminster Abbey. (ibid., 118–19)

– in, that is, a late phase characterised as detachment, as resignation and as common feeling with other artistic geniuses, in whichever field, at the equivalent stage of their lives. Ulrici here appears able, *avant la lettre*, to synthesise the serene and the irascible versions of lateness – or, rather, still more interestingly, to read them as identical. He writes both of Shakespeare's 'bitterness of soul' and of his expectation of 'glorification' after death, 'distaste' for cosmopolitan life leading to rejection of 'worldly pursuits', and he turns, despite his conviction of the finality of *Timon* and prompted, it seems, by the Westminster Abbey memorial, to Prospero's 'revels' speech for his last word. 'I have already alluded', he says, later in the book,

to the fact, that a certain dissatisfaction with their past labours, and indeed with themselves as well as with the whole of human nature – a distaste for the present and a longing for a higher and better existence, in short, a heavenly-home-sickness – usually besets great artistic genius at the evening of life more strongly even than the rest of mankind. (ibid., 245)

This is expressed in a

phase of art which not only raises its head freely into heaven, in order to quicken some vague presentiment or meagre notion of its own infinite grandeur, but also, with the inspired eye of fancy, pierces into the heavenly recesses, to snatch from them the most lively images and similitudes, as well as also the most ardent aspirations. (ibid., 245)

For Ulrici here, disillusion and world-weariness go hand in glove with a desire for translation to the world beyond, producing 'a heavenly-home-sickness', a longing for the afterlife. He thus makes explicit here something that is only implicit in the development of the discourse of late style from the beginning of the nineteenth century yet which underpins the nature of the discourse as an extension of the Romantic understanding of creativity, looking forward both to the Victorian appropriation of the discourse of lateness as validation for creative artists living into old age and to the twentieth-century blurring of the distinctions between *Altersstil* and *Spätstil*. For Ulrici, the artist, as he moves nearer to his heavenly home, begins to catch glimpses of the glory to come, epiphanies of the ultimate sublime that is death, in a cyclical extension of the Romantic belief in the intensity of children's awareness, in close proximity as they are to the sublimity from which the new-born baby emerges into the world. The tragedy of mid-life is the fading of that childhood vision, a decreasing frequency of epiphany. For Romantic poets who died young, the problem never arose, but it became acute – and was seen to be acute by his peers and successors – for Wordsworth, who was never able to recapture the poetic intensity or flexibility of his younger days. Or, as T. S. Eliot later expressed it,

[w]hy are the later long poems of Browning and Swinburne mostly unread? It is, I think, because one gets the essential Browning or Swinburne entire in earlier poems; and in the later, one is reminded of the early freshness which they lack, without being made aware of any compensating new qualities.[52]

Late style, as it emerged, offered a solution to this problem, which became particularly acute, as Eliot implies, for the Romantics' successors – that is, the possibility of a cyclical return to 'early freshness'. As death approaches, so does the sublime, once again epiphany makes itself felt, and the energy of the consequent creativity is akin to that last experienced in youth. The late period, then, for Ulrici, is a time in which 'the inspired eye of fancy, pierces into the heavenly recesses, to snatch from them the most lively images and similitudes, as well as also the most ardent aspirations' (*Dramatic Art*, 245). It is, in other words, the moment at which, after decades of enforced detachment, the creative artist begins once again to feel the proximity of the sublime and thus the impetus for and urgency of new creativity.

The Fifth Period, far from being the end of a linear process, is for Ulrici a cyclical reclamation of the characteristics of the beginning of the artistic career. 'Thus, then', he claims, 'does this *last* period of Shakspeare's dramatic career approach, in its general feature, to the character of the *first*' in the 'profound moral earnestness of his nature, the vivid consciousness and passionate scorn for the power of sin, and the no less vivid faith in God's superintending and retributive providence' which were the hallmarks of his youth and which now manifest themselves once more (ibid., 98). The last phase thus fulfils the career, overriding the frustrations of mid-life:

What the poet was then striving after, from an unconscious impulse only [. . .] now appears no longer a mere desire, but a thing actually accomplished, and replete with all the varied wealth of a profound mind, that has sought much, and found it [. . .] and of a heart which has greatly loved, and deeply suffered. (ibid., 99)

So, he argues, 'the dramas of the last period exhibit the complete Shakspearian master-hand' (ibid.) and *Timon*, far from being irredeemably bleak, 'forms the beautiful close of Shakspeare's poetical career', in which '[w]e distinctly see him abandoning the trifling pursuits and contentions of this life, for calm heavenly meditation' (*Dramatic Art*, 239–40). In the end, then, despite Ulrici's intense emphasis on disillusionment and weariness, his Shakespeare ends his life in a manner almost precisely predictive of Dowden's serene late stylist of thirty years later. It would thus be fair to say that Ulrici, not Dowden, was the originator of the idea of late Shakespeare. Ulrici himself was perhaps not aware that was what he was doing; Dowden, by contrast, consciously constructs the 'Romances'. But Ulrici's grim late Shakespeare, embodied in a final *Timon*, is not fundamentally different from the more familiar serene late Shakespeare celebrated by Dowden and his successors. The same sense ultimately prevails of a genius standing at the brink of heaven. Not that such an *ur*-point is especially needed. The key issue is that Shakespearean lateness, as fully articulated for the first time by Dowden, was itself already somewhat belated, since the idea had been in play for three or four decades by the time Dowden began his account of Shakespeare's 'life and art'. Ulrici's late Shakespeare – a proleptic synthesis of Dowdenesque serenity and Saidean irascibility – in its grim theologising provides not, in the end, the opposite of Dowden's vision but one that is to all intents and purposes identical with it.

As far as Dowden was concerned, however, it was as if Ulrici had never written. Dowden took his impetus not from Ulrici but, as I noted in Chapter 1, from F. J. Furnivall, the founder of the New Shakspere

Society, for whom the ostensible darkness of Ulrici's vision would not have been at all congenial. Schoenbaum is sniffy about Furnivall's vegetarian/ teetotal/spelling-reform persona, but the point is that Furnivall was an enthusiast, an idealist, and he wanted to inspire even as he infuriated. Ulrici finds the most apparently reluctant way to construct the heaven-bound Shakespeare; Furnivall wanted a rather more glorious religion. In his speech at the founding meeting of the New Shakspere Society, Furnivall had expressed his hope that somebody might produce a biography that would provide an emotional explanation for the works, dealing in a 'worthy manner with Shakspere as a whole' and tracking 'the rise and growth of his genius from the boyish romanticism or the sharp young-manishness of his early plays, to the magnificence, the splendour, the divine intuition, which mark his ablest works'.[53] Dowden responded directly to this call. Schoenbaum is quick to spot a conscious (verbal) linkage between Furnivall's prospectus for the Society and Dowden's book and Dowden seems to have drawn his key 'Four Periods', and to a certain extent the nature of those periods, directly from Furnivall, something he implicitly acknowledges by reprinting Furnivall's 'Trial Table of the Order of Shakespeare's Plays' in the original preface to *Shakspere: His Mind and Art* (1875).[54]

This table had first appeared a year earlier in Furnivall's introduction to the English edition of the *Shakespeare Commentaries* by the German scholar G. G. Gervinus, who, as a friend and correspondent of Goethe, provides the clearest link between the emergence of 'late Shakespeare' and the German Romantic sources for ideas of the growth of genius. Gervinus himself divided the career into only three periods, the third of which encompasses all the Jacobean plays and does not offer a distinct 'lastness', so Furnivall's prefatory table pre-empts the discussion to come. Furnivall's fourth period, though it offers the late plays in, for us, the unfamiliar order *Pericles*, *The Two Noble Kinsmen*, *The Tempest*, *Cymbeline*, *The Winter's Tale* and *Henry VIII* – thus ignoring Campbell and the now-habitual association of Shakespeare and Prospero – for the first time assembles all the plays we know as the 'late plays' together as a distinct group. Moreover, he characterises them in a way that seems to lead directly to Dowden's fuller account:

After the darkness came light; after the storm, calm; and in the closing series of his plays [...] he speaks of reconciliation and peace. [...] And thus, forgiven and forgiving, full of the highest wisdom and of peace, at one with family, and friends, and foes, in harmony with Avon's flow and Stratford's level meads, Shakspere closed his life on earth. (Gervinus, *Commentaries*, xl, xlii)

Dowden's key words, 'peace' and 'reconciliation', are thus in place already in Furnivall, though the order of events is a little blurred by the fact that Furnivall has a footnote in his Gervinus introduction recommending Dowden's forthcoming book, implying that he had read it in manuscript. Whichever of them came up with the 'four periods', there is no doubt that Dowden set out to do precisely as Furnivall had urged in his prospectus; equally, there is no doubt that the shape he gave to Shakespeare's career (both through *Shakspere: His Mind and Art* and, as we have seen, through his shorter, vastly more popular Shakespeare *Primer*) had the most substantial impact of any single critical work on the way in which late Shakespeare has been subsequently understood.

Once established, the idea of the late style developed rapidly in mainstream accounts of the life, and Dowden's influence, both in and beyond Shakespeare studies, can hardly, as a result, be overstated. Until Dowden explicitly appropriated for Shakespeare the periodic life-structure already in play half a century earlier in musicology, the idea of the late period was implicit only in the association of Prospero with Shakespeare: his book provided a system by which this association of character and playwright could be extended to an understanding of the last plays as a group providing a redemptive conclusion to the career of the National Poet. It was a model that caught on with astonishing speed, shaping the understanding of the end of the life for critics for decades after him – most notably for Georg Brandes and, as I noted above, Dover Wilson, but also David Masson, Frank Harris and others. By this time, the outlines of the late style had become clear. It was essentially a teleology: each of the last plays, like Shakespeare's career as a whole, culminates in dramatic and therefore personal integration, the playwright's reconciliation with life implicit in the resolutions he provides for his characters, as the equation of 'last' and 'reconciliatory' is made. At the same time, the overall pattern of the career is a necessarily unified cycle, from youth to late return; within this cyclical structure, archaism has a persistent place, as if the return to the early in the life of the playwright is also an epochal return to an earlier time, to a certain primitivism. For Adorno, as we have seen, late work always has an 'archaising tendency', not only looking back to the writer's own past but also introducing folk motifs, atavistic elements, merging the youthful simplicities of both self and nation. The development of the idea of late Shakespeare offers a clear test case for this, underlining the basis in Romanticism of the idea of late style as a return to the early which is at once personal and epochal. In any case, the late style is basically theological, expressing a move away from the corrupting city to the redemptive pastoral which incorporates a final rejection of the theatre. As Drake put it as early as 1817:

> [H]igh in reputation as a poet, favoured by the great and accomplished, and beloved by all who knew him, Shakspeare, after a long residence in the capital, [...] at length sought for leisure and repose on the banks of his native stream. [...]
>
> The Genius of dramatic poetry may sigh over a determination thus early taken! but who shall blame what, from our knowledge of the man, we may justly conceive to have been his predominating motive, the hope that in the bosom of rural peace, aloof from the dissipations and seductions of the stage, he might the better prepare for that event which awaits us all, and which talents, such as his were, can only, from the magnitude of the trust, render more awfully responsible. (*Shakspeare and his Times*, 603–4)

Marking the poet's stepping clear from the 'seductive' profession of theatre, the Shakespearean late phase becomes the most purified form of a writing life which, because the writer in question has for so many years been expressing himself profoundly, is evidence of that profundity in its most mature, transcendent form.

3.3 THE BACKLASH: (POST)SUBJECTIVISM FROM STRACHEY TO BOND

Dowden's influence remains immense. The dominant narrative of late Shakespeare continues broadly to be his, sustained by all the late-play criticism in which the 'romances' stand outside the career as a separate, serene group, perhaps written in retirement or on the verge of retirement by a man who has seen and done pretty much everything and has found a happier place, filled with daughters and rural scenery, well beyond the trauma embodied in the tragedies. 'A commonplace of criticism pictures late Shakespeare sailing into calm waters, finally at peace with himself,' Russell Fraser notes, with his trademark aphoristic dismissiveness. And then he adds: 'But evil darkens his last plays, and you could say he wrote them to still his beating mind.'[55] As so often with critiques of subjectivist reading, Fraser's deliberate echo of Prospero's post-'revels' state of mind reintroduces subjectivism in the second sentence. But he is right: people have indeed suggested that the late Shakespeare is anything but serene. A minority of critics, echoing the grimness of Ulrici in Old-Testament mode but not his unexpected final redemptive turn, have written in this vein, giving Shakespeare a late phase very different from that outlined by Dowden, creating a limited but persistent sub-genre of darker, more

The backlash: (post)subjectivism from Strachey to Bond

irascible readings of the end of the life. After all, as Edward Said has emphasised, by no means all versions of lateness are of the warm and fuzzy kind.

This negative take on the end of the life crops up in particular with those critics who are prepared to acknowledge *The Two Noble Kinsmen*, rather than *The Tempest*, as the last play. Or perhaps it is the other way round: the choice of *The Two Noble Kinsmen* is a way to reinforce the preference for an unreconciled ending to the life. E. Talbot Donaldson, noting his telltale regret that a critic working on Chaucer and Shakespeare has no choice but to address *The Two Noble Kinsmen*, suggests that the 'heavy strain of pessimism' apparent in the play 'appealed to Shakespeare' because, 'nearing the end of his active career, [he] was in a mood different from that which produced *A Midsummer Night's Dream*.'[56] 'Those who have looked most closely at *The Two Noble Kinsmen*', notes Lois Potter in her edition, 'that is, the translators and directors of the play – often claim to find in it an overpowering sense of melancholy which left them in no doubt that it was "written by a man who felt old age close upon him".'[57] She also reports a largely French tradition of negative readings of *The Two Noble Kinsmen*, with roots in Victor Hugo's highly rhetorical Shakespeare biography.[58] Pierre Leyris, for example, sees the play as the marker of the handover from the old Shakespeare to the young Fletcher:

Dans le nouveau théâtre de Blackfriars acquis en outre du Globe par les King's Men [...], nous voyons un Shakespeare vieilli, à la veille de sa retraite à Stratford – où il devait mourir trois ou quatre ans plus tard –, passer graduellement ses pouvoirs en tant que principal auteur de la troupe au beaucoup plus jeune Fletcher, qui allait régner à ce titre de longues années. Il est clair que cette abdication progressive – qui ne commença, cela va sans dire, qu'après *La Tempête* – prit en 1612 et 1613 la forme d'une collaboration littéraire entre les deux hommes.

In the new Blackfriars theatre acquired over and above the Globe by the King's Men, we see an ageing Shakespeare, on the eve of his retirement to Stratford, where he would die three or four years later, gradually passing his status as chief playwright for the company to the much younger Fletcher, who would occupy the role for many years. It is clear that this gradual abdication, which would not begin, it goes without saying, until after *The Tempest*, took in 1612 and 1623 the form of a literary collaboration between the two men.[59]

The ageing Shakespeare, fading back from his achievements, 'abdicates' his powers to Fletcher, their collaborations marking ('it goes without saying') a postinspirational moment. For the French at least, there has been no tabu on negative images of the late Shakespeare.

For anglophone criticism, however, *The Tempest* remains the touchstone, and the upbeat narrative for the end of the life remains powerful. Not that there is no anglophone negative reading of the late plays. On the contrary, there has been a persistent anti-Dowden vein that works precisely by inverting his subjectivism. The doyen of these readings is Lytton Strachey, the first critic to offer a thoroughgoing rejection of Dowden's characterisation of the late Shakespeare as serene, joyful, benign, the consummate artist at the height of his spiritual engagement with his art. For Strachey, things looked very different indeed. In his essay 'Shakespeare's Final Period' (first published in 1906 – it was, wincemakingly, one of his undergraduate essays – though most fully circulated in his 1922 collection *Books and Characters*), Strachey argues with relishable shamelessness that, as far as the late plays are concerned, '[i]t is difficult to resist the conclusion that [Shakespeare] was getting bored. [...] Bored with people, bored with real life, bored with drama, bored, in fact, with everything except poetry and poetical dreams.'[60] Warming to the task of crushing Dowden, he points out the grimness and savagery of the late plays, as well as the harshness of language that, as we have seen, militates against presumptions of serenity: 'nowhere,' he claims, 'does [Shakespeare] verge more often upon a sort of brutality of phrase, a cruel coarseness' ('Final Period', 54). By way of contrast with Dowden's insistence on serenity and reconciliation, he asks of Caliban's lines 'You taught me language, and my profit on't/Is, I know how to curse': 'Is this Caliban addressing Prospero, or Job addressing God?' And he offers his own triumphantly dismissive reply: 'It may be either; but it is not serene, nor benign, nor pastoral, nor "On the Heights"' (ibid., 64). Outspoken this may be, yet, as both G. E. Bentley and Samuel Schoenbaum have rightly observed, Strachey's intervention does not in fact mark a paradigm shift. 'Violently as Dowden and Strachey differ,' Bentley points out, 'they agree in seeking subjective interpretations' (Bentley, 'Blackfriars Theatre', 48). 'Both portraits,' agrees Schoenbaum, 'require us to assume a one-to-one correspondence between what an author writes and his mood at the time,' and he suggests mischievously that '[e]ven the boredom may be a cynic's version of serenity' (*Shakespeare's Lives*, 479).

Strachey, then, did not make the break with subjectivism with which he is frequently credited. The sustained impact of his diatribe, though, is clear – Tony Dawson's essay discussed above is only the most recent, if one of the more entertaining, echoes of the original attack, itself based on a 1939 essay by Theodore Spencer – but it took a decade or more to bite.[61] As the date of the Spencer essay suggests, it was in the late 1930s that the Dowden legacy was most vehemently resisted, that the last period of Shakespeare's life was most fully characterised as a time of decline, readings of the late plays responding, it seems, to the critics' awareness of the slide of western civilisation into war, a development that needs to be compared both with the far more positive readings of late Shakespeare that appeared after 1945 and with the postwar development of theories of late style exemplified in Broch's celebration of 'the music of the infinite' in the last works of great artists. Three essays written in consecutive years, Spencer's being the last, make the mood of the moment apparent. D. G. James, in his *Scepticism and Poetry* of 1937, deliberately echoes Strachey's critique of Dowden, only to undermine both. He seems initially to agree with Dowden, arguing that it was Shakespeare's 'peace of mind which gave us the last plays' and that 'his interest was no longer in [the world]; it was beyond it, and beyond the human', but he immediately retracts this apparent agreement by dismissing the late plays as 'not among the greatest of Shakespeare's plays' and glossing this dismissal by explaining that they are not in fact *plays* at all in his definition of the term, because 'they are no longer [...] of the order of imagination which is "human and dramatic" '.[62] This, he argues, wrenching the spiritual serenity identified by Dowden to an ungenerous otherworldliness, demonstrates that Shakespeare 'is no longer interested in humanity – his interest is elsewhere', that 'poetry is no longer a passion or a necessity to him, and he finally gives it up and goes home', and he adds that 'it is not an accident that Shakespeare's last plays are tortured by a sense of inexpressiveness and failure' (207). The problem is that although Shakespeare had failed in his tragedies to find a fundamental unity in life, he preferred to create his own myth rather than turn to the ready-made but imagination-sapping one provided by Christianity. Yet, James continues, 'he must quickly have come to see the impossibility of what he was trying to do' (210). The plays are, as a result, he argues, 'comparatively formless', revealing 'a failure of expressiveness' apparent in 'the ways in which he repeatedly used a single theme for his purpose', which marks 'a curious lack of versatility for the man who wrote the comedies and tragedies with all their great variety of plot' (210). And he concludes by describing *The Tempest*, almost casually, as a play in which 'humanity is destroyed, and with it poetry' (241). Even Strachey's 'poetry and poetical things', then, as the only remaining aspects of life that do not bore the ageing Shakespeare, are brushed aside.

The following year, H. B. Charlton's *Shakespearian Comedy* pushed this argument a little further. Claiming that the mid-period comedies mark the consummation of Shakespeare's comic writing, he adds that he does not, all the same, mean to forget that towards the end of his days, in the benevolence of his older age, Shakespeare averted his eyes from the abyss of universal tragedy they had pierced, and, fixing them once more on the springs of human joy, he – or rather the poet in him – saw those benign idylls of human charity, the so-called romances, which we know as his *Cymbeline*, his *Winter's Tale* and his *Tempest*.[63]

Charlton's reading thus seems to be shaping up as a standard post-Dowden assessment, reinforced by his description of the late plays as 'glimpses [...] of the ingrained charitableness, the temperamental gentleness, the serene and benevolent tolerance of Shakespeare the mortal' (*Shakespearian Comedy*, 267). But he abruptly changes tack, arguing that the plays' 'benignity must not sentimentalise our judgment into a false appraisement of their dramatic worth' (ibid.). Dowden, it seems, made a basic error in reading the late plays, through the symmetry implied by the phrases 'In the Depths' and 'On the Heights', as in some way equivalent in impact to the great tragedies. This comparative nomenclature simply 'allures one to the delusive slope', Charlton argues, reworking Dowden's spatial metaphors of mountain and tableland, when the evidence makes it clear that the late plays, rather than providing evidence of a spiritual recovery from the crisis that produced the tragedies, in fact mark a falling away of the playwright's abilities. 'There can', after all, he claims,

scarcely be a shadow of doubt that, in the romances, Shakespeare the dramatist is declining in dramatic power. The hand still retains its cunning, the stage-carpenter is still master of his craft, and the poet is still the consummate magician of words. But the dramatist is losing his intuitive sense of the essential stuff of drama, of the impact of man on men and on the things which in the mass made that experience which we call life,

all of which offers the firmest evidence 'of the weakening of Shakespeare's dramatic genius' (*Shakespearian Comedy*, 268–9). The late plays' location at the end of the career does not, he warns, automatically give them aesthetic priority – 'Though the romances are Shakespeare the man's last words on humanity and on destiny, they are not therefore his profoundest words' (ibid., 268) – and he provides a closing judgement of the plays which differs profoundly from that of Dowden and became almost as frequently cited. The late plays, he argues, 'are an old man's compensation for the inescapable harshness of man's portion, a compensation which pleases the more because with the coming of age, something of the terror of the things the dramatist in his strength has hitherto seen has been blunted by the weakening in him of his power of imaginative vision' (ibid., 267). The phrase 'an old man's compensation for the inescapable harshness of man's portion' became a standard anti-Dowden watchword, tying aesthetic judgement of the late plays to the issue of old age and opening up the vexed question of the relationship between *Altersstil* and *Spätstil* to which I will return in Chapter 5.

Schoenbaum's critique of Strachey, it should be noted – that, for all his opposition to Dowden, he sustains the basic subjectivist premise of a one-to-one correspondence between the work and the state of mind of the writer at the time that work was produced – applies also to James and Charlton: they simply invert Dowden's optimistic reading, turning it into something much grimmer. There had, though, been a tradition of genuine anti-subjectivism running parallel to these readings, beginning only a decade or so after Dowden established his periods for the work. For James Halliwell-Phillips, for instance, writing towards the end of his own life, it was 'difficult to treat with seriousness the opinion that the great master of imagination wrote under the direct control of his varying personal temperaments', as if somehow the practical business of theatre never impinged on his creative processes.[64] 'It would thence follow', he argues,

that, when he was selecting a plot, he could have given no heed either to the wishes of the managers or the inclination of the public taste, but was guided in his choice by the necessity of discovering a subject that was adapted for the exposition of his own personal feeling. One wonders, or, rather, there is no necessity for conjecturing, what Heminges and Condell would have thought if they had applied to Shakespeare for a new comedy, and the great dramatist had told them that he could not possibly comply with their wishes, he being then in his Tragic Period. (*Outlines*, vol. 2, 249, n. 1)

He returns to this topic a little later, rejecting the entire subjectivist project, noting (prompted presumably by Dowden but citing Coleridge) that critics

would have us believe that Shakespeare's judgment throughout his dramatic writings was commensurate with his genius, and that, instead of troubling himself to weigh the chances of popularity, he was always working on an artistic and inner-life directed system to which the theatrical views of the day were altogether subordinate (ibid., 342, n. 232),

and that this has resulted, 'amongst other eccentric fancies', in 'the arrangement of his works into definite Periods, each one being considered to represent a separate mental grade' (ibid.). Thus, he continues,

we are instructed by the inventor of this order how to discriminate between the 'negative period of his perfection', and the 'period of beauty', or that of 'grandeur', while the last Period came, as we are informed in the explicit language of what is politely termed *the higher criticism*, 'when the energies of intellect in the cycle of genius were, though in a rich and more potentiated form, becoming predominant over passion and creative self-manifestation'. (ibid.)

All of this, he proceeds, depends upon 'the more than doubtful supposition that neither the managers of the theatre, nor the company of actors, nor the prevailing temper of the audiences, exercised an influence in the matter' (*Outlines*, vol. 2). In such accounts, he argues, '[i]t is implied' that Shakespeare 'was merry when he wrote a comedy, gloomy when he penned a tragedy, tired of the world when he created Prospero, and so on' (ibid. 249, n. 1).

It is from Halliwell-Phillips that C. J. Sisson was working when he made the single most direct critique of subjectivism in his landmark British Academy lecture 'The Mythical Sorrows of Shakespeare', which he gave on 25 April 1934. Sisson makes his position clear from the outset. He begins with a sideswipe at Nazi appropriations of Shakespeare (a grimly current topic at the time he was writing), proceeds to blame 'the general trend of [. . .] interpretative biography' in contemporary Shakespearean analysis on 'the overwhelming deadweight of nineteenth-century criticism of Shakespeare', and connects the two by arguing that it was Friedrich Schlegel who originated 'the Shakespeare who appeals to Nazi Germany as "rather an old-Northern poet than a Christian poet"'.[65] He then picks on one of Schlegel's successors by disingenuously summarising the reading of the late phase offered by Bernhard ten Brink. 'It appears,' Sisson notes, echoing Halliwell-Phillips, 'that in 1607 Shakespeare's brother Edmund died, an event which helped to infuriate him. Fortunately, in 1608 his mother died, an event which restored him to a kindlier mood. So various are the effects of deaths in the family upon a great poet'.[66] And he extends his irony to the larger picture of the life of Shakespeare as outlined by critics such as James and Charlton:

His 'gay' comedies, so redolent of youth, were still occupying him when he was approaching middle age. Yet by the time he has written *The Tempest*, when he was at most forty-seven, he appears suddenly as an old man. He has now retired to Stratford, a statement unsupported by evidence, as is the notion that he ever retired from Stratford, that he ever ceased to continue in touch with Stratford and his family there. And he is now, only seven years after his long-enduring youth, represented as serene, as immovably complacent, as befits his advanced years. (*Mythical Sorrows*, 22)

Sisson thus concludes that '[t]here is something wrong with either this youth, or this old age, or with both' (ibid.), making it is clear that he is most offended by the argument that Shakespeare, at forty-seven, was 'suddenly' an old man. In later life, Sisson to a certain extent retracted the ferocity of his opposition to subjectivism in 'The Mythical Sorrows', acknowledging that 'few now would either accept the full lyrical interpretation of the plays, or deny to them their reflection of the growth and the increasing maturity of a poet's mind through which experience was transmuted into art' (Sisson, *Studies in the Life*, 9). But he had already made his point.

The 1930s, then, witnessed a surge of interest either in the grim late Shakespeare or in a rejection of the association of particular emotional states with phases of the career. As we have seen, however, war changed things, and late-play criticism in the 1940s – in the larger context of a blossoming of assertions of the idea of late style in the postwar period – shifted perspective back to a transcendent, theological (or, perhaps better, posttheological) late period. But Strachey's reading never entirely faded away and his most obvious inheritor in the late twentieth century – sixty or so years on – was Edward Bond, who in his play *Bingo* offers a vignette of the poet in unserene Stratford retirement. Part Two gives us a glimpse (one for which we have been kept waiting) of the Shakespeare of the theatre, getting drunk in a pub with Ben Jonson (Michael Drayton is, as Bond notes in his introduction, omitted from the scene pictured in the usual anecdotes of the Bard's alleged terminal binge) and talking about his work. Bond has merged 1613 and 1616, the year the Globe burned down and the year of Shakespeare's death, and Shakespeare asks how long it took for the theatre to burn and wants to know if there were '[j]okes about my play setting the house on fire'.[67] Jonson, it turns out, has been given an amateur spying mission by the King's Men. 'What are you writing?' he keeps asking, eventually admitting that '[t]he theatre told me to ask.' Later, he spills it out hastily: 'Well, have you got a new play, it has to be a comedy, rebuilding is expensive, they'd like you to invest' (*Bingo*, 48).

Above all, Jonson wants to find out what has drawn Shakespeare back to Stratford at this stage of his life:

JONSON. Down here for the peace and quiet? Find inspiration – look for it, anyway. Work up something spiritual. Refined. Can't get by with scrabbling it off in noisy corners any more. New young men. Competition. Your recent stuff's been pretty peculiar. What was The Winter's Tale about? I ask to be polite. (*Bingo*, 44)

This comic speech offers an amalgam of attitudes to late Shakespeare: irony at the expense of the biographical notion that the playwright retired to Stratford for 'peace and quiet' ('What quiet?' Shakespeare asks, when Jonson jabbers on); Jonson's own distaste for romantic tragicomedy (a 'mouldy tale,' he called *Pericles* in 'Ode to Himself'); the suggestion that the late plays in their unexpected oddness are evidence of a failure to keep up with the '[c]ompetition' provided by the '[n]ew young men'; and the notion of late writing as 'spiritual', 'refined' and, in particular, 'peculiar' ('What was The Winter's Tale about? I ask to be polite').[68] In response, Shakespeare simply repeats Jonson's question back to him: 'What are you writing?' ('What am *I* writing?' responds Jonson, surprised: 'You've never shown any interest before'). A little further on, Jonson describes Shakespeare in a frankly Dowdenesque manner:

Life doesn't seem to touch you, I mean soil you. You walk by on the clean pavement. I climb tall towers to show I'm clever. Others do tricks in the gutter. You are serene. Serene. (ibid., 46)

And again, building his resentment, he blurts out:

I hate your health. I'm sure you'll die in a healthy way. Well at least you're dying. That's incense to scatter on these burning coals. [. . .] So beautiful and simple. You see why I hate you. How have they made you so simple? Tell me, Will? Please. How have they made you so good? You even know when it's time to die. Come down here to die quietly in your garden or an upstairs room. My death will be terrible. I'll linger on in people's way, poor, thick, dirty, empty, a mess. I go on and on, why can't I stop? (ibid., 48)

We see all of this as absurd, as a basic misreading of the man, as a self-pitying imposition from outside: Bond, writing in the 1970s, looks back to Strachey, suggesting that the serenity is an old man's ennui, an early modern alienation from the modes of production and from the savagery of civilised society that will eventually lead to the playwright's suicide. The Shakespeare of the play directly dismisses the Dowden reading: 'Serene. Serene. Is that how they see me? (*He laughs a little.*) I didn't know', adding: 'Serene. How? When you're running from hangers and breakers and killers' (ibid., 56, 57). And later still, as he is dying, he returns to the word in a way that finally dismisses any last vestige of the spiritual late Shakespeare: 'Everything can be stolen, property and qualities of the mind. But stolen things have no value. Pride and arrogance are the same when they're stolen. Even serenity' (ibid., 63).

3.4 'A CERTAIN MASTERY': HENRY JAMES AND THE ELUSIVE LATE SHAKESPEARE

The theology of late style calls for little or no self-awareness on the part of the late stylist. In its purest form, late style simply descends upon the genius: self-consciousness would be interference in predestination, an impossibility. Dowden implies no awareness whatsoever on Shakespeare's part that he was constructing a late style: in fact, the image of Shakespeare he offers is of an artistic consciousness that has moved beyond the material concerns of a career. Bond's thoroughly modern Shakespeare, by contrast, is painfully self-conscious, grimly aware of his position at the end of things – and it is certainly the case that a range of subsequent artists to whom a late style has been attributed, from Henry James to Pablo Picasso, have been highly self-conscious about their own lateness and have expressed this self-consciousness by way of an engagement, explicit or implicit, with the late phases of their predecessors. James agonised over Shakespeare's inexplicable decision abruptly to stop writing at the height of his powers, in his middle years, addressing it repeatedly in his stories. Picasso, who had cited Rembrandt sporadically throughout his career, began suddenly, in the last six or so years of his life, to identify with the late Rembrandt, to demonstrate a certain psychological dependence upon the ageing Old Master, so that the best-known late Picasso self-portrait is very clearly a version of the self-portraits of Rembrandt from the end of his life. Certainly, by the early twentieth century, three things had become clear. The first was that the acquisition of a late style could now be a conscious performance; the second, that Shakespeare was a primary resource for that performance; the third, that the principal gospel of Shakespearean lateness was *The Tempest*, which in the course of the nineteenth century had, as we have seen, become synecdochic for the late plays as a whole.

It is not especially surprising, then, that a writer such as Joseph Conrad – to pick one representative figure spanning the end of the nineteenth century and the beginning of the twentieth – should turn to Shakespeare in the process of constructing his own late phase. Conrad is a doubly resonant figure in the sense both that the critical fortunes of his last novels map the fluctuating status of late style across the twentieth century and that he developed a lifelong fascination with Shakespeare into a specific engagement with Shakespearean lateness. Moreover, the consciously adopted mode of his later novels invites comparisons with Shakespeare's late turn to romance. For Daphna Erdinast-Vulcan, 'whereas in the early phase of Conrad's work, the prototext is myth, which signifies an alternative mode of perception and conduct, the prototext in the late phase is, appropriately enough, the romance, signifying a sense of unreality, fictionality, and illusion'.[69] This sentence offers an exact balance, suggesting no qualitative differential between the early and late writing, but for several decades the late novels were largely eclipsed by the dominance of what is known in

Conrad studies as the 'achievement-and-decline hypothesis', a reductively subjectivist argument first proposed by Thomas C. Moser in 1957, who read Conrad's post-1910 work (that is, the writing produced in the wake of the novelist's breakdown) as the product of tangible decline. 'If this is affirmation', he writes of the later novels, rejecting the previous generation's understanding of late Conrad as embodying a transcendence of the cultural doubts the novelist had expressed in his early and mid-career work and in the process echoing Strachey's reaction to Dowden, 'it rises not out of serene old age but out of a desperate weariness', adding by way of evidence that '[a]ll the characters, young and old, seem very tired, eager to sit or lie down' and that 'the difficulty with which their creator manipulates them indicates clearly the source of their fatigue'.[70] The fortunes of late Conrad have, though, shifted again in the intervening half-century, with a resurgence in critical interest in the late novels in recent years, prompted perhaps by the teleological imperative of the new millennium. As Owen Knowles and Gene Moore note,

[a] newer generation of critics has mounted a [. . .] challenge to Moser's thesis and its influence, either by questioning the sometimes reductive psychoanalytic assumptions underpinning it, or by pointing to ways in which Conrad's later fiction may demand altered critical perspectives, or, more radically, by challenging the basis of canon-formation itself.[71]

These critics include Gary Geddes, Daniel R. Schwartz and Robert Hampson, each of whom has argued that the last novels demonstrate a failure not on Conrad's part but on that of his critics, unable to understand the subtlety of the novelist's late achievement.[72] For Geddes, 'the later novels remind us that Conrad was as unremitting a stylist in prose as he was in seamanship, always scheming for effects, always trying for the extra longitude' (*Later Novels*, 198). They are not, then, these late novels, failures, as had previously been claimed, but are, rather, 'devastatingly bleak portraits of the failure of religious sentiment, intellect, culture, diplomacy, and the instinct for social change' which 'add considerably to our understanding of Conrad's mind, just as they testify to the energy and constant evolution of his art' (ibid., 203, 205). As this makes clear, work on late Conrad, whether for or against, has been consistently subjectivist: Hampson's table-turning observation that the achievement-and-decline hypothesis 'reveals not so much Conrad's imaginative exhaustion as the exhaustion of its own critical assumptions' is therefore especially welcome (*Betrayal*, 251).

For a critic seeking to assess the particular significance of late Shakespeare for late Conrad, the obvious place to turn is *Victory* – a hotly contested late novel, one that Albert Guerard wanted simply 'to drop [...] from the Conrad canon' (*Conrad the Novelist*, 275) – which is based in several ways on *The Tempest*. Its protagonist, Axel Heyst, is a version of Prospero and Shakespearean counterparts can arguably be found for several of the other characters, too. As Hampson notes, Lena is a version of Miranda and Wang appears a synthesis of Caliban ('Don't talk about him. He makes me feel uncomfortable,' says Lena) and of Ariel ('the trick having been performed, Wang vanished from the scene, to materialise presently in front of the house').[73] But such one-to-one assumptions about the relationships between the characters of *Victory* and of *The Tempest* are not important: the point is the ease with which the bones of the Shakespearean play become Conradian coral.[74] And what is especially fascinating about *Victory* is the evidence it offers of Conrad's own awareness of the problem of late style.

The novel, on close examination, is a highly self-conscious piece of late writing. Schomberg, for instance, is the embodiment of lateness gone wrong. 'Forty-five', we are told – or, as Hampson notes, in early drafts of the novel, 'fifty', suggesting that Conrad was a little uncertain about when middle age (and late style, since the two seem, for him, to be inseparable) begins –

is the age of recklessness in many men, as if in defiance of the decay and death waiting with open arms in the sinister valley, at the bottom of the inevitable hill. [...] For every age is fed with illusions, lest men should renounce life early and the human race come to an end. (*Victory*, 131)

Heyst, reflecting on his own imminent end, remembers the last evening he spent with his father:

He had listened. Then, after a silence, he had asked – for he was really young then:
'Is there no guidance?'
His father was in an unexpectedly soft mood on that night, when the moon swam in a cloudless sky over the begrimed shadows of the town.
'You still believe in something, then?' he said in a clear voice which had been growing feeble of late. [...]
'What is one to do, then?' sighed the young man, regarding his father, rigid in the high-backed chair.
'Look on – make no sound,' were the last words of the man who had spent his life in blowing blasts upon a terrible trumpet which had filled heaven and earth with ruins, while mankind went on its way unheeding.
That very night he died in his bed [...]. (194).

It surprises Heyst that his father should choose a watchful silence at the end. Later, though, as he nears his own death, he adopts a similar stance, this time meshing personal lateness with epochal:

'I wonder, Lena,' Heyst said, with a return of his urbane playfulness, 'whether you are just a little child, or whether you represent something as old as the world.'
She surprised Heyst by saying dreamily:
'Well – and what about you?'
'I? I date later – much later. I can't call myself a child, but I am so recent that I may call myself a man of the last hour – or is it the hour before last? I have been out of it so long that I am not certain how far the hands of the clock have moved since – since – '
He glanced at the portrait of his father, exactly above the head of the girl, and as it were ignoring her in its painted austerity of feeling. He did not finish the sentence; but he did not remain silent for long.
'Only what must be avoided are fallacious inferences, my dear Lena – especially at this hour' (343–4).

The relationship between these two wryly apocalyptic passages and the sentiments expressed is underlined by the glance at the portrait of the father. For Heyst, *père et fils*, the last hours require a change of tone, a move away from assertions of agency to an awareness of human subordination to a larger or higher realm – one with which Neumann, for one, would be familiar. The relationship between Heyst and Lena at this moment is that of Prospero and Miranda, and Conrad, no doubt aware of the 'Last Man' tradition running back to Thomas Campbell and Mary Shelley, gives his protagonist in his last hours a stance both at the end of and outside time.

This profound self-consciousness about lateness is Victorian in origin and Shakespeare has a central place in its development. Dowden, trying to make sense of the arbitrariness of the order of presentation of the late plays in the First Folio, made Shakespeare's late period the touchstone. '[I]n the light of the clear and solemn vision of his closing years', he argued, 'all his writings shall be read' (Dowden, *Mind and Art*, 403), his peremptory 'shall' at least as much an instruction as a prediction, and in so doing he expressed the spirit of his age. The Victorians were not, of course, the first culture in history to be aware of the value of the valedictory gesture, to give it moral or theological loading, but they were the first to systematise this awareness in relation to artistic productivity and to establish lateness as a self-reflexive phenomenon, a necessary prerequisite to being-remembered-as-a-genius. Michael Millgate has provided a fascinating account of this phenomenon – the significance of his book manifest in its lightness of touch as much as in its range and depth – in his seminal *Testamentary Acts*, in which he assesses the ways in which a series of Victorian writers 'famous in their own time' – Browning, Tennyson, James and Hardy –

sought in old age to exert some degree of posthumous control over their personal and literary reputations – over the extent and nature of future biographical investigations and exposure, and over the interpretation and textual integrity of their published works.[75]

Millgate lists the various actions taken by these writers, and by others following in their footsteps, to determine the shape of their posthumous reputations:

They have [...] destroyed or selectively preserved such personal papers as diaries, notebooks, manuscripts, and letters; written autobiographies and memoirs; authorized 'official' biographies and even participated in their preparation; revised [...] their earlier works [...]; and reissued those newly refurbished titles in so-called 'collected' editions that were often inclusive only of whatever elderly authorial judgement had deemed worthy of canonicity. (*Testamentary Acts*, 3)

He notes that, though each of the writers with whom he is engaged survived to a good old age, this is not an essential prerequisite of testamentary actions. Rather, he argues, '[v]aledictory gestures are not confined to the elderly': the prospect of death or enforced retirement 'can operate very much like old age itself in shaping what may prove, irrespective of age, to be the final phase of a writer's working life' (ibid., 2). But the passing of a certain amount of time is nonetheless required. Millgate focusses on 'writers to whom literary fame, economic security, personal longevity, and continued physical and mental well-being have granted the opportunity not only to reappraise their own past works and deeds but actively to enforce such a reappraisal' (ibid., 3) – writers, that is, who are aware of, and keen to capitalise upon, their own lateness.

Writing of Hardy, Millgate observes that the ageing novelist 'assumed the mantle of old age like a destiny, settling into longevity as into a role for which he had spent his entire life preparing' (ibid., 110). This involves a strong awareness both of the idea of late writing and of its value to the writer in old age. 'As early as 1906', Millgate notes, citing the *Life and Work*, itself a remarkable gesture, at once 'late' and 'posthumous', Hardy expressed a particular attachment to the late work of composers and painters (ibid.). 'I prefer late Wagner', he announces,

as I prefer late Turner, to early (which I suppose is all wrong in taste), the idiosyncrasies of each master being more strongly shown in these strains. When a man not contented with the grounds of his success goes on and on, and tries to achieve the impossible, then he gets profoundly interesting to me.[76]

The aside – '(which I suppose is all wrong in taste)' – is deliberately provocative: later he notes, irritated, that, in the general view, the great writers 'must almost, like Shelley or Marlowe, be drowned or done to death, or like Keats, die of consumption', arguing that the critics 'forget that in the ancient world no such necessity was recognised; that Homer sang as a blind old man, that Aeschylus wrote his best up to his death at nearly seventy, that the best of Sophocles appeared between his 55th. and 90th. years, that Euripides wrote up to 70' (Hardy, *Life and Works*, 414). He famously echoes this claim in his poem 'An Ancient to Ancients', which appeared in *Late Lyrics and Earlier* of 1922, celebrating the achievements in old age of classical writers:

> And yet, though ours be failing frames,
>   Gentlemen,
> So were some others' history names,
> Who trode their track light-limbed and fast
> As these youth, and not alien
> From enterprise, to their long last,
>   Gentlemen.
> Sophocles, Plato, Socrates,
>   Gentlemen,
> Pythagoras, Thucydides,
> Herodotus, and Homer, – yea,
> Clement, Augustin, Origen,
> Burnt brightlier towards their setting-day,
>   Gentlemen.[77]

Implicit throughout, of course, is Hardy's own considerable productivity in old age. Defending his late shift from prose to poetry, he turns to opera for an instance of the great artistic achiever in old age. 'It may be observed', he notes,

> that in the art-history of the century there was an example staring [the critics] in the face of a similar modulation from one style to another by a great artist. Verdi was the instance, 'that amazing old man' as he was called. Someone of insight wrote concerning him: 'From the ashes of his early popularity, from *Il Trovatore* and its kind, there arose on a sudden a sort of phoenix Verdi. Had he died at Mozart's death-age he would now be practically unknown'. [...] But probably few literary critics discern the solidarity of all the arts. (ibid., 320–1)

Verdi thus serves as proof both of the importance of late work and of the essential connection of that work with old age. Hardy may, as Millgate shows, be an extreme case, but he is representative nonetheless of a series of ageing writers at the turn of the century who carefully rethought and reshaped their work in order to establish for posterity a clear image of their status as authors blessed both with considerable longevity and with a profound and productive late period.

Millgate's interest in this question is first and foremost that of a textual editor, trying both to make sense of and to intensify the problem of 'final intentions' and of the involvement both of the writer and of his or her relatives, friends and disciples in the laundering of the evidence of the artistic life in the wake of death. He acknowledges the polemical pronouncement of G. Thomas Tanselle that an editor may properly choose to edit an earlier version of a text if he considers it 'a more faithful representation of the author's vision', and although he gently mocks this position by noting that Tanselle's proposal 'sounds rather like being invited to choose the most faithful representation of a person's appearance from among a series of photographs taken at widely different ages' (*Testamentary Acts*, 198), he sets out to map the distortions that result from the automatic adoption of texts representing final intentions and thus, in a good number of cases, from the conscious deployment of the discourse of lateness by the writer as an (often highly successful) attempt to dictate hindsight.[78] This process tends to begin with a retrospective, one which is inevitable and perhaps necessary. 'It is through rereading their own work, discovering the hidden meanings sown by their younger selves, that poets grow', argues Lawrence Lipking, a process which becomes more urgent as the poet ages. The combination of that urgency with the long view of the career can produce violent changes.[79] For Lipking,

> [a]s a poet grows old, the way he reads his earlier work often changes. Poems that once seemed full of meaning now retreat into the background, perhaps to be absorbed by anthologies where their fragile unselfconscious life freezes into the classic. Other poems – the ugly ducklings, which have always seemed to belong to someone else – suddenly emerge into the mainstream. And something even stranger can happen. Very often a great old poet begins to regard his poems as possessing no individual interest (at least for him). Even his masterpieces, taken one by one, appear partial, transitory, 'only fragments of a great confession.' [...] Another logic determines such reading: the logic of the whole. (*Life of the Poet*, 65)

This 'other' logic explains the intrinsic problem of the idea of late style manifest in the evidence that, as soon as the discourse entered general consciousness, artists began to manipulate their textual histories, becoming at best complicit in, if not wholly responsible for, a late distortion of their careers, a reshaping of the often random and diverse materials of their output from the perspective of the end with a view to providing a coherent, linear history that would not otherwise be apparent. The 'great confession' becomes the driving force of the career, the official version, the only authorised structure for the life. Late style, seen as a prerequisite if one wishes to be remembered as a genius and established as an individual and *involuntary* phenomenon, ostensibly different in kind from the willed generic self-construction of the Virgilian *rota* (see Chapter 4), turns out in fact to be no different in kind from its classical forebear. Lateness becomes, from this perspective, less a mystical, natural phenomenon than, to deploy Bourdieu's term once more, a position in a consciously shaped trajectory.

Millgate makes abundantly clear that, other than Hardy, the literary figure at the turn of the century most determined to dictate to posterity in his own late phase was also the one most obsessed with late Shakespeare and in particular with *The Tempest*. That figure was Henry James. Far more even than Conrad, James consciously (and anxiously) constructed his own lateness by way of the precedent of Shakespeare. His actions have had a long reach: there is a hint, for instance, as I have already suggested, of his continuing association with *The Tempest* in Simon Palfrey's observation that '[t]here is enough missing from the two post-*Tempest* plays to suggest that Shakespeare knew that a certain mastery had been achieved'. James has of course become in many ways the touchstone of literary lateness for the twentieth century, as critics struggle to interpret both the dense style of his last novels and his magnificently ambivalent final words, which themselves reinforce the evidence that James had repeatedly meditated on and articulated the condition of lateness, doing so in characteristically manipulative and elliptical ways, evoking and evading simultaneously. He has as a result had a quietly efficient impact on the ways in which we continue to imagine Shakespearean lateness – less conspicuous by far than that of Dowden and Strachey, but effective nonetheless, partly as a result of being insinuating rather than bludgeoning. You could even argue, in a sense, that it has subsequently been impossible to separate Shakespearean from Jamesian lateness.

James's prose in his last works implies an equation of late style with both difficulty and epochal lateness. The former raises the question of connoisseurship, which meant so much to James. For Tia DeNora, 'difficulty', as a principal criterion of 'great' work, was constructed in the particular social environment in which the reputation of Beethoven was formed, the opaque, alienating qualities of his late work arguably serving to cement the general connection between late style and the resistance of the art-object to consumption or interpretation and thus its particular appeal to the connoisseur, a connection upon which James capitalised.[80] But there is more to it than this. The self-consciousness of, for instance, *The Golden Bowl* as a classic instance of late writing is embodied not only in the extraordinarily mannered (and consequently much parodied) late James prose style but also in the lightly-drawn but nonetheless resonant expressions of an end-of-era aesthetic that recur throughout the novel, marking James's equation of his own (as he saw it) late epoch and that in which mannerism grew and blossomed. Mannerism, as *The Wings of the Dove* makes clear, both opens up and closes down: it engages, in its exquisite end-of-epoch or, perhaps, postepochal abstraction, the aesthetic attention, providing a moment which in itself marks the beginning of the period that postdates the perfect, thus serving also as a reminder of mortality. For Milly Theale, standing before the Bronzino portrait of a woman startlingly like herself,

> [o]nce more things melted together – the beauty and the history and the facility and the splendid midsummer glow: it was a sort of magnificent maximum, the pink dawn of an apotheosis, coming so curiously soon. What in fact befell was that, as she afterwards made out, it was Lord Mark who said nothing in particular – it was she herself who said all. She couldn't help that – it came; and the reason it came was that she found herself, for the first moment, looking at the mysterious portrait through tears. Perhaps it was her tears that made it just then so strange and fair – as wonderful as he had said: the face of a young woman, all magnificently drawn, down to the hands, and magnificently dressed; a face almost livid in hue, yet handsome in sadness and crowned with a mass of hair, rolled back and high, that must, before fading with time, have had a family resemblance to her own. The lady in question, at all events, with her slightly Michaelangelesque squareness, her eyes of other days, her full lips, her long neck, her recorded jewels, her brocaded and wasted reds, was a very great personage – only unaccompanied by a joy. And she was dead, dead, dead. Milly recognised her exactly in words that had nothing to do with her. 'I shall never be better than this'.[81]

This pivotal moment depends upon an equation of the late Renaissance and a certain belatedness in Edwardian culture, a decadent precision of taste which is also a marker of overliving, and it offers a clear instance of the self-consciousness of James's own late work.[82]

James is both acutely and at the same time ironically conscious of the problem of the requirement for the acquisition of a late phase if one is to be remembered as a great writer. And it is by way of Shakespeare in particular that James constructs his own lateness even while constructing that of Shakespeare himself. The grand literary figure in James's short stories (which, much more consistently than the late novels, address issues of late style) – Vereker in 'The Figure in the Carpet', St George in 'The Lesson of the Master', Faraday in 'The Death of the Lion', above all the unnamed

'Author' in 'The Birthplace' – seems always simultaneously to be both Shakespeare and James. Shakespeare appears to figure, for James, both lateness and a curious prematurity. *The Tempest* embodies a consummate serenity, a 'late manner' wholly achieved, yet it is also infuriatingly early in Shakespeare's life. Russell Fraser, constructing his own impressionistic narrative of the late period, underlines this Jamesian self-construction as the new late Shakespeare:

> Some writers, beset by demons, never lay down the pen, for example Henry James. His hands still performing the act of writing when he died, he wondered at Shakespeare, forsaking 'his muses dear.' But Shakespeare was like his Ariel who longed to be free, and after 1613 wrote no more.
>
> James, the prose Shakespeare, comes up often in this narrative, worthy to stand comparison with an artist even greater than himself. Also, better than any other, he illuminates the difference between old-fashioned Shakespeare and the modern mandarin. 'It is art that *makes* life, makes interests, makes importance [...] and I know of no substitute whatever for the force and beauty of its process.' Mundane Shakespeare could never have said this, but more assured than James, didn't have to. (*Shakespeare: The Later Years*, 247)

Fraser may offer a tendentious view of Shakespeare here (a modern writer out of time), and he appears unaware of the extent to which James's sense of his own lateness was both self-conscious and dependent upon that of Shakespeare, but he is right to underline James's bewilderment at Shakespeare's decision to retire. As I have suggested, this concluding gesture, this renunciation of art, simply outraged James – unable to agree either with Bailey's serene pronouncement that 'gentle William simply wanted in the autumn of his life the peace of Prospero' or, because of the evidence that had accumulated by this time, with Knight's firm assertion that 'Shakespeare never could have contemplated, in health and intellectual vigour, any abandonment of that occupation which constituted his happiness and glory', but wishing it were so – to think that Shakespeare might wilfully have shaped his late period and given up his art prematurely, in middle age, long before his three-score-years-and-ten had run their course. 'What manner of human being was it', James demanded,

> who *could* so, at a given moment, announce his intention of capping his divine flame with a twopenny extinguisher, and who then, the announcement made, could serenely succeed in carrying it out? Were it a question of a flame spent or burning thin, we might feel a little more possessed of matter for comprehension; the fact being, on the contrary, one can only repeat, that the value of The Tempest is, exquisitely, in its refinement of power, its renewed artistic freshness and roundness, its mark as of a distinction unequalled, on the whole (though I admit that we here must take subtle measures), in any predecessor. (James in Lee (ed.), *Complete Works*, xxiv)

Henry James and the elusive late Shakespeare 179

This passage comes, significantly, from the preface James wrote in 1907 to the *Tempest* volume in Sidney Lee's *Complete Works* – which is in itself a remarkable thing since James was fully immersed in his work on the New York Edition at the time and notoriously reluctant to take on competing tasks. It is a measure of his engagement with *The Tempest* that he did so, and with such gusto: replying to the invitation to write the preface, he claimed he would 'challenge this artist – the master and the magician of a thousand masks – and make him drop them, if only for an interval'.[83] As Millgate notes, 'James saw in *The Tempest* – as the supreme product of Shakespeare's maturer years, "the finest flower of his experience" – a flattering analogue for what he confidently expected to be his own culminating achievement' (*Testamentary Acts*, 89). 'Such a masterpiece puts before me', James wrote,

the very act of the momentous conjunction taking place for the poet, at a given hour, between his charged inspiration and his clarified experience: or, as I should perhaps better express it, between his human curiosity and his aesthetic passion. Then, if he happens to have been, all his career, more or less the slave of the former, he yields, by way of a change, to the impulse of the latter, for a magnificent moment, the upper hand. (James in Lee, *Complete Works*, xvi)

For Lauren Cowdery, 'not only does James attribute to [...] Shakespeare perfect artistry and the ability to get outside of himself, what James will call "objectivity," but he also sees in him a perfect integration of secret and public self'.[84] In this last play, for James, Shakespeare 'sinks as deep as we like [...] into [...] the lucid stillness of his style'; the whole play is his 'high testimony to th[e] independent, absolute value of Style'.[85]

This language of 'sinking' in James's work, as Philip Horne has shown in his important account of James's practice as a reviser of his own work, repeatedly invokes *The Tempest*. A 'sunk' picture, for James, was one which had lost its life over time, had 'faded' or 'melted', but which could yet be the recipient of a rejuvenating restoration. Each time he discusses this concept, he does so by way of language drawn from *The Tempest*, of 'pearls', 'eyes' and 'fathom', of the possibility of a 'sea-change', of unexpected rebirth.[86] To 'sink' is, in other words, not so much to die, to drown, as to presage resuscitation, to foreshadow resurgence. The *Tempest* introduction marks, for Cowdery, 'the crest of James's confidence, as, lighthearted, exhilarated and determined, he scours the house of art in search of a better, an ideal, self' ('Transcendent Adventure', 153) – or, more specifically, as he seeks to resurrect his own earlier work through the revision process for the New York Edition, an ostensibly optimistic trajectory, 'sunken' texts revived, a sense of 'something rich and strange' emerging at the end. Yet James's resistance to, his utter incomprehension of, the idea of a voluntary Shakespearean retirement suggests something far less effortless, far more anxiety-inducing. On the 'supposition' that Prospero is a representation of Shakespeare, James writes,

> his retirement to Stratford, to end his days in the care of his property and in oblivion of the theatre, was a course for which his arrangements had already been made. The simplest way to put it, since I have likened him to the musician at the piano, is to say that he had decided upon the compete closing of this instrument, and that in fact he was to proceed to lock it with the sharp click that has reverberated through the ages, and to spend what remained to him of life in walking about a small, squalid country-town with his hands in his pockets and an ear for no music now but the chink of the coin they might turn over there. (James in Lee, *Complete Works*, xxii–xxiii)

As the dismissive last sentence suggests, for James, this state of affairs is simply inconceivable. As Millgate has argued,

> it seems clear that James's implied unreadiness to contemplate the early extinction of his own 'divine flame' derived at least in part from his confident sense (illusory or otherwise) of being at the height not merely of his personal powers but specifically of his power, his ability and licence to determine the future perception of his lifetime's achievement by selecting for the Edition only those works by which he was now prepared to be judged, by using its prefaces to direct the ways in which those chosen works should, in his matured judgement, be read and understood [...] and, above all, by imposing on the entire series those exquisitely developed stylistic preferences that had become in these later years inseparable from his sense of himself as a literary artist. (*Testamentary Acts*, 89–90)

James's resistance to Shakespearean retirement, in other words, manifests itself as an insistence on reshaping his entire *œuvre* on the basis of his sense of his own late selfhood and its distinctive style.

The key text for any analysis of James and the discourse of lateness is a short story from 1893 called 'The Middle Years', which appeared first in *Scribner's Magazine* and then in the 1895 collection entitled, self-consciously enough, *Terminations*. 'The Middle Years' is a story about a writer called Dencombe who is dying in middle age ('You talk strangely of your age. You're not old', says the young doctor, instantly adding a qualifier: 'I speak physiologically'); it is also the name of Dencombe's last novel, which has just, as the story opens, been published. He is characterised as a belated figure, one frustrated above all by the shortage of time:

> What he saw so intensely to-day, what he felt as a nail driven in, was that only now, at the very last, had he come into possession. His development had been abnormally slow, almost grotesquely gradual. He had been hindered and retarded by

experience, and for long periods had only groped his way. It had taken too much of his life to produce too little of his art. The art had come, but it had come after everything else.[87]

He craves a second chance, a supplementary phase to the life he has had before he is forced to 'surrender to silence' ('Middle Years', 68). For Dencombe,

a first existence was too short – long enough only to collect material; so that to fructify, to use the material, one must have a second age, an extension. This extension was what poor Dencombe sighed for. As he turned the last leaves of his volume he murmured: 'Ah, for another go! – ah for a better chance!' (ibid., 57)

His illness reasserts itself and when he emerges from the 'fragments', his sense of the need for more time is stronger still:

It came over him in the long, quiet hours that only with 'The Middle Years' had he taken his flight; only on that day, visited by soundless processions, had he recognised his kingdom. He had had a revelation of his range. (ibid., 65)

Above all, '[w]hat he dreaded was the idea that his reputation should stand on the unfinished' (ibid.). And James makes clear what would be required to deal with that dread: a new lease of life, one that the writer briefly believes, in a dream of romance teleology, might yet be possible: 'He thought of the fairy-tales of science and charmed himself into forgetting that he looked for a magic that was not of this world' ('Middle Years', 68). What he dreams of is a late phase:

Dencombe, soaring again a little on the weak wings of convalescence and still haunted by that happy notion of an organised rescue, found another strain of eloquence to plead the cause of a certain splendid 'last manner', the very citadel, as it would prove, of his reputation, the stronghold into which his real treasure would be gathered. (ibid., 70)

And he describes (in terms James would repeat resonantly three years later when describing the cruelly elusive 'Figure in the Carpet' as 'the string the pearls were strung on') the 'real treasure' of this '"last manner"': 'the precious metals he would dig from the mine, the jewels rare, strings of pearls' (ibid., 70).

But Dencombe is not allowed such a 'last manner'. There is 'an ache that kept him sentient, the probable sacrifice of his "extension", the limit of his course' (ibid., 72). '"The pearl"', he realises at last, '"is the unwritten – the pearl is the unalloyed, the *rest*, the lost!"' (ibid., 74). And, 'sinking steadily', he dies, though not before he has come to the realisation that the late phase itself may be illusory. 'A second chance – *that's* the delusion', he says, despite all his young friend can do to resist his final bleakness: 'There never was to be but one' (ibid., 75). In the end, '[p]oor Dencombe was barely audible, but he had marked with words the virtual end of his first and only chance' (ibid., 76). The anxiety about the place of, even the possibility of, the late style in the novelistic career is one Dencombe appears to share with his creator – and in suggesting this I would of course be succumbing to the very subjectivism against which I am writing here, except that James, in his turn-of-the-century authorial self-consciousness, repeatedly both invites and deflects this association. The description of Dencombe as 'a passionate corrector, a fingerer of style' – 'the last thing he ever arrived at', we are told, 'was a form final for himself' – makes apparent his association with James, wholesale and restless reviser of his texts, as he insists that his reader (his own avid young doctor, keen to see a pre-publication copy of the latest novel) read it that way: 'His ideal would have been to publish secretly, and then, on the published text, treat himself to the terrified revise, sacrificing always a first edition and beginning for posterity and even for the collectors, poor dears, with a second' (ibid., 63). James's own engagement, ironic yet intense, with the modes of production of the work of the famous is thus wholly apparent – as, throughout, is his anxiety that he should have time to perform his own revisions, to achieve the 'splendid last manner' denied to Dencombe. That *The Middle Years* should also be the title of the volume of his memoirs that remained unfinished at James's death underlines both the logic and the irony of his urgency.

James's unease about the apparent dereliction of duty on Shakespeare's part marked by his unnecessarily early retirement and his fear that there might never be, in the end, a late style prompts three questions which are central to the analysis of the history of Shakespearean lateness. Two of these emerge directly from the Shakespeare/James conjunction; the third more generally from James's celebration of the connoisseur and the question of the authentic that is connoisseurship's correlative. The first draws on one of the constituent binaries of the discourse of lateness that I outlined in Chapter 1, the coupling *knowing/involuntary*. James's historical position in the aftermath of Romanticism and in the wake of the establishment of the possessive attitude to authorship that informed his work throughout his life gives him a writerly self-consciousness in relation to late style that had been unavailable to earlier generations. Lipking argues that 'no poet becomes himself without inheriting an idea of what it means to be a poet' (*Life of the Poet*, viii), a magnificent paradox of subjectivity and subjection, but one which changed and developed over successive centuries. Once the production of a late phase had been privileged as a manifestation of genius, it became impossible for any creative artist, as the years progressed, to step outside the paradox of self-will. Thus by the time James reached his own late phase, he knew precisely in what a late phase was meant to consist and what it should mean for his reputation once he was dead (as did others, as Millgate has shown). There has not, in other words, been an innocent, uncomplicit late phase for two centuries – that is, for the entire period during which the concept of the 'late phase' has existed as an articulable phenomenon. But was this the case for Shakespeare? To what extent, if any, could Shakespeare have shared the writerly self-consciousness exemplified by James? I will try to answer this question in the next chapter.

The second goes, for James, hand in glove with the first: it is the question of age embodied in the binary *old age/proximity to death*. We have seen the unease with which analysts of late style negotiate the asymmetry of the ostensibly interchangeable terms *Spätstil* and *Altersstil*; we have seen too Millgate's acknowledgement that late style is not necessarily the style of old age, that it can be either the product of 'the apprehension of death' which 'can operate very much like old age itself in shaping what may prove, irrespective of age, to be the final phase of a writer's working life', or often enough the product in any case of a collaboration between the ageing artist and younger relatives or executors. Again, we have seen, on the one hand, Hardy's resistance to the privileging of the premature deaths of Marlowe, Keats and Shelley and, on the other, Havelock Ellis's effortless equation of the late styles of Shelley and Keats with those of Titian, Rembrandt and Turner, as if stage of life were neither here nor there in an attribution of late style. Yet we have also seen, again and again, the drawing of a direct equation between the old age of certain major artists and the idea of late work, an assumption that the features of late style are in some sense specifically the product of the ageing process. One question that has haunted this book so far, then, is this: is a 'late style' the same as an 'old-age' style? Which in turn leads to a further, more targeted question: to what extent is it fair to call Shakespeare's late style an 'old-age' style? I will address both of these questions in Chapter 5.

The third question, prompted in part by James the connoisseur, is this: to what extent has late Shakespeare become, by way of the particular qualities attributed to it as a paradigmatic instance of late style, primary material for appropriation and reinvention? The qualities I have in mind are most clearly delineated by the binaries *archaic/proleptic* and *individual/ epochal* and impinge substantially on what we have seen to be the underlying question of authenticity raised by studies of late style. We have seen both that Rembrandt is repeatedly presented as a key exemplar of late style and that late style has become a key determinant of authenticity. The National Gallery of Victoria in Melbourne has two paintings long thought to be late Rembrandts. Recently, one of them, an apparent self-portrait called simply 'Rembrandt', has been reclassified by the Rembrandt Project as the product not of the artist's own hand but of unknown members of his studio (his pupils, presumably), who created a series of 'self-portraits' of Rembrandt in the master's late style. This raises a profound and awkward question. To what extent is a late style imitable? If it is, then whose style is it? If a late style can be imitated specifically by the young, can it be considered a *late* style at all? And if late style is, as Ellis, Neumann, Broch and others would have it, universal, something shared between great artists across time and space, then does a given late style belong, as it were, to the particular artist in question – that is, *Rembrandt's* late style – or is it instead a recognisable late style as channelled through a particular artist at the appropriate stage of his life – Rembrandt's *late style*, in other words?

For Adorno, as we have seen, '[t]he maturity of the late works of important artists is not like the ripeness of fruit. As a rule', he argues,

these works are not well rounded, but wrinkled, even fissured. They are apt to lack sweetness, fending off with prickly tartness those interested merely in sampling them. They lack all that harmony which the classicist aesthetic is accustomed to demand from the work of art, showing more traces of history than of growth. (*Beethoven*, 123)

This passage, with its 'as a rule' and the collectivity of its pronouns, suggests that lateness is a phenomenon that transcends the individual, something that happens to 'important artists' whether they will it or not, an unconscious, inevitable phenomenon, 'showing more traces of history than of growth' – lateness, that is, as a product of artistic history, not of self-conscious development. The question, then, is whether a late style can ever be said to 'belong' to a given author or painter. Does Rembrandt own (determine, produce) his late style? Or does *late style* own, determine or produce Rembrandt's work of the 1660s? Absurd as this might seem, a re-reading of Ellis, Neumann, Broch and Adorno does tend to support the notion. The principal irony of lateness thus lies in its formulaic qualities. The premise of the (self-)attribution of a 'late manner' is its status as proof that the individual in question has been/is/ will be viewed in the future as a genius; yet the standard tenets of lateness – serenity, the return to the early, sophistication, difficulty (not all of which are present in any one late manner, of course, but which together form the spectrum of lateness from the spiritual to the irascible) – serve only to de-individualise the alleged 'genius' in question, since if his originality is paradoxically proven by the conventionality of his late style, that originality is thus defined by and subsumed to conventionality. Critics sustaining the discourse of lateness seem implicitly to recognise this, since accepting a general definition of late style but arguing that your particular artist's late style is in some way different from that of others is standard critical rhetoric. In the process, however, the very identity of the late stylist, the identity at its most acute in late work, is paradoxically diffused. James characteristically probes at the heart of this uncertainty by giving the clearest signal of one of the most curious yet persistent developments in the question of late Shakespeare, one which has distinct resonances, as I will show in my last chapter, right up to the present day.

Holding on to the figure of Shakespeare turns out to be remarkably tricky for James, a difficulty made even worse by lateness, a discourse ostensibly designed to individuate and identify. In 'The Lesson of the Master', a short story of a year or so before 'The Middle Years', the great novelist Henry St George (whose oh-so-English surname humorously implies his identification with the saintly Shakespeare, England's National Poet, amplified as it is by his Prospero-like manipulations of the other characters as the story unfolds) is presented as a late stylist.[88] The impressionable, solipsistic Paul Overt (whose surname is also, of course, playful), adopting the position of a Ferdinand, admits to the story's Miranda-figure, Miss Fancourt, that he is 'prostrate before' St George:

> She had an air of earnestness. 'Do you think then he's so perfect?'
> 'Far from it. Some of his later books seem to me of a queerness – !'
> 'Yes, yes – he knows that.'
> Paul Overt stared. 'That they seem to me of a queerness – ?'
> 'Well yes, or at any rate that they're not what they should be. He told me he didn't esteem them. He has told me such wonderful things – he's so interesting'.[89]

As it turns out, St George is deploying this *sprezzatura* stance of self-conscious lateness in order to trick Overt into leaving the country and thus to give himself a free run at the young woman they both desire. The clue lies in the malleability of the resonant word 'sunk' in James's rhetoric:

> 'Shocking enough, it must be, especially to a young fresh mind, full of faith – the spectacle of a man meant for better things sunk at my age in such dishonour.'

St George, in the same contemplative attitude, spoke softly but deliberately, and without perceptible emotion. His tone indeed suggested an impersonal lucidity that was practically cruel – cruel to himself – and made his young friend lay an argumentative hand on his arm. But he went on while his eyes seemed to follow the graces of the eighteenth-century ceiling: 'Look at me well, take my lesson to heart – for it *is* a lesson. Let that good come of it at least that you shudder with your pitiful impression, and that this may help to keep you straight in the future. Don't become in your old age what I have in mine – the depressing, the deplorable illustration of the worship of false gods!'

'What do you mean by your old age?' the young man asked.

'It has made me old. But I like your youth'. ('Lesson of the Master', 238–9)

St George here appears to have the weariness of Strachey's or Bond's late Shakespeare; it is only later that we learn that he has been playacting throughout, a victory of cold experience over naïveté, that both of Overt and of the reader. 'The Lesson of the Master' is a version of *The Tempest* – at least, there is no sign at the end that St George will renege on his intention to give up his writing (though, equally, it is not absolutely stated that he will not do so) – and thus a story of retirement, of the ending of the art of a magus and the opening up of a new lease of life involving a young woman, but the serenity of the Master's voice is both underpinned and undermined by a quite uncomfortable cynicism, as we realise that, even if it is for his own good as a writer (a redrawing of Ferdinand, kept apart from Miranda for the sake of art, 'lest too light winning / Make the prize light'), our young hero has been urbanely tricked out of the woman of his dreams by a sophisticated Great Writer with little in the way either of conscience or of substance whose implicit (mis)identification with Prospero/Shakespeare leaves the reader distinctly unsettled by the end.

In his best-known engagement with Shakespeare, the short story entitled 'The Birthplace' in which he never actually mentions Shakespeare by name, James takes this simultaneous process of identification and dissolution a logical, perhaps even an inevitable, step further. Morris Gedge and his wife, languishing in obscurity in Blackport-on-Dwindle, are invited to become resident wardens of 'the early home of the supreme poet, the Mecca of the English-speaking race'.[90] For Gedge, the intense excitement of the opportunity, as he explains it to his wife, is the chance it gives them to 'live with Him' ('Birthplace', 408), the unnamed, messianically uppercased Author, to have the chance of

'becoming familiar and intimate – for that's what it will come to. We shall just live with Him'.

'Of course – it *is* the beauty'. And she added quite gaily: 'The more we do the more we shall love Him'.

'No doubt – but it's rather awful. The more we *know* Him', Gedge reflected, 'the more we shall love Him. We don't as yet, you see, know Him so very tremendously'. (ibid., 408)

The illusory nature of their stance is hinted at when Isabel Gedge exclaims: 'we shall live as in a fairy-tale' (Birthplace', 407), but they arrive in full belief, struck with 'the wonder of being fairly housed with Him, of treading day and night in the footsteps He had worn' (ibid., 411). As the story unfolds, however, their implicit belief in the Author, faced with the relentless onslaught of literary pilgrims at the door and within the 'Chamber of Birth', begins to waver. In an unexpected internal hermeneutic shift, they become aware that the meaning of the Birthplace resides not in the place itself or in the person commemorated but in those who visit. Gedge 'had never thought of the quality of the place as derived from Them, but from Somebody Else. [. . .] They, in short, seemed to have got into the way of crowding out Him' (ibid., 414). And, gradually, he begins to understand. 'It isn't about Him', he realises, '– nothing's about Him. None of Them care tuppence about Him. The only thing they care about is this empty shell' (ibid., 421), the building, that is, in which the Author was supposedly born. And this realisation develops in a later exchange. His wife, exasperated, asks: 'You would like the relics destroyed, removed? That's all that's wanted!', to which he replies abruptly: 'There *are* no relics' (ibid., 422). And he moves gradually towards the position made inevitable from the start. '[W]e don't know anything about it', he admits, 'About His having been born up there. About anything, really. Not the least scrap that would weigh, in any other connection, as evidence'. 'Don't you think,' his wife asks 'cuttingly',

'that He was born anywhere?'

He hesitated – it was such an edifice to shake. 'Well, we don't know. There's very little *to* know. He covered His tracks as no other human being has ever done'. (ibid., 428)

Finally, in conversation with a sympathetic young American couple, Gedge brings himself to reach the inevitable conclusion. 'There *is* no such Person', he announces (ibid., 439).

As is well known, Henry James, writing to the novelist Violet Hunt in August 1903, acknowledged that he was '"a sort of" haunted by the conviction that the divine William is the biggest and most successful fraud ever practised on a patient world', a line that has been gleefully cited by anti-Stratfordians ever since (though the Baconian sub-group tend, unsurprisingly, to omit the subsequent sentence – 'I can only express my general sense by saying that I find it almost as impossible to conceive that Bacon wrote the plays as to conceive that the man from Stratford, as we know the man from Stratford, did' – along with James's later objections to Bruce Porter's interest in Baconianism as a 'misguided search for a sensation').[91] There had already been a hint of this interest, though not an especially auspicious one for those engaged with the 'authorship question', when the obsessive narrator of 'The Figure in the Carpet' makes a direct, if unintentionally ironic, comparison between his friend's quest for the hidden truth in Vereker's novels and cryptographic readings of Shakespeare:

> He was like nothing, I told him, but the maniacs who embrace some bedlamitical theory of the cryptic character of Shakespeare. To this he replied that if we had had Shakespeare's own word for his being cryptic he would immediately have accepted it. The case there was altogether different – we had nothing but the word of Mr Snooks. I rejoined that I was stupefied to see him attach such importance even to the word of Mr Vereker.[92]

This is gloriously complex, since the comparison serves to underline the degree of identification the story implies between Vereker and Shakespeare while at the same time undermining that identification, not least by way of the humour of the secondary, underlying narrative voice beyond that of the actual narrator. In his own late period, then, James, displaying a perhaps 'bedlamitical' *fin-de-siècle* fascination for the mysticism fundamental to anti-Stratfordianism, dissolves the figure of the late Shakespeare even as he deploys and depends upon it.

The resonances of this, moreover, do not stop with Shakespeare. There is a curious and infinitely telling echo of 'The Birthplace' in James's late travel narrative *The American Scene*, written four or so years later and published in 1907 – the year, as it happens, of the *Tempest* preface – in which he recounts his return to New York, and specifically to Washington Square, to see the house of his birth. After a description of 'the warm smell of the bakery on the corner of Eighth Street', which evokes happy memories of a childhood appreciation of 'doughnuts, cookies, cream-cakes and pies', he moves on to a less happy experience:

> These were the felicities of the backward reach, which, however, had also its melancholy checks and snubs; nowhere quite so sharp as in presence, so to speak, of the rudely, the ruthlessly suppressed birth-house on the other side of the Square. That was where the pretence that nearly nothing was changed had most to come in; for a high, square, impersonal structure, proclaiming its lack of interest with a crudity all its own, so blocks, at the right moment for its own

success, the view of the past, that the effect for me, in Washington Place, was of having been amputated of half my history. The grey and more or less 'hallowed' University building – wasn't it somehow, with a desperate bravery, both castellated and gabled? – has vanished from the earth and vanished with it the two or three adjacent houses, of which the birthplace was one. This was the snub, for the complacency of retrospect, that, whereas the inner sense had positively erected there for its private contemplation a commemorative mural tablet, the very wall that should have borne this inscription had been smashed as for demonstration that tablets, in New York, are unthinkable.[93]

James's use of the resonantly impersonal term 'the birthplace' for his own remembered place of origin inevitably recalls the earlier story, the melancholy humour of James's acknowledgement of his frustration not only with the absence of a commemorative marker but even of a location for that marker, a remnant of the original building, aligning him with the Shakespeare of 'The Birthplace'. As with Shakespeare, so with James: the questionable process of memorialisation leads to a complex relationship with the supposed physical *ur*-point until the author's identity begins to appear distinctly uncertain in the absence of a grounding in the material, in some sort of incontrovertible architectural proof. Novelistic trajectory is thus severely threatened by the myth of the late writer. James himself cannot remember the details of the design of the house next door to where he was born (castellation *and* gabling?), so why should anyone else do better? The tangible proof of the author's existence, even at the point of origin, remains elusive. Paradoxically, then, James's twin obsessions with revision and with late Shakespeare in the end require him to elide the playwright altogether, to revise him into insubstantiality. Late Shakespeare is finally no Shakespeare at all. And late James – the late James whose trajectory is so closely tied to that he has projected for the late Shakespeare – appears no longer to exist either.

CHAPTER 4

Last words/late plays: the possibility and impossibility of late Shakespeare in early modern culture and theatre

Dying men's wordes are ever remarkable.[1]

La poésie doit être faite par tous. Non par un.[2]

I have stated that the idea of late Shakespeare could not, to all intents and purposes, predate Malone's chronology and the subsequent construction of the figure of Shakespeare the author. I have therefore implied that Shakespeare himself could have had no concept of late style and I wish now to explain and qualify this implication in two ways, first of all by considering the significance accorded to the endings of lives – and specifically to last words – in early modern England and then by examining the asymmetrical relationship between the conditions of production in the early modern theatre and those required for the attribution of a late style. I have also begun to argue for another asymmetry, that of, on the one hand, the general idea of late style and, on the other, the specific idea of late Shakespeare, even while claiming that the latter forms a significant constituent part of the former. Late style is a redemptive fantasy of rejuvenation, a manifestation of critical and artistic wish-fulfilment that may at times approximate a biographical truth but which is far more often the product either of the imposition of an understanding of the creative process inimical to the actual conditions in which the art-works in question were produced or of complicity on the part of the artist, consciously producing work that fulfils the criteria for the attribution of a late style. The juxtapositions, transhistorical and transcultural, necessary to the assertion of an overarching concept of lateness must by definition function beyond circumstance, and the danger for any critical reading of late style is the reproduction by the critic of the very manoeuvre he or she wishes to question. Placing Picasso and Shakespeare side by side, as I chose to do in my introduction, is a tendentious move, but it has, I think, heuristic value in offering a reminder of the issues raised by the claim for transhistoricity implicit in an attribution of late style. The Picasso of the

Paris museum, like the Shakespeare outlined by critics from Dowden to Muir, offers a paradigmatic instance of the requirements for such an attribution. Yet the implicit assertion that these two creative artists, working in wholly different media in wholly different material, political, personal and critical contexts – in wholly different artistic eras, in other words – can have even a portion of their work described in such parallel ways must, unless we are to adopt wholesale a Neumannesque other-worldliness, give us pause.

Late styles were celebrated in both Picasso and Shakespeare only after their deaths, yet while Shakespeare can have had no comprehension of the concept of late style as it would later be constituted, Picasso was, by contrast, highly aware of the crucial role his late work would play in entrenching his future reputation. In various ways, he set out, like the Edwardian novelists I addressed in the preceding chapter, self-consciously to construct his own late phase as a way to determine how he would be viewed by posterity – deliberately (as I have noted) reworking in his old age the art of the Old Masters in *their* old age, constructing his own late self-portraits, for instance, in conscious, indeed obsessive, imitation of the late self-portraits of Rembrandt. Picasso, of course, worked in a modern context in which the idea of the artistic career had long been established as a site of contest. Shakespeare too inherited certain ideas of the shape of the artistic career, but these ideas did not include a conception of late style and, in any case, were not models that could be considered, then or now, as relevant or appropriate to an early modern playwright working in a context of collaboration and company repertory and with an understanding of style quite other than that later established by the Romantics as rooted within the personality of the individual artist. If a late style is to be attributed to Shakespeare, certain conditions would need to be in place for him that were unequivocally in place for Picasso – a clarity of chronology, exceptional old age and a particular understanding of authorship and authenticity – and we would need to be able to separate Shakespeare's own grasp of the import of his late plays from the accretion of later critical attitudes. These conditions are, however, unavailable. The process of creation and the level of self-consciousness of this process, needless to say, differ profoundly from early modern playwright to modern artist, so much so that simply to juxtapose them as I have done (and as the discourse of lateness insists on my doing) is in effect absurd. Picasso was acutely aware of the pressure to create and sustain a late phase. He was working within the era of lateness, within an inherited discourse of lateness that substantially drove his work. Shakespeare was not.

We must not, then, be fooled by late-play mythologising into thinking that Shakespeare would have understood that he was carving out what Henry James would in due course, with only partial irony, call 'a certain splendid "late manner" '. The image of Shakespeare's serene and comfortable retirement to Stratford, free from the impositions of professional theatre and surrounded by his loving family, is profoundly false as an objective correlative for the late style. I have argued that, prior to the latter years of the eighteenth century, the idea of late writing as we understand it now did not exist, that it was invented as a by-product of the emergence of the Romantic idea of individual stylistic development and thus of the newly reconstructed direct relationship between life and work. Neither Steevens nor Malone would have recognised as anything other than fanciful Dowden's account of late Shakespearean serenity. Still less could Shakespeare himself have had in mind anything approximating the concept of late style as it later emerged: the idea, bluntly, postdates him by nearly two centuries. To state this is not, however, to claim either that early modern culture attached no significance to last things or to the endings of lives, or that early modern playwrights were unconscious of the shapes that a life, and particularly a writing life, might take. Nor is it to claim that the seeds of the Romantic development of the idea of the progress of the creative individual cannot be found in earlier times. On the contrary, I would argue that subsequent ideas of lateness deriving from German Romantic philosophy fell onto fertile English soil – quite specifically so, as we have seen, in the case of the soil of Stratford-upon-Avon – and, while it is important to emphasise that a concept of late style as it was eventually formulated by Dowden was simply unavailable to Shakespeare and his contemporaries, it is equally important to be aware both of the associations that old age and the proximity of death are likely to have had for him and of the limits of those associations as the premise for a late creative flowering – for, that is, a 'late style'.

Underlying biographers' and critics' treatment of the late plays lies a spectacularly, indeed wilfully, naïve but also entirely unspoken question – did Shakespeare know he was having a late phase? – to which I will try to respond in this chapter. My answer is, as you will have come to expect by now, no. But this is a qualified no, because although I argue that the conditions for early modern playwriting were such that the subjectivism that informs the question – the assumption that art is an expression of self – is asymmetrical both to the possible understandings of artistic productivity available in the early modern period and to the modes of production for early modern theatre – that is, it is both anachronistic and practically inappropriate – I would acknowledge nonetheless that the seeds of the idea of late style (or at least of an idea of late selfhood) can be found in early seventeenth-century English culture and that Shakespeare would thus have had a strong sense both of the possibilities available for the narrative structuring of a life, and especially of a creative life, and of the particular importance of the endings of lives to that structuring process. That this does not add up to an idea of late writing in the modern sense does not mean it can be ignored in a history of lateness.

4.1 PREMODERN ENDINGS

One celebrated account of the impact of the proximity of death on an early modern creative life offers an instructively contradictory blend of fear and hope. Fretting about the grim prospect of his latter days, Michel de Montaigne cites Horace's prayer to Apollo in order to express the hope that, while the physical decline attendant upon old age might be inevitable, its mental counterpart might not necessarily follow:

> *frui paratis et valido mihi,*
> *Latoe, dones, et, precor, integra*
> *cum mente, nec turpem senectam*
> *degere nec cithara carentem.*

Grant, o son of Latona, that I may enjoy what I possess – in good health, I pray you, and with full mental vigour; and may I have an old age that is not lacking in dignity or bereft of music.[3]

Montaigne, like his Roman model, seeks an ending commensurate with the economy of his life, one of creative accumulation, and he fears the merciless erasure of his imaginative powers that senility would entail. As a bulwark against this, he offers his own lifelong mental discipline, expressing a sense of increasing intensity in the experience of being alive:

To enjoy life requires some husbandry. I enjoy it twice as much as others, since the measure of our joy depends on the greater or lesser degree of our attachment to it. Above all now, when I see my span so short, I want to give it more ballast; I want to arrest the swiftness of its passing by the swiftness of my capture, compensating for the speed with which it drains away by the intensity of my enjoyment. The shorter my lease of it, the deeper and fuller I must make it.[4]

As death draws near, so Montaigne's appreciation of the experience of being alive increases and the last years of life take on a certain pitch and intensity. He has husbanded his resources and hopes now to reap the benefit in a keenly felt conclusion to an active intellectual life. At the same time, his sense of the value of the passing of the years in the depth of engagement that marks the last phase of life is offset by the far less comfortable prospect he draws from his classical source, that of 'squalid senility'.

This fear of a final decline is not especially surprising. Montaigne and his contemporaries inherited a classical perception of old age that was ambivalent at best and frequently downright negative about the prospects for the elderly. The Greeks had little regard for old age and would have considered a resurgence of creative energy at the end of life highly improbable. As Emily Wilson has observed, they even had a myth of old age, one that Montaigne probably knew – the story of Eos and Tithonos, in which the immortal Eos asks for eternal life for the mortal she desires but forgets to ask also for eternal youth and is forced to watch her lover fade into horrific shrivelled senility – to underline the horrors of what she calls 'overliving', that is, living beyond the time in which one's being alive has demonstrable value.[5] Perhaps the best-known figure of old age in Greek drama is the ancient protagonist of Sophocles' *Oedipus at Colonus* – a play written in the dramatist's own old age and treated by certain critics (David Grene, for one) as an early instance of late style – in which the Chorus consists of a group of old men who reflect bitterly on their longevity:

> For the long days hold in store
> many things to steer us nearer to pain
> and it's in vain we look for pleasure
> in a life spun out past its given span . . . .
>
> . . . And in the end
> [a man's] lot is to lack all power:
> despised and cast out in friendless old age
> where a man lives with nothing
> but one hardship topping another.[6]

There were alternatives to this depressing view of the effects of ageing such as Cephalus' opinion in Plato's *Republic* that '[f]or those who are civilised and contented, then even old age is only a slight burden'; but, for the most part, old age appeared to the Greeks a marginal and often grotesque parody of life, offering at best a tangibly diminished role to the old.[7]

The Romans offered Montaigne little more encouragement. 'Old age did not automatically marginalise an individual', Karen Cokayne argues, but '[r]espect for old age had to be earned': '[a]n old person could have status, authority and reverence, as long as societal expectations about how life should be lived were fulfilled'.[8] Due to the limitations of the evidence – it is only, as Cokayne notes, 'the Roman upper classes, and mainly men, about whom we have hard evidence' (*Experiencing*, 173) – we cannot know, finally, how the Romans treated the old in everyday life but it is clear, for instance, that the *paterfamilias*, the head of the family, retained a certain authority into old age, though that authority declined as the Empire itself grew old. Still, it was a Roman writer, Cicero, who produced the first apologia for old age, the *De Senectute*, in which the ageing Cato sets out to demonstrate that a vigorous, mentally alert old age is possible, given appropriate diet and mental activity, arguing that the mental faculties do not necessarily fade with age, that the last years of a person's life can be some of the busiest and that in such cases old people never really need notice that they are growing old – and, even if they do, one of the joys of old age is the calming of the passions that drive younger people into error. Plutarch, a Greek in a Roman world, writing more than a century after Cicero in his own old age, developed this argument, addressing in particular the assumption that old people must not be involved in politics; on the contrary, an experienced older member of society had a *duty* to be politically active. The point, for Plutarch, was, in Tim Parkin's words, that 'one must continue one's lifelong good habits in old age and not suddenly try to start from scratch when it is too late'.[9] The downside of this was 'that in the absence of wage labor as the standard way of life and of a retirement age in general life, people were expected simply to go on doing what they had always done until they dropped' (Parkin, *Experience*, 276); the upside that age and experience provide the reason, judgement, bluntness, clarity of mind and common sense necessary for the maintenance of a good polity.

The arguments of Cicero and Plutarch are, though, by no means typical of the literary representation of the latter years of life in the late Republic and early Empire: both are responding to the far more common negative images of the old that characterised both periods.[10] Most obviously, the stock figure of the Senex in New Comedy offers a consistently negative image, as do the portrayals of the old in the satires of Juvenal, say, and Ovid's grim equation of old age and exile, his last years characterised by depression and fear of illness or violence on Tomis, suggests that the last years of a life can involve the loss of much that made that life worthwhile. Exile apart, Roman medicine offers a straightforward logic for this, since old age was understood to be dry and cold, a dessicated version of the healthy mature state when the body's constituent fluids were in balance. Life begins, with the embryo, in moisture and the process of physical maturing is, basically, a drying process that continues until death. The inexorability of this process offered little prospect of the acceleration of intensity in the experience of life that is projected optimistically yet nervously by Montaigne.

The principal premodern way to understand the shape of a life and thus the shape of the end of that life was through the idea of the 'ages of man'. Cicero offers a basic pattern that treats the phases of life as characterised, like the seasons of the year, in certain fixed ways:

Cursus est certus aetatis et una via naturae eaque simplex, suaque cuique parti aetatis tempestivitas est data.

Life's racecourse is fixed; Nature has only a single path and that path is run but once, and to each stage of existence has been allotted its own appropriate quality.[11]

This appears straightforward enough, but as J. A. Burrow has shown, the trope of the ages of man, as it developed from the classical to the early modern, increased in complexity, with a number of different and contradictory systems in competition at any given point in the course of several centuries.[12] Early modern English commentators such as Thomas Fortescue and Henry Cuffe summarise the various options, beginning with a simple three-phase life of youth, maturity and old age, which Cuffe attributes to Aristotle and which still has a certain currency in descriptions of late work as the product of the 'third period':

Aristotle setteth downe onely three distinct ages, *child-hood, flourishing man-age*, and *old-age*; the first plentifully abounding with heat and moisture; the middle age hauing the same two qualities of life, aswell tempered as their nature possibly can be; old age declining and swaruing from that good and moderate temper, and by little and little decaying in both these qualities, till at length they be both of them consumed.[13]

From this simple Aristotelian model emerged a range of increasingly complex patterns, comprising four, six, seven, ten or twelve phases and based on the seasons or the months of the year or the days of God's creation. Among English writers, two of these schemes, the four-part and seven-part options, predominate. But whichever model is chosen, the last period of life is invariably characterised by a visible decline of powers.

For Cuffe, the standard pattern, a physiological model which draws on the body's constituent humours and offers a different understanding of the nature of old age from the Roman drying process, is based on four, rather than three, phases. According to this scheme, originally outlined by Bede, the four ages of man are childhood, youth, maturity and old age.[14]

Childhood is moist and hot, associated with the spring, with blood in the scheme of humours and with the element air; youth is hot and dry, associated with summer, red choler, and with fire; maturity is dry and cold, associated with autumn, black choler and earth; and finally old age is cold and moist, associated with winter, phlegm and water. This offers a remarkably complete and compact scheme of correspondences which allows for variation within each phase – so that the balance of humours within one, for instance, varies with context, time of day or time of year and that a given individual has an orientation more towards one particular humour than to the others – but still retains a satisfying sense of the interconnectedness of creation at each level.[15] This pattern crossed cultural boundaries with ease. Graeco-Arabic medical treatises, for instance, share Bede's four-part structure but offer a different logic for division, as outlined by Avicenna (Ibn Síná):

There are four ages altogether: the age of growth, called the green age, which lasts up to twenty-five; the age of firmness or vigour, which is called youthful and flowering, lasting up to thirty-five or forty; then the age of diminution, when the time of vigour has gone by, but solid strength has not yet been lost, which is called the stooping or elderly age, which lasts until about sixty; then the age of decline, with an obvious loss of strength, which is called the falling, or decrepit age, and lasts up to the end of life.[16]

Here, there is an additional period which postdates old age, but it is a phase of severe decline which ends in death and to which no positive attributes attach.

Where medical writers spoke of four ages, astrologers showed a marked preference for a pattern of seven phases, periods of life that correspond to the seven planets of the solar system and to the particular influences attributed to those planets. Thus, for instance, infancy, the first four years of life, is made changeable by the Moon, whereas manhood (the fifth age, from forty-one to fifty-six) is controlled by Mars, who introduces cares and troubles and makes the mature person begin to be aware of the passing of time. Later manhood, a twelve-year period of thoughtfulness, decorum and renunciation, the sixth age, is influenced by Jupiter and witnesses a general slowing down of the faculties; while the seventh period is old age, which extends from the age of sixty-eight, is governed by Saturn and is characterised by a cooling off and a slowing down and a general decline of faculties. The persistence of this planetary scheme in early modern England is apparent both in Fortescue and in Cuffe – whose version ends with a dual phase of decline, 'old age' and 'crooked age' – and is described with particular verve by Ralegh in his *History of the World*:

[O]ur Infancie is compared to the *Moone*, in which wee seeme onely to live and grow, as Plants; the second age to *Mercurie*, wherein wee are taught and instructed; our third age to *Venus*, the dayes of Love, Desire, and Vanitie; the fourth to the *Sunne*, the strong, flourishing, and beautifull age of mans life; the fifth to *Mars*, in which we seeke honour and victorie, and in which our thoughts travaile to ambitious ends; the sixth age is ascribed to *Iupiter*, in which we beginne to take accompt of our times, iudge of our selves, and grow to the perfection of our understanding; the last and seventh to *Saturne*, wherein our dayes are sad and overcast, and in which we find by deare and lamentable experience, & by the losse which can never be repaired, that of all our vaine passions and affections past, the sorrow only abideth: Our attendants are sicknesses, and variable infirmities, and by how much the more wee are accompanied with plentie, by so much the more greedily is our end desired, whom when *Time* hath made unsociable to others, we become a burthen to our selves: being of no other use, then to hold the riches we have, from our Successors.[17]

This preference for a seven-phase scheme is of course apparent in the best-known of all such descriptions, Jaques's Ages of Man speech in *As You Like It*, an account which, though slightly off-beam in places – Jaques characteristically stresses the negative and depressing aspects of each age, omitting the 'flourishing and beautiful' age governed by the Sun – is nonetheless clearly dependent upon the standard astrological scheme. 'All the world's a stage', he proclaims,

> And all the men and women merely players.
> They have their exits and their entrances,
> And one man in his time plays many parts,
> His acts being seven ages. At first the infant,
> Mewling and puking in the nurse's arms.
> Then the whining schoolboy with his satchel
> And shining morning face, creeping like a snail
> Unwillingly to school. And then the lover,
> Sighing like furnace, with a woeful ballad
> Made to his mistress' eyebrow. Then, a soldier,
> Full of strange oaths, and bearded like the pard,
> Jealous in honour, sudden, and quick in quarrel,
> Seeking the bubble reputation
> Even in the cannon's mouth. And then the justice,
> In fair round belly with good capon lined,
> With eyes severe and beard of formal cut,
> Full of wise saws and modern instances;
> And so he plays his part. The sixth age shifts
> Into the lean and slippered pantaloon,
> With spectacles on nose and pouch on side,
> His youthful hose, well saved, a world too wide

> For his shrunk shank, and his big, manly voice,
> Turning again toward childish treble, pipes
> And whistles in his sound. Last scene of all,
> That ends this strange, eventful history,
> Is second childishness and mere oblivion,
> Sans teeth, sans eyes, sans taste, sans everything.
>
> (*As You Like It*, 2.7.139–65)

Jaques's deliberate omission of the strongest period, the age controlled by the Sun – which in the standard scheme is the fourth age, characterised by seriousness and control – means that he has to make up the numbers by joining Cuffe in splitting the seventh age into two – old age and complete decrepitude – neither of which offers anything more positive than decline until death.

That Cuffe, writing in 1607, and Ralegh, in 1614, happen to book-end the period of Shakespeare's late plays serves to reinforce the currency of the Ages of Man trope for the understanding of human life in general (and in particular of the end of the life). Although a certain amount of respect attached to considerable old age in Jacobean England, no particular privilege was accorded to works produced in old age – 'There is', Keith Thomas noted in his British Academy lecture on age and authority, 'no reason to look back wistfully at the aged in this period' – and we have no sense of the last years of life as marking a period of serene reflection or of the dispensation of wisdom accumulated from a lifetime of experience.[18] Old age offers a return to the early, but only in the negative sense of 'second childishness and mere oblivion' without rational faculties, never of any kind of positive rejuvenation. Dogberry's telling proverbial mis-citing – 'When the age' (he means 'ale') 'is in, the wit is out' – makes this clear enough, playing, as it does, on the interchangeability of old age and alcohol as fuddlers of the brain. There is little, if any, sense, then, in either the classical inheritance or the early modern understanding of the last years of life – at least, that is, of the last years of life defined specifically as old age – of the likelihood of a late resurgence, of an unexpected return of powers at the last.

Old age was not, though, the only basis on which to imagine the ending of a career or of a life. Montaigne's citing of Horace serves as a timely reminder that early modern projections of selfhood – and in particular of artistic selfhood – were always rhetorical, always dependent in complex, self-conscious ways on the classical inheritance. If the construct we know as the 'ages of man' remains asymmetrical to the eventual prescription of the discourse of lateness, then so too do the available patterns for the construction of the life of the 'maker', the poetic *cursus*. As Richard Helgerson argues in *Self-Crowned Laureates*, early modern poets drew on a range of classical models in order to establish a sense of the writerly life, the most celebrated of which is the *rota Virgilii*, the model of the creative life that prescribes a linear three-genre pattern – pastoral, georgic, epic – and is exemplified in the career of the author of the *Eclogues, Georgics* and *Aeneid*. Each of these generic stages has its accompanying ideology and reflects both stylistic and social mobility, culminating in the high style of epic and its ancient associations with ruler and nation. The Virgilian *cursus* is a political cycle, 'an intricately stylized imitation of [... the] mind's re-engagement in the life of the time – in short, of its rallying to the régime'.[19] Available alternatives included Horatian and Ovidian models, offering very different endings from the triumphant conclusion represented by Virgilian epic, with Ovid writing, as I have noted, for the last period of his life in exile and Horace in retirement. But the Virgilian model was the dominant one, as it had been for the Romans; it was also the easiest to replicate in being the most willed, the least contingent, the most available for personal appropriation.

The three early modern writers most clearly associated with the self-conscious structuring of their careers on classical lines are Spenser, Jonson and Milton. Helgerson demonstrates the intensity of their personal projects: 'the ambition not only to write great poems but also to fill the role of the great poet', he argues, 'shaped everything these men wrote', noting that in the process of 'presenting poems, masques, plays, and pamphlets' as evidence of their pursuit of an established model, 'they were always presenting themselves'.[20] Spenser's appropriation of Virgil has primacy: every other attempt to adapt the model involved a response of some kind to this originary Elizabethan self-fashioning. Jonson's turn to Horace was a conscious distancing of his own career from Spenser's overtly Protestant appropriation of the *cursus* – though, as Helgerson points out, 'what we notice most' about Jonson's self-assocation with Horace 'is the poor fit' (*Self-Crowned*, 103) – and Milton's announcement, while still an undergraduate, of his lifelong project – the echoing of Demodocus (that is, of Homer) – was a consciously recuperative Spenserian gesture in a very different political context. In any case, appropriations of these classical models, even at their most self-conscious, rarely matched the original requirements as neatly as their appropriators liked to imply. Generally, the early modern version of the *cursus* adopts elements of more than one of the available classical options, producing a conscious hybrid which also takes into account intermediary figures such as Petrarch. As Helgerson notes, early modern poets – those seeking laureate status, at least – worked 'in opposition to a set of contemporary expectations [...] similar enough to those against which Virgil and Petrarch presented themselves to make those earlier poets usable, but different enough to alter significantly the resulting pattern' (ibid., 26). The point remains, however, that, while both the models themselves and the ways in which they were appropriated varied, the shared feature is the construction of a poetic selfhood on the basis of the constructed poetic selfhood of another.

None of these models, however, despite their obvious rhetorical potential, appears to offer a platform for the future development of the idea of late style. For one thing, the classical understanding of the successful poetic career as a generic development from apprentice forms to mature creative triumph offers at best an awkward correspondence with the actual life-cycle of the poet. The *rota Virgilii* has an implicit human timeframe in that it requires a certain number of years of poetic experience to achieve the move from pastoral to epic; but the culmination of this version of the *cursus*, the completion of the epic, does not coincide with the end of the life but rather with the central life-phase, the period of maturity that precedes decline, a decline which it may in fact induce. Laurence Lipking cites Samuel Johnson's assertion that, '[b]y the general consent of criticks, the first praise of genius is due to the writer of an epick poem, as it requires an assemblage of all the powers which are singly sufficient for other compositions', noting that part of the logic of epic's prestige and its place as the climactic genre is its role in 'challeng[ing] the poet to sing, to plot, to stretch, to suffer; it drains him of all his abilities'.[21] Epic is the ultimate genre and requires the ultimate poetic sacrifice. This offers an explanation for the absence of a postepic genre in the Virgilian model: in writing the epic, it would seem, the poet has used up his creative powers and, whether or not he has the strength left to live on into old age, there is no subsequent, supplementary genre in the classical prescription to match the decline into the vale of years.

There is, in any case, a fundamental mismatch between these classical conceptions of the poetic career and the subjectivist idea of late style as it would subsequently emerge, since the classical prescription projects a *generic*, not a *personal*, path through the writing life. Permanent status as a significant writer would be given to those successfully completing the generic journey: there is no direct relation between the traversing of that path and the progress (in age or emotional development) of the individual life other than a need to store up the requisite poetic experience. The Virgilian model, in other words, makes no attempt to match the *cursus* the poet must follow to the conditions and progress of his actual life: it is, finally, the product of a form of nationalist rhetoric, not of incipient biography. The subjectivism upon which late style is premised – the emergence from within the creative artist of the particular creativity that receives its endorsement in the late resurgence – is a product, as I have argued, of Romantic ideas of style as the outward manifestation of inner development that would have been wholly incomprehensible to an early modern writer straining either to conform to a fixed, external model or to appropriate that model for a particular set of social and political contingencies. A telling by-product of the sheer strength of will shaping the careers of Spenser, Jonson and Milton along classical lines and of the pre- (or, better, over-) determined nature of the *cursus* projected by each is their persistent subsequent exclusion from the ranks of those to whom late styles have been comfortably ascribed.

4.2 THE SHAKESPEAREAN SWAN SONG

The extent to which Shakespeare himself could have had such a sense of the shape of his career is a matter for current debate. There has been a good deal of work in the last few years, including notably Lukas Erne's *Shakespeare as Literary Dramatist*, arguing for Shakespeare's self-conscious literariness, his deliberate involvement in the print process, as a counterweight to the prevalent view that he was an essentially theatrical figure uninterested in literary immortality. Erne's is, however, only one contribution – though a distinctive and significant one – to a process that has been under way for a while. Patrick Cheney, for instance, has for some time proclaimed the thoroughness of the early modern engagement, theatrical as well as poetic, with classical ideas of the career and undoubtedly he is right to do so. To presume, in the teeth of the levels of intertextual awareness that in so many other ways we expect as the norm in the plays of Shakespeare and his contemporaries, that this particular aspect of the classical literary inheritance would simply have passed the playwrights by would appear a wilful evasion of troublesome evidence.[22] As Cheney has shown, not only poets such as Spenser, conscious of their inherited role, but also certain early modern playwrights show distinct signs of an awareness of the available patterns for the writerly life. The list of playwrights who were also poets with pretensions to laureateship is substantial: not only Jonson but also Marlowe, Chapman, Daniel, Drayton and – Cheney argues – Shakespeare. In *Marlowe's Counterfeit Profession*, he demonstrates powerfully that the Romantic assumptions typically made about Marlowe's career – his brilliance defined as reckless, spontaneous, opportunistic, and his premature death implicitly deployed to align him with the later figures of Keats and Shelley – elide the underpinnings of his abbreviated life in received models of the artistic career and thus the particular self-consciousness of his construction of a form of early modern authorship. For Cheney, Marlowe structured his poetic and dramatic output alike in full awareness of the available models, setting himself up quite elaborately as a rival to Spenser, the self-proclaimed poet of English nationhood, and forging a new version of the poetic *cursus* which incorporates dramatic as well as poetic genres. Marlowe, Cheney tells us, 'manages a complex, multigenre idea of a literary career, in direct professional rivalry with England's great national poet, in order to pen a poetics of counter-nationhood' (Cheney, *Marlowe*, 4). Whether this fully addresses Marlowe's function specifically as a *playwright* is perhaps less clear than its strength as an analysis of his self-consciousness as a poet, but this is an issue to which I will return.

In arguing his case, Cheney was responding to and developing the thesis of Helgerson in *Self-Crowned Laureates*, for whom Shakespeare, along with Dekker and Kyd (and, by implication, Heywood, Fletcher, Webster and others), is an exemplar of a third category of writer – neither the would-be laureates who set out to construct a national career on the model of Virgil and his emulators nor the self-consciously amateur poets who modelled themselves on Ovid and his successor Petrarch but rather 'the writers who made their living from the public theater' (*Laureates*, 5), the professional playwrights. These men were aware of the various models for the poetic life but were not in a position directly to engage with them even if they wished to (which is not by any means clear), both because of the responsive nature of the commercial writing they undertook for the acting companies and because they simply did not regard their work for the stage as the equivalent of poetry in the way that Spenser would have understood the term. At the time of his Marlowe book, Cheney appeared still to accept that Shakespeare's chronology does not yield to this kind of analysis; his recent book on the Shakespearean career, however, makes it clear that he was never comfortable with that exclusion. He sets out, by contrast with Helgerson, to demonstrate Shakespeare's self-conscious construction of his *œuvre* not as a mere 'professional' but as 'national poet-playwright' and so to confirm once and for all – implicitly rejecting the Foucauldian analysis of authorship as only one in a range of options for giving order to texts (and thus, in effect, such subsequent developments in criticism of early modern theatre as repertory studies) – that Shakespeare is an *author*, not simply a playwright, offering a kind of synthesis of the Ovidian

Marlowe and Virgilian Spenser he mapped in his two previous monographs and thus a Shakespeare who 'plots his Ovidian narrative [...] in a Virgilian landscape' (Cheney, *Shakespeare*, 245). '[W]hat finally emerges from the canon of plays and poems', Cheney argues, 'is Shakespearean authorship itself', which he defines as 'a literary voice of national authority, a form of national language' (ibid., 47), with a function equally as political, it would seem – for all that it is cut with its Ovidian alternative – as that of the Virgilian *cursus*.

It seems odd, though, in view of the resistance to Romanticism that motivated his spirited dismissal of the received idea of Marlovian 'spontaneity', that Cheney should choose now to read Shakespeare's career in this way, not least because the four-phase pattern he maps for Shakespeare's life appears to bear the genetic stamp not only of the classical models he cites but also, belatedly, of that of early constructions of lateness – not so much those of Ulrici or Dowden, perhaps, as of the early nineteenth-century biographies of composers which we noted as some of the earliest manifestations of the incipient idea of late style. The life, in Cheney's model, consists of three major phases and a supplement, each deriving from the chronology of the printing of Shakespeare's *poetry*, rather than his plays, and each building up a profile for Shakespeare as a self-conscious 'poet-playwright' – that is, a poet first and a playwright second. There is a brief apprentice phase, 1593–4, the period of publication of *Venus and Adonis* and *The Rape of Lucrece*, running, in terms of the dramatic output, from *The Two Gentleman of Verona* to *Richard III*, in which Shakespeare presents himself to the world and sets out to 'overgo' his rival Marlowe in the three key genres of comedy, history and tragedy. There is then a consolidation phase at 'the mid-point of Shakespeare's professional career', 1594–1601, marked by the publication of *The Passionate Pilgrim* and 'The Phoenix and the Turtle', a period that in terms of the theatrical chronology runs from *Love's Labour's Lost* to *Troilus and Cressida* and in which, far from 'abandon[ing] poetry in favor of theatre', Shakespeare in fact 'intensifies their conjunction' (Cheney, *Shakespeare*, 145) in order to forge for the theatre a conscious synthesis of Virgilian and Ovidian poetics. The third and central phase, which runs from *Sir Thomas More* to *Coriolanus* and culminates in 1609, the year of publication both of *Shakespeare's Sonnets* and of *Troilus and Cressida*, represents for Cheney both a further development of Shakespeare's Ovidian career-model and a gradual foregrounding of the poetic over the dramatic. Following this, the fourth and final phase is necessarily supplementary because no more of Shakespeare's poems appeared in his lifetime and thus the logic of Cheney's schema – to ground the progress of the theatre professional in the publication of the work of the poet-author – lacks the requisite base in published poetry. This last period and the critic's reading thus both take on the form of an afterthought, the last fifteen pages of a 283-page book, a brief and somewhat enigmatic epilogue matched to a career-phase read as an extension of established achievements in the poeticising of theatre. Having elided the generic problem presented by the late plays by praising the author's 'constancy' in working in 'the three dramatic forms advertised on the Folio title page', Cheney closes his book by seeking in those plays versions of the figure of the author – notably Autolycus and, inevitably, Prospero – concluding not entirely surprisingly (despite his earlier acknowledgement of the place in the canon of the three collaborative plays that postdate *The Tempest*) with a peroration equating Shakespeare and Prospero as the latter 'releases the art of poetry into the theatre' (ibid., 271, 283). Despite his ready acknowledgement of the post-*Tempest* plays, then, Cheney foregrounds the final and essential conjunction of Prospero and Shakespeare as poets, as self-conscious shapers of their own destiny, suggesting that underlying the contextually prior models for the career, the Ovidian and the Virgilian, which he regards as the basis for the Shakespearean *cursus* is the subsequent idea of late writing, the late turn to the aesthetic which is both a return to early engagements and a glance forward to posterity – that, in other words, there is a later formulation undercutting the impact of those available to Shakespeare's contemporaries.

Cheney's simultaneous awareness of and discomfort with this alignment appears both in his decision, because of the premise in printing history of his argument and thus of the significance of 1609, to exclude *Pericles* from the final Shakespearean phase and thus to break up the usual 'late play' grouping and in the fact that, despite citing Dowden in the context of a discussion of *The Passionate Pilgrim* earlier in the book, he makes no mention in his final chapter of the subjectivist tradition of reading the 'late romances' as both supplementary and climactic. It also appears in his deployment of Katherine Duncan-Jones's argument, in *Ungentle Shakespeare*, that *Troilus and Cressida* and *Shakespeare's Sonnets* are equally 'deeply rooted in an awareness of death, and of the desperate struggle to make one's voice heard before disease destroys both pen and phallus' – or, rather, it appears in the distance he places between his own reading and Duncan-Jones's implication that the publication date, if not the date of composition, makes both play and sonnet-sequence into late work (Duncan-Jones, *Ungentle*, 219). Cheney nonetheless applies the word 'late' to the 1609 poetry and in particular to *A Lover's Complaint*, thus creating further problems for the beleaguered chronology of Shakespearean lateness, as I suggested in Chapter 2, by introducing the poetry (at least the poetry in its published form) into the late-period mix. For Cheney, 'Shakespeare's combined engagement with the works of Spenser and Marlowe in a narrative poem late in his career helps us to redraw our profile of the world's most famed man of the theatre' (Cheney, *Shakespeare*, 264), since '[w]ithin a few years of retirement' Shakespeare 'is working vigorously to reconcile the Virgilian poetry of Spenser with the Ovidian poetry and theatre of Marlowe' (ibid.). 'Reconciliation' now quietly emerges as a key term for the final period. The 1609 volume, Cheney argues, is 'more than simply an isolated publication gotten up during yet another closing of the theatres'; rather, it may be, he suggests,

an announcement for a distinct phase of the career – a late version of the kind of announcement he had made in his prose dedication to *Venus* and *Lucrece* as when (most famously) he promises Southampton that after his 'idle houres' spent in writing *Venus* he will go on to pen 'some graver labour' (*Shakespeare*, 265) –

an announcement marking, that is, 'a supreme art of [. . .] reconciliation' (ibid., 266). Cheney seems here to be both reaching towards and drawing back from the Romantic model of lateness – the latter for the understandable reason that the classical career, generically, impersonally structured as it is, offers a very poor fit with the subjectivism essential to ideas of lateness. This drawing back is arguably inevitable, however, not only because of the awkwardness of the date of publication for the *Sonnets* and *A Lover's Complaint* and thus the inconvenient caesura they form half-way through the timeframe for the late plays, but also because of the considerable resistance of the Shakespearean canon as we know it to any assimilation to the Virgilian model. It is, after all, obvious that major generic elisions would be required in order to argue for a Shakespearean version of the Virgilian *rota*. *The Aeneid* may be a significant source for *The Tempest* (offering a conjunction of latenesses undoubtedly worth exploring) and *The Two Noble Kinsmen* may depend upon Chaucer's *Knight's Tale*, but it would be extremely difficult for a critic to claim that the late plays are a form of epic theatre. Not only is there the immediate and obvious problem of their pastoral tendency – of Shakespeare's concluding his playwriting life, in other words, with the genre associated in the Virgilian model with poetic *beginnings*, not *endings* – but the absence of a sense of authorial coherence in these plays as a group in any case makes life highly frustrating, as we have seen in Chapter 2, for any critic wishing to offer a linear model of Shakespearean authorship with a clearcut conclusion. Cheney accepts that, of the four phases of the Shakespearean career he maps, the last is 'perhaps the least stable [since] one of the six plays is lost and two of the others are collaborations, leaving only three thought to be fully by Shakespeare' (*Shakespeare*, 271). The difficulty this causes him – the impossibility of aligning poetic self-consciousness with collaborative theatrical practice – is apparent not simply in the fact that he discusses this final phase only in a brief epilogue but also because, despite his urge to ground his understanding of Shakespeare's poetic career in contextually appropriate ways, he omits entirely one possible model for the poetic career which he himself mapped with distinction over a decade earlier – that of Spenser himself.

As critics have long observed, despite his Virgilian self-fashioning, Spenser's career does not culminate in epic but rather incorporates a postepic phase, producing a pattern for the poetic life that Isabel MacCaffrey christened the 'formula of out-and-back'.[23] McCaffrey, Paul Alpers and others have read Spenser's later career as a wilful reshaping of the Virgilian model, noting that though Spenser may be the early modern poet most clearly and consciously dependent upon that model – beginning deliberately with pastoral in *The Shepheardes Calender* and going on to forge a national epic in *The Faerie Queene* – he in fact continues to write, against Virgilian logic, in the wake of that epic and his subsequent works, including the 'Mutabilitie Cantos', *Colin Clouts Come Home Againe*, the *Amoretti*, *Epithalamion*, *Fowre Hymnes* and the *Prothalamion*, appear to mark a shift back from epic to a more inward poetry, a 'poetry of private reform'.[24] This has tended to be read as a failure on the poet's part to achieve the aims of his career, a breakdown in the poetic programme caused by his disillusionment with courtly life. For Cheney, however, the post-*Faerie Queene* work represents something quite other than failure. On the contrary, he argues, Spenser deliberately turned to a new model – a Christian model, that is, which redraws and, in its own terms, redeems the classical inheritance – for the close of his career. '[W]e can best explain Spenser's turn from courtly to contemplative poetry in the mid-1590s', argues Cheney, 'not merely in terms of the Elizabethan model of amateur and laureate, but also in terms of the Renaissance model of the divine poet' (*Spenser*, 223–4), the model in question being not Virgil or Ovid, but Augustine.

Augustine's achievement was to negotiate between the requirements of, on the one hand, the Roman career and, on the other, of Christian salvation, replacing the former with the latter but structuring the latter to a certain extent on the pattern of the former, seeking (and thus concluding with) not the earthly fame sought by the Roman careerist but the spiritual fulfilment achieved by the Christian. 'For the *cursus honorum* of the Roman civil service', argues Leo Braudy, Augustine 'substitutes a course of Christian development', partly on the basis of his own experience of running the two paths – the outward, official and secular and the inward, private and spiritual – in parallel for a decade or so of his own life.[25] Cheney argues that Spenser's achievement post-*Faerie Queene* is the 'Christianiz[ing of] the Virgilian Wheel in light of St Augustine and his late-medieval and Renaissance heirs, especially Dante and Du Bartas' (*Spenser*, 34), noting Augustine's particular urge to redeem the classical teleology of epic by emphasising 'the poet's need to end [his] career by turning [. . .] to aged, contemplative, divine poetry' (ibid., 5). For Cheney, the *Fowre Hymnes* in particular mark a reinvention by Spenser of the Virgilian *rota* through the insertion, as he puts it, of a 'final spoke' (ibid., 193). Spenser, having begun with pastoral, makes a conscious decision not to end with epic; rather, he ends deliberately with a volume of divine poetry, thereby for Cheney merging into a single *telos* the *cursi* of Virgil and Augustine, classical fame and Christian salvation, the earthly glory of the Roman poet and the heavenly redemption of the Christian soul. Spenser in this late work thus offers a 'careful imping of the Augustinian career model of Du Bartas (the later turn from courtly to divine poetry) onto the Renaissance version of the Virgilian model popularized by Petrarch (the progression of pastoral, epic and love lyric)' (ibid., 199). Turning in conclusion to *Prothalamion*, Cheney argues – against Helgerson and others, for whom it is a withdrawal, a sign of Spenser's closing disillusionment – that the poem marks a positive ending which involves a turn back to the early, showing Spenser 'at the end of his career engaging precisely in his earlier ideology' (ibid., 227) – in other words, though Cheney never specifies or addresses the discourse or its history, something that sounds a good deal like a classic late gesture. He reads *Prothalamion* in this vein not merely as a defence 'of a past career' but as a 'prophe[cy of] a future career', noting that 'the key to this reading lies in Spenser's management' of a particular symbol of poetic achievement – that of the swan song (ibid., 228).

'The silver swanne doth sing before her dying day / As shee that feeles the deepe delight that is in death', E. K. tells us in the gloss to the *October* eclogue of *The Shepheardes Calender*, lines that he claims are themselves a Spenserian fragment.[26] For Cheney, Spenser's manipulation of the image of the swan – the well-known vision of 'two Swannes of goodly hewe,/[. . .] softly swimming downe along the Lee' – fashions his poem not as a renunciation but as a reaffirmation of his poetic 'flight', a final achievement which, by turning back to the past, offers a glimpse of a time yet to come. Given the potential this image appears to have as an analogue for late Shakespeare, it is very noticeable that Cheney does not try to extend the Augustinian model, as he does with the Ovidian and the Virgilian, from Spenser to Shakespeare – not least, presumably, because of the unhelpful ease with which such a concluding spiritual phase would resolve into the exclusively play-focussed model offered by Ulrici, Dowden and their successors. Moreover, not only does the pastoral mode of the late plays present, as we have seen, a severe obstacle to the imposition of even a Christianised version of the Virgilian *rota* onto the Shakespearean career, but the premises in both Protestantism and politics of the Spenserian model also offer an uncomfortable mismatch for Shakespeare, who is not exactly renowned for his commitment either to Protestantism or to militant politics, least of all in his last plays. Tempting though it must have been, then, to make a move, through Spenser, away from a classical to an early Christian model for the relationship of the late plays to Shakespeare's prior achievement, offering in the process a logic for a reflective sequence following the major tragedies embodying the green space of a Stratford retirement, Cheney commendably refuses to do anything of the sort.

The introduction of Augustine into the question of the shape of the early modern life holds a particular interest nonetheless for the historian of late style, since, as Cheney's deployment of the language of lateness in respect of Spenser suggests, if there is a single early modern model for the career that is most aligned with subsequent ideas of late writing – and particularly with constructions of Shakespearean lateness – it is the Augustinian reorientation of the classical *cursus*, the shift he makes away from the political and poetical to the spiritual. It could in fact be argued that in the Augustinian *rota* lie the earliest seeds of the idea of the late phase. As David Aers pointed out in his timely attack on the apparent assumption of many early modernists that individual selfhood began with *Hamlet*, '[t]he place to which anyone seeking to write a history of interiority and the subject must return is St Augustine's *Confessions*', and he cites as support Charles Taylor's claim that it was Augustine 'who introduced the inwardness of radical reflexivity and bequeathed it to the Western tradition'.[27] At the same time, Augustine offered a pattern both of history and of human lives – his Christian reworking of the Ages of Man – that at first glance leaves little scope for what we would recognise as selfhood. His scheme offered six phases for the life on the pattern of the days of the week, that is, the six days of creation, with the sabbath representing the afterlife. This division is perhaps best described by way of a passage cited by Burrow from the eleventh-century encyclopaedia *Elementarium Doctrinae Rudimentum* of Papias, which has a very explicit and carefully calculated hebdomadal shape:

> The first age of man, called infancy, lasts for seven years. The second age, called boyhood, lasts for another seven up to fourteen. The third, extending for two further sevens up to twenty-eight, is called adolescence. The fourth, consisting of three consecutive seven-year periods, stretches to forty-nine, and is called youth of manhood. The fifth, also consisting of three hebdomads, lasts until seventy and is called 'elder', having fallen away from youth towards old age but not yet reached it. The sixth is man's old age, which is limited to no particular number of years; and this is also called decrepitude.[28]

History follows a pattern that runs parallel to human life. The world, for Augustine, has progressed from its youth in the period from Adam to Noah to its present old age, which will last until the Day of Judgement. But in his redemptive schema, the sixth and last era, *senectus*, both for the individual and for humankind, is not, as in the alternative models, entirely negative. The classical understanding of old age, as we have seen, allowed for a certain respect for the wisdom gained across the course of the life, even as the physical body declined. The point, as so often in classical moral rhetoric, is *tempestivitas*, seasonableness of behaviour, so that while, in Burrow's words, 'the persistence of youthful characteristics into old age must be deplored as at best ridiculous and at worst vicious' (*Ages of Man* 151), expressions of virtue appropriate to seniority should be given the respect they deserve. Augustine, however, goes further than this. As Burrow puts it,

> [f]or the 'exterior' or natural man, [old age] does indeed represent nothing but a decline; but for the 'interior', spiritual man it can and should be an age of spiritual *renovatio*, in which he may recover on his own account that divine image implanted in man on the sixth day of Creation and manifested through Christ in the sixth age of the world. For the Christian may look forward to a seventh age of 'sempiternal rest', corresponding to the seventh, sabbath, day of Creation on which God himself rested. (ibid., 82)

Thus the six-day pattern is really a seven-day pattern, premised on a supplementary, eternal, redemptive phase to follow immediately after death – a virtual last period, in a way. Burrow notes that

> Augustine's vision of *senectus* as a time when 'the interior man is from day to day renewed' – a lofty spiritual conception, to be distinguished from mere respect for the wisdom of the old – proved too much for most of his successors, who were generally content to derive from it a workaday scheme of six natural ages. (ibid.)

Nonetheless, this model has distinct resonance for the historian of late style as arguably the earliest model of the life to posit an upturn at the very end, a final phase which is proleptic of a renewed spiritual existence yet to come. The key difference from the other versions of the 'ages of man' is the distinction between the spiritual and the physical conditions for old age, since the spiritual state of the sixth age is, for Augustine, quite different from its physical counterpart: the soul in fact paradoxically benefits from the decline of the physical self, since 'complete obliteration of the temporal life' may, if addressed appropriately, lead to a translation into a perfect spiritual form 'made in the image and shape of God'.[29] Augustine says no more than this, but the potential application of this account to the discourse of lateness as it eventually emerges is obvious enough, offering as it does a spiritual rejuvenation for the elect even as the physical, material self declines towards death. And it is clear that Augustine's arguments had a long reach. Richard Baxter, in his 1682 *Last Work of a Believer*, assuming a theology in which there is an accumulation of grace across the course of the godly life in tandem with the developing spiritual maturity of the believer, notes that 'even in age, when [...] infirmities of mind increase with infirmities of body, yet Grace can effectually do its work', adding that 'as God hath promised growth of Grace, and flourishing in old age, so in his way we may expect the fulfilling of his promise [and] as Grace increaseth, infirmities and corruptions of the Soul will vanish'.[30] Baxter's underlying Biblical text is Psalm 92, especially verse 14: 'They shall still bring forth fruit in old age; they shall be fat and flourishing.' This might not be true in physical terms, but there is a clear tradition from Augustine onwards of its fundamental spiritual validity.

One potentially productive way in which to make sense of Augustine's model of the creative life – and one that suggests its possible role as an underpinning of future accounts of lateness – is to read it, harking back to the controlling image of *Prothalamion*, as a Christian appropriation of the pervasive classical idea of the swan song. Cheney, reading Spenser's career on the basis of the idea of the 'famous flight' as both avian and Orphic, includes the swan in the range of emblematic birds he considers as images for the poet, noting its role in the origins of lyric poetry (according to Callimachus, swans served as midwives at the birth of Apollo, singing over the pangs of childbirth) but choosing not to pursue the potential of the swan song in relation to the shape of Shakespeare's career, a decision that is curious, perhaps, in view of the playwright's longstanding identity as the 'Swan of Avon'. Originating with the Greeks and Romans and still current in the early modern period, the image of the poet as a bird singing most sweetly in the face of death offers the earliest analogue for what would arguably much later become the idea of late style – that is, for the idea of a resurgence of creative brilliance in the face of death – underpinning, in its celebration of late productivity, Montaigne's increased determination to write as time grows short.

The precise origins of the swan song, though, remain obscure. One early manifestation comes in Aesop's fable 'The Swan Mistaken for a Goose', in which the swan, captured by mistake and about to be butchered, begins to sing prior to its own death, whereupon its voice is recognised and its life saved.[31] This tale offers an analogue for the understanding that seems to have existed in Greek culture that a logical response to the imminence of death is the kind of increase in output experienced by Montaigne, of which Aesop is himself offered as an example. As Gregory Nagy has shown, the counterbalancing of praise and blame was a structural principle of archaic Greek civilisation: the key word αἶνος encompasses the poetry written both for and against a given individual, the former providing that individual with the key heroic attribute of κλέος, or glory, which is embodied in song.[32] The *Life of Aesop* tradition treats Aesop's fables as αἶνος, that is, as tales implying either praise or blame, the poet taking care to interweave the positive and negative, leaving judgement to the listener. As Aesop's unjust execution draws near, however, the emphasis on blame becomes stronger and 'the deployment of interlocking fables is intensified' (*Best of the Achaeans*, 282): in other words, Aesop's output of fables increases as his death comes closer and the fables he creates ensure that the listener will understand that his death is unjust. Emotional restraint and resistance to pain and grief are sustained and the good death is thereby exemplified. The hero, whether warrior or thinker, struggles against the fear of death that all feel; the successful outcome of that struggle will be the perfect death, a moment that should be recorded in song. Socrates' equanimity in the face of death, in the various perspectives offered on it by Plato, provides a clear instance of this long tradition: 'Evidently you think that I have less insight than a swan', Socrates observes wryly to Simmias, 'because when these birds feel that the time has come for them to die, they sing more loudly and sweetly than they have sung in all their lives before, for joy that they are going away into the presence of the god whose servants they are.'[33] The Romans, for their part, echoed this understanding of the role of the swan song, but introduced a note of cynicism. Martial gives the swan's final moments a sophisticated twist, hinting at the self-consciousness of the gesture: 'The swan murmurs sweet songs with a failing tongue, singer of its own funeral dirge.'[34] And Pliny the Elder, writing in 77 CE, bluntly refutes the myth by way of scientific method, noting that '[i]t is stated that at the moment of the swan's death, it gives utterance to a mournful song' and adding: 'but this is an error, in my opinion, at least I have tested the truth of the story on several occasions'.[35]

Fascinatingly, it is the same Pliny who, developing a critique of contemporary accounts of the good life as expressed in the forms of the Greek *encomium* (ἐγκώμιον) – the song or speech in praise of the public dead – and, subsequently, the Roman *laudatio funebris*, makes perhaps the first and certainly one of the most damning of observations about the special status given to late work. 'It is [...] a very singular fact', he observes, 'and one well deserving of remark, that the last works of these artists, their unfinished paintings, in fact, are held in greater admiration than their completed works'; the reason for this, he concludes, is that 'in such works [...] we not only see the outline depicted, and the very thoughts of the artist expressed, but have the composition additionally commended to our notice by the regrets which we must necessarily feel on finding the hand that commenced it arrested by death'.[36] The resonance of this critique is profound. It is by no means an assertion, *avant la lettre*, of late style, but it does look forward two millennia to current debates over late work, especially by such figures as Titian, whose critics remain divided over whether *The Flaying of Marsyas*, for instance, is, on the one hand, a classic example of the loose, abstract brushwork characteristic of late style or, on the other, simply unfinished. The classical swan song is a mythical self-lamentation, an act of proleptic grief performed prior to death by the dying creature, which can only be performed by that creature: a song, moving to others but finally only fully meaningful to the singer, whose harmonies are precisely and only the product of the proximity of death. It is also, as Pliny suggests, potentially deceptive in its privileging of last work.

It was perhaps Roman cynicism which prompted the early modern dilution of the intensity of the conception of the swan song. That nobody has extended the idea of the Swan of Avon to the Shakespeare of the late period may simply be due to the fact that in Shakespeare's own writing the redemptive quality of the swan song appears deracinated, offering little scope as a positive model for a late resurgence. Lucrece is a 'pale swan in her wat'ry nest' who '[b]egins the sad dirge of her certain ending' (*Rape of Lucrece*, ll. 1611–12). For Prince Henry in *King John*, ''Tis strange that death should sing', and he describes himself as

> the cygnet to this pale faint swan,
> Who chants a doleful hymn to his own death,
> And from the organ-pipe of frailty sings
> His soul and body to their lasting rest. (*King John*, 5.7.21–4)

In *The Merchant of Venice*, the song becomes a somewhat ironic consolation in the face of death which separates mortality and musicality: 'Let music sound while he doth make his choice,' commands Portia, wryly handing the responsibility for the harmony to an anonymous band, 'Then if he lose he makes a swanlike end, / Fading in music' (*Merchant*, 3.2). And least optimistic of all is Emilia, dying at the hands of her own husband, announcing in the final moment of *Othello* that she will 'play the swan / And die in music' (5.2.254–5) by echoing Desdemona's willow song in order to taunt her mistress's murder with the truth.

Emilia's death, though, it should be said, is not necessarily as bleak, from a Christian perspective, as it might at first sight seem. 'Moor, she was chaste', she cries,

> She loved thee, cruel Moor.
> So come my soul to bliss as I speak true.
> So, speaking as I think, alas, I die. (5.2.256–8)

Emilia's last words, being truthful, offer the prospect of the translation of her soul to heaven: 'speaking as she thinks' with her last breath gives her hope of the afterlife. What the classical good death lacked, from the early modern Christian perspective, is the potential offered by Augustine's projected seventh day – the possibility, that is, of redemption. Christian writers, unsurprisingly, appropriated the image of the swan song wholesale, converting it into a melody proleptic of the salvation of the singer's soul. This is clear enough in the tradition of publishing the last sermons of especially respected preachers under the explicit motif of the swan song – texts that include, for instance, *Saint Pauls Triumph, Or, Cygnea illa & dulcissima Cantio, That Swan-like and most sweet Song, of that learned and faithfull Servant of God, Mast. John Randall [. . .] Uttered by him [. . .] lately before his death, in the time of his great and heavie Affliction* (London, 1626) or, later, *Cygnea Cantio: Or, the Swan-song, (Being the last Public Discourse), of William Whitaker, D. D.* (London, 1772). Here, the last words of the dying Christian take on a particular significance, offering a point of access to the state of mind of the virtuous self on the verge of the afterlife.

I have already suggested, in Chapter 1, that late style is a form of eschatology. And no doubt early modern preachers would have understood in a very literal way Butterfield's claim that every moment is lived under the threat of death. Last words have an inescapable theological element, holding a profound and particular significance in Christian culture. Christ's last words from the cross – 'Father, forgive them, for they know not what they do'; 'Verily I say unto thee, today thou shalt be with me in Paradise'; 'Woman, behold thy son! [. . .] Behold thy mother!'; 'My God, my God, why hast thou forsaken me?'; 'I thirst'; 'It is finished'; and 'Father, into thy hands I commend my spirit' – have long been, and remain, a significant focus for Christian meditation, regularly cited at the deaths of institutionally significant figures (the sermon preached at the death of Pope John Paul II by the cardinal who was soon to be his successor being only the most notable recent instance). They offer solace in the face of apparent tragedy and provide a coherent textual demonstration of the function of death as fulfilment – seven words echoing the six days of creation and the seventh day of rest and looking forward to the opening of the seven seals at the end of time, all sharing an intense teleology that would be wholly familiar to Augustine.[37] Last words have thus been taken by Christian tradition as evidence of the life to come and late work unquestionably shares much of the significance of last words, even though it reworks the idea in a sharply different philosophical environment. Every articulate person produces last words of a kind, whether or not they are subsequently read as illuminating. But only an élite produces heuristic last words. And it is in early modern interpretations of such heuristic last words, arguably (perhaps particularly in view of the role of later discursive constructions of late style as sublimated theology) that the seeds of late writing can be found.

4.3 LAST WORDS

Last words mattered in early modern England, then, though their precise import was not always clear. They had the quality of the liminal: for the Christian, they marked the transition not from life to extinction but from life to life in another form, a change not unlike a rite of passage within the earthly life. But liminal expression is frequently unsettling. In early modern England, last words were sometimes thought to have prophetic qualities as the expression of a human being on the verge of the afterlife, beginning to acquire a vision of heaven or the future unavailable to those in the midst of life. Yet it is obvious that the import of prophecy is frequently less clear than this. John of Gaunt's dying speech to Richard II – 'Methinks I am a prophet new inspir'd,/And thus expiring do foretell of him' – is an obvious instance:

> O, but they say the tongues of dying men
> Enforce attention, like deep harmony.
> Where words are scarce they are seldom spent in vain,
> For they breathe truth that breathe their words in pain.
> He that no more must say is listened more
> Than they whom youth and ease have taught to glose.
> More are men's ends marked than their lives before.
> (*Richard II*, 2.1.5–11)

Gaunt makes powerful claims here for the efficacy of last words, yet for all its profundity, this speech makes no impact on the behaviour of its on-stage audience, coming across as no more than a list of truisms uttered by an embittered man. Other Shakespearean instances of last words offer an equivalent ambivalence. Hotspur's last speech – 'Oh, I could prophesy' – is cut off just as he appears to be about to say something significant, leaving us uncertain about the status of that unspoken speech. Is it yet another instance, though an abortive one, of the Hotspur bluster? Or is Hotspur's final tragedy that he is not given time to put into words the truth that occurs to him only at the end? Perhaps the most circumscribed last prophetic speech in the canon comes in one of the late collaborations, *Henry VIII*, in the context of Queen Katherine's deathbed vision. 'Saw you not, even now', she asks,

> a blessèd troop
> Invite me to a banquet, whose bright faces
> Cast thousand beams upon me, like the sun?
> They promised me eternal happiness,
> And brought me garlands, Griffith, which I feel
> I am not worthy yet to wear. I shall,
> Assuredly.   (*Henry VIII*, 4.2.87–93)

The enacting of her vision for the audience too ensures that they will perceive her to be in a state of grace, yet her status as a staunch Roman Catholic who appeals to the Pope for intervention in her divorce hearing and her optimism for the future of her daughter Mary in her last speech – in which she 'commends' her to the King's 'goodness', noting that '[s]he is young, and of a noble modest nature' and adding 'I hope she will deserve well' (4.2.132, 136–7) – strike an unavoidably uncomfortable note for listeners at the Globe and hardly assure us either of her clarity of mind or of the efficacy of the words she utters at the end of her life.

The sheer old-fashioned awkwardness of Katherine's vision scene – compounded by her unsettling irascible Catholic saintliness in a play of supposed reformation which makes Cranmer cry and elides Sir (or Saint) Thomas More – marks a faultline between the shifts and the continuities in attitudes to death from the medieval to the early modern. Philippe Ariès has emphasised the gradual defamiliarisation and secularisation of death in western culture in the wake of the early Middle Ages. In the medieval romance, he notes, the dying person is usually forewarned of the imminence of death, providing the time needed to take the appropriate actions: '[D]eath was a ritual organized by the dying person himself, who presided over it and knew its protocol.'[38] For Ariès, this process marks a relative familiarity with the prospect of death, the most important point being 'the simplicity with which the rituals of dying were accepted and carried out, – in a ceremonial manner, yes, but with no theatrics, with no great show of emotion' (*Western Attitudes*, 12–13). The elaborate emotional performances that later came to be part and parcel of the process of dying, culminating in the (to our eyes) excesses of Victorian deathbed scenes, he argues, reflect the increasing estrangement of death in modernity, in which 'a dramatic and personal meaning' is given 'to man's traditional familiarity with death' (ibid., 27), thereby increasing the pain of separation that death brings about. In the process, death became not a transition from this life to another but a grim caesura:

Like the sexual act, death was henceforth increasingly thought of as a transgression which tears man from his daily life, from rational society, from his monotonous work, in order to make him undergo a paroxysm, plunging him into an irrational, violent, and beautiful world. Like the sexual act death for the Marquis de Sade is a break, a rupture. This idea of rupture is something completely new. (ibid., 57–8)

The medieval *artes moriendi* mark the earliest negotiations of this rupture, 'a series of new phenomena which introduced the concern for the individuality of each person into the old idea of the collective destiny of the species' (ibid., 29). These include, *inter alia*,

the portrayal of the Last Judgment at the end of the world; the displacing of this judgment to the end of each life, to the precise moment of death; macabre themes and the interest shown in portrayals of physical decomposition. (ibid., 29)

The intensity of the images that dominated the understanding of death at this time marks, for Ariès, 'a concentration of the mind and senses on the actual moment of physical death' which gradually subsided as the medieval became the early modern.[39]

For seventeenth-century writers such as Jeremy Taylor and Richard Baxter, far more important than how we face death is how we face the life which precedes that death, and they set out to shift the focus of attention away from the art of dying towards the art of living. Baxter, in his *Last Work of a Believer*, exhorts his reader to be aware *at all times* of the imminence of his or her own death:

> Reader, I beseech thee, as ever thou believest that thou must shortly die, retire from the crowd and noise of worldly vanity and vexation: O bethink thee how little a while thou must be here, and have use for honour, and favour, and wealth; and what it is for a soul to pass into heaven or hell, and to dwell among Angels or Devils for ever; And how men should live, and watch, and pray, that are near to such a change as this.[40]

The problem with the art of dying, in other words, is that you have to wait until you are dying in order to demonstrate your skill in it and Baxter is trying to rule out a life that see-saws in its relationship to grace: the late conversion, the deathbed repentance, though dramatic, is precisely what he seeks to avoid. Taylor, in *The Rule and Exercises of Holy Dying* of 1651, a landmark text in the history of death, accepts that 'it is a great art to dye well', but believes that this art is something that should

> be learnt by men in health, by them that can discourse and consider; by those whose understanding, and acts of reason are not abated with fear or pains, and as the greatest part of death is passed by the preceding years of our life, so also in those years are the greatest preparation to it: and he that prepares not for death, before his last sicknesse, is like him that begins to study philosophy when he is going to dispute publikely in the faculty.[41]

The point, for Taylor, is that 'all that a sick and dying man can do is but to exercise those vertues, which he before acquired, and to perfect that repentance which was begun more early' (*Holy Dying*, A5v). In all likelihood, the good death will only be achieved by the person who has lived a life of

> study and skill, time and understanding in the wayes of godlinesse; and it were very vain, to say so much is necessary, and not to suppose more time to learn them, more skill to practise them, more opportunities to desire them, more abilities both of body and mind then can be supposed in a sick, amazed, timerous, and weak person; whose naturall acts are disabled, whose senses are weak, whose discerning faculties are lessened, whose principles are made intricate and intangled, upon whose eye sits a cloud, and the heart is broken with sicknesse, and the liver pierced thorow with sorrows and the strokes of death. (ibid., A5v–A6r)

Thus, argues Taylor, 'the precepts of *dying well*' should 'be part of the studies of them that live in health' because whereas in the case of 'a late and sick-bed repentance', 'if we practise imperfectly once, we shall never recover the errour: for we die but once', for those who begin early enough 'an imperfect study may be supplied by a frequent exercise, and a renewed experience' (ibid., A6r, A5v, A6v). 'For a sick bed', he argues,

is only a school of severe exercise, in which the spirit is tried, and his graces are rehearsed: and the assistances which I have in the following pages given to those vertues which are proper to the state of sicknesse, are such as suppose a man in the state of grace; or they confirm a good man, or they support the weak, or adde degrees, or minister comfort, or prevent an evil, or cure the little mischiefs which are incident to tempted persons in their weaknesse; this is the summe of the present designe, as it relates to dying persons. (ibid., A6v–A7r)

'And therefore', he adds,

I have not inserted any advices proper to old age, but such as are common to it and the state of sicknesse; for I suppose *very old age* to be *a longer sicknesse*, it is labour and sorrow when it goes beyond the common period of nature; but if it be on this side that period, and be healthfull, in the same degree it is so, I reckon it in the accounts of life; and therefore it can have no distinct consideration. (ibid., A7r–v)

For Taylor, then, the grace of the moment of death is not specific to old age; a good death is the result of the grace achieved during life, not of a distinct and abrupt moment at the end.

Despite the best efforts of preachers such as Baxter and Taylor, though, the significance of final moments did not fade away. For Emilia in the last scene of *Othello*, as we have observed, it is crucial that she be heard to speak the truth with her last breath – 'So come my soul to bliss as I speak true' – since silence at this crucial juncture would be enigmatic and might not lead to her salvation. The influence of Foxe's *Acts and Monuments*, for which the manner of the deaths of the Protestant martyrs was such a profound source of propaganda, tended to ensure that these final moments before death were scrutinised with great care. And there was, for Protestants, a particular pressure on last words in the context of the Reformation's rejection of extreme unction and of the second chance offered by purgatory (a grim prospect, but a chance nonetheless). As Craig Koslofsky has noted in his work on rituals of death in Reformation Germany, the model Protestant death required a careful negotiation of the moment of passing. Citing a report of the death of one godly householder, Koslofsky observes that '[a]s one of their most consistent points of doctrine, Protestants rejected the Christian tradition of intercession for the dead and removed the dead from the world of the living', noting that the dead man's brother reported the death as follows:

Then [Hermann] leaned back with his hands on the arms of the chair, closed his eyes and mouth, breathed heavily three times and departed quite gently, (thank the Lord!) like a person falling peacefully asleep. [. . .] And I stood by him and held him by the hands, and prayed *until he had departed*.[42]

It is this last phrase, highlighted by Koslofsky, that is key. 'In his pious account of Hermann's death', Koslofsky notes,

> Gerlach makes clear that their spiritual relationship is severed at the moment Hermann dies. Gerlach reports that he prayed for his brother until Hermann died – beyond death's divide there was, according to the new Protestant doctrine, neither the need nor the possibility of intercession by the living for the dead. Prayers for the dead, a central part of the Christian economy of salvation since the second century, had been made obsolete by the new doctrine of salvation by faith alone. (*Reformation of the Dead*, 2)

This doctrine puts immense pressure on final words, since there can be no redress for error in the afterlife. Moreover, as Jessica Martin has argued, the loss of the 'mechanical efficacy of the ritual' of extreme unction meant that Protestants, 'while feeling an equal need to offer such certainties, were effectively prevented from doing so, and were instead forced to fall back on interpreting the conduct and attitude of each subject to his imminent death'.[43] Last words thus became a porous, complex, interpretatively available resource with which to replace last rites.

It is not, moreover, only in sectarian accounts or in accounts specifically of the deaths of the virtuous that final utterances are foregrounded. Early modern reports of the last words of both the elect and the reprobate – of saints and of sinners alike, of the godly person on his or her deathbed and of the condemned person on the scaffold – place heavy emphasis on final utterances and stand as examples to all. Catholics and Protestants alike appealed to the basic assumption that dying words were privileged. As Peter Lake observes in a discussion of scaffold rhetoric,

> [o]n both sides of the confessional divide the capacity of the felon to face death with equanimity, sure of his or her repentance and therefore assured of Christ's intercession and hence of salvation, was considered to be an acid test of the personal religious profession of the condemned and of the truth of the religious system within which that profession was framed.[44]

'The whole ritual of last dying speeches', Lake argues, 'revolved around the privileged aura attaching to words delivered in the face of death': he notes that 'felons were expected not merely to tell the truth about their crimes but to reveal truths both about their own spiritual condition and about the nature of true religion itself' ('Agency and Appropriation', 241). And he cites William Allen's *True, Sincere, and Modest Defence* to emphasise the close and logical association of truth and the last moments of life. 'It is not probable', writes Allen, 'that such men would against their consciences and against the truth have avouched a falsehood at that instant to the present and everlasting perdition of their souls'.[45] Rarely, if ever, is an assertion of this kind directly explained or defended; it is simply apparent that a person's last words, whatever he or she has done, good or bad, will have a certain efficacy.

Frances Dolan, writing specifically of the last utterances of condemned women and acknowledging Foucault's analysis of the totalising effect of the state ritual of execution, argues nonetheless for an element of agency in scaffold speeches. Lake, in his account of the executions of priests, agrees that 'despite all the totalising pretensions of the parties involved [...] an inexpungible air of dialogue hung over the proceedings' ('Agency and Apprehension', 243). These are useful correctives, but there is no escaping from the ritualisation of last words and the extent to which moments of agency were heavily circumscribed by the formal requirements of the moment is clear enough. As J. A. Sharpe argued in a landmark essay, '[p]ublic executions were carried out in a context of ceremony and ritual' and 'by far the most consistently reported aspect of these rituals, and evidently one which was felt to be of central importance, was the speech delivered from the gallows by the condemned'.[46] Each condemned prisoner 'was expected to make a farewell speech, and usually did so in a very stereotyped form' ('Dying Speeches', 150). For Henry Goodcole, who made a habit of reporting lurid crimes that ended up with an execution,

dying men's wordes are ever remarkable, & their last deeds memorable for succeeding posterities, by them to be instructed, what vertues and vices they followed and imbraced, and by them to learne to imitate that which was good, and to eschew evill. (Goodcole, *True Declaration*, A4r)

Usually, the final speech involved a reflection on the life that had preceded it, a repentance of past sin necessary if last-minute confession and conversion were to be achieved: these are, by definition, the opposite of the lives lived in the awareness of the need for ongoing grace encouraged by Taylor and Baxter. And the efficacy of the ritual enactment of individual salvation at the moment of execution was extended and disseminated through the publication of formulaic gallows literature that was both 'didactic and normative' ('Dying Speeches', 148). Catholics and Protestants alike operated within a narrow framework in which both sides agree that the authenticity of final moments located in the proximity to death of the speaker and that the issue at stake is salvation. We see what Lake calls a 'struggle for narrative control' even if that narrative is in large part pre-scripted. What we hear are ritual expressions, formulaic phrasings. Last words function as reassurance, as social reconstruction, as reassertions of the order of things, which will have been changed, no matter how imperceptibly, by each death; as such, they follow certain prior patterns, conferring status on the utterer. The godly man dying a good death is presumed to be demonstrably one of the elect and thus to be transferring directly from earth to heaven; the condemned man voicing his repentance is accepting the right of the state to punish him on earth in the assumption that his repentance will propel him likewise to heaven. Last words voice a rite of passage, not an ending.

The last sermons of preachers, the dying words of the godly, the ritual speeches of the condemned on the scaffold, deathbed repentances. It is out of these materials, according to Jessica Martin in her invaluable account of Izaak Walton's *Lives*, that the English form of biography developed. For Martin,

> Walton's practice was crucial in shaping modern expectations of what a biography should contain. His work is latent in our views of how a biography should be organized, how seriously it should treat evidence (textual and oral); in how 'literary' an enterprise it should be conceived to be, how seriously it should regard narrative coherence; and most of all in our settled expectation of an intimate relationship between author, reader, and subject. (*Walton's Lives*, ix)

Walton's life-writing, she notes, derived in large part from two connected sources, from Plutarch's *Lives* and from post-Reformation verbal negotiations of death, notably in the form of the funeral sermon – that is, she suggests that English biography as a genre emerged from the particular process of writing the *end* of the exemplary life. This puts commemoration – the life viewed from the end of that life – at the heart of biography from the beginning and it privileges the final moments of the life over the life seen whole. Lives are read from the vantage point of the latter end; earlier events are redrawn from the perspective of that end. Biography, at the point of origin, then, is both derived from final gestures and expressions and fundamentally exemplary, emerging as a form of homily, as an account of a life lived as an embodiment of sermon precepts. Its pre-Christian origins, notably in Plutarch, provide fertile ground for Reformation appropriation, conceived as they were, in Martin's words, 'to provide virtuous matter for the reader's imitation'. The idea of late writing appears a logical outcrop of this, both as critical construction and as creative complicity, offering in each case, it might be argued, an ongoing, sublimated, secularised version of the funeral elegy. Noting Walton's double strategy of investing authority in his own narratorial voice and making 'extensive use of his subjects' own writings', Martin describes the *Lives* as 'attempts at a kind of posthumous autobiography' (ibid., ix, xi), as 'a new form of chronological narrative, where the author was mediating, artfully, the re-creation of the history of a life' (ibid., ix).

To illustrate her contention about the centrality of the end of the life to the understanding of the whole of that life, Martin addresses what she calls 'the century's most politically contentious ecclesiastical "martyrdom"', that is, 'the execution of Laud' (ibid., 131), as it was depicted by Peter Heylyn. She cites in particular Heylyn's theatrically aware defence of the way in which he presents the life of Laud:

> It is a preposterous kind of writing to begin the story of a great mans life, at the houre of his death, a most strange way of setting forth a solemne *Tragedie*, to keepe the *principall Actor* in the *tyring-house* till the play be done, and then to bring him on the stage onely to speake the *Epilogue*, and receive the Plaudites. Yet this must be the scope of the following papers. To write the whole life of [. . .] the Lord Arch-Bishop of Canterbury, would require more time then publique expectation can endure to heare of. (Heylyn, *Briefe Relation*, A2r)

'Posthumous autobiography', as Martin describes early life-writing, is a good description too of the status – the self-conscious status – of this kind of final speech and is indeed, in the multiply-layered sense in which Patricia Parker has described the word, 'preposterous'.[47] As Martin notes, 'Heylyn's talk about shortness of time is pragmatic. [. . .] His martyr's version of Laud's death must get into print at least as fast as rival versions' (*Walton's Lives*, 131). But, she adds, 'rhetorically it works, in that by confining his account to Laud's deportment only in that final act Heylyn implicitly vindicates all his other acts without having to mention them. He died well: he must have lived well' (ibid., 131). What particularly fascinates Martin about the archbishop's death is the very careful attention Laud pays to the textual transmission of his final words to posterity. She notes that 'in the printed account of this sermon, the title-page specifies that it was "all faithfully written by *John Hinde*, whom the Archbishop beseeched him that he would not let any wrong be done him by any phrase in false Copies"'.[48] Martin understands this to mean that on the scaffold itself Laud took the time to safeguard his final text by checking the presence and faithfulness of his stenographer, and she notes that

> the sermon itself is an explicit performance. Laud begins by apologizing to the crowd for using notes, because he knows their critical appreciation is important, but the effect is to highlight his remarkable self-possession. '*Good People*,' he begins, 'You'l pardon my old Memory, and upon so sad occasions as I am come to this place, to make use of my Papers, I dare not trust my self otherwise'. (*Walton's Lives*, 131–2; Laud, *Funerall Sermon*, B1v)

The care taken by Laud to determine the accuracy of reporting of his carefully staged final words could be said to look forward two centuries or more to the self-consciousness of a Hardy or a James in the construction of late style.

The origins of the discourse of lateness and the origins of biography, then, appear, not altogether surprisingly, to be the same. Harold Nicolson defined as two of the 'impure' causes of biography (as opposed to a Platonic, 'pure' cause such as the search for truth) what he called 'the commemorative instinct' (which he ironises as 'the cenotaph urge') and 'the didactic temptation' (that is, hagiography), and it seems clear that the English roots of lateness – that is, those that would develop eventually, a long way down the line, into accounts of the late Shakespeare – intertwine with the roots of biography. Walton's lay transformation of a sacred form takes place through accounts of the end of the life. And it does not seem so very far, perhaps, from Walton to Edward Young's 1759 *Conjectures on Original Composition*, a key document in the history of the idea of genius, and thus to the emergence of the idea of late style along with the development of Romantic biography. For Young, there is little to be looked forward to in old age per se: '[e]vils there are', he accepts, 'which [Fortune's] Smiles cannot prevent, or cure. Among these are the Languors of old Age.'[49] But he is clear about the impact of last words, offering a peroration on the death of Addison, whose serene departing is ample evidence of his genius:

For, after a long, and manly, but vain struggle with his distemper, he dismissed his physicians, and with them all hopes of life: But with his hopes of life he dismissed not his concern for the living, but sent for a youth nearly related, and finely accomplished, but not above being the better for good impressions from a dying friend: He came; but life now glimmering in the socket, the dying friend was silent: After a decent, and proper pause, the youth said, 'Dear Sir! You sent for me: I believe, and I hope, that you have some commands; I shall hold them most sacred': May distant ages not only hear, but feel, the reply! Forcibly grasping the youth's hand, he softly said, 'See in what peace a Christian can die.' He spoke with difficulty, and soon expired. Thro' Grace divine, how great is man? Thro' divine Mercy, how stingless death? Who would not thus expire? (*Conjectures*, 101–2)

For Young, this is an ideal ending, exemplary both as a particular moment of spiritual enlightenment for the dying man's young associate and as a general exhortation to all who read the account:

What an inestimable legacy were those *few dying words* to the youth beloved? What a glorious supplement to his own valuable fragment on the truth of Christianity? What a full demonstration, that his fancy could not feign beyond what his virtue could reach? [...] His compositions are but a noble preface; the grand work is his death: That is a work which is read in heaven: How has it join'd the final approbation of angels to the previous applause of men? [...] If all our men of Genius had *so* breathed their last; if all our men of Genius, like him, had been men of Genius for *eternals*; *then*, had we never been pained by the report of a latter end! (ibid., 102, 104, 105)

In Young's account, the spiritual significance of Addison's last words thus serves also to validate his artistic career and the good Christian death is renegotiated as identical with the death of the artistic genius. For Young, in other words, last words matter more than the end itself and late expression becomes the primary focus for accounts of genius.

None of this, however, even Young's account of the last words of Addison, quite adds up to a conception of late writing in the modern sense. Neither the pre-Romantic understanding of the progress of life in general nor that specifically of the artistic life lends itself readily to the development of a concept of late style. Nonetheless, I would suggest that, although lateness did not emerge as a coherent concept until the early nineteenth century, certain features of what to us are recognisable as component parts of a concept of lateness are already established by Shakespeare's day – though not by any means all, and only as symptoms. It may well be that the ascription of a late style fits the circumstances of a given set of works by a single artist. As I said in my introduction, it is undeniable that certain artists have produced the most astonishing work in old age. But Shakespeare's circumstances are not so comfortably matched to the concept. In fact, the case of Shakespeare arguably serves better as a critique of the concept to which it has been bound than as an exemplar. I have argued that Shakespeare offers neither the clearcut caesura nor the comfortably long life that would make the ascription of a late style straightforward. I now want to turn my attention away from early modern culture in general to the specifics of the early modern stage, to consider the nature of the Shakespearean dramatic *oeuvre* as material for an ascription of late style and to suggest that such an ascription misunderstands the conditions of production for early seventeenth-century theatre. In order to do so, I will once again begin by suggesting an analogy with art history.

4.4 LATE STYLE AND THE CONDITIONS OF THEATRICAL PRODUCTION IN EARLY MODERN LONDON

In Dulwich Picture Gallery in south London is a painting of Jacob's dream that for a very long time was attributed to Rembrandt. When the curators got round to having it cleaned, they found (no doubt to their considerable chagrin) that the signature was not, after all, that of Rembrandt but rather that of one of his pupils. The wall label notes that the painting 'used to be' one of the gallery's 'most loved' pictures until this discovery was made – the implication being that it ceased to be loved once it became clear that the painting was not, after all, by Rembrandt, even though the painting itself had not changed by a single line or brushstroke. What matters, it seems, to the visitor to the gallery is the attribution to Rembrandt, not the actual painting. This is a simple enough, if slightly absurd, reminder of our persistence in reading the work of art exclusively through the artist, in understanding that work solely as the product of an individual rather than of a milieu, a culture, a genre or any input other than the genius of the painter, writer or composer with whom it is associated. Another painting at Dulwich – again involving the name of Rembrandt – provides a more specific focus for this critical insistence on engaging the painter's existence with the work of art. The wall label for the *Portrait of a Young Man* (Bourgeois Bequest, no. 221, acquired in 1811) tells us that

> [d]espite some doubts in the past, recent scholarly opinion has favoured the firm attribution of this sensitive and subtly-lit portrait to Rembrandt. It has the characteristic broad handling of Rembrandt's late style. [...] There has been less agreement about the sitter, but the traditional identification, as Rembrandt's only son Titus, is surely convincing.

In both the senses in which this statement offers attributions, they are clearly uncomfortable or problematic, requiring a degree of hopeful assertion ('favoured' and 'firm' are awkward bedfellows, for one thing), a certain professional optimism in face of the subjective quality of the first attribution – that the painting is an instance of the late Rembrandt style – and the biographical guesswork (enhanced by the use of the word 'tradition') of the second – that the sitter is Rembrandt's son Titus – for which no actual evidence is offered. The acknowledgements of 'some doubts in the past,' of 'less agreement,' of a 'surely convincing' 'traditional identification', taken together, tend to undermine the claim that the work is by Rembrandt (an attribution devoutly to be wished by any art museum, of course) and foreground both the persistence and the discomfort of biographical criticism and the fluidity of the definition and attribution of a late style. As we saw earlier with the Rembrandt/not-Rembrandt 'Self-Portrait' at the National Gallery of Victoria, the association of late style with the question of attribution can be troublesome.

It is typical of work on lateness, as we have seen, that questions of authenticity and of the singular authority of the creator should be foregrounded. Lateness is a particularly intense form of individuation. It is profoundly, exclusively author-focussed. It has no time at all for the 'death of the author'. On the contrary, it reinstates the author through the unique specificity of the late style (even as the acquisition of the universal traits of late style could, as we have noted, be said paradoxically to de-individualise the author by subsuming him to an overarching realm of late abstraction). Kenneth Clark notes of the late reliefs of Donatello – which 'he worked on [...] till his death at the age of eighty' and which Clark argues are the earliest instances of an 'old-age style', in which 'a reckless perspective is used intermittently in order to heighten emotional effect, and the actual modelling (or rather the carving, for almost the whole surface has been cut in the bronze) is as free and expressive as the stroke of a pen in an impassioned drawing' – that, '[a]s with many works of the old-age style', they have moved 'so far outside the humanist norm that an earlier generation of critics questioned their authenticity' (*Artist Grows Old*, 8). This foregrounds the awkwardness of the relationship between late style and attribution that is apparent in the Dulwich wall labels. The extraordinary nature of the late style marks it out powerfully as the work of an individual; at the same time, that extraordinariness, which is apparent in the difference between the late style and the earlier styles, offers a challenge to the idea of individual style and often results in uncertainty over the attribution of late work. The paradox of a given late style would seem to be, then, that its very authenticity as late work – its location after the stylistic caesura that differentiates it from the artist's previous styles – is also what threatens its status as authentic.

A good instance of the difficulty created for critics of Renaissance art by this focus on the individual artist, on the late work as the most intense manifestation of that artist's individuality and thus on the late style as a key factor in the process of attribution, is the question of the studio. Painters such as Titian and Rembrandt worked not in isolation but in studios alongside younger artists training specifically to work in the style or styles – by no means excluding the late style – of the master. It is thus frequently impossible fully to detach that master from his pupils in the way canonicity requires. Walter Liedtke argues that

[t]he painting once thought to be by Rembrandt and now recognized as by one of his pupils is a tribute to the master as teacher, to the actual artist, and to the culture that sustained not only the career of Rembrandt but also the careers of some forty artists who occasionally produced works in his style.[50]

And so, he adds,

[o]ne need hardly be a rabid revisionist to appreciate the pleasure of discovering a painting by Flinck, Fabritius, or another associate of Rembrandt in the

permanent collection of a museum that hopes to present a balanced view of Dutch art. ('Rembrandt', 5)

For Liedtke, it is difficult to ringfence Rembrandt's work in the way post-Romantic criticism would prefer. 'Notwithstanding the poetic interpretation of Rembrandt as an artist who transcended his time, who belongs to all (or some of Western) humankind', he observes,

> it now appears that from about 1630 to about 1670 in the Netherlands there was a fairly widespread interest in the master's approach to the Bible, mythology, history, nature, and humanity. It appears as well that this sympathetic response to his vision was satisfied – as always, in any culture, on different levels of quality and meaning – by at least three dozen painters over a period of about forty years. (ibid.)

Thus the significance of the name 'Rembrandt' is not necessarily adequately delineated by the image of the lone painter. To think this way is not, Liedtke insists, to diminish Rembrandt's astonishing ability and impact but rather to demonstrate the productive reach of that impact in its own time.

Another obvious, earlier case in point – and one which again uncomfortably foregrounds the relationship of late style and the question of attribution – is that of Titian. M. Roy Fisher's *Titian's Assistants During the Later Years* makes it clear that Titian's late work is in a range of ways collaborative. 'More often than not', he notes, 'the products of the painting studios of sixteenth-century Venice represented a group effort', arguing that 'some helpers, no doubt, were limited to participation in the initial stages of picture-making, the grinding of pigments, the priming of canvas, preparation of the cartoon from master drawings, and the final transfer of the design to the canvas', but that, at the same time, others in the studio had a more substantive role, operating 'as specialists, executing landscapes, still life elements, or portraits, the labor on a single canvas often being divided among many hands'.[51] Workshop activity of this kind 'represented an integral factor in the economy of artistic production, for only by means of a division of labour were the leading masters able to meet the relentless demand for pictures' (*Titian's Assistants*, iv). Writing in 1958, prior to the theoretical debates about authorship initiated a decade or so later by Michel Foucault and Roland Barthes, Fisher negotiates carefully with the authority of the master, arguing that 'in the end the work remained – ideally speaking – the creation of the individual artist who generated the prime conception', but adding nonetheless that '[m]uch of the time the assistants acted in such close identification with the master that the final product represented an extension, unadulterated, of the directing intelligence' (ibid., i, v). This formulation requires an adjustment of the scope of authorship so as to incorporate the work of others in the style required by the named painter. It thus challenges the centrality to attributions of late style of the physical impact on the canvas of the individual artist – the generator of 'the prime conception' though not necessarily the actual painter – by way of the materiality of the brushstroke, the application of paint and the resultant textural quality of the painting – all the features, in other words, generally considered to offer the strongest clues to the authenticity of a given late style. Fisher emphasises that the collaborative work performed by the studio artists was taken for granted at the time, citing Ridolfi, who notes simply that '[h]ad not his disciples relieved him of so many labors [...] Titian would never have completed so many works'.[52] Moreover, the identity of the assistant Fisher believes to have been most responsive to Titian's late style offers a nice twist in the tale of the relationship of lateness, authenticity and attribution. He was Palma Il Giovane, a painter who was, at the time he seems to have collaborated with Titian (his involvement, it should be noted, is Fisher's claim rather than documented fact), around twenty years of age and whose name would in any case, somewhat ironically, always insist on his youth. For Fisher, there was 'only one figure' in Titian's studio 'with a mentality receptive to the "late style" and ample abilities to express it', one 'capable of reproducing the highly personal idiom of Titian's late style', and that was Palma (*Titian's Assistants*, xxi, 69). The irony of the reproducibility of Titian's 'unique' late style is reinforced by the identification of the man responsible for the reproduction of that style as a young artist at the very beginning of his career, one who would never be allowed, at least nominally speaking, to grow old.[53]

The involvement of others in the production of the last work of a toweringly canonical artist such as Titian is a significant problem for critics of late work, because late style cannot brook collaboration. For Kenneth Clark, unequivocally and insistently, '[o]ld artists are solitary; like all old people they are bored and irritated by the company of their fellow bipeds and yet find their isolation depressing. They are also suspicious of interference' (*Artist Grows Old*, 8). This claim of Clark's is echoed by David Rosand who, in a special edition of *Art Journal* from 1987 devoted to the question of old-age style, notes that in late work there is typically 'an evident disregard for externals, a kind of isolated self-sufficiency'.[54] This sense of the wilful detachment of the artist from his context and materials serves to underpin the general understanding of late style as transcendent and timeless, as the product of an intersection of artist and phenomenon beyond the confines of context. So it perhaps comes as a surprise to realise that collaboration is in fact a consistent feature of lateness across the range of art-forms within which late styles have been established, causing significant problems for the definition of late style as a manifestation of individual genius beyond the reach of contingency. If there is anything approximating the 'universal' in late style, it seems, it is the likelihood that that work is *not* produced singlehandedly.

Three reasons for collaboration present themselves in narratives of late style: the passing of the baton; the onset of disability and illness; and the impact of artistic success resulting either in the acquisition of disciples or, through the financial security consequent on success, the ability of the artist to employ a helper in various capacities. The last of these might be exemplified by the relationship of Igor Stravinsky and Robert Craft, the younger man providing the impetus for the master to turn, at the end of his life, to a form of composition (that is, to atonalism) that he had ignored or resisted for years, thus becoming instrumental in the shift of focus that resulted in the late style. An instance of a blend of the second and third might be the sharing of the production of the late Matisse cut-outs – when illness made the painter unable to perform the physical task of painting – between Matisse and the assistants who applied paint to paper in colours he specified and who assembled the final works. Another might be the conjunction of Henry James and his amanuensis Theodora Bosanquet, the physiology of old age (James's inability to hold a pen without pain and his consequent shift to dictation) requiring a change of writerly technique with a demonstrable impact upon the writer's style. And a further, slightly different instance – one which offers a certain contextual irony – might be that of Edward Said, whose late account of lateness was assembled posthumously by his friend Michael Wood, as the latter records in his introduction to *On Late Style*:

> The book on late style was unfinished, [. . .] but the materials for it are very rich. [. . .] In what follows I have put together several different sets of materials, but although I have cut and spliced, I have not thought it necessary to write summaries or bridging passages. The words are all Said's. (Wood in Said, *On Late Style*, xviii–xix)

Here the collaboration is not with an assistant but with an executor and it takes place posthumously, yet the textual effect is not dissimilar: Wood's 'assemblage' of disparate extant materials into a single chapter may or may not reflect a late intention on the part of Said, but it is clear all the same that a second writerly influence has directed the shape of the published material. The inexorability of death, of course, frequently means that the only form in which late work can be disseminated is by way of a posthumous collaboration of this kind (another primary instance might be the editorially reconstructed 'last works' of Ernest Hemingway, *The Garden of Eden, The Dangerous Summer* and *True at First Light*, published decades after his death), opening up the highly complex problem, especially in art appreciation, denoted by the binary *finished/unfinished*, a particularly acute issue in studies of the late work of a range of canonical artists, not least Titian.

Such forms of collaboration call for explanation or clarification, which when they are forthcoming invariably reinstate the centrality of the author within a creative process in which the input of others is firmly treated as subordinate (or, at times, insubordinate). The late Shakespearean collaborations offer an obvious case in point, as we have seen already. One of the standard narratives deployed to account for these troublesome, supplementary plays argues that Fletcher's collaborative role in relation to that of the late Shakespeare was the equivalent for Shakespeare of a younger member of the studios of Titian or Bernini or Rembrandt, only in a way more so – a younger coadjutor who was being groomed to take over as principal playwright for the King's Men. For Muir and O'Loughlin, as we have already seen, it was simply a question of practicalities, the master returning to assist his less prolific successor: 'The Shakespearean parts of *Henry VIII, The Two Noble Kinsmen*, and *Cardenio* were presumably written in retirement to help his fellows and John Fletcher to keep up with demand for new plays' (*Voyage to Illyria*, 221 n. 1). There is a twist, though, in some versions of the narrative of the end of Shakespeare's life, such as that humorously offered by Tony Dawson in '*Tempest* in a Teapot' ('Shakespeare's [...] worried partners in The King's Men [...] perhaps asked young Fletcher to do what he could to make the old master's new texts acceptable to their increasingly perplexed audiences') in which Fletcher's role has become that of the sorcerer's apprentice, learning from his master only then to ease him out of his role – a development of, though by no means a complete change from, the attitude of Dowden to the collaborative production of *The Two Noble Kinsmen*, for whom 'the degradation of Shakspere's work by the unclean underplot of Fletcher is painful, and almost intolerable'.[55]

In each of these cases, different as they are, the late work is nonetheless in complex ways partly the direct or indirect product of a form of collaboration, even as, particularly in the case of Shakespeare, that collaboration creates problems of attribution. This is not, of course, the case with Bosanquet, who cannot be read as a primary, active collaborator with the late James in the way that Fletcher is with Shakespeare; yet without her facilitation of a marked change in writing method the recognisable late Jamesian style might not have emerged in the way that it did. Equally, the atonal late Stravinsky works cannot be co-attributed to Craft, even though without his influence Stravinsky would in all probability have sustained his resistance to the style of Schoenberg out of which he, in the event, carved his own late manner. Again, Palma Il Giovane cannot be treated as equal to his master in the production of the Titian late style, no matter the ease with which, according to Fisher, he could reproduce that style. Nonetheless, the fact remains that if a given late style can be found in the work of a young man working as an assistant to the originator of that style, then the supposed intrinsic value of the late brushstroke as a signifier of an interior, authorial signified must come under a certain pressure. In other words, even as the input of the collaborator is played down, there is still evidence of that input's effect. It depends, in the end, of course, upon the extent and nature of the shared activity permitted in the critic's working definition of 'collaboration'. If collaboration is restricted to two people working closely together as acknowledged equals on a work of art they share evenly between them, then late work must either remain outside that definition (unless both collaborators happen to be in their late phases) or must be awkwardly fragmented, the input of the unlate collaborator being excised from consideration. But artistic collaboration is rarely so conveniently defined, rarely so clearcut. And whatever definition is deployed, the question of the involvement in the production of late work by figures other than the artist at the end of his or her career asks awkward questions of the ostensible individuality of a late style, questions artists and critics alike prefer to elide. Joseph Straus, writing what he presents accurately as 'the first [book] to be devoted to Stravinsky's late music' (*Stravinsky's Late Music* xiii), notes that

[i]n the early 1950s, Stravinsky's compositional style began to change and evolve with astonishing rapidity. He abandoned the musical neoclassicism to which he had been committed for the preceding three decades and, with the stimulus provided by his newly gained knowledge of the music of Schoenberg and Webern, launched himself on a remarkable voyage of compositional discovery. (ibid.)

There is nothing at all in this account about Craft, who appears to have been airbrushed out of the picture, relegated to the passive voice of 'newly gained knowledge'. Collaboration, on a permanent collision course with

Late style and theatrical production in early modern London 233

subjectivism, must be sidestepped, it seems, if the attribution of a late style is to succeed.

If it is true both of late work in general and of the late work of Renaissance painters in particular that that work is to a surprising and perhaps uncomfortable degree collaborative, the same is also true – even more so, arguably – of the late work of playwrights writing for the early modern English stage. It would obviously be inappropriate to draw too close a comparison between the Renaissance studio system and Elizabethan/Jacobean theatrical collaboration, but it is clear that collaborative authorship is a thorn in the side of critics of late Shakespeare, who are prepared to jump through a series of hoops in order not to address the issue. It should not, however, be the least bit surprising that Shakespeare wrote plays with others in his 'late period'. As numerous scholars have confirmed, collaboration was standard practice in the early modern theatre. G. E. Bentley provides helpful working statistics. '[W]e can', he acknowledges,

only guess at the precise amount of collaboration involved in the plays, but the evidence shows that it must have been large. We know the titles (often no more) of about 1,500 plays from 1590 to 1642. For about 370 we know nothing at all about the authorship. For the remaining 1,100 or so, we have evidence that between ⅕ and ⅙ contained the work of more than one man as either collaborator, reviser, or provider of additional matter. If we consider the professional dramatists only, this proportion is much too low, for the total includes over 200 amateur plays, which after 1590 were seldom collaborated, and it includes many plays about whose authorship we have only a title-page statement, which tended, as a number of known examples show, to simplify the actual circumstances of composition. Altogether the evidence suggests that it would be reasonable to guess that as many as half of the plays by professional dramatists in the period incorporated the writing at some date of more than one man. In the case of the 282 plays mentioned in Henslowe's diary (far and away the most detailed record of authorship that has come down to us) nearly two-thirds are the work of more than one man.[56]

Bentley elaborates on these figures, noting both the significance of the details of collaborative production offered by Henslowe and the extent to which (the Henslowe evidence suggests) title pages mislead by reducing the headcount of collaborators, and he assesses the various collaborative partnerships – from the best known (Beaumont and Fletcher are usually cited as the prime instance) to the far less so (the team of Dekker, Chettle, Smith, Webster and Heywood, say) – in order to distinguish the prevalent patterns of collaboration. In the process, he readily acknowledges the difficulty of maintaining firm boundaries between simultaneous collaboration per se and the kind of collaborative effort in evidence in the work of revisers or 'reformers' of prior work by others. As he notes, '[f]or the scholar the two are often entangled' and he asks rhetorically: 'in a given text which appears to present the work of more than one man, is the second (or third or fourth) hand that of a collaborator, or of a reviser who may never have known the principal author?' (Bentley, *Profession*, 235). Moreover, Bentley's statistics are arguably in any case a little conservative. Neil Carson, examining Henslowe's accounts, notes that collaborations comprised a remarkable 82% of Admiral's Men plays completed in the spring and summer of 1598 and suggests that this may not be exceptional.[57] Together, these critics make it apparent that collaboration should be taken as a (if not quite *the*) norm in Shakespeare's day. 'Well-known collaborations like those of Beaumont and Fletcher or Middleton and Rowley or Shakespeare and Fletcher', Bentley concludes, 'should not be looked upon as oddities, but as common occurrences in the careers of professional dramatists of the time' (ibid., 234).[58]

Brian Vickers, too, argues that 'collaboration was a normal way of sharing the burden of composition, producing a script more quickly, and taking part in a collective enterprise' (*Shakespeare, Co-Author*, 27). Thus, he notes, '[a]t any one time in Jacobean London, up to thirty dramatists may have been involved in group composition, several occupied with more than one play, changing partners according to the project in hand' (ibid.). This prompts him to look for evidence of the practicalities of the collaborative process or, as he puts it: 'we would like to know how dramatists divided up the writing, once they had jointly sketched out the plot as a whole' (ibid.). 'No issue in Shakespeare studies', he announces in the opening paragraph of *Shakespeare, Co-Author*,

> is more important than determining what he wrote. We cannot form any reliable impression of his work as a dramatist unless we can distinguish his authentic plays from those spuriously ascribed to him, whether by publishers in his own age or by scholars in the four centuries intervening, and unless we can identify those parts of collaborative plays that were written by him together with one or more fellow dramatists. (*Shakespeare, Co-Author*, 3)

The solution to the question posed by collaboration, for Vickers, lies in the properly rigorous separation of the inputs of 'co-authors' into a given play by way of a range of established methods for authorial attribution, of which he provides a valuable survey in his second chapter. These range from the mid-nineteenth-century proposals of Hickson and Spedding about the collaborations of Shakespeare and Fletcher to the revisions and refinements of that work in the analyses of Hoy and, later, Hope; and from the ongoing analyses of the Middleton canon by Lake and Jackson (which have led directly to the extended canon shortly to be enshrined in Gary Taylor's *Oxford Middleton*) to the statistics for pause patterns proposed by Oras and the development of metrical patterns mapped by Tarlinskaja and finally to the more problematic cases represented by the generically insensitive stylometric projects of Morton, Metz and Merriam.[59]

Vickers's book is not, however, simply a survey of attributional method. It is also, both implicitly and explicitly, a counterblast to the development of the idea of collaboration as an early modern theatrical norm by critics working in the wake of Michel Foucault who, in his 1969 essay 'What is an Author?', questioned the commonsense presumption that an author is a creative individual who originates and has control over a work. Rather, Foucault argued, the author should be read differently, not as a creative individual but rather as an organising principle within textual culture, as a way in which, retrospectively, we give order to texts. 'The author', he argued, 'does not precede the works, he is a certain functional principle by which, in our culture, one limits, excludes, and chooses', offering a new definition of authorship as 'the principle of thrift in the proliferation of meaning'.[60] For Foucault, the author need not be understood as a unique personality determining the nature and meaning of the text, but rather as the most significant of the many ways culture has established by which to limit the endlessness of interpretation, a formula that emphasises both the contingency of authorship and the dispersal of authority effected by that contingency. This formulation does not deny the role of the writer in the production of the text, but it suggests that the idea of textual control expressed in the concept of authorship – the assumption that the author controls the meaning of the text – is an inadequate way to address the nature of literary texts. For Vickers, who seems not to understand the detachment of 'author' (rhetorical category) from 'writer' (producer of text) that Foucault's intervention requires, this is an unnecessary muddying of the critical waters, an 'anachronistic conception' of authorship 'deriving from Foucault's constant obsession with the issues of power and powerlessness' which 'as a version of history [...] has nothing to recommend it' (*Shakespeare, Co-Author*, 400). 'As a model for scholarly research into authorship problems in Renaissance drama', he insists, 'it is hard to think of anything more irrelevant, or more destructive' (ibid.). Yet Foucault's understanding of authorship cannot be so easily dismissed in the present study for two reasons: first, because it offers a basic critique of the subjectivism that underpins the idea of late style and, secondly, because the Shakespeare/Fletcher collaborations – always the pivot of any debate over attribution – raise profound questions, as I have already suggested, for the establishment of a specifically *Shakespearean* late style.

The critic who has most fully addressed the implications of early modern theatrical collaboration for the understanding of authorship is Jeffrey Masten.[61] Masten develops Bentley's statistics for collaborative playwriting, arguing that

> in a way that has not been full recognized or conceptualized by scholars trained to organize material within post-Enlightenment paradigms of individuality, authorship, and textual property, collaboration was a prevalent mode of textual production in the sixteenth and seventeenth centuries, only eventually displaced by the mode of singular authorship with which we are more familiar.[62]

Early modern dramatic collaborations, Masten argues, 'strikingly denaturalize the author–text–reader continuum assumed in later methodologies of interpretation' and thus require a more historically specific analysis (Masten, *Textual*, 13). Located as they are

> both at a historical moment prior to the emergence of the author in its modern form and as a mode of textual production that distances the writer(s) from the interpreting audience, collaborative play-texts disperse the authorial voice (or rather, our historically subsequent notion of the authorial voice). Read in the forms in which they were initially circulated, these texts instead exhibit the different configurations of authorities constructing, re-forming, and controlling texts and [...] constraining their interpretation. (ibid.)

For Masten, the term 'collaboration', when applied to the early modern stage, cannot be restricted to the rigorous division of co-adjutors in the production of a given play, no matter how ostensibly foolproof the attributional methods deployed, for the simple reason that the author cannot be viewed as the sole, or perhaps even at times the principal, determinant of the meaning of the text. 'The modern critical model of authorial development that dwells upon "date of composition" and first editions', he argues, extending Bentley's recognition of the difficulty of division between collaboration and revision, 'obscures the extent to which a play revived and reprinted could exert a continuing influence on the "original" playwright himself, as well as other playwrights watching, acting in, or revising the play' (Masten, 'Playwrighting', 376). Thus revision, often held to demonstrate the continuing dominance of the author over his text, may 'figure a *complication* of the authorial self – rather than disclose its ongoing unity of intention' (ibid.). Nor is it simply the engagement of playwrights with texts, whether simultaneously or over a period of decades, that questions the possibility of treating a given set of plays as representative of their author's personality. The actual work a playwright does, Masten argues, runs directly counter to the assumption that an individual style will be detectable for a writer. As he points out,

> a playwright im/personates another (many others) in the process of writing a play-text and thus refracts the supposed singularity of the individual in language. At the same time, he often stages in language the *sense* of distinctive personae, putting 'characteristic' words in another's mouth.[63]

There is, in other words, in theatrical writing always a negotiation of the playwright's voice with those of the characters he creates. Identity is, for Masten, far more fluid than attributionists are prepared to admit: 'In attribution study's terms', he argues, 'textual "habits" are taken [...] to convey or express individual identities', but analyses of this kind 'fail to register the ways in which "habits", however seemingly concrete in a given text, can be broken, emulated, adopted, adapted, thrown off, unintentionally lost, and contextual'.[64]

For Vickers, this is absurd. The individual playwright's voice, he insists, retains its distinctiveness even when collaborators share the delineation of a character. He cites Spedding, who argues that the character of Queen Katherine in *Henry VIII* is tangibly different in scenes by each of the collaborating playwrights. In Fletcher's scene of her encounter with Cardinals Wolsey and Campeius, Spedding argues, referring to an earlier, dramatically explicable alteration of character (that of Buckingham before and after being sentenced to death), 'I found her as much changed as Buckingham was after his sentence, though without any alteration of circumstances to account for an alteration of temper' ('Who Wrote', 119). It is odd, especially considering that Vickers, commendably intolerant as he is of kneejerk disparagements of collaborative work, argues insistently for the possibility of artistic coherence in a co-authored play, that he does not do more to question Spedding's assertion here, since it is not in fact hard to see a perfectly good reason for Katherine's shift of manner in the fact of her exile from both court and husband and the sense of powerlessness that that unwanted position has provoked in her by the time of the scene in question. Moreover, while emphasising the persistence of authorial characteristics within the voice of a given character, Vickers will not brook the possibility of the reverse movement, that from character back onto playwright, which is surely the more likely in collaborative work designed, as Masten argues, in order to give an impression of dramatic coherence, not to allow the audience to perceive the fissures between one authorial contribution and another.

As Tiffany Stern has shown, the early modern play-text was itself in any case far more fragmentary and multiply constructed than we have generally cared, because of the longstanding critical insistence on aesthetic unity, to admit. She argues that plays in this period are best viewed as 'assemblages of different parts – prologues, epilogues, songs, letters, actors' speeches – rather than as consistent, tightly-unified "whole" texts' and that '[f]actors which Shakespeare embraced and which in turn moulded his writing' – that is, the practical, material and commercial nature of the theatrical world to which he belonged – 'are shown to be not additional to the plays but deeply embedded within them'.[65] One such practical, commercial factor, one whose significance has only recently begun to be fully acknowledged by critics, is company repertory. Neil Carson has extended our understanding of collaborative playwriting by demonstrating the intersections of collaboration and company organisation. His study of the evidence in Henslowe's *Diary* of the work of the 'Chettle, Dekker, Heywood syndicate' suggests that '[t]he assumption that collaboration was forced on players and dramatists alike by the pressure of the performance schedule [...] seems unsupported by the evidence', and that '[d]ramatists appear to have formed loose partnerships or syndicates which worked together for short periods and then broke up and reformed into other alliances' (*Companion to Henslowe*, 22). As Heather Hirschfeld notes, the patterns of collaboration apparent in Henslowe 'indicate that writers worked not only in pairs but also, more frequently, in groups of three, four, and even five, and the groups observed hierarchies, as some writers were paid more than others for what appears to be the same amount of work on a play' and that,

> though it is not possible to be sure [...] whether the writers themselves arranged these groupings or whether it was the acting companies or financiers who commissioned them, it is clear that collaborative work for the Admiral's and Worcester's Men [...] was characterized in this period by consistency and repetition.[66]

The writing of professional plays for the early modern stage took place not in isolation from the world, in the imaginary garret of *Shakespeare in Love*, but in the determining context of the repertory, the backbone of early modern commercial theatre and, in the words of Roslyn Knutson, 'a company's most potent commercial instrument'.[67] Alexandra Halasz, in her account of the emergence in pamphlet literature of the early modern public sphere, notes the thoroughgoing intersection of theatre with the world of commerce, citing a speech from Dekker's 1609 pamphlet *The Gull's Hornbook* which is often, as she notes, quoted in analyses of the role of the market in theatrical culture but which, in a context of a reception history of late Shakespeare, acquires additional resonance as an analogue of (perhaps even a source for) Prospero's 'revels' speech in *The Tempest* of a year or so later:

The *Theater* is your Poets Royal-Exchange, upon which, their Muses (y^t are now turnd to Merchants) meeting, barter away that light commodity of words for a lighter ware then words. *Plaudities* and the *Breath* of the great *Beast*, which (like the threatnings of two Cowards) vanish all into aire. *Plaiers* and their *Factors*, who put away the stuffe, and make the best of it they possibly can (as indeed tis their parts so to doe).[68]

Theatre here becomes a marketplace, 'an economy of stage production' mapped 'onto the social status of its audience members' which 'reproduces social relations as an effect of commercialization' (Halasz, *Marketplace*, 180); performance becomes breath which 'vanish[es . . .] into air' and players deal with the 'stuff' of theatre (the 'stuff' that dreams are made on, perhaps) as factors rather than as agents; playwrights 'barter' their 'light commodity of words'. In this context, Halasz argues, 'poets, players, and audiences alike are implicated in [. . .] commerciality' (ibid., 179). And one obvious way in which the commercial nature of early modern theatre manifested itself was through the institution of the company for which the playwrights wrote.

The formation of an acting company is a way to ensure the pace and manner of reproduction of the materials of entertainment by multiplying the agents involved and is thus an institutionalisation of the collaborative process, a practical acknowledgement that theatre is never, by definition, a solo affair. On the contrary, the nature of the early modern company repertory militates in several ways against the idea of individual style – and not only because companies often commissioned collaborative plays. Scott McMillin, Sally-Beth MacLean, Mary Bly and Lucy Munro have all in recent years demonstrated the validity of the idea of a *company* style. McMillin and MacLean note that while '[w]e have always settled for the category of authorship to organize our readings of the drama, while we have reserved the category of acting company to organize our narratives of fact', it is possible that 'a new history of Elizabethan drama *and* theatre might emerge [. . .] from combining criticism, textual study, and factual narrative under the primary category of acting company'.[69] Analysing the work of one company, the Queen's Men, they focus on 'those special characteristics which gave the company its identity – its acting style, its staging methods, its kinds of versification, its sense of what constituted a worthwhile repertory of plays', acknowledging both that this 'amounts to saying that acting companies were responsible for the plays they performed and can be evaluated according to that responsibility' and, where '[n]ormally playwrights are seen as the responsible agents' in the production of a play, '[t]hat acting companies have identities too is not such a familiar idea' (*Queen's Men*).

It is important, however, they argue, to realise the extent to which a given company established in its repertory a 'house style', a distinctive way of doing things, and they turn on its head one of the standard objections to this claim – that company personnel never stayed stable, making the establishment of a fixed identity impossible – by pointing out that

[o]rganizations have reason to develop characteristics of their own *because* they are subject to shifts and losses of personnel, and for a repertory acting company, the stock of older plays, with the style connected to them, must carry through to form the basis of each new season or tour. (ibid.)

'We think it clear', they state,

that each company would have had its own style, its own textual procedures, its own sense of purpose, and its own impact on audiences and other acting companies. To some extent these characteristics would have been shared among the other companies, and sometimes actors moved from one troupe to another. (ibid.)

This sense of a fluid but nonetheless distinctive company style is echoed by Mary Bly in her work on the short-lived King's Revels company at the Whitefriars, one of the companies that failed in the lengthy period of plague-closure after which the bulk of Shakespeare's late plays were written. She argues, on straightforward commercial logic, that 'the plays of the Whitefriars company, written by novice playwrights in circumstances of extreme financial duress, display a similar texture due to the deliberate intent to capture a particular market' (*Queer Virgins*, 28). The nature of the company organisation, she claims, was responsible for the apparent 'homogeneity of Whitefriars plays' and she outlines the specifics of that organisation. The history of the company is one of collective effort: 'All seven extant Whitefriars plays show evidence of collaboration' (ibid., 119). And the playwrights were substantially involved in the day-to-day running of the company:

The King's Revels troupe was not democratically run by players (as we might characterize the King's Men), nor was it autocratically run by a single author (as we might describe the Paul's boys under John Marston). The company was started by two playwrights who later brought in another playwright as a shareholder. Two other playwrights became financially involved, through cosigning loans. Thus five playwrights (Drayton, Barry, Machin, Cooke, and Sharpham) were financially interested in the company's future, beyond the normal interest of a professional like John Day, who necessarily scrambles to place his work when a company 'breaks', or goes bankrupt. (ibid., 36–7)

The Whitefriars company – while by no means typical because of the amateur status of the writers concerned – nonetheless speaks of the interweaving of playwright and company and thus the inseparability of authorising functions within the commercial theatrical world, offering resonances for the understanding of the early modern stage as a whole.

Lucy Munro, writing about a professional repertory, that of the Children of the Queen's Revels, offers a fuller picture of the sharing of responsibility for dramatic creativity, arguing that the company's plays

> were created not only by the dramatists, but also through the ideas and desires of the company's shareholders, licenser, patrons, actors and audience. The repertory system of production, organised around playing companies, created an environment in which texts and ideas were circulated between people from vastly different professions and backgrounds. Companies reacted to the plays performed alongside their own, with influences and sources bouncing back and forth between adult and children's companies alike, just as plays occasionally moved from one theatre to another.[70]

In this context, she observes,

> the production of plays [...] was predicated not only on authorial whim, but also on commercial exigency and on the relationship between individuals within companies. Influential patrons such as Anna of Denmark could find their literary tastes reflected, while the predilections of a paying audience were both mocked and feared. Shareholders might preserve plays which were seen as having been abandoned by their authors [...] or they might take plays to other companies. [...] Company members [...] could contribute to the writing of plays as well as to their performance. [...] The commercial need for freshness and innovation, to see plays 'new vamped', propelled changes within the drama and in the constitution of the theatre repertory. (*Children*, 165)

Thus, she notes,

> [a]lthough we often assume that well-known dramatists such as Jonson, Chapman and Marston bore the primary responsibility for their plays, it seems that little-known figures such as [Queen's Revels] shareholders Kendall, Keysar and Kirkham might have had an equally strong influence on dramatic production. (ibid., 53)

Moreover, she adds, '[w]e need also to be aware of the different functions that various individuals may have had within the company at any one time: Field and Barksted, for instance, should be understood as both actors and dramatists, Marston and Daborne as both dramatists and shareholders' (ibid.). For Munro, the inference to be drawn from this is clear: 'To seek a single voice behind any one play – be it writer, actor or shareholder – vastly underestimates the complexity of the way in which early modern plays reached the stage' (ibid.). In fact, she argues, 'it is unnecessary to look for a prime intelligence behind the plays'; rather, '[i]t is in [a] network of allegiances', she continues, 'that any authority behind or over the plays produced will be discovered' (ibid.). 'Rather than looking for a central controlling presence behind the theatrical performances', she concludes, 'we should think perhaps of a composite authority over a play or series of plays, which is strictly local and limited' (ibid.).

Theatrical production in early modern London was, it seems, intrinsically multiple and collaborative. In Stephen Orgel's words,

[t]he company commissioned the play, usually stipulated the subject, often provided the plot, often parceled it out, scene by scene, to several playwrights. The text thus produced was a working model, which the company then revised as seemed appropriate. The author had little or no say in these revisions: the text belonged to the company, and the authority represented by the text – I am talking now about the *performing* text – is that of the company, the owners, not that of the playwright, the author.[71]

For Peter Stallybrass,

[i]nstead of a single author, we have a network of collaborative relations, normally between two or more writers, between writers and acting companies, between acting companies and printers, between compositors and proofreaders, between printers and censors.[72]

Authorial agency is thus understood to be dispersed across a wide range of intentionalities and agencies, no longer inhering in a single authorial consciousness. As Norman Rabkin noted thirty years ago, writing of Ben Jonson's additions to *The Spanish Tragedy*,

[w]e have [them] and we know that they are the best improvements one could imagine[, yet n]o one [...] has ever managed to find in them the unique Ben Jonson of everything to which he signed his name. His invisibility in those additions points to the fact that makes our study of Elizabethan collaboration almost insuperably difficult: the decorum according to which the collaborator serves not himself but a joint project.[73]

'Hot on the trail of a quirky writer's share in a play', he adds, 'we find ourselves repeatedly foiled by the great Elizabethan disappearing act' ('Problems', 12).

It is this position that Vickers resists so fiercely. And he is right in one way: attributional methods have developed a good deal since Rabkin wrote his fine brief essay on the hermeneutics of collaboration and, within the limits of their positivism, they provide a far more reliable account of the tactics of collaboration than they did in the mid-seventies.[74] Moreover, they perform a highly valuable function in sustaining a close focus on details of verse-form and of word-choice and thus of the building blocks of dramatic verse and prose, the basic materials of any adequate critical analysis, in the process sustaining critical and editorial skills which might otherwise be lost. As Macdonald P. Jackson (whose attributional work has been of immense value to scores of editors of early modern play texts) notes somewhat elegiacally in his *Defining Shakespeare*, 'appreciation of the finer details of blank verse movement has declined, as the metrical statistics [. . .] compiled by the New Shakspere Society and its rivals [. . .] have been forgotten or ignored'.[75] There is no denying that without attributional work of this kind, plays such as *Henry VIII*, for which there is no external evidence of collaboration, would simply not be available to analyses such as that of Masten because they would continue to be treated, by default, as solo work. The two opposed ways of addressing authorship – those of Vickers and Masten – are thus in a certain sense co-dependent. At the same time, a hierarchy of genius is apparent all too often in the work of attribution analysts, undermining their apparent objectivity. A. C. Partridge's 1964 account of Shakespearean orthography offers a good, if flagrant, instance of this. He notes that 'the quest' for the sections of the collaborative plays that can be guaranteed to be Shakespeare's is

the more interesting because a writer of lesser gifts, like Fletcher, even if willing to accommodate his literary personality to that of the master in the interests of unity (of which there is not much evidence in *Henry VIII*), would be quite unconscious of his ingrained grammatical habits.[76]

The *a priori* bias apparent here suggests the limitations of such analyses for the criticism they are designed to enhance, limitations given their *reductio ad absurdum* in the stylometrist Thomas Merriam's recent argument that it is essential to differentiate as accurately as possible between the Shakespeare and Fletcher sections of *Henry VIII* for the simple reason that the former are the work of a Roman Catholic and the latter of a Protestant.[77] More to the point, the very work performed by authorial attribution, underlining, as it does, the collaborative nature of so much early modern drama, leads directly to the questioning of the premises upon which such attribution is performed.

A good case in point is offered by David Nicol, when he considers the case of *Wit at Several Weapons*, a play first published in the 1647 Beaumont and Fletcher Folio but with a far more complex authorial history than this might suggest. As Nicol notes,

> three major authorship analyses have concluded that the play is a revision by Middleton and Rowley of an earlier play, presumably by Fletcher. All three consider the play to be a thorough and wholesale revision, to the extent that Cyrus Hoy questioned the point at which a revision becomes a new play.[78]

Piecing together the evidence, Nicol suggests that the revision projected by the attributionists was probably performed by Middleton and Rowley in 1615 for the latter's company, the Prince's Men, following their merger with Lady Elizabeth's Men, a company which, in turn, had emerged from the ashes of the Queen's Revels company. Fletcher had, Nicol notes, 'written several plays for this earlier company, and it is therefore likely that the original version of *Wit* was one of them' ('Mask of Simplicity', 157). 'When the companies merged', he argues,

> they presumably combined their repertoire, and we can therefore assume that Fletcher's original text of *Wit* fell into Rowley's hands around 1614. Rowley's partnership with Middleton would have begun at the same time, since Middleton had previously written *A Chaste Maid in Cheapside* [1613] for Lady Elizabeth's Men. The likeliest explanation for the genesis of *Wit* is, therefore, that it was an old private theatre play revised by Middleton and Rowley for performance by the new, merged company at the Hope playhouse on Bankside. (ibid.)

The process of revision, however, Nicol argues, was not enough entirely to erase the play's origins:

> We cannot know precisely what the original Fletcher play was like, or what Middleton and Rowley did to it, but the extant text seems at first glance incongruous with the repertoire of a public theatre company. [. . . It is] similar to the city comedies performed by the boys' companies in 1600–10. Like those plays, it is thoroughly unromantic, for the happy ending rewards those who are the most cunning and devious. ('Mask of Simplicity', 156–7)

In other words, the play, though clearly in various ways a Prince's Men product, retains traces of its original role as work for a children's company known for a particular kind of satiric drama. The extant *Wit at Several Weapons*, then, is a collaborative play shaped by the commercial environment for which it was produced and subsequently reproduced and it demonstrates the difficulty, practical and theoretical, of separating out not only the inputs of the three collaborating playwrights but also the impact of the three company repertories through which the play appears to have passed and by which it has been substantially moulded.

Part of the interest of the case of *Wit at Several Weapons* for the student of late Shakespeare, needless to say, is the involvement of Fletcher, who not so very long after writing the first version of *Wit* collaborated with Shakespeare over a period, probably, of eighteen months or so on a total of three plays. How different, we might want to ask, then, are Fletcher's collaborative Queen's Revels plays from his King's Company plays? Or, to ask the same question differently, to what extent did the King's Company repertory change once Fletcher began to write for that company? To what extent are those changes due to Fletcher and to what extent are they due to the Queen's Revels style that he brought with him? And to what extent does a collaborative process of this kind – the construction and reconstruction of a play by three playwrights in a range of different repertory contexts – impinge upon the assumptions implicit in the attribution of a periodic style – a late style, say – to a given playwright? While the Shakespeare/Fletcher collaborations may indeed be 'late' Shakespeare, they are also, as I suggested in Chapter 2, 'early' (or at least earlyish) Fletcher, making uncomfortably apparent the difficulty raised by the evidence of the collaborative nature of early modern drama for the attribution of a late style to any individual playwright in the period – not least, of course, Shakespeare. Collaboration – the engagement of more than one creative subjectivity in the production of a text – even if restricted to the interaction of equal coadjutors, makes the establishment of a late style – a style understood as the product of a particular creative individual at a particular stage of his life – deeply problematic.

Perhaps the simplest way to pursue this question is to examine the last plays of playwrights other than Shakespeare who have, like him, been subsequently accorded the status of genius, but for whom late phases have either never been ascribed or at best only unconvincingly so. John Webster (who, like Middleton and in a certain way Fletcher, was a collaborator of Rowley's) is a good instance of a genius of the early modern theatre to whom a late style has never been attributed. It is not hard to see why, however, since a playwriting life less like the approved individual *cursus* required for an ascription of late style would be hard to imagine. By the end of the 1950s, Webster had been firmly canonised: critics (ignoring for the moment their parallel belief that he was the epitome of the supposed post-Shakespearean, pre-Civil War 'decadence of the drama') had acclaimed him – in just two plays, *The White Devil* and *The Duchess of Malfi* – as reaching as close as anyone to Shakespeare in his tragic achievement. 'John Webster's two tragedies are', as R. W. Dent put it, 'commonly regarded as the finest to be produced by any Jacobean dramatist other than Shakespeare, and hence among the best to be produced by any English playwright of any age.'[79] But it was Dent's own book, *John Webster's Borrowing*, published in 1960, that put this ascription of genius under the severest scrutiny. Dent suggested, to use his own mild phrasing, that it might be 'necessary to revise somewhat our bases for admiring Webster's poetic genius', since he had painstakingly demonstrated that Webster was in fact a consummate and habitual plagiarist (*Borrowing*, 4). Earlier critics had certainly been aware of Webster's occasional indebtedness to others, notably Shakespeare, but they did not see this as exceptional – the occasional unconscious reminiscence or conscious citation, the latter generally viewed as overt homage to the prior writer. For Hereward Price, writing a landmark essay on Webster's imagery in 1955, 'whatever he took he worked into the essential substance of the play'.[80] But Dent demonstrated that Webster's compositional method went much further than this, that something like three-quarters of Webster's lines are in fact traceable to someone writing before him, suggesting, in effect, that it becomes impossible to track down the 'essential substance' of a play composed substantially of the words of others.

Critics prior to Dent were fully aware that early modern writers used commonplace books as an aid to writing, that they would typically jot down passages they admired in whatever they were reading into a kind of diary that they would have to hand when they started their own writing. After all, every early modern writer worked within a rhetorical tradition that recommended, as a key tenet of good practice, the imitation of predecessors – most obviously, of course, of classical predecessors. At the same time, they held to a firm distinction between 'imitation' – that is, working with images bequeathed from forebears but reshaping them into something new and fresh – and 'plagiarism' – that is, copying out wholesale the writing of others and passing it off as their own. Poets such as Ben Jonson spent a deal of time and venom writing poems attacking others – perhaps the most often-cited instance is Robert Greene – for (in Dent's words) 'hastily turning out saleable commodities with a minimum of effort and a maximum of copying' (*Borrowing*, 8). But Webster was always thought of as a slow, careful producer of great art, not a hack copyist like Greene looking for a quick buck. The role of the commonplace book had, all the same, always been apparent in the shape of the *sententiae* that crop up regularly in *The White Devil* and *The Duchess of Malfi*, the moralising rhyming couplets that characters produce in contexts which make them either trite, ironic or compromising, or perhaps all three. Antonio's oft-quoted first speech offers a clear instance of this. Moralising about authority, he observes that

> a prince's court
> Is like a common fountain, whence should flow
> Pure silver drops in general; but if't chance
> Some cursed example poison't near the head,
> Death and diseases through the whole land spread.

The last couplet announces itself, simply by rhyming, as deriving from elsewhere, thereby implying that the rest is Webster's own (editions frequently italicise such rhyming couplets in order to reinforce their difference from the surrounding lines), but, as Dent made clear, it is in fact the entire speech, not just the final couplet, that is drawn from the work of others, taken almost verbatim, that is, either from Elyot's *Image of Governance* (1541) or from Plutarch's *Morals* as translated in 1603 by Philemon Holland. Dent went on to demonstrate the pervasiveness of this practice throughout the five acts of the play, providing charts of representative sections of scenes from the Webster canon to demonstrate the extraordinary extent (to modern eyes, at least) of the borrowing in the major tragedies. Websterian authorship, in the established sense of the word as original composition determined and unified by a personality, was dissolving before the critics' eyes.

Moreover, the teleology of Webster's career takes the problem of the dissolution of authorial selfhood a stage further – and, in the process, provides a useful test case for an analysis of the idea of late style – since it is clear that, rather than emerging from youthful collaboration into full possession of his mature powers, Webster followed a quite different trajectory, his plays in fact becoming more and more collaborative as his theatrical career came to a close, to the extent that the question posed by the title of a recent essay by Jackson – 'Late Webster and His Collaborators: How Many Playwrights Wrote *A Cure for a Cuckold?*' – raises issues over and above the purely attributional, issues we have already considered of the ascription of a late period and the relationship of the recipient of that ascription to collaborating playwrights at different phases of their lives.[81] Noting that the play's 1661 title page attributes it to John Webster and William Rowley, Jackson sets out to demonstrate the unacknowledged involvement also of Thomas Heywood, thereby confirming the claim of the first critic to suggest this might be the case, H. D. Gray.[82] In the process (though this is not his aim), he makes it clear that his description of *A Cure for a Cuckold* as 'late Webster' sits at best uncomfortably with his attributional premise. After all, that attribution depends on whose canon is being described, Webster's or that of one or other of his collaborators. As Jackson reports, the play's early-twentieth-century editor, F. L. Lucas, had noted that '[b]oth of Webster's latest plays show "some strong marks of Heywood's style"', had wondered if the answer to this question was 'that Webster was [...] imitating Heywood or that he was collaborating with him' or that 'one of them [was] revising the other's work', and had, like Gray, concluded, though he lacked clear proof, that Heywood had indeed collaborated on the play.[83] Jackson provides that proof by way of a computational analysis of verbal parallels between the known solo plays of the individual playwrights which shows the statistically high likelihood of Heywood's involvement as an active collaborator, but he does not in the process address the larger issue that the title of his article arguably invites – the question, that is, of the feasibility of the attribution of a body of 'late work' to a group of collaborative playtexts. If *A Cure for a Cuckold* is the work of two or three playwrights, how can it be thought of as 'late Webster'? After all, as we have repeatedly seen, the attribution of a late phase and a late style is a way to distinguish a certain élite of artists from the merely productive, to provide a way to make key individuals stand apart from others; Webster's trajectory, by contrast, is one of increasing collaboration, not increasing individuation. As such, it arguably disables – or at least runs directly counter to – the discourse of lateness. Webster's movement from solo plays constructed from the words of others to collaborations written more or less overtly with others is a logical enough progression, but it also stands as an implicit acknowledgement that authorship – like the idea of honour or the materiality of the flesh in his tragedies – is far more soluble and dispersed than those keen to attribute a late style to a given playwright might care to acknowledge. From commonplace books to collaboration, Webster's techniques of construction in his plays appear as forms of *bricolage*, assemblings of others' texts, others' voices, as he moved from building his plays out of others' words to building plays with others, offering a counter-narrative to the Romantic idea of the maturing of the lone creative genius. He collected quotations, absorbed others' voices and wrote with, round and through others. His 'selfhood' as a playwright is thus remarkably difficult, indeed impossible, to pinpoint and certainly no adequate version of 'late Webster' can readily be isolated. In effect, by the time he stopped writing altogether around 1627, Webster the author had almost entirely dissolved, standing instead as a paradigm of the intertextual, collaborative process that was the production of early modern drama and thus outside the framework of possibility for the attribution of a late style.

Not that this should be surprising. I have already cited (as critics frequently do) John Hoskins's disarming comment on the putting on and taking off of style: 'For my part I have used and outworn six several styles since I was first Fellow of New College, and am yet able to bear the fashion of writing company'.[84] John Florio, addressing the same issue in the prefatory essay to his translation of Montaigne's essays (which Shakespeare knew), asks, 'What doe the best then, but gleane after others harvest? borrow their colours, inherite their possessions? What doe they but translate? perhaps, usurpe? At least, collect?'[85] Florio's understanding of authorship here as the practice of a 'collector' is echoed in a curious commentary on the nature of dramatic style to be found in a scene from the second part of *Return from Parnassus*, a Cambridge University play that satirises the professional stage, with characters commenting on certain playwrights' writerly techniques. For Heather Hirschfeld, discussing this play and the understanding of style it implies, 'the authors of the *Parnassus* plays recognize and categorize writers according to an implicit, assumed sense of what constitutes writerly style; they conflate biographical detail and linguistic proclivities into a measure of authorial "personality"' (*Joint Enterprises*, 25) – yet the impact of the attitude to style apparent in the *Parnassus* plays, I wish to suggest, is in fact quite other than this, the implications of the play's attempt to define a given playwright's style in terms of the styles of others being that style is always in fact *composite*. The character Judicio, for instance, notes the deployment of the commonplace book, which contains '[s]entences gathered out of all kind of Poetts, referred to certaine methodicall heads, profitable for the vse of these times, to rime vpon any occasion at a little warning'.[86] John Marston, similarly, is described by Ingenioso in terms of styles *not* his own:

> Me thinks he is a Ruffian in his stile,
> Withouten bands or garters ornament.
> He quaffs a cup of Frenchmans Helicon,
> Then royster doyster in his oylie tearmes,
> Cutts, thrusts, and foines at whomsoeuer he meets,
> And strewes about Ram-ally meditations.   (1.2.269–74)

Generic, not personal, considerations seem paramount here, the style adopted suiting the shift of tone required for a new scene. The style of 'Marston' is thus a synthesis of styles, of Nicholas Udall's *Ralph Royster*

Doyster (*c.* 1534–41), perhaps the rhetorical style of Montaigne ('Frenchman's Helicon'?) and of another, more basic form of rhetoric, the canting associated with Ram Alley, a lane off Fleet Street once a resort of those fleeing from the law – all of which adds up, for Ingenioso, to a *déclassé* manner. This is not to say that the resultant style is not therefore characteristic of Marston, but rather that the acquisition of a distinctive style is a cumulative, composite process of imitation of the styles of others. Even Ben Jonson, always thought of, then and now, as the most forthrightly distinctive of early modern playwrights, is described, condescendingly, as a *bricoleur*, as a bodger assembling texts as he might have assembled construction materials in his days in the building trade:

A Meere Empyrick, one that getts what he hath by obseruation, and makes onely nature priuy to what he enditeth; so slow an Inuentor, that he were better betake himselfe to his old trade of Bricklaying: a bould whorson, as confident now in making of a booke, as he was in times past in laying of a brick. (1.2.293–99)

In a literalising and downgrading of the process of imitation, style is read as a process of derivation and multiplication and playwriting as work for a bricklayer, not a poet.

This may simply demonstrate the different understandings two critics with basically shared interests can have of lines in the same play, but two things are, at least, clear. One is that Webster, who became more and more collaborative as his career progressed, cannot be taken as an instance of a playwright with a late style defined in the traditional way as a final period of creativity driven internally by the fact of old age or proximity to death. The other is that neither, more to the point, can Jonson himself, the disparaged ex-bricklayer and the primary exemplar when a self-conscious Elizabethan/Jacobean playwright-author is sought. Jonson's last plays, while forming a distinct bloc at the end of his career, do not, despite isolated critical attempts to argue otherwise, comfortably fit received ideas of the stylistic or generic features associated with lateness, and to suggest that they derive from a Jonsonian 'late moment' is to elide their emergence from particular topical circumstances. Jonson, impatient and ambitious, had arguably in any case already used up in mid-life a significant 'late' gesture (one deployed to marked effect, as we have seen, three-hundred-odd years later by Henry James) when he published his collected plays in folio. The 1616 *Works*, though deliberately chronological and ostensibly encyclopaedic, is not 'late work' per se, functioning a little in the way of contemporary ghosted autobiographies of sports stars that conclude in early middle age. In any case, to read the plays on the basis of Jonson's personality in this way is to be complicit in Jonson's own construction of his poetic selfhood, the self-conscious wrenching of a version of authorship apparent in his resistance to the reproduction of his collaborative plays in print. 'I would inform you', he wrote in a note in the 1605 Quarto of *Sejanus His Fall*,

> that this book, in all its numbers, is not the same with that which was acted on the public stage, wherein a second pen had good share: in place of which I have rather chosen to put weaker (and no doubt less pleasing) of mine own, than to defraud so happy a genius of his own right by my loathed usurpation.

As Bentley puts it, 'only Jonson, with his growing preoccupation with posterity, would have gone so far as painstakingly to weed out of the text all the words of his collaborator' (*Profession*, 207). At this stage of his career, Jonson's authorial vista was clear and his dynamic apparent. The circumstances of his late work, however, seem to have been quite different. As Joseph Loewenstein observes, 'while most careers can be mapped as a development, Jonson's may be distinctively mapped in terms of resurgences'; his late period is perhaps best viewed as one of a series of such resurgences rather than as the endpoint of a transcendent teleology.[87]

A major technical problem for analysts of Jonsonian lateness is in any case his obvious distaste for Shakespearean lateness, or at least for the style and nature of the plays written by Shakespeare during the period we consider 'late' – he dismissed them, as we have seen, as '*Tales, Tempests,* and such like *Drolleries*', 'a nest of *Antiques*', 'a concupiscence of *Iigges* and *Dances*', and for him *Pericles* was 'some mouldy tale' – though this has not stopped critics from attempting to shape Jonson's last work as a version of that of Shakespeare. The most thorough attempt so to do is that of Anne Barton, who in her 1984 book *Ben Jonson, Dramatist* argues – despite a disclaimer ('It is emphatically not', she says, 'my intention in this book either to sentimentalize Jonson or to make him over in the image of Shakespeare') – that

> [t]his entire group of plays, heralded by *The Devil Is An Ass* in 1616, represents a late style, a radical re-thinking of both his Elizabethan and his Jacobean comic modes, like that we have come to associate with Shakespeare's late plays. Jonson too ended by writing extreme, self-conscious comedies which, in his case, not only reach back to Elizabethan forms he had once disdained, but re-think some of his own early work.[88]

While she is undoubtedly right that Jonson's Caroline plays are 'works of substance and delight', that '*The New Inn, A Tale of a Tub* and *The Sad Shepherd*, in particular, have been seriously mis-read and underestimated' (*Ben Jonson*, xi) – as Martin Butler has insisted, these plays are by no means the 'dotages' Dryden thought them – and that in various ways these plays rethink aspects of Jonson's earlier work, she arguably herself misreads these plays by treating them as instances of a late style in a direct parallel with Shakespeare.[89] For one thing, while forming a bloc at the end of the career, they do not comfortably fit received ideas of the stylistic or generic features associated with lateness and they are adequately explained neither by mapping them overtly onto the model of late Shakespeare, as Barton implicitly does in reading *A Tale of a Tub*, for instance, as, 'like certain sections of *Pericles, Cymbeline* and *The Winter's Tale* [...] an immensely sophisticated attempt to re-create the atmosphere of early Elizabethan drama', nor by setting them up, with Larry Champion, as an instance of the opposite phenomenon, of the kind of late work that Edward Said would have admired, the last works of a stubborn personality who, 'in character until the end, did not, like Shakespeare via Prospero, break his staff and drown his book'.[90]

For Julie Sanders, readings of this kind, in their insistent focus on the author alone, 'underestimate the [...] topicality' of the Jonsonian late plays 'as well as the continuing exercises in dramatic experimentation' they represent and downplay the extent to which late Jonsonian theatre, with its local thick-description specificity, draws upon and echoes the work of other Caroline playwrights, especially the Blackfriars plays of the very late 1620s and early 1630s.[91] The plays were composed, as Martin Butler notes, 'immediately prior to the recall of the last of Charles's early Parliaments, in March 1629', which was 'a moment in which rapprochement or accommodation, rather than confrontation, might at last have been achieved between the court and the court's critics' ('Late Jonson', 172), a context in which, for Sanders, the emphasis on ideal communities in *The New Inn*, *The Magnetic Lady* and *The Sad Shepherd*, which might easily be read as a connection with late-play pastoralism, appears far less the product of late otherworldliness than a response to and negotiation of tangible political contingencies. For Andrew Stewart, Jonson in *The New Inn*

> unfolds a world in which unity, tolerance and merriment are not just achievable but compulsory. [...] The story told is [...] that of Lovel's education into happiness and the Host's recovery of his wife and family, together with the re-adoption of his title. These are events which are emblematic of the re-discovery of aristocratic responsibility and importance, and were extremely pertinent in the aftermath of Buckingham's death.[92]

'The political situation', Stewart argues, 'must have appeared to be simultaneously in a state of relative harmony and unsettling flux. This was the climate in which Jonson wrote his play, celebrating the rejuvenation and reconciliation of the aristocracy and the incorporation of the disaffected into a newly promising world' ('Some Uses', para. 17).

In the end, then, for Stewart, as for Sanders, the projected relationship between late Shakespeare and late Jonson 'rests, if it rests at all, upon a basis almost too shifting and insubstantial to be perceptible, even with the greatest permissible level of speculation' (ibid., para. 24). Thus late Jonson, rather than embodying a tragicomic transcendence of matters political as the comparison with late Shakespeare implicitly requires, appears instead to be very much the opposite, that is, the product of intersecting political contexts channelled by way of Jonson's own compromised place between social worlds. Arguably, then, for Jonson no more than for Webster, despite the immense difference between their respective trajectories, can a late phase be constructed with any degree of comfort. Shakespeare's remains the stand-alone early modern dramatic 'late period' and it too, as we have seen, offers a remarkably poor fit with received ideas of lateness – though this is hardly surprising since the first move in the establishment of a Shakespearean late phase was the elision of the actual conditions for dramatic production. It is the multiply collaborative model offered by Webster, far more than Jonson's furious, repeated attempts to invent himself as author, that lays bare for us the workings of the early modern stage. It is simply not a model that lends itself to the attribution of a late style.

In the course of this chapter, I have both given and taken away the possibility of ascribing a late style to an early modern playwright. I have argued that in certain aspects of early modern culture we can find the potential for the invention of late style. I have argued too, however, that that potential could only be fulfilled in the context of subsequent developments in the philosophy of creativity, developments I outlined in Chapter 2, notably the construction, at the end of the eighteenth and beginning of the nineteenth centuries, of a notion of individual style and thus the assertion of an intrinsic connection between style and author that was simply unavailable in early modern England. We have seen the value attributed to last words in the period. We have seen too the complexly collaborative process through which early modern plays came into being, the impersonal dispersal of individual authority effected by the commercial process expressed in collaboration and repertory. If last words are to be detected in the so-called 'late plays' of Shakespeare or Jonson or Middleton, they would need to make their way through impossible levels of interference. In the end, I wish to argue, it has become impossible for us to speak of the 'late work' of an early modern playwright. Shakespeare's 'late plays' are, in the sense in which a postromantic critical mindset understands that term – as a statement of a fundamental connection between the state of mind of the playwright in the last period before his death and the nature of the plays produced in that period – not late plays at all.

If there is a model late stylist in the period, it is surely not in any case Shakespeare (or, for that matter, Jonson) but rather his rival (and, for *The Winter's Tale*, principal source) Robert Greene, whose last works embody an entertainingly excessive sense of the significance of the end of life, a form of testamentary work *avant la lettre* that invokes the theological weight of last words in order to demand authorial ascription while at the same time evading it. Perhaps it is this that best characterises late style: a kind of excess, a version of the supplementary but with a heightened degree of impact, over and above the individual canon. Certainly, Greene's 'deathbed' pamphlets have an air of the excessive, perhaps most of all *Greenes Vision: Written at the instant of his death. Conteyning a penitent passion for the folly of his Pen* (1592), in which the dedicatory address ends 'Yours dying. Robert Greene', the mingled self-pity and irascibility of the authorial persona serving to resist the obliteration of that persona 'at the instant of his death'.[93] This dedication appears to confirm both the sense of privilege and the theological import we have seen accruing to last words in the early modern period. 'It was one of the last workes of a wel known Author, therefore I hope it will be the more acceptable', announces Greene, adding in the third person that '[m]anie have published repentaunces under his name, but none more unfeigned then this, being euerie word of his owne: his own phrase, his own method', and then specifying the source of inspiration: 'The experience of many vices brought forth this last vision of vertue' (*Greenes Vision*, A3r). The irony of this final sentence is compounded in the context of the rest, since Greene is a notable exemplar of the problem of authenticity, a prime test case for attributional method. In another of the 'deathbed' pamphlets (the best known of them), *Greene's Groats-worth of witte, bought with a million of Repentance* (1592), Greene warns other playwrights against untrustworthy actors, famously describing Shakespeare as 'an upstart Crow, beautified with our feathers, that with his *Tygers heart wrapt in a Players hyde*, supposes he is as well able to bombast out a blanke verse as the best of you' – that is, as a plagiarist. In the address to the reader, the image of the swan is invoked:

The Swan sings melodiously before death, that in all his life time useth but a jarring sound. *Greene* though able inough to write, yet deeplyer serched with sicknes than ever heeretofore, sendes you his Swanne like songe, for that he feares he shall never againe carroll to you woonted love layes, never again discover to you youths pleasures.[94]

'This is the last I have writ', he announces, 'and I feare me the last I shall writ' (*Groats-worth*, A2v). In this context, it is especially ironic that *Greene's Groats-worth* has recently and convincingly been argued to be the work not of Greene but of Henry Chettle, the swan song displaced and the lateness purely rhetorical.[95] And the complex identity offered here for late writing is further complicated by the image of Greene that appears on the title page of *Greene in Conceipt*, a pamphlet written after his death by John Dickenson, capitalising, like Chettle before him, on the commercial value of the Greene persona that was really only fully established after the author's death, and offsetting the reverence accorded to 'last workes' by offering a farcically excessive version of lateness, as we see the dead writer, pen in hand, sitting up to table, still writing even in his shroud, producing work in what can only be described as the latest of late styles.[96]

The point, of course, is that, though classical and Christian tradition opens up the possibility of a heuristic view of the last words and deeds of the virtuous individual and though Montaigne's anxiety to retain the mental clarity to capitalise on the increasing urgency of productivity at the end of his life suggests an embryonic version of the quest for the 'late manner' we have seen at its anxious zenith in Henry James, the context and conditions for the pre-nineteenth-century understanding of such matters is wholly different from that expressed in the idea of late writing. In any case, the nature of playwriting in early modern England – despite all that Ben Jonson could do to finesse it – was inimical to subjectivism: it was a collective, collaborative process that cannot adequately be represented by the figure of the self-contained individual author. Shakespeare understood the significance of last words perfectly well, but he would have had – could have had – no comprehension of the idea of late writing as it would subsequently be constructed. The image of Greene continuing to write beyond the grave runs back against itself in spectacular manner, since in asserting the ongoing writing persona, the relentless drive to create an identifiable personal style, it in fact demonstrates the detachment of that style from the author in the context of death – lateness 'defin[ing] itself by acknowledging its own death' in Subotnik's words ('Adorno's Diagnosis', 259) – since, by the time he finally achieved the cachet of authorship, Greene was already in his grave and someone else was producing 'his' work.

In a complex way, then, we return, by way of the collaborative conditions within which early modern drama came into being, to Adorno's understanding of late style, to the 'ceding to heteronomy' that he defined as the ultimate achievement of the purportedly autonomous subject, the acceptance that there is no longer, at the ultimate moment, any direct relationship between style and self and that both are in any case the product of external forces, not of the kind of interiority required for an ascription of authorship, and thus of a late style, in the modern sense. That concept was in formation at the time, Jonson being the obvious, though not the only, figure willing it into existence. But it was not yet fully a possibility. In any case, in Adorno's terms, late style militates against its own subjectivist premise. For him, at the late (perhaps at the *latest*) moment, the composer (writer, painter) finally concedes the impossibility of a synthesis of subjective and objective, of self and convention, and it is this recognition which produces the late style, even as it makes that late style in a certain sense impossible, read *as* the late style of a given artist, because it refuses the unifying requirement for such a style. The attribution of a late style paradoxically, then, even as it depends upon the idea of the author, foregrounds the crisis in authorship – especially in the Shakespearean context of a theatrical economy based in collaborative endeavour – insisting as it does on the primacy of subjectivity in the face of the dissolution of that subjectivity. What is left after the deconstruction of selfhood effected in late writing is, as Adorno argues, *convention* – that is, genre, style, form, the rules of the game – not a supplementation or apotheosis of subjectivity. Still believing in a generalised *late style*, a phenomenon reproducible across time, Adorno in the same sentence acknowledges the impossibility of such a style, since the late work can be the product neither, in its conventionality, of a self nor, in its contingency, of the universal and transcendent. The attempt, in other words, to ground an understanding of a given late style either in the individual within whose career that style is detected or in the epoch within which that individual operates can never be adequate. At the same time, the late style remains as a monument to the impossible *idea* of that style.

As a result, it may well be that, in their conventional, archaic, resistant, fragmentary, tragicomic, collaborative supplementarity, the Shakespearean late plays form the most heuristic possible conclusion to the career, representing the impossibility of the identification of a given late style with the trajectory of an early modern playwright and thus of the inappropriateness of the quest to isolate a specifically Shakespearean late style, even when that style appears to be at its most distinct. Generically, stylistically and chronologically, we have seen that the plays resist resolution to a clear, separable, unifiable group, equally appearing to stand apart from what preceded them and to depend upon earlier genres, forms and styles, upon what would have seemed to their first audiences both fashionable and outmoded. For those seeking to celebrate that late style, the plays both turn back to the early in the form of the early canon (Gower in *Pericles*; the source of *The Two Noble Kinsmen* in Chaucer's *Knight's Tale*; that of *The Tempest* in *The Aeneid*) or the early nation or the formation of nations (Cranmer's speech in *Henry VIII*; *The Tempest*'s colonial premises and, again, its Virgilian underpinnings; *Cymbeline*'s dramatisation of the colonisation of Britain) or of the pastoral world that precedes, undercuts or supersedes the courtly (*The Winter's Tale*'s green world, the music of the isle and the illusion of masque in *The Tempest*, the shepherd-masque in *Henry VIII*, all of which are anchored in one way or another in the locus of retirement in Stratford, as opposed to the cosmopolitanism of London) and they look forward, it is alleged, via mannerism, to the fragmentary, abstract modes of modernism.[97] The simultaneous historicity and ahistoricity of this reception is highly striking and in a way fits well enough with the paradoxical premises of the idea of late writing. This self-cancelling simultaneity allows critics to celebrate the late plays as situated beyond the reach of analysis, as powerful instances of art as pure aesthetic, as a transforming, magical force immune to contingency, while at the same time the late style is characterised by a turn towards convention, a sense that it is specifically in the plays' negotiations, of received forms that their identity lies.

I outlined in Chapter 1 certain constituent binaries for the identification of a late style, seeing in those binaries both the origins of and the obstacles to such an identification. The reception history of late Shakespeare demonstrates the antithetical deployment of each of these binaries. For critics at different times in the course of the last century and a half, Shakespeare's late writing has been both *personal* – a style which emerges from the internal life of the playwright, representing a return to the most characteristic motifs and styles of his own earlier life – and *impersonal* – a style which either reflects forces beyond Shakespeare's control, notably the emergence of the modern subject and the inevitability of the establishment of such a style in a creative artist of genius, or is the product of collaboration and/or company repertory. It has been both *involuntary* – a late style of which Shakespeare was channel rather than origin, one that descends willy-nilly on genius – and *knowing* – a late style self-consciously established by Shakespeare on the basis of a version of the classical *rota* as an assertion of his own literariness. It has been both *serene* – a late style marking a period of final calm after the agonies embodied in the tragedies which is most fully expressed in Prospero – and *irascible* – a late style marking a period of weariness or resentful decline in the context of old age and death, most fully embodied also, but on different grounds, in Prospero. It has been both *childlike* – plays which embody a simplification of dramatic engagement and a return to youth both as subject matter and as protagonist – and *difficult* – plays which are characterised by a stylistic jaggedness and harshness unavailable in the rest of the *œuvre*. It has been both *archaic* – a late style embodying a turn to earlier, even atavistic, dramatic forms and themes – and *proleptic* – a late style offering a version of the 'abstractions' of mannerism and thus foreseeing the eventual emergence, centuries ahead, of modernism. And it has served both as *completion* – a late style which is the crowning achievement of the career, fulfilling a curve traceable back to the earliest comedies – and as *supplement* – a late style seen as additional, both in genre, existing over and above the canonical comedies, tragedies and histories of the Folio, and in chronology, as work which postdates the major tragic achievement. The Shakespearean late style is thus in a range of ways both possible and impossible, a distillation of a reception history fundamentally and persistently at odds with itself in respect of the nature of Shakespearean creativity and particularly in respect of the relationship between style and the life of the author.

There is one more constituent binary, one that addresses a key, perhaps *the* key, question in the analysis of the discourse of lateness, that I have not yet mentioned – that of *old age* and *the proximity of death* – and it is that to which I will turn in the next chapter.

CHAPTER 5

How old is 'late'? Late Shakespeare, old age, King Lear

From my sixth year I have had a passion for sketching the form of things. From about the age of fifty I produced a number of designs, yet of all I drew prior to my seventieth year there is truly nothing of any great note. In my seventy-third year I finally apprehended something of the true quality of birds, animals, insects, fishes, and of the vital nature of grasses and trees. Therefore in my eightieth year I shall have made some progress, in my ninetieth I shall have penetrated even further into the deeper meaning of things, in my hundredth year I shall have become truly marvellous, and at one hundred and ten each dot, each line shall surely possess a life of its own. I only beg that gentlemen of sufficiently long life take care to note the truth of my words.[1]

The seventy-one-year-old artist has previously talked of retirement. But that would now seem to have been premature. 'My new concept,' he announced, 'is that I am into my late period. Most artists go potty as they get older: dafter and madder as they get more celibate. So I am consciously going to do that'.[2]

The account by the Japanese artist Hokusai of the relationship of age to creative achievement, which was written in 1834, may belong to a culture quite other than the Western tradition I have been examining in this book, a culture with very different attitudes both to old age and to creativity, but it chimes productively, if somewhat uncomfortably, nonetheless, both in its seriousness and in its apparent irony, with the discourse of lateness that I have mapped by way of Shakespearean reception history. For Hokusai, who was seventy-four at the time of writing, life begins at a hundred and ten, suggesting both the importance of longevity in the creative process and the absurdity of a trajectory that is humanly impossible. Peter Blake arguably sets himself up as Hokusai's postmodern counterpart, announcing, both amusingly and with considerable self-consciousness, the commencement of his own 'late period' at the age of seventy-one. For both artists, lateness and longevity operate hand in glove. After all, if there is a single essential prerequisite for the attribution of a late style, logic suggests, it must be old age. Thus it bothers Shakespeareans beyond measure that Shakespeare was not actually *old* when he wrote his late plays. For Henry James, it was, as we have seen, an outrage that Shakespeare could have chosen to retire before his time. 'What manner of human being was it', he demanded, appalled, 'who *could* so, at a given moment, announce his intention of capping his divine flame with a twopenny extinguisher, and who then, the announcement made, could serenely succeed in carrying it out?' It is, for James, simply incomprehensible that a creative artist of Shakespeare's calibre could choose to stop working before the contingencies of age should force him to do so. And this frustration is by no means restricted to Henry James. The question of age has undermined subjectivist criticism of the late plays with sufficient consistency that the disjuncture between 'late' Shakespeare and 'old-age' Shakespeare has been and still is regularly, even systematically, elided. In this chapter, I wish to address the one remaining major issue in the analysis of late style that I have yet fully to broach – that of the relationship of late writing to old age – by way of the problem posed by Shakespeare's middle-aged late phase and by the effects on the interpretation of Shakespearean drama of the critical desire for Shakespeare himself to be convincingly old. In the final chapter, I will address the perhaps unexpected utility that this middle-aged Shakespearean late phase has acquired, through the identification of Shakespeare with one of his late-play characters, for the construction of the careers and selfhoods of certain twentieth- and twenty-first-century actors and directors. But first of all I wish to examine the question of the relationship – or, rather, the absence of relationship, the lack of identity – between two phenomena generally assumed to be identical – *Spätstil* and *Altersstil*, 'late style' and 'old-age style' – and to consider the particular impact of that lack on the critical analysis not of the last plays themselves but rather of a play in the Shakespeare canon that, by way both of its generic markers and of the date of its primary moment of composition, appears to lie outside the late-play group yet which has, in effect and for various reasons, been treated *as if it were* a late play.

5.1 OLD-AGE STYLE

Hugo Munsterberg's celebration of artistic creativity in old age, *The Crown of Life*, offers a clear instance of the critical blind spot that is apparent in the conflation of 'old-age style' with 'late style'. Munsterberg focusses for the most part on painters and sculptors, only occasionally citing practitioners in other genres (he mentions Beethoven, Goethe and Tennyson, but only briefly). He does, however, cite Shakespeare, quoting Jaques's ages-of-man speech – '[t]here is probably no gloomier assessment in literature', he proposes, 'of the close of our earthly existence' – and observing that, though the 'most famous depictions [of old age] are found in Shakespeare's plays', the playwright himself 'never experienced these years, since he died in 1616 at fifty-two' (*Crown of Life*, 6, 5). Yet, in a classic instance of the slippage that seems naturally to occur when critics celebrate Shakespearean lateness, Munsterberg appears a few pages later to have forgotten this basic biographical point when describing the *Rondanini Pietà* of Michelangelo as the 'ultimate statement on the part of the aged genius similar to Beethoven's late quartets or Shakespeare's last plays, in which the aged artist transcends artistic conventions and gives expression to his most profound and personal sentiments' (ibid., 18). Shakespeare, unfortunately both for Munsterberg and for the universal claims of the idea, is, as we have seen, in various ways a remarkably poor exemplar of the phenomenon of late style. He was not, after all, actually 'aged' when he wrote the late plays, nor did he know (as far as we are aware, in the absence of any proof of prophetic powers or precise medical prognostication) that he had only three more years to live after (co-)writing the last of them, and in any case – to shift the terms of discussion away from the limitations imposed by subjectivism – the conditions of production of the plays we think of, in our practical but provisional way, as 'his' late plays militate, as I argued in the previous chapter, against their subsumption to the autobiographical understanding of 'late work' as it has been established since the middle of the nineteenth century. The idea of 'late Shakespeare', rooted as it is both in anti-theatricalism and in a fundamental anachronism, continues to limit our understanding of and engagement with the final plays. Yet, despite these considerable obstacles, the last plays continue to be cited as a (sometimes even the) classic instance of late writing.

For many critics, there is a default assumption that a late style must be the product of longevity. Hajo Düchting, for instance, offers a representative description of a late work by Miró:

The painting *Woman III* (1965) shows a transparent figure, who looks more like an insect than a human being, against a splotchy, multi-coloured surface. The artist's elementary brush-strokes followed a strong, inner impulse, with a raw energy that was left unrefined and without further rational processing. The elementary symbols are only loosely connected, without any congruence that could be justified in aesthetic terms, and yet they have preserved that 'anthropomorphic' character which dominates the whole of this series and which can also be found in man's early incantations and projections of his anxieties. Perhaps it was with these 'wild' pictures, in particular, that Miró achieved a degree of intensity and emotional depth that was totally new to him and could only be attained at the end of a very long life – a life in which he had set himself the aim of fathoming the very roots of life, against all conventions and obligations. (Düchting in Erben, *Joan Miró*, 228)

Düchting here effectively restates, though without irony, Hokusai's assertion that it is only at the end of the longest of lives that a certain depth of artistic insight can be achieved: insight that is apparent in the work's 'elementary [...] energy', which resists the rational and engages instead with a kind of artistic atavism (a version of the 'childhood of art' invoked by the Musée Picasso wall label), repeating primitive 'incantations' and resisting the 'conventions and obligations' of its own age. This kind of work 'could only be attained at the end of a very long life': there can be no substitute for longevity. The late stylist is always also, then, in Hermann Broch's words, 'the artist of old age', the late style 'the style of old age' ('Mythical', 12, 13); likewise, for Erich Neumann, late work is invariably the work of 'aged masters' ('Art and Time', 103). For Munsterberg, too, this is a given. 'It would seem', he observes, 'that most people reach the peak of their creativity relatively early in life, with their best work the product of their youth and early adulthood. However, there are others, including men of extraordinary genius like Michelangelo and Titian, who produced some of their finest work late in life' (*Crown of Life*, 7). 'Many additional examples could be cited from other fields', he continues, listing three:

Sophocles, who wrote *Oedipus Coloneus* when he was eighty-nine; Verdi, who produced some of his most outstanding operas during his seventies; and Beethoven, who wrote his late quartets at the very end of his life. In all these cases, old age, far from diminishing the creative power of the artists, seems to have deepened and strengthened it, giving their work a profundity and expressive quality that their early art did not possess. (ibid.)

This old-age style, he adds, 'is characterized by a transcendent quality and a reduction of forms to their very essence' (ibid.). He acknowledges that some artists, 'having exhausted themselves, either petered out or stopped creating altogether', but he insists that old age has been the 'period when some of the greatest figures produced their best work' (*Crown of Life*, 1), thereby providing a distinct gauge of genius. And he is noticeably careful to avoid using the term 'late style', preferring 'old-age style' throughout, the only exception to this rule being his discussion of what he considers (*pace* the Paris wall label) a failure to achieve a style of the kind he is celebrating, that of Picasso. This preference is due in part to the self-consciousness with which he writes in the wake of (that is, both echoing and resisting) Kenneth Clark's seminal work on old-age style, *The Artist Grows Old*.

The view of creativity in old age upon which Clark insists is a darker, far less optimistic one than that of Munsterberg. He offers an anatomy of lateness that incorporates resignation, pain, pessimism and resentment alongside – and much more prominently than – mystery, transcendence, beauty and freedom from the constraints of convention. He is more specific than Munsterberg about the final style itself, writing of the 'reckless freedom of facture' and the 'uninterrupted fullness' of the 'old-age style', and he attempts, restricting himself to the media of painting and sculpture, to summarise its features, which include

> [a] sense of isolation, a feeling of holy rage, developing into what I have called transcendental pessimism; a mistrust of reason, a belief in instinct. And in a few rare instances the old-age myth of classical antiquity – the feeling that the crimes and follies of mankind must be accepted with resignation. All this is revealed by the imagery of old men's pictures, and to some extent by the treatment. If we consider old-age art from a more narrowly stylistic point of view, we find a retreat from realism, an impatience with established technique and a craving for complete unity of treatment, as if the picture were an organism in which every member shared in the life of the whole. (*Artist Grows Old*, 21–2)

Though he grudgingly acknowledges the possibility of a 'gentle, dreamlike departure from reality' such as that to be found, he argues, in the last paintings of Claude, Clark's is for the most part a ferocious view of the art of the old: he rejects out of hand 'the conventional picture of a golden old age' (ibid., 1), preferring to emphasise the solitariness, mistrust and rage of those who continue creating into great age. Moreover, he differentiates between the prospects for the elderly in the field of fine art and what he sees as the lack of equivalent possibilities for ageing poets or composers, writing of the inevitable 'decline in the poetic faculty in old age' and coldly noting that '[t]he number of poets who have written memorable verse over the age of seventy is very small indeed' (ibid., 1–2). Happily for painters and sculptors (and thus happily for Clark, whose field happens to be painting and sculpture), they do not, '[f]or some reason which is rather hard to analyse, [...] suffer from the same loss of creative power that afflicts writers' (ibid., 5), though he considers it 'evident that those [artists] who have retained their creative powers into old age take a very poor view of human life, and develop as their only defence a kind of transcendental pessimism' (ibid., 6). 'We need only,' he adds, 'think of the eyes that look out on us from the late self-portraits of Rembrandt to realise how deeply this great lover of life became disenchanted by life' (ibid.). As David Rosand has put it, '[i]f the aging artist achieves a remarkable mastery of his medium over the course of a long professional life, so that expressive potential seems almost limitless, he must nonetheless submit to the constraining fact of his own deteriorating body, constant reminder of his mortality.'[3] For Clark, the awareness of, and fury at, the inevitability of deterioration is the driving force behind all significant late styles.

Munsterberg reacts to this grim view by reiterating the canonical belief that old-age style embodies a certain serenity, a sense of fulfilment and peace. In a broad-brush survey of ideas about ageing, he suggests that while certain artistic individuals – he cites Swift, de Beauvoir and Hamsun – have experienced old age 'as a purely negative phenomenon', many cultures, eastern and western, have seen old age on the contrary as 'a meaningful [...] phase of human existence [with] its own character and its own value' (*Crown of Life*, 5, 3). He cites the conviction of Carl Jung – himself a 'living example' of late creativity, since he worked actively right up to his death at eighty-six – that a human being 'would certainly not grow to be seventy or eighty years old if this longevity had no meaning for the species to which he belongs', and he repeats the rhetorical question this prompts on Jung's part: 'Could by any chance *culture* be the meaning and purpose of the second half of life?'[4] Late creativity thus appears a basic human tendency, the manifestation of the cultural value of a long life, of a life freed from the troubles and obligations of earlier life-stages by the inevitable slowing down attendant upon ageing and by a certain turning inward which, in a handful of privileged cases, also involves an extraordinary outward expression in art. Old age is thus intrinsically a benefit for, not a burden upon, cultural life, and psychoanalysis appears to support Munsterberg's argument that truly great artists tend to find a new lease of positive creative life in their last years.

The picture, however, is not quite as clear as this might suggest, since the status of old age in relation to the earlier stages of life is in fact a point of contention among psychoanalysts. For Jung, deploying a metaphor of sunrise and sunset (and rephrasing the late Romantic reclamation of the latter years as a turning back towards the sublimity out of which we emerge when we are born), old age and the earliest years of a person's life are in certain significant ways surprisingly similar, not though because age brings a debilitating 'second childhood' *sans* everything but because both are characterised – in a way middle age, fraught with practical problems and obligations, is not – by 'submersion in unconscious psychic happenings', periods of time in which the inner life, latching on to certain archetypes, dominates the conscious. 'Since the mind of a child grows out of the unconscious', Jung argues, 'its psychic processes [...] are not as difficult to discern as those of a very old person who has plunged again into the unconscious, and who progressively vanishes with it' (*Modern Man*, 116). This seems to offer the possibility of a last phase in which creativity responds to the archetypal underpinnings of culture, carving out a brief productive space prior to the obliteration of personality by the forces of the unconscious. For the anthropological psychoanalyst Erik Erikson, on the other hand, old age is not so much a return to the impulses of childhood as the completion of a life-pattern that, having begun in hope, concludes in wisdom. Erikson crisply maps out the stages of life, acknowledging that the sensual is paramount both at the beginning and at the end but arguing that, where in infancy the principal psychosocial crises are those of simple trust and mistrust, by the eighth and final stage of life the primary struggle is between integrity and despair and the individual hopes to have developed the attribute that Erikson calls 'wisdom', that is, an 'informed and detached concern with life itself in the face of death itself', whose 'antipathic counterpart' is the 'disdain' that results from a sense of helplessness in the face of death.[5] Jung and Erikson thus between them offer a modern version of the medieval and early modern 'ages of man' patterns that I addressed in the previous chapter – schematic, generally applicable models of the ageing process – and both Jung's idea of 'progressive vanishing' and Erikson's sense of the likely prominence of a concluding 'disdain' in all but the most self-controlled seem to echo the negativity of the bulk of those early models. Certainly, the prescriptiveness of their claims (especially those of Erikson) seems to limit the range of possibilities for creativity in old age.

One potentially productive way to develop the work of Jung and Erikson, however (and one designed in part to address the limitations of both), is offered by 'literary gerontologists' such as Kathleen Woodward, whose early book on the late work of American modernist poets – in which she resisted the received idea that American poets do not 'age well' by arguing that, 'while most of the English Romantics [...] burnt themselves out when they were young', Eliot, Pound, Stevens and Williams 'reached into old age with intellectual vigor and poetic force' – ushered in a career-long engagement with creativity in old age.[6] Not, she acknowledges, that she 'set out consciously to write a book on aging and poetry, although this is just what has emerged' (Woodward, *At Last*, ix). Partly, it was simply a question of taste. 'Some seven years ago', she reports, while reading the poetry of Wallace Stevens, I found myself drawn to his last poems, preferring them to the early poems [...] at a time when his last poems had received comparatively little critical attention and the early poems were canonized. I decided to study them in the context of the entire body of Stevens' work to discover if I could account for a development over time. (ibid., ix–x)

In order to do so, she turned to the archetypal model of Erich Neumann, reading the late poems of Stevens and his peers as instances of access to a creative realm beyond the material and temporal. 'Although I am not sure', she admits,

in what way historical realities are ever transcended in a work of art, I do understand, and accept, what Neumann points to. The poems of Stevens, Eliot, Pound, and Williams do possess an orphic quality, a timeless dimension, which links them with what can only be called the age-old wisdom of humanity. (ibid., 17–18)

Her debt to Neumann (and therefore to Jung) is obvious as she outlines what she sees as the persistent features of old-age style, which include 'disengagement', 'a solitude of the self', a certain rapprochement with tradition, an 'orphic and sacramental' silence or 'still point [...] that lets in symbolism', a movement towards closure, and a turn to archetype – in particular to that of the 'Wise Old Man' which for Neumann is the central cultural paradigm. And she concludes her account with a kind of peroration:

The late poems of these poets embody that which is lacking in our culture. The pursuit of the eternal – which is indeed what Pound, Eliot, and Williams, and even Stevens were devoted to – cannot be submitted to the coarse test of pragmatism. Contemplation, [Hannah] Arendt insists, is not the same as thought and reasoning. Contemplation is absolute quiet. Contemplation has as its goal beholding the truth. Wisdom has its source in solitude, although to be in solitude is to be with one's self, a partner. The still point. 'Every movement,' she writes, 'the movements of body and soul as well as of speech and reasoning, must cease before truth. Truth, be it the ancient truth of Being or the Christian truth of the Living God, can reveal itself only in complete human stillness.' And these meditative poems testify to the nobility of the life of the mind as the quintessential human activity. (ibid., 175)

The language of this statement – especially the resonances of 'the still point' – make clear how dependent Woodward's earliest analysis of late work is both on the language of the modernist poets she is reading and on the large theological or paratheological claims of Neumann. At the same time, her recognition of the problems set up by his blithe assertions of transcendence underlines the development already taking place in her work as she turns away from generalisation about late-style wisdom to the empiricism offered by the discipline of humanistic gerontology.

Practitioners in this emerging field seek an interdisciplinary synthesis of socio-medical science 'with the materials and methods of the humanities' (ibid., ix), arguing that, while '[g]erontological knowledge making remains dominated by the paradigm of modern science and its various expressions in the social and medical sciences, [... t]his situation must change if gerontology is to fulfill its real potential' (Cole, Kastenbaum and Ray, *Handbook*, xi). In other words, the discipline emerged not primarily in order to apply empirical methodology to questions customarily addressed by the humanities but rather the reverse: to seek humanistic perspectives on issues normally considered the domain of science. Nonetheless, the potential of this work for the humanities would appear considerable, not least for the study of late style.[7] For Woodward and others working in this field, the features of late writing or late painting have their origins in observable phenomena which are characteristic of old age. Woodward derives the term 'disengagement', for instance, which describes the old person's tendency to back away from social obligation, to acquire a certain distance from the motivations and interests of the young or middle-aged, and which she uses to account for particular features of the ageing poets she addresses in her first book, from one of 'two competing theories of successful aging: the "activity" theory and the "disengagement" theory' (Woodward, *At Last*, 23 n. 8). For the latter, the old person's gradual detachment from the mainstream social world should not necessarily be viewed as regrettable but as 'a distinct phase in the psychosocial development of the individual' through which 'society prepares for the disruption in the social fabric that death inevitably brings, and the individual readies himself for the personal crisis of death' (ibid.). The process of withdrawal in fact 'promotes the health of a culture as well as the spiritual realization of the individual'.[8]

Similarly, in a later essay, Woodward turns to Robert Butler's idea of the 'life-review', his term for the tendency of the old to look back over, and reach conclusions about, the course of their lives, in order to develop an account of the nature of late style.[9] 'To age', in Nietzsche's words, 'there pertains an appropriate senile occupation, that of looking back, of reckoning up, of closing accounts, of seeking consolation through remembering what has been.'[10] Butler formalises this observation by 'postulat[ing] the universal occurrence in older people of an inner experience or mental process of reviewing one's life' and proposing

that this process helps account for increased reminiscence in the aged, that it contributes to the occurrence of certain late-life disorders, particularly depression, and that it participates in the evolution of such characteristics as candor, serenity, and wisdom among certain of the aged. ('Life Review', 65)

The endpoint, for Butler, is psychological integration:

> I conceive of the life review as a naturally occurring, universal mental process characterized by the progressive return to consciousness of past experiences, and, particularly, the resurgence of unresolved conflicts; simultaneously, and normally, these revived experiences and conflicts can be surveyed and reintegrated. (ibid., 66)

The appeal of a study of this kind for literary critics, art-historians and musicologicists seeking scientific support for claims about the principal characteristics of late style or for foregrounding the process of revision in creative old age is obvious.[11]

Work within humanistic gerontology with equal interest for students of late style might also include, for instance (to move beyond Woodward's particular choices), Dean Keith Simonton's statistical accounts of the 'swan-song phenomenon' or, in the centrality they accord to questions of convention, the extensions across the whole life-cycle by his successors of Jean Piaget's analyses of childhood cognition. Once a child has learned to speak, Piaget claimed, it goes through three developmental stages of reasoning: the intuitive, the concrete operational and the formal operational. In other words, there is a change around the age of seven as the child acquires the logical ability to classify, to infer and to quantify the concrete; there is then a further change in adolescence that enables the individual to form hypotheses and to consider the implications of those hypotheses by testing them against experience. Lawrence Kohlberg, extending this account across the full life-span, describes six 'moral' stages that operate alongside and then beyond Piaget's 'logical' stages, noting that '[m]any individuals are at a higher logical stage than the parallel moral stage, but essentially none are at a higher moral stage than their logical stage'.[12] He divides his six moral stages into three pairs or 'levels' on the basis of their relations to social engagement and expectation:

> The preconventional level is the level of most children under 9, some adolescents, and many adolescent and adult criminal offenders. The conventional level is the level of most adolescents and adults in our society and in other societies. The postconventional level is reached by a minority of adults and is usually reached only after the age of 20. (*Moral Development*, 172)

Implicit in this structure, quite clearly, is a sense both of moral development across the life-span and of a degree of equivalence between increasing age and progression up the levels. Thus Kohlberg's fifth and, particularly, sixth moral stages offer possibilities that can only be fulfilled in later life by a minority of people, and his implication that the final phase requires a move beyond convention offers a potentially productive contrast with the perspective of Adorno, for whom late style works both *with* and *against* convention.

Kohlberg's six-stage pattern, however, contrasts with the bulk of studies of intellectual and creative functioning in old age which extrapolate with less optimism from Piaget's analyses of childhood development, reading 'adulthood and aging as a period of loss and regression in biological adaptability and cognitive abilities' and suggesting a trajectory for cognition that is fundamentally inimical to the idea of late style, one in which 'the apex of thinking in terms of complex cognition–emotion integrations is not in late life, but rather around midlife'.[13] Such analyses appear to do little more than provide, like Jung and Erikson, a contemporary scientific restatement of the ages-of-man model for the trajectory of human life and, in response, scholars with a particular interest in the relations of ageing and creativity tend to look for exceptions and alternatives. Dean Keith Simonton, acknowledging the evidence that 'productivity in creative endeavors is closely approximated by a curvilinear *inverted backward-J* age function' – that is, that 'creative output rises fairly rapidly to a single peak, after which a gradual decline sets in' – wonders nonetheless how what he calls the 'swan-song effect' might be quantified and negotiated against this general pattern of decline.'[14] Addressing this in an essay on late music, he sets out a method for analysis, taking 1,919 musical compositions by 172 composers from Halsey's catalogue of recorded classical music and assessing them on the basis of seven criteria: melodic originality (as judged by 'a computerized content analysis of the two-note transition frequencies for the first six notes after transposing each theme into a C tonic'), melodic variation (that is, 'the standard deviation of the melodic originality scores for all themes'), repertoire popularity (based on a wide range of record-buying guides, anthologies, concert guides and library record and score guides), aesthetic significance (as derived from Halsey's 'ratings . . . on a 5-point scale from *a masterpiece* to *flawed or insubstantial*'), listener accessibility (as drawn again from Halsey, this time on a different five-point scale, one which runs from '*work commands attention*' to '*austere, esoteric, or too arbitrary for most listeners*'), performance duration and thematic size.[15] The conclusion he reaches after computational analysis of the chosen material on the basis of these criteria is that, statistically, 'last-works effects are substantively significant' ('Swan-Song', 228). 'Composers in their final years', he argues, extrapolating from his analysis, 'seem to concentrate on producing masterworks that will permanently establish their reputation, doing so by creating works of a concise directness, as revealed by the brevity and melodic simplicity of their concluding pieces', from which he concludes that '[t]he swan song is perhaps more an expression of resignation, even contentment, than despair or tragedy' (ibid., 227). And, he adds, '[c]onsistent with this interpretation is the fact that melodic originality drops the most precipitously right before death' (ibid.). Developing this observation, he suggests that '[l]ast-works effects may be found in almost any creative activity, a universality based on the fundamental fact that creators, like everyone else, must somehow cope with death' and that '[o]ne vehicle for such coping is the career's swan song' ('Swan-Song', 229). Late work, then, is, in the most direct way, work produced in the shadow of death.

The attractions of Simonton's material for critics are obvious in that he provides statistical data in support of the existence of a tangible late style, something frequently observed but never formally isolated and defined. But the drawbacks of his work are equally apparent. His criteria are, to say the least, highly unlikely to convince a musicologist (or for that matter an informed listener to classical music) of his understanding of the nature of musical achievement: he accepts without discussion, for instance, Halsey's risible assumption that 'good' music will always be popular and accessible, not austere or esoteric. Moreover, he makes no distinction between ideas of 'universal' late style and the deliberate, self-conscious production of 'masterworks that will permanently establish [the] reputation' of a given artist – that is, of what Michael Millgate calls 'testamentary acts'. He thus seems to lack several of the controls essential for any convincing scientific assessment of the question of late creativity. The discomfort of the juxtaposition of disciplines required by humanistic gerontology is thus as clear in analyses such as Simonton's as is the potential of that juxtaposition for enhancing, or at least for contextualising, critical accounts of late style. Few scholars in the humanities would be likely to endorse the methods deployed by Simonton and his peers. At the same time, there is no question that humanistic gerontology provides examples of good practice for anyone working on late creativity, not the least of which is the care with which its practitioners differentiate between the varying experiences of ageing across cultures. To claim that being old is essentially the same without regard to time and geography – as many critics who correlate late style and old-age style and read both as transcultural and transhistorical in their application implicitly do – would be as absurd as to insist that the experience of being a woman is the same in all historical, cultural or political environments, a patriarchal truism that feminist criticism has worked hard and successfully to dispel.[16] The section in Cole, Kastenbaum and Ray's *Handbook of the Humanities and Aging* on the varying understandings of old age across a range of disciplines and cultures, while limited in scope by its unapologetic orientation towards a solely American demographic, serves nonetheless as a valuable corrective to the transcendent assumptions of Neumann and Broch (even of Adorno) and their inheritors.[17]

The fact remains, however, that humanistic gerontologists by definition identify late style as a specific manifestation of old age, as a phenomenon produced by the conditions – social, psychological and physiological – of the latter phases of the ageing process; and in the end, it seems, there are two options for critics: to treat late style either as a *product* or as a *transcendence* of old age – that is, to see late work as something that emerges either from ageing or from the overcoming of ageing. Either way, lateness is primarily debated in its specific relation to old age. The problem with this is that, as we have seen, by no means all celebrated late styles are the product of an ageing artist. Even Simonton's arguments for the swan song, emerging as they do from research specifically on 'the connection between personal age and creative achievement', do not take age per se into account ('Swan-Song', 217). For him, as we have seen, the primary relationship is not that of late style and old age but of late style and *death*. 'Last-works effects', he argues, 'hinge not on the creator's chronological or even career age but rather on the perceived proximity of death' (ibid., 218) – an assertion that makes the relationship of his work to gerontology appear, paradoxically, incidental. Late styles have been attributed to artists, writers and composers at a wide range of ages, from the twenties to the nineties (even, echoing Hokusai, into the hundreds), and these attributions raise a fundamental question – perhaps *the* fundamental question – in the study of the discourse of lateness. Is *Altersstil* the same as *Spätstil*? Or is there a demonstrable difference? And to what extent – not least in view of the specific work done by humanistic gerontology – is the attribution of a late style to an individual who has not reached old age a problem for the discourse as a whole?

5.2 OLD-AGE STYLE WITHOUT OLD AGE

A straightforward instance of the difficulties raised by the habitual critical conflation of old-age style and late style is provided by Robert Spaethling when he makes a direct comparison between the late styles of Goethe and Mozart. He describes both as a form of *Altersstil* and then defends his claim as follows:

Goethe was eighty years old when he wrote the 'Dornburger Gedichte', a poetic summing up tinted by the consciousness of his ripe age. Mozart was all of thirty-five when he composed the B-flat Major concerto, far too early for a summing up, but life had worn down his fragile body, and the composer knew it. The 'Requiem', and even more the story surrounding it, are indications that Mozart knew his time had come. His last piano concerto expresses that knowledge, the poignancy of it, and the relief.[18]

In Spaethling's account, Mozart provides a clear instance of the life of the genius culminating in a burst of transcendent productivity shortly before death, yet that death comes far too soon for a credible attribution of old-age style and a good deal of work is required in order to confirm the comparison with the ageing Goethe. This is, as we have seen, work that had been done from the very beginning. For Ulïbïshev, first describing a late phase for Mozart, the composer 'died young because his vital forces were exhausted by producing works of superhuman quality: the genius that produced this work was ageing and could achieve no more, and his premature death was the condition of, and the price to be paid for, such work' (Ulïbïshev, *Mozart*, 424). The work of literary gerontologists such as Woodward assumes, as we have seen, that late style and old-age style are synonymous, and it seeks an understanding of the nature of late style through empirical observation of psychological and behavioural developments in old age. Critics such as Clark and Munsterberg begin from the same basic premise – that 'late' artists are always also 'old'. Yet the example of Mozart provokes a wholly different question, that of the attribution of a late style to creative artists who have died not in old age but in youth or middle age. A sufficient number of the principal exemplars repeatedly cited, as it turns out, lack the one apparently key requirement for an attribution of old-age style – that is, old age itself – to cause severe problems for any account that assumes the identity of *Spätstil* and *Altersstil*.

Havelock Ellis, as I noted in Chapter 1, lists as two of his classic instances of late writing Shelley and Keats, neither of whom, of course, reached anything even approximating old age, and without specifying his reasons he deliberately juxtaposes both with Shakespeare. 'Look', he insists,

at the last plays of Shakespeare, so loose and undramatic, so flowing or so broken, so full of exquisite music of the spirit more than of poetic form, of a heavenly atmosphere refined beyond any that was ever breathed on earth and yet so humanly tender; or at Shelley, who completed a large cycle of art in a short time, and wrote at last, in the 'Witch of Atlas,' only with water and fire; or, within a yet greater and yet shorter cycle, trace the evolution of the ideals of Keats. (*Impressions*, 7)

Ellis's use of the word 'cycle' here echoes Coleridge's account of the last of the Shakespearean 'æras' – 'when the Energies of Intellect in the cycle of Genius were tho' in a richer and potenziated form becoming predominant over Passion and creative Self-modification' – and depends upon ideas of completeness, of the inevitable, but heightened and abbreviated, shape of a life (see Chapter 3, 146). It is for Shelley and Keats at the end of their brief lives as it is for the ageing Rembrandt or Rodin: the final works embody a heightened, climactic outcropping of creativity which is the direct product of the poets' proximity to death. There has been in criticism of these poets an urge to find in the briefest of careers a kind of abbreviated teleology, an artistic trajectory that maps the symptoms of lateness onto a drastically foreshortened chronology. The *reductio ad absurdum* of this tendency is Alexander Crawford's account of the last poems of Keats. Crawford, writing in 1931, is intent on providing Keats with the trajectory, even in so curtailed a career (four years), of a genius, refusing to accept that his poems are all in effect juvenilia and attempting to delineate within that tiny *œuvre* a subset of later, mature works against which to gauge the early. 'The period of Keats's poetic activity was so brief', he argues, 'that casual readers have been inclined to think that his work was all of a piece.'[19] However, he adds, '[a]ll careful readers of Keats [. . .] now realize the truth of Palgrave's words when he said that there was a "tropical rapidity of growth in the mind and poems of Keats," and that with him "months count like the years of advance in case of ordinary mortals"'.[20] In fact, Crawford argues,

[t]he real genius of Keats should be sought in his best and most mature work, and by that part of his work which he himself thought the most complete expression of himself. [. . . W]e should estimate Keats finally and chiefly by the work of the last wonderful year of his life, and more particularly by the poems and letters of his last active period, the marvellous spring and summer of 1819. (*Genius of Keats*, 7)

It is in this, 'the real Keats of the last period', for Crawford, that the poet's true genius can be found (ibid., 8).

Crawford's argument, in all of its question-begging compression, is, to be fair, only an extreme version of what is in fact a standard, if mostly unspoken, critical assumption – that, for a tiny élite of creative artists 'who completed a large cycle of art in a short time', the rules of human development do not apply, that for these short-lived geniuses a late style can emerge decades before the onset of old age. Quite contrary to the claims of Woodward and the humanistic gerontologists, it appears to be not old age itself but proximity to death at *any* age – along, perhaps, with an awareness of that proximity – that is the key to late style. 'Late style' and 'old-age style' are not, after all, it seems, synonymous, and one of Hermann Broch's achievements, as we have seen, was to expand the concept of *Altersstil* beyond its limiting association with old age. He argues that, while a certain consummate stylistic transcendence can be realised 'only by the artist of old age', there are many artists – most artists – who, no matter how long they live, remain 'bound to [a] conventional vocabulary' ('Mythical', 12). This kind of artist,

> though he may enlarge his art more and more, reaching a boundless abundance, is never able to achieve his real goal: one cannot capture the universe by snaring its atoms one by one; one can only capture it by showing its basic and essential principles, its basic, and one might even say, its mathematical structure. And here the abstractism of such ultimate principles joins hands with the abstractism of the technical problem: this union constitutes the 'style of old age'. (ibid., 12–13)

Broch explains that '[t]he artist who has reached such a point is beyond art', that '[h]e still produces art, but all the minor and specific problems, with which art in its worldly phase usually deals, have lost interest for him', and thus that 'his abstractism is [...] very near to that of myth' (ibid.). Broch is careful to detach the late style from the specifics of chronology, arguing that

> [t]he 'style of old age' is not always a product of the years; it is a gift implanted with his other gifts in the artist, ripening, it may be, with time, often blossoming before its season under the foreshadow of death, or unfolding of itself even before the approach of age or death. ('Mythical', 10)

Broch's, then, is not in fact a style of old age understood in the obvious way (he is careful always to put the term 'old-age style' in parentheses) nor even necessarily a late style where lateness is defined as proximity to death: Brochian lateness is, in the end, an epochal as much as an individual phenomenon.[21] The possession of a late style marks the artist out as especially gifted, as someone with the creative genius to look beyond the surface of things and beyond the specificity of his moment; it is not a direct product of the ageing process.

Adorno too, at first sight, seems to equate late style with the style of old age, only in fact to move, like Broch, in a quite different direction. 'There is a statement by Goethe,' he notes, 'to the effect that ageing is a gradual stepping back from appearances,' and he claims that Beethoven's late quartets 'conform entirely to Goethe's dictum' (*Beethoven*, 188). In the quartets, he argues, there is a similar effect, 'something like the paring away of the sensuous, a spiritualization, as if the whole world of sensuous appearance were reduced in advance to the appearance of something spiritual' (ibid.). This said, however, it rapidly becomes clear that his understanding of late style is not tied to old age per se. Beethoven's late style, he argues, in keeping with his insistent rejection of the subjective, is not simply a reaction of a person who has grown old, or even of one who, having gone deaf, no longer has full mastery of the sensuous material. Beethoven *was* still fully able to write works conforming to the classicist ideal of his middle phase, and he *did* so in some of the most famous works of precisely this late phase. (*Beethoven*, 191)

In other words, late style is not a direct product of the stage the individual has reached in the life-cycle. For both Adorno and Broch, the point is the development of the individual cycle within the larger cycle of history. Both in their different ways present lateness as universal and transcultural, as something applicable to a handful of extraordinarily accomplished artists across time and circumstance – as, in other words, a natural phenomenon which would have been equally recognisable to Sophocles or to Shakespeare as to their twentieth-century successors – yet it is, at the same time, perfectly clear that their understanding of late style is shaped and determined by their own historical moment. Adorno reads Beethoven's late style as a fragment of resistance to the general effacement of art by modern history, an apocalyptic understanding hardly surprising in the writing of a cultural critic whose best-known pronouncement is that '[t]o write poetry after Auschwitz is barbaric'.[22] As Rose Subotnik observes, Adorno was 'driven by [...] tormenting experience: a view from the inside of how an incomparably civilized intellectual heritage could lead with apparent continuity, and even necessity, to total barbarism', and she notes how (happily) difficult it is to recreate 'the sense of apocalyptic immediacy needed to appreciate fully the moral anguish behind Adorno's music criticism' ('Adorno's Diagnosis', 244). In a certain way, Adorno, as Said has noted, 'uses the model of late Beethoven to come to terms with an ending', an ending which is both his own and that of the bourgeois epoch.[23] There is a clear element of the theological in his thinking, as there is, finally, in all arguments about late style. In the music of Schoenberg – the music that late Beethoven prefigures both in its effects and in its sheer seriousness – Adorno finds that '[t]he shocks of incomprehension, emitted by artistic technique in the age of its meaninglessness, undergo a sudden change', a change through which '[t]hey illuminate the meaningless world', an effort to which modern music 'sacrifices itself', taking upon itself 'all the darkness and guilt of the world'.[24]

Late style is, then, theological or, perhaps better, a marker of the impossibility of theology. For Broch, the modernist moment culminating in the Second World War marks a shattering of convention:

It need not be stressed again that, owing to its loss of religious centrality, the present world, at least of the West (although the East surely has not remained untouched), has entered a state of complete disintegration of values, a state in which each single value is in conflict with every other one, trying to dominate them all. The apocalyptic events of the last decades are nothing but the unavoidable outcome of such a dissolution. ('Mythical', 27)

In this context, one of self-consciously dramatised history, *all* art manifests the style normally associated only with old age and all artists (all geniuses, at least), not just the chronologically old, unavoidably adopt a late style: 'this epoch of disintegration imposes on them the style of old age, the style of the essential, the style of the abstract' (ibid., 28). Broch thus conflates individual and epochal 'old age', viewing modernity as in itself a late moment and reading certain of modernism's characteristics (simplicity, myth, primitivism) as identical with the features of late style. The art of Picasso offers a clear instance of a style which is the product of epochal rupture and is thus inescapably a late style:

> Picasso's development is paradigmatic of these processes, all the more so since he achieved in one work a real and perhaps the first full expression of our time: this is 'Guernica,' a picture so abstract that it could even renounce all color, a picture expressing horror, sorrow, mourning – nothing else, and for this very reason the strongest rebellion against the evil. (ibid.)

Guernica is, of course, by no means an instance of late Picasso. The point is that Picasso's abstractism is, for Broch, intrinsically an old-age style: the artist's actual age has become irrelevant and a work from mid-career can openly be cited as an instance of late style. This produces a kind of generic ecumenism:

> The striking relationship between the arts on the basis of their common abstractism, their common style of old age, this hallmark of our epoch is the cause of the inner relationship between artists like Picasso, Stravinsky and Joyce. This relationship is not only striking in itself but also by reason of the parallelism through which the style of old age was imposed on these men, even in their rather early years. ('Mythical', 29)

Modernism is thus indistinguishable, for Broch, from the style of old age. And the style of old age does not only emerge in the work of an artist who has reached his own old age.

Said echoes Broch in seeing modernism itself as a 'late-style phenomenon' in its tendency to return both to 'ancient myth or antique forms such as the epic or ancient religious ritual' and to a rather more recent and specific past, that of Romanticism, a period viewed by Heine and others in instant hindsight – that is, in the wake of the deaths of Goethe and Hegel in 1832 and 1833 respectively – as a time of extraordinary artistic production (*die Kunstperiode*).[25] Broch viewed his own historical moment, the postwar period, not as a fundamental break with the past but as a cyclical return, noting that the two key nineteenth-century exemplars of late style had produced their late work at just such a moment of personal and epochal intersection. 'In the case of Beethoven and Goethe', he argued, 'it was not only their personal genius [...] which compelled them toward a new style, they were enjoined to it by their epoch, in which the closed values were already being shattered' (ibid., 24). Romanticism, for Broch, was a privileged moment in the history of late style in its combination of creative and sociopolitical paradigm shifts; the modernist period culminating in the Second World War marked an equivalent moment in the cycle of history. Hegel's reconstruction of all art as a thing of the past in a sense provokes the association of late art with a certain prophetic quality since, in this historical levelling, modern art is no less a thing of the past than is the art against which it defines itself as modern. Late style, in this reading, opens up a synchronic window that elides both historical difference and the timebound material contexts of artistic production and can thus be seen, in all its earlier manifestations, as a kind of proleptic modernism. At the same time, Broch's argument for congruence between mid-twentieth-century cultural disintegration and the conditions in which late Beethoven or late Goethe were forged serves to underline not a kind of transcendent synchrony but, on the one hand, the failure of historicity intrinsic to the idea of late style and, on the other, its timebound origins in the early nineteenth century.

Thus if German Romanticism was responsible for the invention of late style, then German modernism was in a sense responsible for its reinvention. In its expression of the immanence of apocalypse, late style became everyday style, the style of the last days which are always upon us. In the process, it ceased to be what it was for Ulïbïshev or for Lenz – that is, the expression of subjectivity at the extreme edge of life – becoming instead something impersonal and epochal. At the same time, the danger of the specificity with which Adorno and Broch both map their historical moment, arguing that late style and certain characteristic stylistic aspects of modernism are one and the same, is obvious, namely that they thereby tip the diachronic study of late style into crisis precisely because it can only understand individual late styles prior to modernism as the precursors of – as prophetic of – modernism and therefore jeopardise their historicity. For Adorno, as we have seen, what is fascinating about late Beethoven, what makes the late style so pivotal, is its embodiment, a century too soon, of the critique of classical music that was only fully effected in the work of Schoenberg. As Subotnik puts it,

Schoenberg's music represents merely the inevitable last stages of a process which first became manifest in Beethoven's late style, the severing of subjective freedom from objective reality. Thus, implicit in Beethoven's late style, as Adorno analyzes it, is the eventual dissolution of all the values that made bourgeois humanism the hope of a human civilization. ('Adorno's Diagnosis', 245)

Schoenberg's music thus marks, for Adorno, the end of history: '[T]he whole history of music from Beethoven's late period to Schoenberg's represents at once the winding down of human history and a prolegomenon to the music of a post-historical world' (ibid., 245–6). Adorno's critique, then, defines late style as a marker within history of the inevitability of the end of history; it also threatens to elide the distinction between Romanticism and modernism and thus the historically specific conditions for the production of the idea of lateness in the early nineteenth century.

Conversely, the danger with Adorno's occasional tendency to generalise about 'the late style of all great artists' is that it undermines the specificity of his choice as exemplars of Beethoven and Schoenberg, i.e. of the representative Romantic and the representative Modern (the representative *forward-looking* Modern, that is, as opposed to Stravinsky who, for Adorno, writing well before the latter's own late twelve-tone experimentation, looks back insistently to the classical era). After all, if every late style shares these features, then late style must represent something other than an expression of the failure of art in the modern world, since some instances of late style generally conceived must entirely predate the modern – Sophocles being the standard instance of this. The twentieth-century theorising of lateness thus enters its own crisis, since no late work can be assessed without reference to modernism, yet to argue that there is a transhistorical line of modernist art that runs right back to Sophocles would be absurd in the wildness of its ahistoricity. Sam Smiles has written of the frustration faced by Turner scholars when they see Turner's late style casually addressed as proleptic Impressionism, as if that alleged future orientation were the only validation for Turner's stylistic experiments.[26] The danger is that the modernist understanding of lateness, even while ostensibly celebrating late style, serves to invalidate it. Yet just as modernism could only acquire its understanding of late style by way of Romanticism, so we cannot now read late style except through the lens of modernism. The abstraction associated with late style is impossible to separate from modern abstract art, leaving late Titian, late Rembrandt and late Goya as undifferentiated precursors of the modern moment. And the turn back to the early that is characteristic of descriptions of late style might perhaps be read in reverse, not as a self-conscious return but as evidence that the early foresaw the late.

The contingency and complicity of self-consciousness, of the modern urge to establish a late phase as proof for posterity of the passing of genius, is thus dissolved into a claim of prophecy.

Late style is, in the end, then, not directly connected to, or produced by, old age; it is, rather, a means of policing the borders of the canon, of sorting the chosen from the rest. It is in his characterisation of 'old-age style' as a mythic language that the full extent – and the *impersonality* – of Broch's understanding of lateness becomes apparent. In his hands, late style has ceased to be the product of the last days of an individual, becoming instead a descriptor for an epochal phenomenon. For Said, developing Broch's insight, Beethoven's last quartets are not simply 'late' in the sense that they derive from the last years of the composer's life; they are 'late to the extent that they are beyond their own time, ahead of it in terms of daring and startling newness, later than it in that they describe a return or homecoming to realms forgotten or left behind by the relentless forward march of history'.[27] Late writing is thus out-of-time writing, art which reaches both before and after its moment. Late works, which are only incidentally late in relation to the career of the artist, are late – or perhaps better, *belated* – also in relation to the era in which he writes. This is a stance derived ultimately, as I have suggested, from Hegel: that one can only ever understand experience with hindsight and that one is thus always already belated in one's engagement with the universe. As such, it demonstrates the tradition within which Broch, and Neumann alongside him, worked. It also makes clear how far the concept of lateness had come by the mid-twentieth century from its origins as the apparently straightforward observation of a shift of style in the work of a celebrated artist late in life, and it underlines the fundamental tension in the discourse of lateness between the individual and the epochal. In Erikson's words, 'individual life is the coincidence of but one life cycle with but one segment of history; and all human integrity stands or falls with the one style of integrity of which one partakes' (*Life Cycle*, 65–6) – that is, a given late style will be the product of its era far more than of the creative individual associated with that style.

We have come a long way from Kenneth Clark's structural assumption that late style and old-age style are one and the same. As an epochal phenomenon, lateness may in fact have little, if anything, to do with the individual life-cycle at all. At the same time, the evidence frequently appears to resist this claim. It is perfectly obvious that the vast bulk of attributed late styles do indeed coincide with the last years of long-lived artists: the Shelleys and Mozarts are relatively few compared to the Titians, Rembrandts and

Verdis. It is also obvious that those late styles which do not coincide with old age per se often reflect circumstances which approximate or *stand in for* old age. Artistic production is, after all, never free from physical or mental contingency. On the contrary, it is often very clearly both the product and the by-product of materialities of various kinds. Sometimes medical conditions enforce stylistic shifts, as we have seen. Matisse turned from painting to pasting, or instructing his assistants to paste, paper to paper. Henry James was forced by the onset of carpal tunnel syndrome or 'writer's cramp' to shift from writing by hand to dictating to an amanuensis. It was another amanuensis, Eric Fenby, who enabled Frederick Delius, blind and paralysed by syphilis, to write his late music. In each of these cases, illness in combination with collaboration of one kind or another, not the transcendence of a free individual beyond contingency, resulted in a late style. To what extent, then, we need to ask, is late writing the product not of old age per se but of illness or other contingencies which produce the *effect* of old age?

The work of Paul Klee provides a particular test case for this question. For Klee, two sets of circumstances, one historical, the other medical (the latter probably brought on by the former), seem to have determined the double caesura of his late phase. At the end of 1933, when he was fifty-three, Klee and his wife fled Germany: he had had his work defamed by the Nazis and had been suspended from his job at the Düsseldorf Academy and it was clearly time to depart. The couple went to Switzerland, specifically to Bern, where Klee had been brought up. This moment provides a clear, unquestionable 'cleavage' in Klee's existence that appears to mark the start of his late phase; the major exhibition devoted to defining late Klee that took place in 2003 thus began with his work from 1933 onwards. However, as the show's curators readily acknowledged, a couple of years after his departure from Germany Klee fell ill: he was confined to bed for the bulk of the second half of 1935 and was rarely, if ever, free of the effects of illness from then on until his death seven years later, in June 1940, at the age of sixty. Medical problems thus create an alternative, second caesura within his work, with 1937, the year of the onset of his final illness and also the year in which he fully established the style generally considered his late style 'with its combination of luminous backgrounds and a semiotic language of black bars', marking the change.[28] For Matthias Bärmann, it is thus impossible to separate emigration, illness and the creative process in late Klee. He chooses instead to picture *levels* of lateness, an initial level produced by exile, a further by illness – the latter, he argues, 'even more than emigration, caus[ing] a deep caesura in his work, the last phase of which began in

1937' – though he reads the particular nature of scleroderma, the disorder which eventually killed the artist, 'an incurable autoimmune disease of the connective tissue', as an internalised version of exile.[29] '[H]is own body turned against itself', writes Bärmann, leaving Klee 'in a paradoxical situation, being at once in exile and at home, a stranger in his own land – and even in his own body' ('As if', 13). This second caesura produced what Bärmann calls 'a veritable explosive unleashing of creative energy and inspiration', with Klee apparently deriving 'a paradoxical vitality from the conscious, profound process of coming to terms with disease and the approach of death, a vitality that significantly transformed his art' (ibid.). In this period, he produced works which 'exhibit the late style of black symbols, reduced forms that convey an impression of the archaic', and in which Klee 'develops a broad, energy-charged range of devices, extending from delicate pencil lines to brushstrokes of elemental concision and impact' (ibid.), while at the same time there is a shift from 'the coherent strokes predominant until the mid-thirties to more fragmented configurations', a change marked by 'discontinuous patterns and textures' and 'an antagonistic interplay of open and self-contained formal elements' ('As if', 15).

There is thus in the analysis of late Klee a tension between the two contexual delimiters of lateness: exile due to Nazism (1933–1940), on the one hand, and illness (1937–1940), on the other. The two are, for Bärmann, intertwined because the illness was a direct result of the trauma of exile, but they mark different kinds of lateness, with the second phase privileged because of the extraordinary productivity that characterises it. In both cases, and despite the 2003 exhibition's insistence on a teleology of 'fulfilment', the late work appears to be the direct product of contingencies rather than of some kind of redemptive transhistoricity. It is impossible, finally, to separate Klee's late style from his particular circumstances, from the political crisis that forced him to leave his home and from the increasing illness that seems to have been the direct result of exile. These circumstances appear to have provoked a late style relatively early, at the age of fifty-three (the first sub-phase) or of fifty-seven (the second sub-phase). Nonetheless, old age itself appears relatively incidental – illness, not old age itself, appears to be the primary influence on the work – though it is of course a fact that as artists grow older they are more likely to suffer from various ailments. And there is one illness in particular which is itself frequently (perhaps even absurdly) difficult – even impossible – to distinguish from late style, a disease which is specifically associated with old age.

The American poet George Oppen published a final collection of verse, *Primitive*, in 1978. These poems bear many of the hallmarks of 'late writing' as it has been established since the middle of the nineteenth century: fragmentation, difficulty, mythic simplicity of subject matter, an engagement with the past, especially childhood. Even the title is typical of twentieth-century lateness. A characteristic instance of his work in this collection is 'The Tongues', which exemplifies many of these features:

> *The Tongues*
> of appearance
> speak in the unchosen
> journey immense
> journey there is loss in denying
> that force the moments the years
> even of death lost
> in denying
> that force the words
> out of that whirlwind his
> and not his strange
> words surround him

It is hard to read a poem such as this and not see Oppen's last writings as a classic instance of late work, as the abstract, fragmented product of a poet immersed in convention even as he rejects convention, making myth even as that mythmaking is under threat. At the same time, it is equally hard for critics not to read *Primitive* in the context of the one crucial biographical fact that dominates discussion of Oppen's final work, namely that he wrote these poems two or three years after the symptoms of Alzheimer's disease had first begun to appear. Critics have yet to agree – as is the case also with the late paintings of Willem de Kooning, another sufferer from Alzheimer's – about the status of the last work, whether it is the way it is because of the writer's control over his material or because of the writer's *loss* of control over that material and over his own mental and creative processes. Is Alzheimer's in some way a *cause* of late style? Or does it displace late style?

The answer to this should, one would think, be obvious. Alzheimer's arrests creativity; it neither facilitates nor, least of all, enhances it. The *New Oxford Textbook of Psychiatry* defines dementia, of which Alzheimer's disease is 'one cause', as 'a progressive cognitive decline in multiple areas', the 'core clinical symptom' of which is 'cognitive impairment'.[30] In other words, the impact of Alzheimer's runs directly counter to the last stages of the progression of cognition as outlined by Kohlberg *et al.* and certainly counter to Simonton's 'secondary peak'. Alzheimer's manifests itself in the shape of what are known as the '4As': amnesia (memory loss – 'early and inevitable' – beginning with short-term memory and progressing to long-term), aphasia (difficulties with word-finding become problems with syntax and eventually with speech in general), agnosia (difficulties with recognising objects and sometimes even one's own face) and apraxia (difficulties with complex tasks, most obviously, to begin with, dressing and cooking). In addition, '[v]isuospatial difficulties commonly occur in the middle stages of the disorder and may result in topographical disorientation, wandering, and becoming lost' and '[d]ifficulties with calculation, attention, and cognitive planning all occur' (*New Oxford Textbook*, 389). As this suggests, the cognitive decline provoked by the disease is matched by functional deterioration, a loss that leads in time to the need for full-time care.

All of these symptoms appear guaranteed drastically and progressively to reduce artistic capability, yet in the cases both of Oppen and of de Kooning the very same marks have been read by critics both as evidence of Alzheimer's and as evidence of a genuine late style, the art itself treated as a valiant struggle to maintain creativity in the face of imminent darkness. It is as if, in late style, there is no clear way to differentiate between creativity and decline. For Mark Stevens and Annalyn Swan in their recent biography of de Kooning, citing neurologists working specifically on Alzheimer's, it is very difficult 'to chart the effects of dementia' on a creative artist.[31] This is in part because of what is known as 'procedural memory', that is, the 'unconscious memory that governs complex motor acts' and which thus 'governs the movement of the hand while painting or playing a musical instrument' (*De Kooning*, 615). 'Part of the mind', notes one of the specialists, Donald Douglas, 'can work at a depth that is not verbal, or memory. [...] It doesn't even use the same brain mechanisms' (interview reported ibid.). In other words, it is not impossible that, at certain moments even in the middle stage of his illness, de Kooning's late style emerged from the chaos of his Alzheimer's, even as his mind's functionality inexorably deteriorated.

The point of the cases of Oppen and de Kooning within the problematics of the discourse of lateness is not, however, the particular details of Alzheimer's as a disease and its impact on creativity but the general question of two relationships, that between late style and extra-stylistic contingency and that between late style and old age. Contrary to popular belief, Alzheimer's is not a disease of old age per se; it is not identical with senility. The original subject of Alois Alzheimer's work on the disease was in fact a woman in middle age. Head injuries, strokes and carbon monoxide poisoning can all cause dementia in people at any age, though the bulk of sufferers are, unsurprisingly, the elderly. But the crisis Alzheimer's causes for late-style studies lies precisely in its specific association in people's minds with old age, since despite the evidence for the impact of various medical, psychological and material influences on the late styles of a range of writers, artists and composers, critics continue to treat late style as a specific product of old age itself, viewed solely as a phase in the normal lifespan. At the same time, these critics seem happy, as we have seen, to include in the ranks of late stylists creative artists who did not reach old age, whose final phase occurs well before the age usually considered to be old. What does seem to happen in these cases, however, as we have seen, is that the critic feels obliged to address the artist *as if he were* old, to ignore the chronological age of the subject of an attribution of lateness and to construct instead a series of supporting premises for that attribution. A late stylist, it seems, must be *considered* old, *treated as* an old man, even if he is not (or particularly if he is not) actually *old*. And the best-known late stylist who was not actually old when he produced his late work is Shakespeare.

5.3 SHAKESPEARE'S MIDDLE YEARS

For many (perhaps most) critics, the Shakespeare of the late plays – and in particular the Shakespeare of *The Tempest* – is an old man. I have already cited H. B. Charlton's influential assertion that the plays

are an old man's compensation for the inescapable harshness of man's portion, a compensation which pleases the more because with the coming of age, something of the terror of the things the dramatist in his strength has hitherto seen has been blunted by the weakening in him of his power of imaginative vision (*Shakespearean Comedy*, 267)

and it is clear that Charlton is by no means alone in this assumption. For Marco Mincoff,

Shakespeare's last complete drama creates the impression of being very much an old man's play. The central figure is an elderly man, very much aware of his age, whose every third thought is of death, and who regards this life as a transient dream. But more than that, there is also a general lack of tension, the lack of any deep interest in the personages, and the slightly bitter but calmly resigned recognition that the brave new world of the young is an illusion. (*Things Supernatural*, 118)

Strindberg, likewise, argues that in *The Tempest*,

the aging man's need for peace, summing up, and coming to terms with existence after a rather difficult life find their expression. [. . .] It is almost as if he had begun living on the other side, and has tried to depict a better world as man has conceived it in his dreams. [... T]he play is Shakespeare's final confession, view of life, farewell, thanks, and prayer. [...] He feels the end approaching; he is about to wake from the instructive dream that is called life.[32]

And he adds:

That is really how it is when one gets on in life; if one looks back at what one has lived through, it is so terrible one hardly believes it is real, and the best that had a sort of reality slowly dissolves as if it were smoke. (*Letters*, 203)

And if this is true of *The Tempest*, it is even more so of *The Two Noble Kinsmen*. As Tony Dawson observes, for many critics Shakespeare the collaborator is 'the old master', quietly being sidelined by 'young Fletcher' ('*Tempest* in a Teapot', 63), a contrast which implies a larger age-gap than the fifteen years that actually separated the two playwrights. Theodore Spencer, describing the Shakespearean sections of the final collaboration as 'static' and 'stiff', argues that '[t]hey have a deliberate yet vague grandeur, a remote and half-exhausted exaltation', that 'they are expressed through a clotted rhetoric that is the poetry of an old man who has finished with action', and that they contrast markedly with the obviously more youthful Fletcher scenes (Spencer, '*The Two Noble Kinsmen*', 276). 'Their style', he insists, 'is the style of old age, and the imagery is an old man's imagery' (ibid.). And it is not just critics who see the late Shakespeare in this way; theatre professionals do so too. For the director Digby Day, in similar vein, the *Kinsmen* was 'written by a man who felt old age close upon him' (Day in Potter, *Two Noble Kinsmen*, 13). And Sir John Gielgud, reflecting later on his experience of playing Shakespeare in Bond's *Bingo*, notes 'that the play seemed finally to suggest that Shakespeare became a rather bitter businessman in his old age'.[33] The Shakespeare of the last phase, it seems, is unquestionably an old man.

The problem is that this is not true. Shakespeare was not old when he wrote either *The Tempest* or his share of *The Two Noble Kinsmen* or, for that matter, when he died. He was in fact only forty-three (give or take six months) when he began work on *Pericles*, the first of the so-called 'late plays', and forty-nine when he finished work on the *Kinsmen* – middle-aged, certainly, and tangibly further through life than either Shelley or Keats when they wrote their last poems, but nonetheless, as Ellis tacitly acknowledges by way of juxtaposition, nearer in age to both than to, say, Sophocles or Verdi. Henry James, bewildered by the retirement, noted that, '[w]ritten as it must have been [...] before the age of forty-seven', *The Tempest* 'has that rare value of the richly mature genius who, by our present measure of growth and fulness, was still young enough to have had in him a world of life' (James in Lee, *Complete Works*, xii). Kenneth Muir, commenting on Charlton's 'old man's consolation', observes wryly that '[w]e may pass over the assumption that Shakespeare at the age of forty-five was declining into dotage, though those of us who have passed that age may feel that our minds are not yet beginning to decay' (Muir, *Last Periods*, 59). Nobody can deny Shakespeare's calendar age at the time of the late plays, in other words, but it is the understanding of the significance of that age – of its place within the Jacobean life-cycle – that varies widely. For James, the Shakespeare of the late plays was still decidedly middle-aged; for Charlton, he was already an old man.

In arguing for an ageing Shakespeare, scholars often lean on the common misconception that because mortality levels were so much higher in Shakespeare's day and life expectancy at birth so much lower, old age began earlier then than it does now. This was not, however, the case. Certainly, *average* life expectancy in Jacobean England fluctuated between thirty and forty (it seems to have been somewhere between forty and forty-one in 1606), but this figure is heavily influenced by the appallingly high proportion of deaths in infancy and because of the various diseases – notably the plague, which killed John Fletcher, for one – for which cures had not yet been found, not because the cells of the body (or of the brain) wore out any more quickly than they do now.[34] Herbert Howarth, while describing the late plays as evidence of 'an old man's pleasure in understanding human behaviour', admits that there is a larger myth in play, one that he is frankly prepared to endorse, despite his recognition of its inadequacy.[35] '[E]veryone who comments on the late plays subscribes to one myth or another', he points out, disarmingly, 'and I like', he says, 'the myth that the Elizabethans and Jacobeans did everything earlier than we do: took degrees earlier, married earlier, campaigned earlier, rotted earlier' (*Tiger's Heart*, 143). 'Indeed', he continues, 'the historian Creighton Gilbert has recently maintained, and fortified the claim with evidence, that the myth is truth. Shakespeare had led a busy existence. It is fair to the facts to call him an old man at 48.'[36] Myths can of course have their value and their defenders, but more recent studies suggest that in the early seventeenth century men were neither old nor viewed as old in their forties. Certainly, as Janet Roebuck notes, the question of old age was more one of 'function, or lack of it, than a question of precise calendar years'.[37] She proceeds to explain that

[t]he aged were those who were infirm, frail, and suffering incapacities of body or mind to the extent that they could no longer fully support or take care of themselves, *and who also* gave the appearance of being old. The assumption was that people could be advancing in years, or they could be incapable of supporting

themselves, but it was only when the two conditions came together in one person that that person was considered 'old' by the authorities. ('When', 417)

Old age was thus a flexible conjunction of calendar age and infirmity, and it is important to remember this flexibility in establishing an understanding of the perception of ageing in the seventeenth century. In Chapter 4, I discussed early modern attitudes to old age, demonstrating the variability of the ages-of-man patterns that structured thinking about the latter stages of life. As Lynn Botelho and Pat Thane point out, 'old age is a highly nuanced process, one that is culturally embedded and not merely biological'.[38] You are old, in other words, not when you reach a particular age but when you are considered old by others within your culture.

That said, in Jacobean England, associations were nonetheless made with certain calendar ages. Keith Thomas notes that 'sixty had long become stylized as the age of incipient decrepitude': '[a]t sixty a man ceased to be liable to compulsory service under the labour laws or to prosecution for vagrancy [and] he was no longer obliged to attend the court leet or to do military service' (Thomas, 'Age', 237). John Taylor the Water Poet (himself fifty-seven at the time and not to die until he was seventy-two) underlines the contemporary significance of this figure when he notes in his pamphlet *The Olde, Old, Very Olde Man* that at the time of the birth of Thomas Parr – still living, Taylor claims, at the decidedly ripe old age of 152 – 'there was no Register' and adds that

> The Register was ninty seven yeares since
> Giv'n by th'eight *Henry* ...
> ... in the thirtieth yeare of that Kings raigne;
> So old *Parr* now, was almost an old man,
> Neere sixty ere the Register began.[39]

Nearing sixty, Parr was 'almost' old; by 152, there is no 'almost' about it. Not that we need Taylor to tell us about unequivocal old age, since we know from Shakespeare's own plays how old a really old man is. Lear says that he is 'a very foolish fond old man,/Fourscore and upward, not an hour more nor less', adding heartrendingly: 'And to deal plainly,/I fear I am not in my perfect mind, (*King Lear [F]*, 4.6.53–6). There is nothing to suggest that Shakespeare, around half Lear's splendidly vague age when writing his first 'late play', was either old or in anything other than 'perfect mind'.[40] Thomas Fuller, writing later in the century about the 'silver-tongued' preacher Henry Smith, notes that '[t]he wonder of his worth is increased by the consideration of his tender Age, dying very young' – 'very young' in this instance being forty-one.[41] Shakespeare, writing *Pericles* at forty-three, cannot simultaneously be both 'very young' and an old man. 'There is', as Sisson put it in 'The Mythical Sorrows', 'something wrong with either this youth, or this old age, or with both' (22).

Still, it is not unreasonable to suppose that by 1609 or 1610 Shakespeare might have begun to be uncomfortably aware of the relative proximity of death. Stephen Greenblatt, in *Will in the World*, while acknowledging the evidence that Shakespeare made business trips to London as late as 1614, suggests (with a slight touch of the Howarths) that the burning down of the first Globe the previous year might have prompted in the playwright reflections upon mortality. The playhouse's 'fragility', he suggests, 'was one sign among many that Shakespeare, reaching his fiftieth birthday in 1614, could read in himself and in his world', noting in particular that '[h]is brother Gilbert died in 1612, at the age of forty-five [and that] a year later his brother Richard died just shy of his fortieth birthday'.[42] 'For us', Greenblatt adds, 'fifty is an age of undiminished vigor, and even then it was hardly ancient, but Shakespeare seems to have thought of himself as well struck in years' (*Will in the World*, 382). This could of course be true, though Sisson's anti-subjectivist irony, which I cited in Chapter 3, remains salutary: 'It appears that in 1607 Shakespeare's brother Edmund died, an event which helped to infuriate him. Fortunately, in 1608 his mother died, an event which restored him to a kindlier mood. So various are the effects of deaths in the family upon a great poet' ('Mythical Sorrows', 9). Mortality rates nonetheless make it clear enough that, in Ralph Houlbrooke's words, 'the majority of those who survived childhood died before they reached 60'.[43] Still, it depends a little on how you look at it, on how the individual responded. Houlbrooke makes the same point slightly differently elsewhere. 'A mean figure', he notes, 'based on the experience of twelve parishes with very good registers suggests that [...] adults who reached the age of 30 could look forward to another twenty-eight or thirty years of life in early modern times'.[44] Put this way, it would arguably be a little premature of Shakespeare to begin to fret about the end of his life at forty-three.

Something, the subjectivists argue, must have happened to prompt such thoughts. E. K. Chambers, extrapolating from Dowden, offers the simplest, if vaguest, solution. For him,

[t]he profound cleavage in Shakespeare's mental history about 1607–1608 must have been due to some spiritual crisis the nature of which it is only possible dimly to conjecture; some such process as that which in the psychology of religion bears the name of conversion; or perhaps some sickness of the brain which left him an old man, freed at last from the fever of speculation and well disposed to spend the afternoon of life in unexacting and agreeable dreams.[45]

I argued in Chapter 2 that this 'profound cleavage' is harder to identify than critics often suppose; its supposed cause is even more so: as a starting point for further conjectures, it appears less than convincing. For Edward Bond in *Bingo*, it is less a crisis than a pervasive *ennui* that makes Shakespeare feel old –

JUDITH   You'll get old sitting there all day.
SHAKESPEARE   I *am* old.
JUDITH   You used to be so busy. Striding about. Laughing. It's all gone. You look so tired these days (*Bingo*, 26)

– an *ennui* that appears to mark at least as much the end of an epoch as of an individual – or perhaps both: the end of the 'age of Shakespeare'. And for Kenneth Clark, whatever age Shakespeare was when he wrote the late plays, he was exhausted and thus, artistically speaking, old. He offers some initial comparisons. 'Mr Henry Moore', he notes (writing in 1970),

is seventy-three, but neither in himself nor in his carving is there the slightest sign of old age. Matisse became bed-ridden, but his art remained as fresh as a daisy. Conversely, Beethoven was under fifty when he entered what critics agree to call his last period, and the quartets, written when he was fifty-five, are classic examples of the old-age style in their freedom from established forms and their mixture of remoteness and urgent personal appeal. (*Artist Grows Old*, 23–4)

And seeking 'other examples of an old-age style in a great artist under fifty for which there is no such simple explanation', he turns from fine and plastic art or music to Shakespeare. 'How', he asks, 'do we explain Shakespeare's last four plays?', noting that '[c]ritics tend to write of them as if they were the work of an old man, although Shakespeare was in his middle forties when he wrote them', and adding that he considers that '*Pericles*, *Cymbeline*, and *The Winter's Tale* do indeed show some of the negative characteristics of the old-age style – the impatience, the recklessness, the bitterness', 'symptoms', he senses, 'of exhaustion rather than of a new direction' (ibid., 24). Thus he argues that

Lytton Strachey's notorious judgement that 'Shakespeare in his last years was half enchanted by visions of beauty and half bored to death,' although it has been rejected with horror by most scholars of Shakespeare, seems to me substantially true. No man has ever burnt himself up more gloriously. But *The Tempest* does seem to show some characteristics that only an artist who has lived his life could give. Far more than the earlier plays it creates a private world of the imagination. Shakespeare, who had in the past written so immediately for his actors and his audiences, now seems to be writing only for himself. (ibid.)

'Prospero's last speech', he adds decisively, 'could surely not have been written by a young man, even the young Shakespeare' (ibid.).

It need not, of course, as we have seen in the case of Klee, be a purely spiritual crisis that provokes premature ageing. Ben Jonson, reflecting at fifty-four on the impact of his stroke, moodily observed of himself that 'thy nerves be shrunk and blood be cold/Ere years have made thee old' (Jonson, 'Ode', ll. 45–6). And it is of course possible – despite the lack of actual evidence for medical difficulties until the drawing up of the will in January 1616 and the counter-evidence that, at least as late as the end of 1614, he was in good enough health to make journeys to London on business with the future of his property, and presumably of himself, firmly in mind – that around the time of the late plays Shakespeare too was beginning to feel the effects of incipient ill health. There is an entertaining, if not always entirely honourable, tradition in Shakespeare biography which makes apparent biographers' urge to find in illness an alternative to old age as the impetus for the late writing. A recent instance is Katherine Duncan-Jones's engaging, forthright biography *Ungentle Shakespeare*, in which she suggests that, around the time of the writing of *Pericles* (a play that, after all, suggestively dwells on the topic of brothels), Shakespeare may have contracted syphilis, thereby providing him with a tangible sense of his own mortality and pushing him into premature old age. She emphasises both his friendship with his *Pericles* collaborator George Wilkins and the location of Wilkins's house – Turnmill Street was notorious for its brothels – in order to argue that the combination of 'disturbingly graphic images of sweating tubs and venereal infection' in both *Troilus and Cressida* and *Shakespeares Sonnets* (both, as we have seen, published in 1609) and the 'repeated gestures of retrospection and valediction in the late work [. . .] support[s] a supposition that Shakespeare's visits to Turnmill Street had left him with an unwanted legacy of infection' (*Ungentle Shakespeare*, 224).

In giving the late Shakespeare this 'legacy of infection', Duncan-Jones may be recalling Peter Whelan's 1996 play about Shakespeare's last days, *The Herbal Bed*:

JOHN   That night, when you had out the Venetian turpentine potion and the lead box . . . and the rest . . . you intended them for him, didn't you? [. . .]
SUSANNA   It's what I thought he had then, yes.
JOHN   You must know . . . he's far beyond that now.[46]

Whelan, in turn, may have drawn on Anthony Burgess's characteristically scurrilous, inventive fictional biography *Nothing Like the Sun*: 'There he is, John Hall, the quality's own physician, my son-in-law. He surveys me frowning, pursing his lips, stroking his beard. Little time to go now, he thinks; perhaps in tomorrow's early hours. He will record nothing of his father-in-law's disease in his notebooks. [...] His father-in-law's disease was one only to be whispered about.'[47] These writers have no doubt what finished Shakespeare off. Hedging her 'supposition', though, Duncan-Jones adds, mischievously, that 'it makes little difference whether, from about 1608, he was indeed venereally infected, or whether he merely thought he was' (*Ungentle Shakespeare*, 224). The point is that by this time he was feeling distinctly less than robust, and Duncan-Jones elides this with the burning down of the Globe ('While younger King's Men playwrights picked themselves up and started again, Shakespeare, increasingly tired and unwell, opted out') in order to argue that, though 'in the event Shakespeare turned out to be considerably longer-lived than most males in his family [... i]ntimations of impending mortality appear to colour all of the late plays' retrospections' (ibid.). Syphilis thus becomes metonymic of the contingent possibilities – the various options offered over the years, from straightforward weariness to progressive, fatal illness – for the alleged decline of the playwright in his last years and can be read directly into the final plays. Facilitating this decline, Whelan compresses the three years between the late collaborations and the death, ending his play with Susanna 'admit[ting] that she suspected her father of having gonorrhea' and bringing the curtain down to the sound of offstage voices carrying her father in a chair:

JOHN (*off*)   Easy ... take the legs ... gently.
RAFE (*off*)   Turn him now ...
JOHN (*off*)   Gently ... gently .... (*Herbal Bed*, 120, 123)

He sets the play in June 1613, ignoring the evidence of the recorded London visit the following year and making it clear both that Shakespeare has been ill for some time – certainly while writing the late plays – and that he is already in Stratford at the time of the burning of the Globe.

Syphilis and gonorrhoea are possibilities, if such are needed, as indeed are the scores of other illnesses for which there was no cure in Jacobean England. One, at least, however, can be discounted as the prompt for the Shakespearean late phase – and not just because Shakespeare was not yet, or indeed ever, old – and that is Alzheimer's. In his discussion with Stevens and Swan about de Kooning's dementia, the neurologist Donald Douglas, addressing the question of procedural memory, the lingering on in the sufferer of certain deeply embedded movements and thus of certain physical skills, makes a telling comparison between the likely impact of Alzheimer's on a writer and on a painter:

Were Shakespeare suffering from Alzheimer's, posits Douglas, he could not have written his plays, because of their verbal and psychological complexity. But Picasso might have continued to paint because the complex language of painting was almost instinctual with him. 'It is considered one effect of some manifestations of dementia that once somebody learns a language, he doesn't forget the whole thing so easily', says Douglas. 'What happened yesterday, however, is a different matter'. (*De Kooning*, 615)

Douglas reports that the particular complex, creative verbal skills relied upon by a writer are especially hard hit by the onset of dementia; certain kinds of physical movement, on the other hand, including that required to make a characteristic brushstroke, are less so. It would seem, then, at least in regard to Alzheimer's and its possible relationship with late style, that assumptions about the symmetry across disciplines of the manifestations of lateness are decidedly problematic, that certain contingent late styles are possible in one kind of creativity and not in others. At least one provoker and destroyer of the possibility of late work, in other words, discriminates in favour of painting and against writing. Kenneth Clark's argument that, as far as late style is concerned, different rules apply to different artistic media, that '[p]ainters and sculptors tend to live much longer than writers or musicians', and that, unlike the latter, 'their work shows no sign of old age till their last years' (a characteristically tendentious claim that would have come as a surprise to Thomas Hardy, for one), thus meshes curiously with Douglas's account of the disciplinary relativity of the impact on creativity of Alzheimer's (*Ages of Man*, 23).

Which brings us back – inevitably, it seems – to old age. As Douglas's casual comparison implies, making, as it does, a firm correlation between the Shakespeare of the last plays and the ageing Picasso of the late style, commentators appear unable, despite the fact that Shakespeare, whatever his state of mind or health, was not actually old, to resist associating his late style with old age. This is frequently more implicit than explicit in criticism, though perhaps the most thoroughgoing recent critical attempt to make Shakespeare old before his time is that of Maurice Hunt. Writing of *The Tempest*, Hunt notes that '[t]he physical stooping that old age enforces is mentioned in the play [. . .], and it figures in the graphic hooping and bending that Prospero literally and figuratively inflicts upon Ferdinand and other characters on his island', and he adds that, while

[a]t the time he wrote *The Tempest*, Shakespeare was probably forty-seven years old, apparently too young to be regarded as Prospero's alter ego in this respect [. . .] the valedictory nature of certain of Prospero's speeches, and of *The Tempest* as

a whole, has encouraged generations of playgoers and readers to suspect that at moments Shakespeare saw himself in Prospero – a gifted but aged man.[48]

As support for this conventional reading, Hunt cites Elizabeth Bieman's argument for the widening of the identification of Shakespeare and Prospero to the other allegedly ageing male figures of his late plays, notably Leontes. Bieman reports the association by Jungian psychoanalysts of two archetypal male figures, the *puer*, the eternal youth, and the *senex*, the ancient wise man, noting that '[t]he *puer*-driven man who does not come to know the anima within, his internal principle of love, life, inspiration, will come under the *senex* years before his time' and demonstrating that the characterisation of Leontes in particular exemplifies this pattern.[49] Hunt, summarising, claims that

Shakespeare's representation of this Jungian pattern and final integration in *The Winter's Tale* implies that, as aging playwright, he was able to achieve personally a similar integration (which then made possible his creations of the pattern and its transcendence in the characters Leontes and Prospero). (*Laboured Art*, 274–5)

Thus, he argues, eliding effortlessly, 'Shakespeare's late creative work fashioned a self with whom he could live', one which grew 'out of the aging playwright's desire to cram as much as possible within his last creative years' and thus 'fueled' his late writing (ibid., 275).

This account, placed alongside that of Douglas, underlines the ongoing importance of old age for critics in the attribution of a late style to Shakespeare. In the process, it foregrounds an unavoidable problem: that, no matter how often the question is finessed by way of unsupported claims for 'Shakespeare's sense of himself as aging artist' (ibid., 275), the key late stylist in anglophone literary culture, the one to whom pretty much every subsequent writer in English has looked as a model for lateness, was not, at the time at which he wrote the plays belonging to his supposed 'late period', an old man. We are thus given a stark choice. Either late style and old-age style have to be distinguished and the conclusion reached that an artist can have a late style in middle age. Or if old-age style and late style are synonymous, then, since Shakespeare was not old, he cannot have had a late style, in which case either the basis upon which the late plays have been read for at least a century and a half must be rejected or else means must be found to reclaim old age for the late plays, to insinuate old age back into those plays. And what better vehicle for a reclamation of this kind than a play about old age – a play, moreover, considered by many to be the finest play in the entire canon – that can be repositioned heuristically as a late play?

5.4 'I HAVE A JOURNEY, SIR, SHORTLY TO GO': *KING LEAR* AS A LATE PLAY

'Why begin with *Lear*?' (Ruth Nevo)

'I have a journey, sir, shortly to go'. At the end of Act 5, Kent confirms the tragic grimness of *King Lear* by refusing service to the reconstituted state and projecting instead his ongoing fealty to his dead master in the imminence of his own self-willed death. This service, projected through the metaphor of a journey, looks away generically from tragedy towards the wandering tendency of romance even while at the same time implying an extended tragic *dénouement* beyond Act 5, a double generic impetus that has prompted a good deal of interpretation. For critics of romance, *King Lear*, despite the ostensible savagery of its conclusion, is of peculiar interest. Helen Cooper, for instance, concludes *The English Romance in Time* [...] *from Geoffrey of Monmouth to the Death of Shakespeare* not, as you might expect, with *The Tempest* (or even, distinguished Chaucerian that she is, with *The Two Noble Kinsmen*) but with *Lear*, noting that, beneath the surface of the play, '[t]he known story of Lear promises an ending like that Shakespeare was to give *Pericles* and *Cymbeline* and the *Winter's Tale*, where father and daughter rediscover each other in a powerful invocation of harmony and a promise of a better future' (406). *King Lear*, in other words, even as it fails to achieve a redemptive late-play ending, gestures towards those plays. In suggesting a connection of this kind between *King Lear* and the late plays, Cooper is sustaining a critical tradition. As we have already seen, for critics in the mid-twentieth century keen to read Shakespeare's late writing as evidence not of abrupt caesura but of continuity with his mid-period work, above all with the mature tragedies, *Lear* became the most significant play in the canon beyond the confines of the late plays themselves, acting as the harbinger within the tragic grouping of the redemptive genre yet to come. The curious position of *King Lear* in relation to the late plays is thus, I wish to suggest, one of the more interesting, and perhaps unexpectedly productive, side-effects of the conflation of old-age style and late style in Shakespearean criticism.

At the beginning of this book, I cited Edward Said's claim that classic late serenity is to be found 'in Shakespeare's late romances like *The Tempest*, *The Winter's Tale* and *Cymbeline* [...] where, to borrow from another context, ripeness is all' (*On Late Style*, 40). The subject of Said's focus is 'late romance', then, but the borrowing is not from an actual late play but from *King Lear* – Edgar's bleak observation to his blind father in Act 5 which is often read not as moment-specific but as a general comment on the experience of old age, especially that of Lear himself, across the course of the play. Lear, it seems from Said's conflation, reinserts into the late plays the ripeness, the note of genuine old age, that is missing from those plays. For William Kerrigan, though, as for many other critics, that note is not in fact missing in the first place: for him, *The Tempest*, in particular, is both 'an old man's play' and 'a play about becoming an old man'.[50] Yet, though the figure of Prospero is indeed near-uniformly represented, in Stephen Orgel's words, as 'a benign wizard, elderly, serene and majestic', there is in fact, as Orgel points out, very little in the play to suggest that Prospero is actually ancient – Miranda is, after all, only fifteen, and when he describes her to Ferdinand as 'a third of mine own life' (4.1.3), one of his possible meanings is that bringing her up has taken up a third of his lifetime, which makes him a mere forty-five – and he 'only *declares* himself old when his daughter is ready to marry', a declaration in which, in Orgel's perceptive phrase, '[t]here is surely more dramatic psychology [...] than physiology'.[51] Prospero need not, in other words, *pace* Kerrigan *et al.*, be old at all, whereas the considerable old age of King Lear, on the other hand, is crucial to the logic of the play whose protagonist he is. In a sense, the problems created for Shakespearean criticism by the presumption of identity between late style and old-age style can be summarised chiastically by way of these two plays: Lear is old but *King Lear* is not a late play, whereas *The Tempest* is a late play but Prospero is not old. The incorporation of *King Lear* into discussion of Shakespearean lateness might therefore have a certain heuristic value for critics wishing to read the late plays as plays of old age.

The term 'late plays' has been used in very deliberate ways, as I have argued, to set up a post-tragic narrative for Shakespeare. Dowden created his category of 'romances' precisely to mark this caesura. Both *Timon of Athens* and *Antony and Cleopatra*, tangibly different generically and tonally from *Pericles* or *The Winter's Tale* yet only preceding them by a short period of time, can readily be deployed by critics in order to sustain this position – though even this is not perhaps quite as clearcut as might be expected, since the protagonist of *Timon* shares his disillusioned exit from society with Pericles and *Antony and Cleopatra*, with its geographical expansiveness and negotiation of non-Roman *romanitas*, can be aligned in several ways with *Cymbeline*. But *Coriolanus* most distinctly cannot be used in this way, despite unavoidably postdating *Pericles*, and neither can *King Lear*, which Shakespeare appears to have revised, according to

Gary Taylor, in the midst of writing the late plays. Yet, despite the provocative decision by the editors of the Oxford Shakespeare to incorporate a separate, later text for Folio *Lear* into the middle of the late period, book after book on the last plays – even the atypical ones, such as that of Richards and Knowles, which fully integrate the post-*Tempest* collaborations into the late-play group – exclude tragedies of any kind from their narrative of Shakespearean lateness. We do not, in other words, open a book on the late plays expecting to see essays on *Coriolanus*. That said, Richard Tobias and Paul Zolbrod's collection *Shakespeare's Late Plays* does include essays on both *Timon* and *Lear*, despite the fact that, in his introduction, Zolbrod specifically and conventionally sets the grimness of *Othello* against the 'transcend[ing]' of the 'dark vision' effected in *The Tempest* 'which marks the absolute distance of Shakespeare's movement away from darkness and despair', thereby firmly distinguishing between tragedy and late play.[52] And the unreconstructed logic of the inclusion of *Timon* is clear enough at the end of Michael Tinker's essay when he manages somehow to find forgiveness and a bringing of 'humanity back to the world' in the play's ending.[53] There is no explanation given, however, for the presence in the collection of an essay on *King Lear*.[54]

Lear has in fact been treated for decades as something of an exception to the rule of the rigorous exclusion of tragedies from the late phase. E. M. W. Tillyard, as I have already noted in Chapter 2, reading the last plays not as a new turn but as an extension of what he calls the 'tragic pattern', rejects the conception of tragedy as stoic resistance to implacable circumstance (or rather argues that, while this narrative might work adequately for Webster, it does not adequately address Shakespeare's version of the genre) and argues that tragedy necessarily encompasses both destruction and regeneration, echoing Dover Wilson's belief that '[t]he Lear that dies is not a Lear defiant, but a Lear redeemed. His education is complete, his regeneration accomplished' (Tillyard, *Last*, 17). For Wilson Knight, Lear, 'at the last instant of racked mortality', catches a glimpse of a 'smiling destiny' despite all the grimness, thereby pre-empting the dénouement of romance (Knight, *Wheel*, 192). And perhaps the most explicit statement of the connection between *Lear* and the late plays is that of Cyrus Hoy in his 1978 essay on family relationships in the romances. He begins by noting that '[b]ehind all the fathers and daughters in Shakespeare's romances are the most affecting father and daughter he ever drew, Lear and Cordelia', and he proceeds to stake out his belief both in the essential continuity of the tragedies and the late plays and in the centrality of *King Lear* to that continuity:

Shakespeare's tragedies are the necessary prelude to the romances; the romances are inconceivable without the tragedies; and among the tragedies, *King Lear* stands out for a number of reasons, not the least of which concerns its protagonist's relation to women. Lear is a father with daughters, not a son with a mother (as in *Hamlet* or *Coriolanus*), or a husband with a wife (as in *Othello* or *Macbeth*), or a lover with a mistress who is both more and less to him than a wife (as in *Antony and Cleopatra*).[55]

For Hoy, Shakespeare's principal interest – obsession, even – in the late plays is the male negotiation of the female other as monster or as paragon. Thus he argues that

[a]ll Shakespeare's work from *Lear* to the end of his career seems to be generated by the tensions between two powerful imaginative efforts: on the one hand, to free the self from bondage to the kind of female monsters most horrifically embodied in Goneril and Regan, and on the other hand to replace the sense of female monstrosity with [. . .] an ideal of femininity on whom the imagination can bestow its tenderest sentiments, without the distractions of sexual desire. ('Fathers and Daughters', 81, 84)

Foregrounding polarities, with the 'horrific' Goneril and Regan set against the 'ideal' Cordelia, Hoy establishes *Lear* as the play in which the dominant thematic interests of the late plays first break surface, marking the triumph of the ideal over the monstrous. 'One suspects', he writes, 'that Shakespeare was attracted to the romance form at least in part for the freedom it gave him to create an atmosphere in which other idolized daughters – Marina, Imogen, Perdita, Miranda – could endure' (ibid., 78). Thus, *King Lear* represents 'the beginning of the imaginative way that will lead to *Pericles*, *Cymbeline*, *The Winter's Tale* and *The Tempest*' (ibid., 77).

Ruth Nevo responds to this claim by glancing back at the very beginning of the career and noting both that *Titus Andronicus* offers 'the sensational pathos' of the protagonist's 'archaic father and abused and mutilated daughter' and that in *The Comedy of Errors* critics find 'the whole wandering romance story of vicissitude and family reunion which structures the later plays' and she asks a simple but pointed question of critics such as Hoy who insist on seeing in *King Lear* the *ur*-point of the romances: 'why begin with *Lear*?' (*Other Language*, 2). Yet, for her antagonists, the connections between *Lear* and the late plays are patent. For Derek Traversi, in particular, as I suggested in Chapter 2, *King Lear*, 'in so many ways Shakespeare's central masterpiece', is the pivotal play in the canon, marking the most 'complete [. . .] integration of plot and character' (*Last Phase*, 14), and he sees the late plays as a logical extension of the supreme achievement of *Lear*. Tempests are central to his argument, permitting a thematic connection between *Lear* and the late plays to be expressed in action. 'It is clear', he claims, that the set of related events [...] placed, as its turning-point, at the centre of the play contains all the typical contrasts – between tempest and succeeding calm, birth and death, mortality and healing – which go to make up the symbolic unity of the last plays; they provide, from now on in increasing measure, a framework for the pattern of interdependent imagery by which the play attains its full poetic life. (ibid., 25–6)

'This pattern begins to take shape', he argues, 'when Pericles evokes, in terms that once more remind us of *Lear*, the tempest by which his ship is threatened' (ibid., 26). With *King Lear*, for Traversi,

[t]here is a very real sense [...] in which the whole action of the tragedy might be described as a projection of the conflicting issues supremely present in the mind of the central figure. [...] The personal conflicts of the tragic hero are projected into the dramatic action, itself conventional [...] both are unified as expressions of an inclusive creative impulse by the threads of related imagery, repeated or contrasted, which underlie the complete development. (ibid., 14, 17–18)

'From this state of affairs', he argues, 'it is an easy and natural step to the deliberate abandonment of realism which is apparent in the last plays' (ibid., 18). In other words, as Robert Speaight phrases it, '*Lear* is not Shakespeare's last word, but it is the overture to his last act'.[56]

Kenneth Muir, in *Last Periods*, takes a slightly different tack, drawing an instructive parallel between *King Lear* and the late work of Strindberg and setting both up as instances of what he sees as a kind of second-rung or unachieved lateness. For Muir, Strindberg, who appeared to have established a proper late serenity towards the end of his life (in, for instance, *Easter*), lapsed from that mood when writing *The Ghost Sonata*. He cites the view of Arkenholz the student ('Jesus Christ descended into hell! – that was his journey on earth, this madhouse, this reformatory, this charnel house the earth') as that of Strindberg himself and suggests that 'Strindberg's view of the world seems to be not unlike that of the mad Lear', adding that '[j]ust as with Shakespeare's mad folk we have "reason and impertinency mixed, Reason in madness", so with Strindberg we have a distorted picture of life, which is nevertheless at moments poignant and profound'.[57] *King Lear* thus becomes, for Muir, a kind of late play but one which is limited by the writer's failure to achieve the serenity necessary for true lateness. For Strindberg, a play such as *The Ghost Sonata* was a backward step from the personal peace he had already briefly experienced, a peace not, sadly, to be recaptured: he 'remained to the end of his life an obsessed and tortured figure, and although he struggled in his last period towards forgiveness and reconciliation he only achieved them momentarily' (*Last Periods*, 27–8). For Shakespeare, by contrast, the last period would in due course bring the serenity denied to his later counterpart. The implication of the comparison is that *Lear* stands as a kind of failed proto-late play, a play with the hallmarks of lateness but not yet the clarity of vision required for lateness to operate its magical transformations upon the writer's larger perspective. This reading persists in later essays such as that of Coppélia Kahn, for whom the play's final destructive patriarchalism, its relentless obliteration of women, requires Shakespeare to 're-imagine a world in his last plays' in which this does not have to be the case – in, that is, 'the world of pastoral tragicomedy and romance, the genres of wish-fulfilment, rather than the tragic world of *King Lear*'.[58] Here, once again, even as *Lear* is distinguished from the late plays, it retains the quality of overture.

Readings of *Lear* as redemptive tragedy did not survive the combined impact of the Second World War and Cold War. R. A. Foakes, in his comparative study of the critical reputations of *Hamlet* and *King Lear*, notes that even as *Lear* 'regained' in the mid-twentieth century the 'ascendency in critical esteem' it had held in the days of Hazlitt and Keats but which had in the intervening years been transferred by and large to *Hamlet*, it also 'changed its nature almost overnight'.[59] 'The main tradition of criticism up to the 1950s', he reports,

> had interpreted the play as concerned with Lear's pilgrimage to redemption, as he finds himself and is 'saved' at the end, but in the 1960s the play became Shakespeare's bleakest and most despairing vision of suffering, all hints of consolation undermined or denied. (*Hamlet versus Lear*, 3–4)

Interestingly, in the context of a discussion of old age, Foakes attributes this shift to changes in political culture, both in the USA and in Britain, from the midpoint of the twentieth century. '[U]ntil the 1950s', he argues, *King Lear* was read either

> as a tragedy of personal relations between father and daughter, or as a grand metaphysical play about Lear's pilgrimage to discover his soul. All this changed after 1960, since when *King Lear* has come to seem richly significant in political terms, in a world in which old men have held on to and abused power, often in corrupt or arbitrary ways. (ibid., 6)

For Foakes, there is a direct correlation between Lear's blindness to the misrule that brings about his and others' downfall and the politics of the Cold War and post-Cold War period. Commenting on responses to Peter Brook's archetypally bleak interpretation in his 1962 production, one heavily influenced by Jan Kott's existential reading of the play as a precursor of Beckett, Foakes notes that even those who found Brook's reading too grim, too monolithic and, in the end, too far from what they felt to be Shakespeare's original conception nonetheless recognised that history had necessarily influenced the way in which critics and audiences responded to the play, that the experience of war and its aftermath in the twentieth century meant that it was impossible to read the play in the same way again.[60] 'Even Maynard Mack', Foakes reports, 'who dismissed Brook's version as having little to do with "the play Shakespeare wrote", nevertheless acknowledged that the experience of Auschwitz and two world wars had altered our perception of the play' (*Hamlet versus Lear*, 60). And Foakes notes that Brook specifically adjusted his production to match changed circumstances and perceptions:

[he] made more specific political connections when his production toured in Hungary: there Lear became 'the figure of old Europe, tired, and feeling, as almost every country in Europe does, that after the events of the last 50 years people have borne enough'. In interviews Brook also specifically linked Lear to contemporary old men who wielded political power in a rather dictatorial way, de Gaulle and Adenauer, and said, 'One could easily see in Lear the incarnation of the process that takes place within a certain form of Stalinism'. After such knowledge, what forgiveness? (ibid.)

'It would seem', Foakes concludes wryly, 'that the recapturing of a sense of something positive at the play's end would have to take a new form, not a glowing sense of redemption' (ibid.).

This 'new form', I would argue, turned out to be the reassertion in the 1980s of the suggestion made at various times in the history of Shakespeare scholarship that the textual differences between the two extant versions of *King Lear* mean that each might usefully be considered independently, not, as had been habitual ever since Shakespearean editing began, conflated into one comprehensive text.[61] This does not seem, at first sight, an especially productive line of inquiry for a study of the idea of late writing. Yet the separation of the two texts of *Lear* and the dating of the later Folio text to 1610, I wish to suggest, is designed, perhaps un- or subconsciously, to reclaim the play's alleged affinity with late Shakespeare – in effect to remake it as a late play. This, at least in part, can be held to explain both the willingness with which so many critics have accepted the arguments of Gary Taylor for the two-text *King Lear* – that is, for the separation of Q *Lear* from F *Lear* as distinct, equally valid texts – and, at the same time, for the preference of most Shakespeareans who have acknowledged the distinction between Quarto and Folio *Lear* for the latter.

Not that Taylor was first off the mark in returning to the question of the *Lear* text. Michael Warren, with whom Taylor collaborated on the landmark volume, *The Division of the Kingdoms*, had already analysed the characterisation of Albany and of Edgar on the assumption of Shakespearean revision.[62] And Steven Urkowitz argued two years later that the differences between Quarto and Folio *Lear* needed to be seen as authorial revision, claiming that 'the Folio text represents a careful and dramatically sensitive revision of the Quarto; and that the revision could have been made by no one other than Shakespeare himself'.[63] For Urkowitz, these revisions were made soon after the first writing of the play, in the gap between the creation of the text that was preserved in the Quarto and the play's first performance and were primarily made with performance in mind: he argues that 'the Folio is Shakespeare's final version' (*Shakespeare's Revision*, 147). Taylor, writing shortly afterwards, agrees with Urkowitz's claim for Shakespearean revision but not with his assumptions both about the non-'final' nature of the Quarto text and about the timing of the revision. Why, he asks, 'would anyone setting out to rework *King Lear* begin from a copy of Q1?' – a key question in explicating the nature of the changes – and he proceeds to offer a possible scenario, one which deliberately extends the timeframe presumed by Urkowitz.[64] 'Sometime after 1603', Taylor suggests,

> Shakespeare began to spend less time in London acting, and more time in Stratford with his family. If, at some point in or after 1608, he had decided to revise *Lear* during one of these sojourns in Stratford, he could hardly have taken the prompt-book with him: the company might need it in his absence, or he might lose it, and in any case he had no advance guarantee that the company would approve of his mutilating it. If he could not take the prompt-book, and could not take the foul papers (which had been sold), the only text of his play he could have taken with him was an exemplar of Q1 – printed, he would have known, from his own foul papers. He could annotate, revise, blot, and dirty a copy of Q1 as much as he wanted, without committing himself or the King's Men to anything; and if, when he had finished, the result seemed to him worth presenting to his fellow sharers as a new version of the play, then at some point he or someone else would have had to transcribe a new fair copy from Shakespeare's own heavily marked-up exemplar of Q1. ('Date and Authorship', 365)

Though he acknowledges the absence of external proof for this assertion, Taylor believes his reconstruction of events to be 'what actually happened' (ibid., 366). His point is that the two texts *both* represent 'what the author regarded, at the time, as the play's final form, and both [...] presumably received full theatrical production by Shakespeare's company in Shakespeare's lifetime' (ibid., 429). Thus the Folio represents not simply evidence of immediate theatrical adjustments to a stable original 'but a new version of the play, and one begun from an exemplar of Q1' (ibid., 366). This, he argues, 'provides a simple explanation for the complex and apparently conflicting evidence as to the nature of the Folio copy – evidence impossible to account for on the assumption that there was only ever one 'true' text of Shakespeare's play' (ibid.). More to the point, he adds, 'this evidence firmly dates the Folio redaction sometime after the publication of Q1, in January 1608' (ibid.).

Taylor's enthusiasm for his argument is apparent in the slippage from his early acknowledgement of the absence of clear proof to his later assertion that the evidence he has provided is 'firm'. He looks to the texts themselves for this evidence, seeking parallels with other Shakespearean texts both in their use of source material and in matters of vocabulary. As far as source-materials are concerned, Taylor searches for parallels between the Folio changes and 'works which Shakespeare is believed, on other grounds, to have read between 1605 and the end of his career, concentrating on the areas or passages in those books which seem to have immediately influenced the later plays' ('Date and Authorship', 377). Though he finds 'no parallels with any of the sources for [. . .] Shakespeare's last five plays: *Cymbeline, The Tempest, Henry VIII*, the lost *Cardenio*, and *The Two Noble Kinsmen*', he argues, this does not mean that 'such parallels nowhere exist'; he 'may simply have missed them, or failed to cast [his] net sufficiently wide' (ibid.). But he does admit that source-material alone does not offer adequate evidence. 'On the other hand', he reports, 'the same kind of search did turn up several interesting verbal parallels with the sources of the group of plays from *Macbeth* to *The Winter's Tale*' (Taylor, 377), and it is to these verbal parallels that he turns his attention. The vocabulary of the Quarto, he argues, 'tends to confirm a date of original composition between *Othello* and *Macbeth*, either just before or just after *Timon of Athens*' ('Date and Authorship', 388). The 'vocabulary unique to the Folio', on the other hand,

would appear to have been written later than Q, or by another writer. It does not have significant links (as Q does) with the plays from *As You Like It* to *Othello*; its strongest links are with the four plays *The Winter's Tale, Cymbeline, The Tempest* and *Henry VIII*. The excess of links between the Folio-only material and these four last plays would happen by chance only about one time in two hundred. (ibid., 388–89)

And to these statistical tests he adds as reinforcement both a topical reference – the line 'No heretics burn'd', he argues, from the Fool's

Merlin speech, 'is unlikely to have been written after 14 December 1611, when Edward Wightman was condemned to death for heresy' – and a theatrical argument – 'the revision presumes the use of act intervals, and hence post-dates the purchase of the Blackfriars in August 1608'.[65] Thus, he argues, '[o]n the traditional hypothesis, of a single version of *Lear* composed in 1605 or 1606, th[e] remarkable link between *Lear* and the late romances is quite inexplicable'; it would, however, he adds, 'be a natural consequence of Shakespeare's having extensively revised the play at some point after *Coriolanus* and before *Cymbeline*' (ibid., 389). And he concludes that, taken together, this evidence is sufficient to

suggest that the revision of *Lear* took place after *Coriolanus* and before *Cymbeline*: after Shakespeare's last tragedy, heavily concerned with war and politics, and just before another foray via Holinshed into early British history. The bibliographical evidence, of initial revision directly on to a copy of Q1, is consonant with this date, as is the absence of clear Folio links with the sources of the original composition (approximately four years earlier). So is the evidence of vocabulary.[66]

For Taylor, then, it is apparent that Folio *Lear* was a revision, performed upon a copy of the Quarto, by Shakespeare himself, one that took place in 1610 or thereabouts, in the midst not of the period of the 'mature tragedies', of which *Lear* is arguably the very finest, but of the Shakespearean late phase.

Throughout his analysis, Taylor appears intent on remaking *King Lear* as a late play. As far as the evidence is concerned, he is noticeably keener to emphasise the vocabulary tests, which suggest a close relationship between Folio *Lear* and the late plays, than the source-material tests, which do not. And in proposing his preferred narrative for the process of revision, he invokes the longstanding tradition that the last plays were written in Stratford tranquillity – not precisely in retirement, but in the gradual transition to retirement. Around the time of James I's accession, he claims, 'Shakespeare began to spend less time in London acting, and more time in Stratford with his family', positing that 'at some point in or after 1608' he might have 'decided to revise *Lear* during one of these sojourns in Stratford' ('Date and Authorship', 365). At the same time, he deploys a version of Bentley's theatrical argument that the move to the Blackfriars was the impetus for the particular shape and nature of the late plays (see above, 96–7). Furthermore, a little later, discussing the pattern of revision in Folio *Lear*, he appears directly to echo the Christian-redemptive readings of mid-century critics such as Knight:

In strengthening Edgar the Folio [. . .] strengthens the promise of moral continuity after the tragedy. Naturally, that promise remains subordinate to the crushing present pain of Cordelia's death, and Lear's; the undertaste of hope arguably only sharpens the bitterness. But in giving greater emphasis to the young promising survivor Edgar, the Folio clearly complements the new emotional complexity evident in Lear's own unaltered final moments. That complexity in its turn has been anticipated and prepared by Folio alterations elsewhere in Lear's own part and in the final scene. (ibid., 427)

Thus, he notes,

[i]n Q, we can compare Lear's final moments either with Gloucester's, whose heart 'burst smilingly', or with Edgar's description of the despairing Kent, bellowing with grief, then recounting 'the most pitious tale ... That euer eare receiued' until his 'strings of life, / Began to cracke' [...]. The Quarto makes Lear's death unmistakably closer, emotionally as well as temporally, to the second of these two moments. It is as though an audience were being offered a preview of two potential, alternative endings to the play: one like Gloucester's, in which Lear would be restored to his kingdom, and die exhausted by past grief and present joy – or one like Kent's, in agony unrelieved by hope. The old *Leir* play would have encouraged audiences to expect the first; Shakespeare instead – in the Quarto – gave them the second. (ibid.)

But, he proceeds,

the Folio cuts this description of Kent entirely, and at the same time makes Lear's death strikingly similar to Gloucester's, with the essential and painful difference that Lear's final reunion with his dearest child remains as illusory (in this world) as Gloucester's is real. (ibid.)

For Taylor, this illusion does not change the fundamental difference between the texts, does not entirely obliterate the 'sense of hope, transcendence, spiritual consolation [that] the Folio ending nevertheless surely offers' (ibid.,). 'Nor', he adds,

should this surprise us if, as I have suggested, the Folio redaction dates from 1609–10. A. C. Bradley once wondered what *King Lear* would have been like if Shakespeare had taken up the story later in his career, for instance at about the time when he was writing *Cymbeline*; the answer has, I think, been staring us in the face for three and a half centuries, in the form of the Folio text. Certainly, the interrelated changes in the Folio's dramatization of the ending of *King Lear* produce an effect strikingly similar to the resonant emotional complexity of the most memorable scenes in *The Winter's Tale* and *Cymbeline*. (ibid.)

Thus *King Lear* becomes, in its Folio form, a play which offers a striking congruence with the late plays. Taylor's aim here, in insisting on the relationship of Folio *Lear* to the late plays, is of course not to extend and renew the Shakespearean late phase but to demonstrate that the Folio text represents a later revision by Shakespeare himself of his own play.

His foregrounding of the connection with the late plays is thus performed instrumentally in order to place a good number of years between Quarto and Folio *Lear* and to underline the distinct and subsequent nature of the latter. But by reading his argument in reverse we can see that the secondary effect, arguably unintended, is to make Folio *Lear*, in a certain sense, into a late play. In the excavation of arguments for the association of late-play tranquillity and early retirement to Stratford and in the emphasis on the development of the redemptive possibilities Taylor finds in the Folio text, I wish to suggest, is the urge to associate *Lear*, the play of old age, with the late plays.

The revisions to the text of *Lear* do not, of course, need not be read as changes made for personal reasons or for posterity but rather as changes made for practical, professional or political reasons. In the course of his essay on the dating, Taylor does acknowledge, as we have seen, one possible institutional reason for the revision he posits, suggesting that 'an occasion' for Shakespeare's revision of *Lear* might have been 'the opening of the Blackfriars, in the winter of 1609–10' ('Date and Authorship', 428). That opening', he acknowledges,

> would not of course have compelled Shakespeare to revise any of his plays; but it might have *permitted* it, the opportunity to advertise the play as 'with additions and revisions' compensating for the trouble involved in preparing a new promptbook and new actors' parts. [...] For both Shakespeare and the company, the opening of the Blackfriars would have provided an opportunity [...]. (ibid.)

Having offered in this way a material, practical reason for the revision, however, Taylor reverts to subjectivism – to, that is, personal preoccupations and motivations on the part of the playwright as the fundamental reasons for stylistic change and revision – and, in the process, turns once again to the late plays. 'Why Shakespeare might have wished to return to the subject we will never know', he admits,

> [b]ut his preoccupation with fathers and daughters in the late romances – particularly his return in *Cymbeline* to early British history, and to the story of a daughter who disobeys her father, marries, sojourns in the wilderness, and returns at the end in the company of an invading (but eventually defeated) army – hardly make a return to *King Lear* psychologically implausible. (ibid.)

This idea of revision by the playwright himself, despite its ostensible multiplication and fragmentation of both text and authorship, in fact sustains a subjectivist sense that the logic of interpretation must always be based in the psychology of the playwright. Moreover, the emphasis on the relationship of *Lear* with the late plays is in fact underlined by the institutional factor too, since, as we have seen, critics have frequently cited the move to the Blackfriars as one of the primary factors in the late-play caesura (see Chapter 2, 96–9). In other words, the reoccupation of the Blackfriars prompted two outcroppings of Shakespearean creativity: the late plays and the revised *Lear*. Even the theatrical, institutional impetus Taylor suggests for the Folio revisions, then, matching as it does one of the principal arguments for the difference of the late plays from the other plays in the Shakespeare canon, turns us back to the late phase. Underpinning the critical emphasis on the *authorial* nature of the revisions to the text of *Lear* is the shadow of the late plays, because such revision allows Shakespeare to be responsible for the increased redemptive quality of the Folio text and thus its unexpected tonal proximity to the late plays. What critics do not want to find is that the changes were made by someone else – like the additions to *Doctor Faustus* or *The Spanish Tragedy*, say – since that would undermine the subjectivist understanding of the development of style upon which the reading of the conjunction of Folio *Lear* and the late plays is premised.

Is Folio *King Lear*, then, in the end, an instance of 'late writing'? Is Folio *Lear* a 'maturer' text than Quarto *Lear*? Is it representative of the supposed shift in Shakespearean thinking marked traditionally by the late-play caesura? All of this assumes that Shakespeare shared the perception of a Henry James about the concept of the career, which, as I showed in Chapter 4, he cannot have done. But it is a persistently appealing thought both for critics and for editors, this career-mindedness, suggesting the extent to which certain residual critical attitudes (the assumption of singular authorship as an anterior category) inform an ostensibly new, theorised form of editing (revision studies): working on revision, in other words, is still working within the paradigm of the author. It could be argued that *Lear* critics wish to read the play as a late play, that much of the discussion about the differences between Quarto and Folio *Lear* – and in particular the late dating, to 1610, of Folio *Lear* – is dependent upon an unvoiced desire to make this play about an old man an old man's play, a kind of grim counterpart to, or forerunner of, the retirement motif of *The Tempest*. If Shakespeare writes a play about old age, in other words, it must be associated as closely as possible with the plays which embody that old age dramatically – that is, the late plays. It may be, then, that the arguments in favour of creating two distinct texts for *Lear* – one from 1606 or so in the middle of the mature tragedies, the other from 1610 or 1611 in the middle of the late plays – and the choice of the editors of the Oxford Shakespeare to provide both of these texts yet not to include both Q2 and F *Hamlet* or Q and F *Othello* were due at least in part to the additional impetus provided by the semi-conscious desire to reconfirm

Lear as the pivot between the tragedies and late plays. As if to underline this, the editors of the Oxford Shakespeare in their second edition of 2005 provocatively (yet, for the most part, silently) expand the compass of the late-play group by a little chronological readjustment, drawing *All's Well That Ends Well* into the fold by moving it, without explanation or precise dating, to a position just prior to *Pericles* and printing Folio *Lear* not immediately after the Quarto text between *Timon* and *Macbeth* as in the first edition – located, in other words, in both textual forms, firmly with the tragedies – but, more appropriately in view of their understanding of the chronology, between *The Winter's Tale* and *Cymbeline*, thereby not only disrupting the usually smooth succession of the four 'principal' late plays but extending the impact of their originary dating of Folio *Lear* to 1610. This abrupt introduction of *All's Well* and Folio *Lear* into the late phase serves as a valuable reminder of the limitations of the dating of the Shakespeare canon and of the inadequacy of traditional assumptions about the clarity of the late-play caesura; at the same time, it broadens and alters the set of plays thought of as the late plays in such a way, arguably, as to undermine the category. Paradoxically, then, in a classic instance of the counter-productive logic of the supplement, an attempt to bolster the Shakespearean late period, to extend and sustain it, serves to disrupt and disperse it instead. The subjectivism that underpins the chronological relocation of Folio *King Lear* serves only to undermine the impact of that relocation.

In any case, the critical preference for Folio over Quarto *Lear* is problematic for a simple, if profoundly awkward, reason – namely, that it is not at all clear that the later version of the play is the nearer in tone to the late plays. It could in fact be said – indeed it has frequently been said – that Folio *Lear* is the more formally tragic of the two versions. Like Taylor, John Jones, addressing the question of revision in his *Shakespeare at Work*, reads the Folio text as Shakespeare's later thoughts – not quite as late, though: for Jones, the revisions were made 'perhaps three years' after the first telling of the story, at the outset of the late phase – but reaches the opposite conclusion.[67] Jones cites the Quarto's Scene 17, omitted in its entirety from the Folio text, in which Kent and an anonymous gentleman discuss Cordelia's reaction to news about her father's madness, noting the language of the gentleman's report:

> ... now and then an ample tear trilled down
> Her delicate cheek ....

>   ... Patience and sorrow strove
> Who should express her goodliest. You have seen
> Sunshine and rain at once; her smiles and tears
> Were like, a better way. Those happy smilets
> That played on her ripe lip seemed not to know
> What guests were in her eyes, which parted thence
> As pearls from diamonds dropped. In brief,
> Sorrow would be a rarity most beloved
> If all could so become it. [...]
>   [...] There she shook
> The holy water from her heavenly eyes
> And clamour mastered, then away she started
> To deal with grief alone.
>   (Quarto, Sc. 17, 13–14, 17–25, 30–3)

Jones describes the shock of these lines, the static stylisation which seems at odds with the 'supple warmth' of the play's tragic discourse, and he asks: 'where to go to find anything like it?'. His answer, given immediately, is 'to the late Romances, to *Cymbeline*, *The Winter's Tale*, *The Tempest*, and especially to Marina in *Pericles*', and, by way of support, he cites Pericles' lines describing his daughter at the moment of recognition:

>   Yet thou doest look
> Like patience gazing on kings' graves, and smiling
> Extremity out of act   (*Pericles*, Sc. 21, 126–8)

and

>   thou look'st
> Modest as justice, and thou seem'st a palace
> For the crowned truth to dwell in.   (Sc. 21, 109–11)

Jones's point in noting these parallels of expression and tone is that both characters, Cordelia and Marina, are 'romance heroines' and that 'the *something wrong* that has been felt through the centuries over the death of Cordelia stems from Shakespeare's breach of his own romance conventions' (Jones, 210). Immediately acknowledging the preposterousness (in Patricia Parker's sense of the term – or, in *Lear* vocabulary, the handy-dandyness) of this, Jones states his case directly, if counter-intuitively:

> I am saying that a convention has been breached which has not yet been established. In other words, the Quarto text of *Lear*, written three or four years before Shakespeare turned to Romance, is a work which has got out of phase. It was born before its time. (*Shakespeare at Work*, 210)

Thus, for Jones, Quarto *Lear* proleptically incorporates a certain late-play quality which Shakespeare, revising, excises from the Folio because, by that time, with the late plays under way, he sees, with the clarity of hindsight, that his original version of *King Lear* was already drifting away from tragedy and towards romance, a drift he seeks to arrest and reverse through the process of revision.

Not that Jones believes Shakespeare succeeded in this aim. 'The enterprise', he suggests, 'was doomed from the start', since 'Cordelia's first word, that famous "Nothing", presents the masklike impenetrability of the romance heroine': '"Nothing" is both her first word and the play's first move in a projection of Cordelia which links her once more with Marina in *Pericles*' (ibid., 211–12). Nevertheless, despite the hopelessness of the task, despite the late-play quality of Cordelia, both intrinsic and proleptic,

[t]aking the surgeon's knife to an entire scene, as Shakespeare did, thus expunging the baroque iconization of Cordelia's smiles and tears, shows resolve. [. . .] It looks radical enough and yet is better understood as a bold stroke in the making of a second version when the only answer, again from the tragic standpoint, was another play. (ibid., 213)

Jones proceeds to map out the other changes on the basis he has established, as excisions of romance material incorporated ahead of its moment into Quarto *Lear*. One such change comes about in the vignette of the King's awakening in 4.6 (Q's Scene 21), from which the character of the Doctor and his line 'Please you draw near. Louder the music there!' (*Q*, 21.23) are cut and the loss addressed in the Folio text with the insertion of a stage direction: '*Enter King Lear asleep, in a chair carried by his servants*' (*F*, 4.6.20 SD). 'What has happened', explains Jones,

is that the unconscious King is now being brought down stage among the other characters, so there is no longer any need or point in asking anybody to draw near, meaning to come towards him. He is being brought to them, whereas in Quarto he was lying up stage on a couch or bed within the kind of space that housed innumerable chamber encounters

in Shakespeare's other plays ('Shakespeare at Work', 213–14). At the same time, the removal of 'the tacit stage direction', the half-line demanding louder music, 'tells us that Shakespeare had wanted Lear's awakening to be accompanied by music, and Folio proves that he changed his mind' (ibid., 214). For Jones, these changes are coherent: they mark 'an attempt, at once local and far-reaching' on Shakespeare's part 'to turn the play round from Romance to Tragedy' due to his recognition, in revising hindsight, that music of this kind is closely tied to the 'mystical renewals and restorations' of romance. 'The Quarto Lear rises from his bed as from his grave, in a father and daughter scene almost embarrassingly like that towards the end of *Pericles*', Jones observes, and it is this alignment that Shakespeare seeks to excise by way of his cut.

Jones's argument thus reverses Taylor's implication that Folio *Lear* has become, in a certain way, a late play, turning the play in Quarto into a 'Proto-Romance' and in Folio into a reassertion of tragedy. And it foregrounds the neat inversion in the argument Taylor is obliged to make by his implicit recognition of a future counter-argument when, in the process of demonstrating the late dating of the Folio text, he discusses the differences between certain significant moments in Q and F, not least the moment of Lear's awakening. Recognising that the omission of passages with obvious late-play resonance makes F look *less*, not more, like a late play – as he would of course prefer in order to consolidate the lateness and deliberateness of the process of revision – Taylor finds an ingenious rhetorical solution. The Folio text's staging, he argues,

> facilitates an audience's attention to the dramatic, emotional, and intellectual heart of the scene: Lear's reactions of awakening, and his recognition of Cordelia. Excising the music serves the same function: it leaves the silences truly silent, filled only with the deep specific emotions of three characters rather than the generalised ready-made emotion of off-stage instruments. The 'meer stage convenience' makes the scene harder on the performers by making its success entirely dependent on their resources, rather than those of the music room. As a result, the Folio makes up in painful actuality for what it loses in moody musicality. ('Date and Authorship', 413)

By contrast, the Quarto text 'emphasizes symbolic properties – an attendant doctor, music, Lear rising from his bed like a man from his grave – at the expense of the central dramatic relationship' (ibid.). Thus, though

> [n]o one would wish to deny the pertinence of these symbols, or their parallels in Shakespeare's late plays; one can understand their attraction for critics primarily committed to literary rather than dramatic values. Nevertheless, they remain peripheral to this scene: Shakespeare exploits their resonances much more fully and dramatically in *Pericles*, *The Winter's Tale*, and *Cymbeline*. To accept F's directions here one need only assume that Shakespeare, in 1606, decided that he would develop the dramatic potential of literal and figurative rebirth in future plays, and so altered the staging of this scene in *Lear*. (ibid.)

Taylor manages in this way to make the *lack* of similarity of the revision to the late plays part of the logic of dating the revision to the period of those plays. At the same time, he is forced to acknowledge in advance the argument that Jones eventually makes, that the Folio bears the marks of Shakespeare's 'purging *Lear* of romance elements' ('Shakespeare at Work', 211). Taylor's implicit argument for the late dating of Folio

Lear, that it has in effect become a late play, thus runs into considerable turbulence.

Not that this especially matters. These debates have, after all, been in circulation for two decades now. And, certainly, I have no wish to criticise Gary Taylor, whose iconoclastic input into the *Oxford Shakespeare* gave the moribund field of Shakespearean editing a wholly deserved kick from which it is still both recoiling and benefiting, and whose desire to find connections between Folio *Lear* and the late plays was in any case a by-product of his arguments for Shakespearean revision, not evidence of an urge to renew the redemptive readings of the mid-century. The point for the present study is the receptive context for arguments (of which Taylor's is the fullest) for the late dating of Folio *Lear*, indicative as it is of the pervasiveness of the discourse of lateness across the full range of Shakespearean studies. Critics have, by and large, embraced the 1610 date – and the two-text solution that such a date, such a gap between first writing and revision, requires – yet they have been far more reluctant (at least until Ann Thompson and Neil Taylor's Arden 3 *Hamlet*) to embrace separate texts of Quarto and Folio texts of *Hamlet* or of *Othello* than they have of *Lear*.[68] This is in part, I have been arguing, because of the difference in critical perception of *King Lear* from those other tragedies, because of the longstanding tradition of treating *Lear* as the harbinger of romance and of the relative ease with which this play of old age can be aligned with plays from the very end of the career. The late dating of the Folio text thus allows the revival of the mid-century continuity critics' urge to read *King Lear* as the pivotal play, the play in which the advance signs of the late period can be seen, to treat it as (almost) a late play, a critical trajectory elegantly extended by Jones. It suggests, in the process, that the *idea* of late Shakespeare predetermines the *constitution* of late Shakespeare, that we accept into that category only material that enhances, develops or confirms our preconceived sense of that category. The discourse of lateness thus, in effect, presides over questions of Shakespearean chronology and of the Shakespearean text beyond the immediate bounds of the late plays themselves. This outward tendency is immediately apparent when, acknowledging the boldness of his claim for Quarto *Lear* as 'Proto-Romance', John Jones searches elsewhere for support and finds it in other instances of late-style prolepsis:

What can compare with this? We are looking, with an eye ranging across the arts and through the centuries – through millennia! – for something like Dickens's last fling and vigorous fresh turn in *Edwin Drood*, but it must be much bigger, more startling than *Drood*, and unlike *Drood* it must be finished. Moreover, the creative shift at the end must be understood, with hindsight, to declare itself by muddying or distorting some earlier work. [. . .] The *Ajax* of Sophocles, apparently a middle-period tragedy, is beset with uncomfortable cross-patterns which suggest an earth tremor running ahead of those two prodigies of his extreme old age, the *Philoctetes* and the second *Oedipus* play. [. . .] Racine and Goethe lack the sharp ferocity of contrast between earlier and last. Goya? Beethoven? These are nearer home, especially the ungrateful spiky fugue writing – for example, of the *Hammerklavier* and the Opus 102 cello sonatas, which do not altogether belong to where Beethoven is because they are giving weird insights into where he will be. ('Shakespeare at Work', 211)

This is beautifully expressed, but the basic transhistoricity and the rhetorical ('Goya? Beethoven?') and aphoristic qualities ('Racine and Goethe lack the sharp ferocity of contrast between earlier and last') of Jones's sudden outward turn to parallel cases – in a work of criticism otherwise directed firmly inward, performed by way of the acutest of close readings – underlines its fundamental premise in the discourse of lateness, in questions of caesura and continuity that will by now be wholly familiar.

If *King Lear* becomes an honorary late play, a 'Proto-Romance', then, by the same token, reversing the polarities, it offers a noticeably darker, more tragic version of late Shakespeare, one which has appealed to some. *Bingo*, Edward Bond's play about the end of Shakespeare's life, set against the problem of Shakespeare's failure to resist the enclosure at Welcombe and thus implicitly against uncomfortable questions of human 'accommodation', is far more clearly a version of *King Lear* than it is of *The Tempest*, the play to which you might expect Bond to turn for his dramatisation of the ageing playwright. Though in his brief introduction Bond does not mention any of the late plays, he does refer to *King Lear*. 'My account rather flatters Shakespeare', Bond suggests:

If he didn't end in the way shown in the play, then he was a reactionary blimp or some other fool. The only more charitable account is that he was unaware or senile. But I admit that I'm not really interested in Shakespeare's true biography in the way a historian might be. Part of the play is about the relationship between any writer and his society. [. . .] Shakespeare created Lear, who is the most radical of all social critics. But Lear's insight is expressed as madness or hysteria. Why? I suppose partly because that was the only coherent way it could have been expressed at that time. (*Bingo*, 4)

Bond's Shakespeare, both 'senile' and 'old before [his] time' (*Lear (F)*, 1.5.41; *(Q)*, Sc. 5.41), is a version of Lear, struggling with a daughter who wants him to go away, back to where he came from, to his 'interesting friends' (Bingo, 34) and supported by an Old Woman who is, as Bond's introduction states, a version of Shakespeare's other daughter – 'I gave the more comforting and

King Lear *as a late play*

strengthening role that I think Susanna played in his life', Bond noted, 'to an old woman servant. I did this for my own dramatic convenience' (ibid., 3) – and who is both a Regan, living in one of his houses, and a Cordelia, trying to keep him from harm. After the Young Woman (an alternative version of Cordelia) has been hanged, and with her beheaded corpse in full view on stage like that of Cloten in *Cymbeline*, Shakespeare speaks like Lear on the heath:

SHAKESPEARE   What does it cost to stay alive? I'm stupefied at the suffering I've seen. The shapes huddled in misery that twitch away when you step over them. Women with shopping bags stepping over pools of blood. What it costs to starve people. The chatter of those who hand over prisoners. The smile of men who see no further than the end of a knife. Stupefied. How can I go back to that? What can I do there? I talk to myself now. I know no one will ever listen. [. . .] [. . .] They stand under the gallows and ask if it rains. Terrible. Terrible. What is the right question? I said be still. I quietened the storms inside me. But the storm breaks outside. To have usurped the place of god, and lied. . ..
OLD WOMAN   Why torment yo'self? You'm never harmed no –
SHAKESPEARE   And my daughter?
OLD WOMAN   No, no. Yo' yont named for cruelty. They say yo'm a generous man. Yo' looked arter me an' father. Give us one a your houses t' live in. (*Bingo*, 40–1)

This is not *Lear* as a late play defined as such both by renegotiated date and redemptive qualities, but rather, in Strachey's sense, the last work of a tired, disillusioned man. Certainly, it is not the redemptive *Lear* of the continuity critics.

The point about the association of *King Lear* with the late plays is that the conjunction, unfounded though it appears to be, works both ways. Not only does it redeem the bleakness of the tragedy by associating it proleptically with a later Shakespearean experiment in redemptive generic form, it also operates to import into the late plays the imprimatur of old age. Prospero, contrary to modern theatrical tradition, is not, as we have seen, old (or, at least, he need not be old), and neither is Pericles, who has also been through hell, certainly, but only for the sixteen years that have taken him from naïve, restless youth to traumatised middle age. But placing Prospero and Pericles alongside the ageing Lear makes them, as it were, *implicitly* old, makes any critical or theatrical assumption that they are aged seem entirely appropriate. Not only does the tacit incorporation of *King Lear* into the late plays offer a glimpse of a salvation that is not in fact available, then, it also implicitly turns the late plays into something they are not – plays of old age, written by an allegedly 'ageing' playwright who was not in fact 'old' at all.

5.5 KINGS AND DESPERATE MEN

It is arguably in the theatre, even more than in criticism, that the most sustained productive affinity between *King Lear* and the late plays, and in particular between *Lear* and *The Tempest*, can be found, one that is established by way of the actors who play the central roles of Lear and Prospero. In the final chapter, I will discuss certain significant performances of the latter – 'performances' not only in the theatrical sense but also in the critical sense of 'performativity', that is, of interpretations of the role that have served to establish a subject-position for the actor in question – but it is useful briefly to preface that discussion with the acknowledgement that *King Lear* has, because of the old age and the trajectory across the play of its principal character, acquired a role – a justificatory, redemptive role – as a vehicle for the triumphant return to the stage of actors who have plumbed the depths, for whom ripeness has finally been achieved despite all that the storm of public exposure can inflict. The most obvious recent instance is that of Robert Stephens, who played Lear in Adrian Noble's powerful Royal Shakespeare Company production at Stratford in 1993, two years before his death. Stephens had been a prominent figure in the early years of the National Theatre at the Old Vic and had been seen as the natural heir of Olivier, an actor of immense natural talent and of self-consciously 'hell-raising', 'heroic' status, but his departure from the National in 1970, the break-up of his marriage to Maggie Smith in 1973 and the alcoholism that was both cause and effect of these events tipped his career into the doldrums (he never achieved the cinematic fame of peers such as Richard Burton), and it was not until he was cast as Falstaff and then as Lear by the RSC in the early nineties that he returned to the stage, his superb performances underlining the opportunities that had been lost.

For Peter Holland, in Stephens the RSC had reclaimed an actor who 'possessed the role with an authority as absolute as Lear's own rule': it was, in fact, partly Stephens's availability to play the role that prompted Noble to direct a production of *Lear*.[69] Stephens's absolute authority is quite specifically enhanced by the tangible evidence in his nightly performances of the toll taken by the intervening years and is addressed by the critic, lightly but significantly, in autobiographical terms. 'When a teenager', writes Holland,

I remember complaining, with all the arrogance of youth, of the fluffs and doubles in Schnabel's recordings of Beethoven's piano sonatas. 'Ah but', a far wiser mentor told me, 'never mind about the few wrong notes. Just listen to all the right ones.' It was appropriate advice for Stephens' Lear. There were many lines fluffed and

rewritten – on some nights many more than others. Sometimes the new lines were nonsensical; sometimes the metre went haywire as a result. Certainly there were nights when, for Shakespeare scholars, the fluffs loomed large and troubling. But then Shakespeare scholars are by their very nature a pedantic breed. And one would have had to be, like the onstage audience Lear addresses at the end of the play, 'men of stones' not to be wrenchingly moved by Stephens' Lear.
(*English Shakespeares*, 167–8)

There is a direct association here of actor and character – one only truly observable (the momentary turn to autobiography implies) by a critic who has also lived a little – that underpins the power of the performance. 'If with John Wood's Lear, in [Nicholas Hytner's] production in 1990 [...] one could not help but observe the technique that was producing the effects, admiring the actor's skills that created the emotional charge of the performance', Holland writes with his customary style, 'with Stephens it seemed wrong to hold oneself removed, observing how he did it. If this Lear did not make one weep, no performance ever would' (ibid., 168). Some of those tears were clearly shed for Stephens as much as for Lear himself, tears that acknowledged the necessity of the lived experience of the depths (to echo Dowden's terms) before the heights can be fully attained. Stephens himself echoes Dowden in his autobiography, both when he says of playing Lear that 'it's the pinnacle, the mountain top. You can see everything from up there' and, more poignantly, in the lines with which he concludes the book: 'Think of me as a tree that has nearly been axed through, but the sap has found a way of working its way up. The tree, miraculously, still stands. The roots which have held me in place go down deep. And I've still got people telling me about the dreams to come' (*Knight Errant*, 181, 190). Traversi's recognition of the close association between *Lear* and the last period thus acquires a new dimension: the play being performed may be a tragedy, but the performance is pure late play.

Orson Welles, turning to Shakespeare for his own late films as he did throughout his career, began towards the end of his life to make a film of *Lear* that was never completed, with himself as Lear, Oja Kodar as Cordelia and Abb Dickson, a magician, as the Fool. In a six-minute proposal for the film, taped for prospective producers, Welles explained his plans, emphasising that he intended to produce a film – an 'almost ferociously down-to-earth' film – about old age:

[W]hat is truly important is not that the tragic hero is an old king but that he's an old man. [...] *King Lear* is about death and the approach of death, and about power and the loss of power, and about love. In our consumer society we are encouraged to forget that we will ever die, and old age can be postponed by the right face cream. And when it finally does come, we're encouraged to look forward to a long and lovely sunset.[70]

And he continues:

> 'Old age', said Charles de Gaulle, 'old age is a shipwreck' – and he knew whereof he spoke. [. . .] When old age tempts or forces a man to give away the very source of his ascendancy over the young – his power – it's they, the young, who are the tyrants and he, who was all-powerful, becomes a pensioner.

The autobiographical element in this – Welles was seventy by this time and soon to die, and he had for several years been finding it near-impossible to attract funding for film projects – is obvious, as is the implicit equation of Lear and Prospero as 'shipwrecked' old men giving up the source of their ascendancy.

In an article in *The Guardian* in 2006 addressing the apparent impossibility of creating a convincing film version of *King Lear*, Dominic Dromgoole, Mark Rylance's successor as artistic director of Shakespeare's Globe, echoes Welles's perspective on the play – though he notes, wryly, that Welles 'made a television version when young, and spent much of the rest of his life offering his drinking companions parts in his final, definitive and never made version' – and, at the same time, makes a further connection between *Lear* and the late plays, especially, once more, *The Tempest*.[71] 'The fully successful film version of *King Lear*', he argues, 'remains something of a holy grail. Just as the title part, with its precipitate trajectory from rugged magnificence to naked fragility, remains the ultimate challenge for actors, so the whole play defies the ability of anyone but the best to match it.' 'And yet', he points out, despite this, 'directors continue to gravitate towards it – particularly towards the end of their careers.' This, he points out, is not surprising since 'the play was written by a man coming to the end of his own career as an actor and producer' – an implicit late dating apparently implying Folio rather than Quarto *Lear* – adding that

> *Lear* has an application for all different forms of senescence, but it has a particular sharpness for the waning powers of the film director. As shark-like young producers circle their prey, and in Goneril and Regan fashion strip them of their retinue – 'What need you 50 million for your next film? Why 25? Why for that matter 12 or 5?' – the old director feels the sharp teeth of ingratitude dragging them under.

Ageing directors here become fathers and those wishing to displace them their ungrateful daughters. And in Dromgoole's subsequent observation that '[t]here are few modern positions as close in its freedom and sway to the medieval king as that of the film director; and the image of the magus clinging to his power remains pertinent', we see the early modern become the medieval and *King Lear* become *The Tempest*, the old director a 'magus clinging to his power', as the circle of subjectivism is extended from the actor inhabiting the role to the man (the gendering is, as ever within the discourse of lateness, strictly male) directing, and thus in a certain way sharing, that inhabitation. Moreover, in the trajectory Dromgoole outlines, the director becomes Shakespeare himself – late Shakespeare, that is, the 'man coming to the end of his own career', the playwright of the late plays, into whose ranks *King Lear* has become wholly absorbed.

Orson Welles – fascinatingly, in the context of the conjunction of 'old age' and 'shipwreck' in his quotation from de Gaulle – never actually played Prospero but he is reported by Peter Conrad to have merged *King Lear* and *The Tempest* in his memory: 'During the 1970s he remembered planning a version of [*The Tempest*] with designs by the surrealist painter Pavel Tchelitchev; it was actually *King Lear* that they briefly worked on in 1937.'[72] This suggests the ease with which, as plays firmly associated with old age, *The Tempest* and *Lear* become almost indistinguishable for actors and directors towards the end of their lives, each play reduced to its subjectivist function as the expression both of the ageing Shakespeare and of the ageing actor/director. In each of these cases, that of the actor, that of the director and that of the commentator, the play of old age and harsh experience becomes a vehicle for self-fashioning, for the validation of longevity and survival through interpretation and appreciation of certain Shakespearean roles. In the concluding chapter, I wish to turn away from *King Lear*, the honorary late play, to *The Tempest*, the play most completely associated in the minds of actors, directors, critics and the general public with the ageing Shakespeare, in order to demonstrate the function the play has acquired as the primary vehicle both for the contemporary discourse of lateness in the theatre and for the detachment of that discourse from the limitations of its traditional association with old age.

CHAPTER 6

The Tempest *and the uses of late Shakespeare in the theatre: Gielgud, Rylance, Prospero*

> I'm going to revive Prospero next year in *The Tempest* which is another role I love playing and you can do that pretty well until you're ninety so I can have another bash at that one.[1]

> The play was, of course, Shakespeare's swansong.[2]

> If *The Tempest* did not exist, it would be necessary to invent it.[3]

I have argued that, almost as soon as the discourse of lateness was established as a concept within the general culture of creativity, it became subject to certain complicities; that 'genuine' lateness became impossible to distinguish from 'knowing' lateness, from lateness striven for and assumed by a given artist. Henry James's 'Middle Years', as I have shown, makes this clear, and the late James's engagement – indeed, obsession – with the Shakespearean late phase and in particular with *The Tempest* as the supreme embodiment of late Shakespeare demonstrates Shakespeare's centrality to the idea of late style as it developed in twentieth-century literary culture as the poetic counterpart to late Beethoven in musicology and late Rembrandt in art history. I have noted, too, that Edward Said's turn to the analysis of late style coincided with his own later years and terminal illness. Late Shakespeare has also, unsurprisingly, been an object of particular interest for critics late in life, who demonstrate a susceptibility to the extension of subjectivism offered by the idea of late writing, from the association of the late author with the late work to that of the late critic with the late author.[4] The Bulgarian Shakespearean Marco Mincoff, for instance, turned quite deliberately to the late plays in his own last decade and, as Boika Sokolova notes in an appreciation, Mincoff's *Things Supernatural and Causeless* was published, after delays due to his refusal to bend to political imperatives, 'a few days before his death' (*Things Supernatural*, 127), and is thus late work in at least two senses. In describing the book as 'a rich and complex work executed with the creative command of Prospero before he broke his staff', Sokolova makes explicit the extension of the identification of Shakespeare and his island-duke to the late-play critic (ibid., 127). Most critics seeking to identify with Shakespeare and Prospero do so in the Dowden vein, as indeed does Sokolova in her commentary. Mincoff's version of the late Shakespeare, however, resists the resurgence considered characteristic of a fully fledged late phase. He offers a depressed, ageing Shakespeare who, even in *The Tempest*, lacks the brilliance of his earlier years. There is, for Mincoff, a 'general lack of tension, the lack of any deep interest in most of the personages, and the slightly bitter but calmly resigned recognition that the brave new world of the young is an illusion' (ibid., 118). Mincoff's late Shakespeare has neither the purity of the serene artist 'on the heights' nor the admirable intransigence of a resistant late stylist in the Said vein: if he has an obvious forebear, it is Strachey's bored genius, tired of both life and art.

Mincoff's identification with Prospero is clear enough, if only made explicit in Sokolova's commentary. A classic instance of this identification which needs no such commentary is provided by Kenneth Muir, whose *Last Periods of Shakespeare, Racine, and Ibsen* is, as has been apparent throughout this book, a landmark text in the history of the relationship of late Shakespeare to the larger question of late style. Muir's personal investment in Shakespearean lateness is at its clearest, however, not in a publication but in a performance. In March 1974, just prior to Muir's retirement as King Alfred Professor of English Literature at the University of Liverpool, the English Society presented a staff/student production of *The Tempest*, with what was, in its way and with a little hindsight, a quietly star-studded cast.[5] It was directed by Nicholas Shrimpton, now a Fellow of Lady Margaret Hall, Oxford, and it featured, *inter alios*, Nicholas Grene, now Professor of English at Trinity College Dublin as Alonso, David Liddiment, BBC Trustee and former Director of Programmes at ITV playing Francisco, and Hermione Lee, now Goldsmiths' Professor of English Literature at the University of Oxford, in the role of Miranda. And the part of Prospero was played by Kenneth Muir himself, consciously inhabiting the role most closely associated with Shakespeare as a means of marking his own retirement from a post whose previous incumbents had included A. C. Bradley and Walter Ralegh and thus underlining in a very practical way his assertion in *Last Periods* thirteen years earlier that if *The Tempest* is thought of not only as 'a masterpiece in its own right' but also as 'the epilog to a life's work, its significance is immeasurably increased' (*Last Periods*, 115).[6]

My aim in this chapter, extending the analysis of the subjectivist engagement of actor and role we have seen with *King Lear*, is to emphasise the persistent desire, not only of critics but also of others engaged professionally with the Shakespearean text, to deploy Prospero as a figure both of the late Shakespeare and of the late career in general, a deployment which is part of a process of self-fashioning conducted through the discourse of lateness. In this concluding chapter, then, I aim to demonstrate three things: the ongoing utility of the idea of late Shakespeare right up to the present (I close with events that took place in the latter half of 2006); the value it has for postmodernism; and thus the apparent effortlessness with which the baton of lateness has been passed to the current cultural epoch, and the particular manifestation of the discourse of late Shakespeare in the contemporary theatre.

6.1 THEATRE OF COMPLICITY

In an interview with Philippe Büttner transcribed in the catalogue for the 2003 exhibition of late Klee I discussed briefly in Chapter 5, whose sub-title 'Fulfilment in the Late Work' makes explicit its particular redemptive teleology, the art collector Ernst Beyeler reflects on his habit of collecting late work. 'I have always', he recalls, 'had a special preference for late works, because they represent a kind of summing-up of an artist's lifework.'[7] And he proceeds to outline the classic symptoms of late style familiar from the accounts of Ellis, Neumann, Broch and the Picasso Museum wall label, assuming the 'greatness' of the artist and the particular character of the work as a kind of summing up, an easing of conventional expectations, as having a tendency towards prolepsis as well as a certain inwardness and concentration:

> With great artists, this phase often brings a relaxation of previous structures that can have a visionary character and encourage future developments, as with Cézanne or Monet and abstraction. Another characteristic of significant late works lies in the artists' ability to combine a final burst of energy with a certain detachment. They no longer require any "input," but instead are able to concentrate on creating solely out of their own personal perception. Monet, for instance, was no longer particularly aware of what was going on around him during his final years. He just kept on working in his studio, as if obsessed. (Beyeler in Bärmann *et al.*, *Paul Klee*, 25)

This will be, by now, a familiar enough story. Yet even as he emphasises the self-containment of the artist, his standing outside both of the material and of contingency, Beyeler also acknowledges the impact of external influences on the late style. Klee's late work, he notes, 'underwent a marvellous intensification, to which his illness contributed not a little – from finest structures to a profoundly expressive tragic tendency, a dramatic vision into other worlds', and he suggests that while 'one might say that in his exile in Bern, Klee was able to draw on his rich inner storehouse of imagery', it is true too that

> he was also subject to crucial late influences and impressions. For instance, there was his visit to the Prado exhibition held in Geneva in 1939, when its works were shown there due to the war. But what perhaps impressed him most of all was seeing the Picasso retrospective in Zurich, in the year 1932. And ultimately he was able to artistically digest these impressions better than, say, Ernst Ludwig Kirchner, who in one of his later periods was unable to deal confidently with the influence of that incomparable master, Picasso. Nor was he the only artist to fail in this regard. It really took someone like Klee, with his skills, to absorb Picasso and derive enrichment from him. (ibid.)

In an article on the photographer Nan Goldin in the *Observer Magazine* at the time of her 2002 Whitechapel Gallery exhibition, Sheryl Garratt noted that '[i]t wasn't until her big 1986 retrospective at the Whitney that she noticed recurring themes in her work: people looking outside from the inside, women in water'.[8] 'I have no idea why', she reports Goldin as saying, 'There's no theory behind it. I don't want to analyse it. I just accept that I've always photographed women in water' (Goldin in Garratt, 'The Dark Room', 15). Beyeler similarly notes the impact on artists of retrospectives – of, that is, the display of an artist's works to date in roughly chronological order – and not only retrospectives of their own work, but also those of others. For him, the anxieties and the possibilities produced by the impact of the retrospective divides a successful late phase from an unsuccessful one. Klee, for instance, had enough composure and command not to be daunted by seeing Picasso's overall *œuvre*, whereas Kirchner was outfaced by the same experience. Beyeler thus, even as he expresses the transcendence of the late style, also somewhat grudgingly acknowledges the impact of contingencies too, of the intrusion of the styles of others, offering a negotiation or synthesis of the two to explain the origins of late Klee. On the one hand, he claims, Klee 'lived in a higher, spiritual world, thanks to which he was able to overcome the strokes of fate of the final years. On the other hand, the political developments and his illness also brought about an increasing concision and focus in his work' (Beyeler in Bärmann *et al.*, *Paul Klee*, 31). For Beyeler, then, even as he invokes the transcendent understanding of late style that we have seen at its purest, its most unquestioningly mystical, in Neumann, there is a clear sense in which the caesura that marks the end of the middle style and the beginning of the late can have an external as well as an internal impetus. We have seen this, of course, in discussing the question of old age.

Contingency, then, enters into conflict with subjectivism, with the presumption that the late style emerges from the interior of the artist – is a marker of that artist's genius at the phase of full accomplishment – and it raises a further spectre in the house of lateness in the form of complicity. The idea of 'late style' was invented to attest to a phenomenon that was universal (to a handful of geniuses, that is) and involuntary: late style was what came upon you, or welled up from within you, if you were a genius, in the face of the imminence of death. But as soon as the idea became established critically, it became impossible to differentiate between an 'authentic' late style, that is, a late style which is the *unmediated*, unsought result of a genius in old age or near death, and a *complicit* late style, constructed deliberately by an artist so that he or she might be remembered as a genius by those coming later. Once the concept exists, it becomes impossible to differentiate between these two forms of lateness. As we have seen, this process arguably achieved its high-water mark with Victorian writers such as Robert Browning and Henry James, who deliberately set out, in their 'testamentary acts', to construct clearly delineated late periods to ensure that future generations would recognise them as geniuses.[9]

There are other kinds of complicity in operation, too, for which the artist cannot be held responsible. In his interview with Büttner, Beyeler, whose collection is especially rich in late Klees, speaks, as we have seen, of his 'special preference for late works', because this is because 'they represent a kind of summing-up of an artist's lifework' (Beyeler in Bärmann *et al.*, *Paul Klee*, 25). At the same time, he frankly acknowledges the early material premise for this preference. 'One should not forget', he observes, that in the early 1960s when he started collecting,

> the late Matisse and the late Klee were simply considerably less expensive. Matisse's "papiers découpés," for instance, initially cost quite little, but people weren't prepared to pay even that, not even in the case of Klee. But although the financial aspect may have been important to me, these late works meant taking a risk; other people could have acquired them as well. David Thompson, the collector, also bought some of Klee's late works in New York, because they were cheaper. (ibid., 27)

Büttner notes that '[n]owadays the reverse tends to be true', and Beyeler happily agrees: 'Yes, the late Matisse, too, is now very, very expensive. At the time, it represented a chance – late work as a chance!' and he adds that the increase in the valuation of late style was, at best, gradual:

> By the way, it also took a very long time for the late work of Cézanne to find acceptance. Back then there was a great discussion in Basel about the very late *Cabanon de Jourdan*, of 1906, which in the end could not remain in Basel. But the late Monet and the late Picasso were controversial for a long time as well. (ibid.)

It is at moments such as this that the aficionado and the owner of a gratifyingly valuable art collection converge, and it demonstrates the inescapability of the contingent in the appreciation of the aesthetic – one that we have already seen in the Rembrandt project's declassification of late collaborative 'self-portraits'.

Not all collections of late work represent a purely financial basis for privileging late work, however. The two Paris museums, the Rodin and the Picasso, as we have seen, mark the direct engagement of the artist with the question of the retrospective, with the posthumous reputation and value of the work. They are, in Millgate's terms, 'testamentary acts', the artist's own bequest as a permanent public statement of status, each comprising the personal collection of the artist left to the state (in Picasso's case partly as a way to avoid death duties) and designed to memorialise the life and work of figures who will, by definition, be remembered as geniuses. Both are grand instances of the deliberate, self-conscious end-of-life gesture that confirms the artist's status for posterity. Rodin was especially keen to ensure that the state turned his life's work into a museum housed in his favourite property; after some uncertainty about the work itself, the state chose to accept the gift and the gesture. It was from that point inevitable that Rodin's work would be remembered as that of a genius, and it was arguably equally inevitable that a visitor such as Ellis, with the unusual opportunity to see the full range of the artist's work across his life, should see a clear linear dynamic in that life, culminating in the ultimate expression of individual genius, a late period.

Of the Shakespearean late plays, it is *The Tempest*, as will by now be entirely clear, that has acquired the status of archetypal late Shakespeare. For Dowden, whatever the actual order of plays, *The Tempest* was morally the last. 'It is The Tempest', he tells us, 'which gives its most perfect expression to the spirit that breathes through [the] plays which bring to an end the dramatic career of Shakspere; and therefore for us it is Shakspere's latest play' (Dowden, *Mind and Art*, 380). A century or so later, Muir, even while dismissing Dowden as 'naïve', finds a different way to say the same thing: 'If *The Tempest* did not exist', he argues, it would be necessary to invent it. It is the natural culmination of the plays of the final period. All the themes which found partial expression in the other romances are in it completely achieved. In the others the happy endings depend on a series of curious chances; but in *The Tempest* accident is virtually eliminated. [. . . I]t was [. . .] the expression of the prevailing mood of Shakespeare's last period. (*Last Periods*, 51)

It is thus *The Tempest*, far more than any other late play, that has been consistently taken to stand metonymically for Shakespearean lateness and it is to this play, far more than to any other, as we have seen in the case of James, Conrad and others, that those intent on appropriating late Shakespeare for the establishment of their own version of lateness tend to turn.

The autobiographical status afforded to *The Tempest* in relation to Shakespeare is, it should immediately be noted, by no means unique as an instance of the establishment of a given work as a synecdoche for its creator: it is in fact characteristic of the work of art that is held to be the very last work of any artist to whom a late style is attributed. An obvious parallel case is, once again, that of Rembrandt. A fairly full range of paintings (though, after the work of attribution done in the late twentieth century, far fewer than was once the case) is described by critics as 'late Rembrandt', and his self-portraits in particular are taken as evidence of his state of mind at the end of his life. As Mariët Westermann points out, '[c]ollectively, Rembrandt's presentations of himself in old age – their number alone is striking – are largely responsible for his reputation as a lone and defiant artist, with wisdom born of adversity, and these paintings depend on their rough surfaces for their full effect.'[10] One group of paintings, overtly autobiographical, thus serves to confirm a standard reading of the late artist as solitary, wise and defiant, producing work characterised by its loose facture. But it is not to a self-portrait, but to a work that is *not* overtly autobiographical that critics tend to turn in their need for a single final redemptive work. Westermann describes it thus:

The painting Rembrandt left incomplete on his easel when he died confirms the image of a painter stubbornly dedicated to picturing the miraculous insight of which the human soul is capable. In *Simeon Holding the Christ Child*, begun for Otto van Cattenburch, Rembrandt returned to a theme that had occupied him since the 1630s. [. . .] As [Simeon] took the baby in his arms he praised God and said 'Now Lord, let your servant go in peace, after your word.' Simeon's eyes are shrouded in apparent blindness, but his inner vision is unimpaired. (*Rembrandt*, 316)

The *nunc dimittis* functions here as the final redemptive gesture of the genius, old and physically diminished but still with an undimmed artistic vision, creating a direct association of Rembrandt with Simeon, the ageing believer given final peace by the revelation of salvation, which is hard to resist, emotionally, for the critic. Simeon's vision thus stands synecdochically for that of the late Rembrandt, who moves finally beyond the 'defiance' of so much of his late work to a serene teleology.

Yet the casual clause with which Westermann begins her paragraph masks a more wilful history than she would care to acknowledge. Simon Schama notes that there were no fewer than thirteen paintings left in Rembrandt's studio after his death 'which Steeman the notary judged to be "unfinished" ' – 'But then', he adds, 'how would he, or anyone else still alive, know?'[11] Moreover, he notes, the efforts of those who survived Rembrandt to 'complete' these 'unfinished' pictures – Arendt de Gelder, for instance, who, says Schama, 'continued to fly in the face of fashion by persevering in Rembrandt's late style' – only serve to confuse the picture further, offering completions that are in fact collaborations (perhaps posthumous collaborations), adaptations or even falsifications (*Rembrandt's Eyes*, 683). Yet Schama himself, having noted the artificiality of the posthumous reconstruction of the artist's final days, succumbs to the very practice he uncovers, working steadily through a series of paintings which *can* be dated before turning to the two he treats as the very last – *The Return of the Prodigal Son* and *Simeon in the Temple with the Christ Child* – thereby offering an apparently confirmed chronological narrative which is really a fine evocation of lateness with its Christian underpinnings revealed, giving Rembrandt in his last, closeted, fading days a path towards redemption and concluding with the words of the *nunc dimittis*:

Everything from the conventions of *Simeon in the Temple* pictures – rabbis; Temple Column; priests – has been effaced save Simeon himself, the Virgin, and the infant Messiah. The background is a shadowy void, but all three figures seem to swim in a luminous mist, a hazy penumbra of illumination that Rembrandt has contrived by making the paint granular, like finely pulverized crystal, applied not with the slapping force of his old age but with a filigree delicacy, as if with a sponge or finely spun gauze. The old man's cradling hands are immense, held rigid as if in deepest prayer. His face, closed off from the world in an ecstatic trance, glimmers with unearthly brilliance. Behind his heavy lids he has, at last, seen the light of salvation, and is able, at last, to declare, 'Lord, now lettest thou thy servant depart in peace'. (ibid., 686)

Schama's book, which, he announces in his 'author's note' on questions of authenticity, is 'about the painter's long journey to singularity' (ibid., 703), offers an adherence to the author, to the painter himself, which drives his elegant and evocative account of the paintings, insistently subsuming the work to the life or deploying the work to make sense of the life and the life to make sense of the work. The narrative he provides of the last seven or so years of Rembrandt's life is thus exemplary both as a biographical account and as an instance of the persistence of the discourse of lateness. And the particular emphasis he places on *Simeon Holding the Christ Child* as Rembrandt's last painting is an instance of the urge, emerging from the biographical impulses of commemoration and hagiography, to find a redemptive last work for the exemplary artist. Shakespeare's *nunc dimittis*, in turn, as he steps away from the theatre towards the green fields of Stratford and final peace, is Prospero's speech of book-drowning.

The longevity of the idea of late work or late style has, as we have seen, embedded it deeply in our culture and it continues to exert an influence on our understanding of 'great' artists even as we recognise the inadequacy of the subjectivism that underpins it. In this context, the key issue becomes not the value or otherwise of the concept of lateness but its utility – that is, the *uses* to which it has been, and is still being, put. I wish to suggest in this final chapter that it is in the theatre that the purest current form of the deployment of the discourse of lateness can be found. As I suggested in Chapter 5 in respect of *King Lear*, actors and directors seem often to feel an urgent need (partly, presumably, as a result of the continuing reliance on Stanislavsky in drama schools) to be at one with playwright and character, and *The Tempest* brings out both the best and the worst in this tendency amongst Shakespeareans. I want to look in the rest of this chapter at two instances of the utility of lateness for postmodern performance, one from the last decade of the twentieth century, the other from the first decade of the twenty-first – those of Sir John Gielgud and Mark Rylance. Each deploys the identification of Prospero as Shakespeare in order to establish a shape and a logic for his own career, the latter in part working with materials provided by the former. In the process, both demonstrate the utility of the concept of late style for successful Shakespearean theatre professionals in their quest for an individual identity that is nonetheless negotiated carefully in relation to tradition. Both articulate their own sense of an ending – of a very personal ending – by way of *The Tempest*, developing the opportunity the play offers for projecting a coherence – expressed both as linear and as cyclical – for the theatrical life. In each case, *The Tempest*, once described by the theatre critic Irving Wardle as 'that serene ritual of reunions and farewells', becomes the site for the theatre professional both to capitalise upon and to reinvent the idea of late style.[12]

6.2 LATENESS AND THE MID-LIFE CRISIS

Travelling by train a year or two ago on the east coast of Spain and bored with the novel I was reading, I turned instead, in the teeth of my ignorance of Spanish, to the free onboard magazine. Flicking through it, I found to my surprise an interview with a successful director of Shakespeare, Helena Pimenta, who, it seemed, had recently both translated and directed *The Tempest* and toured it throughout Spain. The article appeared to emphasise above all the importance of Shakespearean chronology for the director's engagement with the play. Translating later with the help of a friend, I became intrigued by the connection drawn by Pimenta between the trajectory of her own career and that of Shakespeare. It seems that, a decade earlier, she had planned to direct a production of *The Tempest* but had abandoned the project early on. Now she was finally returning to it. The interviewer asks her why she had postponed it for so long. She replies:

> When I first planned to stage *The Tempest* it was after I had won the National Theatre Prize for *A Midsummer Night's Dream* in 1993, a moment of great excitement and delight for me. Things had been going remarkably well: I felt fully understood by the public and very much loved, and when I confronted *The Tempest* I realised that here was a work of great maturity compared with *A Midsummer Night's Dream*, which is a work of Shakespeare's first period, his youth.[13]

Clearly, this 'confrontation' was traumatic, revealing the different states of mind required to direct the two plays, and in reply to the interviewer's follow-up question – 'What difference is there between the Helena Pimenta of *A Midsummer Night's Dream* and the current one?' – she indicates a shift in her sense of her own selfhood:

> The difference is that I accept that there is a bad side to human nature which I innocently believed it was easier to resist. Now I don't deny it, but I believe in certain antidotes which, were we to use them, would allow us to develop the good side of human nature (which is also there) in a way that would be more beneficial for everyone. (Valle, 'Helena Pimenta', 22)

For Pimenta, the distance between the Athenian wood and Prospero's island is measured in emotional maturity, as the internal technologies of selfhood, operating to minimise the impact of the world, also open themselves, through the experience of her engagement with the two plays, one early, one late, to a more general utility.

The interviewer, though, seems slightly to misunderstand her, suggesting that '[w]hat you say implies that late Shakespeare is more pessimistic', something she firmly denies:

> No. But I'd say, as do several critics, that in Shakespeare's last phase is his beginning. He is a man who in his old age is younger than ever, because he is full of vitality and his aesthetic ideas are sound. But to understand this you have to go through certain phases of life yourself. I'm not saying that I've passed through all of my own personal or theatrical periods, but I have lived long enough to have some understanding. There were concepts that I could understand intellectually but not spiritually or emotionally. [. . .] I needed to be in a later moment when I had acquired a more established and secure line in directing and confronting the actors' efforts. Because *The Tempest* is a work stripped down to its essence, free from ornamentation. (ibid.)

Pimenta makes certain classic assumptions here both about the Shakespearean late plays and about the overarching idea of late style. Underpinning her engagement with the play is her awareness both of its chronological location at the very end of Shakespeare's career and of the significance of that chronology: *The Tempest* is a play of 'maturity' where *A Midsummer Night's Dream* is not. Thus the only way truly to understand a given Shakespeare play, it seems, is to achieve roughly the same level of life-experience as Shakespeare at the moment of composition. As a result, she finds, it is only now, in middle age, that she can begin to comprehend the play. She does not need to be *precisely* Shakespeare's age, but she does need to have had enough experience of life, to have passed through more than one period of her own career, in order to reach the point at which she is emotionally equipped to direct it. This is, at least in part, because of the supposed simplicity, the nakedness, of *The Tempest*, a play 'free from ornamentation', a play which completes the circle and draws us back towards the playwright's early years, embodying the late stylist's last period of golden, clarified productivity. This chronological awareness appears to prompt her to articulate a conservative narrative for *The Tempest*, not only relying on its lateness in Shakespeare's career for the basis of her understanding but also invoking a reading more familiar from the early twentieth century than the early twenty-first in which, through his recognition both of the difficulty of suppressing evil and of a certain kinship with his slave Caliban, a benign Prospero succeeds in finding a solution of benefit not only to himself but to all the characters.

Certain assumptions, then, lie behind Pimenta's understanding of *The Tempest*: that in order fully to engage with a given dramatic text, it is necessary for the director to be aware of, and to try to reproduce, the stage

Lateness and the mid-life crisis

of the playwright's life that that text represents; and that there is a particular quality to *The Tempest* as the play that marks the very end of the career not just of any playwright but of William Shakespeare. These assumptions seem to me to underscore the often frustrating mismatch between contemporary engagements with Shakespeare in the theatre and in criticism, and they illuminate the peculiar resonance that Shakespeare's late plays, and in particular *The Tempest*, have acquired for theatre professionals as they seek structural validation for their own lives and careers. It is the appropriation of Shakespearean lateness as a vehicle for the self-conscious structuring of theatrical careers, then, to which I will now turn.

Discussing his 1988 production of *The Tempest*, the celebrated Japanese Shakespeare director Yukio Ninagawa offers a highly personal narrative to explain the intensity and appropriateness of his engagement with the play. 'Some suggested', he reports, that

> the Bermudas would be the best setting, and that I should travel abroad for fresh inspiration. I hate travelling, and I was not really anxious to go, but I did. However, I didn't feel good and just stayed in the hotel for two whole days thinking about the setting for the play: should the exiles' setting be the Bermudas? A South Pacific island? An island where convicts were exiled? Then I thought Sado Island in Japan should be the place! Zeami (the Shakespeare of Noh theatre) was exiled there. For the Japanese, Sado Island is also a place where convicts were sent. [...] With this decision made, I came back to Japan, then set straight off to Sado Island. I discovered there are thirty-two ancient Noh stages on the island, all of them open to the elements. The roofing was of straw and the whole stage shuttered because disused.[14]

This remarkable discovery gave him the basis for a sharply defined and appropriate reshaping of the play's context, but for some reason his mood did not fully lift. '[W]hen I was directing *The Tempest*', he admits, 'I was slightly depressed', describing this wryly as '[t]he usual mid-life crisis' (Interview, 213). 'That's the way I was', he admits,

> not seeing anyone and thinking about retirement. My own situation at that time seemed to relate to Prospero's thoughts in the play when he says, 'Our revels now are ended.' I was convinced that I had lost my talent for directing and that this would be my last chance to make a successful production. If it failed, I would retire. (ibid., 213–14)

Established already as a postmodern, globalised interpreter of Shakespeare, Ariel-like in his ability to circumnavigate the world with his productions (despite his professed hatred of travelling), aware of the scholarship that has connected William Strachey's shipwreck narrative with Ariel's reference to the 'still-vex'd Bermoothës', and interested specifically in the issue of exile, Ninagawa begins his engagement with the play by reconnoitring Bermuda as a logical possible location for his production. His visit was disastrous, though, in part because of his sense that so literal a locational choice would undermine the necessary process of re-engaging the play with Japanese theatrical culture. His brainwave – the choice of an ex-prison island off the coast of Japan – is the result of an identification which is also a transposition, that of Zeami, the most celebrated writer of classical Noh theatre, with Shakespeare, the most celebrated writer of the western theatrical tradition. To his surprise and satisfaction, Ninagawa's choice appears to be confirmed by theatre history when he arrives on the island and discovers a series of disused Noh theatres which are ideal for his purposes, implicitly allowing him to produce a play written for a long-gone English stage in a space that could arguably be read as its Japanese counterpart.

At this point in the narrative, however, a further identification and a further transposition take place, affecting his experience of directing the play. His account suggests explicitly (and histrionically) that he was at this time undergoing a 'mid-life crisis' – he was fifty-two when he began planning the production – and seriously considering retiring from the theatre, and he is clear that this emotional situation markedly affected his engagement with the play. Aware as he was of the critical association of Prospero with Shakespeare and of both with the idea of retirement, he was able to instil a sense of crisis into the production, a sense of crisis which is also a sense of *lastness*. Echoing Prospero's most frequently quoted speech – most frequently quoted, that is, out of context – he dramatises his own identification with both Shakespeare and Prospero: 'My own situation at that time seemed to relate to Prospero's thoughts in the play when he says, "Our revels now are ended."' 'I was convinced', he says, 'that I had lost my talent for directing and that this would be my last chance to make a successful production. If it failed, I would retire.' Ninagawa's conception of the play, channelled by way of the subjectivist reading of Prospero's 'revels' speech as Shakespeare's own statement of the ephemeral nature of the theatrical life, thus allows him to develop through his own mid-life anxiety a sense of identification between Shakespeare, Prospero, Zeami and himself, thereby sustaining the tradition of Shakespearean lateness and at the same time extending that tradition to Japanese theatre history. This both echoes and runs counter to Helena Pimenta's 'confrontation' with *The Tempest*. It echoes her experience in the sense that both directors associate themselves with Shakespeare and Prospero; it contradicts, however, her sense of the need for a period of years between first addressing the play and finally reaching the stage of life at which an appropriately mature approach can be taken to direction. Ninagawa's first encounter with *The Tempest* comes in middle age and his engagement with the play is instantaneous. While Pimenta too agrees that middle age is old enough, she adds the need for perspective. And it is her sense of *The Tempest*, highlighted by the contrast with that of Ninagawa, as a play which demands a sustained structural relationship across a period of years that seems to me to chime most clearly with its function in the lives of two of its most prominent British interpreters in the last hundred or so years.

6.3 PERFORMING LATE SELFHOOD: GIELGUD, PROSPERO, SHAKESPEARE

By far the most sustained engagement of any theatre professional in the twentieth century with *The Tempest* and specifically with the role of Prospero was that of Sir John Gielgud. When he died in 2000 at the age of ninety-six, the leading London theatre critic Michael Billington, writing in *The Guardian* about the great actor's life on the stage, singled out his 1957 Stratford Prospero as a 'classic example of Gielgud's ability to redefine a role. In place of the usual pontificating Prospero, four times as old as his brother, we got an irascible, moody, half-naked figure who delayed, until the last possible moment, the access of benevolence and charity.'[15] Billington also pointed out that Gielgud 'never ceased dreaming of making a movie of *The Tempest*, [to be] directed by Ingmar Bergman, though in the end he had to settle for Peter Greenaway's *Prospero's Books*'. Billington's phrase 'settle for' does not, it seems to me, simply serve as disparagement of Greenaway as a film-maker in comparison with the great Bergman; it can also be read as a comment on the development – or, perhaps better, the decline – in Gielgud's interpretation (or inhabitation) of the role of Prospero between the mid-century stage production and the turn-of-the-century film. Gielgud gradually *became* Prospero over the course of his lifetime, and that becoming paradoxically involved an interpretative regression, a retraction of early radicalism, that is, arguably, the inevitable result of a close identification with Shakespearean lateness over time.

One of the slipperiest issues in the history of the construction of lateness is, as we have seen, that of age. As far as the lateness embodied in *The Tempest* is concerned, tradition – the same tradition that equates Prospero and Shakespeare – has given its answer: Prospero is 'a benign wizard, elderly, serene and majestic' (Orgel, *Tempest*, 79). Yet, as I suggested in Chapter 5, it is not at all necessary for Prospero to be so venerable (see above, 295). Nor has he always been portrayed on stage as an old man. Nineteenth-century representations offered Prospero in a variety of guises: some are Christ-like and thus reasonably youthful; T. Howard's bare etchings of 1827 make him an early-middle-aged, stoical Erasmus-figure or an Italian Renaissance Man, with Miranda clearly very young indeed; others propose a Lear-like character, ageing and wild-eyed; others a figure classical and stern; yet others an oriental mage with a turban, his cell like a richly appointed tent; and in early nineteenth-century German illustrations, he is made to look medieval, like a Tennysonian Arthur, especially in illustrations by Moritz Retzsch.[16] Yet by the later nineteenth and twentieth centuries (that is, once the identification of Shakespeare with Prospero had become a presumption), Prospero on the stage was invariably white-haired and bearded like Gandalf. Gielgud drove a coach and horses through this tradition. As Orgel observes, the 1957 production singled out by Billington, though itself relatively early in Gielgud's long career, was by no means his first *Tempest* or his first Prospero. He in fact played the role four times prior to *Prospero's Books*, developing it in different ways as he matured, with probably only three constants – his wholly distinctive, measured voice, his curiously priestlike stage presence, and his habit of never looking at Ariel while speaking to him, maintaining the impression of the spirit as a product of his imagination. His characterisation of Prospero, however, changed a great deal.

He first played the part in 1930 for Harcourt Williams at the Old Vic as a twenty-six-year-old, 'looking like Dante, without a beard', as he later said, and returned to it ten years later, directed by George Devine and Marius Goring, again at the Old Vic, in a performance described as 'very far from the usual mixture of Father Christmas, a Colonial Bishop, and the President of the Magician's Union [in] a clearly arresting picture of a virile Renaissance notable (no dotard) who has "a daily beauty in his life" as well as magical powers'.[17] The 1957 production for Peter Brook at Stratford and then at Drury Lane was thus his third Prospero, played, in his amused words, 'as a sort of El Greco hermit with very short hair' (*Hit or Miss*, 109), in a manner notable for his portrayal of a depressed and isolated Prospero in exile whose internal turmoil shaped the island as a grim dreamscape of caves and undergrowth and whose turn to reconciliation at the end was noticeably reluctant. Even at this stage, a quarter of a century on from his first Prospero, Gielgud was clearly still in the prime of life, both vocally and physically supple, and certainly 'no dotard'. In two ways, then, this Prospero broke with tradition: Gielgud was, for the third time now, younger than the expected norm and, following the lead of Michael Hordern at the Old Vic three years earlier, he was not the usual serene wizard but rather a brooding obsessive – except that where Hordern's dark Prospero of 1954 had been rejected by critics as insufficiently 'poetic', Gielgud's natural sense and weighting of the verse seems to have carried the reading effortlessly.

Thereafter Gielgud left the role alone for nearly twenty years, returning to it only in 1974 for the emergent National Theatre company, once again at the Old Vic, in Peter Hall's first production as the company's Director. Clearly he felt a little limited by Hall's vision of the role. 'He wanted me,' reported Gielgud, 'to look like Dr Dee, the Elizabethan alchemist, and persuaded me to wear a beard and spectacles and voluminous robes, so that I felt very swaddled and confined' (ibid.). He acknowledges that '[i]n some ways this is right for Prospero', but tellingly adds: 'I was anxious to show him as a man who had lived with nature for many years' (ibid.). This anxiety marks a turning point in the development of the Gielgud Prospero as he moves towards the particular vision of the role and of the play with which we are familiar from Pimenta, as one that makes sense only with the passing of the years. The time that has gone by since his first Prospero marks the transition from Gielgud the mould-breaker to Gielgud the institution, and his performance follows suit, taking its cue now from age and status. For Robert Cushman, writing in *The Observer*, in the 1974 production Gielgud, who has built up an unassailable ownership of Prospero through the sustained nature of his performance, finally 'sets his seal on the role forever', as if no other interpretation will again be possible.[18] And he notes casually that Gielgud's next appearance on the London stage would be in Edward Bond's *Bingo*, in which he was to play Shakespeare in his Stratford retirement – a move the critic describes as 'logical' in the wake of this definitive Prospero. (A parallel, if extreme, logic seemed to be in operation at the BBC in 1991 when, in the immediate wake of his performance as Prospero in *Prospero's Books*, Gielgud was cast, in a radio adaptation of the Book of Genesis, as God.) The tradition is fulfilled, then, in Gielgud and approved by the theatre critics: by the age of seventy he had made the roles of both Prospero and Shakespeare his, uniting the strands of the play's inheritance.

By this time, Gielgud's Prospero had become, to use Orgel's term, 'normative' – a performance characterised as '[e]xpressive, intellectual, fastidious [. . .] built around the setpieces, [and giving] great emphasis to the richness and beauty of the verse throughout' (Orgel, *Tempest*, 80). Orgel's description dates from the 1980s and thus from the years between the

Gielgud/Hall production and Gielgud's last Prospero in Peter Greenaway's 1991 film *Prospero's Books*, but his description is decidedly prescient of the film performance – or rather it makes clear that the Prospero familiar to those of us who have to rely on *Prospero's Books* rather than the stage productions for our sense of Gielgud's interpretation of the role is one with roots far back in the actor's career.[19] Certainly the film displays – indeed it relentlessly foregrounds – each of the features Orgel describes: Gielgud's magnificent, melodic intonation, the calm precision with which he enunciates his lines, the astonishing clarity of the voice in old age, plus an overwhelming emphasis (harking back to pre-twentieth-century traditions of spectacular staging) on large-scale set-pieces and on visuals as sumptuous as the language and the delivery. It has thus solidified, in the minds at least of arthouse cinema-goers, the late Gielgud Prospero, exemplifying film's tendency to fossilise performance in a way that the stage, by definition, cannot.

The film is something Gielgud had wanted to make for years: 'Prospero has been a favourite part of mine and it would be a wonderful thing to do at the end of one's career, because it is so obviously Shakespeare's last work – the end of his career.'[20] Yet it took him a remarkably long time to realise this dream. In his account of his life as a Shakespearean actor, he expresses his bewilderment:

I had always had a great ambition to film *The Tempest*, but I could not find a director until I happened to meet Peter Greenaway. I had been fascinated by his films, especially *The Draughtsman's Contract*, which I saw two or three times. He was a completely new personality, as you could feel from the way in which his films were photographed and acted. (*Hit or Miss*, 111)

No director seemed to want to touch it (except for Derek Jarman, who asked Gielgud to be in his radical reworking of *The Tempest*, a request that Gielgud turned down because, as he delicately put it, 'I didn't care for his ideas'). His autobiography lists those he tried to recruit for the project, quite a roll-call of greats: Kurosawa, Strehler, Brook, Resnais, above all Bergman – but they all said no.[21] Greenaway, however, having already cast and worked with Gielgud in a television film of Dante's *Inferno*, took up the idea with gusto, going so far as to suggest that Gielgud play, or at least speak, not only Prospero but all the other parts too (at least, that is, until the final scenes of release and reconciliation).

The upshot is an extraordinary film. Neil Forsyth offers a helpful description:

Peter Greenaway's 'spell-stopped' film [. . .] with its frames within frames, its 'high charms', its rendering of the tempest-tossed ship as a child's toy galleon and the water world as a boy's fantasy of omnipotence as he pisses, is a baroque, dense, claustrophobically rich tribute to the connection of magician and playmaker.[22]

Greenaway makes clear the inseparability of Shakespeare and Prospero (he 'sees Prospero not just as the master manipulator of people and events but as their prime originator'), who is seen to be writing the play throughout:

On his island of exile, Prospero plans a drama to right the wrongs done to him. He invents characters to flesh out his imaginary fantasy to steer his enemies into his power, writes their dialogue, and having written it, he speaks the lines aloud, shaping the characters so powerfully through the words that they are conjured before us.[23]

Gielgud becomes the third figure in an indivisible trinity: 'it is intended that there should be much deliberate cross-identification between Prospero, Shakespeare and Gielgud', writes Greenaway, making clear that this merging is premised on their shared lateness:

Prospero is the last major role that Shakespeare invented, reputedly, in the last complete play he wrote, and there is much, both in the character and in the play, that can be understood as a leave-taking of the theatre and a farewell to role-playing and the manufacturing of illusion through words – not insignificant perhaps when Gielgud's seventy-year career on stage is considered. (*Prospero's Books*, 9)

The equation of character and actor with playwright is made explicit both at the beginning of the film, as we see Prospero both write and speak the first word, and at the end, when the calligraphic manuscript he has been producing is 'revealed' as *The Tempest*, the play for which nineteen blank pages have been left at the beginning of the otherwise complete First Folio that is volume 24 ('Thirty-Six Plays') in his vast library.

Despite Greenaway's acknowledgement of 'more than a few apparently conflicting facets of [Prospero's] personality – not all of them particularly praiseworthy' (*Prospero's Books*, 12), a good deal of directorial effort goes into creating a consistent, controlled, finally benign characterisation of the mage. Greenaway carefully cuts most of the lines that have led historicist critics to read Prospero as an insecure, colonising tyrant – pretty much all the lines, in fact, on which *Tempest* criticism since the mid-eighties has depended – leaving behind only those sections of the text that support the image of Prospero as benign and serene – the sections, in other words, that Dowden deployed to produce his late Shakespeare – and emphasising the reasonableness of his behaviour in the face of childish resistance. In section 40 of the script, for instance, Prospero adopts 'a pose of anger that he enacts largely for Ariel's benefit' and Ariel is 'shamed into a more reasonably accurate version of the truth'; again, in section 43, Prospero 'is amused, but he doesn't show it to Caliban – he feigns indignation and, standing tall, puts on a frightening display of wrath' (ibid., 87, 96). Prospero's irascibility is thus soothed down to a mere 'pose of anger'. In the midst of the film's beautiful, crowded screens, Gielgud walks (he does a great deal of walking throughout), calm and detached, intoning not only his own lines but everyone else's in that expressive, precise, fastidious manner that Orgel has described. And behind Gielgud every step of the way, expressing himself throughout by way of Gielgud's Prospero, is the director, Greenaway. As the actor notes admiringly in his account of the filming:

Above all, I was greatly impressed by his control. A very quiet man who never raises his voice, he walked about the studio all day long, never sat down, and seemed to work equally easily with the sound man who was British, the lighting man who was French, all the crew who were of mixed nationalities, including a lot of Dutchmen, and the whole cast, extras of every nationality, all very obedient, even when working overtime. They did not seem to mind taking all their clothes off to play the visionary and mythological characters. Unlike the atmosphere on most film sets, no one ever had to shout for quiet; there was no hammering or tantrums or bad behaviour. The whole thing was wonderfully organised. (*Hit or Miss*, 117)

This emphasis on Greenaway's endless walking, on his ability to control a range of personalities and nationalities so that they become unquestioningly obedient, on the absence of any behaviour in poor taste and on the way in which the whole is organised and controlled embodies both Gielgud's Prospero and a conservative reading of *The Tempest* in which the outcome is the product of the calm, patient word of a well-mannered controller and all is 'harmonious charmingly'. Greenaway coyly describes the way he uses 'paintbox' technology to create the dominant images of the film as 'a nicely tuned conceit to illuminate the role of deception implied by Prospero's magic and by the illusion and deception practised by a playwright [. . .] and maybe by a film-maker in the manufacture of cinema' (*Prospero's Books*, 33). In this way, Greenaway, while repeatedly, if somewhat disingenuously, emphasising the centrality of Gielgud to the play's conception – '[t]he proposition to make a film of *The Tempest* came from Sir John Gielgud and th[e] film-script was devised for his playing of Prospero' (ibid., 9) – in fact deploys Gielgud in the film as a surrogate for himself, as aged actor and middle-aged director simultaneously become Prospero-as-Shakespeare, writing the play and controlling the action.

Prospero's Books received mixed reviews ('the trouble is', one critic felt, 'that Greenaway, unlike Shakespeare, never bothers to make it clear who anybody is'), but Gielgud seems not to have been too concerned about this, perhaps because he is, as Greenaway himself acknowledged, 'the still, calm figure in the midst of all my pyrotechnical extravagance – whatever else is going on in the film, it is always Gielgud you watch'.[24] Gielgud himself acknowledged that, while 'the film is original and fascinating, [it is also] very over-elaborate' (*Hit or Miss*, 117), but he was reported to 'have no Prospero-like regrets [. . .] consider[ing] Greenaway's film to be both a summary of his career and a formal farewell to it' and thus seeing his own performance as largely detachable from its context, placed into the framework of the film rather than integrally connected with it.[25] Yet, while the film's limitations may indeed have been primarily the result of Greenaway's vision of the play, it is clear that as Gielgud grew old, so his Prospero aged with him, transmuting into a reading that is very different from the radicalism of his embodiment of the role in early performances. As Greenaway's insinuation of himself into the equation suggests, however, it is not necessary to reach old age in order to deploy *The Tempest* to such career-shaping ends. The impetus of lateness, as we have seen with Pimenta and Ninagawa, can provoke certain kinds of essentialism and their consequences at any age. In order to demonstrate this, I will turn now to another, current actor – celebrated, like Gielgud, as an extraordinary talent from the moment he left RADA – who has found in Prospero and *The Tempest* a structural principle for his theatrical life.

6.4 AUTHORSHIP AND AUTHENTICITY: RYLANCE, PROSPERO, SHAKESPEARE

The 2005 season at Shakespeare's Globe Theatre in London marked a clear break from the habit adopted in previous years of basing the season's play choices, or at least the choice of lead play starring Mark Rylance, the theatre's Artistic Director, on a quadricentennial. In 2002, for instance, *Twelfth Night* had been the main offering, with Rylance as Olivia, performed both at the Globe and at the Middle Temple Hall, where it was played in 1602; in 2003, it was *Measure for Measure*, a disguised-ruler play associated with the accession of James I in 1603, in which Rylance played Duke Vincentio. But the 2005 summer season saw the abrupt dropping of the anniversary concept, offering three Shakespearean late plays, including *The Tempest*, along with a reworking of a Plautus play considered to be one of its sources. Though identified officially as 'The Season of the World and Underworld', it was in fact a celebration of Mark Rylance's final summer after ten years as Artistic Director of Shakespeare's Globe, the reconstructed Elizabethan theatre created out of the sheer relentless willpower and dedicated fundraising of the American actor Sam Wanamaker which opened up the potential of the Bankside as a centre for London tourism, paving the way for Tate Modern, the Millennium Bridge and the revival of the immediate south side of the Thames. Rylance's ten-year tenure had had its moments of controversy, to be sure, but the Globe had unquestionably, for all that its detractors said against it, been a considerable success under his leadership, with audience statistics to make the average West End manager deeply envious. As the NPR announcer put it on *Morning Edition* at the time of Rylance's final US tour,

[c]ritics predicted that [the reconstructed Globe] would end up being no more than a 'heritage museum' for William Shakespeare's work, with its historically accurate open thatched roof, circular stage, period instruments and men portraying female characters. But the daring and innovative Mark Rylance was named artistic director, and the pairing has turned into a winning combination, with crowds and critics declaring Shakespeare's Globe Theatre a success.[26]

Leaving as he was at the height of his success, Rylance knew his departure would be a cause of mourning for many. With this sense of security, he could break with the anniversary pattern, fast-forwarding five years to 1610, in order to structure his exit from the Globe by way of identification with the late Shakespeare.

Having been reminded, perhaps, of the *The Tempest*'s function as a 'ritual of farewell' by Iain McDiarmid's choice of the play and of the role of Prospero for himself as the last production at the Almeida Theatre in Islington, North London, before its closure for rebuilding at the end of 2000 or, less recently but more resonantly, by the decision of Peter Hall – who had, as we have seen, directed Gielgud as Prospero for his very first production as Director of the National Theatre – to mark the final year of his tenure at the National in 1988 by including *The Tempest* in a season of late Shakespeare plays (alongside *Cymbeline* and *The Winter's Tale*), Rylance chose *The Tempest* as the centrepiece of his last season at the Globe, casting himself as Prospero in a three-man production which also featured three non-speaking female dancers.[27] 'Given that *The Tempest* traditionally is viewed by scholars as Shakespeare's valediction to the stage', noted Ray Schultz, as did several reviewers, 'it seems fitting that Rylance would choose its central character of Prospero, the deposed duke and reluctant magician, as his own valediction to the post he held for ten years', though adding that 'some of Carroll's theories' – Tim Carroll, that is, 'Master of Play' for the production – of 'the theatre's magical and healing capacity [. . .] may read better on paper'.[28] The extent to which these theories were in fact Rylance's rather than the director's is clear from Carroll's programme note. Asked how the idea for the production arose, he explains: 'When Mark Rylance asked me: 'Do you fancy doing *The Tempest* with three actors?' I was surprised to hear myself saying 'Yes' straight away'.[29] And he goes on to explain his interest in perhaps unexpected terms that demonstrate why he has been Rylance's preferred director:

I felt sure my impulse to say 'Yes' must spring from some feeling of recognition. In fact, the moment I thought any more about it I saw what it was. The three-actor idea had appealed to me because it reflected a striking truth about the play: it has a trinity at its very heart. On either side of the central character, Prospero, holding him in a kind of magnetic tension, are the opposing forces of Ariel and Caliban – air and earth, or, as Jung might say, spirit and soul. While Ariel might be said to represent imagination and the mind, Caliban belongs to the darker realm of the appetite, especially to those physical drives that we often seek to suppress in ourselves. (Carroll in *Tempest* programme, 26)

Not only, then, is Carroll unusually happy to subordinate himself to the directorial notions of his principal actor, he is also keen to ensure Prospero's (that is, Rylance's) absolute centrality to the production and to address the play in the Artistic Director's own preferred terms, a blend of alchemical mysticism and Jungian psychology. This approach to *The Tempest* perhaps has its roots in Rylance's early experience of acting in Ron Daniels's 1982 production for the RSC, in which his 'quicksilver Ariel' and Bob Peck's 'earthy Caliban' became, according to one reviewer, 'extensions of Prospero's own personality'.[30] But it is also, more directly, the product of the impact on Rylance's thinking of his encounter with Peter Dawkins, founder-director of two institutions, the Francis Bacon Research Trust (which argues for Bacon's authorship of the plays in the Shakespeare canon) and the Zoence Academy (which, according to the author's note in his most recent book, 'provides a training course in a synthesis of the western wisdom traditions, sacred architecture, landscape cosmology and geomancy'), who has written a series of books on the alchemical significance of the plays, entitled *The Wisdom of Shakespeare*.[31] Rylance, who notes in his foreword to Dawkins's *The Shakespeare Enigma* that he has 'not approached a Shakespeare play since meeting Peter without his thoughts in my mind' – has written of *The Tempest* as

a drama which draws heavily on [. . .] the Hermetic thinking that had thrived in Florence when Ficino worked on the ancient texts of Plato and Plotinus, and which subsequently exercised an influence on a great deal of writing in Elizabeth's England. The play describes the initiation of the characters through imaginary experience. [...] I find myself asking whether this initiation through the imagination is what Shakespeare thought of his plays as effecting in the Globe.[32]

Dawkins's writings on the play expand this emphasis on rites of initiation (his first publication was entitled 'The Pattern of Initiation in the Evolution of Human Consciousness') with reference to the 'alchemical progress of humanity' and to the life-cycles of the elements in the quest for a spiritual balance embodied in a master or mage, reading the play in its historical moment as 'a Rosicrucian work'.[33] These views are expressed in the 2005 programme by way of quotations not, as it happens, from Dawkins himself but from a book called *Prospero's Island: The Secret Alchemy at the Heart of 'The Tempest'* – which Rylance places 'at the top of [his] list of profoundly insightful and practically useful books for the actor and lover of Shakespeare' – by Jungian psychotherapist Noel Cobb, who asks: 'What is [*The Tempest*] if not the impeccable culmination of Shakespeare's life-work, the final distillation of a theme which had occupied him [since the start of his career]: the vital necessity of earthiness as a counterbalance to intellect?'[34]

The programme, then, while occluding the production's premise in the idea of lateness by focussing on *The Tempest*'s alleged mystical resonances, its counterpointing of air and earth, spirit and soul, nevertheless quietly hints at that premise by treating the play specifically as 'the impeccable culmination of Shakespeare's life-work'. For it is clear that, in a range of ways, Rylance's farewell *Tempest* brought both his career as an actor and his specific experience of the Globe full circle, marking the conclusion to a clearly delineated period in his life. Trained at RADA, where he will have been keenly aware of his famous precursors – not least, of course, John Gielgud – he worked first at the Glasgow Citizens' Theatre in 1980 before joining the RSC two years later to play alongside Derek Jacobi's Prospero as Ariel in the Daniels production (in a certain sense reprising this role the following year when playing Peter Pan in the RSC's non-Shakespearean money-spinner). He left the RSC shortly afterwards and performed in a variety of contexts, mostly in London, before returning to the company in 1988 to play both Romeo and, most importantly, a pyjama-clad Hamlet in a memorably brilliant, landmark performance that brought him accolades far and wide as the production toured the UK, Ireland and in due course the United States. There was an immediacy, an intensity, a sheer charisma to his acting that brought out the superlatives: as Al Pacino is alleged to have said, 'Mark Rylance plays Shakespeare like Shakespeare wrote it for him the night before.' Back in 1984, however, Rylance, keen to explore alternative 'ways of communicating Shakespeare', had formed an acting company called the London Theatre of Imagination, 'the aim of which was to explore working without a director', touring an *Othello* which played in London at the Bear Gardens on the Bankside, the precursor of Shakespeare's Globe, at that time a museum and education centre containing a small theatre on the Elizabethan thrust-stage model.[35] In 1990 he and his wife Claire Van Kampen, who had been music director at both the RSC and the National Theatre, formed a successor company called Phoebus' Cart, and the following year they created a production of *The Tempest*, with Rylance this time playing not Ariel but Prospero, for which they once again found a performance space on the Bankside.[36]

The production toured during the summer of 1991 to two outdoor sites associated with Rylance's belief in mysticism and specifically his interest in the psychic significance of ley lines: Corfe Castle in Dorset and the Rollright Stone Circle in Oxfordshire.[37] For their London venue, the company turned again to the Globe project, this time performing on the site on which the reconstructed Globe would in due course be built (two hundred yards or so north-west of the site of the original theatre) but which was at that time dormant. For Rylance, the Globe site was the ideal location in the capital because of its potential congruence with the previous venues:

[T]he *Tempest* project was, like the Globe, an attempt to draw a community into a very old structure, in this case the Rollright Stone Circle. [. . .] For our London performances, we didn't want an indoor space, but an outdoor circular space of similar dimensions to those of the Stone Circle. Here was a site of such space, with the same near-one-hundred-foot dimensions and north-eastern orientation.[38]

The 2005 *Tempest* programme – citing Michael Maier's alchemical treatise *Atalanta Fugiens*, from which Van Kampen drew some of the production's music – illustrates the place of the figure of the circle at the start and finish of the geometrical process that leads towards the ultimate goal of alchemy: 'Make from the male and female a circle, then a square, afterwards a triangle, from which make a circle, and thou shalt have the Philosopher's Stone.'[39] Rylance has suggested the potential spiritual and emotional value of the theatre's congruence with this alchemical geometry by citing an Elizabethan figure considered (as the 1974 Gielgud/Hall production implied through costuming) to be a possible original for Prospero:

Dr John Dee, the great scholar who taught Lord Leicester, the first patron of a professional playing company in Elizabethan England, described the worlds of desire, thought and action by employing a sun or circle, a moon or triangle, and a cross or square: his famous *Monas Hieroglyphica*. The Globe, this roughly circular theatre, with its roughly square stage, two thirds revealed and one third hidden behind the *frons scenae*, and its huge triangular gable supported on the pillars of Hercules, may help us tap into the meaning of Shakespeare in new and powerful ways. (Rylance in Mulryne and Shewring, *Shakespeare's Globe* 175)

The 1991 production, expressly conforming to this geometry ('I did a production of *The Tempest*', Rylance said to an interviewer three years later, unrolling a diagram: 'see, this is a chart of the alchemical process...'), occupied, within the circular site on which the theatre would be built, four stages or altars (at least one of which consisted of an upright triangle) located at the points of the compass, and the audience sat on the ground or promenaded between the stages in a manner predictive of the experience of attending the rebuilt Globe as a 'groundling'.[40] The production also featured dancers from Northern Ballet, representing the four elements, who were on stage throughout in a manner reminiscent of the four naked women dancers omnipresent in *Prospero's Books* (though, the venue being open to the actual elements, they were clothed).

In acting Prospero in *The Tempest* for his final season at the Globe, Rylance was consciously looking back to that 1991 production – and not only because of the apparent parallels with Peter Hall, who had not only, as I have noted, marked the end of his time as Director of the National Theatre in 1988 with a late-play season crowned with *The Tempest* but had also begun his tenure by directing Gielgud as Prospero in 1974. There is a photograph of Rylance early in the programme, a bearded Prospero as he was again in 2005, in earnest conference with Sam Wanamaker, with the four-stage set, laid out on the foundations of the current theatre, in the background, and he made direct reference to the earlier *Tempest* in his farewell speech following the very last performance of the 2005 production, pointing (at the end of this season of 'World and Underworld') to its erstwhile location beneath the stage. The self-consciousness of the final season, then, was tacit but unmistakeable. The choice of the late plays in general, and of *The Tempest* in particular, was made not only to suggest the completion of the initiation ritual Rylance believes the play to represent – which Van Kampen describes in her programme note as 'Prospero's alchemical journey of division, transformation and unification' – but to round off his decade at the Globe: to celebrate his achievement as Artistic Director, to mark the end of his era and to suggest that his departure coincides with the conclusion of the theatre's decade of 'initiation'.[41] As reinforcement and duplication of the claim implicit in his choice of *The*

Tempest as the season's centrepiece and as an embodiment of his ongoing emphasis on the serious import of the playful*ness* of theatre, Rylance included alongside it a tongue-in-cheek production of a new play called *The Storm*, or rather a new version by Peter Oswald of an old play, Plautus' *The Rope* – of which Shakespeare's *Tempest* is, in Ruth Nevo's words, 'a palimpsest' – which begins with a tempest and a shipwreck and focusses on a father/daughter relationship.[42] The production – a kind of carnivalesque alternative to *The Tempest*, also directed by Carroll, with music by Van Kampen, and featuring the members of the *Tempest* cast – not only incorporated a series of props drawn from earlier Globe productions, each carefully chosen to remind those of the audience who had attended previous seasons of the highlights of the Rylance era, but also featured Mark Rylance himself acting several roles, including the Prospero-figure Daemones, and most notably at one point playing himself as Artistic Director, taking comic revenge in various ways on his critics.[43]

Rylance's final season *Tempest* was, as it happens, quietly reminiscent not only of the 1991 production but also of *Prospero's Books*, both in its reduction of the play's speaking parts to a limited number of voices – and in the end to the voice of Prospero alone – and in its visual echoes of the film through some of the movements and postures of the women dancers who remained onstage throughout. Moreover, not only were the film's four Ariels, according to Greenaway, designed to represent the elements (as had the dancers in the 1991 production), but the consciously postmodern collage of images that makes up the crowded visuals and represents the materials Greenaway imagines an early modern mage would need for his work incorporates a series of items that chime with the concerns of the Globe production: early modern mathematical figures including cubes, pyramids and spheres (from 'A Harsh Book of Geometry' and, later, 'The Book of Universal Cosmography'), 'measurements of [. . .] statues of Hermes, Venus and Hercules' and street plans of Atlantis ('Love of Ruins'), and games of astronomy, the cabbala, the stars and magic ('The Book of Games'), as well as instances of Rosicrucian symbolism (Greenaway, *Prospero's Books*, 17–25).

That there should be connections of this kind between *Prospero's Books* and Rylance's productions, especially the one from the same year as the film, is hardly surprising, however, in view of the fact that the role of Ferdinand in the film was played by the young Mark Rylance himself, his part in the film mostly silent, spoken, like everyone else's, by Gielgud, as Greenaway wanted. It was only his fourth screen appearance (earlier in the same year he had won a BBC Radio Times Award for Best Newcomer for his role alongside Pete Postlethwaite in Gillies MacKinnon's *The Grass Arena*) and his name, unlike that, say, of Isabelle Pasco playing Miranda, does not appear prior to the film's title in the opening credits. But Greenaway, in casting him as Prospero/Gielgud's dynastic successor, could presumably see his star potential. It is possible that, observing Greenaway's deployment of mystical images as simply one factor in a postmodern collage of visual materials in the construction of his cinematic *Tempest*, Rylance was stimulated to create a theatrical *Tempest* that would take the play's supposed mystical resonances more seriously. Whatever the precise nature of the connection between *Prospero's Books* and the four-stage outdoor *Tempest* of the same year, the distance covered between Rylance's early role as a silent Ferdinand and his eventual dual role both as a Prospero speaking others' lines and as Artistic Director of the Globe became very clear in the 2005 production as he deployed the culture of lateness in his self-dramatisation as actor-manager.

It is this *Prospero's Books* connection that provides the most fascinating twist of all, because Rylance's persistence in identifying himself with Prospero arguably sets up a quite deliberate echo. Where his near-exact contemporary Kenneth Branagh, in consciously choosing *Henry V* as the subject of his first Shakespeare film as both star and director, was making a clear statement of his self-appointed status as a Laurence Olivier for the end of the twentieth century, Rylance – through the centrality of *The Tempest* to his vision of Shakespeare and through the continuity and development that can be seen from his role in *Prospero's Books* to the 2005 farewell season at the Globe – arguably situates himself as the new Gielgud. Opening the first full Globe season in 1999 with a quadricentennial *Henry V*, with himself in the title role and Richard Olivier, Laurence's son, as director, Rylance might in fact have been seen to be challenging Branagh for that particular crown from the alternative, deliberately reiterative, anti-technological context of the Globe, but if so, he soon changed tack, turning instead to Gielgud and *The Tempest*.[44] This shift, established already as an implicit act of heredity through *Prospero's Books*, in which Rylance-Ferdinand will inherit the dukedom of Gielgud-Prospero, emerged quite naturally from the centrality of *The Tempest* to Rylance's vision of Shakespeare the mystic.

At the same time, Rylance's timing of his engagement with *The Tempest* also marks his *difference* from Gielgud. What connects his attitude to the late Shakespeare with that of Pimenta or of Ninagawa – and what distinguishes all three from Gielgud (or at least from the Gielgud of *Prospero's Books* as opposed to the Gielgud Prosperos of 1930, 1940, 1957 and 1974) – is that each of these figures is approaching the imaginary Shakespeare of *The Tempest* not in old age but *in mid-life*. Gielgud completes the development of his Prospero by performing the part at the last very late in life, as a genuinely old man, the embodiment of the traditional image of late Shakespeare in sage serenity; Rylance, on the other hand, performs Prospero-as-Shakespeare at the age of forty-five – and thus at roughly the same age as Shakespeare when he wrote *The Tempest*. In so doing, Rylance reshapes the concept of lateness underpinning the logic of his Globe farewell by associating it not with the entire life and career of an individual but rather with that individual only in his association with a particular institution – that is, not with the entire life of Mark Rylance from childhood to old age but with the period of his tenure as Artistic Director of the Globe. This reworks the discourse of lateness as a malleable organising principle for characterising and mythologising a portion of a life as defined in association with an institution – in this case, Rylance's period as the Globe's own Prospero, its central creative talent – which is not necessarily the concluding portion of that life. In the process Rylance both becomes and resists becoming Shakespeare. By creating his own late phase in mid-career in order to mark the end not of his life but of his Globe period, he detaches the concept of lateness from the old age which underpins the standard image of the late Shakespeare and, by retiring from the Globe with a crowning performance as Prospero at the age of forty-five, he rewrites Shakespearean lateness as the product of what Henry James would call 'the middle years' in a move ironically commensurate – since it underlines the lack of fit between Shakespeare's experience of life in 1610 and the image that has subsequently been constructed for him as a man who has reached retiring age – with the Globe's project to recreate the original conditions for production of the plays. One of the major achievements of Rylance's farewell season as the Globe's Artistic Director, then, is the deniability of the premise of that farewell season. By retiring in middle age, he absorbs and at the same time rejects the structural principle of lateness, becoming Shakespeare as he becomes Prospero and yet rejecting the image of the aged magus for whom every third thought is death.

Moreover, in a further *coup*, the programme's emphasis on alchemy and occult philosophy, which offers a logic for the season ostensibly quite other than its underlying premise in the idea of lateness, in fact turns out to reinforce and justify that premise. The opening extract from Noel Cobb runs as follows: 'Shakespeare, like some strange Western incarnation of a

Taoist sage, walked a path which sought harmony between that which is above us and that which is below. This is largely why he has come to represent, for our culture, the idea of wholeness, the complete individual' (18). In his farewell speech after the last performance of the 2005 *Tempest*, Rylance, as I have noted, referred to the 1991 production on the Globe site: specifically and resonantly, he described his final-season return to the play in the round space of the Globe as 'the completion of a circle'. This brings together his repeated foregrounding of the cyclical and the circular in the quest for the alchemical marriage of earth and spirit with the idea of lateness as the rounded conclusion to the career of a genius. It thus encourages us to recognise in Rylance's Globe decade an exemplary instance of a process of completion that is the outcome of the 'path' also taken by both Prospero and Shakespeare, offering a triple identification – of character, playwright and performer – as each finally achieves spiritual and personal fulfilment.[45]

The underlying irony of all this – and the basic plot-twist it offers in the ongoing story of late Shakespeare, a twist that turns us back to the Henry James of 'The Birthplace' – is that Mark Rylance, as is generally known, does not accept that the person he calls 'the man from Stratford' actually wrote the plays. Rylance is both a Friend of the Francis Bacon Research Trust (founder-director Peter Dawkins) and Chairman of the Shakespearean Authorship Trust (of which Dawkins is a trustee), an organisation that describes itself as 'dedicated to open and friendly enquiry into the question of the authorship of Shakespeare's plays and poems' and which

> wishes to create a forum where the authorship of the plays and poems can be discussed courteously and rationally and from a variety of different perspectives, in the knowledge that conflicting and even opposing viewpoints can offer equally valid insights into the works.[46]

'We know so little about the actor from Stratford,' Rylance explains in his foreword to Dawkins's *Wisdom of Shakespeare in 'The Tempest'*, 'and what we do know – the petty law suits against poachers for example – doesn't marry naturally with the deep compassion, wit and philosophical insight of the plays' (Dawkins, *Wisdom*, xxi). He himself leans towards Bacon, but is open to other suggestions.[47] In a 1994 interview with Lawrence Gerald, a Bacon devotee keen to hear his views on the 'authorship question' ('I had already known', notes Gerald, 'that he was a Baconian but I wanted to hear him say so on tape [though] Mark was trying to lay low with me on this as he was the leading candidate for director of the Globe Theatre at the time'), Rylance describes his first encounters with Dawkins and the Francis Bacon Research Trust, whose double engagement with Bacon and mysticism drew him in:

> I found with Peter Dawkins of the Francis Bacon Research Trust that they were talking about esoteric traditions, that alchemy, the Kabalah, the Hermetic teachings which Frances A. Yates writes very intricately about in her books, and the Celtic major cycles, the Druidic, the Celtic traditions here, all these kind of hidden traditions that can kind of be stretched back to Egypt. And I found in them a description of a form of the movement through Hamlet that I was experiencing as an actor.[48]

He explains the appeal of the Bacon attribution:

> I suppose it's particularly helpful to me also to realize that there's a consciousness behind the plays which is not just about making money, which is the general motivation that I hear of Stratfordians. [...] I find with Francis Bacon [...] someone who was connected with these schools of thought, and someone who had a motivation that equals the scope of the comedy and the tragedy in the plays.

And he continues:

> I don't mind who you think wrote the plays. [...] It's an intuitive exercise to do a Shakespeare play and to go through a Shakespeare play. Well, likewise, the authorship question: whoever you believe wrote the plays, they covered their tracks bloody well. [...] So even the Stratford man, you've got to say, why did he leave us only about eleven facts about himself? So whoever you believe wrote the plays, they felt it was important to mask them, to mask the identity, the personality of the author. And to name them, I guess, to name them Shakespeare, which to me is a literal translation of the goddess of wisdom, the Greek goddess of wisdom, Pallas Athena. So even Mr. Shaksper, if he wrote the plays, changed his name to Shakespeare and showed a great consciousness, and I think a proper sense of naming the author of the plays as an inspired source, as coming from an inspired source, into someone who was obviously able to write and able to observe the nature around him in order to encapsulate these really miraculous, miraculous plays. But to me I find Francis Bacon the most likely candidate to be the author.

Or rather, he adds a little later, echoing Dawkins's arguments in *The Shakespeare Enigma*,

> when I say that I believe Francis Bacon wrote it, my personal belief is that he wrote that with a lot of other people helping, good pens as he called them. And I believe that [...] Devere was involved. I believe there were a lot of people involved in these works, [...] [p]eople who were collecting – I think Sir Water Raleigh and others who came back with information about travels abroad.

Picking up on the rhetoric of academic attribution and collaboration studies, Rylance creates a multiple authorship focussed on Bacon which can encompass a number of candidates and stand as a metaphor for inclusiveness and openness, with which academic pedantry and stubbornness can be contrasted. A decade later, the farewell *Tempest* programme included a page on the issue of authorship, reassuring the audience-member that '[w]hoever you believe Shakespeare to be – Protestant or Catholic, the son of a butcher or glover – you are welcome here at the Globe' (8), thus both implying that believing in a single historical Shakespeare is restrictive and exclusive and carefully aligning the issue of authorship with the Globe's trademark policy of making theatre available to as wide an audience as possible through its pricing of 'groundling' tickets, its local outreach schemes, and its strong education programme.[49]

The enthusiasm of the outgoing Artistic Director of Shakespeare's Globe for alternative authorship claims while aligning himself, through Prospero, with Shakespeare – though acting the part for the 2005 production in clothing and a tall hat modelled on images not of Shakespeare but of Bacon – marks what can perhaps best be described as a postmodern development in the utility of the discourse of lateness – postmodern, that is, in its eclecticism, its juxtaposition of tradition and innovation and its partially concealed conservatism.[50] In a frankly brilliant double manoeuvre, lateness is simultaneously deployed and dissolved – without the man, after all, you cannot have the man's late period – evaporating at the exact moment of identification of Shakespeare and Rylance and leaving only the latter in full view. His adoption of the strategies of subjectivism while denying the identity of the subject; his enacting of a traditional, subjectivist reading of *The Tempest* presented as radical by way of a mystical engagement with theatre rooted in a New Age version of late Romantic nostalgia; his deployment – made in part ironic through his ongoing emphasis on comedy and on *play* as the centrepiece of performance – of an institution which recreates a past while acknowledging that past's impossibility: all this make him undeniably a postmodern performer – indeed, it probably makes him a postmodern performance.

In the process, moreover, he sustains a twentieth-century theatrical tradition, since the two other celebrated British Shakespearean actors most frequently associated with an interest in the 'authorship question' are none other than the two Prosperos alongside whom Rylance played before he himself became Prospero – Sir Derek Jacobi and Sir John Gielgud. Both have, as it happens, endorsed the claim of the earl of Oxford rather than of Rylance's preferred claimant, Bacon. Gielgud was one of a group of prominent figures (including, *inter alios*, Sigmund Freud and Orson Welles) who announced themselves swayed in part or whole by the arguments of the poignantly named J. Thomas Looney in his 1920 book *Shakespeare Identified*.[51] Jacobi, for his part, wrote to thank the delegates to the 2005 Shakespeare Authorship Studies Conference, an Oxfordian organisation, for giving him an award for artistic excellence, acknowledging his 'grave doubts [. . .] of the validity of the Stratford man's claim to have written some of the greatest literature the world has produced' and stating that in his opinion the real author 'is most likely to have been Edward de Vere'.[52] Whichever candidate is chosen, however, the impetus to resist both documentary evidence and scholarly consensus is the same and, through his chairmanship of the all-embracing Shakespearean Authorship Trust and thus his apparent openness to all possible identities bar (despite the Trust's rhetoric) one, Rylance arguably in any case subsumes the positions of both Jacobi and Gielgud.

Working with the discourse of lateness, then, Rylance has deployed the career of Gielgud as an organising principle for his own, both asserting his status as the obvious successor – Ferdinand maturing to become Duke of Milan at Prospero's death – and reinstating the late conservatism of Gielgud's final Prospero while reclaiming the energies of the innovative Prosperos of Gielgud's early and mid-career. At the same time, by inhabiting the character of Prospero only (so far, at least) in his own early and mid-career, he has avoided the interpretative decline, the fossilising, that is arguably the inevitable result of a close identification with Shakespearean lateness over an entire lifetime. His 2005 *Tempest* emerges from a pattern of thought identical with that of the 1991 version – a vision just as essentialist in its premises, just as dependent upon an understanding of the play as the embodiment of a totalising spiritual philosophy, as it was fourteen years earlier. There has simply not been time for the premise of the performance to change as did that of Gielgud between 1930 and 1991. Moreover, echoing Gielgud's denial of the existence of the historical Shakespeare while at the same time playing Prospero at the age the historical Shakespeare had reached when writing the late plays enables a last brilliant double *coup*, not only allowing Rylance to challenge the tradition of the aged professional playing Prospero (and so to claim the role as his own three or four decades early) but also clearing the decks of the intrusion of a historical personality and thus enabling him to subsume Shakespeare himself for the occasion of his own (early) retirement from the Globe. In the process, he provides the clearest contemporary instance of the sustained utility of the idea of late Shakespeare, his anti-Stratfordianism extending a twentieth-century tradition – of actors playing Prospero as Shakespeare while denying Shakespeare's authorship of the plays – into the twenty-first century.[53]

6.5 POSTSCRIPT: LATE STYLE IN AUSTRALIA: BELL, PROSPERO, SHAKESPEARE

I completed this book in August 2006 as a Visiting Fellow at the Humanities Research Centre of the Australian National University in Canberra. Two weeks before I returned to London, the Bell Shakespeare Company, Australia's most established company dedicated to performing works from the Shakespeare canon, brought their latest production – a *Tempest* starring ex-RSC actor John Bell, their founder and principal artist, as Prospero – to the Canberra Theatre in a pared-down travelling production with minimal set and effects. Writing a preview article in the *Canberra Times*, Helen Musa addressed the production, predictably enough, in relation to Bell's age – he was sixty-five – beginning by citing the book-drowning speech of 'the ageing magician Prospero' but noting that 'just because John Bell is playing Prospero [. . .] it doesn't mean he is about to [. . .] retire':

> 'No way', as an invigorated Bell tells me as he plunges into a preview of *The Tempest* at the Victorian Arts Centre, 'I'm not going anywhere'.
> And why should he? Founder of his own Bell Shakespeare Company in 1990, he's no stranger to Prospero, and has done it twice before – once in 1990, under the direction of Neil Armfield, and once with Jim Sharman in a production that came to Canberra in 1997. 'Anyway, John Gielgud did it three or four times', he adds, 'so it's nonsense to say it's my swansong' (Musa, 6).

She expands on this theme:

> The play was, of course, *Shakespeare*'s swansong. Though he may have collaborated on a couple more works, *The Tempest* is his last masterpiece, after which he packed his bags and retired in comfort to Stratford-on-Avon. Not for long, Bell observes: he retired at 49 and was dead by 52. (ibid.; my italics)

Noting that this 'early retirement has teased scholarly minds', Musa asks in presumably unconscious homage to Henry James: 'Why would a brilliant writer, producer and director at the very height of his power [. . .] throw it all in?' The ageing but 'invigorated' Bell, though denying any desire to retire, offers a characteristically autobiographical suggestion:

> [T]he choice to retire early and rich was open to the Bard: he had made his pile, by contrast with Bell, who, having chosen the way of 'straight' theatre rather than,

say, Broadway musicals, has lived modestly throughout his career. Bell even channelled his $50,000 Keating Creative Arts Fellowship straight back into his company. So the question of retirement is, to him, notional, whereas to Shakespeare it was possible. (ibid.)

While the production has the shape of a retirement gesture, in other words, circumstances do not permit its resolution into fact.

The parallels with Rylance and, especially (as Bell himself is keen to point out), Gielgud are, of course, obvious – the Gielgud/Prospero relationship reworked through a close personal identification by a star actor both with his predecessors and with Shakespeare himself – and they become still clearer as the various other interviews Bell gave about the production, especially that with Clara Iaccarino in *The Sydney Morning Herald*. The central point of comparison is Bell's track-record over the years as Prospero. 'The first time' that he 'performed the role of Prospero, directed by Neil Armfield', Iaccarino notes, 'it was all about the rage', and Musa reinforces this, reporting that '[i]n his first go at the part, a tempest raged inside Prospero, giving his interpretation an angry edge'.[54] This was in 1990 at the Belvoir Street Theatre in Sydney. His second Prospero was similar, though rage modulated into anxiety. 'Propelled by the great magician's quest for revenge', we learn, 'he maintained the angst when he reprised the role for Jim Sharman's Bell Shakespeare production almost 10 years ago' (Iaccarino). 'The second time,' Musa amplifies, 'he found himself overwhelmed with grief at his loss of power and the impending loss of his daughter – in short, it was an angst-ridden interpretation' (Musa, 7). The connection between these two performances is clear enough: 'These early Prosperos didn't want to relinquish their power base and refused to let go'. 'But now', we learn,

the man who has spent 44 years breathing life into the works of his beloved Shakespeare says his third incarnation of *The Tempest*'s conjurer has mellowed. Not that he was ever a particularly angry man, but Bell says this Prospero is more benevolent and reflects his present state of mind. (Iaccarino)

'The age I am now', he explains, 'there's a kind of resignation about letting go and a relief of letting go. [I'm] mellower, more resigned to getting old, to passing on to the next generation' (Iaccarino). Throughout, the centrality to the production of Bell as personality is overt (as it is in his choice to employ in Peter Evans a young, relatively inexperienced director). Bell has a comfortable familiarity with the role:

Bell has done the research, already knows the lines and says reprising the role of Prospero is 'like putting on a pair of old slippers'. As Shakespeare's last play, *The*

Tempest is said to embody the spirit of the Bard in the character of Prospero, a claim Bell doesn't contest. As he performs the role he says it is helpful to think he is 'really speaking Shakespeare's thoughts and playing his feelings'. 'The parallels are too obvious to be ignored', Bell says, 'a great magician leaving his island, going into retirement, giving up his art. It seems pretty obvious to me'. (Iaccarino)

The implicit identification of Shakespeare and Bell, which has simmered throughout both interviews, refusal to retire notwithstanding, now becomes clearer in two ways, professional and domestic, which are connected with each other through the motif of the father. Bell, we are told – who is, in the slightly tendentious words of the interviewer, 'often dubbed the father of theatre in Australia' – 'shares deep parallels with Shakespeare. Like Shakespeare, Bell runs his own company, acts and directs', though, admittedly, 'he has never fancied himself as a writer'. Above all, he is a company man: 'His company', we are told, is Bell's 'whole life' – though this is immediately qualified by the merging of his theatrical life with his family life:

He admits it makes life easier having a family so entrenched in acting and theatrical pursuits. His wife, Anna Volska, directed Bell Shakespeare's latest regional touring production of *The Merchant Of Venice*; daughter Hilary writes for stage and screen; and Lucy is pursuing her acting career. His four grandchildren share centre stage and are also responsible for a mellowing Bell.

'It's really difficult', Bell admits, 'to separate one's life from one's work. The more you integrate them the more satisfying it is'. Subjectivism thus operates in reverse; if Shakespeare's personal life – including his baffling decision to retire – remains unexplained, that of his surrogate – Bell/Prospero/Shakespeare – need not and, fittingly enough for a late-play appropriation, daughters find themselves (in the rhetoric of the article, at least) 'centre stage'.

As Bell made clear in a radio interview a year earlier, there is one other role still unquestionably available to him:

I've pretty well done the great Shakespeare roles and I'm too old now to play many of them again. I could do another King Lear some time – it is tempting to because it is such an extraordinary play – and I'm going to revive Prospero next year in *The Tempest* which is another role I love playing and you can do that pretty well until you're 90 so I can have another bash at that one. (*Sunday Profile* interview)

The Gielgud identification was clearly there from the start. More to the point, Bell acknowledges that perhaps the last great Shakespearean role left to him at his age is Lear, before resolutely turning the tables on the relentless focus on endings: 'Now I guess that's probably about it, you know, but I would certainly, haven't ruled myself out of doing more new plays, Australian plays. There just simply hasn't been the time in my career to do much of that but again I wouldn't knock out the possibility' (ibid). This combination of patriarchy, *The Tempest*, *King Lear* and the possibility of a resurgence as an actor and promoter of new Australian plays as a kind of return to roots makes it clear that Bell is performing a version of lateness in direct contrast to the recent, politicised tradition of 'Reconciliation Shakespeare' – productions, that is, which deploy *The Tempest*'s celebrated colonial roots in order to address the relationship between indigenous and Anglo-European Australian history and to foreground the experience of Aborigines in the history of modern Australia. Finessing the pressing question of retirement through the deliberate adoption of the persona of Prospero who could in any case, he notes, be a whole range of ages – 'Bell has been doing his calculations', Musa announces, 'and he's figured out that with Prospero's daughter Miranda in her teens, he could be in his late 30s, or as old as 80' (Musa, 6) – he deploys the prospect of performing in new Australian plays as a version of the simultaneous looking back and looking forward characteristic of late style, more specifically perhaps as a late return from postcolonial exile, metaphorically speaking, to home turf.[55] His Prospero thus operates with a high degree of self-consciousness within the parameters established by Gielgud and developed by Rylance over the same period of years as Bell, who negotiates the central issues of identity, age, professional status and retirement through a series of performances over time, adding the extra element of his own negotiations as an Australian actor with England's national poet – a version perhaps (one might, a touch mischievously, suggest) of Shakespeare's own negotiation with the Virgil of *The Aeneid* in *The Tempest*. In so doing, his adopted role as testamentary act(or) allows him a clear place in the performative tradition of celebrated theatre professionals identifying with Prospero that is arguably the most current manifestation of the discourse of Shakespearean lateness.

Notes

INTRODUCTION

1. *The Life and Letters of Sir Henry Wotton*, ed. Logan Pearsall Smith, 2 vols. (Oxford: Clarendon Press, 1907), 2: 33.
2. *Richard II*, 2.1.11. This and all subsequent citations from Shakespeare's plays are taken from Stanley Wells, Gary Taylor, John Jowett and William Montgomery (eds.), *William Shakespeare: The Complete Works*, Second Edition (Oxford: Clarendon Press, 2005).
3. Anthony B. Dawson, '*Tempest* in a Teapot: Critics, Evaluation, Ideology', in Maurice Charney (ed.), *"Bad" Shakespeare: Revaluations of the Shakespeare Canon* (Rutherford: Fairleigh Dickinson University Press, 1988), 61–73 (hereafter 'Dawson').
4. Dawson is here echoing Theodore Spencer, who imagined 'a deputation calling on Shakespeare – it is not an agreeable thought – to suggest that, all things considered, it would be wise to go home and write no more'; see Spencer, 'The Two Noble Kinsmen', *Modern Philology* 36 (1939), 255–76 (257).
5. Kenneth Clark, *The Artist Grows Old*, The Rede Lecture 1970 (Cambridge University Press, 1972), 19.
6. See, *inter alia*, Stephen G. Greenblatt, *Marvelous Possessions: The Wonder of the New World* (Chicago: University of Chicago Press, 1992); T. G. Bishop, *Shakespeare and the Theatre of Wonder* (Cambridge University Press, 1996); Peter G. Platt, *Reason Diminished: Shakespeare and the Marvelous* (Lincoln: University of Nebraska Press, 1997); and, most recently, Daniel Fusch, 'Wonder and Ceremonies of Waking in Shakespeare's Late Plays', *Mediterranean Studies* 14 (2005), 125–47.
7. Sidney Lee (ed.), *The Complete Works of William Shakespeare*, vol. 16, *The Tempest*, with a special introduction by Henry James, 'Renaissance Edition' (London: Harrap, 1907), ix–xxxii (xx); reprinted in Henry James, *Literary Criticism*, ed. Leon Edel, with Mark Wilson (New York: The Library of America, 1984), 1205–20.
8. A notable, if extreme, recent instance of the appropriation of the late plays for a particular ideological purpose is Stephen W. Smith and Travis Curtright's *Shakespeare's Last Plays: Essays in Literature and Politics* (Lanham, MD: Lexington Books, 2002), in which the editors set up the late plays as exemplary texts for

demonstrating the limitations, as they see them, of recent critical approaches, notably cultural materialism, feminism and 'local reading'. One of the contributors, R. V. Young, describing such approaches as fundamentally 'anti-intellectual', suggests with ponderous irony that, since a 'materialist critic ascribes the phenomenon of literature to the interaction of social forces,' it would surely make sense to 'cut out the middleman and [...] go straight to [...] the political scientist or the sociologist', adding that the problems of the limitations of such an approach are 'especially acute for the literary critic dealing with Shakespeare's late romances, which are among his most elusive and ethereal plays' ('"Fresh piece of excellent witchcraft": Contemporary Theory and Shakespeare's Romances,' in Smith and Curtright, *Shakespeare's Last Plays*, 217–38 (234, 218)). '[N]owhere', he proceeds, 'does the odd combination of outrageous conjecture and reductive banality, which are so much a part of the enterprise of new historicism and cultural materialism, emerge so blatantly' ('Fresh piece', 218).

9. Robert Butler, 'The Life Review: An Interpretation of Reminiscence in the Aged', *Psychiatry* 26 (1963), 65–76 (66), reprinted in Bernice L. Neugarten (ed.), *Middle Age and Aging: A Reader in Social Psychology* (Chicago: University of Chicago Press, 1968), 486–96.

10. See Thomas R. Cole, Robert Kastenbaum and Ruth E. Ray (eds.), *Handbook of the Humanities and Aging*, Second Edition (New York: Springer, 2000). In order to map developments in the field, see also the first edition: Thomas R. Cole, David D. Van Tassel and Robert Kastenbaum, *Handbook of the Humanities and Aging* (New York: Springer, 1992); and see Chapter 5, 267–71.

11. Havelock Ellis, *Impressions and Comments*, Third (and Final) Series, 1920–1923 (Boston: Houghton Mifflin, 1924), 6. I am grateful to both John Stokes and Max Saunders for bringing Ellis to my attention.

12. C. J. Sisson, *The Mythical Sorrows of Shakespeare*, Annual Shakespeare Lecture of the British Academy, Proceedings of the British Academy, Vol. 20 (London: Milford, 1934); C. J. Sisson, 'Studies in the Life and Environment of Shakespeare since 1900', *Shakespeare Survey* 3 (1950), 1–12 (9).

13. Catherine M. Soussloff, 'Old Age and Old-Age Style in the "Lives" of Artists: Gianlorenzo Bernini', *Art Journal* 46 (1987), 115–121.

14. Kathleen Woodward notes the work yet to be done on this subject: 'Just as for feminists, experience has been an important touchstone, so for those of us committed to age studies, the tension between discourses of age and experiences of aging requires exploration'; see Woodward, 'Introduction', in Woodward (ed.), *Figuring Age: Women, Bodies, Generations* (Bloomington: Indiana University Press, 1999), ix–xxix (x).

15. Edward Said, *On Late Style* (London: Bloomsbury, 2006); see also my review in *TLS*, September 29, 2006, 30.

16. Karen Painter and Thomas Crow, *Late Thoughts: Reflections on Artists and Composers at Work*, Issues and Debates 14 (Los Angeles: Getty Publications, 2006).

17. Sam Smiles, *The Late Work of Artists*, forthcoming. Professor Smiles, taking Turner as his paradigm case, examines the development of the idea of late style in the history of art and establishes a genealogy for the concept.

18. Ian Bent (ed.), *Music Analysis in the Nineteenth Century*, vol. 1, *Fugue, Form and Style* (Cambridge University Press, 1994).
19. Maynard Solomon, *Late Beethoven: Music, Thought, Imagination* (Berkeley and Los Angeles: University of California, Press, 2003); Joseph N. Straus, *Stravinsky's Late Music*, Cambridge Studies in Music Theory and Analysis 16 (Cambridge University Press, 2001).
20. The concert was the UK première of the *Suite on Verses of Michelangelo*, performed by John Shirley-Quirk with the Royal Liverpool Philharmonic Orchestra and women's choir conducted by Sir Charles Groves, 16 April 1977.
21. On *Sanditon* as fragmented and problematically 'buoyant' late writing, see Clara Tuite, *Romantic Austen: Sexual Politics and the Literary Canon* (Cambridge University Press, 2002), 156–91. I'm grateful to Kate Newey for pointing me to Tuite.
22. For the works, see the exhibition catalogue: Alain Blondel and Ingried Brugger, *Tamara de Lempicka* (London: Royal Academy of Arts, 2004).
23. The case of Emily Kngwarreye presents the opposite problem. Can a career lasting less than a decade and commencing in the artist's late seventies have, or comprise, a late phase?
24. Kathleen Woodward, *Aging and its Discontents: Freud and Other Fictions* (Bloomington: Indiana University Press, 1991), 192; see below, 265–8.
25. Sigmund Freud, *The Interpretation of Dreams*, in *The Standard Edition of the Complete Psychological Works of Sigmund Freud*, trans. and gen. ed. James Strachey in collaboration with Anna Freud, vol. 5 (London: The Hogarth Press, 1953), 457.
26. Freud, 'Femininity', in *Standard Edition*, vol. 22 (1964), 134–5.
27. Hélène Cixous, 'The Author in Truth', in *Coming to Writing and Other Essays: Hélène Cixous*, ed. Deborah Jenson (Cambridge, MA and London: Harvard University Press, 1991), 136–181 (136).
28. Hélène Cixous, 'The Last Painting or the Portrait of God', in *Coming to Writing*, 104–131 (115).
29. Edward Dowden, '*Middlemarch* and *Daniel Deronda*,' *Contemporary Review* 29 (February 1877), 348–69 (361).

1 SHAKESPEARE AND THE IDEA OF LATE WRITING: AUTHORSHIP IN THE PROXIMITY OF DEATH

1. Edith Wharton on the death of Henry James: 'His dying was slow and harrowing. The final stroke had been preceded by one or two premonitory ones, each causing a diminution just marked enough for the still conscious intelligence to register it, and the sense of disintegration must have been tragically intensified to a man like James, who had so often and deeply pondered on it, so intently watched for its first symptoms. He is said to have told his old friend Lady Prothero, when she saw him after the first stroke, that in the very act of falling (he was dressing at the time) he heard in the room a voice which was distinctly, it seemed not his own, saying: "So here it is at last, the distinguished thing". The phrase is too beautifully

characteristic not to be recorded. He saw the distinguished thing coming, faced it, and received it with words worthy of all his dealings with life', in Wharton, *A Backward Glance* (New York: Appleton-Century, 1934), 366–7.
2. *Richard II*, 2.1.5–6.
3. Musée Picasso, Paris 4, visited March 2002. The catalogue is *Le dernier Picasso, 1953–1973*, ed. Marie-Laure Bernadac, Isabelle Monod-Fontaine and David Sylvester (Paris: Editions du Centre Pompidou, 1988). It is worth noting that by no means all art critics would agree with this celebratory account. For Hugo Munsterberg, for instance, echoing John Berger and Clement Greenberg (the first of whom, at least, expressed his opinions on Picasso's late style decades before the artist actually died), the output of Picasso's later years 'lacked any real merit', offering a mere 'decorative playfulness' rather than the 'tension and expressive power' he associates with a true old-age style, and he includes his discussion of Picasso in a chapter entitled 'Past the Peak' – a very different viewpoint indeed from that offered by the final room of the Musée Picasso. See Hugo Munsterberg, *The Crown of Life: Artistic Creativity in Old Age* (New York: Harcourt Brace Jovanovich, 1983), 183.
4. See Pierre Bourdieu, *The Field of Cultural Production: Essays on Art and Literature*, ed. Randal Johnson (Cambridge: Polity, 1993), 136, 189 (also, in a slightly different vein, 104).
5. This was uncomfortably showcased by way of cinematic cliché in *Conspiracy*, a 2001 BBC/HBO film about the Wannsee conference (the meeting in 1942 at which the Holocaust was bureaucratically initiated), in which Kenneth Branagh played SS leader Reinhard Heydrich, the sophistication of whose evil was represented by his connoisseur's appreciation not only of the music of Schubert but specifically of that composer's late work.
6. Joseph N. Straus, *Stravinsky's Late Music* (Cambridge University Press, 2001), xiii.
7. Thomas Mann plays games with the question of the return to the early: 'The house and its surroundings in which Adrian later as a mature man settled down [. . .] were a most extraordinary likeness and reproduction of his childhood home; in other words, the scene of his later days bore a curious resemblance to that of his early ones. I never spoke to Adrian about this whole singular and very obvious parallel. I did not want to do so in the beginning, and later I no longer wanted to. I never cared for the phenomenon. [. . .] Was that artificial 'return' simply a whim? I cannot think so': Thomas Mann, *Doctor Faustus*, trans. H. T. Lowe-Porter (Harmondsworth: Penguin, 1968; first published in German 1947), 30–1.
8. Erich Neumann, 'Art and Time', in *Art and the Creative Unconscious: Four Essays*, trans. Ralph Manheim (Princeton University Press, 1959; originally published in German 1954), 81–134 (106).
9. Ibid., 103. 'Numinosum', meaning a mystical or religious experience with a source beyond oneself, is the Jungian version of a term coined by Rudolf Otto – the 'numinous' – to describe the 'holy', i.e. that which is wholly other; see Otto, *The Idea of the Holy*, trans. John W. Harvey (London: Oxford University Press, 1923), esp. 5–7.

10. Hermann Broch, 'The Style of the Mythical Age', introductory essay to Rachel Bespaloff, *On The Iliad*, trans. Mary McCarthy (New York: Pantheon, 1947), 11.
11. Some of Adorno's writing on late Beethoven predates and some of it postdates Broch's and Neumann's work, ranging from a 1934 essay (first published in 1937 and later collected in *Moments musicaux*) to a radio interview from 1966, though he probably reached his widest audience through his ghost-writing of the Kretschmar (or, better, Kretzschmar, to retain the echo of Nietzsche lost in the anglicised spelling) lectures in Thomas Mann's 1947 *Doctor Faustus*. On Adorno and lateness, see Said, *On Late Style*, esp. 3–24, a section reworked from Said's essay, 'Adorno as Lateness Itself', in Nigel Gibson and Andrew Rubin (eds.), *Adorno: A Critical Reader* (Oxford: Blackwell, 2002), 193–208; on Adorno and Mann, see *On Late Style*, 8–9.
12. Theodor W. Adorno, *Beethoven: The Philosophy of Music. Fragments and Texts*, ed. Rolf Tiedemann, trans. Edmund Jephcott (Cambridge: Polity, 1998; first published in German 1993).
13. On Adorno and mediation, see Max Paddison, *Adorno's Aesthetics of Music* (Cambridge University Press, 1993), esp. Chapter 3.
14. Rose Rosengard Subotnik, 'Adorno's Diagnosis of Beethoven's Late Style: Early Symptom of a Fatal Condition', *Journal of the American Musicological Society* 29 (1976), 251–3 (254).
15. Theodor W. Adorno, *Aesthetic Theory*, trans. C. Lenhardt, ed. Gretel Adorno and Rolf Tiedemann (London: Routledge & Kegan Paul, 1984), 67.
16. Herbert Butterfield, *Christianity and History* (London: Bell, 1949), 121. As is, I'm sure, true for many others, my attention was drawn to Butterfield by Frank Kermode's *Sense of an Ending: Studies in the Theory of Fiction* (New York: Oxford University Press, 2000 'with a New Epilogue'; first published 1967). For a gentle modification of Butterfield's aphorism, see D. Rudolf Bultmann, *History and Eschatology* (Edinburgh: University of Edinburgh Press, 1957), 154.
17. Kenneth Muir, *Last Periods of Shakespeare, Racine, and Ibsen* (Liverpool University Press, 1961), 8 (hereafter, 'Muir').
18. Edward Said, 'Thoughts on Late Style', *London Review of Books* 26 (5 August, 2004), 3–7; see also Said, *On Late Style*, 148.
19. Anon., *Notes on Goethe Extracted from the Bibliothèque Universelle de Génève*, in Sarah Austin, *Characteristics of Goethe*, 3 vols. (London, 1833), 3: 1–96 (81–2).
20. Edward Said, 'Untimely Meditations,' review of Maynard Solomon, *Late Beethoven: Music, Thought, Imagination*, in *The Nation* 277 (September 2003), 38–42 (38).
21. Said, 'Untimely', 40; see also *On Late Style*, 6–7.
22. Jacqueline Rose, 'More writing to be done: Jacqueline Rose remembers Edward Said', *The Observer*, 5 October 2003, seen online at http://books.guardian.co.uk/news/articles/0,6109,1055838,00.html.
23. J. W. Mackail, 'The Note of Shakespeare's Romances' in Mackail, *Lectures on Poetry* (London: Longmans, Green, 1911), 208–30 (230).
24. Edward Dowden, *Shakspere: A Critical Study of his Mind and Art* (London: Henry S. King, 1875), 379. On Dowden's life and career, see Kathryn R. Ludwigson, *Edward Dowden* (New York: Twayne, 1973).

25. Edward Dowden, *Shakspere*, Literature Primers (London: Macmillan, 1877), 58, 59.
26. Walter Raleigh, *Shakespeare*, English Men of Letters (London: Macmillan, 1926), 212. I am grateful to Kevin de Ornellas for directing me to Raleigh's comments on Shakespearean lateness.
27. There have been several overviews of the state of late-play criticism over the last half-century including Hallett Smith, 'Shakespeare's Romances', *Huntington Library Quarterly* 27 (1964), 279–87; Philip Edwards, 'The Late Comedies', in Stanley Wells (ed.), *Shakespeare: Select Bibliographical Guides* (Oxford University Press, 1973); F. David Hoeniger, 'Shakespeare's Romances Since 1958: A Retrospect', *Shakespeare Survey* 29 (1976), 1–10; Norman Sanders, 'An Overview of Critical Approaches to the Romances', in Carol McGinnis Kay and Henry E. Jacobs (eds.), *Shakespeare's Romances Reconsidered* (Lincoln, NE: University of Nebraska Press, 1978), 1–10; and Boika Sokolova, *Shakespeare's Romances as Interrogative Texts: Their Alienation Strategies and Ideology* (Lampeter and Lewiston, NY: Edwin Mellen Press, 1992), 4–13.
28. Russ McDonald, *Shakespeare's Late Style* (Cambridge University Press, 2006), 9.
29. Cyrus Hoy, *The Hyacinth Room: An Investigation into the Nature of Comedy, Tragedy, & Tragicomedy* (London: Chatto & Windus, 1964), 300 (hereafter 'Hoy').
30. See, *inter alia*, Northrop Frye, *Anatomy of Criticism* (Princeton University Press, 1957) and *A Natural Perspective: The Development of Shakespearean Comedy and Romance* (New York: Columbia University Press, 1965); G. Wilson Knight, *The Shakespearian Tempest* (London: Oxford University Press, 1932) and *The Crown of Life* (London: Oxford University Press, 1947), and, by way of commentary, Philip Edwards, 'Wilson Knight and Shakespeare's Last Plays', in John M. Mucciolo (ed.) with Steven J. Doloff and Edward A. Rauchut, *Shakespeare's Universe: Renaissance Ideas and Conventions: Essays in Honor of W. R. Elton* (Aldershot: Scolar Press, 1996), 258–67.
31. The less forgiving prewar critics include D. G. James and H. B. Charlton, whose work I discuss in Chapter 3: see 163–5.
32. Kiernan Ryan (ed.), *Shakespeare: The Last Plays* (London: Longman, 1999), 1.
33. Walter Benjamin, 'The Storyteller: Reflections on the Works of Nikolai Leskov', in *Illuminations*, ed. Hannah Arendt, trans. Harry Zohn (London: Cape, 1970), 100. I'm grateful to Howard Marchitello for commenting closely on this chapter and for pointing me to Benjamin.

2 THE SHAKESPEAREAN CAESURA: GENRE, CHRONOLOGY, STYLE

1. Kenneth Muir, *Shakespeare's Comic Sequence* (Liverpool University Press, 1979), 148.
2. G. K. Hunter, 'The Social Function of Annotation', in Ann Thompson and Gordon McMullan (eds.), *In Arden: Editing Shakespeare. Essays in Honour of Richard Proudfoot* (London: Arden Shakespeare, 2003), 180; Dowden, *Mind*

and Art, 403 (the lack of italics for play-titles is his). On the question of the literary intentions of the Folio, see Lukas Erne, *Shakespeare as Literary Dramatist* (Cambridge University Press, 2003) and, by contrast, David Scott Kastan, *Shakespeare After Theory* (New York: Routledge, 1999), 59–92, and, more fully, *Shakespeare and the Book* (Cambridge University Press, 2001), 50–78. See also Chapter 4, 202ff.

3. E. M. W. Tillyard, *Shakespeare's Last Plays* (London: Chatto & Windus, 1938); Robert Ornstein, *Shakespeare's Comedies: From Roman Farce to Romantic Mystery* (Cranbury, NJ: Associated University Presses, 1986); Robert Henke, *Pastoral Transformations: Italian Tragicomedy and Shakespeare's Late Plays* (Newark: University of Delaware Press, 1997).

4. Derek Traversi, *Shakespeare: The Last Phase* (London: Hollis & Carter, 1954); Frank Kermode, *William Shakespeare: The Final Plays*, Writers and Their Work (London: Longman, 1963); Douglas L. Peterson, *Time, Tide, and Tempest: A Study of Shakespeare's Romances* (San Marino, CA: Huntington Library, 1973); Ruth Nevo, *Shakespeare's Other Language* (New York: Methuen, 1987); Marco Mincoff, *Things Supernatural and Causeless: Shakespearean Romance* (Newark: University of Delaware Press, 1992; first published Sofia, 1987); Robert M. Adams, *Shakespeare: The Four Romances* (New York: W. W. Norton, 1989); Maurice Hunt, *Shakespeare's Romance of the Word* (Lewisburg, PA: Bucknell University Press, 1990); Cynthia Marshall, *Shakespearean Eschatology: Last Things and Last Plays* (Carbondale and Edwardsville: Southern Illinois University Press, 1991); Simon Palfrey, *Late Shakespeare: A New World of Words* (Oxford: Clarendon Press, 1997). Kermode discusses *The Two Noble Kinsmen*, too, though he concludes that it 'is best thought of as a play by Fletcher to which Shakespeare contributed' (*Final Plays*, 52), rather than an integral part of the 'final plays'. Hunt, writing in 1990, mentions *Henry VIII* once in passing, with no reference to its place in the chronology, and *The Two Noble Kinsmen* not at all. Marshall, writing a year later, mentions neither.

5. See Coleridge's 1811–12 lecture on *The Tempest*, where (at least in Collier's report of the lecture) he describes the play as 'a specimen of the romantic drama'; see Terence Hawkes (ed.), *Coleridge on Shakespeare* (Harmondsworth: Penguin, 1969), 224; and see William Hazlitt, *Characters of Shakespear's Plays* (London: Reynell, 1817), 1, where he describes *Cymbeline* as 'a dramatic romance'.

6. E. C. Pettet, *Shakespeare and the Romance Tradition*, with an introduction by H. S. Bennet (London: Staples Press, 1949); Northrop Frye, *A Natural Perspective: The Development of Shakespearean Comedy and Romance* (New York: Columbia University Press, 1965); Stanley Wells, 'Shakespeare and Romance', in John Russell Brown and Bernard Harris (eds.), *Later Shakespeare*, Stratford-upon-Avon Studies 8 (London: Arnold, 1966), 49–79; Howard Felperin, *Shakespearean Romance* (Princeton University Press, 1972); Barbara A. Mowat, *The Dramaturgy of Shakespeare's Romances* (Athens: University of Georgia Press, 1977); Robert Uphaus, *Beyond Tragedy: Structure and Experience in Shakespeare's Romances* (Lexington: The University Press of Kentucky, 1981).

7. See also Richard Hillman, '*The Tempest* as Romance and Anti-Romance', *University of Toronto Quarterly* 55 (1985–6), 141–60.
8. Elizabeth Bieman, *William Shakespeare: The Romances*, Twayne's English Authors Series 478 (Boston: Twayne, 1990), 2 (hereafter, 'Bieman').
9. Alison Thorne (ed.), *Shakespeare's Romances*, 'New Casebooks' (Basingstoke: Palgrave Macmillan, 2003), 3–4 (hereafter, 'Thome').
10. Barbara A. Mowat, '"What's in a Name?" Tragicomedy, Romance, or Late Comedy', in Richard Dutton and Jean E. Howard (eds.), *A Companion to Shakespeare's Works*, 4 vols, vol. 4: *The Poems, Problem Comedies, Late Plays* (Oxford: Blackwell, 2003), 129–49 (hereafter, 'Mowat'). On the 1606 production of *Mucedorus*, see Richard T. Thornberry, 'A Seventeenth-Century Revival of *Mucedorus* in London Before 1610', *Shakespeare Quarterly* 28 (1977), 362–4.
11. Helen Cooper, *The English Romance in Time: Transforming Motifs from Geoffrey of Monmouth to the Death of Shakespeare* (Oxford University Press, 2004; hereafter 'Cooper').
12. See Hans Robert Jauss, *Towards an Aesthetic of Reception*, trans. Timothy Bahti (Minneapolis: University of Minnesota Press, 1982), 22–4; Thorne, 4.
13. Barbara Fuchs, *Romance* (London: Routledge, 2004), 1–2.
14. Diana T. Childress, 'Are Shakespeare's Late Plays Really Romances?', in Richard C. Tobias and Paul G. Zolbrod (eds.), *Shakespeare's Late Plays: Essays in Honor of Charles Crow* (Athens: Ohio University Press, 1974), 44–55 (45).
15. Robert Henke, *Pastoral Transformations: Italian Tragicomedy and Shakespeare's Late Plays* (Newark: University of Delaware Press, 1997), 40.
16. Gary Schmidgall, *Shakespeare and the Courtly Aesthetic* (Berkeley and Los Angeles: University of California Press, 1981), xv.
17. Ashley Thorndike, *The Influence of Beaumont and Fletcher on Shakspere* (Worcester, MA: Wood, 1901); Marvin T. Herrick, *Tragicomedy: Its Origins and Development in Italy, France, and England* (Urbana: University of Illinois Press, 1955); Frank H. Ristine, *English Tragicomedy: Its Origin and History* (New York: Russell & Russell, 1963); Joan Hartwig, *Shakespeare's Tragicomic Vision* (Baton Rouge: Louisiana State University Press, 1972); Verna A. Foster, *The Name and Nature of Tragicomedy* (Aldershot: Ashgate, 2004). Guarini's theories are expounded in his *Compendio della poesia tragicomica, tratto dai duo Verati, per opera dell'autore del pastor fido, colla giunta di molte cose spettanti all'arte* (Venice, 1601), but the first attack on Guarini appeared, long before he had published either his pastoral tragicomedy *Il Pastor Fido* or the *Compendio*, in Giason Denores's *Discorsi di Iason DeNores intorno à que' principii, cause, et accrescimenti, che la comedia, la tragedia, et il poema eroico ricevono dalla philosophia morale, e civile, e da' governatori delle repubbliche* (Padua, 1586).
18. See Gordon McMullan and Jonathan Hope (eds.), *The Politics of Tragicomedy: Shakespeare and After* (London: Routledge, 1991), 2–7.
19. Ben Jonson, 'The Induction on the Stage' to *Bartholomew Fair*, in C. H. Herford, Percy Simpson and Evelyn Simpson (eds.), *Ben Jonson*, 11 vols. (1925–52), vol. 6 (Oxford: Clarendon Press, 1938), 16.

20. David Norbrook, '"What Cares These Roarers for the Name of King?" Language and Utopia in *The Tempest*', in McMullan and Hope, 21–54 (24).
21. David M. Bergeron, 'The Politics and Technology of Spectacle in the Late Plays', in Dutton and Howard, *Companion*, 194–215 (213).
22. In any case, as Jonathan Hope and I argued in our introduction to *The Politics of Tragicomedy*, 1–7, Fletcher's prefatory note, 'To the Reader', to the quarto of *The Faithful Shepheredess* does not represent the form of tragicomedy as it subsequently developed in his work with Beaumont and, later, Massinger and/or others, which is at best obliquely related to pastoral and frequently not at all.
23. Childress, 'Late Plays', 44–55. See also Jonathan Hartwell, '"Skill in the Construction": Dramaturgy, Ideology, and Interpretation in Shakespeare's Late Plays,' unpublished PhD thesis, University of Birmingham (2003), Ch. 1.
24. A. D. Nuttall, *William Shakespeare: The Winter's Tale*, Studies in English Literature 26 (London: Arnold, 1966), 10.
25. Nosworthy, the Arden 2 editor, felt that 'the only claim that can be advanced with real confidence is that *Cymbeline* falls within the range 1606–1611'; see William Shakespeare, *Cymbeline*, ed. J. M. Nosworthy, The Arden Shakespeare (London: Methuen, 1955), xvii. The Oxford editors are more precise, but not much more. There was a court performance of *The Tempest* on 1 November 1611, but it is generally dated in relation to Strachey's narrative of the Bermuda voyage, which first became available in England in late 1610.
26. On the details of the dating, see Suzanne Gossett (ed.), *Pericles*, The Arden Shakespeare (London: Thomson Learning, 2004), 54–62.
27. Philip Edwards, *Shakespeare: A Writer's Progress* (Oxford University Press, 1987), 178. In arguing for the lastness of *Cymbeline*, Edwards demonstrates a preference for a Shakespearean conclusion in national history which arguably aligns him with Knight. J. W. Mackail had also argued for *Cymbeline*'s status as 'the latest of the romances', though rather coyly refusing to say why ('for several reasons into which it is not possible to enter here') (Mackail, 223).
28. 'Q' [Sir Arthur Quiller-Couch], 'General Introduction', in Quiller-Couch and John Dover Wilson (eds.), *The Tempest*, The New Shakespeare (Cambridge University Press, 1921), xxvii.
29. Larry S. Champion, *The Evolution of Shakespeare's Comedy: A Study in Dramatic Perspective* (Cambridge, MA: Harvard University Press, 1970), 97.
30. See Barroll, *Politics, Plague, and Shakespeare's Theatre: The Stuart Years* (Ithaca: Cornell University Press, 1991), 172–209 (esp. 205), on dating the late plays.
31. Valerie Wayne, 'Dating *Cymbeline* with the help of Arbella Stuart', paper submitted to SAA seminar, April 2006, which will form part of the introduction to her forthcoming Arden *Cymbeline*. I'm grateful to Professor Wayne for letting me see this paper and other material towards her edition. See also Paul Reyher, 'La date de "Cymbelyne"', *Revue Anglo-Américaine* (June 1925), 428–30.
32. G. Wilson Knight, *The Crown of Life: Essays in Interpretation of Shakespeare's Final Plays* (London: Oxford University Press, 1947), 336.

33. Tillyard, *Last*, 17; J. Dover Wilson, *Six Tragedies of Shakespeare: An Introduction for the Plain Man*, Workers' Educational Association Outlines (London: Longman, 1929), 46; Wilson, *The Essential Shakespeare: A Biographical Adventure* (Cambridge University Press, 1932), 126; G. Wilson Knight, *The Wheel of Fire: Essays in Interpretation of Shakespeare's Sombre Tragedies* (London: Oxford University Press, 1930), 226, 192.
34. McDonald, *Shakespeare's Late Style*, 181. Professor McDonald, with considerable generosity, handed me the typescript of his book as it went to press. That I travelled twenty-four thousand miles or so in its company is a testimony to its significance for my own work on Shakespeare and lateness.
35. Lawrence Danson, *Shakespeare's Dramatic Genres*, Oxford Shakespeare Topics (Oxford University Press, 2000), 7.
36. See Brian Vickers, *Shakespeare, Co-Author: A Historical Study of Five Collaborative Plays* (Oxford University Press, 2002), 44–134.
37. See William Shakespeare and John Fletcher, *Henry VIII*, ed. Gordon McMullan, The Arden Shakespeare (London: Thomson Learning, 2000), 180.
38. Sir William H. Bailey, *Henry the VIII. and the Last Work of Shakespeare* (Inaugural Address, Manchester Shakespeare Society, 21 October 1902), 6.
39. E. M. W. Tillyard, *Shakespeare's History Plays* (London: Chatto & Windus, 1944; reprinted Penguin, 1962), 8.
40. Kenneth Muir and Sean O'Loughlin, *The Voyage to Illyria: A New Study of Shakespeare* (London: Methuen, 1937), 221 n. 1.
41. Robert Adams, *Shakespeare: The Four Romances* (New York: Norton, c. 1989), 3.
42. Cynthia Marshall, *Last Things and Last Plays: Shakespearean Eschatology* (Carbondale: Southern Illinois University Press, 1991), xiv.
43. Shakespeare's lack of commitment to collaboration with Fletcher is dramatised in a play written by the critic Horace Howard Furness. 'I cannot, nor I will not write at *thy* behest', says the ageing Shakespeare with a combination of haughtiness and weariness: 'I told thee, Jack, I was sick at heart with all of this' – 'this' being the task of writing *The Two Noble Kinsmen*. See Furness, *The Gloss of Youth: An Imaginary Episode in the Lives of William Shakespeare and John Fletcher* (Philadelphia: Lippincott, 1920), 15, 16. The date given for this conversation is April 1615. In the course of the short play, Shakespeare meets a far worthier Jack/John to be his poetic replacement in the person of the boy Milton, who is friends with another young lad named Oliver Cromwell.
44. William Shakespeare, *King Henry VIII*, ed. R. A. Foakes, The Arden Shakespeare (London: Methuen, 1957), xvii–xxvi; but see also Foakes's 'Postscript, 1962' in the reprint.
45. John Fletcher and William Shakespeare, *The Two Noble Kinsmen*, ed. Lois Potter, The Arden Shakespeare (Walton-on-Thames: Thomas Nelson, 1997), 13, 14.
46. See William Shakespeare and John Fletcher, *Cardenio, or, The Second Maiden's Tragedy*, ed. Charles Hamilton (Lakewood, CO: Glenbridge, c. 1994). Hamilton's claim that *The Second Maiden's Tragedy* is in fact the lost

Cardenio has not been accepted by scholars; the play appears in the forthcoming *Oxford Middleton*, general editor Gary Taylor.
47. Jenifer Richards and James Knowles (eds.), *Shakespeare's Late Plays: New Readings* (Edinburgh University Press, 1999).
48. Curiously, Traversi inverts his own argument when seeking to dismiss Fletcher's role: 'The parallels with Fletcher, indeed, in so far as they exist, make themselves felt most strongly at the moment in which Shakespeare (as in certain scenes of *Cymbeline*) is least himself' (*Last Phase*, 1). A high degree of flexibility in the critical understanding of authorial selfhood is clearly required in order to account for the collaborations.
49. Ashley Thorndike, *The Influence of Beaumont and Fletcher on Shakspere* (Worcester, MA: Oliver B. Wood, 1901).
50. See Thorndike's discussion at 152–60.
51. On collaborative playwriting as a norm in early modern London, see Chapter 4, 233–4.
52. Harley Granville-Barker, *Prefaces to Shakespeare, Second Series* (London: Sidgwick & Jackson, 1930), '*Cymbeline*', 234.
53. G. E. Bentley, 'Shakespeare and the Blackfriars Theatre', *Shakespeare Survey* 1 (1948), 38–50 (46).
54. Andrew Gurr, '*The Tempest*'s Tempest at Blackfriars', *Shakespeare Survey* 41 (1988), 91–102 (92).
55. On *Henry VIII* and the Globe fire, see McMullan (ed.), *Henry VIII*, 57–63.
56. Irwin Smith, *Shakespeare's Blackfriars Playhouse: Its History and Design* (London: Peter Owen, 1966), 220–42.
57. John Jowett, 'New Created Creatures: Ralph Crane and the Stage Directions in *The Tempest*', *Shakespeare Survey* 36 (1983), 107–20.
58. Tiffany Stern, *Making Shakespeare: From Stage to Page* (London: Routledge, 2004), 29. Cf., though, Simon Palfrey, who notes that 'the closest [Shakespeare's work] gets' to the kinds of play written for the children at the Blackfriars 'is probably *Henry VIII*' (*Late Shakespeare*, 29). Whether plays were altered to suit the different theatres is unclear, despite Gurr's claim that Shakespeare's 'Globe plays transplanted to the Blackfriars unchanged, as his Blackfriars plays transplanted to the Globe'; see Andrew Gurr, *Playgoing in Shakespeare's London*, Second Edition (Cambridge University Press, 1996), 173.
59. On the influence of court drama on the late plays, see Schmidgall; also, A. C. Kirsch, '*Cymbeline* and Coterie Dramaturgy', *ELH* 34 (1967), 285–306, writes of the last plays in the context of the 'operatic' conventions exploited by Marston, Fletcher and Jonson' (Bibliog Guide, 164); and see Richard Proudfoot, 'Shakespeare and the New Dramatists of the King's Men, 1606–1613', in John Russell Brown and Bernard Harris (eds.), *Later Shakespeare*, Stratford-upon-Avon Studies 8 (London: Arnold, 1966), 235–61.
60. Leeds Barroll, *Politics, Plague, and Shakespeare's Theater: The Stuart Years* (Ithaca, NY: Cornell University Press, 1991), ix; Mary Bly, *Queer Virgins and*

Virgin Queans on the Early Modern Stage (New York: Oxford University Press, 2000), 129.
61. See the immensely helpful chart in Barroll, *Politics, Plague*, 173.
62. Patrick Cheney, *Shakespeare, National Poet-Playwright* (Cambridge: Cambridge University Press, 2004), 200; Duncan-Jones, *Ungentle Shakespeare: Scenes from his Life* (London: Arden Shakespeare, 2001), 219–22.
63. On the dating, see William Shakespeare, *Coriolanus*, ed. Lee Bliss, The New Cambridge Shakespeare (Cambridge University Press, 2000), 1–7, 17–27; see also E. C. Pettet, '*Coriolanus* and the Midlands Insurrection of 1607', *Shakespeare Survey* 3 (1950), 34–42.
64. On the Blackfriars repertory prior to its reoccupation by the King's Men, see Lucy Munro, *Children of the Queen's Revels: A Jacobean Theatre Repertory* (Cambridge University Press, 2005), esp. 55–95 and 134–63 on non-tragicomic plays.
65. Samuel Schoenbaum, *Shakespeare: A Documentary Life* (Oxford: Clarendon Press, 1975), 211.
66. Mariët Westermann, *Rembrandt* (London: Phaidon, 2000), 304, 292.
67. 'Vele jaren agter den anderen heeft hy het met schilderen zoo drok gehad dat de menschen lang naar hunne stukken moesten wagten, niettegenstaande dat hy met zyn werk vaardig voortging, inzonderheit in zyn laatsten tyd, toen het 'er, van na by bezien, uitzag of het met een Metzelaars truffel was aangesmeert. Waarom hy de menschen, als zy op zyn schilderkamer kwamen, en zyn werk van dichteby wilden bekyken, te rug trok, zeggende: *de reuk van de verf zou u verleeven*. Ook wort'er getuigt dat hy eens een pourtret geschildert heeft daar de verf zoodanig dik op lag, datmen de schildery by de neus van de grondt konde opligten. Dus zietmen ook gesteente en paerlen, op Borstcieraden en Tulbanden door hem zoo verheven geschildert al even of ze gebootzeerd waren, door welke wyze van behandelen zyne stukken, zelf in wydenafstant, kragtig uitkomen': in Arnold van Houbraken, *De Groote Schouburgh der Nederlantsche Konstschilders en Schilderessen*, 3 vols. (Amsterdam, 1718), vol. I, 269. My thanks to Sanne Parlevliet.
68. Simon Schama, *Rembrandt's Eyes* (Harmondsworth: Allen Lane/The Penguin Press, 1999), 666–7.
69. Hajo Düchting in Walter Erben, *Joan Miró 1893–1983: The Man and His Work, With a Commentary on Miró's Late Works and Notes on his Paintings by Hajo Düchting* (Cologne: Taschen, 1998), 231
70. Philip Edwards, 'Shakespeare's Romances: 1900–1957', *Shakespeare Survey* 11 (1958), 1–18.
71. William Shakespeare, *The Winter's Tale*, ed. S. L. Bethell (Oxford University Press, 1956), 19.
72. See, for instance, Keir Elam, 'Early Modern Syntax and Late Shakespearean Rhetoric', in C. Nocera Avila, N. Pantaleo and D. Pizzini (eds.), *Early Modern English: Trends, Forms and Texts* (Fasano: Schena Editore, 1992), 61–80.
73. F. C. Tinkler, '*Cymbeline*', *Scrutiny* 7 (1938–9), 5–20.
74. Brian Gibbons, *Shakespeare and Multiplicity* (Cambridge University Press, 1993), 23.

366 *Notes to pages 117–31*

75. John Porter Houston, *Shakespearean Sentences: A Study in Style and Syntax* (Baton Rouge: Louisiana State University Press, 1988), 198.
76. A. C. Bradley, *Shakespearean Tragedy: Lectures on* Hamlet, Othello, King Lear, Macbeth (London: Macmillan, 1904), 68.
77. George T. Wright, *Shakespeare's Metrical Art* (Berkeley: University of California Press, 1988), xi.
78. James Sutherland, 'The Language of the Last Plays', in John Garrett (ed.), *More Talking of Shakespeare* (London: Longmans Green, 1959), 144–58.
79. Anne Barton, 'Leontes and the Spider: Language and Speaker in Shakespeare's Last Plays' in *Essays, Mainly Shakespearean* (Cambridge University Press, 1994), 161–81 (168, 169); Bethell, *Winter's Tale*, 22–3; Charles Olson, 'Quantity in Verse, and Shakespeare's Late Plays', in Robert Creeley (ed.), *Selected Writings of Charles Olson* (New York: New Directions, 1966), 37.
80. John Hoskins, *Directions for Speech and Style*, ed. Hoyt H. Hudson, Princeton Studies in English 12 (Princeton University Press, 1935), 39.
81. Russ McDonald, 'Poetry and Plot in *The Winter's Tale*', *Shakespeare Quarterly* 36 (1985), 315–29 (317).

3 THE INVENTION OF LATE SHAKESPEARE: SUBJECTIVISM AND ITS DISCONTENTS

1. Ralph Waldo Emerson, *Shakespeare, or The Poet*, in Joseph Slater and Douglas Emory Wilson (gen. eds.), *The Collected Works of Ralph Waldo Emerson*, vol. 4: *Representative Men: Seven Lectures*, ed. Douglas Emory Wilson (Cambridge MA: Belknap Press of Harvard University Press, 1987), 107–25 (119, 120).
2. [Peter Heylyn,] *A Briefe Relation of the Death and Sufferings of the Most Reverend and Renowned Prelate the L. Archbishop of Canterbury* (Oxford, 1644), A2r.
3. *Hamlet*, 2.2.205–6.
4. Alexander Pope (ed.), *The Works of Shakespear*, 6 vols. (London, 1725), vii.
5. Margreta de Grazia, *Shakespeare Verbatim: The Reproduction of Authenticity and the 1790 Apparatus* (Oxford: Clarendon Press, 1991).
6. Augustus William Schlegel, *A Course of Lectures on Dramatic Art and Literature*, trans. John Black, 2 vols. (London, 1815), vol. 2, 153–4; Charlemont letter cited in S. Schoenbaum, *Shakespeare's Lives*, new edition (Oxford University Press, 1993), 114.
7. Hardin Craig, 'Preface', in *The Complete Works of Shakespeare*, ed. Craig and David Bevington, revised edition (Glenview, IL: Scott, Foresman & Co., 1973), n.p.
8. William Winstanley, *The Lives of the Most Famous English Poets* (London, 1686), 130–33; Gerard Langbaine, *An Account of the English Dramatick Poets* (Oxford, 1691), 2F3r–2G3r; Nicholas Rowe (ed.), *The Works of Mr. William Shakespear*, 6 vols. (London, 1709), i–xl.
9. Edmond Malone, *An Attempt to Ascertain the Order in which the Plays Attributed to Shakspeare Were Written*, in *The Plays of William Shakspeare*,

ed. Samuel Johnson and George Steevens, 2nd edn, 6 vols. (London, 1778), vol. 1, 280, note o.
10. Malone in Johnson and Steevens, *Plays*, vol. 1, 344.
11. The first critic to name *The Tempest* as the last play had been John Holt who, in 1749, following a conjectural topical logic in which he triangulated the weddings of Princess Elizabeth and Frederick, Elector Palatine and of the earl of Essex and Frances Howard, New World reports, and the introduction to Ben Jonson's *Bartholomew Fair*, dated it to 1614. See John Holt, *An Attempte to Rescue that Aunciente, English Poet, and Play-wrighte, Maister Williaume Shakespere; from the Many Errours, faulsely charged on him, by Certaine New-fangled Wittes (Remarks on The Tempest)* (London, 1749), esp. 17–18.
12. John Gilbert Cooper, *Letters Concerning Taste* (London, 1755), 101.
13. Thomas Campbell (ed.), *The Dramatic Works of William Shakspeare*, 2 vols. (London, 1838), lxiii.
14. Thomas Carlyle, *On Heroes, Hero-Worship and the Heroic in History* (1841), notes and introduction by Michael K. Goldberg, ed. Michael K. Goldberg, Joel J. Brattin and Mark Engel (Berkeley and Los Angeles: University of California Press, 1993), 94.
15. William Poel, 126th meeting of the New Shakspere Society, 10 June 1887.
16. Bailey, *Henry the VIII. and the Last Work of Shakespeare*, 4, 5.
17. Joseph Warton, *The Enthusiast: or the Lover of Nature* (London, 1765), 12–13. See Jonathan Bate, 'Shakespeare and Original Genius', in Penelope Murray (ed.), *Genius: The History of an Idea* (Oxford: Blackwell, 1989), 76–97 (83).
18. Jonathan Bate, *The Genius of Shakespeare* (London: Picador, 1997), 161.
19. Furnivall in *The New Shakspere Society's Transactions* (London, 1874), vi–vii.
20. On landscape, genius and the idea of biography, see Kay Dian Kriz, *The Idea of the English Landscape Painter: Genius as Alibi in the Early Nineteenth Century* (New Haven & London: Yale University Press for The Paul Mellon Centre for Studies in British Art, 1997), who notes of the reception of Turner's early landscapes that 'a turn to biography is consistent with the production of a form of landscape painting that relies upon the singular sensibility and intellect of the artistic individual as the means of revealing to a national public its own essential nature', adding that '[t]he key to the native landscape genius's ability to function at one and the same time as an autonomous subject, insulated from the vitiation of a market-oriented society, and also as a social subject who represents the ideals of that society, is contingent upon the way in which individual autonomy is socially regulated. The elision of the artist's character – his singular capacity to feel, to recognise, and to represent the essence of the landscape – with the symbolic character of the domestic landscape as the locus of individual and national freedom, fixes the individuality of the native genius firmly within the domain of the social' (140–41).
21. Edmond Malone (ed.), *Supplement to the Edition of Shakspeare's Plays Published in 1778*, 2 vols. (London, 1780), I: 654.

22. Giorgio Vasari, *The Lives of the Artists* [1568], trans. Julia Conaway Bondanella and Peter Bondanella, 'The World's Classics' (Oxford University Press, 1991), 503–4.
23. Private communication.
24. 'Le genre humain dans son ensemble a grandi, s'est développé, a mûri comme un de nous. Il a été enfant, il a été homme; nous assistons maintenant à son imposante vieillesse [... N]ous allons essayer de démêler, d'après la forme de celle-ci, quel a dû être le caractère de l'autre, à ces trois grands âges du monde: les temps primitifs, les temps antiques, les temps modernes': Victor Hugo, *Cromwell: Drame* (Paris: Ambroise Dupont, 1828), Préface, iii, iv.
25. Denis Diderot and Jean le Rond d'Alembert, *L'Encyclopédie ou Dictionnaire raisonné des sciences, des arts et des métiers, par une société de gens de lettres* (Paris: Le Breton, 1751–72; suppl. 1776–7; index 1780), vol. 12 (1765), 37.
26. Much of my account of lives of composers by early nineteenth-century biographers derives, as I noted in my introduction, from Ian Bent's immensely valuable annotated anthology, *Music Analysis in the Nineteenth Century*, vol. 1, *Fugue, Form and Style*, esp. 253ff., which I recommend wholeheartedly to anyone interested in the development of the concept of personal style.
27. Giuseppe Baini, *Memorie storico-critiche della vita e delle opere di Giovanni Pierluigi da Palestrina*, 2 vols. (Rome: Dalla Societa Tipografia, 1828), 422–3; translation taken from Bent, *Fugue, Form*, 272.
28. Alexandre Oulibicheff (Alexander Dmitryevich Ulïbïshev), *Nouvelle Biographie de Mozart suivie d'un aperçu sur l'histoire générale de la musique* (Moscow: Auguste Semen, 1843), 452, 424: 'Les six derniers mois de la vie de Mozart, furent une époque de fécondité surhumaine et d'angélique inspiration. [...] / Il partait, parce que sa mission était terminée; il quittait son art, mais non pas avant d'en avoir atteint les sommités les plus hautes. [...] Jeune, il cessait de vivre, parce que ses forces vitales avaient été dépensées à la production d'œuvres surhumaines, pour ainsi dire, dont le génie vieillissant n'eût plus été capable, et dont une fin précoce était nécessairement la condition et le prix' (my translation).
29. 'Nous venons d'ajouter, en parlant du Requiem, que la mort du compositeur tient presqu'autant de place que sa vie, dans les annales de la musique. Et, en effet, cette longue agonie de Mozart, n'a-t-elle pas marqué d'un cachet de sublimité religieuse ou d'idéalisme transcendant [...] la Flûte magique et son ouverture, Titus et le Requiem; ouvrages qui [...] commencent à une pièce détachée, l'*Ave verum Corpus* [...] un chant très simple, mais mélodieux et bien phrasé [...] De la musique toute moderne, diriez-vous, à la première vue. Oui, mais la plus hautement ecclésiastique qu'il soit possible d'entendre [...] quelle gravité sacerdotale et pourtant quelle béatitude séraphique! (Ulïbïshev, *Mozart*, 452–3).
30. This said, there are nonetheless a couple of slight hints in Baini's account of late Palestrina of the characteristics of the later understanding of lateness. Palestrina's tenth style, for Baini, was 'a blend of the second, eighth and ninth' (Bent, *Fugue, Form*, 279), that is, a combination of the most recent

Notes to pages 143–8 369

achievement with a glance back at a very early style; and the description of the last style – in which 'the words and meanings, though still distinctly intelligible, acquire that penetrating quality which persuades and moves as it delights, armed only with melody and harmony' – perhaps looks forward to the transcendent serenity said later to be characteristic of late work.

31. I am grateful to Emma Sutton for sparking off this train of thought, but I should add immediately that she is not responsible for any errors in my exposition.

32. Georg W. F. Hegel, *Introductory Lectures on Aesthetics* (1823–9), trans. Bernard Bosanquet (1886), ed. Michael Inwood (Harmondsworth: Penguin, 1993), 32–3; Goethe, conversation with Eckermann, 11 March 1828, in Johann Wolfgang Goethe, *Gedenkausgabe der Werke, Briefe und Gespräche*, ed. Ernst Beutler, 24 vols. (Zurich: Artemis Verlag, 1948–54), vol. 24: Johann Peter Eckermann, *Gespräche mit Goethe in den letzten Jahren seines Lebens* (1948), 677–8. On Goethe's late energy, see, e.g., G. H. Lewes, *The Life and Works of Goethe*, 2 vols. (London, 1855), vol. 2, 415: 'It is evident [...] there was abundant life in the old Jupiter, whose frame was still massive and erect; whose brow had scarcely a wrinkle of old age; whose head was still as free from baldness as ever; and whose large brown eyes had still that flashing splendour which distinguished them.'

33. I am grateful to Alice Hunt for proposing that Coleridge's pattern is that of the five-act play.

34. See Samuel Taylor Coleridge, *Shakespearean Criticism*, 2 vols, ed. Thomas Middleton Raysor (London: Dent, 1960), vol 1, 211–12.

35. Samuel Taylor Coleridge, *Lectures 1808–1819: On Literature*, ed. R. A. Foakes, 2 vols., comprising vol. 5 of *The Collected Works of Samuel Taylor Coleridge*, gen. ed. Kathleen Coburn, associate ed. Bart Winer (London: Routledge and Kegan Paul/Princeton University Press, 1987), vol. 1, 373–5.

36. Nathan Drake, *Shakspeare and his Times*, 2 vols. (London, 1817), vol. 1, 261–2.

37. William L. Pressly, *A Catalogue of Paintings in the Folger Shakespeare Library: 'As Imagination Bodies Forth'* (New Haven: Yale University Press, 1993), 312.

38. *The Plays of William Shakespeare*, 8 vols. (London: Bellamy & Robarts, 1791), vol. 3.

39. For representative illustrations of *The Tempest*, see Marcia Pointon, "Representing The Tempest in Boydell's Shakespeare Gallery", in Walter Pape and Frederick Burwick (eds.), *The Boydell Shakespeare Gallery* (Bottrop: Peter Pomp, 1996), 103–11. I'm grateful to Georgianna Ziegler and Erin Blake of the Folger Shakespeare Library for generously giving me a range of insights into the history of Shakespeare illustration.

40. '[U]nd daß er den schönen, unwiderstehlich anziehenden Schein, den er selbst hervorgezaubert, wenn er anders wollte, unerbittlich vernichten könnte': August Wilhelm Schlegel, *Vorlesungen über dramatische Kunst und Literatur*, in Schlegel, *Kritische Schriften und Briefe*, ed. Edgar Lohner, 7 vols. (Stuttgart: Kohlhammer, 1962–74), vol. 6 (i.e. vol. 2 of the *Vorlesungen*), 137; thanks to Bernhard Klein for the translation.

41. Ibid., 176. Verplanck, in his 1847 edition, explains the difficulty of dating *The Tempest* by recourse to the idea of revision. He argues rather that Shakespeare revised the play towards the end of his life and that is it due '[t]o this circumstance [...] that the whole piece came to be regarded as its author's final work on retiring from the public field; while in reality that was true only of some of its nobler strains, and of the prophetic allusions at the end, which have stamped upon the drama the last impress of its author's genius, and left it as his farewell to the "rough magic," the "heavenly music," and the "airy charms," which had for years obeyed the biddings of his so potent art"': Gulian C. Verplanck (ed.), *Shakespeare's Plays*, 3 vols. (New York: Harper, 1847), vol. 2, *Tempest*, 5. This manages simultaneously to affirm the possibility of conscious farewell and reject that of a less 'serious' post-tragic phase, and it looks forward to the theories of revision which, combined with distaste for collaboration, would be deployed to marginalise the post-*Tempest* plays.
42. Thomas Campbell, 'The Last Man', *New Monthly Magazine* 8 (1823), 272–3; Mary Shelley, *The Last Man* (London, 1826); George Gordon Byron, 'Darkness', in *The Complete Poetical Works of Lord Byron*, ed. Jerome McGann, 7 vols. (Oxford: Clarendon, 1980–91), vol. 4, 40–3; Thomas Beddoes, *The Last Man*, in *The Poetical Works of Thomas Lovell Beddoes*, ed. Edmund Gosse, 2 vols. (London: J.M. Dent, 1890), vol. 2, 255–68. Beddoes was mortified when he saw Campbell's poem in print, pre-empting, as it did, the publication of his play: neither had known of the other's work.
43. Fiona Stafford, *The Last of the Race: The Growth of a Myth from Milton to Darwin* (Oxford: Clarendon Press, 1994); A. J. Sanbrook, 'A Romantic Theme: The Last Man', *Forum for Modern Language Studies* 2 (1966), 25–33; Lee Sterrenberg, 'The Last Man: Anatomy of Failed Revolutions', *Nineteenth Century Fiction* 33 (1978), 324–47.
44. *Last of the Race*, 230. In addition to the 'last man' works listed at n. 42, see Jean-Baptiste Cousin de Grainville, *Le Dernier Homme*, translated as *The Last Man*, 2 vols. (London, 1806) and John Martin's painting 'The Last Man' (1849) in the Walker Art Gallery, Liverpool.
45. Private communication. I am grateful to Dr Lodge for suggesting the relevance of last-man discourse. Hood's remarkable poem, 'The Last Man', was first published in his *Whims & Oddities in Prose and Verse* (London: Lupton Relfe, 1826).
46. Joseph Hunter, *A Disquisition on the Scene, Origin, Date, Etc. Etc. of Shakespeare's Tempest* (London, 1839), 63.
47. *Disquisition*, 63. Schoenbaum notes that Campbell seemed happy to withdraw his suggestion: 'On 12 December 1839 he thanked Hunter for a presentation copy of the *Disquisition* and made an extraordinary recantation: "You have [he wrote] demolished my comparison between Shakespeare finishing his career with the Tempest & Prospero throwing his magic wand into the sea – with so much truth and urbanity – that I make you welcome to your victory – ". But publicly he kept silent'; see S[amuel] Schoenbaum, *Shakespeare's Lives*, 2nd edition (Oxford University Press, 1993), 230.

48. Henry N. Hudson (ed.), *The Complete Works of William Shakespeare*, 20 vols., Harvard Edition (Boston, MA: Ginn, Heath, 1881), vol. 7, 6.
49. Charles Knight (ed.), *The Comedies, Histories, Tragedies, and Poems of William Shakspere*, 6 vols. (London: Knight, 1842), vol. 4, 126.
50. Charles Knight, *William Shakspere: A Biography* (London, 1843), 526.
51. Hermann Ulrici, *Shakespeare's Dramatic Art: and his Relation to Calderon and Goethe* (London: Chapman, 1846), 98. I am grateful to John Jowett for drawing my attention to the importance of Ulrici for this narrative.
52. T. S. Eliot, *On Poetry and Poets* (New York: Farrar, Straus and Cudahy, 1957), 297.
53. F. J. Furnivall, 'Introduction' to G. G. Gervinus, *Shakespeare Commentaries*, trans. F. E. Bunnèt (London: Smith, Elder & Co., 1875), xix.
54. 'That Dowden was responding specifically to Furnivall's prospectus is illustrated by the fact that he takes from it, with due acknowledgment, the word "youngmanishness" as a descriptive term appropriate to the First Period' (*Shakespeare's Lives*, 355).
55. Russell Fraser, *Shakespeare: The Later Years* (New York: Columbia University Press, 1992), 222.
56. E. Talbot Donaldson, *The Swan at the Well: Shakespeare Reading Chaucer* (New Haven: Yale University Press, 1985), 53.
57. Potter, *Two Noble Kinsmen*, 13, citing Richard Digby Day, programme note for production of the play, York Theatre Royal, 1973.
58. Victor Hugo, *Œuvres complètes de William Shakespeare*, 15 vols., *Les Apocryphes*, 3 vols. (Paris, 1866), vol. 1, 85; Leyris, 'Chant de cygne' (see next note); P. Constant, report on a production of the translation by Réaud at Courneuve, in M. T. Jones-Davies (ed.), *Société (Française Shakespeare: Actes du Congrès 1979* (1980), 30.
59. Pierre Leyris, 'Le chant de cygne de Shakespeare,' *La Nouvelle Revue Française* 215 (1970), 44–57 (44). My translation.
60. Lytton Strachey, 'Shakespeare's Final Period,' in *Book and Characters, French and English* (London: Chatto & Windus, 1922), 47–64 (60).
61. See Introduction, note 4.
62. D. G. James, 'The Failure of the Ballad-Makers,' Chapter 7 of *Scepticism and Poetry: An Essay on the Poetic Imagination* (London: Allen & Unwin, 1937), 207, 241, 207.
63. H. B. Charlton, *Shakespearian Comedy* (London: Methuen, 1938), 267.
64. J. O. Halliwell-Phillips, *Outlines of the Life of Shakespeare*, 11th edition, 2 vols. (London: Longmans, Green, 1907), vol. 2, 249, n. 1.
65. C. J. Sisson, *The Mythical Sorrows of Shakespeare*, 'Annual Shakespeare Lecture of the British Academy, From the Proceedings of the British Academy', vol. 20 (London: Milford, 1934), 5–6, 7.
66. Ibid., 9. For the account Sisson is parodying, see Bernhard ten Brink, *Shakspere. Fünf Vorlesungen aus dem Nachlass von B. ten Brink* (Strassberg, 1983), translated as ten Brink, *Five Lectures on Shakespeare*, trans. Julia Franklin (London: Bell, 1895).

67. Edward Bond, *Bingo: Scenes of Money and Death*, in *Plays: Three* (London: Methuen Drama, 1987), 1–66 (43).
68. Ben Jonson, 'Ode to Himself', in C. H. Herford and Percy and Evelyn Simpson (eds.), *Ben Jonson*, 11 vols. (Oxford: Clarendon Press, 1925–52), vol. 6, 492–3.
69. Daphna Erdinast-Vulcan, *Joseph Conrad and the Modern Temper* (Oxford: Clarendon Press, 1991), 139.
70. Thomas C. Moser, *Joseph Conrad: Achievement and Decline* (Cambridge, MA: Harvard University Press, 1957), 178. The idea of Conrad's 'decline' was first suggested by John Galsworthy in his *Castles in Spain, and Other Screeds* (London: Heinemann, 1927) – 'He was very tired toward the end; he wore himself clean out. To judge him by the tired work is absurd' (81) – and amplified in Douglas Hewitt, *Conrad: A Reassessment* (Cambridge: Bowes and Bowes, 1952) and Albert Guerard, *Conrad the Novelist* (Cambridge, MA: Harvard University Press, 1958). For the earlier 'affirmation' argument, see M. C. Bradbrook, *Joseph Conrad: England's Polish Genius* (Cambridge University Press, 1941); Paul L. Wiley, *Conrad's Measure of Man* (Madison: University of Wisconsin Press, 1954); and Walter Francis Wright, *Romance and Tragedy in Joseph Conrad* (Lincoln: University of Nebraska Press, 1949).
71. Owen Knowles and Gene M. Moore, *Oxford Reader's Companion to Conrad* (Oxford University Press, 2000), 1.
72. Gary Geddes, *Conrad's Later Novels* (Montreal: McGill-Queen's University Press, 1980); Daniel R. Schwarz, *Conrad: The Later Fiction* (London: Macmillan, 1982); Robert Hampson, *Joseph Conrad: Betrayal and Identity* (London: Macmillan, 1992). See also Ian Watt, 'The Decline of the Decline: Notes on Conrad's Reputation,' in Watt, *Essays on Conrad* (Cambridge University Press, 2000), 170–85.
73. Joseph Conrad, *Victory*, ed. Robert Hampson (Harmondsworth: Penguin, 1989), 212, 207. See also Donald Dilke, 'The Tempest of Axel Heyst', *Nineteenth Century Fiction* 17 (1962), 95–113; David Lodge, 'Conrad's *Victory* and *The Tempest*: An Amplification', *Modern Language Review* 59 (1964), 195–9; Adam Gillon, *Conrad and Shakespeare and Other Essays* (New York: Astra Books, 1976), 41–141, esp. 85–116; John Batchelor, 'Conrad and Shakespeare', *L'Epoque Conradienne* 18 (1992), 125–52.
74. Gillon extends the range of the Shakespearean debt, noting that '[t]he tonality, the dramatic, symbolic and ironic orchestration of *Victory* suggest affinities not only with *The Tempest* but also with *Hamlet, King Lear, Macbeth, Othello*, to mention the major plays – all testifying to the overwhelming impact of Shakespeare on Conrad, at the time of his writing the novel (Gillon, 85). His analysis nonetheless makes clear the centrality of *The Tempest* as the principal Shakespearean influence on the novel's shape and engagement with its material.
75. Michael Millgate, *Testamentary Acts: Browning, Tennyson, James, Hardy* (Oxford: Clarendon Press, 1992), 2.
76. Thomas Hardy, *The Life and Work of Thomas Hardy: An Edition on New Principles of the Materials [...] Published over the Name of Florence Emily Hardy*, ed. Michael Millgate (Basingstoke: Macmillan, 1984), 354.

77. Thomas Hardy, 'An Ancient to Ancients', from *Late Lyrics and Earlier* (1922), in Samuel Hynes (ed.), *The Complete Poetical Works of Thomas Hardy*, 3 vols. (Oxford: Clarendon Press, 1982–5), vol. 2, 483.
78. G. Thomas Tanselle, 'The Editorial Problem of Final Authorial Intention', *Studies in Bibliography* 29 (1976), 167–211 (195). A good instance of the primacy of 'final intentions' is the remarkable difficulty found by anyone trying currently to buy non-New York Edition texts of Henry James's early novels, the late revised versions being near-universally preferred by publishers as 'authoritative'.
79. Lawrence Lipking, *The Life of the Poet: Beginning and Ending Poetic Careers* (Chicago: University of Chicago Press, 1981), xiii.
80. See Tia DeNora, *Beethoven and the Construction of Genius: Musical Politics in Vienna, 1792–1803* (Berkeley and Los Angeles: University of California Press, 1995).
81. Henry James, *The Wings of the Dove* (London: Constable, 1902), 182–3.
82. On the significance of the Bronzino, see Denis Flannery, *Henry James: A Certain Illusion* (Aldershot: Ashgate, 2000), 182–4.
83. It was a Boston printer, William Dana Orcutt, rather than Lee himself, who asked James to write the preface. The phrasing reappears in the introduction itself: 'The man himself, in the Plays, we directly touch, to my consciousness, positively nowhere: we are dealing too perpetually with the artist, the monster and the magician of a thousand masks, not one of which we feel him drop long enough to gratify with the breath of the interval that strained attention in us which would be yet, so quickened, ready to become deeper still' (James in Lee, *Complete Works*, xv). James's response and the writing of the introduction are discussed in William T. Stafford, 'James Examines Shakespeare: Notes on the Nature of Genius', *PMLA* 73 (1958), 123–28 (esp. 124).
84. Lauren T. Cowdery, 'Henry James and the "Transcendent Adventure": The Search for the Self in the Introduction to *The Tempest*,' *The Henry James Review* 3 (1982), 145–53 (147). On James and the *Tempest* preface, see, in addition to Stafford and Cowdery, Leon Edel, *Henry James: The Master* (Philadelphia: Lippincott, 1972), 148–9; Nina Schwartz, 'The Master Lesson: James Reading Shakespeare', *The Henry James Review* 12 (1991), 69–83; Neil Chilton, 'Conceptions of a Beautiful Crisis: Henry James's Reading of *The Tempest*', *The Henry James Review* 26 (2005), 218–28; and Peter Rawlings, *Henry James and the Abuse of the Past* (Basingstoke: Palgrave Macmillan, 2005).
85. James, *Literary Criticism*, 1212, 1209.
86. See Philip Horne, *Henry James and Revision: The New York Edition* (Oxford: Clarendon Press, 1990), 86–90.
87. Henry James, 'The Middle Years', in Leon Edel (ed.), *The Complete Tales of Henry James*, 12 vols. (London: Hart-Davis, 1964), vol. 9 (1892–1898), 66, 57.
88. On the Shakespearean resonances of 'The Lesson of the Master', see Horne, *Revision*, 312–14.
89. Henry James, 'The Lesson of the Master,' in Edel (ed.), *Complete Tales of Henry James*, vol. 7, 229.

90. Henry James, 'The Birthplace', in Edel (ed.), *Complete Tales*, vol. 11, 405.
91. *The Letters of Henry James*, ed. Percy Lubbock, 2 vols. (London: Macmillan, 1920), vol. 1, 432 and vol. 2, 171. In his letter to Porter, James refers to what Lubbock notes were 'certain Baconian clues to the authorship of Shakespeare's plays' as 'the most provincial *bêtises'* (vol. 2, 171). I'm grateful to James Shapiro for this reference.
92. Henry James, 'The Figure in the Carpet', in Edel (ed.), *Complete Tales*, vol. 9, 291–2.
93. Henry James, *The American Scene*, in *Collected Travel Writings: Great Britain and America* (New York: Library of America, 1993), 351–736 (431). I am indebted to Philip Horne for this reference.

4 LAST WORDS/LATE PLAYS: THE POSSIBILITY AND IMPOSSIBILITY OF LATE SHAKESPEARE IN EARLY MODERN CULTURE AND THEATRE

1. Henry Goodcole, *A True Declaration of the Happy Conversion, Contrition and Christian Preparation of Francis Robinson, Gentleman, Who for Counterfeiting the Great Seale of England Was Drawen, Hang'd and Quartered at Charing Crosse, on Friday Last, Being the Thirteenth Day of November 1618* (London, 1618), A4r.
2. Isidore Ducasse, also known as Lautréamont, 'Poésies II' in *Poésies and Complete Miscellanea*, ed. and trans. Alexis Lykiard (London: Allison & Busby, 1978), 76.
3. Horace, *Odes*, I: 31, ll. 17–20, in *Odes and Epodes*, ed. and trans. Niall Rudd, The Loeb Classical Library (Cambridge, MA: Harvard University Press, 2004), 80–1.
4. Michel de Montaigne, *The Essays of Michel de Montaigne*, trans. and ed. M. A. Screech (Harmondsworth: Penguin, 1991), III. 13: 'On Experience', 1263.
5. Emily Wilson, *Mocked with Death: Tragic Overliving from Sophocles to Milton* (Baltimore: Johns Hopkins University Press, 2004), 2.
6. Sophocles, *Oedipus at Colonus*, trans. Eamon Grennan and Rachel Kitzinger, The Greek Tragedy in New Translations (Oxford University Press, 2005), ll. 1339–42, 1354–8.
7. Plato, *The Republic*, ed. G. R. F. Ferrari, trans. Tom Griffith (Cambridge University Press, 2000), 3 (Book 1, section 329). Robert Garland notes that the Greek treatment of the old varied in relation to the prevalent political culture: '[o]ligarchic regimes', he explains, 'display a natural inclination towards gerontocracy, whereas democracies reveal the opposite tendency'; see Garland, *The Greek Way of Life: From Conception to Old Age* (London: Duckworth, 1990), 244. See also the optimism of Bessie E. Richardson, *Old Age Among the Ancient Greeks: The Greek Portrayal of Old Age in Literature, Art and Inscriptions* (Baltimore: Johns Hopkins Press, 1933), countered by more recent accounts, including M. S. Haynes, 'The Supposedly Golden Age for the Aged in Ancient Greece (A Study of Literary Concepts of Old Age)', *The Gerontologist* 2 (1962), 93–8, G. S. Kirk, 'Old Age and Maturity in Ancient

Greece', *Eranos Jahrbücher* 40 (1971), 123–58, and Garland, *Greek Way of Life*. For a helpful overview specifically of literary representations of old age, see Thomas M. Falkner and Judith de Luce (eds.), *Old Age in Greek and Latin Literature* (Albany: State University of New York Press, 1989). I am grateful to Tim Duff for conversations about old age in classical Greece and Rome.

8. Karen Cokayne, *Experiencing Old Age in Ancient Rome* (London: Routledge, 2003), 179.
9. Tim G. Parkin, *Old Age in the Roman World: A Cultural and Social History* (Baltimore: Johns Hopkins University Press, 2003), 75. See also 67–8.
10. For a full, and slightly depressing, list of negative images, see ibid., 76–89.
11. Cicero, *De Senectute*, ed. and trans. W. A. Falconer (Cambridge, MA: Harvard University Press, 1923), x. 33.
12. See J. A. Burrow, *The Ages of Man: A Study in Medieval Writing and Thought* (Oxford: Clarendon Press, 1986).
13. Henry Cuffe, *The Difference of the Ages of Mans Life: Together with the Originall causes, Progresse, and End thereof* (London, 1607), 116 (I2^v).
14. See Bede, *De Temporum Ratione*, in *Bedae Opera de Temporibus*, ed. C. W. Jones (Cambridge, MA: The Mediaeval Academy of America, 1943), 246–8.
15. For the clearest outline of the doctrine of the four humours, see Raymond Klibansky, Erwin Panofsky and Fritz Saxl, *Saturn and Melancholy: Studies in the History of Natural Philosophy, Religion and Art* (London: Thomas Nelson, 1964), 3–15.
16. 'Aetates in universum sunt quatuor: nempe aetas incrementi, viridis vocata, quae extenditur usque ad vigesimum quintum annum; aetas consistentiae, sive vigoris, quae iuvenilis, & florida appellatur, ad trigesimum quintum, aut quadragesimum annum excurrens: deinde aetas decrementi, cum iam vigoris tempus excessit, nec dum tamen virium robur amittitur, aetas vergens, & senilis appellata, quae durat usque ad sexagesimum fere annum: postremo aetas decrementi cum manifesto virium lapsu, quae praeceps, & decrepita dicitur, & extenditur ad finem vitae': [Husain Ibn 'Abd Allah, Abu 'Ali, called Ibn Síná, or] Avicenna, *Canon* (Vicenza, 1611), Fen. 1, Lib. 1, Cap. 3, 'De Temperamentis Aetatum', D4r. My translation.
17. Sir Walter Ralegh, *History of the World* (London, 1621), Part 1, Bk. 1, Chap. 2, Sect. 5, Civ.
18. Keith Thomas, 'Age and Authority in Early Modern England,' *Proceedings of the British Academy* 62 (1976), 205–48 (234, 245).
19. John S. Coolidge, 'Great Things and Small: The Virgilian Progression', *Comparative Literature* 17 (1965), 1–23 (13).
20. Richard Helgerson, *Self-Crowned Laureates: Spenser, Jonson, Milton, and the Literary System* (Berkeley: University of California Press, 1983), 1–2.
21. Samuel Johnson, 'Milton', in *The Lives of the Most Eminent English Poets; with Critical Observations on their Works*, ed. Roger Lonsdale, 2 vols. (Oxford: Clarendon Press, 2006), I: 242–95 (282); Lipking, *Life of the Poet*, 68.
22. Patrick Cheney, *Marlowe's Counterfeit Profession: Ovid, Spenser, Counter-Nationhood* (Toronto: University of Toronto Press, 1997); see also Patrick

Cheney and Frederick A. de Armas (eds.), *European Literary Careers: The Author from Antiquity to the Renaissance* (Toronto: University of Toronto Press, 2002). That the process began prior to the early modern period is clear from Michael A. Calabrese's *Chaucer's Ovidian Arts of Love* (Gainesville: University Press of Florida, 1994).
23. Isabel G. MacCaffrey, *Spenser's Allegory: The Anatomy of Imagination* (Princeton University Press, 1976), 366.
24. Patrick Cheney, *Spenser's Famous Flight: A Renaissance Idea of a Literary Career* (Toronto: University of Toronto Press, 1993), 5; see also Paul Alpers, 'Spenser's Late Pastorals', *ELH* 56 (1989), 797–817.
25. Leo Braudy, *The Frenzy of Renown: Fame and its History* (New York: Oxford University Press, 1986), 161.
26. Edmund Spenser, *The Shepheardes Calender*, gloss to line 90, in Spenser, *Poetical Works*, ed. J. C. Smith and E. de Selincourt (Oxford University Press, 1912), 415–67 (459).
27. David Aers, 'A Whisper in the Ear of Early Modernists; or, Reflections on Literary Critics Writing the "History of the Subject"', in Aers (ed.), *Culture and History 1350–1600: Essays on English Communities, Identities and Writing* (Hemel Hempstead: Harvester Wheatsheaf, 1992), 177–202 (182); Charles Taylor, *Sources of the Self: The Making of Modern Identity* (Cambridge University Press, 1989), 131.
28. Papias, *Elementarium* (Milan, 1476), *Aetas*, in V. de Angeli (ed.), *Papiae Elementarum*, Littera A, II: *Aequus–Anniferme*, Testi e Documenti per lo Studio dell'Antichita (Milan: Cisalpino-Goliardica, 1978), 110. The translation is from Burrow, *Ages of Man*, 85.
29. According to Augustine, 'sextam omnimodae mutationis in aeternam vitam, et usque ad totam oblivionem vitae temporalis transeuntem in perfectam formam, quae facta est ad imaginem et similitudinem Dei. Septima enim jam quies aeterna est, et nullis aetatibus distinguenda beatitudo perpetua': Augustine, *De Vera Religione*, Book 1, Ch. 26, in *Patrologia Latina*, vol. 34, cols. 143–4 (online resource accessed 25 January 2007, British Library).
30. Richard Baxter, *The Last Work of a Believer. His Passing-Prayer, recommending his departing Spirit to Christ to be Received by him* (London, 1682), A2v.
31. Aesop, *The Complete Fables*, trans. Olivia and Robert Temple (Harmondsworth: Penguin Classics, 1998), 127.
32. Gregory Nagy, *The Best of the Achaeans: Concepts of the Hero in Archaic Greek Poetry*, revised edition (Baltimore: Johns Hopkins University Press, 1999; first edn 1979).
33. Plato, *Phaedo*, 84d–85a, in *The Last Days of Socrates: Euthyphro, Apology, Crito, Phaedo*, trans. Hugh Tredennick and Harold Tarrant (Harmondsworth: Penguin, 2003; first published 1954), 155.
34. See Martial, *Epigrams*, ed. and trans. D. R. Shackleton Bailey, 3 vols., Loeb Classical Library (Cambridge, MA: Harvard University Press, 1993), 202: Book 13, epigram 77. The translator in this particular edition, though,

mistranslates *defecta* as 'flattering' and seems to miss the point of the self-reflexive nature of the epigram.
35. Pliny the Elder, *Natural History*, Book 10, Chapter 32, in *The Natural History of Pliny*, trans. John Bostock and H. T. Riley, 6 vols., Bohn's Classical Library (London: Bohn, 1855–7), vol. 2, 503.
36. Pliny, *Natural History*, Book 35, Chapter 40, ibid., vol. 6, 280–1.
37. See 'Homily of His Eminence Cardinal Joseph Ratzinger' at the Funeral Mass of the Roman Pontiff John Paul II, St Peter's Square, 8 April 2005, http://www.vatican.va/gpII/documents/homily-card-ratzinger_20050408_en.html.
38. Philippe Ariès, *Western Attitudes Toward Death: From the Middle Ages to the Present*, trans. Patricia M. Ranum (London: Marion Boyars, 1976; first published Johns Hopkins University Press, 1974), 11.
39. Philippe Ariès, *The Hour of Our Death*, trans. Helen Weaver (Harmondsworth: Penguin, 1981; first published Paris: Editions du Seuil, 1977), 297.
40. Richard Baxter, *The Last Work of a Believer. His Passing-Prayer, recommending his departing Spirit to Christ to be Received by him* (London, 1682), a1r–v.
41. Jeremy Taylor, *The Rule and Exercises of Holy Dying* (London, 1651), A5r–v.
42. Craig M. Koslofsky, *The Reformation of the Dead: Death and Ritual in Early Modern Germany, 1450–1700* (London: Macmillan, 2000), 2.
43. Jessica Martin, *Walton's Lives: Conformist Commemorations and the Rise of Biography* (Oxford University Press, 2001), 136.
44. Peter Lake, 'Agency and Appropriation at the Foot of the Gallows: Catholics (and Puritans) Confront (and Constitute) the English State', in Peter Lake with Michael Questier, *The Antichrist's Lewd Hat: Protestants, Papists and Players in Post-Reformation England* (New Haven: Yale University Press, 2002), 229–280 (241).
45. William Allen, *A True Sincere and Modest Defence of English Catholiques that suffer for their Faith at home and abrode* (Rouen, 1584), B6v.
46. J.A. Sharpe, ' "Last Dying Speeches": Religion, Ideology and Public Execution in Seventeenth-Century England', *Past and Present* 107 (1985), 144–67 (146, 150).
47. See Patricia Parker, 'Preposterous Estates, Preposterous Events: From Late to Early Shakespeare', in Parker, *Shakespeare from the Margins: Language, Culture, Context* (Chicago: University of Chicago Press, 1996), 20–55.
48. *Walton's Lives*, 131. See William Laud, *The Archbishop of Canterbury's Speech or, His Funerall Sermon, Preacht by Himself on the Scaffold on Tower-Hill, on Friday the 10. of Ianuary, 1644* (London, 1644), title page.
49. [Edward Young,] *Conjectures on Original Composition* (London, 1759), 8–9. I am grateful to Markman Ellis for sending me to Young.
50. Walter Liedtke, 'Rembrandt and the Rembrandt Style in the Seventeenth Century', in Hubert von Sonnenburg, Walter Liedtke *et al.*, *Rembrandt/Not Rembrandt in the Metropolitan Museum of Art: Aspects of Connoisseurship*, 2 vols.: vol. 1, Hubert von Sonnenburg, *Paintings: Problems and Issues*; vol. 2, Walter Liedtke, Carolyn Logan, Nadine M. Orenstein and Stephanie S. Dickey, *Paintings, Drawings, and Prints:*

Art-Historical Perspectives (New York: Metropolitan Museum of Art, 1995), vol. 2, 3–39 (5).
51. M. Roy Fisher, *Titian's Assistants During the Later Years* (New York: Garland, 1977), i, v.
52. Ibid., v; 'Ne haverebbe già Titiano tante opere condotte à fine, se da Discepoli non fosse stato tal'hor sollevato dalle fatiche', Carlo Ridolfi, *Le maraviglie dell'arte*, ed. Detlev von Hadeln, 2 vols. (Berlin: Grote, 1914–24), vol. 1, 225.
53. On Palma Il Giovane's role in relation to the late Titian, see Fisher, *Titian's Assistants*, 43–114.
54. David Rosand, 'Editor's Statement: Style and the Aging Artist', *Art Journal* 46 (1987), 91–3 (91).
55. Dowden, *Mind and Art*, 405; on ways of imagining Shakespearean collaboration, see Charles H. Frey, 'Collaborating with Shakespeare: After the Final Play', in Frey (ed.), *Shakespeare, Fletcher and* The Two Noble Kinsmen (Columbia: University of Missouri Press, 1989), 31–44, esp. 31–2.
56. G. E. Bentley, *The Profession of Dramatist in Shakespeare's Time 1590–1642* (Princeton University Press, 1971), 199.
57. Neil Carson, *A Companion to Henslowe's Diary* (Cambridge University Press, 1988), 57.
58. Bentley, *Profession*, 234; see also Neil Carson, 'Collaborative Playwriting: The Chettle, Dekker, Heywood Syndicate', *Theatre Research International* 14 (1989), 13–23 (14–15).
59. See Vickers, *Shakespeare, Co-Author*, 44–134. See also Samuel Hickson, 'The Shares of Shakspere and Fletcher in *The Two Noble Kinsmen*', *Transactions of the New Shakspere Society* 1 (1874), 25–61 (first published as a review essay on *The Two Noble Kinsmen* in 1847); James Spedding, 'Who Wrote Shakspere's *Henry VIII*?', *Gentleman's Magazine* 178, ns 34 (1850), 115–23; Cyrus Hoy, 'The Shares of Fletcher and his Collaborators in the Beaumont and Fletcher Canon (I)', *Studies in Bibliography* 8 (1956), 129–46; II, *SB* 9 (1957), 143–62; III, *SB* 11 (1958), 85–106; IV, *SB* 12 (1959), 91–116; V, *SB* 13 (1960), 77–108; VI, *SB* 14 (1961), 45–67; VII, *SB* 15 (1962), 71–90; Jonathan Hope, *The Authorship of Shakespeare's Plays: A Socio-Linguistic Study* (Cambridge University Press, 1994); Peter J. Lake, *The Canon of Thomas Middleton's Plays* (Cambridge University Press, 1975); MacDonald P. Jackson, *Studies in Attribution: Middleton and Shakespeare* (Salzburg University Press, 1979); Ants Oras, *Pause Patterns in Elizabethan and Jacobean Drama: An Experiment in Prosody*, University of Florida Monographs, 3 (Gainesville: University Press of Florida, 1960); Marina Tarlinskaja, *Shakespeare's Verse: Iambic Pentameter and the Poet's Idiosyncrasies* (New York: Peter Lang, 1987); A. Q. Morton, 'Stylometry vs. "Stylometry"', *Shakespeare Newsletter* 34 (1984), 5; G. H. Metz, 'Disputed Shakespearean Texts and Stylometric Analysis', *Text* 2 (1985), 149–71; and Thomas Merriam, '*Pericles* I–II Revisited and Considerations Concerning Literary Medium as a Systematic Factor in Stylometry', *Notes and Queries* 237 (1992), 341–5.
60. For Foucault's originary formulation, see his essay "What is an Author?", translated in Josué V. Harari (ed.), *Textual Strategies: Perspectives in*

Post-Structuralist Criticism (Ithaca: Cornell University Press, 1979), 141–60; see also, as an early point in the development of the idea of the 'author-function', Roland Barthes's 1960 essay 'Authors and Writers' in Susan Sontag (ed.), *A Barthes Reader* (London: Jonathan Cape, 1982), 185–93.

61. Vickers devotes a thirty-five page, small-print appendix to attacking Masten's 'preoccupation with Foucauldian theory' and his 'queering of the English language' (*Shakespeare, Co-Author*, 537). I should acknowledge a personal interest in this debate, since my Arden edition of Shakespeare and Fletcher's *Henry VIII* has also been a target for one of Vickers's characteristically intemperate attacks (see ibid., 397–402).
62. Jeffrey Masten, *Textual Intercourse: Collaboration, Authorship, and Sexualities in Renaissance Drama* (Cambridge University Press, 1997), 4.
63. Masten, "Beaumont and/or Fletcher," 342.
64. Jeffrey Masten, 'More or Less: Editing the Collaborative', *Shakespeare Studies* 29 (2001), 109–131 (115).
65. Tiffany Stern, *Making Shakespeare: From Stage to Page*, 'Accents on Shakespeare' (London: Routledge, 2004), 160.
66. Heather Anne Hirschfeld, *Joint Enterprises: Collaborative Drama and the Institutionalization of the English Renaissance Theater* (Amherst: University of Massachusetts Press, 2004), 18.
67. Roslyn Lander Knutson, *Playing Companies and Commerce in Shakespeare's Time* (Cambridge University Press, 2001), 56. See also Knutson's *The Repertory of Shakespeare's Company, 1594–1613* (Fayetteville: University of Arkansas Press, 1991), which prompted much of the recent work on the significance of repertory in our understanding of early modern playwriting. See also Andrew Gurr's two major contributions to the field, *The Shakespearean Playing Companies* (Oxford: Clarendon Press, 1996) and *The Shakespeare Company, 1594–1642* (Cambridge University Press, 2004).
68. Thomas Dekker, *The Guls Horne-booke* (1609), E2r. This passage is cited (with one or two minor transcription errors) by Halasz, *The Marketplace of Print: Pamphlets and the Public Sphere in Early Modern England* (Cambridge University Press, 1997), 179; also by Jean-Christophe Agnew, *Worlds Apart: The Market and the Theater in Anglo-American Thought, 1550–1750* (Cambridge University Press, 1986), 118–19, and Douglas Bruster, *Drama and the Market in the Age of Shakespeare* (Cambridge University Press, 1992), 1–28.
69. Scott McMillin and Sally-Beth MacLean, *The Queen's Men and their Plays* (Cambridge University Press, 1998), xiii.
70. Lucy Munro, *The Children of the Queen's Revels: A Jacobean Theatre Repertory* (Cambridge University Press, 2005), 165.
71. Stephen Orgel, 'What is a Text?' in David Scott Kastan and Peter Stallybrass (eds.), *Staging the Renaissance: Reinterpretations of Elizabethan and Jacobean Drama* (New York: Routledge, 1991), 83–7 (84).
72. Peter Stallybrass, 'Shakespeare, the Individual, and the Text', in Lawrence Grossberg, Cary Nelson and Paula Treichler (eds.), *Cultural Studies* (New York: Routledge, 1992), 593–610 (601). On this subject, see also Douglas A.

Brooks, *From Playhouse to Printing House: Drama and Authorship in Early Modern England* (Cambridge University Press, 2000).

73. Norman Rabkin, 'Problems in the Study of Collaboration', *Research Opportunities in Renaissance Drama* 19 (1976), 7–13 (12).
74. Good examples of the developments that have taken place in attributional method since the 1970s include the work of Hope (*Authorship*) and Jackson, notably in his *Defining Shakespeare*: Pericles *as Test Case* (Oxford University Press, 2003). And Vickers's survey in *Shakespeare, Co-Author* provides a useful sense of the refinement of a range of methods, particularly in view of the scope offered by the shift from manual counting of relevant features to computational analyses.
75. Jackson, *Defining Shakespeare*: Pericles *as Test Case*, 59.
76. A. C. Partridge, *Orthography in Shakespeare and Elizabethan Drama: A Study of Colloquial Contractions, Elision, Prosody and Punctuation* (London: Arnold, 1964), 144.
77. Tom Merriam, *The Identity of Shakespeare in* Henry VIII, Renaissance Monographs 32 (Tokyo: The Renaissance Institute, Sophia University, 2005).
78. See Nicol's unpublished doctoral thesis, 'The Mask of Simplicity: Religion, Politics and Dramaturgy in the Plays of William Rowley' (University of Central England, 2002), 156. On the authorship of *Wit at Several Weapons*, see Hoy, 'The Shares of Fletcher and his Collaborators in the Beaumont and Fletcher Canon (V)', *SB* 13 (1960), 77–108, esp. 89–92; MacD[onald] P. Jackson, *Studies in Attribution: Middleton and Shakespeare*, Salzburg Studies in English Literature (Salzburg: Institut für Anglistik und Americanistik, 1979), 125–7; and David J. Lake, *The Canon of Thomas Middleton's Plays: Internal Evidence for the Major Problems of Authorship* (Cambridge University Press, 1975), 198–214.
79. R. W. Dent, *John Webster's Borrowing* (Berkeley and Los Angeles: University of California Press, 1960), 3.
80. Hereward T. Price, 'The Function of Imagery in Webster', *PMLA* 70 (1955), 717–39 (719).
81. MacD. P. Jackson, 'Late Webster and His Collaborators: How Many Playwrights Wrote *A Cure for a Cuckold*?', *Papers of the Bibliographical Society of America* 95 (2001), 295–313.
82. H. D. Gray, ' "A Cure for a Cuckold" by Heywood, Rowley and Webster', *Modern Language Review* 22 (1927), 389–97.
83. F. L. Lucas (ed.), *The Complete Works of John Webster*, 4 vols. (London: Chatto & Windus, 1927), vol. 3, 12.
84. John Hoskins, *Directions for Speech and Style*, ed. Hoyt H. Hudson, Princeton Studies in English no. 12 (Princeton University Press, 1935), 39.
85. John Florio, 'To the curteous Reader', in *The Essayes of Morall, Politike and Millitarie Discourses of Lo: Michaell de Montaigne* (London, 1603), A5r.
86. *The Second Part of the Return from Parnassus*, 1.1.198–201, in J. B. Leishman (ed.), *The Three Parnassus Plays (1598–1601)* (London: Nicholson & Watson, 1949), 215–367.

87. Joseph Loewenstein, *Ben Jonson and Possessive Authorship* (Cambridge University Press, 2002), 123.
88. Anne Barton, *Ben Jonson, dramatist* (Cambridge University Press, 1984), x.
89. Martin Butler, 'Late Jonson', in McMullan and Hope (eds.), *The Politics of Tragicomedy*, 168–88.
90. Barton, *Ben Jonson*, 322; Larry S. Champion, *Ben Jonson's 'Dotages': A Reconsideration of the Late Plays* (Lexington: University of Kentucky Press, 1967), 140.
91. Julie Sanders, 'Print, Popular Culture, Consumption and Commodification in *The Staple of News*,' in Julie Sanders, with Kate Chedgzoy and Susan Wiseman (eds.), *Refashioning Ben Jonson: Gender, Politics and the Jonsonian Canon* (Basingstoke: Macmillan, 1998), 183–207 (183). See also Butler, 'Late Jonson'; Helen Ostovich, 'The Appropriation of Pleasure in *The Magnetic Lady*', *Studies in English Literature, 1500–1900* 34 (1994), 425–42; Sanders, ' "The Day's Sports Devised in the Inn": Jonson's *The New Inn* and Theatrical Politics', *Modern Language Review* 91 (1996), 545–60; and Part Three of Sanders's *Ben Jonson's Theatrical Republics* (Basingstoke: Macmillan, 1998).
92. Andrew Stewart, 'Some Uses for Romance: Shakespeare's *Cymbeline* and Jonson's *The New Inn*,' *Renaissance Forum* 3 (1998), www.hull.ac.uk/renforum/v3no1/stewart.htm, para. 17.
93. *Greenes Vision: Written at the instant of his death. Conteyning a penitent passion for the folly of his Pen* (1592), A4v.
94. *Greenes Groats-worth of witte, bought with a million of Repentance. . . . Written before his death and published at his dyeing request* (1592), A2v.
95. See John Jowett, 'Johannes Factotum: Henry Chettle and *Greene's Groatsworth of Wit*,' *Papers of the Bibliographical Society of America* 87 (1993), 453–86; see also Warren B. Austin, *A Computer-Aided Technique for Stylistic Discrimination: The Authorship of 'Greene's Groatsworth of Wit'* (Washington, D.C.: US Department of Health, Education and Welfare, 1969) and, more recently, D. Allen Carroll (ed.), *Greene's Groatsworth of Wit* (Binghamton, NY: Medieval & Renaissance Texts & Studies, 1994), 1–32.
96. J[ohn] D[ickenson], *Greene in Conceipt. New raised from his grave to write the Tragique Historie of faire Valeria of London . . . Received and reported by I. D.* (1598). Katherine Duncan-Jones, in *Ungentle Shakespeare*, suggests a correlation between Greene and late Shakespeare: 'If [. . .] he was now suffering from one of Greene's shaming 'life-style' diseases, it would not be surprising if he felt dispirited and demoralized, even to the extent of inviting an identification of his own writing with that of a ridiculous hack, a recycler of trite and sensational romance narrative – while also no doubt hoping to achieve further popular success by doing so' (230).
97. For Barbara Everett in a recent essay, resurrecting an earlier argument by Cyrus Hoy, Shakespeare's 'late drama surely reflects tendencies of that very conscious Mannerism which art historians have seen as succeeding High Renaissance art, in a shift that foreshadows Modernism's rebellion against and ironizing of nineteenth-century aesthetic values. The distortions of these

tragicomedies are at least within the same world as the work of Bronzino and Parmigianino': ' "By the rough seas reft": How the "badness" of the *Pericles* Quarto may be of Shakespeare's making', *TLS*, 11 August 2006, 13–16 (15); see also Hoy, 'Jacobean Tragedy and the Mannerist Style', *Shakespeare Survey* 26 (1973), 49–67, for whom 'Shakespeare's last plays represent the culmination of the mannerist style in Jacobean drama' (66).

5 HOW OLD IS 'LATE'? LATE SHAKESPEARE, OLD AGE, KING LEAR

1. Autobiographical note by Hokusai Katsushika – who by this time called himself Gakyô-*rôjin* (the Old Man Mad about Painting) – in the colophon to Series I and Series II of *The Hundred View of Mount Fuji* (Edo [i.e. Tokyo], 1834 & 1835), cited in Richard Lane, *Hokusai: Life and Work* (London: Barrie & Jenkins, 1989), 232. For Lane, '[i]t would certainly have been no surprise if Hokusai from his mid-70s should have faltered in energy if not in imagination. But the fact is that what books he did in this late period were good ones; and many of his best paintings date from his 80s' (257).
2. Charlotte Higgins, 'It was 37 years ago today – and Sgt Pepper cover has still failed to pay', interview with Peter Blake, *The Guardian*, 3rd June 2004, http://books.guardian.co.uk/hay/story/0,1230413,00.html, accessed 25th January 2007.
3. David Rosand, 'Editor's Statement: Style and the Aging Artist', *Art Journal* 46 (1987), 91–3 (92).
4. C. J. Jung, *Modern Man in Search of a Soul* (New York: Harcourt Brace and World, 1933), 125; my italics.
5. Erik H. Erikson, *The Life Cycle Completed: A Review* (New York: W. W. Norton, 1982), 61. See also Erik Erikson, Joan M. Erikson and Helen Q. Kivnick, *Vital Involvement in Old Age* (New York: W. W. Norton, 1986).
6. Kathleen Woodward, *At Last, the Real Distinguished Thing: The Late Poems of Eliot, Pound, Stevens, and Williams* (Columbus: Ohio State University Press, 1980), 4; see also Kathleen Woodward and Murray M. Schwartz (eds.), *Memory and Desire: Aging – Literature – Psychoanalysis* (Bloomington: Indiana University Press, 1986); Kathleen Woodward, *Aging and its Discontents: Freud and Other Fictions* (Bloomington: Indiana University Press, 1991); and David Van Tassel, *Aging, Death, and the Completion of Being* (Philadelphia: University of Pennsylvania Press, 1979).
7. A recent instance of such work with particular relevance for the current project is Erin Campbell (ed.), *Growing Old in Early Modern Europe: Cultural Representations* (Aldershot: Ashgate, 2006), esp. the essay by Philip D. Collington, 'Sans Wife: Sexual Anxiety and the Old Man in Shakespeare', 185–207.
8. See Elaine Cumming and William Henry, *Growing Old: The Process of Disengagement* (New York: Basic Books, 1961).

9. Kathleen Woodward, 'The Mirror Stage of Old Age', in Woodward and Schwartz, *Memory and Desire*, 97–113 (108); see my Introduction, 9.
10. Friedrich Nietzsche, 'On the Uses and Disadvantages of History for Life' (1874), in *Untimely Meditations*, trans. R. J. Hollingdale, introduction by J. P. Stern (Cambridge University Press, 1983), 57–124 (101).
11. A good instance of Butler's appeal to literary critics is Judith de Luce's argument that the last poems of Ovid exhibit all the signs of the 'life review' as, 'exiled at fifty' and thus 'without the support of family or friends', he assesses his existence up to that point; see de Luce, 'Ovid as an Idiographic Study of Creativity and Old Age', in Falkner and de Luce, *Old Age in Greek and Latin Literature*, 195–216 (210).
12. Lawrence Kohlberg, *The Psychology of Moral Development: The Nature and Validity of Moral Stages*, vol. 2 of *Essays in Moral Development* (San Francisco: Harper and Row, 1984), 171.
13. Gisela Labouvie Vief, *Psyche and Eros: Mind and Gender in the Life Course* (Cambridge University Press, 1994), 2; Labouvie-Vief, 'Positive Development in Later Life', in Cole, Kastenbaum and Ray, *Handbook of the Humanities and Ageing*, 365–80 (371).
14. Dean Keith Simonton, 'The Swan-Song Phenomenon: Last-Works Effects for 172 Classical Composers', in Simonton, *Genius and Creativity: Selected Papers* (Greenwich, CT: Ablex, 1997), 217–30 (217); first published in *Psychology and Aging* 4 (1989), 42–7.
15. Ibid., 219–20. Simonton has conducted extensive analyses both of the aesthetic qualities of art-works and of the interrelations of ageing and creativity. These include, *inter alia*, 'Age and Literary Creativity: A Cross-Cultural and Transhistorical Survey', *Journal of Cross-Cultural Psychology* 6 (1975), 259–77; 'Creative Productivity, Age, and Stress: A Biographical Time-Series Analysis of 10 Classical Composers', *Journal of Personality and Social Psychology* 35 (1977), 791–804; 'Dramatic Greatness and Content: A Quantitative Study of 81 Athenian and Shakespearean Plays', *Empirical Studies of the Arts* 1 (1983), 109–23; 'Musical Aesthetics and Creativity in Beethoven: A Computer Analysis of 105 Compositions', *Empirical Studies of the Arts* 15 (1987), 87–104. See also his *Greatness: Who Makes History and Why?* (New York: The Guilford Press, 1994), 203–11.
16. See Anne M. Wyatt-Brown and Janice Rossen (eds.), *Aging and Gender in Literature: Studies in Creativity* (Charlottesville: University Press of Virginia, 1993), Part III.
17. Part I, 'Disciplinary Approaches', in Cole, Kastenbaum and Ray, *Handbook*, 1–180.
18. Robert Spaethling, *Music and Mozart in the Life of Goethe* (Columbia, SC: Camden House, 1987), 170.
19. Alexander W. Crawford, *The Genius of Keats: An Interpretation* (London: Stockwell, 1931), 13.
20. Ibid., 13; Francis T. Palgrave, *The Poetical Works of John Keats*, Golden Treasury (London: Macmillan, 1884), 274.

21. Robert Butler's account of the 'life-review' endorses this. While, he argues, 'the life review is more commonly observed in the aged because of the actual nearness of life's termination', '[t]he relation of the life-review process to thoughts of death is reflected in the fact that it occurs not only in the elderly but also in younger persons who expect death – for example, the fatally ill or the condemned.... The life-review, Janus-like, involves facing death as well as looking back. Lot's wife, in the Bible, and Orpheus, in Greek mythology, embodied an association of the ideas of looking death in the face and looking back' (Butler, 'Life Review', 67).
22. Theodor W. Adorno, 'Cultural Criticism and Society', in *Prisms*, trans. Samuel and Sherry Weber (London: Spearman, 1967), 17–34 (34).
23. Edward Said, 'Thoughts on Late Style', *London Review of Books* 26: 15 (5 August 2004), 3–7 (5).
24. Theodor W. Adorno, *Philosophy of Modern Music*, trans. Anne G. Mitchell and Wesley V. Bloomster (London: Sheed & Ward, 1973; first published in German, 1948), 133.
25. Said, *On Late Style*, 135. On the development of German studies in this period, see Pier Carlo Bontempelli, *Knowledge, Power, and Discipline: German Studies and National Identity*, trans. Gabriele Poole (Minneapolis: University of Minnesota Press, 2003).
26. Sam Smiles, *J. M. W. Turner: The Making of a Modern Artist* (Manchester University Press, 2007), *passim*.
27. Edward W. Said, 'Untimely Meditations', *The Nation*, September 1/8, 2003, 38–42 (38); reprinted in *On Late Style*, 135.
28. Matthias Bärmann, Ernst Beyeler, Stefan Frey and Ulrich Krempel, *Paul Klee. Death and Fire. Fulfillment in the Late Work* (Bern: Benteli Verlag, 2003), 9.
29. Matthias Bärmann, '"As if it concerned myself": Emigration, Illness and the Creative Process in Paul Klee's Last Years', in Bärmann *et al.*, *Paul Klee*, 10–23 (13, 11, 13).
30. *New Oxford Textbook of Psychiatry*, ed. Michael G. Gelder, Juan J. López-Ibor and Nancy Andreason, 2 vols. (Oxford University Press, 2000), vol. 1, 388.
31. Mark Stevens and Annalyn Swan, *De Kooning: An American Master* (New York: Knopf, 2005), 615.
32. August Strindberg, *Letters to The Intimate Theatre*, trans. Walter Johnson (London: Owen, 1967), 202–3. I'm grateful to Sophie Ratcliffe for pointing out this passage to me.
33. John Gielgud, with John Miller, *Shakespeare: Hit or Miss?* (London: Sidgwick & Jackson, 1991), 103.
34. Ralph Houlbrooke, *Death, Religion, and the Family in England, 1480–1750* (Oxford: Clarendon Press, 1998), 7; for a detailed account and graphs, see E. A. Wrigley and R. S. Schofield, with contributions from Ronald Lee and Jim Oeppen, *The Population History of England, 1541–1871: A Reconstruction* (Cambridge University Press, 1989; first published by Arnold, 1981), 528–9.
35. Herbert Howarth, *The Tiger's Heart: Eight Essays on Shakespeare* (New York: Oxford University Press, 1970), 145.

36. Ibid., 143. See also Creighton Gilbert, 'When did a Renaissance Man Grow Old?' *Studies in the Renaissance* 14 (1967), 7–42.
37. Janet Roebuck, 'When Does Old Age Begin? The Evolution of the English Definition', *Journal of Social History* 12 (1979), 416–28 (417).
38. Lynn Botelho and Pat Thane (eds.), *Women and Aging in British Society Since 1500* (New York: Longman, 2001), 3.
39. John Taylor, *The Olde, Old, Very Olde Man: Or The Age and long Life of Thomas Par* (London, 1635), D4v. William Harvey was called in to dissect Parr's body at his death, not so much to question the alleged age as to see what might have ensured such longevity, whether diet or wholesome air; see Thomas, 'Age', 235.
40. The phrase 'not an hour more nor less' is one of the Folio additions.
41. Thomas Fuller, *The Church History of Britain* (London, 1655), Book 9: 142.
42. Stephen Greenblatt, *Will in the World: How Shakespeare Became Shakespeare* (London: Cape, 2004), 382.
43. Houlbrooke, *Death*, 8.
44. Ibid., 8. Houlbrooke cites Wrigley and Schofield, who offer a table of actuarial figures for 'Expectation of life at 30' in fifty-year periods from 1550 to 1799. For the period 1600–49, the figure for men is 29.8 (Wrigley and Schofield, *Population History*, 250).
45. E. K. Chambers, *Shakespeare: A Survey* (London: Sidgwick and Jackson, 1925), 293.
46. Peter Whelan, *The Herbal Bed* (London: Warner/Chappell Plays, 1996), 120.
47. Anthony Burgess, *Nothing Like the Sun: A Story of Shakespeare's Love-Life* (London: Heinemann, 1964), 230–1.
48. Maurice Hunt, *Shakespeare's Labored Art: Stir, Work, and the Late Plays* (New York: Peter Lang, 1995), 274.
49. Bieman, *The Romances*, 79. Hunt also cites in support of his argument David Brailow, 'Prospero's "Old Brain": The Old Man as Metaphor in *The Tempest*', *Shakespeare Studies* 14 (1981), 285–303, and William Kerrigan, 'Life's Iamb: The Scansion of Late Creativity in the Culture of the Renaissance,' in Kathleen Woodward and Murray M. Schwartz (eds), *Aging–Literature–Psychoanalysis* (Bloomington: Indiana University Press, 1986), 168–91, esp. 172–80.
50. William Kerrigan, 'Life's Iamb: The Scansion of Late Creativity in the Culture of the Renaissance', in Woodward and Schwartz, *Memory and Desire*, 168–91. Kerrigan's essay is ambitious and productive; it will be clear, though, that we differ over several essentials: 'I am interested in authors, in the odd chains of psychic works that result in great art, and like everyone so inclined I wish we knew more about Shakespeare. There were daughters, of course, and he is said to have contracted his fatal illness celebrating the wedding of the youngest one. Possibly, in the case of *The Tempest*, that is enough to know' (179).
51. William Shakespeare, *The Tempest*, ed. Stephen Orgel, The World's Classics (Oxford University Press, 1994), 79, 80. Robert Stephens, in his autobiography, says the same thing: '[I said] that as his daughter should be about eighteen years old, maximum, Prospero should be no older than his mid-forties, fifty

top. I didn't see him as some old magician at all, but very violent and vengeful'; see Stephens, with Michael Coveney, *Knight Errant: Memoirs of a Vagabond Actor* (London: Hodder and Stoughton, 1995), 176.
52. Paul G. Zolbrod, 'From Iago to Prospero: An Introductory Essay', in Tobias and Zolbrod, *Shakespeare's Late plays* 1–13 (12, 10).
53. Michael Tinker, 'Theme in *Timon of Athens*,' ibid., 76–88 (88).
54. That is, Alex Newell's 'Early Modern English Idiom in a Prose Passage from *King Lear*', ibid., 56–75.
55. Cyrus Hoy, 'Fathers and Daughters in Shakespeare's Romances', in Carol McGinnis Kay and Henry E. Jacobs (eds.), *Shakespeare's Romances Reconsidered* (Lincoln: University of Nebraska Press, 1978), 77–90 (77).
56. Robert Speaight, *Nature in Shakespearian Tragedy* (London: Hollis & Carter, 1955), 89. Speaight's view was restated, with political context, two decades later by Glynne Wickham in his essay 'From Tragedy to Tragicomedy: *King Lear* as Prologue,' *Shakespeare Survey* 26 (1973), 33–48.
57. August Strindberg, *A Dream Play and Four Chamber Plays*, trans. Walter Johnson (Seattle: University of Washington Press, 1973), 227; Muir, *Last Periods*, 27.
58. Coppélia Kahn, 'The Absent Mother in *King Lear*', in Margaret W. Ferguson, Maureen Quilligan and Nancy J. Vickers (eds.), *Rewriting the Renaissance: The Discourses of Sexual Difference in Early Modern Europe* (Chicago: University of Chicago Press, 1986), 33–49 (49).
59. R. A. Foakes, *Hamlet versus Lear: Cultural Politics and Shakespeare's Art* (Cambridge University Press, 1993), 3.
60. See Jan Kott, '*King Lear*, or Endgame', in *Shakespeare Our Contemporary*, trans Boleslaw Taborski (London: Methuen, 1964), 101–37.
61. This is not the place for a full bibliography of work done on the textual question in *King Lear*, but those who argued that Folio *Lear* might represent evidence of authorial revision include Samuel Johnson, Charles Knight and Howard Staunton in their editions, along with, *inter alios*, R. H. Cunningham, 'The Revision of *King Lear*', *Modern Language Review* 5 (1910), 445–53; Madeleine Doran, *The Text of* King Lear (Stanford University Press, 1931); and E. A. J. Honigmann, *The Stability of Shakespeare's Text* (London: Arnold, 1965). See also, for contrary views, the following: Alice Walker, '*King Lear* – the 1608 Quarto', *Modern Language Review* 47 (1952), 376–8; G. I. Duthie (ed.), *Shakespeare's 'King Lear': A Critical Edition* (Oxford University Press, 1949); and Leo Kirschbaum, *The True Text of* King Lear (Baltimore: Johns Hopkins University Press, 1945); also the anti-two-text essay by Ann R. Meyer, 'Shakespeare's Art and the Texts of *King Lear*', *Studies in Bibliography* 47 (1994), 128–46.
62. Gary Taylor and Michael Warren (eds.), *The Division of the Kingdoms: Shakespeare's Two Versions of* King Lear (Oxford: Clarendon Press, 1983); Michael Warren, 'Quarto and Folio *King Lear* and the Interpretation of Albany and Edgar', in David Bevington and Jay Halio (eds.), *Shakespeare, Pattern of Excelling Nature* (Newark: University of Delaware Press, 1978), 95–107.

63. Steven Urkowitz, *Shakespeare's Revision of* King Lear (Princeton University Press, 1980), 3.
64. Gary Taylor, '*King Lear*: The Date and Authorship of the Folio Version', in Taylor and Warren, *The Division of the Kingdoms*, 351–468 (365).
65. Stanley Wells and Gary Taylor, with John Jowett and William Montgomery, *William Shakespeare: A Textual Companion* (Oxford: Clarendon Press, 1987), 131; Gary Taylor, 'The Structure of Performance: Act-Intervals in the London Theatres, 1576–1642', in Taylor and John Jowett, *Shakespeare Reshaped 1606–1623* (Oxford: Clarendon Press, 1993), 3–50.
66. Taylor, 'Date and Authorship', 386. On the connections of *King Lear* and *Cymbeline*, see also Irving Ribner, 'Shakespeare and Legendary History: *Lear* and *Cymbeline*', *Shakespeare Quarterly* 7 (1956), 47–52.
67. John Jones, *Shakespeare at Work* (Oxford: Clarendon Press, 1995), 208. I'm grateful to Simon Palfrey for drawing Jones's book to my attention, not only because of its eventual value for this chapter but also because it is a thoroughly good read.
68. William Shakespeare, *Hamlet*, ed. Ann Thompson and Neil Taylor, The Arden Shakespeare (London: Thomson Learning, 2006) and *Hamlet: The Texts of 1603 and 1623*, ed. Ann Thompson and Neil Taylor, The Arden Shakespeare (London: Thomson Learning, 2006). On this point, see Grace Ioppolo, *Revising Shakespeare* (Cambridge, MA: Harvard University Press, 1991), esp. 184.
69. Peter Holland, *English Shakespeares: Shakespeare on the English Stage in the 1990s* (Cambridge University Press, 1997), 167.
70. Orson Welles, proposal for a film of *King Lear*, http://www.wellesnet.com/?p=40, accessed 20 January 2007.
71. Dominic Dromgoole, 'Kings and Desperate Men', *The Guardian*, March 2, 2006, http://film.guardian.co.uk/features/featurepages/0,,1721283,00.html, accessed 19 January 2007.
72. Peter Conrad, *Orson Welles: The Stories of his Life* (London: Faber, 2003), 347. Conrad argues that, as '[i]n his early life, Welles skirted the role of Hamlet', so '[a]t the end of it, he also avoided playing Prospero', but immediately qualifies this: 'Though Welles bypassed *The Tempest*, he crept up on it by roundabout means. *The Immortal Story* in 1968 and *F for Fake* in 1973 were reflections on Shakespeare's play, and in both he played a would-be Prospero' (ibid.).

6 THE TEMPEST AND THE USES OF LATE SHAKESPEARE IN THE THEATRE: GIELGUD, RYLANCE, PROSPERO

1. John Bell, interview for ABC's *Sunday Profile*, 4 November 2005.
2. Helen Musa, 'Bell's Still Weaving his Magic on Stage', 'Panorama' arts insert, *The Canberra Times*, 12 August 2006, 6–7 (6).
3. Muir, *Last Periods*, 51.

4. I can't resist pointing out that the directness of the critical investment in late Shakespeare is perhaps most apparent in the number of Shakespeareans who have daughters or granddaughters named Miranda, Marina, Imogen or Perdita.
5. I'm grateful to Ann Thompson for letting me see the programme/cast list for the production.
6. It is worth noting that, despite having edited *King Lear* for the second Arden series, Muir turned nonetheless not to Lear but to Prospero for his retirement performance.
7. [Philippe Büttner,] ' "A Blue Glow": A Conversation with Ernst Beyeler about Paul Klee's Late Work', in Bärmann *et al.*, *Paul Klee*, 24–31 (25).
8. Sheryl Garratt, 'The Dark Room,' *Observer Magazine* 6 January 2002, 10–15 (15).
9. Michael Millgate, *Testamentary Acts* (Oxford: Clarendon Press, 1992).
10. Westermann, *Rembrandt*, 310.
11. Schama, *Rembrandt's Eyes* 683.
12. Irving Wardle, review of the Peter Hall/Gielgud *Tempest* for the National Theatre at the Old Vic, *The Times*, 6 March 1974.
13. Soledad Valle, 'Helena Pimenta: A propósito de Shakespeare', *Paisajes* 174 (April 2005), 20–4 (22). Thanks are due to Paula de Pando for her assistance with the translation: any infelicities of phrasing are of course mine, not hers.
14. 'Interview with Ninagawa Yukio', in Minami Ryuta, Ian Carruthers and John Gillies (eds.), *Performing Shakespeare in Japan* (Cambridge University Press, 2001), 208–19 (213–14).
15. Michael Billington, 'Walking a Tightrope to Great Acting', *The Guardian* 23 March 2000.
16. Descriptions drawn from the mostly unsourceable cuttings in Folger Library Shakespeare Scrapbook (Flat), 18th–19th century, vol. 36 (Temp.).
17. Ibid., 109; unspecified review by Ivor Brown, cited in Gielgud, *Hit or Miss* 17.
18. Robert Cushman, *Observer*, 10 March 1974.
19. *Prospero's Books* (1991), a film by Peter Greenaway, Allarts/Cinea/Camera One/Penta co-production in association with Elsevier Vendex Film/Film Four International/VPRO/Canal Plus and NHK, produced by Kees Kasander and Denis Wigman, music by Michael Nyman, directed by Peter Greenaway.
20. Gyles Brandreth, *John Gielgud: An Actor's Life* (Stroud, Gloucestershire: Sutton Publishing, 2000), 138.
21. Arguably, Resnais had in a sense already created a film around Gielgud's Prospero in casting him as Clive Langham in his 1977 film *Providence*, which perhaps explains both why Resnais was not interested in making a *Tempest* film and why Gielgud had hoped he might be. Greenaway has expressed his admiration for the films of Resnais. On the books and on the relationship of *Prospero's Books* and *Providence*, see Amy Lawrence, *The Films of Peter Greenaway*, Cambridge Film Classics (Cambridge University Press, 1997), 140–64.
22. Neil Forsyth, 'Shakespeare the Illusionist: Filming the Supernatural,' in Russell Jackson (ed.), *The Cambridge Companion to Shakespeare on Film* (Cambridge University Press, 2000), 274–94 (291).

23. Peter Greenaway, *Prospero's Books: A Film of Shakespeare's 'The Tempest'* (London: Chatto and Windus, 1991), 9.
24. Sheridan Morley, *John G: The Authorised Biography of John Gielgud* (London: Hodder and Stoughton, 2001), 432.
25. Peter Conrad in the *New York Times*, cited in Morley, *John G.*, 434.
26. 'Morning Edition', National Public Radio, 29 November, 2005.
27. *The Tempest* could be considered an odd choice, coming as it did relatively soon after the production starring Vanessa Redgrave as Prospero in 2000, especially since the late play most obviously missing from the 2005 season was *Cymbeline*, omitted presumably because it had been part of the 2001 season. Of the remaining late plays, *The Two Noble Kinsmen* was produced in 2000 alongside the Redgrave *Tempest* and Mark Rylance's return to *Hamlet*; *Henry VIII* remains the only late play not so far produced at the reconstructed theatre, perhaps because it would bring uncomfortable echoes of the burning down of the first Globe in 1613. Of the other two plays in the 2005 season, *Pericles* and *The Winter's Tale*, the former offered unplanned evidence of Rylance's skill and versatility as an actor: when Corin Redgrave (brother of Vanessa), playing Pericles, was taken ill early in the run, Rylance stepped in, learning the part in next to no time and performing it with his habitual effortlessness and commitment.
28. Ray Schultz, review of the Globe *Tempest*, 19 May 2005, *Theatre Journal* 58 (2006), 314–16. See also, for instance, Paul Taylor in *The Independent*, 20 May 2005: 'A couple of years ago, while writing a profile of this great actor-manager, I canvassed the opinion of a number of leading directors and performers. They were unanimously of the view that only one man could have launched Shakespeare's Globe and made it such a thriving theatrical concern. That man is Mark Rylance, the theatre's first artistic director. At the end of this, his 10th year at the Globe, he will pass the baton on to a successor. There's a symbolic edge, then, to the fact that he inaugurates the 2005 season with a portrayal of Prospero, the magician and surrogate-director, who resigns by breaking his staff and renouncing his magic powers.'
29. Tim Carroll, 'Master Piece I: Direction', programme note, *The Tempest*, Shakespeare's Globe Theatre, 6 May–2 October 2005, 26.
30. Review of Ron Daniels's RSC production, *Oxford Mail*, 12 August 1982, cited in William Shakespeare, *The Tempest*, ed. Virginia Mason Vaughan and Alden T. Vaughan The Arden Shakespeare (London: Thomson Learning, 1999), 115.
31. Peter Dawkins, 'About the Author', in *The Shakespeare Enigma* (London: Polair, 2004), a book which 'updates' the argument for Bacon's authorship of the plays by arguing that the plays were written collaboratively by a Rosicrucian group under the direction of Bacon 'in the manner of a Renaissance studio' (Dawkins, *Enigma*, 414); Dawkins, *The Wisdom of Shakespeare in 'The Tempest'* (Warwickshire: I. C. Media Productions, 2000), part of his 'Wisdom of Shakespeare series' which has so far also covered *As You Like It*, *Julius Caesar*, *The Merchant of Venice*, and *Twelfth Night*.
32. Mark Rylance, Foreword to Dawkins, *Enigma*, xii; Rylance, 'Playing the Globe: Artistic Policy and Practice', in J. R. Mulryne and Margaret

Shewring (eds.), Andrew Gurr (advisory ed.), *Shakespeare's Globe Rebuilt* (Cambridge University Press, 1997), 169–76 (174). In his *Enigma* foreword, Rylance recalls first hearing of alchemical ideas at one of Dawkins's Francis Bacon Research Trust meetings: 'Most important to me ... was the exploration of how the psyche changes, using patterns of initiation from the European Hermetic Tradition, such as Alchemy, the Cabala, and the Eleusinian, Dionysian and Bardic mystery schools of the Greeks and Celts. I began to sense patterns of movement in the structure of the plays ... which helped me to discover richer movements from one scene or act to another' (ix).

33. Peter Dawkins, 'The Pattern of Initiation in Human Consciousness', *Francis Bacon Research Trust Journal* 1/1 (1981); Dawkins, *Wisdom*, 212.

34. Rylance, programme note, *Tempest*, 18; Noel Cobb, *Prospero's Island: The Secret Alchemy at the Heart of 'The Tempest'* (London: Coventure, 1984), 13, also cited in Globe *Tempest* programme, 19. This question is the opening sentence of Cobb's introduction.

35. This seems to have been when Rylance first came to the attention of Sam Wanamaker: 'Sam said we could use the Globe site, which was dormant at the time, a big, wet hole in the ground, so long as it cost him nothing. [...] Sam and I shared a similar desire to explore old structures for new theatre, but I did not then foresee that I would be invited to join the Artistic Directorate or subsequently be chosen as Artistic Director': see Rylance in Mulryne and Shewring, *Shakespeare's Globe*, 169.

36. The commitment of Rylance and Van Kampen to Phoebus' Cart and specifically to the *Tempest* is clear enough in his description of the production as 'a project which my wife and I had mortgaged our flat to complete' (ibid., 169).

37. The existence of ley lines – the principle for the choice of performance venues for the 1991 *Tempest* – was first suggested in 1921 by the amateur archaeologist Alfred Watkins and discussed initially in his *Early British Trackways* (Hereford: The Watkins Meter Co., 1922) and then more fully in *The Old Straight Track: Its Mounds, Beacons, Moats, Sites, and Mark Stones* (London: Methuen, 1925). Ley lines are alleged alignments of places of archaeological or geographical significance, from stone circles and mounds to wells and ponds, which Watkins understood as lines of sight allowing ancient Britons to navigate when Britain was mostly heavily forested; for the most part, the connecting landmarks are circular. Anthropological explanations argue for the astronomical or religious significance of the lines; sceptics respond by pointing out the mathematical ease with which random points can be made to align and treat ley lines as pseudoscience. Since the 1930s, ley lines have been given mystical significance by a range of writers, from Nazi researchers into ancient Teutonic rituals to occultists such as Dion Fortune, friend and correspondent of Aleister Crowley, who incorporated them into her synthesis of psychoanalysis, Hermeticism and Freemasonry. Broadly speaking, ley lines are held by New Age interpreters to resonate certain kinds of psychic energy and to be connected to the practices of dowsing and geomancy. Corfe Castle and the Rollright Stones have both been identified as being situated on ley lines or the

conjunctions of ley lines (Watkins discusses the Rollright Circle briefly in *The Old Straight Track*, 171–2).

38. Rylance in Mulryne and Shewring, *Shakespeare's Globe*, 169. Cobb explains the significance of the figure of the circle: 'Like any image, the circle has no absolutely fixed psychological meaning. Rather, it resembles an inviting tree at dusk, giving shelter to many meanings which come to roost like birds from different directions. Thus, what we are dealing with is a clustering of sense. The circle, as C. G. Jung has so amply demonstrated, is everywhere a symbol of wholeness – and thus a hieroglyph for the self. The magician's circle, the stone circles of the ancients, the witches' circle of conjuration and the holy circle of religious dance and ritual are all ringing ripples of this archetypal circle. The circle protects, but it also contains; it excludes, yet it provides the space for integration' (Cobb, *Prospero's Island*, 177). Dawkins, in turn, emphasises in *The Wisdom of Shakespeare in 'The Tempest'* the role of cycles in the alchemical process, offering a diagram mapping the play's development by way of the life-cycles of the four elements Earth, Water, Air and Fire.

39. Michael Maier, *Atalanta Fugiens, hoc est Emblemata Nova de Secretis Naturae Chymica* (Oppenheim, 1618), M3^r; the quotation in the programme is translated from Maier's Latin. Maier was a physician, composer, hermetic philosopher, and counsellor to the Holy Roman Emperor Rudolf II. Rudolf died in 1612, and his tendency to ignore matters of state in favour of occult studies makes him a possible original for Prospero: see David Scott Kastan, ' "The Duke of Milan / And his Brave Son": Old Histories and New in *The Tempest*', in *Shakespeare After Theory* (New York: Routledge, 1999), 183–97, esp. 192–4.

40. Mark Rylance, interview with Lawrence Gerald, 1994, http://www.sirbacon.org/markrylance.htm.

41. Claire Van Kampen, 'Master Piece II: Music', in *Tempest* programme, 28.

42. This foregrounding of the concept of play is made explicit in the book Rylance published on the early Globe productions: Mark Rylance, *Play: A Recollection in Pictures and Words of the First Five Years of Play at Shakespeare's Globe Theatre* (London: Shakespeare's Globe Publications, 2003).

43. Oswald wrote both other instances of new writing performed at the Globe during Rylance's tenure: his play *Augustine's Oak* and his adaptation of Apuleius' *Golden Ass*.

44. Rylance perhaps hinted at the Olivier inheritance in his 1994 interview with Lawrence Gerald, in which, reflecting on his experiences acting in Stratford in 1988, he notes that 'I was experiencing something in the Hamlet performances which we were doing four times a week, and four times Romeo at that time, so there was a certain kind of energy generated in the performance [. . .] the whole cast had come off and said to me, "Oh, it was really good tonight. Why was it, you know, so good?" And you hear that going back to Laurence Olivier, you know, these great performances. He never understood why. And, of course, in a certain sense you don't want to define why': see http://www.sirbacon.org/markrylance.htm.

45. Rylance in Mulryne and Shewring, *Shakespeare's Globe*, 172.

46. See the Trust's website at http://www.shakespeareanauthorshiptrust.org.uk.
47. See, for instance, the interview by William S. Niederkorn, 'To Be or Not to Be William Shakespeare', *New York Times*, 21 August 2004: 'Mr. Rylance said, "There's just so much evidence that you cannot write Bacon out of these plays [...]. With Oxford ... what I've read – the comparisons of his life with Hamlet's life, the wildness, the fact that he's very much complimented for comedy – I find it difficult for the moment to completely remove Oxford from the writing of these plays." The candidacy of Marlowe "is interesting to me because of his relationship to Mary Sidney and because of the early days of the Shakespeare work [...] and that leads me mostly into the idea of collaboration and group work"'.
48. See http://www.sirbacon.org/markrylance.htm, as above at notes 40 and 44.
49. The care with which this alignment has been effected is clear from Rylance's foreword to Dawkins's *Shakespeare Enigma*, in which he describes one of the achievements of his time at the Globe: 'In 1996 I became the Artistic Director and had to take great care not to alarm with my authorship questions. [...] It is a great sign of the times that the discussion is now much less offensive. And indeed my fellows at the Globe, who all hold their own personal views about the authorship, have agreed we are an institution that welcomes all forms of interest in Shakespeare and hopes to refine and develop the questions about the authorship in the same way that we have refined and developed the questions about his amphitheatre' (Enigma, xii).
50. I'm grateful to Helen Hackett for identifying the Baconian hat.
51. J. Thomas Looney, *'Shakespeare' Identified in Edward de Vere, the Seventeenth Earl of Oxford* (London: Cecil Palmer, 1920).
52. Sir Derek Jacobi, quoted from http://www.deverestudies.org/articles/jacobi.cfm.
53. As it happens, the very last Globe production featuring Mark Rylance was not technically the 2005 Tempest, because in the wake of that final performance at the Globe itself the company went on a tour of the USA not with *The Tempest* but with a revival of the 2003 *Measure for Measure*. Arguably, though, the lateness tradition is confirmed by the fact that Rylance played Duke Vincentio. As Cyrus Hoy pointed out decades ago, the Duke is a kind of proto-Prospero: 'Prospero's earlier avatar', he argues, 'is the Duke in *Measure for Measure*: he conducts *The Tempest* as the Duke presides over the action of his play, though with a surer hand and to deeper ends'. See Hoy, 'Fathers and Daughters in Shakespeare's Romances', in Carol McGinnis Kay and Henry E. Jacobs (eds.), *Shakespeare's Romances Reconsidered* (Lincoln: University of Nebraska Press, 1978), 90.
54. Clara Iaccarino, review of the Bell Shakespeare Company production of *The Tempest* (subtitled 'More mellow now, John Bell has diffused the rage for his third Prospero'), *Sydney Morning Herald*, 4 September 2006, accessed at http://www.smh.com.au/news/arts-reviews/the-tempest/2006/09/04/1; Musa, 7. Neil Armfield, artistic director of the Belvoir Street Theatre in Sydney, returned to *The Tempest* only four years later as part of the theatre's

tenth anniversary celebrations, in a production that featured a young Cate Blanchett as Miranda and Kevin Smith, an Aboriginal actor, playing Caliban, a choice that inevitably caused controversy. The Queensland and Melbourne Theatre Companies under Simon Phillips developed this postcolonial-Australian interpretative tradition in 1997 with a consciously antipodean *Tempest*, in which John Stanton played Prospero as a Captain-Cook-era figure.

55. On 'Reconciliation Shakespeare', see Elizabeth Schafer, 'Reconciliation Shakespeare? Aboriginal Presence in Australian Shakespeare Production', in Elizabeth Schafer and Susan Bradley Smith (eds.), *Playing Shakespeare: Australian Theatre and the International Stage* (Amsterdam: Rodopi, 2003), 63–78; see also Sue Tweg, 'Dream On: A 'Reconciliation' *Tempest* in 2001', *Contemporary Theatre Review* 14 (2004), 45–52. My thanks to Penny Gay for kindly reading and commenting on my discussion of Bell's *Tempest* at precisely no notice.

Index

Achilles Tatius 70
Adams, Robert 68, 90
Addison, Joseph 134, 224, 225
Admiral's Men 234, 238
Adorno, Theodor W. 14, 15, 32–44, 46–7, 56, 65, 66, 103, 105, 125, 141, 142, 159, 184, 255–6, 269, 271, 274, 275, 277–8, 358 n. 11
Aers, David 209
Aesop 212
'Ages of Man' 196–9, 209–11
Allen, William 220
Almeida Theatre, London 338
Alpers, Paul 207
Altersstil 10, 26, 156, 165, 183, 271, 272, 274
Alzheimer's disease 282, 291–2
Amadis de Gaule 71
Anguissola, Sofonisba 20
Anna of Denmark 241
anti-Stratfordianism 187, 188, 346–9
archetypes 9, 31, 32, 33
Arden Shakespeare 3, 80, 81, 92
Arendt, Hannah 266
Ariès, Philippe 217
Aristotle 196
Armfield, Neil 350, 351
ars moriendi 217–19
Augustine 207–11, 214, 215
Auschwitz 275, 300
Austen, Jane 18
Australian National University 350
authenticity 27, 88, 129, 226–30, 254, 322, 325
authorship 88, 226, 231–58, 346–50
autobiography 1, 26, 324
Avicenna (Ibn Síná, i.e. Husain Ibn 'Abd Allah, Abu 'Ali) 197

Bach, Johann Sebastian 31, 33, 35, 40, 49, 109
Bacon, Sir Francis 188, 339, 346–8
Bailey, Sir William 89, 134, 178
Baini, Giuseppe 139–42
Barker, Harley Granville 95–6

Barksted, William 241
Bärmann, Matthias 280–1, 322
Barroll, Leeds 81, 99–101, 103
Barry, Lording 240
Barthes, Roland 228
Bartók, Béla 31
Barton, Anne 121, 251–2
Bate, Jonathan 11, 134–5
Baxter, Richard 211, 217–19, 221
BBC (British Broadcasting Corporation) 344
Bear Gardens Museum 341
Beaumont, Francis, and John Fletcher 75, 84, 94–5, 100, 101, 233, 234, 243
 A King and No King 100
 The Maid's Tragedy 100
 Philaster 71, 84, 94, 95, 100
Beddoes, Thomas 150
Bede 197
Beethoven, Ludwig van 2, 13, 14, 15, 21, 27, 33, 35, 36–45, 46, 48–9, 51, 55, 62, 65, 66, 85, 103, 105, 109, 114, 125, 142–4, 176, 261, 274, 275, 277, 278, 279, 289, 312, 314, 318
Bell, John 318, 350–3
Bell Shakespeare Company 350, 351, 352
Belvoir Street Theatre, Sydney 351
Benjamin, Walter 38, 62
Bent, Ian 14, 138, 139
Bentley, G. E. 96–7, 162, 233, 234, 236, 251, 303
Bergeron, David 76
Bergman, Ingmar 331, 334
Bernini, Giovanni Lorenzo 11, 14, 231
Bethell, S. L. 111–12, 115
Bevis of Hampton 70, 71
Beyeler, Ernst 320–2
Bieman, Elizabeth 70, 73, 75, 293
Billington, Michael 331–2
biography 3, 6, 26, 37, 48, 90, 138, 222–4
Blackfriars Theatre 95–9, 102, 103, 105, 161, 252, 303, 305, 306
Blake, Peter 259
Blake, William 55

394

Index

Bliss, Lee 102
Bloch, Ernst 60
Bly, Mary 12, 99, 239, 240–1
Boas, F. S. 81
Bond, Edward 167–8, 169, 186, 285, 289, 312–13, 333
Bosanquet, Theodora 230
Botelho, Lynn 287
Botticelli, Sandro 55
Bourdieu, Pierre 25, 176
Bradley, A. C. 117, 131, 304, 319
Branagh, Kenneth 344
Brandes, Georg 159
Braudy, Leo 208
Briggs, Julia 92
Broch, Hermann 32–6, 44, 55, 56, 65, 108–9, 110, 163, 184, 262, 271, 273, 274, 275–7, 279, 320
Brook, Peter 299–300, 332, 334
Browning, Robert 156, 173, 322
Burgess, Anthony 290
Burrow, J. A. 196, 210
Burton, Richard 314
Butler, Martin 251, 252
Butler, Robert 9, 85, 266, 267–8
Butterfield, Herbert 42, 215
Büttner, Philippe 320, 322
Byron, George 54, 150

caesura 35, 39, 41, 43, 65–125, 280, 281, 306, 307, 312, 322
Callimachus 211
Campbell, Thomas 132, 147–8, 149–51, 153, 158, 172
Carlyle, Thomas 133
Carroll, Tim 338–9, 343
Carson, Neil 234, 238
Castle of Perseverance, The 70
Celestina, La 71
Cézanne, Paul 30, 320, 323
Chambers, E. K. 288
Champion, Larry 80, 81, 252
Chapman, George 202, 241
  Bussy d'Ambois 102
Charles I, King of England 252
Charlton, H. B. 163–5, 166, 284, 286
Chaucer, Geoffrey 70, 71–3, 161
  Knight's Tale 73, 85, 206, 257
Cheney, Patrick 12, 102, 202–9
Chettle, Henry 233, 238, 255
Childress, Diana 72–3
chronology 65, 66, 78–104, 128–32, 138, 203, 258, 274, 321, 327, 328
Cixous, Hélène 20–1
Clark, Kenneth 6, 12, 14, 227, 229, 263, 272, 279, 289, 292
Claude Lorrain 263

Cobb, Noel 340, 345
coda 26
Cokayne, Karen 194
Cole, Thomas 9, 267, 270
Coleridge, Samuel Taylor 69, 136, 144–7, 152, 153, 165, 272
collaboration 88–95, 207, 230–8, 242–51, 253, 256, 257, 325, 347
Collier, John Payne 132
Condell, Henry 1, 165, 166–7
connoisseurship 6, 27
Conrad, Joseph 169–72, 176, 324
  Victory 170–2
Conrad, Peter 317
contingency 26, 34, 65, 99, 256, 257, 279, 280–1, 283, 292, 322
Cooper, Helen 71–3, 294
Cooper, John Gilbert 132
Corfe Castle, Dorset 341
Cowdery, Lauren 179
Craig, Hardin 130
Craig, William Marshall 148
Craft, Robert 230, 232
Crane, Ralph 117
Crawford, Alexander 273
Crow, Thomas 14
Cuffe, Henry 196, 197, 199
Cushman, Robert 333

Daborne, Robert 241
Daniel, Samuel 75, 202
Daniels, Ron 339
Danson, Lawrence 86
Dante Alighieri 208, 332, 334
Dawkins, Peter 339–40, 346–9
Dawkins, Richard 71
Dawson, Anthony B. 1, 4, 79, 80, 162, 231, 285
Day, Digby 285
Day, John 241
de Beauvoir, Simone 264
Dee, John 333, 341
de Grazia, Margreta 11, 129
de Helder, Arendt 325
de Kooning, Willem 282, 291
de Vere, Edward 349
Dekker, Thomas 203, 233, 238
  The Gull's Hornbook 238
Delius, Frederick 280
DeNora, Tia 176
Dent, R. W. 245–7
Derrida, Jacques 16
Devine, George 332
Dickens, Charles 311
Dickenson, John 255
Diderot, Denis 137–8, 140

discourse of lateness 5, 68, 127, 326, 348
Dolan, Frances 221
Dollimore, Jonathan 8
Donaldson, E. Talbot 161
Donatello (Donato di Niccolò di Betto Bardi) 227
Douglas, Donald 283, 291–2, 293
Dowden, Edward 16, 22, 66–9, 79, 81, 94, 96, 101, 103, 104, 123, 127, 131, 135, 136, 146, 153, 157–9, 160, 162, 163, 164–5, 168, 169, 170, 172, 176, 191, 192, 204, 205, 209, 231, 288, 295, 315, 319, 323, 335
Drake, Nathan 146, 160
Drayton, Michael 167, 202, 240
Dromgoole, Dominic 316–17
Dryden, John 251
Du Bartas, Guillaume de Salluste 208
Düchting, Hajo 107, 261
Dulwich Picture Gallery 225, 227
Duncan-Jones, Katherine 102, 205, 290–1
Dutton, Richard 70

eclogue 25
Edwards, Philip 79, 110
Eliot, George 21–2, 51, 265, 266
Eliot, T. S. 156, 265
Elyot, Thomas 247
Ellis, Havelock 10, 28–32, 43, 46, 55, 68, 107, 110, 183, 184, 272, 285, 320, 323
Emerson, Ralph Waldo 127
epic 25, 27
Erdinast-Vulcan, Daphna 169
Erikson, Erik 265, 269, 279
Erne, Lukas 12, 202
eschatology 3, 10, 277
Evans, Peter 351
Everett, Barbara 381 n. 97
Everyman 70

Felperin, Howard 69, 71, 74
feminism 20–1, 270
Fenby, Eric 280
Fétis, François-Joseph 142–4
Fichte, Johann Gottlieb 138
Ficino, Marsilio 339
Field, Nathan 241
Fisher, M. Roy 228–9
Fletcher, John 2, 4, 75, 88–91, 110, 203, 231–2, 235, 237, 243, 244–5, 285, 286
   The Faithful Shepherdess 76
Florio, John 249
Floris and Blancheflour 71
Foakes, R. A. 92, 299–300
Forman, Simon 79
Forsyth, Neil 334
Fortescue, Thomas 196, 197

Foster, Verna 74
Foucault, Michel 203, 228, 235
Foxe, John 219
France 27
Fraser, Russell 54, 90, 92, 94, 160, 178
Freud, Sigmund 16, 19, 77, 86, 348
Frye, Northrop 56, 69
Fuchs, Barbara 71
Fuller, Thomas 287
Furness, Horace Howard 95, 96
Furnivall, F. J. 52, 135, 157–9

Garratt, Sheryl 321
Gawain and the Green Knight 71
Geddes, Gary 170
Genet, Jean 20
genius 16, 25, 27, 42, 45, 128, 134, 183, 201, 225, 230, 243, 257, 272, 274, 279, 285, 322, 346
genre 25, 63, 66–78, 86
Geoffrey of Monmouth 71
Gerald, Lawrence 346
gerontology 6, 9, 266–71, 272, 273
Gervinus, G. G. 158–9
German critical culture 2, 26, 192, 277
Gibbons, Brian 117
Gielgud, Sir John 64, 285, 326, 331–7, 340, 341, 344, 348–9, 350, 351, 352, 353
Gilbert, Creighton 286
Glasgow Citizens' Theatre 340
Globe Theatre 3, 81, 97–9, 133, 161, 167, 288, 291; *see also* Shakespeare's Globe Theatre
Goethe, Johann Wolfgang von 13, 33, 35, 45, 47, 49, 52, 109, 138, 144, 158, 261, 271–2, 274, 276, 277, 312
Goldin, Nan 321
Goodcole, Henry 190, 221
Goring, Marius 332
Gossett, Philip 14
Gossett, Suzanne 125
Gower, John 70
Goya, Francisco 14, 35, 45, 49, 312
Grainville, Jean-Baptiste Cousin de 150
Gray, H. D. 247–8
Greece 16, 27, 194, 212
Greenaway, Peter 331, 334–7, 343–4
   The Draughtsman's Contract 334
   Prospero's Books 331, 332, 333, 334–6, 343–5
Greenblatt, Stephen J. 288
Greene, Robert 246, 254–5
Grene, David 12, 55, 194
Grene, Nicholas 319
Guarini, Giambattista 74–6
Guerard, Albert 171
Gurr, Andrew 97–9
Guy of Warwick 32–6, 70

Index

Halasz, Alexandra 238, 239
Hall, Peter 333, 338, 341, 342
Halliwell-Phillips, James Orchard 134, 165–6
Hals, Frans 35
Halsey, Richard Sweeney 269–70
Hamilton, Charles 92
Hampson, Robert 170, 171
Hamsun, Knut 264
Hardy, Thomas 173–4, 183, 224, 292
Harris, Frank 159
Hartwig, Joan 74
Hazlitt, William 69, 299
Hegel, Georg Wilhelm Friedrich 143, 144, 150, 276, 277, 279
Heine, Heinrich 276
Helgerson, Richard 199, 200, 203, 208
Heliodorus 70
Hemmings, John 1, 165
Hemingway, Ernest 231
Henke, Robert 68, 73, 74, 76, 77
Henslowe, Philip 233–4, 238
Hermeticism 339, 347, 390 n. 37
Herrick, Marvin T. 74
Heylyn, Peter 127, 223
Heywood, Thomas 203, 233, 238, 247–8
Hickson, Samuel 234
Hirschfeld, Heather 249
Hodgdon, Barbara 12
Hokusai Katsushika 259, 261, 262, 271
Holinshed, Raphael 98
Holland, Peter 314–15
Holland, Philemon 247
Homer 144, 200
Hood, Thomas 150
Hope playhouse 244
Hope, Jonathan 234
Horace 193, 199, 200
Hordern, Michael 333
Horne, Philip 179
Hoskins, John 122, 249
Houbraken, Arnold van 105
Houlbrooke, Ralph 288
Houston, John Porter 117, 121, 122
Howard, Jean E. 70
Howarth, Herbert 286, 288
Hoy, Cyrus 55, 56, 234, 244, 296, 297
Hudson, Henry 151, 152
Hugo, Victor 137, 161
Hunt, Maurice 68, 109–10, 292–3
Hunt, Violet 187
Hunter, G. K. 67
Hunter, Joseph 151–2
Hytner, Nicholas 315

Iaccarino, Clara 351
Ibsen, Henrik 55

Jackson, MacDonald P. 234, 243, 247, 248
Jacobi, Sir Derek 340, 348–9
James I, King of England (VI of Scotland) 99, 303, 337
James, D. G. 74, 163, 165, 166
James, Henry 8, 17, 27–8, 45, 61, 127, 134, 152, 169, 173, 176–89, 192, 224, 230, 250, 255, 260, 280, 286, 306, 322, 324, 345, 346, 350
 The American Scene 188
 'The Birthplace' 134, 178, 186–7, 188, 346
 'The Death of the Lion' 177
 'The Figure in the Carpet' 177, 181, 188
 The Golden Bowl 93, 177
 'The Lesson of the Master' 177, 185–6
 'The Middle Years' 180–2, 318
 New York Edition 28, 179, 180
 Terminations 180
 The Wings of the Dove 177
Jarman, Derek 334
Jauss, Hans-Robert 71
Johnson, Samuel 201
Jones, John 307–12
Jonson, Ben 30, 76, 90, 129, 134, 167–8, 200, 202, 241, 242, 246, 250–6, 290
 Bartholomew Fair 76
 The Devil is an Ass 251
 'late Jonson' 250–3
 The Magnetic Lady 252
 The New Inn 251, 252
 The Sad Shepherd 251, 252
 Sejanus 251
 A Tale of a Tub 251, 252
 Works 129, 250
Jowett, John 98
Joyce, James 276
Jung, Carl 19–20, 32, 33, 264–6, 269, 293, 339, 340
Juvenal 195

Kafka, Franz 20
Kahn, Coppélia 299
Kastenbaum, Robert 9, 267, 270
Keats, John 30, 174, 183, 203, 272, 273, 285, 299
Kendall, Thomas 241
Kermode, Frank 12, 68
Kerrigan, William 295
Keysar, Robert 241
King's Men 1, 76, 91, 96, 100, 101, 103, 105, 117, 161, 167, 231, 240, 245, 291, 301
King's Revels Company 99, 100, 240
Kirchner, Ernst Ludwig 321
Kirkham, Edward 241

Klee, Paul 14, 107, 280–1, 290, 320–2
Kngwarreye, Emily Kame 9
Knight, Charles 152–3, 178
Knight, G. Wilson 56, 82–4, 87, 296, 303
Knowles, James 92, 296
Knowles, Owen 170
Knutson, Roslyn 12, 238
Kohlberg, Lawrence 268–9, 282
Kollwitz, Käthe 20
Koslofsky, Craig 219–20
Kott, Jan 299
Kurosawa, Akira 334
Kyd, Thomas 203
  The Spanish Tragedy 242, 306

Lady Elizabeth's Men 244
Lake, David J. 234
Lake, Peter 220, 221
Lampedusa, Giuseppe Tomasi di 49
Langbaine, Gerard 130
late style
  and convention 35–9, 256, 257, 269, 282
  and death 10, 27, 28, 31, 38, 41, 45, 255, 270, 271, 272, 273, 322
  as abstract 26, 29, 35, 44, 46, 108, 111, 274, 278, 282, 320
  as archaising 40–1, 44, 45, 159, 256, 258, 262, 276, 281
  as canonical 11, 279
  as complicit 45, 65, 175, 279, 322
  as critique of middle style 39
  as difficult 26, 31, 44, 45, 49, 115, 184, 258, 282
  as epochal 26, 44, 45, 256, 274, 275, 276, 277, 279, 279
  as exile 49, 280, 281
  as fragmentary 228, 232, 275, 281, 282
  as individual 44, 45, 226, 227, 228, 232, 256, 274, 275, 276, 279
  as irascible 38, 40, 45, 49, 258, 263
  as looseness of facture 24, 26, 44, 105–8
  as product of illness 230, 280–4
  as proleptic 26, 44, 45, 258, 277, 311
  as resistant 13, 256
  as return to childhood/return to early 18, 40, 45, 184, 258, 263, 278, 282
  as serene 13, 31, 44, 45, 46, 48, 49, 53–4, 57, 184, 257, 264, 299, 319, 325, 345
  as spiritual 18, 133
  as supplementary 2, 26, 29, 45, 256, 258
  as transcendent 27, 31–6, 44, 65, 253, 256, 262, 266, 267–8, 271, 272, 274, 277, 321
  as universal 5, 230, 256, 270, 322
  emergence of 5
  gendering of 17–19, 65
  impersonality of 279

  in music 14–15, 269–70, 318
  in art 14–15, 291–2, 318, 320–3, 324–53
Laud, William 223–4
Lautréamont (Isidore Lucien Ducasse) 190
Lee, Hermione 319
Lee, Sidney 179
Lempicka, Tamara de 18
Lenz, Wilhelm von 142–4, 277
Leyris, Pierre 161
Liddiment, David 319
Liedtke, Walter 227, 228
Lipking, Laurence 12, 175, 182, 201
Liverpool 15, 319
Lodge, Sara 150
Loewenstein, Joseph 251
Longus 70
Looney, J. Thomas 349
Lucas, F. L. 248
Lukács, Georg 38

MacCaffrey, Isabel 207
McDiarmid, Iain 338
McDonald, Russ 6, 55, 85
MacKinnon, Gillies 344
MacLean, Sally-Beth 12, 239–40
McMillin, Scott 12, 239–40
Machin, Lewis 240
Mack, Maynard 300
Mackail, J. W. 50, 116
Maier, Michael 341
Malone, Edmond 96, 127, 128–34, 136, 146, 147, 148, 152, 190, 192
Malory, Sir Thomas 70, 71
mannerism 177, 257, 258, 381 n. 97
Marlowe, Christopher 54, 174, 183, 202–4, 206
  Doctor Faustus 306
Marshall, Cynthia 68
Marston, John 75, 240, 241, 249–50
Martial 212
Martin, Jessica 220, 222–3
Martin, John 150
Marx, Karl 16
Masson, David 159
Masten, Jeffrey 11, 236–7, 243
Matisse, Henri 230, 280, 289, 322
Merriam, Thomas 235, 243
Metz, G. Harold 235
Michelangelo di Lodovico Buonarroti Simoni 10, 15, 29, 30, 55, 77, 138, 261, 262
middle age 10, 63, 171, 178, 180, 250, 264, 284–93, 328, 329, 331, 345
Middleton, Thomas 234, 244–5, 253
  A Chaste Maid in Cheapside 244
Millgate, Michael 12, 172–6, 179, 180, 270, 323

Index

Milton, John 25, 134, 150, 200, 202
  Paradise Lost 25
Mincoff, Marco 68, 90, 94, 284, 318–19
Miró, Joan 107, 261, 262
modernism 257, 258, 265, 276, 277, 278, 381 n. 97
Monet, Claude 30, 320, 323
Montaigne, Michel de 193–4, 199, 212, 249, 250, 255
Moore, Gene 170
Morton, A. Q. 235
Moser, Thomas C. 170
Mowat, Barbara 69, 70, 73, 78
Mozart, Wolfgang Amadeus 2, 13, 15, 45, 54, 140–4, 271–2, 279
Muir, Kenneth 12, 46, 55–7, 65, 68, 81, 89, 125, 191, 231, 285, 298, 318, 319–20, 323
Mulryne, Ronnie 342
Mundus et Infans 70
Munro, Lucy 12, 102, 239, 241–2
Munsterberg, Hugo 14, 260–4, 272, 357 n. 3
Musa, Helen 318, 350, 351, 353
Musée Picasso (Paris) 24, 26, 28, 43, 44, 191, 262, 320, 323

Nagy, Gregory 212
National Gallery of Victoria, Melbourne 226
National Theatre, London 314, 333, 338, 341, 342
Nietzsche, Friedrich 266–71
Neumann, Erich 32–6, 43, 44, 55, 56, 60, 66, 124, 184, 262, 266, 271, 279, 320
Nevo, Ruth 68, 77, 85–6, 123, 343
new formalism 7, 354–355 n. 8
New Historicism 7
New Shakspere Society 52, 157, 158, 243
Nicol, David 243–4
Nicolson, Harold 224
Ninagawa, Yukio 329–31, 344
Noble, Adrian 314
Noh 330
Norbrook, David 76
Northern Ballet 342
Nosworthy, J. M. 80–1
NPR (National Public Radio, USA) 338
Nunc Dimittis 324, 325, 326
Nuttall, A. D. 77, 78

O'Loughlin, Sean 231
old age 8–10, 24, 25, 26, 27, 45, 85, 108, 194–9, 210, 258, 259–317, 322, 331
Old Vic Theatre 314, 332–3
Olivier, Sir Laurence 314, 344
Olivier, Richard 344
Olson, Charles 122
Oppen, George 281, 282, 283

Oras, Ants 235
Orgel, Stephen 242, 295, 331, 332, 333–4, 336
Ornstein, Robert 68
Oswald, Peter 343
Ovid 195, 200, 203, 205, 206, 207
Oxford Shakespeare, The 78, 79, 81, 90, 101, 296, 306, 307, 311
Oxfordianism 349

Pacino, Al 340
Painter, Karen 14
Palestrina, Giovanni Pierluigi da 139–42
Palfrey, Simon 68, 93, 176
Palma Il Giovane 229, 232
Papias 210
Parker, Patricia 128, 308
Parkin, Tim 195
Parr, Thomas 287
Partridge, A. C. 243
Pasco, Isabelle 344
pastoral 25
Paul's boys 240
Peck, Bob 339
Peterson, Douglas 68
Petrarch 200, 201, 203, 208
Pettet, E. C. 69
Piaget, Jean 268–9
Picasso, Pablo 2, 13, 14, 26, 43, 44, 77, 85, 169, 190–1, 263, 276, 292, 321, 323
Pimenta, Helena 327–8, 333, 344
plague 99–101, 240
Plato 194, 212, 339
Plautus 337, 343
Pliny the Elder 213
Plotinus 339
Plutarch 195, 222, 247
Poel, William 133
Pollard, Alfred 52
Pope, Alexander 25, 129
Porter, Bruce 188
Postlethwaite, Pete 344
Potter, Lois 92, 161
Pound, Ezra 265, 266
Pressly, William 147
Price, Hereward T. 246
Pride of Life 70
Prince's Men 244
Protestantism 200, 209, 219–20, 221, 348
Proudfoot, Richard 124
psychoanalysis 19–20, 86, 390 n. 37

Queen's Revels, Children of 100, 241–2, 244–5
Quiller-Couch, Sir Arthur 80

Rabkin, Norman 242
Racine, Jean 55, 312
RADA (Royal Academy of Dramatic Art) 337, 340
Ralegh, Sir Walter 197, 199
Raleigh, Sir Walter 54, 319
Randall, John 214
Raphael (Raffaelo Sanzio) 138, 139
Ray, Ruth 9, 267, 270
reception history 6, 16
Rembrandt Harmensz. van Rijn 8, 13, 14, 20, 27, 27, 30, 33, 35, 49, 79, 104, 105–7, 169, 183, 184, 191, 225–6, 231, 263, 273, 279, 318, 323, 324
   Return of the Prodigal Son 325
   Simeon Holding the Christ Child 324, 325, 326
repertory 238–41, 253, 257
Resnais, Alain 334
Retsch, Moritz 332
Return from Parnassus, The Second Part of 249–50
revision 28, 85, 86, 236, 306, 311
Richards, Jennifer 92, 296
Ridolfi, Carlo 229
Ristine, Frank 74, 75
Rodin, Auguste 28–9, 46, 77, 273, 323
Roebuck, Janet 286
Rollright Stone Circle, Oxfordshire 341
romance 50, 66, 69–74, 77, 152, 217, 294, 309–10
Romanticism 2, 16, 128, 137, 138, 148, 150, 156, 159, 182, 192, 202, 206, 248, 264, 265, 276, 277, 278, 348
Rome 16, 194–6, 212
Rosand, David 229, 264
Rose, Jacqueline 49
Rosicrucianism 340, 343
Rossini, Gioachino 14
Rowe, Nicholas 130
Rowley, William 234, 244–5, 247
Royal Shakespeare Company (RSC) 314, 339, 340–1, 350
Rubens, Peter Paul 106
Ryan, Kiernan 60, 67
Rylance, Mark 61, 64, 316, 326, 337–49, 351

Said, Edward 10, 13, 15, 36, 46–7, 85, 114–15, 153, 161, 230, 252, 276, 279, 294, 295, 318, 319
Sanbrook, A. J. 150
Sanders, Julie 252, 253
Schama, Simon 106–7, 325–6
Schelling, Friedrich Wilhelm Joseph von 52, 138, 146
Schiller, Friedrich 144
Schindler, Anton 142–4
Schlegel, August Wilhelm 129, 148, 149, 151
Schlegel, Friedrich 166
Schlosser, Johann 142–3, 144
Schmidgall, Gary 73
Schoenbaum, Samuel 11, 12, 103, 105, 128, 158, 162
Schoenberg, Arnold 24, 28, 40, 43, 232, 275, 277, 278
Schultz, Ray 338
Schwartz, Daniel R. 170
Shaffer, Peter 15, 140
Shakespeare, William
   All's Well That Ends Well 81, 101, 124, 307
   Antony and Cleopatra 101, 103, 109, 118, 119, 146, 153, 295, 297
   As You Like It 198, 302
   Cardenio 4, 59, 67, 87, 91, 92, 101, 103, 231, 302
   The Comedy of Errors 74, 85, 297
   Coriolanus 101–3, 109, 118, 119, 125, 153, 295, 296, 297, 303
   Cymbeline 1, 4, 49, 57, 59, 67, 67, 76, 77, 79–81, 87, 88, 90, 91, 95, 100–1, 109–24, 125, 149, 152, 153, 158, 252, 257, 289, 294, 295, 297, 302, 303, 304, 305, 307, 308, 310, 313, 338
   First Folio 67, 95, 98–9, 104, 105–7, 117, 129, 172, 258, 300–11, 335
   Hamlet 56, 77, 78, 94, 131, 148, 209, 297, 299, 306, 311, 340, 347
   Henry IV, Pt 1 68, 216
   Henry IV, Pt 2 68
   Henry V 3, 68
   Henry VI plays 68
   Henry VIII (All Is True) 3–4, 15, 58, 59, 67, 77, 85, 87–92, 101, 109, 115, 120, 124, 135, 152, 153, 158, 216, 231, 237, 243, 257, 302
   Julius Caesar 146, 153
   King John 3, 153, 213
   King Lear 53, 56, 78, 101, 123, 154, 287, 294–317, 326, 352–3
   Love's Labours Lost 77, 123, 204
   A Lover's Complaint 205, 206
   Macbeth 79, 92, 101, 118, 119, 123, 148, 152, 153, 297, 302, 307
   Measure for Measure 75, 78, 93, 146, 153, 337
   The Merchant of Venice 214, 352
   A Midsummer Night's Dream 74, 85, 148, 161, 327, 328
   monument, Westminster Abbey 147, 155
   Much Ado About Nothing 75, 199
   Othello 78, 101, 153, 214, 219, 296, 297, 302, 306, 311, 341
   The Passionate Pilgrim 204, 205
   'The Phoenix and the Turtle' 204
   Pericles 4, 11, 54, 57, 58, 59, 67, 68, 74, 75, 77, 79–81, 85, 87, 90–5, 100–3, 109–24, 125, 152, 158, 168, 205, 251, 252, 257, 285, 287, 289, 290, 294, 295, 297, 307, 308, 310
   The Rape of Lucrece 204, 206, 213

Index

Richard II 1, 24, 28, 68, 119, 216
Richard III 68, 204
Romeo and Juliet 340
Shakespeares Sonnets 101, 102, 204, 205, 206, 290
Sir Thomas More 78, 204
The Tempest 1–4, 7, 8, 40, 48, 49, 55, 57, 59, 67, 69, 73–81, 85, 87–91, 100–4, 109–24, 133, 148–9, 152–3, 158, 161–2, 163, 169, 171, 176, 178–80, 188, 205, 206, 231, 239, 257, 284–5, 289, 292, 294, 295, 296, 297, 302, 306, 308, 312, 316, 317, 318–23, 326–53
Timon of Athens 53, 78, 101, 102, 109, 119, 123, 157, 295, 296, 302, 307
Titus Andronicus 297
Troilus and Cressida 75, 78, 101, 102, 146, 152, 153, 204, 205, 290
Twelfth Night 78, 81, 131–3, 148, 149, 337
The Two Gentlemen of Verona 123, 204
The Two Noble Kinsmen 4, 57, 58, 59, 67, 72–4, 75, 77, 85, 87–92, 101, 103, 109, 114, 120, 124, 135, 158, 161, 206, 231, 257, 285, 294, 302
Venus and Adonis 204, 206
The Winter's Tale 1, 4, 49, 53, 57, 59, 67, 77, 79–81, 87, 90, 100–1, 109–24, 149, 152, 153, 158, 168, 205, 252, 254, 257, 289, 293, 294, 295, 297, 302, 304, 307, 308, 310, 338
Shakespeare's Globe Theatre 3, 316, 337–49, *see also* Globe Theatre
Sharman, Jim 350, 351
Sharpe, J. A. 221
Sharpham, Edward 240
Shelley, Mary 149, 172
Shelley, Percy Bysshe 30, 31, 45, 54, 174, 183, 203, 272, 279, 285
Shewring, Margaret 342
Shostakovich, Dmitri 15, 15, 16
Shrimpton, Nicholas 319
Sidney, Sir Philip 71
Simonton, Dean Keith 268–71, 282
Sisson, C. J. 10, 11, 54, 165, 166–7, 288
Smiles, Sam 14, 137, 278
Smith, Henry 287
Smith, Irwin 97
Smith, Maggie 314
Smith, Wentworth 233
Sokolova, Boika 318–19
Solomon, Maynard 14, 48
Sophocles 45, 49, 55, 194, 262, 275, 278, 285, 312
Sousloff, Catherine 11, 14
Spaethling, Robert 271, 272
Spätstil 10, 26, 156, 165, 183, 272
Spedding, James 89, 234, 237
Speaight, Robert 298
Spencer, Theodore 162, 163, 285

Spenser, Edmund 71, 200, 202, 203, 204, 206, 207–9, 211
Amoretti 207
Colin Clouts Come Home Againe 207
Epithalamion 207
The Faerie Queene 71, 207, 208
Fowre Hymnes 207, 208
'Mutabilitie Cantos' 207
Prothalamion 207, 208, 211
The Shepheardes Calender 207, 208
Stafford, Fiona 150
Stallybrass, Peter 242
Stanislavsky, Konstantin Sergeyevich 326
Stationers' Register 79, 103
Steevens, George 136, 192
Stephens, Robert 314–15
Stern, Tiffany 99, 238
Sterrenberg, Lee 150
Stevens, Mark 283, 291
Stevens, Wallace 265, 266
Stewart, Andrew 252, 253
Strachey, Giles Lytton 54, 96, 131, 162–3, 167, 168, 170, 176, 186, 289, 313, 319
Strachey, William 132, 329
Stratford-upon-Avon 91, 95, 96, 103, 104, 130, 155, 158, 161, 167, 180, 188, 192, 209, 257, 291, 301, 303, 305, 314, 326, 331, 332, 333, 346, 347, 350
Straus, Joseph N. 14, 232
Strauss, Richard 8
Stravinsky, Igor 14, 27, 28, 230, 232, 276, 278
Strehler, Giorgio 334
Strindberg, August 55, 56, 284, 298
Stuart, Arbella 81
style 6, 109–25
subjectivism 4, 37, 38, 79, 96, 99, 122, 288, 305, 307, 317, 318, 322, 326, 352
Subotnik, Rose 39, 41, 255, 275, 277
Sutherland, James 120
Swan, Annalyn 283, 291
swan song 211–14, 254–5, 270, 318, 350
Swift, Jonathan 264
Swinburne, Algernon Charles 156
synchrony 9, 27, 277

Tanselle, G. Thomas 175
Tarlinskaja, Marina 235
Taylor, Charles 209, 310–11
Taylor, Gary 235, 296, 300, 301–6, 307
Taylor, Jeremy 217–19, 221
Taylor, John (the Water Poet) 287
Taylor, Neil 311
Tchelitchev, Pavel 317
Tegg, Thomas 148
teleology 6, 25, 247, 251, 273, 281, 320, 325
ten Brink, Bernhard 166

Tennyson, Alfred Lord 89, 173, 261, 332
testamentary acts 172, 254, 270, 322, 323
Thane, Pat 287
theatre history 6
Theobald, Lewis
  Double Falsehood 92
theology 68, 214–15, 254, 275
Thomas, Keith 199, 287
Thompson, Ann 311
Thorndike, Ashley 74, 94–5, 100, 364 n. 58
Thorne, Alison 68, 70, 71
Thurston, John 148
Tiedemann, Rolf 36, 43, 65, 103, 105
Tillyard, E.M.W. 68, 69, 82–4, 87, 89, 296
Tinker, Michael 296
Tinkler, F. C. 116
Titian (Tiziano Vecelli) 5, 13, 14–15, 29, 31, 33, 35, 45, 49, 107, 136, 138, 183, 213, 231, 232, 262, 279
Tobias, Richard 296
tragicomedy 74–8, 94, 253, 256
Traversi, Derek 68, 82–4, 87, 92, 110, 115–16, 297–8, 315
Turner, J. M. W. 13, 14, 21, 30, 31, 51, 173, 183, 278

Udall, Nicholas 249
unity 66
Ulïbïshev, Alexander 140–4, 272, 277
Ulrici, Hermann 153–7, 160, 204, 209
Uphaus, Robert 69
Urkowitz, Steven 301

Van Kampen, Claire 341, 342, 343
Vasari, Giorgio 5, 13, 136–7, 139
Verdi, Giuseppe 174, 279, 285
Vickers, Brian 88, 234–7, 242–3
Victorian Arts Centre 350
Virgil 14, 25, 26, 142, 200, 201, 203, 204, 206, 353
  Aeneid 200, 206, 257, 353
  Eclogues 200
  Georgics 200
  rota Virgilii 25, 27, 50, 176, 200, 201, 204, 205, 206, 207, 208, 209, 257

Wagner, Richard 173
Walton, Izaak 222–4

Wanamaker, Sam 338, 342
Wardle, Irving 326
Warren, Michael 301
Warton, Joseph 134
Watkins, Alfred 390 n. 37
Wayne, Valerie 81
Webern, Anton 232
Webster, John 30, 203, 233, 253, 296
  A Cure for a Cuckold 247, 248
  The Duchess of Malfi 245, 246
  The White Devil 245, 246
Wells, H. G. 150
Wells, Stanley 69
Welles, Orson 315–17, 348
Westermann, Mariët 104–5, 324, 325
Wharton, Edith 24
Whelan, Peter 290, 291
Whitaker, William 214
Whitechapel Gallery 321
Wightman, Edward 303
Wilkins, George 4, 91, 92–3, 110, 290
Williams, Harcourt 332
Williams, William Carlos 265, 266
Wilson, Emily 194
Wilson, J. Dover 83–4, 135, 159, 296
Wilson, Richard 92
Winstanley, William 130
Wit at Several Weapons 243–5
Wolfe, Thomas 35
Wood, John 315
Wood, Michael 48, 230
Woodward, Kathleen 9, 19, 265–8, 272, 273
Woolf, Virginia 18
Wordsworth, William 54, 156
Wotton, Sir Henry 1, 3
Wright, George T. 118–20

Xenophon 70

Yates, Frances A. 347
Yeats, W. B. 46, 49, 77, 115
Young, Edward 224–5

Zeami Motokiyo 330
Zoence Academy 339
Zolbrod, Paul 296